This book comprises papers examir
theory given at the Sixth World (
Barcelona in August 1990. This is the latest in a series of collections which
cover the most active fields in economic theory over a five-year period. With
papers from the world's leading specialists, this book gives the reader a
unique survey of the most recent advances in economic theory.

Econometric Society Monographs No. 21

Advances in economic theory
Sixth World Congress
Volume II

Econometric Society Monographs

Editors:
Avinash Dixit   *Princeton University*
Alberto Holly   *Université de Lausanne*

The Econometric Society is an international society for the advancement of economic theory in relation to statistics and mathematics. The Econometric Society Monograph Series is designed to promote the publication of original research contributions of high quality in mathematical economics and theoretical and applied econometrics.

Advances in economic theory Sixth World Congress
Volume II

Edited by

JEAN-JACQUES LAFFONT

Universite des Sciences Sociales de Toulouse

CAMBRIDGE
UNIVERSITY PRESS

Published by the Press Syndicate of the University of Cambridge
The Pitt Building, Trumpington Street, Cambridge CB2 1RP
40 West 20th Street, New York, NY 10011–4211, USA
10 Stamford Road, Oakleigh, Melbourne 3166, Australia

First published 1992
First paperback edition 1995

Printed in Great Britain at the University Press, Cambridge

A catalogue record for this book is available from the British Library

Library of Congress cataloguing in publication data
Econometric Society. World Congress (6th: 1990: Barcelona, Spain)
Advances in economic theory: Sixth World Congress / edited by
Jean-Jacques Laffont.
    p.   cm. – (Econometric Society monographs: no. 21)
ISBN 0 521 43019 4
1. Economics – Congresses. I. Laffont, Jean-Jacques, 1947–
II. Title. III. Series.
HB21.E23 1992
330'.01'5195 – dc20   91–26036 CIP

ISBN 0 521 43019 4 hardback
ISBN 0 521 48460 X paperback

VN

Contents

Contributors

Larry Epstein
Department of Economics, University
    of Toronto

Milton Harris
Graduate School of Business,
    University of Chicago

Artur Raviv
Kellog Graduate School of
    Management, Northwestern
    University

Jean Tirole
Department of Economics,
    Massachusetts Institute of
    Technology

Patrick Bolton
Laboratoire d'Econometrie de l'Ecole
    Polytechnique, Paris

Darrell Duffie
Graduate School of Business,
    Stanford University

David Cass
Department of Economics, University
    of Pennsylvania

Roger Guesnerie
DELTA, Ecole des Hautes Etudes en
    Sciences Sociales

Michael Woodford
Graduate School of Business,
    University of Chicago

Larry Jones
Kellog School of Management,
    Northwestern University

Andreu Mas-Colell
Department of Economics, Harvard
    University

Editor's preface

This book, *Advances in economic theory – Sixth World Congress* contains invited papers as well as discussions presented at symposia of the Sixth World Congress of the Econometric Society in Barcelona, Spain, August 1990. The topics, the speakers and the discussants were chosen by the Program Committee. The purpose of symposia was to survey important recent developments in economic theory. An accompanying volume in econometrics is edited by Christopher Sims. All manuscripts were received by the end of February 1991.

Jean-Jacques Laffont

Chairman of the Program
Committee for Economic Theory
of the Sixth World Congress
of the Econometric Society

CHAPTER 1

Behavior under risk: recent developments in theory and applications

Larry G. Epstein*

1 INTRODUCTION

In the last decade a number of new theories have been proposed to explain individual behavior under risk where, following Knight (1921), risk is defined as randomness with a known probability distribution. Some of these theories are formally atemporal and generalize the classical expected utility model of choice. Their development was inspired primarily by the growing body of laboratory evidence regarding static or one-shot choices, that has cast doubt upon the descriptive validity of the expected utility model. Other theories are explicitly intertemporal and generalize the time-additive expected utility model which is standard in capital theory. The noted laboratory evidence also provides some motivation for this work since it is clearly desirable that a theory of intertemporal utility, when restricted to static gambles, be consistent with the evidence.

The capacity to explain behavior in the laboratory is one criterion that might be applied to a theory of choice under risk. At least as important, however, is that the theory be useful as an engine of inquiry into standard market-based economic questions. The expected utility model has proven extremely successful in this respect. By application of now standard techniques, modelers have been able to derive a rich set of predictions in a variety of contexts. Moreover, a substantial body of non-experimental evidence has been shown to conform well to the expected utility hypothesis. The ultimate influence of the new theories on the profession at large will probably depend on whether they can match the elegance and power of expected utility as a tool of analysis and whether they can significantly improve the explanation of non-experimental evidence. In order to cast light upon these questions, I will survey some of the new theories of choice and their applications to a number of standard problems in macro-economics, finance, and game theory.

The limitations and objectives of this chapter should be made clear at the outset. First, I will emphasize economic applications and, where it exists, market-based evidence. The theories themselves will be described only to the extent necessary to understand the applications. This is particularly so for the formally atemporal theories, since there already exist a number of excellent surveys dealing with them and their relation to laboratory evidence (Machina, 1983a, 1987; Sugden, 1986; Weber and Camerer, 1987; Fishburn, 1988; Karni and Schmeidler, forthcoming; Camerer, 1989b). Second, a number of papers have demonstrated that many results, in diverse areas of economic analysis, are robust to generalizations of expected utility. In contrast, I will focus below primarily on those instances in the literature where it has been shown that the added flexibility provided by the generalization of expected utility "makes a difference" because it delivers either

1   added analytical power and consequently new theoretical insights, or
2   interesting new testable implications regarding market behavior.

It will be useful to distinguish between *static* or 1-shot choice problems and *dynamic* choice problems. Typically, in dynamic problems a number of decisions are made subject to different information as a result of the resolution of some risks, and thus the issue of consistent choice arises. Within dynamic problems distinguish further between *intertemporal* choice, where consumption sequences are the objects of choice and source of utility – as in capital theory – and *sequential* choice, where terminal wealth is the source of utility. In a sequential problem there are several stages at which decisions are made but the entire process involves so little time that consumption/savings plans may be reasonably viewed as fixed. Alternatively, the multistage nature of a decision problem could be due exclusively to the way in which the problem is perceived by the individual. In that case, no real time passes as the stages are traversed, but the problem is still sequential. Many games fit into the sequential choice framework.

In order to better achieve the objective stated earlier, I will emphasize the literature on dynamic choice with non-expected utility preferences. Static choice will be discussed primarily in order to facilitate understanding of the theory and applications of dynamic choice. Specifically, the chapter proceeds as follows. The next section describes some atemporal theories and applications. Intertemporal utility theory is reviewed in section 3 and then section 4 describes applications to consumption theory and asset pricing. Finally, section 5 considers sequential choice and then how received game theory is affected by generalized specifications of utility. The first part of section 5 parallels closely and relies upon section 3.

2   STATIC CHOICE

A decision problem under risk is static if all decisions must be made at a single point in time and dynamic otherwise. The bulk of the laboratory evidence cited earlier is based on static choice behavior. Accordingly, the generalizations of expected utility that have been developed to explain that evidence have been formulated and analyzed primarily from the perspective of static choice problems. In fact, these new theories are strictly speaking inapplicable to dynamic choice problems, since they invariably specify a **single** utility function rather than, as would be needed, a **sequence** of utility functions, one for each decision time. This section describes some of these static theories and some results that they have produced. A primary objective, however, is to lay the groundwork for the following sections where it is shown how these theories may be extended and applied to dynamic choice settings.

The objects of choice are lotteries, where a lottery is represented by a cumulative distribution function (cdf) over R^n, or by the underlying random variable, or by a probability measure on some more general space of outcomes. Utility functions are defined over lotteries. I will concentrate on the case of real-valued outcomes; extensions to more general prizes are available in the cited references.

2.1   Generalized expected utility analysis

The standard description of choice from a set of feasible lotteries is based on the maximization of an expected utility function, or equivalently, of a function that is "linear in probabilities." Machina (1982b) points out that, just as in ordinary calculus, analysis of linear functions can be readily extended to the analysis of "locally linear" or "smooth" functions in such a way that many of the techniques of expected utility analysis apply to suitably smooth utility functions.

Formally, Machina considers the set $D[a,b]$ of cdf's defined on a bounded interval $[a,b]$ and restricts the utility function V to be Fréchet differentiable with respect to the L^1 metric, $||F - F_0|| \equiv \int_a^b |F(x) - F_0(x)| dx$. Such differentiability is equivalent to V being "locally expected utility or linear in probabilities." To be precise, there exists $u: [a,b] \times D[a,b] \to R^1$ with $u(\cdot;F)$ absolutely continuous for all F, such that throughout the domain:

$$V(F) - V(F_0) = \int_a^b u(x;F_0) d(F(x) - F_0(x)) + o(||F - F_0||), \quad (2.1.1)$$

where $o(|x|)/|x| \to 0$ as $|x| \to 0$. Consider the probability simplex for three-outcome lotteries (figure 1.1), where the outcomes are fixed and

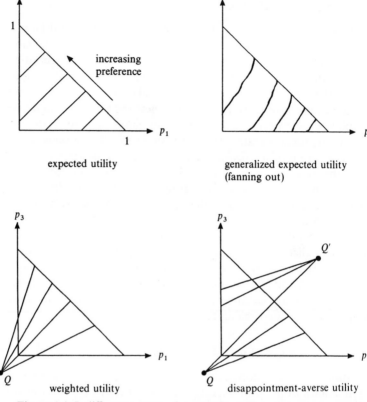

Figure 1.1 Indifference curves for gambles with outcomes $x_1 < x_2 < x_3$ and probabilities $p_1, p_2, p_3, p_2 = 1 - p_1 - p_3$.

different points in the triangle represent different probability vectors and hence different lotteries. For expected utility functions indifference curves in the simplex are parallel straight lines, while for generalized expected utility functions indifference curves are generally non-linear but they have unique tangent lines everywhere.

The function $u(\cdot; F_0)$ is V's *local utility function* at F_0. If it does not depend on F_0 then expected utility is obtained globally. Even in general, however, there is a strong similarity to expected utility analysis in that the monotonicity and concavity of $u(\cdot; F_0)$ for all F_0 are equivalent to the global increasingness and risk aversion of V respectively. These and other results derived by Machina are based on a fundamental insight of generalized expected utility analysis: as in ordinary calculus, one can use integration to "piece together" qualitative results regarding differential (local) situations to derive qualitative non-differential (global) results.[1] Formally, let $\{F_\alpha : \alpha \varepsilon [0,1]\}$ be a path such that for each $\alpha^* \varepsilon [0,1]$, $||F_\alpha - F_{\alpha^*}||/|\alpha - \alpha^*|$ is bounded in α for α near α^*, e.g., $||F_\alpha - F_{\alpha^*}||$ is differentiable in α at $\alpha = \alpha^*$. Then:

$$\frac{d}{d\alpha} V(F_\alpha)\bigg|_{\alpha^*} = \frac{d}{d\alpha} \left[\int u(x; F_{\alpha^*}) dF_\alpha(x) \right]\bigg|_{\alpha^*} \qquad (2.1.2)$$

and hence, under the conditions of the Fundamental Theorem of Calculus:

$$V(F_1) - V(F_0) = \int_0^1 \frac{d}{d\alpha} \left[\int u(x; F_{\alpha^*}) dF_\alpha(x) \right]\bigg|_{\alpha^*} d\alpha^*. \qquad (2.1.3)$$

If the sign of the integrand on the right side is uniform across α^*, then the same sign will be shared by the left side.

There exist theoretical arguments for postulating a Fréchet differentiable but non-linear utility function. Such a specification can be justified if F represents a delayed risk (Machina, 1984) or if V represents group preference and F represents a gamble which is to be shared optimally among members of the group, each of whom may conform with the expected utility model (Machina, 1989b).

On the other hand, the assumption of Fréchet differentiability is not innocuous. For example, the disappointment averse utility functions defined in section 2.3 are not Fréchet differentiable. For another example, Chew, Karni, and Safra (1987) show that rank-dependent expected utility functions (see Quiggin, 1982; Yaari, 1987; Segal, 1989 for definitions and axiomatizations) are generally not Fréchet differentiable. Fortunately, the former authors show that the weaker property of Gâteaux differentiability is sufficient to provide a notion of a local utility function and subsequently Machina's (1982b) main results. (Other notions of smoothness are exploited in Chew and Nishimura, forthcoming; Chew, Epstein, and Zilcha, 1988; Wang, 1991.)

Another important contribution of Machina (1982b) is the formulation of a hypothesis regarding utility, called Hypothesis II, that is shown to be closely connected to consistency with Allais-type behavior and with the laboratory-based empirical patterns that have come to be known as the common consequence and common ratio effects. Hypothesis II states that indifference curves *fan out* as shown in figure 1.1, or that they become steeper as one moves upward along any vertical line. The opposite pattern is referred to as *fanning in*. A natural and important question, to be addressed in section 4.5, is whether Hypothesis II is useful in explaining market data.

2.2   Betweenness-conforming utility

For the sake of greater specificity, it is desirable to restrict utility functions by more than a smoothness requirement. There are a number of alternative axiomatically based generalizations of expected utility theory that have been developed, but the one which seems to me to strike the optimal balance between generality and tractability, at least for the applications that I will consider, is the *betweenness* theory due to Chew (1983, 1989), Fishburn (1983), and Dekel (1986).[2] The cornerstone axiom imposes the following requirement on a preference ordering of cumulative distribution functions, where $\sim$ denotes indifference:

Betweenness: If $F \sim G$, then $\alpha F + (1 - \alpha)G \sim F$ for all $\alpha \varepsilon(0,1)$.

The relation between this axiom and the independence axiom ($F \sim G \Rightarrow \alpha F + (1 - \alpha)H \sim \alpha G + (1 - \alpha)H$) is clarified by their respective implications for indifference curves in the probability simplex corresponding to three outcome lotteries. Under betweenness, indifference curves are straight lines but not necessarily parallel (see the two examples in the bottom half of figure 1.1).[3]

Betweenness delivers (given some other specified axioms) an elegant and tractable functional form for the representing utility function V. In sections 3 and 4 it will be convenient to work with the *certainty equivalent* representation of utility μ, where, for any F, $\mu(F)$ is defined implicitly by:

$$V(\delta_{\mu(F)}) = V(F). \tag{2.2.1}$$

Here δ_x denotes the cdf corresponding to the lottery with the certain outcome x. Consequently, $\mu(F)$ equals that amount of money which, if received with certainty, would be indifferent to the lottery F. If the preference ordering satisfies betweenness and other standard assumptions, then there exists a function $H: R^2 \to R^1$, with $H(x,x) \equiv 0$, such that $\mu(F)$ is defined implicitly as the unique solution to:

$$\int H(x,\mu(F))dF(x) = 0, \tag{2.2.2}$$

for each cumulative distribution function F in the domain of μ. If H is increasing and concave in its first argument and decreasing in its second argument, then μ is increasing in the sense of first-order stochastic dominance and risk averse in the sense of being averse to mean-preserving spreads (see footnote 4). Expected utility is obtained if H is specialized to $H(x,z) \equiv v(x) - v(z)$.

The above functional structure provides a perspective on the relation with expected utility functions. Suppose that F^* is an optimum according to

μ in some feasible set D. If H is decreasing in its second argument, then $\mu(F) \leq \mu(F^*) \Rightarrow$

$$\int H(x,\mu(F^*))dF(x) \leq 0 = \int H(x,\mu(F^*))dF^*(x) \; \forall F\varepsilon D,$$

or

$$F^* \varepsilon \; \text{argmax} \left\{ \int H(x,\mu(F^*))dF(x) : F\varepsilon D \right\}. \tag{2.2.3}$$

That is, F^* is also optimal according to the expected utility function with von Neumann–Morgenstern index $H(\cdot,\mu(F^*))$. Of course (2.2.3) does not imply that betweenness conforming functions are empirically indistinguishable from expected utility functions, since $H(\cdot,\mu(F^*))$ generally varies with F^* and hence with the feasible set D. However (2.2.3) and the fact that $H(\cdot,\mu(F^*))$ depends on F^* only through its utility level help to explain why betweenness functions retain much of the tractability of expected utility as demonstrated in both sections 4 and 5.

When H is sufficiently differentiable, a similar point can be made by reference to (2.1.2)–(2.1.3) since then μ is Fréchet differentiable with local utility function:

$$u(x,F) = -H(x,\mu(F))/\int H_2(y,\mu(F))dF(y), \tag{2.2.4}$$

for which the local measure of risk aversion $-u_{11}(x,F)/u_1(x,F)$ depends on F via $\mu(F)$. But, as mentioned earlier, there are interesting examples of betweenness-conforming utility functions (see (2.3.6)) that are not Fréchet differentiable and thus the more general perspective provided by (2.2.3) is useful. In conjunction with the underlying functional form (2.2.2), it also suggests the alternative and possibly more illuminating name "implicit expected utility functions," first used by Dekel (1986), for betweenness-conforming utility functions.

2.3 Parametric functional forms

Two parametric specializations of (2.2.2) will be described here, both in order to clarify further the nature and variety of betweenness-satisfying utility functions and also because they will be applied in section 4.5. For empirical tractability and consistent with the existing empirical asset pricing literature, the hypothesis of *constant relative risk aversion* is adopted for μ, i.e.:

$$\mu(F_{\lambda\tilde{x}}) = \lambda\mu(F_{\tilde{x}}) \text{ for all } \lambda > 0, \tag{2.3.1}$$

where $F_{\lambda\tilde{x}}$ and $F_{\tilde{x}}$ denote the cdf's for the random variables $\lambda\tilde{x}$ and $\tilde{x}$.

Restrict attention to cdf's on R^1_{++}. Given the above assumption, the functional structure in (2.2.2) simplifies to:

$$\int \phi(x/\mu(F))dF(x)=0, \tag{2.3.2}$$

where $\phi(x)\equiv H(x,1)$ and so ϕ is increasing and concave on an appropriate subset of R^1_{++} with $\phi(1)=0$.[4]

For the first parametric functional form let:[5]

$$\phi(x)=x^\delta(x^\alpha-1)/\alpha, \qquad \alpha\neq 0, \qquad \alpha+2\delta<1. \tag{2.3.3}$$

This leads to the constant relative risk averse specialization of Chew's (1983) *weighted utility* having the explicit representation:

$$\mu_{wu}(F)=\left\{\int x^{\alpha+\delta}dF(x)/\int x^\delta dF(x)\right\}^{1/\alpha}. \tag{2.3.4}$$

Expected utility is obtained if $\delta=0$. (To obtain the limiting form corresponding to $\alpha=0$, use the fact that $(x^\alpha-1)/\alpha\to\log x$ as $\alpha\to 0$; similarly for other functional forms below.)

Under the restriction $\alpha+2\delta<1$, ϕ in (2.3.3) is both increasing and concave in a neighborhood of 1, from which it follows (see footnote 4) that there exists an interval $[a,b]$ containing 1 such that μ_{wu} is monotone and risk averse on $D[a,b]$. Under some auxiliary assumptions, μ_{wu} is well-behaved in this sense for all cdf's having finite mean and support in the positive real line. Those assumptions are:

$$
\begin{array}{lll}
\text{(i)} & \delta=0 & \text{and } \alpha<1, \qquad\text{or} \\
\text{(ii)} & \delta<0 & \text{and } 0<\alpha+\delta<1, \text{ or} \\
\text{(iii)} & 0<\delta<1 & \text{and } \alpha+\delta<0.
\end{array}
\tag{2.3.5}
$$

For weighted utility, indifference curves in the three-outcome probability simplex all emanate from a single point which is at infinity in the expected utility special case. The case of fanning out is shown in figure 1.1 and corresponds to $\delta<0$, but fanning in occurs if $\delta>0$ when the point of projection is on the north-east side of the triangle.

An alternative generalization of expected utility is obtained by choosing ϕ to satisfy:

$$\phi(x)=\begin{bmatrix}(x^\alpha-1)/\alpha, & x\leq 1 \\ A(x^\alpha-1)/\alpha, & x\geq 1\end{bmatrix} \tag{2.3.6}$$

where $\alpha<1$ and $0<A\leq 1$. This leads to the constant relative risk averse specialization of Gul's (1991) *disappointment averse* utility functions. The certainty equivalent μ_{da} is defined implicitly by:

$$\mu_{da}^{\alpha}(F)/\alpha = \int x^{\alpha}dF(x)/\alpha + (A^{-1}-1)\int_{x<\mu_{da}(F)} [(x^{\alpha}-\mu_{da}^{\alpha}(F))/\alpha]dF(x). \quad (2.3.7)$$

If $A=1$, one obtains the common homogeneous expected utility function. Smaller values for A reflect an aversion to disappointment in the following sense: refer to an outcome as disappointing if it is worse than expected in the sense of being smaller than the certainty equivalent of the lottery. When $A<1$ disappointing outcomes generate negative values for the second integral on the right side of (2.3.7), producing a smaller certainty equivalent value than if $A=1$.

The indifference map for μ_{da}, shown in figure 1.1, features two distinct sources of projection Q and Q' both of which recede to infinity as $A \to 1$. Indifference curves fan out in the lower part of the triangle and otherwise fan in. It is interesting to note in this regard that the behavioral evidence supporting fanning out is weaker in the upper triangle than in the lower region. (See Conlisk, 1989, for example.) Finally, with regard to the domain of μ_{da} note that ϕ is increasing and concave on $(0,\infty)$ and refer to footnote 4.

The weighted utility and disappointment averse functional forms have several properties in common. First, they have both been used to explain laboratory-based evidence against expected utility theory. Secondly, they both constitute single parameter extensions of the common constant relative risk averse expected utility specification. Moreover, they retain the tractability of the latter for empirical work (section 4.5) and thus allow some econometric evidence to be brought to bear upon the significance of the independence axiom or the fanning out property for market data. Finally, for each functional form there is a simple qualitative relation between the parameters and the degree of risk aversion. To elaborate, say that the certainty equivalent μ^* is *more risk averse than* μ if $\mu^*(F) \leq \mu(F)$ everywhere.[6] Then for μ_{wu} risk aversion decreases with α and δ and for μ_{da} it decreases with α and A.

However, the functions μ_{wu} and μ_{da} differ from one another in the way in which they evaluate small gambles. Since this difference will be of some importance in the subsequent discussion of asset pricing models, I move now to an examination of risk premia for small gambles.

2.4 First-order risk aversion

Let π be the risk premium associated with an actuarially fair gamble $t\tilde{\varepsilon}$ and initial non-stochastic wealth x. Thus the decision-maker is indifferent between the gamble $x + t\tilde{\varepsilon}$ and the sure prospect $x - \pi$. Following Segal and Spivak (1990), say that the utility function exhibits *first-order* (resp.

second-order) risk aversion if, for all x and for all $\tilde{\varepsilon}$ with non-zero and finite variance, π is of the order of t (resp. t^2) as $t \to 0$. In that sense, the risk premium for a small gamble is proportional to the standard deviation of the gamble under first-order risk aversion, rather than to its variance as in the more familiar case of second-order risk aversion. A useful graphical representation is possible in outcome space in the case of binary gambles. As portrayed in figure 1.2, given second-order risk aversion the indifference curve is tangent to the actuarially fair market line at certainty, reflecting risk neutrality to the first order. In the case of first-order risk aversion, there is a kink at the certainty line.

Expected utility functions generally exhibit second-order risk aversion. In the twice differentiable case, this is reflected by the famous Arrow–Pratt formula for the premium associated with a small gamble. More generally, kinks along the certainty line are rare in that an increasing and concave function can fail to be differentiable at only a countable number of points. In particular, second-order risk aversion applies if the von Neumann–Morgenstern index is homogeneous of any degree. More generally, the constant relative risk averse weighted utility function μ_{wu} also exhibits second-order risk aversion. On the other hand, the disappointment averse form is first-order risk averse if $A < 1$; the absolute slopes of the indifference curve in figure 1.2 on either side of the certainty point c are $A^{-1}p_1/p_2$ and Ap_1/p_2 where p_1 and p_2 are the probabilities of the two outcomes.

In terms of usefulness of first-order risk aversion, Segal and Spivak (1990) point out a number of empirical implications which seem consistent with observation. For example, there is a lesser tendency to diversify towards a risky asset while holding a safe asset.[7] More precisely, such diversification is optimal under second-order risk aversion if the mean excess return to the risky asset is positive, while a sufficiently large mean excess return is necessary for diversification given first-order risk aversion. More generally, only for second-order risk aversion is it true that any favorable bet is desirable at a sufficiently small scale, i.e., any favorable market line through the certainty point c in figure 1.2 lies above the indifference curve shown somewhere near c.

There is a sense in which kinks along the certainty line are typical for community utility functions in a multiperson model with incomplete markets. Consider two individuals with monotonic preferences and an aggregate gamble which is shared according to a given inefficient allocation rule. Let the representative aggregate gamble have equally likely outcomes e_1 and e_2. Individual preference orderings over individual gambles induce an ordering of aggregate gambles for each agent. Thus for each wealth level e, we can define $I(e)$ as the boundary of $\{(e_1, e_2)$: each individual prefers

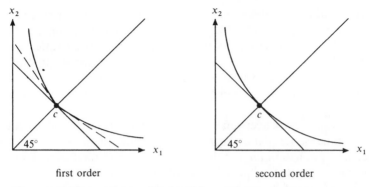

first order   second order

Figure 1.2 First and second-order risk aversion

(e_1, e_2) to $(e,e)\}$. Then $I(e)$ is a form of community indifference curve through (e,e), such that (under specified assumptions) points that lie above it are Pareto superior to (e,e). Because of the inefficiency of the given allocation rule, it will typically be the case that $I(e)$ will be kinked at certainty as in figure 1.2, even if both agents are expected utility maximizers. (This will be true, for example, if one agent receives the fraction $\alpha_i \varepsilon (0,1)$ of the aggregate endowment in state i, $i = 1,2$, $\alpha_1 \neq \alpha_2$, if the remaining endowments are allocated to the other agent and if their common von Neumann–Morgenstern index is not logarithmic.)

Finally, I would like to describe a separate argument, based on functional form flexibility, for being interested in first-order risk aversion. As has already been noted, for reasons of tractability the assumption of constant relative risk aversion is common in the asset pricing literature, particularly in empirical studies such as those cited in section 4. Thus let a decision-maker have constant relative risk aversion and suppose further that he is an expected utility maximizer. Following Kandel and Stambaugh (1990), consider how such an individual would evaluate binary symmetric gambles with outcomes $x \pm \varepsilon$. For concreteness, let $x = 75,000$. If relative risk aversion is 2, the individual would pay "only" 0.83 to avoid the "small" gamble corresponding to $\varepsilon = 250$, while the willingness to pay rises to 12.48 if relative risk aversion equals 30. But with the larger degree of risk aversion he would pay 1,091.17 to avoid the moderately sized gamble with $\varepsilon = 2,500$ and 23,790.52 to avoid the large gamble having $\varepsilon = 25,000$. The "reason" for these implications of the common homogeneous expected utility function is that it is risk neutral to the first order. Thus it can generate a plausible risk premium for small gambles only if the coefficient of relative risk aversion is so large that the implied risk premium for large gambles is unrealistically large. Epstein and Zin (1990b) show how a first-order risk averse utility function is better able to model "plausible" risk attitudes over a broad range of gamble sizes. For a numerical illustration, let $v(x) = \log x$ and $A = 5/6$. Then to avoid the three gambles above, the decision-maker would be willing to pay 22.50, 265.50, 6,373.57 respectively. Collectively, these certainty equivalent values seem more plausible on introspective grounds than those obtainable from any homogeneous expected utility function.

First-order risk aversion is of interest below in attempting to fit aggregate US time series data. That is because the smoothness of aggregate consumption data implies that the evaluation of small gambles is critical, while frequently the "plausibility" of a utility function is judged informally on the basis of its ranking of "real-life" moderate or large gambles. To develop this intuition, it is first necessary to consider the problem of intertemporal choice and the integration of the above atemporal theories into a temporal framework. Then their potential role in helping to explain time series data can be considered. Before proceeding with that principal thrust of this survey, however, I will mention briefly some results which have been derived using generalized utility functions in static choice settings.

2.5 Results

Many of the results which have been derived with the above utility functions in static choice settings are direct extensions of well-known propositions from expected utility theory. For the reasons indicated earlier through (2.2.3) for betweenness functions and (2.1.2)–(2.1.3) for "smooth" functions, many of the useful theoretical properties and behavioral implications of expected utility are preserved. These include the Arrow–Pratt characterization of comparative risk aversion across individuals (Machina, 1982b), the Ross characterization of comparative risk aversion (Machina and Nielsen, 1987), the Kihlstrom–Mirman characterization of comparative multivariate risk aversion (Karni, 1989), and the Rothschild–Stiglitz and Diamond–Stiglitz comparative statistics predictions regarding the effects of changing risk (Machina, 1989c and Chew and Nishimura, forthcoming).

Such robustness led Machina (1982b, p. 279) to state that even without the independence axiom "the implications and predictions of theoretical studies which use expected utility analysis typically will be valid, provided preferences are smooth." Subsequently, the displayed robustness of expected utility predictions has been interpreted as a defense of expected utility analysis; for example, see the finance textbook by Huang and Litzenberger (1988, p. 16). However, there are important examples where there is a payoff to considering a broader class of preferences. Sections 4 and 5 show that in dynamic choice settings, including an intertemporal asset pricing framework, generalizations of the expected utility model can be advantageous for both theoretical and empirical work.

In static choice models, advantageous applications of generalized utility functions have been made to address the Friedman–Savage observations on insurance and lotteries (Machina, 1982b), formulate and apply strong notions of declining risk aversion (Machina, 1982a and Epstein, 1985), provide an explanation of individual investor behavior in the stock market (Shefrin and Statman, 1984, 1985), clarify the foundations of axiomatic Nash bargaining theory (Rubinstein, Safra, and Thomson, 1990), and contribute to the theory of social choice and inequality measurement (Fishburn, 1988; Yaari, 1988; and Chew and Epstein, 1989b).

3   INTERTEMPORAL UTILITY

This section is concerned with utility functions defined on infinite horizon stochastic consumption programs, with a primary focus being on recursive utilities. When restricted to *timeless gambles*, i.e., those for which all uncertainty is resolved before further consumptions/savings decisions are made, recursive utility coincides with one of the atemporal certainty equivalent functions discussed in section 2. Even if the ranking of timeless gambles conforms with expected utility theory, however, the temporal resolution of consumption risk may matter. Hence recursive utility functions generally do not agree with intertemporal expected utility theory on the domain of consumption programs.

A primary motivation for this work is the desire to disentangle intertemporal substitution from risk aversion as explained in section 3.1. One way in which this has been accomplished, via recursive intertemporal utility functions, is described in section 3.3, after the important issue of intertemporal consistency has been clarified in section 3.2. Some normative issues are considered next.

3.1   Risk aversion and intertemporal substitution

In much of received capital theory it is assumed that the ranking of intertemporal stochastic consumption programs $\tilde{c} = (\tilde{c}_0, \tilde{c}_1, \ldots)$ may be represented by a function of the form:

$$V(\tilde{c}) = E_0 \sum_0^\infty \beta^t u(\tilde{c}_t). \tag{3.1.1}$$

Here $\tilde{c}_t$ denotes random scalar consumption at time t, $0 < \beta < 1$ is the rate of discount and E_0 denotes the expected value operator conditional upon period 0 information (see section 3.2 for some measure-theoretic details). A property of the felicity function u which is of particular interest is its curvature as measured by $-cu''(c)/u'(c)$. This elasticity is often referred to as the measure of relative risk aversion (with respect to consumption gambles in any single period). It is also inversely related to the willingness to substitute consumption across time. For example, in the case of the homogeneous specification:

$$u(c) = \begin{bmatrix} c^\rho/\rho, & \rho \neq 0 \\ \log c, & \rho = 0, \end{bmatrix} \tag{3.1.2}$$

the constant elasticity of intertemporal substitution σ equals $(1-\rho)^{-1}$, while the measure of risk aversion equals $(1-\rho)$. Thus a precise inverse relation between intertemporal substitutability and risk aversion is imposed a priori.

Such a restriction is unfortunate firstly because risk aversion and substitution correspond to two conceptually distinct aspects of preference – one concerns the attitude toward the variation in consumption across states of the world (at a given time) while the other is concerned with variations across time (in the absence of risk). Some economists might conjecture that the pairings (high risk aversion, low substitution) and (low risk aversion, high substitution) would be more common empirically than the other possibilities, i.e., either one strongly dislikes "change" or one does not. But the validity of the conjecture cannot be determined unless the a priori constraint can be relaxed. Besides, the standard functional form (3.1.1) goes even further since it imposes a quantitative relation between the measures of substitution and risk aversion.

A consequence of this inflexibility of the additive expected utility specification is that the effects of increased risk aversion in the model under study cannot be determined. A comparative statics analysis based upon a change in the curvature of the felicity function u does not admit an unambiguous interpretation since both intertemporal substitutability and risk aversion are changed in this way. Lucas (1978, p. 1441) points this out in attempting to understand the determinants of equilibrium asset prices. There are many other theoretical contexts in which the effects of greater risk aversion are of interest.

In the empirical literature also, this inflexibility has been of concern. As described further in section 4.1, expected utility, representative agent optimizing models have not performed well in explaining asset returns and aggregate consumption data and the noted inflexibility of the utility specification has been suggested as one possible reason. For example,

Grossman, Melino, and Shiller (1987) claim that the data suggest that two parameters are needed in place of the single parameter ρ. The situation is reminiscent of that prevailing in demand theory when the Cobb-Douglas or even CES functional forms were the dominant specifications for utility. The severe constraints imposed by these specifications on the pattern of substitution across commodities led to the adoption of more "flexible" forms such as the Generalized Leontief or Translog. Similarly, it would be desirable to have more flexible functional forms that are empirically tractable for the study of consumption and asset return data.

Move from considering risks that are confined to consumption in a single period to the more relevant case of multiperiod risks. For the reasons given by Kihlstrom and Mirman (1974, pp. 365–6), comparisons of risk aversion should be restricted to preferences with a given ordering of deterministic programs. Thus the best that can be hoped for is a class of utility functions for which it is possible to change the degree of risk aversion without affecting the preference ranking of deterministic consumption paths.[8] One possibility is to apply the Kihlstrom and Mirman (1974) approach to multicommodity risk aversion that retains the expected utility framework and considers ordinally equivalent von Neumann–Morgenstern indices. For example, let h be increasing and concave and define:

$$V^*(\tilde{c}) \equiv E_0 h\left[\sum_0^\infty \beta^t u(\tilde{c}_t)\right].$$

The functions V^* and V agree ordinally on deterministic programs but V^* is *more risk averse than* V in the sense that any gamble $(\tilde{c}_0, \tilde{c}_1, \dots)$ that would be rejected by V in favor of some deterministic program, would also be rejected by V^*. (This notion of comparative risk aversion for intertemporal utility functions is adopted throughout the paper; it is consistent with the definition of "more risk averse than" for certainty equivalents described in section 2.3, but see footnote 6.) Moreover, if h is strictly concave then there exist gambles that would be rejected by V^* but accepted by V.

However, this approach encounters serious difficulties in a temporal framework with discounting. Thus I feel that a separation of substitution from risk aversion that is likely to be useful in the applied contexts considered below is achievable only outside the expected utility framework.

To see the nature of the difficulties, consider an individual with the function V^* who arrives at period T and contemplates the remaining future. If previous consumption levels were $\bar{c}_0, \dots, \bar{c}_{T-1}$ and if tastes are not changing (see below for a definition), then the utility function for the remaining future is:

$$V^{*T} = E_T h \left[\sum_0^{T-1} \beta^t u(\bar{c}_t) + \sum_T^\infty \beta^t u(\tilde{c}_t) \right],$$

where E_T is the expected value operator conditional upon period T information. Suppose that h does not have constant absolute risk aversion (that case will be covered below), then risk attitudes at T depend implausibly upon the past in that the risk premium for a small gamble in c_T is affected more by a small change in $\bar{c}_0$ than by a corresponding change in $\bar{c}_{T-1}$, locally near $\bar{c}_0 = \ldots = \bar{c}_{T-1}$. This follows readily upon examination of the Arrow–Pratt absolute risk aversion measure for period T consumption risks (see Epstein and Zin, 1989, p. 951). Such implausible dependence upon the past is not limited to the case where the von Neumann–Morgenstern index is additively separable across time. For example, in a similar fashion one can show that it prevails also if the felicity function u in each period t depends upon finitely many lagged values of consumption, or if it is a function of c_t and z_t, where $z_t = \delta \sum_0^\infty (1-\delta)^i c_{t-i}$ and $1 - \delta < \beta$.

Further limitations of the Kihlstrom and Mirman approach emerge if we suppose that time begins at $-\infty$. Let $s_t = (\ldots, c_{t-2}, c_{t-1})$ denote the history at t. Suppose that the von Neumann–Morgenstern index $v(\cdot; s)$ represents the intertemporal ordering $\gtrsim_s$ at any time t if $s_t = s$. In such an environment it is both natural and common to assume that preferences are *stationary* – they can vary through time but only because the consumption history does.[9] It can be shown that the von Neumann–Morgenstern index $v(c_t, c_{t+1}, \ldots; s_t)$ implies stationarity of preferences if and only if there exist suitable functions A and B, $B > 0$, such that for all t:

$$v(c_t, c_{t+1}, \ldots; s_t) = A(c_t; s_t) + B(c_t; s_t) v(c_{t+1}, \ldots; s_{t+1}). \tag{3.1.3}$$

Suppose also that there is positive discounting along globally constant paths, in the sense that for all c:

$$B(c, s(c)) < 1,$$

where $s(c) \equiv (c, c, \ldots)$. Such discounting could be inferred from common continuity assumptions.

Now consider whether comparative risk-aversion analysis is possible within the class of stationary expected utility functions; that is, if v satisfies (3.1.3) and if $v^*(\cdot) = h(v(\cdot))$ for some increasing and strictly concave h, can v^* satisfy a similar relation? Assuming twice differentiability, an implication of (3.1.3) is that for $\tau > t$:

$$\frac{-v_{c_\tau c_\tau}}{v_{c_\tau}}(c_t,\ldots,c_\tau,\ldots;s_t)=\frac{-v_{c_\tau c_\tau}}{v_{c_\tau}}(c_\tau,c_{\tau+1},\ldots;s_\tau) \qquad (3.1.4)$$

and similarly for v^*. If the Arrow–Pratt measure for period τ risks is computed for $v^*(\cdot)=h(v(\cdot))$ via the chain rule, if the appropriate forms of (3.1.4) are applied, and if a constant path at level c is considered, then $B(c,s(c))=1$ is implied, contradicting positive discounting.

Though these arguments do not prove that the expected utility framework is inadequate in all temporal settings, I believe they do provide a prima facie case for exploring more general utility functions. Selden (1978) was the first to propose a generalization that achieves a separation between risk and certainty preferences. Some discussion of his approach appears in the next section.

3.2   Intertemporal consistency

A central and often misunderstood property of intertemporal utility functions is intertemporal consistency, which I now clarify following Johnsen and Donaldson (1985). This discussion will be useful also for understanding the work on sequential choice with non-expected utility preferences (section 5).

First define consumption programs somewhat more formally. Let (Ω,F,P) be a probability space and $\{F_t:t\geq 0\}$ an increasing filtration of sub σ-algebras of F that represents the information structure. A consumption program $(\tilde{c}_0,\tilde{c}_1,\ldots,\tilde{c}_t,\ldots)$ is a sequence of random variables such that each $\tilde{c}_t$ is F_t-measurable. Frequently, consumption will be restricted to be a positive scalar but occasionally a vector of consumption goods within each period will be allowed. When the tilde is deleted, the corresponding variable is deterministic. Give $T\geq 0$, an event $I_T\varepsilon F_T$ and a consumption program as above, $(\tilde{c}_T,\tilde{c}_{T+1},\ldots|I_T)$ denotes the consumption program whose i^{th} component, $i=0,1,\ldots$, is $\tilde{c}_{T+i}|I_T$, the restriction of $\tilde{c}_{T+i}$ to $I_T\subseteq\Omega$.

Consider a time $T>0$, an event $I_T\varepsilon F_T$ of positive probability and two programs $\tilde{c}=(\tilde{c}_0,\tilde{c}_1,\ldots,\tilde{c}_T,\tilde{c}_{T+1},\ldots)$ and $\tilde{c}'=(\tilde{c}_0,\tilde{c}_1,\ldots,\tilde{c}'_T,\tilde{c}'_{T+1},\ldots)$ that agree on $\Omega\backslash I_T$ (see figure 1.3 for a simple example). If $\tilde{c}$ is ranked better than $\tilde{c}'$ at time 0, then *intertemporal consistency* of preferences requires that the continuation $(\tilde{c}_T,\tilde{c}_{T+1},\ldots|I_T)$ be preferred to $(\tilde{c}'_T,\tilde{c}'_{T+1},\ldots|I_T)$ at (T,I_T). Otherwise, the choice made at 0 would with positive probability be reversed. Evidently, whether or not consistency prevails depends upon which utility function dictates choice at (T,I_T).

Consider the corresponding situation when there is no risk and let V be the utility function at time 0. The natural specification for the utility function at T, in the absence of changing tastes, is the restriction

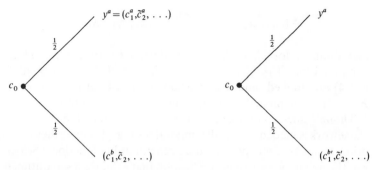

Figure 1.3 Two consumption programs

$V^T(\cdot) \equiv V(c_0, \dots, c_{T-1}, \cdot)$, where $c_0, \dots, c_{T-1}$ are the consumption levels actually experienced in the interim periods. Intertemporal consistency obtains trivially since:

$$V(c_0, \dots, c_{t-1}, c_T, \dots) > V(c_0, \dots, c_{T-1}, c_T', \dots)$$

and

$$V^T(c_T, \dots) \qquad\qquad > V^T(c_T', \dots)$$

are equivalent statements.

This argument has a counterpart in the case of risk. For example, consider the two programs represented by the probability trees in figure 1.3. The specification of utility at the lower node at $t=1$ that corresponds to constant tastes is the restriction $V^{1,b}(\cdot) = V(c_0, y^a, \cdot)$, where equality is modulo ordinal equivalence and where the notation introduced above has been modified in the obvious way. (In general, *constant tastes* will refer to the case where intermediate utility functions are defined as the obvious restrictions of the initial V. Otherwise, I'll speak of *changing tastes*.) Precisely as in the certainty case, the choice between the two consumption programs shown will be identical whether it is made at $t=0$ or at the lower node at $t=1$; that is, intertemporal consistency is ensured if tastes are constant.

It is noteworthy, however, that $V^{1,b}$ may depend through y^a on consumption alternatives that were *ex ante* possible at $t=0$ but which were never realized. Such dependence is not irrational, e.g., it could arise through feelings of disappointment or relief at the failure of some potential outcomes to be realized. Nevertheless, ruling out dependence on unrealized alternatives provides an intuitively appealing way to narrow down the class of admissible intertemporal utility functions and thereby add both predictive power and tractability. Therefore, say that V is *weakly recursive* if

$V^{1,b}$ above, and more generally the restrictions of V at each intermediate time and state, are independent (up to ordinal equivalence) of unrealized alternatives. This property is weaker than the separability across states exhibited by intertemporal expected utility functions. [10] Under weak recursivity, the constant tastes specification and the concomitant intertemporal consistency are uncontroversial.

With the above terminology in place, it may be useful at this point to refer to figure 1.4 which outlines three approaches to the specification of intertemporal utility functions along with their main features. Two approaches feature constant tastes and thus dynamic consistency. The route corresponding to the middle branch, that assumes weak recursivity, has been by far the most productive to date and will be the focus of the remaining discussion of intertemporal utility and applications.

Changing tastes, corresponding to the branch on the left, usually arises from the assumption that at each time T the individual acts as though time begins anew – she disregards past and unrealized parts of the consumption program and uses the original utility function V to evaluate the future, i.e., in figure 1.3, $V^{1,b}(\cdot)$ is ordinally equivalent to $V(\cdot)$. As first elucidated by Strotz (1956), changing tastes, or the intertemporal inconsistency of preferences, poses problems for the modeler in describing behavior. The notion of sophisticated planning (Pollak, 1968) may be adapted to the present context to describe a consistent course of action (Chew and Epstein, 1990), but this approach has not yet delivered any interesting new empirical implications for consumption and asset returns.

As a further illustration, consider the following functional form due to Selden and Stux (1978) which is a multiperiod extension of Selden (1978):

$$V(\tilde{c}_0, \tilde{c}_1, \ldots) = \sum_0^\infty \beta^t u(\hat{c}_t), \qquad \hat{c}_t \equiv v^{-1} E_0 v(\tilde{c}_t). \tag{3.2.1}$$

This functional structure is appealing on several grounds. It reflects a seemingly natural algorithm for computing utility – first, each random consumption level is replaced by its certainty equivalent and second, the intertemporal utility of the sequence of certainty equivalents is computed by the common additive function. Moreover, a separation between certainty and risk preferences is possible in that aversion to multiperiod risks can be increased by suitably changing v while keeping β and u fixed. In addition, note that the certainty equivalent could be redefined using a betweenness-conforming function, for example, in order to accommodate Allais-type behavior.

However, the Selden and Stux function violates weak recursivity. Thus the constant tastes assumption would necessarily impose dependence of

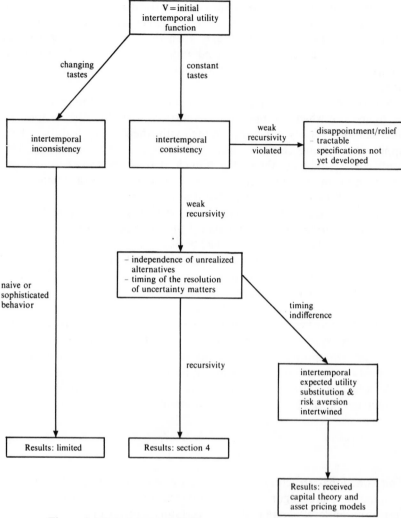

Figure 1.4 Intertemporal Utility

preferences upon unrealized alternatives. In particular, under constant tastes, period T preferences would continue to be based upon certainty equivalents $\hat{c}_t$ computed according to period 0 information. In fact, where the function has been employed (Attansio and Weber, 1989; Hall, 1985; Zin, 1987) it is assumed that the utility function at any time T is computed as above except that the expected values are computed conditional upon period T information, i.e., tastes change as risk resolves. Moreover, the hypothesis of naive behavior is adopted in these studies – inconsistencies are assumed to be ignored by the decision-maker who continually revises plans.

3.3   Recursive utility

Under weak recursivity and constant tastes, preferences are dynamically consistent and independent of unrealized alternatives. In the interest of still greater specificity and tractability, restrict utility further. Require that preferences be independent also of realized past consumption levels and further that V itself dictate choice at any intermediate time, e.g., in figure 1.3, require that $V(c_0, y^a, \cdot)$ be ordinally equivalent to $V(\cdot)$. Call V *recursive* if it satisfies these requirements.[11] Under recursivity, stationary dynamic programming techniques are applicable to specified optimization problems in such a way that state variables reflecting past consumption are unnecessary (see section 4).

Recursive utility functions may be constructed by means of the following recursive functional relation:[12]

$$V_t = W(c_t, \mu_t), \qquad t \geq 0, \tag{3.3.1}$$

where $V_t = V(c_t, \tilde{c}_{t+1}, \ldots | I_t)$ is intertemporal utility beginning at t, $\mu_t = \mu(\tilde{V}_{t+1} | I_t)$ is the certainty equivalent of the distribution of future utility $\tilde{V}_{t+1}$ conditional upon period t information, and W is called an *aggregator* function since it aggregates current consumption c_t with an index of the future to determine current utility. The function W is such that $W(c, \cdot)$ is increasing.

The certainty equivalent function μ assigns to each real valued random variable $\tilde{x}$ a certainty equivalent value. Require that μ be increasing in the sense of first-order stochastic dominance and that $\mu(\tilde{x}) = x$ if $\tilde{x}$ equals x with certainty. Then (3.3.1) restricted to deterministic consumption programs coincides with the Koopmans (1960) structure:

$$V_t = W(c_t, V_{t+1}), \qquad t \geq 0,$$

which generalizes the common intertemporally additive utility function (corresponding to $W(c, z) = u(c) + \beta z$) by endogenizing the discount factor $W_2(c_t, V_{t+1})$.

A broader special case applicable to stochastic programs arises if μ has the expected utility form:

$$\mu_{eu}(\tilde{x}) = h^{-1} E h(\tilde{x}), \tag{3.3.2}$$

for some increasing h. Then (3.3.1) corresponds to a special case of the structure studied in a finite horizon framework by Kreps and Porteus

(1978). A further parametric specialization (see (4.2.2) and (4.2.3) below) has been proposed and applied by several researchers (Epstein and Zin, 1989; Weil, 1990a; Farmer, 1990; Kocherlakota (1987)). Note that generally, even given (3.3.2), preferences over consumption programs do not conform with intertemporal expected utility theory since they are not indifferent to the way in which risk resolves over time (see section 3.4).

It is apparent from (3.3.1) how a degree of separation is achieved between substitution and risk aversion. Certainty preferences are determined by W alone. Thus only risk attitudes are affected by a change in μ. In particular, let $\mu^*(\tilde{x}) \leq \mu(\tilde{x})$ for all $\tilde{x}$ and suppose that V^* is the intertemporal utility function corresponding to W and μ^*. Then V^* is more risk averse than V (Chew and Epstein, 1990b).[13]

Though μ is applied to utility gambles, it is intimately related to the induced preference ordering over timeless wealth gambles. For example, if intertemporal utility is linearly homogeneous as is the case if W is linearly homogeneous and μ exhibits constant relative risk aversion, then $\mu(\tilde{x})$ represents the preference ordering over timeless wealth gambles $\tilde{x}$ (Epstein and Zin, 1989, p. 956). For another example, if μ satisfies betweenness then so does the ordering of timeless wealth gambles.[14] Moreover, choices amongst timeless gambles constitute the laboratory evidence regarding atemporal expected utility and its generalizations. Thus it is appropriate to use μ as the route through which these atemporal theories are integrated into the temporal framework and the possible links between the laboratory evidence and intertemporal market behavior are investigated. Any of the functions discussed in section 2 are admissible.

In the next section, I will offer a normative argument for restricting μ to the betweenness class. From a descriptive perspective, Duffie and Epstein (1991a) provide some insight into the specifications for μ that might prove useful. They formulate the continuous time counterpart to (3.3.1), under a smoothness assumption for μ. (Fréchet differentiability, with a sufficiently smooth local utility function, is sufficient to imply such smoothness.) In (3.3.1), μ is applied to the conditional distribution of $\tilde{V}_{t+1}$ given period t information. In a continuous environment, this conditional distribution has a small variance if the period corresponds to a short interval of time. Thus the only aspect of μ that is relevant is how it evaluates small gambles about certainty. The continuous time result is that smooth certainty equivalents are *observationally equivalent* to one another if they agree in their evaluations of infinitesimal gambles about certainty, and if only choices between Brownian consumption processes are observable. In particular, a Fréchet differentiable specification for μ, which satisfies the additional regularity conditions typically assumed by Machina (1982b), is empirically indistinguishable from an expected utility form (3.3.2) within the standard diffusion models of asset prices. The above suggests also that there may be little empirical gain in generalizing from μ_{e_u} to another smooth specification for μ if one is dealing with time series data, such as for aggregate U.S. consumption, having a small conditional variance. In terms of intertemporal utility functions, it is being suggested that there may be little advantage in generalizing from the structure studied by Kreps and Porteus (1978) to the class of recursive utility functions having a suitability differentiable certainty equivalent. The economic essence of the smoothness property that underlies the noted observational equivalence appears to be that of second-order risk aversion, but that remains a conjecture.

3.4   Some normative considerations

The next section will demonstrate the tractability and power of recursive utility for addressing some central questions in macroeconomics and finance. Here I examine further the rationality of recursive utility, which examination was started above with the description of its underlying axioms. I do this to assuage concerns that recursive utility may have logical implications for behavior that are obviously contradicted by observation and also to describe a normative argument for restricting the class of recursive utility functions.

Recursive utility functions are generally not indifferent to the way in which risk resolves over time in the sense of Kreps and Porteus (1978).[15] Given the expected utility certainty equivalent (3.3.2), define $U_t(\cdot) \equiv h(V_t(\cdot))$ and the new aggregator $\hat{W}(c,\cdot) \equiv hW(c,h^{-1}(\cdot))$. Then (see footnote 13), $U_t = \hat{W}(c_t, E_t \tilde{U}_{t+1})$, from which it follows that late (early) resolution is preferred if $\hat{W}(c,\cdot)$ is concave (convex). (This is readily verified for the consumption programs in figure 1.5; for the general case see Kreps and Porteus, 1978.) Thus recursive utilities generally distinguish between the consumption programs in figure 1.5, unlike the case for (3.1.1) or for any other intertemporal expected utility function. Moreover, such indifference to timing is exactly the property of preference which is being dropped in generalizing from expected to recursive (or weakly recursive) utility functions (Kreps and Porteus, 1978; Chew and Epstein, 1989a, 1991), as indicated in figure 1.4.[16]

Introspection suggests that one might care about the temporal resolution of risk even in the absence of any implications for planning. For example, early resolution might be preferred by a "nervous" or "edgy" person who does not like living with risk, while an affinity for surprises could lead to the opposite preference. An individual might also prefer to defer resolution in order to continue to "consume" the hope for or illusion of a favorable outcome for a risky prospect. Kreps and Porteus (1978) offer other

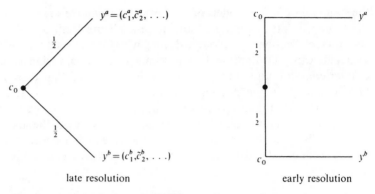

late resolution   early resolution

Figure 1.5 Temporal resolution

supporting arguments. Supporting anecdotal evidence exists, as does some laboratory-based evidence (Cook, 1989). Unfortunately, casual observation of market behavior is not informative. Market choices generally reflect both the planning advantages of early resolution, e.g., of income risk, and the psychic costs or benefits of the corresponding early resolution of consumption risk which are the focus here.

Suppose that the risk to be resolved is which of two indifferent alternatives will be realized, e.g., $V(y^a) = V(y^b)$ in figure 1.5. Then the psychic costs or benefits of early resolution are less apparent and timing indifference is plausible. Say that utility satisfies *quasi-timing indifference* if in all such circumstances there is indifference to the timing of resolution. This reasonable property restricts the class of recursive utility functions to those for which the certainty equivalent μ in (3.3.1) satisfies betweenness (Chew and Epstein, 1989a, 1991). (See section 4.5 for a separate argument in support of betweenness based upon empirical tractability.)

To this point the discussion has dealt with individual preferences and behavior and thus, ideally, individual level data should be used to investigate and apply recursive (or other) utility functions empirically. However, since aggregate data are much more readily available and also call for "explanation," the applications in the coming section are confined to them. Consequently, the utility function in question is hypothesized for a representative agent. Since the latter is fictional, the relevance of rationality and the normative properties of various functional form specifications becomes clouded. The existence of the representative agent and her utility should ideally be deduced via an appropriate aggregation theorem. In principle, the derived utility function need not possess all of the rationality properties considered important at the level of the individual. However, aggregation can be justified theoretically only under stringent conditions and, moreover, tractability is a serious concern. For example, recall the complete markets justification for aggregation (Constantinides, 1982) and suppose that individual utility functions are recursive. The representative agent's function V is an optimized weighted average of the individual functions $V^1, \ldots, V^N$; more precisely, for some utility weights $\lambda_1, \ldots, \lambda_N$:

$$V(\tilde{c}_0, \tilde{c}_1, \ldots) = \max \left\{ \sum_{i=1}^{N} \lambda_i V^i(\tilde{c}_0^i, \tilde{c}_1^i, \ldots) : \sum_{i=1}^{N} \tilde{c}_t^i \leq \tilde{c}_t \forall t \right\}.$$

Then V is generally not even weakly recursive. Moreover, the representative agent "works" in the complete markets case only if constant tastes are assumed for her. But then the dependence of preferences on unrealized alternatives might render the model untractable.

We are left with the familiar "excuse" for representative agent modeling, namely the current lack of a superior alternative. Moreover, it is useful to treat the representative agent as though she were real, since that allows us to organize observations in terms of familiar microeconomic principles and notions.

4   CONSUMPTION AND ASSET RETURNS

This section describes applications of recursive utility to both theoretical and empirical issues in macroeconomics and finance dealing with aggregate consumption and asset pricing. It begins by considering the consumption/savings and portfolio behavior of an agent having a recursive utility function and operating in a standard competitive and stationary environment. The Euler equations for the optimal intertemporal plan serve as the basis for all of the results below. When the agent is taken to be a representative agent for the economy, the Euler equations define relations between aggregate consumption and rates of return that must hold in a rational expectations equilibrium. In particular, they determine the equilibrium prices of the assets. Before describing the applications of recursive utility to the issues that have been of concern in this literature, the first subsection provides as background a brief review of the relevant results and limitations of the standard expected utility model.

4.1   Background

In the standard model with intertemporal expected utility function (3.1.1)–(3.1.2), the Euler equations take the following familiar form:

$$\beta E_t \left[\left[\frac{\tilde{c}_{t+1}}{c_t} \right]^{\rho - 1} \tilde{r}_{i,t+1} \right] = 1, \qquad i = 1, \ldots, N, \tag{4.1.1}$$

where $\tilde{r}_{i,t+1}$ is the gross real return to the ith asset (see Lucas, 1978, for example). These equations generalize to the stochastic context the equality of the marginal rate of substitution and marginal rate of transformation that characterizes optimal consumption/savings behavior under certainty. Subtracting the ith equation from the jth leads to the following relations that characterize an optimal portfolio allocation:

$$E_t\left[\left[\frac{\tilde{c}_{t+1}}{c_t}\right]^{\rho-1}(\tilde{r}_{i,t+1}-\tilde{r}_{j,t+1})\right]=0, \qquad i,j=1,\ldots,N.$$

If, for expository convenience, the first asset is taken to be riskless, then one obtains a form of Breeden's (1979) consumption-based restrictions on asset returns, whereby:

$$E_t[\tilde{r}_{i,t+1}-r_{1,t+1}]=K_t\text{cov}_t\left[-\left[\frac{\tilde{c}_{t+1}}{c_t}\right]^{\rho-1},\tilde{r}_{i,t+1}\right], \qquad (4.1.2)$$

where $K_t^{-1}\equiv E_t[\tilde{c}_{t+1}/c_t)^{\rho-1}]$ and $\text{cov}_t(\cdot,\cdot)$ is the covariance conditional upon period t information. Thus, conditional on available information, the mean excess return to each asset is proportional to its systematic risk, which in turn is measured by the covariance of its return with an increasing function of the consumption growth rate.

Unfortunately, (4.1.1) and (4.1.2) do not accurately represent the relation between asset returns and aggregate per capita consumption observed in the U.S. For example, when confronted with time series data, (4.1.1) has been rejected statistically by Hansen and Singleton (1983) and Grossman, Melino and Shiller (1987) and on less formal grounds by Grossman and Shiller (1981) and Mehra and Prescott (1985). Furthermore, Mankiw and Shapiro (1986) have shown that, contrary to (4.1.2), cross-sectional mean returns are related much more closely to covariances with the return on the aggregate stock market than to covariances with aggregate consumption.

To a large degree, the research on intertemporal non-expected utility functions has been motivated by the desire to see whether the above empirical shortcomings can be ameliorated by a more general specification of utility for the representative agent.[17] Thus in this section the standard model is modified by specifying that the utility function of the agent is recursive. A consequence is that the associated Euler equations generalize (4.1.1) and take the form:

$$E_t[\text{IMRS}_{t,t+1}\cdot\tilde{r}_{i,t+1}]=1, \qquad i=1,\ldots,N, \qquad (4.1.3)$$

where $\text{IMRS}_{t,t+1}$ is a suitably defined intertemporal marginal rate of substitution between consumption at t and $t+1$ (see Hansen and Jagannathan, 1991 for a general formulation of models of asset returns in terms of such marginal rates of substitution). For several models described below, the associated IMRS depends on more than just aggregate consumption. However, it can be computed from data given a parametrization of intertemporal utility and thus (4.1.3) is empirically tractable. Moreover, (4.1.2) may be adjusted to reflect the corresponding new model of the cross-sectional variation of excess mean returns given by:

$$E_t[\tilde{r}_{i,t+1} - r_{1,t+1}] = K_t^* \text{cov}_t[-\text{IMRS}_{t,t+1}, \tilde{r}_{i,t+1}], \qquad (4.1.4)$$

where $K_t^{*-1} \equiv E_t[\text{IMRS}_{t,t+1}]$.

As discussed in section 3, there are also theoretical considerations that motivate generalizations of intertemporal expected utility theory. Below (see section 4.7) the theoretical gains from the disentanglement of substitution and risk aversion are demonstrated in the context of a Lucas (1978) style general equilibrium endowment economy. Under the expected utility specification (3.1.1)–(3.1.2), the ex-dividend price P_t of an asset paying dividend $\tilde{d}_t$ in each period t, can be derived by substituting $(\tilde{P}_{t+1} + \tilde{d}_{t+1})/P_t$ for $\tilde{r}_{i,t+1}$ in (4.1.1), yielding the recursive relation:

$$P_t = \beta E_t \left[\left[\frac{\tilde{c}_{t+1}}{c_t} \right]^{\rho-1} (\tilde{P}_{t+1} + \tilde{d}_{t+1}) \right]. \qquad (4.1.5)$$

Recursive substitution and imposition of a transversality condition deliver the formula:

$$P_t = E_t \sum_{s=1}^{\infty} \beta^s (\tilde{c}_{t+s}/c_t)^{\rho-1} \tilde{d}_{t+s},$$

whereby the price is the expected value of the discounted sum of future dividends. Comparative statics analysis of these formulae typically have ambiguous interpretations because of the dual role played by the parameter ρ, thus preventing a clear understanding of the determinants of equilibrium asset prices. In contrast, for recursive utility, (4.1.3) produces the following generalization of (4.1.5):

$$P_t = E_t[\text{IMRS}_{t,t+1}(\tilde{P}_{t+1} + \tilde{d}_{t+1})]. \qquad (4.1.6)$$

For some parametric forms of recursive utility, the marginal rate of substitution involves separate substitution and risk aversion parameters, thus permitting more illuminating comparative statics analyses to be conducted.

The standard utility function (3.1.1) is separable across time and across states of the world. The results in the coming subsection are due primarily to the relaxation of state separability, though time non-separability underlies the restriction (4.6.3) on asset returns. It should be noted that time non-separability due to habits or the durability of goods has been examined extensively in the empirical macro/finance literature (see Singleton, 1990; Constantinides, 1990; Heaton, 1991, for example). The utility functions used in these studies extend (3.1.1) in that the felicity function in period t depends also on lagged values of consumption; consequently they are weakly recursive but not recursive. A separation between substitution and risk aversion is *not* delivered in this way (see footnote 9 and the surrounding discussion in section 3.1), nor are any of the new asset pricing models described below. Of course, it is an empirical question, that is still unresolved, as to whether time or state non-separability is more useful in explaining aggregate data. Neither is it clear yet which form of time non-separability is most useful.

4.2   Euler equations

Suppose there are N assets with the vector of gross real returns $\tilde{r}_{t+1} = (\tilde{r}_{1,t+1}, \ldots, \tilde{r}_{N,t+1})$ over the interval $[t, t+1]$. Denote the fraction of total real wealth held in the jth asset in period t by $\omega_{j,t}$ and the N-vector of portfolio weights by ω_t. Let wealth evolve according to the process:

$$\tilde{x}_{t+1} = (x_t - c_t)\omega_t'\tilde{r}_{t+1}, \qquad x_0 > 0 \text{ given.} \tag{4.2.1}$$

Denote by $J(I,x)$ the value of the agent's intertemporal optimization problem beginning with wealth x and information variable I used to predict future rates of return. Suppose the recursive utility function is represented by the aggregator W and certainty equivalent function μ. The latter is taken in the beginning of this section to be of the expected utility form (3.3.2). Then J should solve the Bellman equation:

$$J(I_t, x_t) = \text{Max } W(c_t, h^{-1}E_t[hJ(\tilde{I}_{t+1}, (x_t - c_t)\omega_t'\tilde{r}_{t+1})]), \tag{4.2.2}$$

because of the recursive relation (3.3.1).[18] If J, W, and h are suitably smooth, then the envelope theorem and first-order conditions for the Bellman equation can be used to derive Euler equations for the intertemporal optimization problem. Such a straightforward attack at the above level of generality proves unsatisfactory, however, since the Euler equations (more particularly, the appropriate IMRS from (4.1.3)), invariably involve the unobservable value function. To generate empirically useful results, the utility function must be restricted further.

One powerful assumption is that intertemporal utility is homothetic, i.e., the common rescaling of two consumption programs does not affect their relative ranking. (An alternative assumption is described in the context of the multicommodity asset pricing model below.) Duffie and Epstein (1991b) derive the implications of homotheticity in a continuous-time setting. Here, to simplify and facilitate interpretation, specialize further to the following convenient functional forms:

$$W(c,z) = \begin{cases} ((1-\beta)c^\rho + \beta z^\rho)^{1/\rho} & , \quad 0 \neq \rho < 1 \\ \exp((1-\beta)\log c + \beta \log z), & \rho = 0, \end{cases} \tag{4.2.3}$$

$$\mu(\tilde{x}) = \begin{cases} (E\tilde{x}^\alpha)^{1/\alpha} & , \quad 0 \neq \alpha < 1 \\ \exp(E\log \tilde{x}), & \alpha = 0. \end{cases} \tag{4.2.4}$$

The utility of deterministic programs is evaluated by a CES function with elasticity of substitution $\sigma = (1-\rho)^{-1}$ and rate of time preference $\beta^{-1} - 1 > 0$. Aversion toward intertemporal consumption gambles increases as α falls. In addition, $1 - \alpha$ equals the degree of relative risk aversion with respect to timeless wealth gambles (see footnote 14 and the discussion leading to it). The common specification (3.1.1)–(3.1.2) corresponds to the special case $\alpha = \rho$.

If $\alpha > (<)\rho$, then a preference for late (early) resolution of consumption risk is implied (section 3.4). However, even if there is a psychic cost associated with the early resolution of consumption risk, early resolution of rate of return risks provides planning advantages that could outweigh the associated psychic costs. As an example where closed-form solutions are possible, consider the case of a single asset ($N = 1$) with rates of return $\tilde{r}_t$ that are identically and independently distributed like $\tilde{r}$ over time. The value function for the associated planning problem coincides with that implied by the deterministic problem where the rate of return is constant at the certainty equivalent level $(E\tilde{r}^\alpha)^{1/\alpha}$. Thus maximum intertemporal utility is $x_0(1-\beta)^{1/\rho}[1 - \beta^{1/(1-\rho)}(E\tilde{r}^\alpha)^{\rho/\alpha(1-\rho)}]^{(\rho-1)/\rho}$. Next suppose that the entire sequence of rates of return $(r_1,\ldots,r_t,\ldots)$ is revealed at $t=0$ before any consumption decisions are made and evaluate maximum utility from the perspective of an instant preceding 0 when the sequence that will be revealed is not yet known. Maximum utility in this case of early resolution is $x_0(1-\beta)^{1/\rho}\left[E\left(\sum_0^\infty \beta^{t/(1-\rho)}(\tilde{r}_1\tilde{r}_2 \ldots \tilde{r}_{t+1})^{\rho/(1-\rho)} \right)^{\alpha(1-\rho)/\rho} \right]^{1/\alpha}$.

It follows that the early resolution of rate of return risk is preferred if and only if $\rho(1+\alpha) \geq \alpha$, or equivalently, $\sigma + (1-\alpha) \geq 2$. This is compatible with the condition $\sigma(1-\alpha) < 1$, which corresponds to a preference for the late resolution of consumption risk.

With the above functional forms, the Euler equations for $\rho \neq 0$ are:

$$E_t\left[\left(\beta^{1/\rho}\left[\frac{\tilde{c}_{t+1}}{c_t} \right]^{(\rho-1)/\rho} \tilde{M}_{t+1}^{1/\rho} \right)^\alpha - 1 \right] \bigg/ \alpha = 0 \text{ and}$$

$$E_t\left[\left[\frac{\tilde{c}_{t+1}}{c_t} \right]^{\alpha(\rho-1)/\rho} \tilde{M}_{t+1}^{(\alpha-\rho)/\rho}(\tilde{r}_{i,t+1} - \tilde{r}_{j,t+1}) \right] = 0 \qquad i,j = ,\ldots,N, \tag{4.2.5}$$

where $\tilde{M}_{t+1} \equiv \omega_t^{*'} \tilde{r}_{t+1}$ is the return to the optimal portfolio and where $(x^\alpha - 1)/\alpha$ stands for $\log x$ when $\alpha = 0$.[19] The familiar Euler equations (4.1.1), analysed by Hansen and Singleton (1983) for example, are obtained if $\alpha = \rho$. A corresponding set of Euler equations involving only "observables," is not available without additional assumptions if $\rho = 0$ and $\alpha \neq 0$.[20] Henceforth, $\rho \neq 0$ is assumed unless explicitly stated otherwise. Note that, if $\alpha \neq 0$, the Euler equations can be rewritten in the equivalent and sometimes more convenient form:

$$E_t \left[\beta^{\alpha/\rho} \left[\frac{\tilde{c}_{t+1}}{c_t} \right]^{\alpha(\rho-1)/\rho} \tilde{M}_{t+1}^{(\alpha-\rho)/\alpha} \tilde{r}_{i,t+1} \right] = 1, \qquad i = 1, \ldots, N, \quad (4.2.5')$$

which is the special case of (4.1.3) in which:

$$\text{IMRS}_{t,t+1} = \beta^{\alpha/\rho} (\tilde{c}_{t+1}/c_t)^{\alpha(\rho-1)/\rho} \tilde{M}_{t+1}^{(\alpha-\rho)/\rho}. \tag{4.2.6}$$

Since the utility function is homothetic, if it is assumed that it is also common to each agent in the economy and if common information is also assumed, then demand aggregation in the sense of Gorman (1953) holds. In this way theoretical justification can be provided for the existence of a representative agent and for the application of (4.2.5) to aggregate data.

Some applications of the above Euler equations will now be described.

4.3   Consumption

The study of consumption in the rational expectations school of macroeconomics is commonly based on the Euler equation characterization of optimal consumption and empirical tests of it. Hall's (1978) random walk hypothesis and its generalizations (Hall, 1988; Hansen and Singleton, 1983) have assumed expected utility function specifications. The resulting inability to separately identify substitution and risk aversion poses a problem since, as Hall (1988, p. 339) notes, the magnitude of the intertemporal substitution effect of a change in the expected real interest "is one of the central questions of macroeconomics." Identification is not an issue if it is believed that the elasticity of substitution σ and the degree of relative risk aversion are in fact reciprocals of one another as in the conventional homogeneous specification. But then estimates of σ near 0 such as found by Hall imply an incredibly large degree of risk aversion.

Epstein and Zin (1991a) show that the Euler equations (4.2.5) identify both α and ρ when the Generalized Method of Moments (GMM) estimation procedure is applied to monthly post-war US data on NYSE stock returns, treasury bills, and various measures of per capital consumption expenditures. The performance of the model varies with the choice of instrumental variables and also with the measure adopted for consumption. For some choices the expected utility restriction $\alpha = \rho$ is rejected and the general model cannot be rejected. For a study based on Israeli data see Bufman and Leiderman (1990), who report results favorable to the recursive utility model.

Hall and other researchers have based their empirical analyses on a linear relation between consumption growth and individual asset returns and have interpreted the parameter multiplying the asset return as σ. Qualified justification for such an analysis can be provided as follows (see also Attanasio and Weber, 1989): define $\tilde{z}_{t+1} \equiv \beta^{1/\rho}(\tilde{c}_{t+1}/c_t)^{(\rho-1)/\rho}\tilde{M}_{t+1}^{1/\rho}$. After taking logarithms, the first Euler equation above can be transformed into the relation:

$$\log(\tilde{c}_{t+1}/c_t) = k + \sigma \log \tilde{M}_{t+1} + (1-\sigma)E_t \log \tilde{z}_{t+1} + \tilde{\varepsilon}_{t+1},$$

where k is a constant, $E_t[(\tilde{z}_{t+1}^\alpha - 1)/\alpha] = 0$ and $E_t \tilde{\varepsilon}_{t+1} = 0$. If $E_t \log \tilde{z}_{t+1}$ is constant through time, then the desired linear regression equation is obtained and σ can be estimated consistently by instrumental variables techniques. A similar equation, where the return to any single asset replaces the market return on the right side, can be obtained by analogous arguments.

It is intuitive that the relationship between consumption growth and the real interest rate is governed by the intertemporal substitution aspect of preferences. Intuition may not be clear or correct in slightly modified models, however. Consider the framework of Hall (1978) where the return to saving r is deterministic and constant and suppose that there is an exogenous stochastic stream of payments to inelastically supplied labour. The conventional Euler equation is:

$$\beta r E_t[u'(\tilde{c}_{t+1})/u'(c_t)] = 1. \tag{4.3.1}$$

Does the curvature of u represent intertemporal substitution or risk aversion? Under a functional form specification for recursive utility, based on exponential rather than power functions as in (4.2.3)–(4.2.4), Epstein (1991) points out that an appropriate form of (4.3.1) applies and that it is risk aversion, rather than substitution, that is embodied in u.

Weil (1990c) uses yet another parametric specification of recursive utility to study behavior given a constant interest rate and undiversifiable labor income risk. He shows that a CES form for the aggregator W and a constant absolute risk aversion form for μ are particularly well suited to the analysis of the determinants of precautionary savings.

Finally, it is worth noting a difficulty with the implementation of the extended Euler equations or a linear regression equation derived from them – the measurement of consumption. In the conventional model, the use of any component of consumption, such as non-durables consumption for example, can be justified theoretically by the assumption that the intertemporal von Neumann–Morgenstern index is additively separable between the selected component and the rest of consumption. A comparable argument does not exist in the recursive utility model, however, and the use of a comprehensive measure of consumption is required by the theory.

4.4   A two-factor asset pricing model

The two principal models in finance for explaining excess mean returns are the consumption-based CAPM of Lucas (1978) and Breeden (1979) and the market-portfolio-based CAPM. In one systematic risk of an asset is measured by covariance of its return with consumption growth and in the other by covariance with the return to the market. It is evident from the portfolio allocation equation in (4.2.5) (see also (4.1.4) and (4.2.6)) that for recursive utility functions, both consumption and the market return enter into the covariance that defines systematic risk. Roughly speaking, $\tilde{c}_{t+1}$ and $\tilde{M}_{t+1}$ both enter into the marginal rate of substitution in (4.2.6) because the marginal rate of substitution between c_t and consumption in a specified state I_{t+1} at $t+1$ depends upon both consumption levels and, given the non-separabilities present when $\alpha \neq \rho$, upon future intertemporal utility $J(I_{t+1}, x_{t+1})$. The market return acts as a proxy for J.

If there is a riskless asset with return r_{t+1}^f over the interval $[t, t+1]$, then for each risky asset:

$$
E_t[\tilde{r}_{i,t+1} - r_{t+1}^f] = \frac{\alpha(1-\rho)}{\rho} \text{cov}_t\left(\frac{\tilde{c}_{t+1}}{c_t}, \tilde{r}_{i,t+1}\right)
$$
$$
+ \frac{\rho - \alpha}{\rho} \text{cov}_t(\tilde{M}_{t+1}, \tilde{r}_{i,t+1}). \tag{4.4.1}
$$

Duffie and Epstein (1991b) derive the counterpart of this equation in a continuous time framework. Alternatively, the equation can be derived from (4.1.2) as an approximation via a joint lognormality assumption for consumption growth and asset returns (Epstein and Zin, 1991a); in that case, one half of the conditional variance of $\tilde{r}_{i,t+1}$ must be subtracted from the right side. The consumption-CAPM follows if $\alpha = \rho$, but in general a linear combination of the two common asset pricing models obtains. For empirical evidence regarding this 2-factor model based on a cross-sectional analysis of various securities, see Mankiw and Shapiro (1986) and Giovannini and Weil (1989); for evidence that considers time series data as well, see Bollerslev, Engle, and Wooldridge (1988), Epstein and Zin

(1991a), and Bufman and Leiderman (1990). Overall the evidence suggests that the market covariance is the more important, but that both factors are statistically significant.

Motivated by the problems in measuring consumption, Campbell (1990) adopts auxiliary assumptions in order to substitute out consumption from the asset pricing model. In his model, covariance with consumption growth is replaced by the covariance with news about the discounted value of all future market returns.

4.5   Non-expected utility for timeless wealth gambles

To this point the results described have been based mostly on the expected utility certainty equivalent (4.2.4). Since, as discussed in section 3.3, the certainty equivalent μ represents the ranking of timeless wealth gambles and since choices amongst such gambles constitute the laboratory evidence regarding atemporal expected utility theory, it is of interest to determine the theoretical and/or empirical gains from admitting more general specifications for μ. In particular, can such generalizations improve the explanation of the consumption and asset return data that have been studied and do the market data and laboratory evidence indicate similar deviations from an expected utility form for μ?

These questions can be addressed by taking μ to be a betweenness-conforming function (sections 2.2 and 2.3). Suppose further that μ has constant relative risk aversion and is represented by the function ϕ as in (2.3.2). If the CES form for the aggregator is also retained, then Epstein and Zin (1989) show that the Euler equations (4.2.5) generalize to:

$$E_t\left[\phi\left(\beta^{1/\rho}\left[\frac{\tilde{c}_{t+1}}{c_t}\right]^{(\rho-1)/\rho}\tilde{M}_{t+1}^{1/\rho}\right)\right]=0 \quad \text{and} \quad (4.5.1)$$

$$E_t\left[\phi'\left(\beta^{1/\rho}\left[\frac{\tilde{c}_{t+1}}{c_t}\right]^{(\rho-1)/\rho}\tilde{M}_{t+1}^{1/\rho}\right)\cdot\left[\frac{\tilde{c}_{t+1}}{\tilde{M}_{t+1}}\right]^{(\rho-1)/\rho}\cdot(\tilde{r}_{i,t+1}-\tilde{r}_{j,t+1})\right]=0.$$

It is noteworthy that these equations are as tractable as the earlier ones; for example, generalized method of moments estimation is applicable once a functional form is specified for ϕ. This feature seems to be due to the considerable affinity already noted between expected utility and betweenness orderings. While other suitably differentiable specifications for μ can generate first-order conditions for the portfolio allocation, those equations are much less attractive for estimation purposes since they generally require functional form assumptions about the distribution describing consumption and asset returns.[21]

Two convenient parametric forms for ϕ, corresponding to weighted utility and disappointment averse utility, are given by (2.3.3) and (2.3.6).[22] Each defines a single parameter extension of the expected utility certainty equivalent (4.2.4), but they differ from one another in that only disappointment averse utility satisfies first-order risk aversion (section 2.4). In light of the observational equivalence result of Duffie and Epstein (1991a) described in section 3.3 and the smoothness of US aggregate consumption data, one might therefore expect that the generalization to weighted utility would be of little help in explaining US monthly data, but that the disappointment averse functional form could move the theory significantly closer to observed behavior. Preliminary evidence reported by Epstein and Zin (1991b) supports these conjectures.

It is conceivable that the weighted utility form would prove more valuable in explaining data from more volatile economies. In any case, it is evident that a number of new functional forms have been added to the tool kit of the empiricist interested in fitting consumption and asset return data.

Another demonstration of the usefulness of a non-expected utility certainty equivalent is provided by the discussion of the equity premium puzzle in section 4.7.

4.6   Multicommodity asset pricing

The Euler equations (4.2.5) were generalized above by adopting more general specifications for the certainty equivalent. Now consider an alternative generalization which has the following motivation: according to the wealth accumulation equation (4.2.1), all income is investment income. Thus the agent's portfolio presumably includes human capital and other non-traded assets, which renders the return to the aggregate portfolio $\tilde{M}_{t+1}$ unobservable, i.e., the Roll (1977) critique of CAPM is relevant here. (In practice, the market return is sometimes measured as an index of the returns to stocks traded on the New York Stock Exchange.)

Epstein and Zin (1990b) in discrete time and Duffie and Epstein (1991b) in continuous time describe a model in which endogenous labor supply may be incorporated and in which returns to non-traded assets are not needed for empirical implementation. Reconsider a recursive utility function with general aggregator W and expected utility certainty equivalent μ_{eu} from (3.3.2), but let consumption at time t be a vector $(c_t, q_t) \varepsilon R_+^1 \times R_+^L, L \geq 1$. The first good is the numeraire; the remaining relative prices are denoted p_t. One of the components of q_t could represent leisure and the corresponding component of p_t would be the real wage rate. The real wealth accumulation equation is:

$$\tilde{x}_{t+1} = (x_t - c_t - p_t' q_t + y_t) \omega_t' \tilde{r}_{t+1},$$

where y_t represents exogenous income which includes the value of skill and time endowments, and where ω_t and $\tilde{r}_{t+1}$ refer to traded assets only.

As mentioned earlier, recursive utility models generate first-order conditions that may be difficult to implement empirically because they contain the unobserved value function. But in a multicommodity context that unobservability may be overcome as follows: an intratemporal optimality condition for the agent is:

$$\frac{W_{q_l}}{W_c}(c_t,q_t,\mu_t) = P_{l,t}, l=1,\ldots,L, \qquad (4.6.1)$$

where μ_t is the certainty equivalent of the $(t+1)$ period value function given period t information. The ratio on the left is the marginal rate of substitution between c_t and $q_{l,t}$. In the standard specification (replacing c by (c,q) in (3.1.1)), this marginal rate of substitution is independent of μ_t since (c_t,q_t) is weakly separable from consumption at all times $t' \neq t$. Consider the opposite assumption in the form of the following: there exists at least one $l\varepsilon\{1,\ldots,L\}$ such that for each (c,q) the function:

$$\Psi(\cdot) \equiv \frac{W_{q_l}}{W_c}(c,q,\cdot)$$

is strictly monotonic and hence invertible. In that case refer to q_l as being *invertibly non-separable from c*. Given such non-separability, μ_t can be uniquely recovered from the lth intratemporal equation in (4.6.1).

Epstein and Zin (1990b) show how this permits the derivation of Euler equations of the form:

$$E_t[f(z_t,\tilde{z}_{t+1})\tilde{r}_{i,t+1}] = 1, \qquad i=1,\ldots,N, \qquad (4.6.2)$$

for some function f derived from W and μ, where $z_t \equiv (c_t,q_t,p_{l,t})$. In continuous time, Duffie and Epstein derive the counterpart of the following model of excess mean returns:

$$E_t[\tilde{r}_{i,t+1} - r^f_{t+1}] = K_c(t)\text{cov}_t\left(\frac{\tilde{c}_{t+1}}{c_t},\tilde{r}_{i,t+1}\right) + \sum_{k=1}^{L} K_k(t)\text{cov}_t\left(\frac{\tilde{q}_{k,t+1}}{q_{k,t}},\tilde{r}_{i,t+1}\right)$$

$$+ K^*_l(t)\text{cov}_t\left(\frac{\tilde{p}_{l,t+1}}{p_{l,t}},\tilde{r}_{i,t+1}\right), \qquad i=1,\ldots,N, \qquad (4.6.3)$$

where l is any index such that q_l is invertibly non-separable from c, which non-separability permits the price p_l to serve as a proxy for future utility. Since the coefficients K_c, K_k, and K^*_l do not depend on the asset i, it might be possible to apply (4.6.3) to a cross-section of securities. The significance of the price covariance term would provide support for the model based on invertible non-separability and against the standard utility specification where (4.6.3) applies with $K_l^* \equiv 0$ for any l. There is no empirical evidence available yet regarding (4.6.2) or (4.6.3).

Since the assumption of invertible non-separability is an assumption regarding W, it restricts certainty preferences rather than μ or attitudes towards timeless wealth gambles. In fact, the cited papers show that it can be accommodated by an intertemporal expected utility ordering in which the von Neumann–Morgenstern index has the Uzawa (1968) functional form. Such a specification has:

$$W(c,q,\phi) = u(c,q) + B(c,q)\phi, \qquad \mu(\tilde{x}) = E\tilde{x}.$$

Thus a non-expected utility function would not be implied (nor would it be contradicted) by the significance of a price beta in the regression suggested by (4.6.3). However, I will outline a modified multicommodity model in which a non-expected utility ordering for intertemporal gambles is an essential ingredient.

A feature of (4.6.3) is that only a single price beta appears on the right side, though l can correspond to any good that satisfies the requisite invertible non-separability. The modified model requires $L \geq 2$ and provides justification for having two price betas appearing simultaneously. Thus the joint significance of two price betas in the obvious cross-sectional regression would indicate a non-expected utility ordering. It will be evident to the reader how to extend the model further to admit more than two price betas.

Consider an extension of (3.3.1) whereby for some function W with $W(c,q,\cdot,\cdot)$ increasing:

$$V_t = W(c_t,q_t,\mu_t,v_t), \qquad t \geq 0, \tag{4.6.4}$$

where $\mu_t = \mu(\tilde{V}_{t+1})$ and $v_t = v(\tilde{V}_{t+1})$ represent conditional certainty equivalents of $\tilde{V}_{t+1}$ computed according to the two distinct certainty equivalent functions μ and v. If the last two arguments of W are weakly separable from (c_t,q_t), then μ_t and v_t can be aggregated into a single certainty equivalent and the recursive structure (3.3.1) is obtained. In the absence of such weak separability, recursivity is violated by V.[23] Weak recursivity is always satisfied, however, and under the constant tastes hypothesis intertemporal consistency prevails and dynamic programming is applicable with the obvious Bellman equation.

The intratemporal optimality conditions are the counterparts of (4.6.1). They involve the two unobservables μ_t and v_t. Thus it is natural to introduce the following terminology and ensuing assumption: say that $(q_l,q_{l'})$ is *invertibly non-separable from c* if for each (c,q) the vector-valued function Ψ:

$$\Psi(\cdot) \equiv \left(\frac{W_{q_l}}{W_c}(c,q,\cdot), \frac{W_{q_{l'}}}{W_c}(c,q,\cdot) \right)$$

is invertible. Suppose that $\exists l, l' \varepsilon \{1, \ldots, L\}$ such that this non-separability obtains. Then μ_t and v_t can be recovered from the appropriate intratemporal optimality conditions. Consequently, by extending the arguments in Epstein and Zin (1990b) and in Duffie and Epstein (1991b), counterparts to (4.6.2) and (4.6.3) can be derived.[24] In the latter, precisely two price betas appear, corresponding to l and l'.

As an example which is particularly relevant to continuous time, restrict attention to non-negative random variables and let:

$$\mu(\tilde{x}) = (E\tilde{x}^2)^{1/2} \quad \text{and} \quad v(\tilde{x}) = E\tilde{x}.$$

Note that the mean $m(\cdot)$ and variance $\text{var}(\cdot)$ are expressible as:

$$m(\tilde{x}) = v(\tilde{x}), \quad \text{var}(\tilde{x}) = \mu^2(\tilde{x}) - v^2(\tilde{x}).$$

Since the latter equations define a one-to-one relation between $(\mu(\tilde{x}), v(\tilde{x}))$ and $(m(\tilde{x}), \text{var}(\tilde{x}))$, (4.6.4) can be expressed equivalently as:

$$V_t = \hat{W}(c_t, q_t, m(\tilde{V}_{t+1}), \text{var}(\tilde{V}_{t+1})), \tag{4.6.4'}$$

for suitable $\tilde{W}$. It is immediate that $(q_l, q_{l'})$ is invertibly non-separable from c if:

$$\frac{\tilde{W}_{q_l}}{\tilde{W}_c}(c, q, \cdot, \cdot) \nearrow m \text{ and } \nearrow \text{var},$$

$$\frac{\tilde{W}_{q_{l'}}}{\tilde{W}_c}(c, q, \cdot, \cdot) \nearrow m \text{ and } \searrow \text{var}.$$

In words, a brighter expected future or increased uncertainty about the future shift preferences toward q_l and away from the numeraire, given fixed levels of the other commodities. On the other hand, the mean and variance of future prospects work in opposite directions in affecting the marginal rate of substitution between $q_{l'}$ and c.

4.7   Asset prices in general equilibrium

Now consider some general equilibrium issues. First, it seems that recursive utility defines a natural class of preferences for dynamic general equilibrium theory. Since intertemporal consistency obtains, so does the non-market reopening property typically assumed in the standard Arrow–Debreu model of contingent commodity markets. Donaldson and Selden (1981) and Johnsen and Donaldson (1985) have discussed the link between preferences and the reopening of markets.

Next consider Lucas' (1978) endowment model modified so that the utility function V of the representative agent is recursive and corresponds to the functional form specifications (4.2.3)–(4.2.4). If an asset pays dividend $\tilde{d}_t$ in period t, then substitution of $(\tilde{P}_{t+1} + \tilde{d}_{t+1})/P_t$ for $\tilde{r}_{i,t+1}$ in the Euler equation (4.2.5′) implies that the equilibrium exdividend price P_t must satisfy:

$$P_t = \beta^{\alpha/\rho} E_t \left[\left[\frac{\tilde{c}_{t+1}}{c_t} \right]^{\alpha(\rho-1)/\rho} \tilde{M}_{t+1}^{(\alpha-\rho)/\rho} (\tilde{P}_{t+1} + \tilde{d}_{t+1}) \right], \text{ for all } t. \quad (4.7.1)$$

In particular, the price p_t^* of aggregate equity or claims to the endowment process satisfies:

$$(p_t^*)^{\alpha/\rho} = \beta_t^{\alpha/\rho} E \left[\left[\frac{\tilde{c}_{t+1}}{c_t} \right]^{\alpha(\rho-1)/\rho} (\tilde{p}_{t+1}^* + \tilde{c}_{t+1})^{\alpha/\rho} \right], \quad (4.7.2)$$

where $\tilde{M}_{t+1} = (\tilde{p}_{t+1}^* + \tilde{c}_{t+1})/p_t^*$ has been substituted.[25]

Consider the effects on the price of equity of a change in the degree of risk aversion as represented by α. Following Epstein (1988), if the endowment and thus also consumption levels are i.i.d., then $p_t^* = K c_t^{1-\rho}$, where K is the unique solution to $K^{\alpha/\rho} = \beta^{\alpha/\rho} E[(\tilde{c}^\rho + K)^{\alpha/\rho}]$. Thus the period t price increases (falls) as risk aversion increases if the elasticity of intertemporal substitution σ is less (greater) than 1. The intuition is clear. At fixed prices, an increase in risk aversion acts to reduce the certainty equivalent of the return $\tilde{M}_{t+1}$ to savings. The effect on behavior is similar to the consequence of a lower rate of return in a deterministic model. If $\sigma < (> 1)$, the dominant income (substitution) effect implies reduced (enhanced) present consumption and an increased (reduced) demand for securities. Thus the price of equity is forced to rise (fall).[26] Results of comparable sharpness and intuitive clarity are possible for other comparative statics exercises, e.g., the consequences of changes in the consumption endowment process. However, the clarity is lost if α and ρ are constrained to be equal as in the conventional model.

Next consider the term structure of interest rates. In order to obtain closed-form solutions, assume that $\rho = 0$ (i.e., $\sigma = 1$). The pricing formula (4.7.1) does not apply in this case but an alternative formula can be derived if it is assumed that consumption growth rates $\tilde{y}_{t+1} \equiv \tilde{c}_{t+1}/c_t$ follow the autoregressive process:

$$\log \tilde{y}_{t+1} = \lambda \log y_t + \delta + v \tilde{\varepsilon}_{t+1},$$

where $\beta|\lambda| < 1$, and the ε_t's are white-noise normal variates. Consider the appropriate form of the Bellman equation (4.2.2) for the representative agent's optimization problem. Since the intertemporal utility function V is linearly homogeneous, the corresponding value function is linearly homogeneous in wealth. Then the first-order conditions for the Bellman equation imply that optimal consumption equals the fraction $(1-\beta)$ of current wealth. Since wealth evolves according to $\tilde{x}_{t+1} = (x_t - c_t)\tilde{M}_{t+1}$, it follows that $\tilde{y}_{t+1} = \beta\tilde{M}_{t+1}$. Thus the equilibrium market return follows the process:

$$\log\tilde{M}_{t+1} = \lambda\log M_t + \delta + (\lambda - 1)\log\beta + v\tilde{\varepsilon}_{t+1}.$$

The implied lognormality can be exploited to derive an explicit solution for the value function, with $I_t = M_t$, of the form:

$$J(M_t, x_t) = kM_t^\theta x_t, \qquad \theta \equiv \lambda\beta/(1 - \lambda\beta).$$

Finally, we obtain the following counterpart to the first-order conditions in (4.2.5) for optimal portfolio allocation:

$$\mathrm{E}_t[\tilde{M}_{t+1}^{\alpha\theta + \alpha - 1}(\tilde{r}_{i,t+1} - \tilde{r}_{j,t+1})] = 0.$$

The latter equation can be used to price any asset. In particular, let $P_{t,t+1}$ be the price in period t of a one period pure discount bond. Then:

$$P_{t,t+1} = \mathrm{E}_t[\tilde{M}_{t+1}^{\alpha\theta + \alpha - 1}]/\mathrm{E}_t[\tilde{M}_{t+1}^{\alpha\theta + \alpha}],$$

which implies, after integrating, that the interest rate $r_t \equiv P_{t,t+1}^{-1}$ satisfies the autoregressive model:

$$\log\tilde{r}_{t+1} = \lambda\log r_t + K + \alpha v^2(1 - \lambda)(1 - \lambda\beta)^{-1} + \lambda v\tilde{\varepsilon}_{t+1},$$

for some constant K that does not depend on α. Under expected utility, $\alpha = 0$ necessarily. With α free, however, it can be deduced that: (i) the conditional mean of the interest rate decreases (increases) with risk aversion if $\lambda < (>)1$ and is independent of risk aversion in the unit root case $\lambda = 1$; (ii) the conditional variance of the interest rate does not depend upon the degree of risk aversion.

Similarly, if $P_{t,T}$ denotes the price at t of a discount bond promising one unit of consumption at T, then:

$$P_{t,T} = \mathrm{E}_t[\tilde{M}_{t+1}^{\alpha\theta + \alpha - 1}\tilde{P}_{t+1,T}]/\mathrm{E}_t[\tilde{M}_{t+1}^{\alpha\theta + \alpha}],$$

which implies that:

$$P_{t,T} = B(t,T)M_t^{A(t,T)},$$

where A and B are explicitly determinable functions of t and T. Define by $(T-t)\log R(r_t,t,T) = -\log P_{t,T}$ the yield-to-maturity of a bond maturing at T given the interest rate r_t at t. It is a straightforward matter to show that an increase in risk aversion reduces the yield for bonds of all maturities if $\lambda \geq -1$. In addition, the slope of the yield curve decreases with risk aversion if $\lambda \geq 0$.

A separate and important question concerning the Lucas economy is whether preferences, including both intertemporal substitutability and risk aversion, are recoverable from a *single* dynamic equilibrium; in particular, could an observer of equilibrium consumption and asset prices in a *given* economy distinguish between the intertemporal expected utility case ($\alpha = \rho$) and the more general recursive case $\alpha \neq \rho$? If not, then the more general model does not provide any additional power for explaining time series from a single economy. Kocherlakota (1990) has shown that, if consumption growth rates are i.i.d., then indeed none of the parameters β, ρ, and α is uniquely determined and the recursive utility model based on (4.2.3)–(4.2.4) is observationally equivalent to the standard model.[27] In fact, if consumption growth rates are i.i.d., then the price of aggregate equity satisfies $p_t^* = K c_t$, where K is a constant that combines β, α, and ρ. The intuition underlying such observational equivalence is clear. Asset prices at t reflect marginal rates of substitution at the conditional consumption program faced by the agent at time t. If that program does not vary sufficiently with t, as in the i.i.d. case, then marginal rates of substitution will be delivered only on a limited domain. The i.i.d. case is analogous to the situation in demand theory where a single price/quantity data point cannot be used to pin down the underlying utility function. This intuition suggests that observational equivalence should be a problem only for a "small" set of consumption processes. Wang (1990) proves a number of results that confirm this intuition. In particular, he shows that the following is true generically in the space of finite state, first-order Markov processes for consumption growth rates: the function describing the equilibrium price of equity in an economy with the Kreps–Porteus utility (4.2.3)–(4.2.4) and $\alpha \neq \rho$ is distinct from that implied by any intertemporally additive expected utility function satisfying specified technical conditions.

Finally, in an empirical vein, consider the equity premium puzzle posed by Mehra and Prescott (1985). They argue that the general equilibrium implications of the representative agent, expected additive utility model, sensibly restricted with regard to the degree of risk aversion, are inconsistant with the historically observed low average real rate of return on debt and large risk premium for equity in the US Weil (1989) and Kochkerlakota (1990) have shown that the generalization of utility to the recursive form (4.2.3)–(4.2.4) does not improve matters. It is intuitive, once again in light of the smoothness of aggregate consumption, that the "order" of risk aversion should be important here. Indeed, Epstein and Zin (1990a) have shown that a partial resolution of the puzzle is achieved with a first-order risk-averse specification for the certainty equivalent μ. As noted earlier, such a specification can produce a sizeable risk premium for a small gamble without implying implausibly large premia for larger gambles. Note that first-order risk aversion precludes μ from being expected utility based. Thus it **requires** that choices amongst timeless wealth gambles violate expected utility. First-order risk aversion can be accommodated readily, however, within the betweenness theory via the disappointment averse functional form, for example (see sections 2.3 and 2.4).

5   SEQUENTIAL CHOICE AND GAME THEORY

Many dynamic decision problems are reasonably viewed as taking place over short intervals of time during which consumption/savings plans can be taken to be fixed. The source of utility is terminal wealth rather than a consumption sequence. Such decision problems are called sequential. It may be convenient to think of such problems as being faced at $t \geq 0$ and extending over a small subinterval of $[t, t+1]$. In contrast, recall the static problems considered earlier of the one-shot choice at t between timeless wealth lotteries. Alternatively, the multistage nature of a decision problem could be due exclusively to the way in which the problem is perceived by the individual. In that case no real time passes as the stages are traversed but the problem is still sequential.

This section begins by discussing how agents who do not maximize expected utility behave in sequential choice settings. As in the intertemporal setting, dynamic consistency is an important issue and it can be understood here in similar terms. The discussion of sequential choice behavior provides a useful perspective on the research into game theory with non-expected utility preferences, which is reviewed in the second subsection.

5.1   Sequential choice

Frequently risks are resolved gradually over time and hence the objects of choice are compound or multistage lotteries. An example is the two-stage lottery $(F_1, p_1; \ldots; F_n, p_n)$, where each F_i occurs with probability p_i in the first stage and F_i is a cumulative distribution function representing the simple wealth lottery to be played in the second stage. If there is no risk in the first stage, $(F, 1)$ may be written simply as F.

An example of a sequential choice problem, that will serve as the vehicle for the discussion, is portrayed in figure 1.6a by means of the standard decision tree diagram. Circles denote chance nodes and squares denote decision nodes. Think of the agent making a choice at the first decision node and formulating a contingent choice for the second node. The choice is essentially between the compound lotteries $(I, 1)$, $(F, p; H, 1-p)$ and $(G, p; H, 1-p)$, and is presumably based on the utility function for compound lotteries. If the second decision node is reached, one may wonder

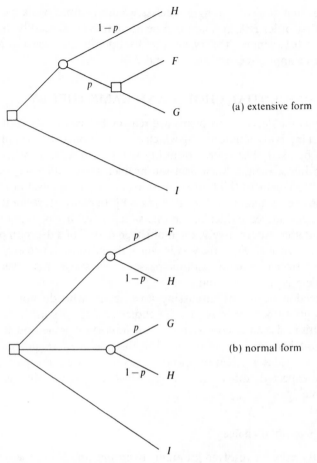

Figure 1.6 Decision trees

whether the contingent plan will be carried out. If so, preferences will be said to be dynamically consistent. If the contingent choice made at the first node is binding, then the decision problem facing the agent is the normal form problem in figure 1.6b. The latter is a one-shot choice problem for which dynamic consistency is not an issue. It is important for what follows to note that the normal form problem is defined as the choice between the two-stage lotteries $(I,1)$, $(F,p;H,1-p)$, and $(G,p;H,1-p)$ rather than between the simple lotteries I, $pF+(1-p)H$ and $pG+(1-p)H$. With the chosen definition, dynamic inconsistency is the only potential reason for different choices in the normal and extensive decision problems.

Whether or not consistency prevails depends upon the utility function for simple lotteries that determines choice at the second node. Denote by v^1 and v^2 the utility functions that apply at nodes 1 and 2. The usual starting point for their specification is a given utility function v for simple lotteries, which will be assumed to be strictly increasing in the sense of first-degree stochastic dominance; v could belong to the betweenness class or be Fréchet differentiable (section 2). The three principal routes that have been followed to move from v to v^1 and v^2 are outlined in figure 1.7, along with their main features.[28] It should be evident that the main points apply much more generally than the particular problem in figure 1.6.

Most commonly it is argued that, since the entire decision problem is assumed to occur over a short time interval, the individual is indifferent to the way in which risk is resolved over time. That is, for all compound lotteries:

$$(F_1,p_1;\ldots;F_n p_n) \sim (\Sigma p_i F_i, 1).$$

Given this reduction of compound lotteries axiom (ROCLA), the utility function v^1 that applies at the first decision node is simply:

$$v^1(F_1,p_1;\ldots;F_n,p_n) \equiv v(\Sigma p_i F_i). \tag{5.1.1}$$

It remains to define utility functions for subsequent nodes or more particularly, for the second decision node in figure 1.6a. The situation is similar to that for intertemporal utility discussed in section 3.2. Drawing the obvious parallels, refer to the constant tastes specification as the one where v^2 is defined as the restriction of v^1:

$$v^2(\cdot) = v^1(\cdot,p;H,1-p), \tag{5.1.2}$$

where equality is modulo ordinal equivalence. Machina (1989a) provides detailed and forceful arguments to support this specification, as well as references to antecedents in the literature. It implies dynamic consistency and also that, unless v is expected utility, preferences at the second node depend upon the unrealized alternative H, due possibly to psychological considerations such as relief or disappointment. Thus backward induction or "rolling back," where decisions at each node are made without reference to "what might have been," is not applicable.[29] Finally, the extensive form decision problem is identified by the agent with the associated normal form (figure 1.6b) which amounts under ROCLA to a static problem of choice between I, $pF + (1-p)H$ and $pG + (1-p)H$.

Any deviation from (5.1.2) implies changing tastes along the decision tree. For example, suppose that:

$$v^2(\cdot) \equiv v(\cdot), \tag{5.1.3}$$

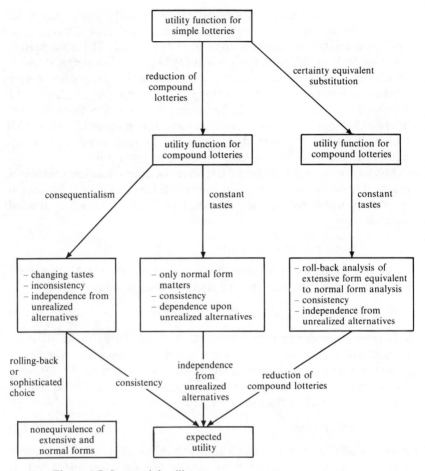

Figure 1.7 Sequential utility

which is the predominant specification for sequential choice problems (e.g., Raiffa, 1968) and is termed *consequentialism* by Machina following Hammond (1988, 1989).[30] According to (5.1.3), the choice between F and G at node 2 is made as though the rest of the tree did not exist, whereas from the perspective of decision node 1 and v^1, the presence of H generally influences the contingent choice between F and G. This change in tastes leads to a dynamic inconsistency for any F, G, H, and p for which the conditions of the independence axiom are violated by v, e.g., if:

$$v(F) > v(G) \text{ and } v(pF + (1-p)H) < v(pG + (1-p)H). \qquad (5.1.4)$$

This dynamic interpretation of violations of the independence axiom is the basis for the widely held view that non-expected utility preferences must be dynamically inconsistent.

One prescription for behavior in such a situation is to solve the extensive form problem by "rolling back," letting v^2 determine the contingent choice at the second node, thus determining the opportunity set to which v^1 is applied. (The corresponding behavior in the intertemporal setting was termed sophisticated in section 3.2.) Given (5.1.4), such a procedure implies that the choice at node 1 is between I and $pF + (1-p)H$. In most cases such rolling back of decision trees does not produce a lottery that is optimal in the normal form (Hazen, 1987). In those cases, the decision-maker would be willing to pay a positive price for the ability to commit to the contingent choices dictated by v^1, since such commitment would mean that the normal form problem is the one being faced.[31]

There is a third approach to the modeling of the sequential choice behavior of non-expected utility maximizers. In this approach, advocated by Segal (1990), the reduction of compound lotteries axiom is dropped, reflecting the frequent finding in the psychology literature that a compound lottery is perceived differently if it is reduced to a single stage. In a series of papers, referenced in his (1990) paper, Segal argues that dropping ROCLA can lead to a unified explanation of a range of behavioral evidence, thus bolstering the argument against the adoption of ROCLA in descriptive modeling.

As an alternative to (5.1.1), extend v to the domain of compound lotteries by means of *certainty equivalent substitution*, i.e., by declaring the compound lottery $(F_1,p_1;\ldots;F_n,p_n)$ to be indifferent to the simple lottery $\Sigma p_i\delta_{x_i}$, where each x_i is the certainty equivalent of F_i with respect to v, i.e.:

$$v(\delta_{x_i}) = v(F_i). \tag{5.1.5}$$

In short, v^1 is defined by (5.1.5) and:

$$v^1(F_1,p_1;\ldots;F_n,p_n) \equiv v(\Sigma p_i\delta_{x_i}). \tag{5.1.6}$$

Note the algorithmic appeal of this way of evaluating compound lotteries and the parallel with recursive intertemporal utility. Finally, the function v^2 is specified according to (5.1.2) to reflect constant tastes.

These utility specifications have the following immediate implications. First, $v^2(\cdot) = v(\cdot)$ up to ordinal equivalence, so that unrealized alternatives do not affect preferences. Second, dynamic consistency obtains since:

$$v^2(F) \geq v^2(G) \Leftrightarrow v^1(F,p;H,1-p) \geq v^1(G,p;H,1-p).$$

(The fact that $v(\cdot)$ is strictly increasing is important here.) Thus roll-back analysis of the extensive form delivers a compound lottery that is optimal in the normal form. (However, this statement is false if by the normal form one means the choice between the simple lotteries I, $pF + (1 - p)H$ and $pG + (1 - p)H$.)

A variety of normative arguments have been applied in an attempt to differentiate between the three approaches outlined above. For example, under consequentialism, sophisticated behavior cannot be rationalized by a preference ordering (Hammond, 1976, 1989) unless v is an expected utility function. Machina (1989a) argues in favor of his constant tastes specification in part by drawing the analogy with the implications of non-separability for intertemporal choice under certainty. Finally, when the duration of a choice problem is short, or conceptual rather than real, the reduction of compound lotteries axiom has considerable normative appeal. On the other hand, violation of the axiom might be understood as reflecting a utility or disutility of gambling. It is for this reason that von Neumann and Morgenstern (1953, p. 632) identify the relaxation of the reduction axiom as an important direction for the extension of their theory of games.

One might also try to exploit the obvious analogy with the analysis of intertemporal choice behavior to differentiate between the three approaches. There is some merit to maintaining consistency across the two contexts with respect to constant versus changing tests, for example. On the other hand, if recursive utility is specified in the intertemporal context, it does not follow that its counterpart for sequential choice, Segal's certainty equivalent substitution approach, is the only sensible one to adopt here. It is clearly plausible that the attitude towards the way in which a multistage lottery is resolved as the stages are traversed depends upon whether time is conceptual or real.

It is consistent with the emphasis throughout this chapter to argue that the differentiation being discussed should be made on the basis of "usefulness" in standard sequential choice models. The following section will outline some recent applications of the above three modeling approaches to the study of strategic interactions between agents.[32] Unlike the case for intertemporal choice modeling, however, the research on applied sequential choice models has not yet delivered a convincing demonstration of the superiority of any of the three approaches.

One final point regarding the modeling of general sequential choice problems deserves attention. As mentioned, in all three approaches the starting point is a utility function v for simple lotteries. It is interesting to note that none of these approaches directly imply restrictions on the set of acceptable specifications for v. However, some restrictions are forthcoming under additional assumptions regarding the nature of sequential choice. Under consequentialism (and the reduction of compound lotteries) v must be expected utility if dynamic consistency is demanded. In the context of

Machina's approach to sequential choice Gul and Lantto (1990) describe arguments that rule out all but betweenness-satisfying functions v. A complementary argument in support of betweenness, that applies to all three approaches under discussion, follows from the requirement of consistency between the modeling of intertemporal and sequential choice. In sections 3.4 and 4.5, it was suggested that a betweenness-conforming specification for the certainty equivalent is advantageous in the context of recursive intertemporal utility functions. Such a specification corresponds to the hypothesis that the derived utility function for timeless wealth gambles satisfies betweenness. However, that derived utility function is naturally identified with the function v.

5.2   Game theory

The theory of games has been one of the most important areas of application for expected utility theory. Therefore, to demonstrate the comparable usefulness of non-expected utility theories, it is important to show that the theory of strategic interactions between agents can be extended to incorporate broader definitions of individual rationality. The research in this area is still at an early stage in its development. Accordingly the summary to follow is relatively brief.[33]

Following Crawford (1990), consider a two-person normal form game of complete information. The players, R and C, have finite sets of pure strategies and corresponding probability simplices Σ_R and Σ_C representing sets of mixed strategies. A combination of mixed strategies induces a probability distribution of monetary outcomes for each player and preferences over such lotteries are represented by the utility functions v_R and v_C. A *Nash equilibrium* is a pair of mixed strategies $(p^*,q^*)\varepsilon\Sigma_R \times \Sigma_C$ such that each is a best response to the other. Note that the specification of payoffs is in monetary terms, rather than in utility terms as is customary in the expected utility framework. This is advantageous since it permits the separation of the game structure from players' preferences over monetary gambles.

The primitive utility functions v_R and v_C and the mapping from $\Sigma_R \times \Sigma_C$ into monetary gambles induce utility functions $\hat{v}_R$ and $\hat{v}_C$ on $\Sigma_R \times \Sigma_C$ which represent preferences over strategy pairs. It is well-known (see Debreu, 1952, for example) that a Nash equilibrium exists if $\hat{v}_R$ and $\hat{v}_C$ are each quasiconcave in own probability vectors for each given choice of opponents' strategies. Moreover, $\hat{v}_R(\cdot,q)$ is quasiconcave on $\Sigma_R \forall q\varepsilon\Sigma_C$ if and only if v_R is quasiconcave on (a suitable subdomain of) probability distributions over monetary outcomes, i.e., "better-than" sets in probability triangles corresponding to monetary outcomes are convex. A similar statement applies to v_C and $\hat{v}_C$. Thus existence of an equilibrium is ensured if v_R and v_C are both quasiconcave and *a fortiori* if both satisfy betweenness, which is the conjunction of quasiconcavity and quasiconvexity. In general, however, an equilibrium may fail to exist because the players may be unwilling to randomize. For example, under strict quasiconvexity, for any mixed strategy of C, R will strictly prefer at least one of his pure strategies. Thus an equilibrium does not exist if there is no pure strategy equilibrium. Technically the difficulty is that best reply correspondences need not be convex-valued.

I have argued in earlier sections that the restriction to betweenness-satisfying utility functions represents an attractive balance between generality and tractability, and the discussion of game theory will bolster this view. Nevertheless, it is desirable to have a theory of strategic interaction that is not limited by assumptions such as the independence axiom, the betweenness axiom or quasiconcavity in probabilities, which should be viewed as empirically refutable hypotheses rather than tenets of individual rationality. Moreover, there exists some laboratory evidence contradicting betweenness, with the violations divided roughly equally between quasiconcavity and quasiconvexity (see footnote 3).

To accommodate more general preferences, Crawford adapts from Aumann (1987) the notion of an *equilibrium in beliefs*, which is a pair (P^*, Q^*) such that: P^* and Q^* are probability distributions on Σ_C and Σ_R respectively, that represent beliefs about opponents' strategy choices; and $P^*(Q^*)$ assigns positive probability only to those mixed strategies of C(R) that are optimal responses for him given his beliefs. The beliefs equilibrium concept has three attractive features. First, such an equilibrium exists whenever utility functions are continuous. This is so because, if players' utility functions are transformed to make them quasiconcave by replacing "better-than" sets by their convex hulls, then each Nash equilibrium of the convexified game defines an equilibrium in beliefs for the original game. For the second feature note that, if $(p^*, q^*)\varepsilon\Sigma_R \times \Sigma_C$ is a Nash equilibrium, then the pair of beliefs which assign probability 1 to (p^*, q^*) constitutes a beliefs equilibrium. Conversely, assuming the reduction of compound lotteries axiom, any probability distribution on Σ_R (or Σ_C) defines a unique element of Σ_R (or Σ_C). (Modulo this identification, Crawford shows that any beliefs equilibrium is also a Nash equilibrium given the quasiconcavity of utility.) In this sense, the notion of equilibrium in beliefs coincides with Nash equilibrium given quasiconcavity. Finally, in a beliefs equilibrium explicit randomization on the part of agents is necessary only if it is desired, i.e., if utility is strictly quasiconcave in probabilities. If both players have quasiconvex utility functions, then each chooses a pure strategy, with no attempt to randomize, but there is uncertainty about the opponent's choice (see also Harsanyi, 1973).

Dekel, Safra, and Segal (1991) offer an interesting perspective on Crawford's analysis and an alternative approach to modeling normal form games. They argue that, since the opponent's strategy is generally mixed, each player must rank alternative two-stage lotteries in choosing a mixed strategy. For example, let r_{ij} be the monetary payoff to R if he plays his i^{th} pure strategy and C plays his j^{th} pure strategy, $i = 1, \ldots, m$ and $j = 1, \ldots, n$. Then, if C plays $q = (q_1, \ldots, q_n)\varepsilon\Sigma_C$ and if R views himself as playing first, R's choice of $p\varepsilon\Sigma_R$ implies the two-stage lottery in which the simple lottery $(r_{i1}, q_1; \ldots; r_{in}, q_n)$ is obtained with probability $p_i, i = 1, \ldots, m$. Crawford implicitly assumes that R employs the reduction of compound lotteries axiom to reduce the compound lottery to a simple lottery, which is then evaluated by the utility function v_R. Dekel, Safra, and Segal assume instead that each agent uses the certainty equivalent substitution procedure described in section 5.1 to evaluate compound lotteries. Under the assumptions that each player views himself as moving first and that v_R and v_C are continuous and strictly increasing in the sense of first-degree stochastic dominance, they prove that a Nash equilibrium exists. Each best reply set is convex, even if the utility functions are quasiconvex, since it equals the convex hull of the collection of pure strategies that are best replies. On the other hand, if each player perceives himself as moving second, in which case the pair of strategies (p,q) leads to the compound lottery for R in which $(r_{1j}, p_1; \ldots; r_{mj}, p_m)$ is encountered with probability $q_j, j = 1, \ldots, n$, then convex-valued best response correspondences can be guaranteed only if both players are expected utility maximizers. Thus it remains to find an equilibrium concept (perhaps a variation of the beliefs equilibrium) that can be applied under alternative assumptions about individual perceptions.

The Dekel, Safra, and Segal analysis draws attention to the distinction between normal and extensive form modeling of games that is one of the principal lessons that has emerged from the extension beyond the expected utility framework. Define the normal form of the above game as in Crawford (1990) whereby, because of the reduction axiom, the strategy pair (p,q) produces a simple monetary lottery for each player. Then the preceding paragraph points to the loss of information in restricting attention to the normal form and consequently to the need for extensive form analysis. On the other hand, if reduction is not imposed in the definition of the normal form, so that (p,q) produces a two-stage monetary lottery, then two different normal forms are being discussed in the preceding paragraph and attention is drawn rather to the proper definition of the normal form. (The parallel issue in the context of individual choice problems was mentioned in section 5.1.) Note that the distinction between the alternative definitions of the normal form is immaterial if reduction of compound lotteries is imposed at the level of preferences.

The explicit formulation of players' choices in terms of compound lotteries calls attention to the sequential nature of individual decision problems and therefore to the issue of dynamic consistency. If explicit randomization is actually undertaken, then each player has two non-trivial decisions to make – first, which mixed strategy to employ and second, whether or not to play the pure strategy that is delivered by the chosen randomization. In light of the discussion in the preceding section, it is evident that consistency is guaranteed in Crawford's analysis if Machina's view of sequential choice behavior is adopted. It is also guaranteed in the analysis of Dekel, Safra, and Segal, since they employ the certainty equivalent substitution approach to sequential choice.

Under consequentialism, however, consistency is potentially a problem if quasiconvexity is violated. This is because a decision-maker with strictly quasiconcave utility may choose to randomize over two non-different lotteries F and G and then renege if confronted with the outcome of the inferior alternative.[34] Even if F and G are equally attractive, the decision-maker may prefer to randomize again rather than accepting either F or G. Crawford assumes these problems away by supposing that players commit themselves to abide by the outcome of the mixed strategy. He argues that the ability to make such commitments is implicit in the assumption that the players can use mixed strategies. Viewed in this light, the preceding discussion of consistency is more properly reinterpreted as the comparison of behavior in different extensive form games having the same normal form.

The related issues of dynamic consistency and the equivalence of normal and extensive forms have been considered in the context of auction games. Suppose that bidders behave non-cooperatively and that their valuations of the auctioned object are private and independent. Consider a Dutch or descending-bid auction and a first-price sealed-bid auction. The corresponding games have identical (reduced) normal forms and produce the identical outcomes under expected utility (Milgrom and Weber, 1982; Milgrom, 1989). But more generally, they produce different outcomes assuming consequentialism, because of the dynamic inconsistency present in the Dutch auction. To elaborate, consider a bidder in the Dutch auction with monetary valuation of the auctioned object equal to r. Suppose the price has fallen to $b+1 < r$ and that the individual is deciding whether to claim the object at that price or at the "next" price b. Either choice implies a lottery which can be represented by a point in the probability simplex corresponding to outcomes $0, r-b-1$ and $r-b$. Denote these lotteries by F^{b+1} and F^b (where $F^{b+1} = \delta_{r-b-1}$ and F^b is a mixture of δ_0 and δ_{r-b}). On the other hand, consider the same bidder at the start of the Dutch auction, or in the sealed-bid auction, comparing the same two bids. In this case, either choice entails the additional risk, having probability α say, that someone else will bid more than $b+1$. Thus the relevant comparison is between the lotteries $(1-\alpha)F^b + \alpha\delta_0$ and $(1-\alpha)F^{b+1} + \alpha\delta_0$. If the independence axiom is satisfied, F^b is chosen in the former case if and only if $(1-\alpha)F^b + \alpha\delta_0$ is chosen in the latter comparison, but not so more generally. Indeed, if indifference curves fan out as portrayed for weighted utility in figure 1.1, then the individual could offer b in the first-price auction and $b+1$ in the Dutch auction once the price has fallen to that level. (Note that the chord in the probability simplex connecting F^b and F^{b+1} is parallel to that connecting $(1-\alpha)F^b + \alpha\delta_0$ and $(1-\alpha)F^{b+1} + \alpha\delta_0$.) If indifference curves fan in, the lower bid would occur in the Dutch auction.

Karni and Safra (1989a) show that dynamic consistency is a problem also in the English auction under the consequentialist view of sequential choice if the object being sold is a lottery. In (1989b), these authors posit sophisticated behavior and assume that bidders restrict attention to strategies that will actually be carried out. Formally, Karni and Safra adapt Selten's (1975) trick (see his "agent's normal form") of regarding the same bidder at different decision nodes as distinct players. Then they consider the Bayesian–Nash equilibrium of the resulting game of incomplete information. Under the assumption that utility functions are quasiconcave, they establish the existence of an equilibrium, which they show to be value-revealing if and only if betweenness is satisfied.

To this point, the discussion of games has concentrated on the consequentialist and certainty equivalent substitution approaches to sequential choice. If Machina's (1989a) approach is adopted, then the discussion in the last section implies immediately that only the normal form matters and that dynamic consistency generally prevails. However, the approach conflicts with the principle of backwards induction (see also footnote 29).

In summary, the literature on game theory with general preferences has just begun to tackle the problem of formulating a satisfactory equilibrium concept. The modeling of strategic rationality depends upon which of the three approaches to modeling individual sequential choice behavior outlined in figure 1.7 is adopted. Regardless of the approach that is adopted, however, it has been shown that one of the following features of received game theory must be abandoned if utility functions do not conform to expected utility theory: the applicability of backwards induction, or the equivalence of normal and extensive forms in games of perfect recall, at least where the normal form is defined in the usual way in terms of simple rather than multistage payoff lotteries. As for applications, the literature has produced some new predictions regarding the equivalences, efficiency, and demand-revealing properties of common auctions. It remains to be seen whether non-expected utility preferences will deliver interesting new predictions in other contexts.

Notes

* I am grateful to the Social Sciences and Humanities Research Council of Canada for financial support. I am especially indebted to Darrell Duffie, Angelo Melino, Michael Peters, and Uzi Segal for valuable discussions and comments. This draft has also benefited from suggestions by Eddy Dekel, Ingrid Peters-Fransen, Jerry Green, Carolyn Pitchik, Zvi Safra, A. Siow, Tan Wang, and Philippe Weil.

1 For certain quantitative empirical exercises, however, there is a substantial difference in tractability between Fréchet differentiable functions and expected utility functions (see footnote 21).

2 The reader is referred to the surveys cited in the introduction for descriptions of other classes of utility functions and appropriate references. Some notable models include rank-dependent expected or anticipated utility (references given above), the non-transitive regret theory (Bell, 1982; Loomes and Sugden, 1982) and the closely related skew-symmetric-bilinear utility theory (Fishburn, 1982). Some studies that have applied these models are listed below, but these alternative models are not particularly useful for the applications in sections 4 and 5. The same comment applies to prospect theory (Kahneman and Tversky, 1979). The latter also suffers, in comparison with expected utility and the other models mentioned, from more ambiguous predictions because of the lack of a precise theory of the framing and editing processes.

3 See the cited sources on betweenness and the surveys mentioned in the introduction for a discussion of the extent to which the betweenness axiom is compatible with the behavioral evidence against independence. There have also been some attempts to examine directly the descriptive validity of betweenness in the laboratory. See Camerer (1989a,b) and the references and discussions in Machina (1985), Crawford (1990), and Chew, Epstein, and Segal (1991).

4 Conversely, given such a function ϕ defined on $[a,b]$, $0 < a < 1 < b < \infty$, equation (2.3.2) defines a monotone and risk averse μ on $D[a,b]$, the set of cdf's on $[a,b]$. If ϕ is defined and well-behaved on $(0,\infty)$, then μ is well-defined, monotone, and risk averse on the set of all cdf's on R_{++}^1 having finite mean. For example, to show risk aversion let G be a mean preserving spread of F. Then:

$$\int \phi(x/\mu(F))dF(x) = 0 = \int \phi(x/\mu(G))dG(x)$$

$$\leq \int \phi(x/\mu(G))dF(x) \Rightarrow \mu(F) \geq \mu(G).$$

See Epstein and Zin (1991b) for further details. These facts can be applied to deduce the domains of the certainty equivalent functions corresponding to (2.3.3) and (2.3.6) below.

5 Chew (1989) axiomatizes the family of semi-weighted utility functions, a subset of the betweenness class containing both of the parametric classes to follow.

6 This notion of comparative risk aversion for certainty equivalent functions is

employed in the analysis of intertemporal utility (section 3.3). Machina (1982b, p. 299) formulates and analyzes a stronger notion.

7 Related inhibitions to trade also appear in Gilboa and Schmeidler (1989), Bewley (1989), and Dow and Werlang (1992). Kinks in indifference curves are critical there also, but the kinks reflect aversion to uncertainty (randomness with unknown probability) rather than aversion to risk.

8 If only single period risks are considered, then the functional form (3.2.1), which is based upon research by Larry Selden, provides a complete separation between substitution and risk aversion in that it is possible also to change the ranking of deterministic programs without affecting risk aversion.

9 More precisely, stationarity requires that for all t and consumption programs, and for all events $I \varepsilon F_{t+1}$ (see the notation introduced in section 3.2):

$$(c_t, \tilde{c}_{t+1}, \tilde{c}_{t+2}, \ldots | I) \underset{s_t}{\gtrless} (c_t, \tilde{c}'_{t+1}, \tilde{c}'_{t+2}, \ldots | I) \quad \Leftrightarrow$$

$$(\tilde{c}_{t+1}, \tilde{c}_{t+2}, \ldots | I) \underset{(s_t, c_t)}{\gtrless} (\tilde{c}'_{t+1}, \tilde{c}'_{t+2}, \ldots | I).$$

Stationarity is assumed without exception (to my knowledge) in both the theoretical and empirical literature on capital theory that employ the framework of an infinitely lived agent. This is true in particular of the habit-formation literature, for which some references are provided in section 4.1. Epstein (1983) considers stationarity in the case where consumption histories do not influence preferences and derives the appropriate specialization of (3.13).

10 Weak recursivity can be defined more formally as follows: let $\tilde{c}$, $\tilde{c}'$, $\tilde{c}^*$ and $\tilde{c}^{**}$ be four consumption programs and $T > 0$. For any $I \varepsilon F_T$, denote by $(\tilde{c}|I, \tilde{c}^*|\Omega \backslash I)$ the consumption program in which period t consumption is $\tilde{c}_t(\omega)$ if $\omega \varepsilon I$ and $\tilde{c}^*_t(\omega)$ if $\omega \varepsilon \Omega \backslash I$; and similarly for other combinations of the above programs. Weak recursivity requires that $\forall I_T \varepsilon F_T$, if:

$$V(\tilde{c}|I, \tilde{c}^*|\Omega \backslash I) \geq V(\tilde{c}'|I, \tilde{c}^*|\Omega \backslash I) \quad \forall I_T \supseteq I \varepsilon F_T,$$

then the same should be true if $\tilde{c}^*$ is replaced by $\tilde{c}^{**}$. An intertemporal expected utility function satisfies the stronger condition that $\forall I_T \varepsilon F_T$, if:

$$V(\tilde{c}|I_T, \tilde{c}^*|\Omega \backslash I_T) \geq V(\tilde{c}'|I_T, \tilde{c}^*|\Omega \backslash I_T),$$

then the inequality is true also if $\tilde{c}^*$ is replaced by $\tilde{c}^{**}$. To see the difference between these conditions in the context of figure 1.3 would require that a third alternative be added at $t = 1$. For further elaboration in the context of a two-period model see Johnsen and Donaldson (1985, pp. 1454–5).

11 Recursivity requires that $\forall \tilde{c}, \tilde{c}', \tilde{c}^*, T > 0$ and $I_T \varepsilon F_T$:

$$V(\tilde{c}|I, \tilde{c}^*|\Omega \backslash I) \geq V(\tilde{c}'|I, \tilde{c}^*|\Omega \backslash I) \quad \forall I_T \supseteq I \varepsilon F_T,$$

if and only if:

$$V(\tilde{c}_T, \tilde{c}_{T+1}, \ldots | I) \geq V(\tilde{c}'_T, \tilde{c}'_{T+1}, \ldots | I) \quad \forall I_T \supseteq I \varepsilon F_T.$$

12 Working in a domain of probability measures rather than random variables, Chew and Epstein (1991) show that (3.3.1) is characterized by a slightly strengthened form of recursivity. Note that (3.3.1) implies stationarity in the sense of section 3.1, footnote 9.

13 There are several (W,μ) pairs that represent the same intertemporal preference ordering. If $V^{**}=g(V)$ is ordinally equivalent to V then V^{**}, W^{**}, and μ^{**} satisfy the appropriate form of (3.3.1) if $W^{**}(c,z)\equiv gW(c,g^{-1}(z))$ and $\mu^{**}(\tilde{x})=g(\mu(g^{-1}(\tilde{x})))$. But if, as here, the aggregator is held fixed, then the certainty equivalent function corresponds uniquely to the intertemporal preference ordering.

14 Let J be the value function corresponding to V and the intertemporal optimization problem. Then timeless wealth gambles $\tilde{x}$ are evaluated by $\mu(J(\tilde{x}))$. For most of the axiomatic generalizations of expected utility that have been developed recently, including the betweenness theory, $\mu(\cdot)$ lies in the given axiomatic class if and only if $\mu(J(\cdot))$ does. Finally, if J and its inverse both satisfy Lipschitz conditions, then $\mu(\cdot)$ is Fréchet differentiable if and only if $\mu(J(\cdot))$ is.

15 Indeed, Kreps and Porteus studied recursive utility functions **because** they implied non-indifference to temporal resolution. On the other hand, the more recent attention that has been afforded these functions has been motivated more by the separation they deliver between substitution and risk aversion.

16 Figure 1.4 also indicates (in the right branch) that dynamic consistency and timing indifference can be achieved simultaneously, but at the cost of allowing dependence upon unrealized alternatives. Any utility function V, which depends only on the joint distribution of the $\tilde{c}_t$'s, is indifferent to the temporal resolution of risk.

17 The utility specification is not the only potential cause of the empirical failures. Some studies have focused on the consequences of generalizing the standard model by incorporating heterogeneous agents and incomplete markets. See Marcet and Singleton (1990) and Weil (1990b), for example.

18 A general analysis of dynamic programming with recursive utility is not yet available. Some supporting arguments for the homogeneous functional forms below are provided in Epstein and Zin (1989). Streufert (1990b) and Ma (forthcoming) contain some results for more general cases.

19 See Epstein and Zin (1989) for details and also for a proof that there exists a utility function V, defined on a suitable domain, that satisfies recursive relation (3.3.1) for the specified W and μ. Existence theorems comparable in generality to those available in the certainty case (Streufert (1990a)) are not yet available. But see Streufert (1990b) and Ma (forthcoming).

20 See the discussion of term structure in section 4.4 for an example of such additional assumptions. It is shown there that optimal consumption is myopic when $\rho=0$. The non-myopic nature of optimal consumption when $\rho\neq0$ is essential in the derivation of (4.2.5) (see Epstein and Zin, 1989).

21 If μ is Fréchet differentiable with local utility function u, the first-order conditions for portfolio choice take the form:

$$E_t[u_1(\tilde{z}_{t+1};F_t^*)\cdot(\tilde{r}_{i,t+1}-\tilde{r}_{j,t+1})]=0,$$

where $\tilde{z}_{t+1} \equiv (\tilde{c}_{t+1}/c_t)^{(\rho-1)/\rho} \tilde{M}_{t+1}^{1/\rho}$ and F_t^* is the conditional cdf of $\tilde{z}_{t+1}$. Generalized method of moments estimation is not applicable since F_t^* is not observed. Only if a parametric form is assumed for F_t^* can the integrand be computed, given specified values for all unknown parameters. On the other hand, if μ satisfies betweenness, then, because of (2.2.4), u_1 can be replaced in the above expectation by $H_1(z_{t+1}, \mu(\tilde{z}_{t+1}|I_t))$ which depends on F_t^* only via $\mu_t^* = \mu(\tilde{z}_{t+1}|I_t)$. Epstein and Zin (1989) show how μ_t^* can be expressed in terms of observables by suitably exploiting the Bellman equation. Thus the specialization to a betweenness-conforming certainty equivalent is advantageous for empirical tractability.

22 For the disappointment averse specification, ϕ is not differentiable at 1, but under specified assumptions on the distribution of consumption and asset returns that is of no consequence in (4.5.1). See Epstein and Zin (1991a).

23 The following component property of recursivity is violated: for all consumption programs:

$$V(y_0, \tilde{y}_1, \tilde{y}_2, \ldots) \geq V(y_0, \tilde{y}_1', \tilde{y}_2', \ldots) \quad \langle = \rangle$$
$$V(y_0', \tilde{y}_1, \tilde{y}_2, \ldots) \geq V(y_0', \tilde{y}_1', \tilde{y}_2', \ldots), \quad \text{where} \quad y_t \equiv (c_t, q_t).$$

24 Theorems guaranteeing that utility is well-defined by the recursive equation (4.6.4) or its continuous time counterpart are not yet available. However, if existence of utility is assumed, the remaining arguments in the cited papers are readily extended.

25 The papers cited below provide some results regarding the existence of an equilibrium in the representative agent economy with the CES specialization of recursive utility. Ma (forthcoming) provides an existence result for a heterogeneous agent economy with recursive utilities by extending Duffie, Geanakoplos, Mas-Colell, and McLennan (1988).

26 Similar intuition was validated formally by Kihlstrom and Mirman (1974, pp. 378–80) and Selden (1979) with respect to the behavior of an individual facing exogenous prices and operating in a two-period environment.

27 Kocherlakota's observational equivalence result for an i.i.d. environment should be distinguished from the Duffie and Epstein (1991a) result for continuous time Brownian (but not necessarily i.i.d.) environments, described in section 3.3. Kocherlakota is concerned with observational equivalence with intertemporal expected utility, while Duffie and Epstein are concerned with whether one could detect if the ordering of timeless wealth gambles (i.e., the certainty equivalent μ) violates expected utility theory.

28 There is an evident parallel between the discussion of intertemporal choice (based on figure 1.4) and that of sequential choice (based on figure 1.7). Roughly speaking, the latter can be viewed as the special case of intertemporal choice where there is no discounting, consumption is perfectly substitutable across time, and, possibly, the horizon is finite. But the parallel is imperfect. For example, the usual starting point in the sequential framework is a utility function defined over simple, rather than over multistage, lotteries. Moreover, the associated literatures have developed independently and employ different terminology. Thus a brief separate treatment of sequential choice is provided.

29 Mention should be made of the related modeling of psychological factors in

strategic situations by Geanakoplos, Pearce, and Stacchetti (1989), who also point out the inapplicability of backwards induction in their context.

30 There is some disagreement about the proper definition of consequences and hence of consequentialism. See Hammond (1989, pp. 1447–8) and Machina (1989a, section 6.6).

31 In single-person decision problems, the ability to commit, in the sense of guaranteeing that v^1 dictate all choices, is always (weakly) preferable according to v^1. However, Fershtman, Safra, and Vincent (1990) show that in strategic situations an agent may strictly prefer not to commit in this way. Roughly, entering into a game with utility function v^2 rather than v^1 may produce an equilibrium payoff to the player which is preferred by v^1.

32 See Karni and Safra (1990) for a single-agent sequential choice problem corresponding to optimal search. They adopt the consequentialist approach and propose a form of sophisticated behavior to resolve the dynamic inconsistency.

33 In addition to the studies referred to below, mention should be made of Fishburn and Rosenthal (1986). They study Nash equilibrium in finite non-cooperative games where players have skew-symmetric-bilinear utility functions and thus are non-transitive. Also, recall the paper on axiomatic bargaining theory by Rubinstein, Safra, and Thomson, cited in section 2.5.

34 See Green (1987) for a related argument that an agent who violates quasiconvexity can be exploited.

References

Attanasio, O.P. and G. Weber (1989), "Intertemporal Substitution, Risk Aversion and the Euler Equation for Consumption," *Economic Journal* (supplement), 99: 59–73.

Aumann, R.J. (1987), "Correlated Equilibrium as an Expression of Bayesian Rationality," *Econometrica*, 55: 1–18.

Bell, D. (1982), "Regret in Decision Making Under Uncertainty," *Operations Research*, 30: 961–81.

Bewley, T. (1989), "Market Innovation and Entrepreneurship: A Knightian View," Paper 905, Cowles Foundation.

Bollerslev, T., R.F. Engle, and J.M. Wooldridge (1988), "A Capital Asset Pricing Model with Time-Varying Covariances," *Journal of Political Economy*, 96: 116–31.

Breeden, D. (1979), "An Intertemporal Asset Pricing Model with Stochastic Consumption and Investment," *Journal of Financial Economics*, 7: 265–96.

Breeden, D., M.R. Gibbons, and R.H. Litzenberger (1989), "Empirical Tests of the Consumption-Oriented CAPM," *Journal of Finance*, 44: 231–62.

Bufman, G. and L. Leiderman (1990), "Consumption and Asset Returns Under Non-Expected Utility," *Economic Letters*, 34: 231–5.

Camerer, C.F. (1989a), "An Experimental Test of Several Generalized Utility Theories," *Journal of Risk and Uncertainty*, 2: 61–104.

(1989b), "Recent Tests of Generalizations of Expected Utility Theory," Mimeo, Wharton School.

Campbell, J.Y. (1990), "Intertemporal Asset Pricing Without Consumption," Working Paper 119, Woodrow Wilson School, Princeton University.

Chew, S.H. (1983), "A Generalization of the Quasilinear Mean with Applications to the Measurement of Income Inequality and Decision Theory Resolving the Allais Paradox," *Econometrica*, 51: 1065–92.

(1989), "Axiomatic Utility Theories with the Betweenness Property," *Annals of Operations Research*, 19: 273–98.

Chew, S.H. and L.G. Epstein (1989a), "The Structure of Preferences and Attitudes Towards the Timing of the Resolution of Uncertainty," *International Economic Review*, 30: 103–17.

(1989b), "Axiomatic Rank-Dependent Means," *Annals of Operations Research*, 19: 299–309.

(1990a), "Non-Expected Utility Preferences in a Temporal Framework with an Application to Consumption-Savings Behavior," *Journal of Economic Theory*, 50: 54–81.

(1991), "Recursive Utility Under Uncertainty," in A. Khan and N. Yannelis (eds), *Equilibrium Theory with an Infinite Number of Commodities*, Springer Verlag.

Chew, S.H., L.G. Epstein, and U. Segal (1991), "Mixture Symmetry and Quadratic Utility," *Econometrica*, 59: 139–64.

Chew, S.H., L.G. Epstein, and I. Zilcha (1988), "A Correspondence Theorem Between Expected Utility and Smooth Utility," *Journal of Economic Theory*, 46: 186–93.

Chew, S.H., E. Karni, and Z. Safra (1987), "Risk Aversion in the Theory of Expected Utility with Rank Dependent Probabilities," *Journal of Economic Theory*, 42: 370–81.

Chew, S.H. and N. Nishimura (forthcoming), "Differentiability, Comparative Statics and Non-Expected Utility Preferences," *Journal of Economic Theory*.

Conlisk, J. (1989), "Three Variants on the Allais Example," *American Economic Review*, 79: 392–407.

Constantinides, G.M. (1982), "Intertemporal Asset Pricing with Heterogeneous Consumers and Demand Aggregation," *Journal of Business*, 55: 253–67.

(1990), "Habit Formation: A Resolution of the Equity Premium Puzzle," *Journal of Political Economy*, 98: 519–43.

Cook, V.T. (1989), "The Effects of Temporal Resolution on the Overall Utility and Suspense of Risky Monetary and Survival Gambles," Ph.D. Dissertation, Department of Psychology, McGill University.

Cox, J., J. Ingersoll, and S. Ross (1985), "A Theory of the Term Structure of Interest Rates," *Econometrica*, 53: 385–408.

Crawford, V. (1990), "Equilibrium Without Independence," *Journal of Economic Theory*, 50: 127–54.

Debreu, G. (1952), "A Social Equilibrium Existence Theorem," *Proceedings of the National Academy of Sciences*, 38: 886–93.

Dekel, E. (1986), "An Axiomatic Characterization of Preferences under Uncertainty," *Journal of Economic Theory*, 40: 304–18.

Dekel, E., Z. Safra, and U. Segal (1991), "Existence and Dynamic Consistency of Nash Equilibrium with Non-Expected Utility Preferences," *Journal of Economic Theory*, 55: 229–46.

Donaldson, J. and L. Selden (1981), "Arrow-Debreu Preferences and the Reopening of Contingent Claims Markets," *Economic Letters*, 8: 209–16.

Dow, J. and S.R. Werlang (1992), "Uncertainty Aversion and the Optimal Choice of Portfolio," *Econometrica*, 60: 197–204.

Duffie, D. and L.G. Epstein (1991a), "Stochastic Differential Utility," Research Paper 1078, Graduate School of Business, Stanford University; forthcoming in *Econometrica*.

(1991b), "Asset Pricing with Stochastic Differential Utility," Working Paper 9122, University of Toronto; forthcoming in *Review of Financial Studies*.

Duffie, D., J. Geanakoplos, A. Mas-Colell, and A. McLennan (1988), "Stationary Markov Equilibria," mimeo.

Epstein, L.G. (1983), "Stationary Cardinal Utility and Optimal Growth Under Uncertainty," *Journal of Economic Theory*, 31: 133–52.

(1985), "Decreasing Risk Aversion and Mean-Variance Analysis," *Econometrica*, 53: 945–61.

(1988), "Risk Aversion and Asset Prices," *Journal of Monetary Economics*, 22: 179–92.

(1991), "Discussion of 'Substitution Over Time in Consumption and Work'," in L. McKenzie and S. Zamagni (eds), *"Value and Capital" Fifty Years Later*, London: Macmillan, pp. 268–78.

Epstein, L.G. and S.E. Zin (1989), "Substitution, Risk Aversion and the Temporal Behavior of Consumption and Asset Returns: A Theoretical Framework," *Econometrica*, 57: 937–69.

(1990a), "'First-Order' Risk Aversion and the Equity Premium Puzzle," *Journal of Monetary Economics*, 26: 387–407.

(1990b), "Consumption, Labor Supply and Portfolio Choice with Time and State Non-Separable Utility," mimeo, University of Toronto.

(1991a), "Substitution, Risk Aversion and the Temporal Behavior of Consumption and Asset Returns: An Empirical Analysis," *Journal of Political Economy*, 99: 263–86.

(1991b), "The Independence Axiom and Asset Returns," NBER Technical Working Paper 109.

Farmer, R.E.A. (1990), "RINCE Preferences," *Quarterly Journal of Economics*, 105: 43–60.

Fershtman, C., Z. Safra, and D. Vincent (1990), "Delayed Agreements and Non-Expected Utility," Discussion Paper 867, Kellogg School, Northwestern University.

Fishburn, P. (1982), "Nontransitive Measurable Utility," *Journal of Mathematical Psychology*, 26: 31–67.

(1983), "Transitive Measurable Utility," *Journal of Economic Theory*, 31: 293–317.

(1988), *Nonlinear Preference and Utility Theory*. Baltimore: Johns Hopkins University Press.

Fishburn, P. and R. Rosenthal (1986), "Noncooperative Games and Nontransitive Preferences," *Mathematical Social Sciences*, 12: 1–7.

Geanakoplos, J., D. Pearce, and E. Stacchetti (1989), "Psychological Games and Sequential Rationality," *Games and Economic Behavior*, 1: 60–79.

Gilboa, I. and D. Schmeidler (1989), "Maxmin Expected Utility with Non-Unique Prior," *Journal of Mathematical Economics*, 18: 141–53.

Giovannini, A. and P. Weil (1989), "Risk Aversion and Intertemporal Substitution in the Capital Asset Pricing Model," NBER Working Paper 2824.

Gorman, W.M. (1953), "Community Preference Fields," *Econometrica*, 21: 63–80.

Green, J. (1987), " 'Making Book Against Oneself,' The Independence Axiom and Nonlinear Utility Theory," *Quarterly Journal of Economics*, 102: 785–96.

Grossman, S., A. Melino, and R. Shiller (1987), "Estimating the Continuous-Time Consumption-Based Asset-Pricing Model," *Journal of Business and Economic Statistics*, 5: 315–27.

Grossman, S. and R. Shiller (1981), "The Determinants of the Variability of Stock Market Prices," *American Economic Review*, 71: 222–7.

Gul, F. (1991), "A Theory of Disappointment Aversion," *Econometrica*, 59: 667–86.

Gul, F. and O. Lantto (1990), "Betweenness Satisfying Preferences and Dynamic Choice," *Journal of Economic Theory*, 52: 162–77.

Hall, Robert E. (1978), "Stochastic Implications of the Life Cycle-Permanent Income Hypothesis: Theory and Evidence," *Journal of Political Economy*, 86: 971–87.

(1985), "Real Interest and Consumption," NBER Working Paper 1694.

(1988), "Intertemporal Substitution in Consumption," *Journal of Political Economy*, 96: 339–57.

Hammond, P. (1976), "Changing Tastes and Coherent Dynamic Choice," *Review of Economic Studies*, 43: 159–73.

(1988), "Consequentialist Foundations for Expected Utility," *Theory and Decision*, 25: 25–78.

(1989), "Consistent Plans, Consequentialism, and Expected Utility," *Econometrica*, 57: 1445–9.

Hansen, L.P. and R. Jagannathan (1991), "Implications of Security Market Data for Models of Dynamic Economies," *Journal of Political Economy*, 99:225–62.

Hansen, L.P. and K. Singleton (1982), "Generalized Instrumental Variables Estimation of Nonlinear Rational Expectations Models," *Econometrica*, 50: 1269–86.

(1983), "Stochastic Consumption, Risk Aversion, and the Temporal Behavior of Asset Returns," *Journal of Political Economy*, 91: 249–65.

Harsanyi, J.C. (1973), "Games with Randomly Distributed Payoffs: A New Rationale for Mixed Strategy Equilibrium Points," *International Journal of Game Theory*, 2: 1–23.

Hazen, G. (1987), "Does Rolling Back Decision Trees Really Require the Independence Axiom?" *Management Science*, 33: 807–9.

Heaton, J. (1988), "An Empirical Investigation of Asset Pricing with Temporally Dependent Preference Specifications," Working Paper 3245-91, Sloan School, MIT.

Huang, C.F. and R.H. Litzenberger (1988), *Foundations for Financial Economics*, New York: North-Holland.

Johnsen, T.H. and J.B. Donaldson (1985), "The Structure of Intertemporal Preferences under Uncertainty and Time Consistent Plans," *Econometrica*, 53: 1451–8.

Kahneman, D. and A. Tversky (1979), "Prospect Theory: An Analysis of Decision Under Risk," *Econometrica*, 47: 263–91.

Kandel, S. and R.F. Stambaugh (1990), "Asset Returns and Intertemporal Preferences," NBER Working Paper 3633.

Karni, E. (1988), "On the Equivalence Between Descending Bid Auctions and First Price Sealed Bid Auctions," *Theory and Decision*, 25: 211–17.

    (1989), "Generalized Expected Utility Analysis of Multivariate Risk Aversion," *International Economic Review*, 30: 297–305.

Karni, E. and Z. Safra (1989a), "Dynamic Consistency, Revelations in Auctions and the Structure of Preferences," *Review of Economic Studies*, 56: 421–33.

    (1989b): "Ascending Bid Auctions with Behaviorally Consistent Bidders," *Annals of Operations Research*, 19: 435–46.

    (1990), "Behaviorally Consistent Optimal Stopping Rules," *Journal of Economic Theory*, 51: 391–401.

Karni, E. and D. Schmeidler (forthcoming), "Utility Theory with Uncertainty," in W. Hildenbrand and H. Sonnenschein (eds), *Handbook of Mathematical Economics*, vol. IV.

Kihlstrom, R.E. and L.J. Mirman (1974), "Risk Aversion with Many Commodities," *Journal of Economic Theory*, 8: 361–88.

Knight, F. (1921), *Risk, Uncertainty and Profit*, Boston: Houghton Mifflin.

Kocherlakota, N. (1987), "State Nonseparability: Theory and Empirical Implications," Ph.D. Thesis, University of Chicago.

    (1990), "Disentangling the Coefficient of Relative Risk Aversion from the Elasticity of Intertemporal Substitution: An Irrelevance Result," *Journal of Finance*, 45: 175–90.

Koopmans, T.C. (1960), "Stationary Ordinal Utility and Impatience," *Econometrica*, 28: 287–309.

Kreps, D.M. and E.L. Porteus (1978), "Temporal Resolution of Uncertainty and Dynamic Choice Theory," *Econometrica*, 46: 185–200.

    (1979), "Temporal von Neumann-Morgenstern and Induced Preferences," *Journal of Economic Theory*, 20: 81–109.

Loomes, G. and R. Sugden (1982), "Regret Theory: An Alternative Theory of Rational Choice Under Uncertainty," *Economic Journal*, 92: 805–24.

Lucas, R.E. (1978), "Asset Prices in an Exchange Economy," *Econometrica*, 46: 1426–45.

Ma, C. (forthcoming), "Market Equilibrium with Heterogeneous Agents and Recursive Utility," *Economic Theory*.

Machina, M.J. (1982a), "A Stronger Characterization of Declining Risk Aversion," *Econometrica*, 50: 1069–79.

(1982b), "'Expected Utility' Analysis Without the Independence Axiom," *Econometrica*, 50: 277–323.

(1983a), "The Economic Theory of Individual Behavior Towards Risk: Theory, Evidence and New Directions," Stanford University, IMSSS Technical Report #433.

(1983b), "Generalized Expected Utility Analysis and the Nature of Observed Violations of the Independence Axiom," in B. Stigum and F. Wenstop (eds), *Foundations of Utility and Risk Theory with Applications*, Dordrecht, Holland: D. Reidel Publishing Co.

(1984), "Temporal Risk and the Nature of Induced Preferences," *Journal of Economic Theory*, 33: 199–231.

(1985), "Stochastic Choice Functions Generated from Deterministic Preferences over Lotteries," *Economic Journal*, 95: 575–94.

(1987), "Choice Under Uncertainty: Problems Solved and Unsolved," *Journal of Economic Perspectives*, 1: 121–54.

(1989a), "Dynamic Consistency and Non-Expected Utility Models of Choice Under Uncertainty," *Journal of Economic Literature*, 27: 1622–68.

(1989b), "The Behavior of Risk Sharers," unpublished.

(1989c), "Comparative Statics and Non-Expected Utility Preferences," *Journal of Economic Theory*, 47: 393–405.

Machina, M.J. and W. Nielsen (1987), "The Ross Measure of Risk Aversion: Strengthening and Extension," *Econometrica*, 55: 1139–49.

Mankiw, N.G. and M.D. Shapiro (1986), "Risk and Return: Consumption Beta Versus Market Beta," *Review of Economics and Statistics*, 68: 452–9.

Marcet, A. and K.J. Singleton (1990), "Equilibrium Asset Prices and Savings of Heterogeneous Agents in the Presence of Portfolio Constraints," mimeo, Carnegie Mellor University.

Mehra, R. and E. Prescott (1985), "The Equity Premium: A Puzzle," *Journal of Monetary Economics*, 15: 145–61.

Merton, R.C. (1973), "An Intertemporal Capital Asset Pricing Model," *Econometrica*, 41: 867–87.

Milgrom, P.R. (1989), "Auctions and Bidding: A Primer," *Journal of Economic Perspectives*, 3: 3–22.

Milgrom, P.R. and R.J. Weber (1982), "A Theory of Auctions and Competitive Bidding," *Econometrica*, 50: 1089–22.

von Neumann, J. and O. Morgenstern (1953), *Theory of Games and Economic Behavior*, 3rd edition, Princeton: Princeton University Press.

Pollak, R.A. (1968), "Consistent Planning," *Review of Economic Studies*, 35: 201–8.

Quiggin, J. (1982), "A Theory of Anticipated Utility," *Journal of Economic Behavior and Organization*, 3: 323–43.

Raiffa, H. (1968), *Decision Analysis: Introductory Lectures on Choices Under Uncertainty*, Reading, MA: Addison-Wesley.

Roll, R. (1977), "A Critique of the Asset Pricing Theory's Tests: Part I: On Past and Potential Testability of the Theory," *Journal of Financial Economics*, 4: 129–76.

Rubinstein, A., Z. Safra, and W. Thomson (1990): "On the Interpretation of the Nash Bargaining Solution and Its Extension to Non-Expected Utility Preferences," Working Paper 24-90, Tel Aviv University.

Segal, U. (1989), "Axiomatic Representation of Expected Utility with Rank-Dependent Probabilities," *Annals of Operations Research*, 19: 359–73.

(1990), "Two-Stage Lotteries Without the Reduction Axiom," *Econometrica*, 58: 349–77.

Segal, U. and A. Spivak (1990), "First-Order versus Second-Order Risk Aversion," *Journal of Economic Theory*, 51: 111–25.

Selden, L. (1978), "A New Representation of Preference over 'Certain × Uncertain' Consumption Pairs: The 'Ordinal Certainty Equivalent' Hypothesis," *Econometrica*, 46: 1045–60.

(1979), "An OCE Analysis of the Effect of Uncertainty on Saving Under Risk Preference Independence," *Review of Economic Studies*, 46: 73–82.

Selden, L. and I. Stux (1978), "Consumption Trees, OCE Utility and the Consumption/Savings Decision," mimeo, Columbia University.

Selten, R. (1975), "Reexamination of the Perfectness Concept for Equilibrium Points in Extensive Games," *International Journal of Game Theory*, 4: 25–55.

Shefrin, H.M. and M. Statman (1984), "Explaining Investor Preference for Cash Dividends," *Journal of Financial Economics*, 13: 253–82.

(1985): "The Disposition to Sell Winners Too Early and Ride Losers Too Long: Theory and Evidence," *Journal of Finance*, 40: 777–92.

Singleton, K.J. (1990), "Specification and Estimation of Intertemporal Asset Pricing Models," in B. Friedman and F. Hahn (eds.), *Handbook in Monetary Economics*, New York: North-Holland, pp. 583–623.

Streufert, P.A. (1990a), "Stationary Recursive Utility and Dynamic Programming under the Assumption of Biconvergence," *Review of Economic Studies*, 57: 79–98.

(1990b), "Stochastic Dynamic Programming Under the Assumption of Biconvergence," mimeo, University of Wisconsin.

Strotz, R.H. (1956), "Myopia and Inconsistency in Dynamic Utility Maximization," *Review of Economic Studies*, 23: 165–80.

Sugden, R. (1986), "New Developments in the Theory of Choice Under Uncertainty," *Bulletin of Economic Reserves*, 38: 1–24. Reprinted in *Surveys in the Economics of Uncertainty*, in J. Hey and P. Lambert (ed.), Oxford: Basil Blackwell.

Svensson, L.E.O. (1989), "Portfolio Choice with Non-Expected Utility in Continuous Time," *Economic Letters*, 30: 313–17.

Uzawa, H. (1968), "Time Preference, the Consumption Function and Optimum Asset Holdings," in J.N. Wolfe (ed.), *Value, Capital and Growth: Papers in Honour of Sir John Hicks*. Chicago: Aldine.

Wang, S.S. (1990), "The Recoverability of Risk Aversion and Intertemporal Substitution," Ph.D. Thesis, University of Toronto.

Wang, T. (1991), "Lp-Fréchet Differentiable Preference and Local Utility Analysis," mimeo, University of Toronto; forthcoming in *Journal of Economic Theory*.

Weber, M. and C. Camerer (1987), "Recent Developments in Modelling Preferences Under Risk," *OR Spektrum*, 9: 129–51.

Weber, R.J. (1982), "The Allais Paradox, Dutch Auctions and Alpha-Utility Theory," Kellogg School of Management, mimeo, Northwestern University.

Weil, P. (1989), "The Equity Premium Puzzle and the Risk Free Rate Puzzle," *Journal of Monetary Economics*, 24: 401–22.

(1990a), "Non-Expected Utility in Macroeconomics," *Quarterly Journal of Economics*, 105: 29–42.

(1990b), "Equilibrium Asset Prices with Undiversifiable Labor Income Risk," mimeo, Harvard University.

(1990c), "Precautionary Savings and the Permanent Income Hypothesis," mimeo, Harvard University.

Yaari, M.E. (1987), "The Dual Theory of Choice Under Risk," *Econometrica*, 55: 95–115.

(1988), "A Controversial Proposal Concerning Inequality Measurement," *Journal of Economic Theory*, 44: 381–96.

Zin, S. (1987), "Intertemporal Substitution, Risk and the Time Series Behavior of Consumption and Asset Returns," Ph.D. Thesis, University of Toronto.

CHAPTER 2

Financial contracting theory

Milton Harris and Artur Raviv*

One of the oldest and most important questions in corporate finance is what determines how firms finance their investments and operations. This question has been referred to as the "capital structure" problem. The modern theory of capital structure began with the celebrated paper of Modigliani and Miller (1958). Here Modigliani and Miller (MM) pointed the direction that such theories must take by showing under what conditions capital structure is irrelevant. Since then, many economists have followed the path mapped by MM. Now, some thirty years later it seems appropriate to take stock of where this research stands and where it is going. Our goal in this survey is to synthesize the *recent* literature, summarize its results, relate these to the known empirical evidence, and suggest promising avenues for future research.[1]

Capital structure theories have traditionally been concerned with what determines the relative amounts issued by firms of various given securities, mainly debt and equity. A much deeper question, however, is what determines the specific form of the contract (security) under which investors supply funds to the firm. Investors provide such funds with the expectation of sharing in the returns generated by the firms' investments. Therefore, financial contract design must resolve the problem of allocating the cash flows generated to investors. For example, debt contracts generally promise a fixed payment not contingent on firm performance. If the firm fails to make this payment, returns to debtholders are negotiated under the bankruptcy law of the relevant jurisdiction. Equity contracts specify that the holders share the residual returns after debtholders are paid, subject to limited liability. Returns to be allocated by financial contracts depend, however, on decisions made within the firm such as choice of project, assignment of personnel, day-to-day operating decisions, etc. As a result, returns depend on who is in control of these activities. Consequently, the problem of designing financial contracts includes the assignment of control rights as well as the allocation of cash flows. Debt contracts, for example, allocate no control rights except when the firm is in bankruptcy. Again, in this situation, the rights of debtholders are determined by bankruptcy law. Equity contracts typically allocate proportional voting rights (one-share–one-vote).[2] Which issues may be voted on and the majority rule to be applied are generally specified by the corporate charter. The charter is thus an implicit part of every financial contract.[3] In general, we see that the security design problem encompasses both the allocation of cash flows and control rights.

Having been largely ignored by financial economists for thirty years, the more fundamental issue of security design has recently been the subject of increasing attention in the literature. In this paper, we include these developments and relate them to each other and to the traditional capital structure literature. In what follows we reserve the phrase "traditional capital structure" for those theories that take debt and equity as the exogenous securities. The phrase "security design" is used to refer to models in which the financial contracts are at least partly endogenous.

Our goal of synthesizing the recent literature is, however, too ambitious to result in a careful understanding of the state of financial contracting research. Consequently, we have chosen to narrow the scope of our inquiry. First, we focus on financial contracting *theory*. Although we discuss the empirical literature as it relates to the predictions of theory, we make no attempt to give a comprehensive survey of this literature. We simply take the empirical results at face value and do not review or criticize the methods used in these papers. Second, we arbitrarily exclude theories based primarily on tax considerations. While such theories are undoubtedly of great empirical importance, we believe that they have been adequately surveyed.[4] Moreover, tax-based research is not our comparative advantage. Third, we systematically exclude certain topics that, while related to financial contracting theory, focus on issues that are narrower than the ones we consider here. These include literature dealing with the call or conversion of securities, dividend theories, bond covenants and maturity, bankruptcy law, pricing and method of issuance of new securities, and preferred stock. In short, we concentrate on non-tax-driven financial contracting theories.

Although the above considerations exclude many papers, a fairly large literature remains. To highlight the current state of the art, we consider mainly papers written since 1980. The only exception to this statement is the inclusion of papers written in the mid to late 1970s that serve as the foundation for the more recent literature. A diligent search of both published and unpublished research, meeting the above criteria, resulted in over 150 papers. Obviously, we could not survey all these papers here in detail. Consequently, we were forced to pick and choose those papers that, in our opinion, are the most important or the most representative of a given stream of research. Naturally, this selection process is biased by our own tastes and interests. Thus we tend to emphasize papers based on the economics of information, incentives, and contracting. We apologize to those authors whose papers were left out or were not given the attention the authors believe them to deserve.

In organizing the survey, several options were available. One approach which has proved fruitful in other areas is to construct or identify a very general model and then examine how existing models specialize this framework. This approach has the advantage of showing clearly the interrelationships among models. In the case of financial contracting, however, the set of features one must include in such a general model is so large and complicated, that the resulting structure would not yield clear insights. A related approach is to ask what issues might be resolved by theories of financial contracting. This "wish list" would include questions such as what is the effect on capital structure of changes in the volatility of cash flows, firm size, elasticity of demand for the product, the extent of insider private information, etc. The survey would then proceed to document the answers available in the literature. The problem with organizing the survey in this way is that often a single model addresses several issues. Such a model would then require discussion in several places. Moreover, a closely related model focusing on a different issue would be presented separately, making a comparison of the two models difficult to exposit. Because of these difficulties, we have chosen instead to organize our survey based on the forces that determine capital structure.

Grouping models based on the force driving capital structure allows discussion of the model to be consolidated in one place and facilitates an examination of the relationships among similar models. We have identified four categories of determinants of capital structure. These are the desire to:

> ameliorate conflicts of interest among various groups with claims to the firm's resources, including managers (the agency approach),
> convey private information to capital markets or mitigate adverse selection effects (the asymmetric information approach),
> influence the nature of products or competition in the product/input market, or
> affect the outcome of corporate control contests.

Each of these four categories is discussed in a separate section. Many of the papers we survey fit well in more than one category. We include these in the category corresponding to the most important driving force of the model.

In each topic, we start with the traditional capital structure theories then discuss the security design literature. After a brief overview of the papers surveyed and their relation to each other, we describe in some detail the central papers and their results. This is generally followed by a discussion of related extensions. Note that we do not exposit all the subtleties of even the models on which we focus the most attention. Instead we try to present the main idea in its most stripped-down form. Each section concludes with a summary of the main implications of the models surveyed in the section. Finally, we collect these results and compare them to the available evidence. Since each section is self-contained, readers not interested in the entire survey can pick and choose sections. Moreover, the summary subsection in each of sections 1 through 4 can also be read independently. Readers interested only in the overall summary and conclusions should read sections 5 and 6.

Briefly, our conclusions are as follows. First, the models surveyed have identified a large number of *potential* determinants of capital structure. The empirical work so far has not, however, sorted out which of these are important in various contexts. Second, the theory has identified a relatively small number of "general principles." Several properties of the debt contract have important implications for determining capital structure. These are the bankruptcy provision, convexity of payoffs of levered equity, the effect of debt on managerial equity ownership, and the relative insensitivity of debt payoffs to firm performance. In addition, some important insights for designing securities are that securities should not have "cheap votes," that debt can force payout via the threat of bankruptcy, and that securities can make corporate control contingent on firm performance. Third, the empirical evidence is largely consistent with the theory, although there are a few instances where the evidence seems to contradict certain models. These inconsistencies cannot, however, be regarded as conclusive, because the empirical studies were not designed specifically to test the models and were, therefore, not careful about satisfying the *ceteris paribus* conditions. With regard to further theoretical work, it appears that models relating to products and inputs and the security design area are underexplored, while the asymmetric information approach has reached the point of diminishing returns. Finally, with regard to further empirical work, it seems essential that empirical studies concentrate on testing particular models or classes of models in an attempt to discover the most important determinants of capital structure in given environments.

The plan of the Chapter is as follows. In section 1, we discuss models based on agency costs. Models using asymmetric information are considered in section 2. Interactions of capital structure with behavior in the product or input market or with characteristics of products or inputs are taken up in

section 3. Section 4 surveys models based on corporate control considerations. In section 5, we summarize the theoretical results and compare them
with the evidence. Finally, our conclusions are presented in section 6.

1   MODELS BASED ON AGENCY COSTS

A significant fraction of the effort of researchers over the last ten years has
been devoted to models in which financial contracts are determined by
agency costs, i.e., costs due to conflicts of interest. Research in this area was
initiated by Jensen and Meckling (1976) building on earlier work of Fama
and Miller (1972). They consider frictions arising from features of standard
debt and equity contracts. The security design literature, beginning with
Townsend (1979), attempts to derive contracts that optimally resolve
conflicts between outside investors and managers.

1.1   Traditional agency models

Jensen and Meckling (1976) identify two types of conflicts of interest.
Conflicts between shareholders and managers arise, because managers
hold less than 100 percent of the residual claim. Consequently, they do not
capture the entire gain from their profit enhancement activities, but they do
bear the entire cost of these activities. For example, managers can invest
less effort in managing firm resources and may be able to transfer firm
resources to their own, personal benefit, e.g., by consuming "perquisites"
such as corporate jets, plush offices, building "empires," etc. The manager
bears the entire cost of refraining from these activities but captures only a
fraction of the gain. As a result managers overindulge in these pursuits
relative to the level that would maximize firm value. This inefficiency is
reduced the larger is the fraction of the firm's equity owned by the manager.
Holding constant the manager's absolute investment in the firm, increases
in the fraction of the firm financed by debt increase the manager's share of
the equity and mitigate the loss from the conflict between the manager and
shareholders. Moreover, as pointed out by Jensen (1986), since debt
commits the firm to pay out cash, it reduces the amount of "free" cash
available to managers to engage in the type of pursuits mentioned above.
This mitigation of the conflicts between managers and equityholders
constitutes the benefit of debt financing.[5]

Conflicts between debtholders and equityholders arise, because the debt
contract gives equityholders an incentive to invest suboptimally.[6] More
specifically, the debt contract provides that, if an investment yields large
returns, well above the face value of the debt, equityholders capture most of

the gain. If, however, the investment fails, because of limited liability, debtholders bear the consequences. As a result, equityholders may benefit from "going for broke," i.e., investing in very risky projects, even if they are value decreasing. Such investments result in a decrease in the value of the debt. The loss in value of the equity from the poor investment can be more than offset by the gain in equity value captured at the expense of debtholders. Equityholders bear this cost to debtholders, however, when the debt is issued if the debtholders correctly anticipate equityholders' future behavior. In this case, equityholders receive less for the debt than they otherwise would. Thus, the cost of the incentive to invest in value decreasing projects created by debt is borne by the equityholders who issue the debt. This effect, generally called the "asset substitution effect," is an agency cost of debt financing.[7]

Jensen and Meckling argue that an optimal capital structure can be obtained by trading off the agency cost of debt against the benefit of debt as previously described.[8] A number of implications follow. First, one would expect bond contracts to include features that attempt to prevent asset substitution, such as interest coverage requirements, prohibitions against investments in new, unrelated lines of business, etc. Second, industries in which the opportunities for asset substitution are more limited will have higher debt levels, *ceteris paribus*. Thus, for example, the theory predicts that regulated public utilities, banks, and firms in mature industries with few growth opportunities will be more highly levered. Third, firms for which slow or even negative growth is optimal and that have large cash inflows from operations should have more debt. Large cash inflows without good investment prospects create the resources to consume perquisites, build empires, overpay subordinates, etc. Increasing debt reduces the amount of "free cash" and increases the manager's fractional ownership of the residual claim. According to Jensen (1989) industries with these characteristics today include steel, chemicals, brewing, tobacco, television and radio broadcasting, and wood and paper products. The theory predicts that these industries should be characterized by high leverage.

All the theories based on agency problems surveyed in the remainder of this section use one of the conflicts introduced by Jensen and Meckling as a starting point. Consequently, we classify these papers into two subsections corresponding to the conflict between equityholders and managers and the conflict between equityholders and debtholders.

Conflicts between equityholders and managers

The two papers surveyed in this subsection share a common concern with manager–shareholder conflicts but differ according to the specific way in which this conflict arises. More importantly, they also differ in how debt alleviates the problem and in the disadvantages of debt.

In Harris and Raviv (1990) and Stulz (1991), managers and investors disagree over an operating decision. In particular, in Harris and Raviv managers are assumed to want always to continue the firm's current operations even if liquidation of the firm is preferred by investors. In Stulz, managers are assumed to want always to invest all available funds even if paying out cash is better for investors. In both cases, it is assumed that the conflict cannot be resolved through contracts based on cash flow and investment expenditure. Debt mitigates the problem in the Harris and Raviv model by giving investors (debtholders) the option to force liquidation if cash flows are poor. In Stulz, as in Jensen (1986), debt payments reduce free cash flow. Capital structure is determined by trading off these benefits of debt against costs of debt. In Harris and Raviv, the assertion of control by investors through bankruptcy entails costs related to the production of information, used in the liquidation decision, about the firm's prospects. The cost of debt in Stulz's model is that debt payments may more than exhaust "free" cash, reducing the funds available for profitable investment. This comparison of Harris and Raviv and Stulz is summarized in table 2.1 where the relationship of these two models to Jensen and Meckling (1976) and Jensen (1986) is also shown.[9]

The optimal capital structure in Harris and Raviv trades off improved liquidation decisions versus higher investigation costs. A larger debt level improves the liquidation decision because it makes default more likely. In the absence of default, incumbent management is assumed not to liquidate the firm even if the assets are worth more in their next best alternative use. Following a default, however, investors control the liquidation decision, and they expend resources to obtain additional information pertinent to this decision. Since investors choose an optimal liquidation decision based on their information, default improves this decision. More frequent default, however, is more costly as resources are expended investigating the firm when it is in default.

The Harris and Raviv model predicts that firms with higher liquidation value, e.g., those with tangible assets, and/or firms with lower investigation costs will have more debt, will be more likely to default, but will have higher market value than similar firms with lower liquidation value and/or higher investigation costs. The intuition for the higher debt level is that increases in liquidation value make it more likely that liquidation is the best strategy. Therefore information is more useful and a higher debt level is called for. Similarly, decreases in investigation costs also increase the value of default resulting in more debt. The increase in debt results in higher default probability. Harris and Raviv also obtain results on whether a firm in

Table 2.1. *Comparison of agency models based on manager–shareholder conflicts*

Model	Conflict	Benefit of debt	Cost of debt
Jensen and Meckling (1976)	Managerial perquisites	Increase managerial ownership	Asset substitution
Jensen (1986)	Overinvestment	Reduce free cash	Unspecified
Harris and Raviv (1990)	Failure to liquidate	Allows investors option to liquidate	Investigation costs
Stulz (1991)	Overinvestment	Reduce free cash	Underinvestment

bankruptcy is reorganized or liquidated. They show that the probability of being reorganized decreases with liquidation value and is independent of investigation costs. Using a constant-returns-to-scale assumption they show that the debt level relative to expected firm income, default probability, bond yield, and the probability of reorganization, are independent of firm size. Combining these results, Harris and Raviv argue that higher leverage can be expected to be associated with larger firm value, higher debt level relative to expected income, and lower probability of reorganization following default.

The optimal capital structure in Stulz is determined by trading off the benefit of debt in preventing investment in value decreasing projects against the cost of debt in preventing investment in value increasing projects. Thus, as in Jensen (1986), firms with an abundance of good investment opportunities can be expected to have low debt levels relative to firms in mature, slow-growth, cash-rich industries. Moreover, Stulz argues that, in general, managers will be reluctant to implement the optimal debt levels but are more likely to do so the greater is the threat of takeover. Thus firms more likely to be takeover targets can be expected to have more debt, *ceteris paribus*, while firms with antitakeover measures will have less debt. Finally, firms whose value increasing investment opportunities create more value than the value decreasing ones destroy will have less debt than firms in the opposite situation. The reason is that such firms are primarily concerned with not losing the value creating opportunities.[10]

Conflicts between equityholders and debtholders

This subsection surveys two papers in which reputation moderates the asset substitution problem, i.e., the incentive of levered equityholders to choose risky, negative net-present-value investments.[11] Diamond (1989) and Hirshleifer and Thakor (1989) show how managers of firms have an incentive to pursue relatively safe projects out of reputational considerations.[12]

Diamond's model is concerned with a firm's reputation for choosing projects that assure debt repayment. There are two possible investment projects: a safe, positive NPV project and a risky, negative NPV project. The risky project can have one of two payoffs ("success" or "failure"). Both projects require the same initial investment which must be financed by debt. A firm can be of three, initially observationally equivalent types. One type has access only to the safe project, one type has access only to the risky project, and one type has access to both. Since investors cannot distinguish the firms *ex ante*, the initial lending rate reflects their beliefs about the projects chosen by firms on average. Returns from the safe project suffice to pay the debtholders (even if the firm is believed by investors to have only the risky project), but returns from the risky project allow repayment only if the project is successful.

Because of the asset substitution problem, if the firm has a choice of projects, myopic maximization of equity value (e.g., in a one-period situation) would lead the firm to choose the risky project. If the firm can convince lenders it has only the safe project, however, it will enjoy a lower lending rate. Since lenders can observe only a firm's default history, it is possible for a firm to build a reputation for having only the safe project by not defaulting. The longer the firm's history of repaying its debt, the better is its reputation, and the lower is its borrowing cost. Therefore, older, more established firms, find it optimal to choose the safe project, i.e., not engage in asset substitution, to avoid losing a valuable reputation. Young firms with little reputation may choose the risky project. If they survive without a default, they will eventually switch to the safe project. As a result, firms with long track records will have lower default rates and lower costs of debt than firms with brief histories. Although the amount of debt is fixed in Diamond's model, it is plausible than an extension of the model would yield the result that younger firms have less debt than older ones, other things equal.

Managers may also have an incentive to pursue relatively safe projects out of a concern for *their* reputations. Hirshleifer and Thakor consider a manager who has a choice of two projects, each with only two outcomes, success or failure. Failure means the same for both projects, but from the point of view of the shareholders, the high-risk–high-return project yields both higher expected returns and higher returns if it succeeds. Suppose that from the point of view of the manager's reputation, however, success on the two projects is equivalent, i.e., the managerial labor market can only distinguish "success" *versus* "failure". Thus the manager maximizes probability of success while shareholders prefer expected return. If the safer project has a higher probability of success, the manager will choose it even if the other project is better for the equityholders. This behavior of managers, reduces the agency cost of debt. Thus, if managers are susceptible to such a reputation effect, the firm may be expected to have more debt than otherwise. Hirshleifer and Thakor argue that managers of firms more likely to be takeover targets are more susceptible to the reputation effect. Such firms can be expected to have more debt, *ceteris paribus*. Conversely, firms that have adopted antitakeover measures will use less debt, other things equal.

1.2 Security design based on agency problems

In this section we consider security design models that approach the issue from the point of view of resolving agency problems between managers and outside investors. These papers address only the allocation of cash flows to securities. The common basic framework involves a manager who can keep any income not paid out to outside investors. The firm requires outside financing, however, so the problem to be solved is to design an optimal contract (financial security) for which outside investors are willing to pay what is required. The papers surveyed in this section differ in the way in which the manager is induced to pay the contractually specified amount. Their common conclusion is that debt is an optimal financing contract in such environments. In some cases, the solution also involves outside equity.

Townsend (1979) was the first to address this issue.[13] He assumes that contracts with outside investors can depend on income if and only if a verification cost is incurred. A contract must specify for each payout to investors, whether income is verified. The set of verified payouts is called the verification region. If the payout is in the verification region, the contract specifies a total payment (including the amount already paid out) that depends on actual income. We assume that the manager is risk neutral. Contracts are designed to minimize verification costs while raising the required revenue from outside investors. Several results regarding the structure of the optimal contract follow.

First, whenever income is *not* verified, actual payout is a constant, independent of income. Given any contract, among payouts in the non-verification region, the manager will choose the smallest regardless of income.

Second, any payout in the verification region must be less than the minimum payout in the non-verification region. Otherwise, the manager would make the minimum payment in the non-verification region.

Third, the optimal contract will specify that all income in excess of verification costs be paid out in the verification region, i.e., when income is verified, the manager obtains a net payoff of zero. Otherwise, to obtain the same expected payout to the investor, the verification region would need to be larger. To understand this in somewhat more detail, consider any contract. From this contract, we can construct a new one in which all income above verification costs is paid out in the verification region. The new contract is preferred by the manager while the investor is indifferent between them. To construct this contract, suppose F is the fixed payment on the old contract's non-verification region. For this contract, if income is less than F, then it is verified. For the new contract, let the verification region be the set of incomes below F', where $F' \leq F$. Note that, if income is not verified under the old contract, it must exceed F and hence is not verified under the new contract either. Thus the new verification region is smaller than the old one. Also assume that, under the new contract, all income in excess of verification costs is paid out in the verification region. First suppose $F' = F$. For any income that is not verified under either contract, the new contract pays out the same as the old. For any income that is verified under either contract, the new contract pays at least as much (since it pays everything available). For any income that is verified under the old contract but not under the new one, the new contract pays F' which exceeds the payment under the old contract by the second result, above. Consequently, we have shown that the verification region under the new contract is no larger than that under the old. Also, the payment to the investor is always at least as large under the new contract and is strictly larger for any income which is verified under the old contract but not fully paid out. This implies that F' can be chosen to be smaller than F and still keep the investor indifferent. This enlarges the non-verification region. Consequently, although the investor is indifferent between the two contracts, the manager prefers the new contract since the expected payout to the investor is the same and the new contract has a smaller verification region (hence lower verification costs).

Fourth, the verification region must be the interval from zero to some payout, say F. Moreover, whenever income is above F, the manager will choose to pay F. To see this, let F be the minimum payout in the non-verification region. The second result states that the verification region is contained in $[0,F]$. But, if $z\in[0,F]$, z must be verified since F is the smallest unverified payout. Also, for any income $y \geq F$, if the manager paid less than F, he would be left with nothing since the payout would be verified and (from the third result) all income would be paid out. If he paid F, he would be left with $y - F \geq 0$. Thus, if feasible the manager pays out F.

Taking these four results together, we conclude that, for some number F, payout is F if income is above F, and otherwise, all income is paid out. That is, the optimal contract is debt of face value F.

Another, related approach, is provided by Diamond (1984). Diamond retains the basic framework of Townsend, i.e., the manager can consume any income not paid out, but he assumes that income cannot be used in a contract, even at a cost. Instead, Diamond assumes that a (non-pecuniary) penalty can be imposed on the manager as a function of what he pays out. This penalty is a dead-weight cost, like the verification cost of Townsend, since investors do not benefit from the manager's loss. It is not paid from firm income. Examples include loss of reputation or time spent in bankruptcy proceedings. The penalty determines how much the manager pays out to investors as a function of true income. The object is to design an optimal penalty function that maximizes the manager's expected payoff subject to the constraint that the resulting payout is sufficient to compensate investors for putting up the required capital. We can show that the solution to this problem also involves a debt contract.

One observation is immediate, namely, that the manager will pay out an amount that minimizes his total cost, i.e., the total of the payout and the penalty, subject to not paying out more than income. Consider any penalty contract. Suppose that, ignoring the income constraint, the payout that minimizes total cost to the manager under this contract is F, and the minimum cost (F plus penalty) is h. Since the penalty is non-negative, $F \leq h$. Note that whenever income is at least F, the manager will pay out F. Now consider a new penalty function such that the manager's total cost is F for payouts not above F, and his cost equals the payout for payouts above F. That is, the penalty for payouts below F is simply the difference between the payout and F, and the penalty for payouts above F is zero. Under this new contract, whenever income is at least F, the manager will pay F just as under the old contract. Whenever income is below F, he is indifferent among all feasible payouts (his total cost is F regardless of payout). We can assume he will pay out the entire income. Under the new contract, the manager pays out the same as before when income is above F and pays out everything when income is below F. Thus, he pays out at least as much under the new contract as under the old one for each income level. Also, under the new contract, the manager's total cost is always F (if income is less than F, his payout plus penalty is F, and if income is above F, he pays out F and incurs no penalty). Under the old contract, however, the manager's *minimum* total cost is $h \geq F$. Thus, under the new contract, both the manager and investors are better off.

We can conclude that any optimal contract has the property that, for some constant F, income is entirely paid out if it is below F, while F is paid out if income is above F. Thus, as in Townsend (1979), the optimal contract involves debt.

Two additional papers that exploit the assumption that inside equity owners (managers) can appropriate to themselves any income not paid out are Bolton and Scharfstein (1990) and Hart and Moore (1989). In both models, managers make payments to investors to avoid liquidation of the firm (instead of through verification or because of penalties). In Bolton and Scharfstein, the firm needs external financing in two periods. Investors can withhold funds in the second period based on payout in the first period. Bolton and Scharfstein show that an optimal contract involves withholding funding in the second period for sure if payout is low in the first and providing funding for sure if payout is sufficiently high.[14] In Hart and Moore, the firm needs external financing for a project whose returns accrue over several periods. Outside investors are allowed to force the firm to liquidate and can seize the proceeds from liquidation (but not other income). Since liquidation is assumed to be suboptimal, optimal contracts minimize the probability of liquidation subject to raising the required external funds. The resulting contract provides an initial investment by outsiders (which can exceed the amount required) and for a sequence of fixed payments. If the actual payment is less than the one called for, renegotiation occurs and can result in liquidation or rescheduling of payments.

Townsend (1979), Diamond (1984), Gale and Hellwig (1985), Bolton and Scharfstein (1990), and Hart and Moore (1989) all obtain the result that debt is an optimal contract in situations in which managers can appropriate to themselves income not paid out. The models differ in how outside investors capture the firm in bankruptcy. In Townsend and Gale and Hellwig, investors acquire income through costly verification. In Diamond, investors induce the manager to turn over the entire income to them by preventing him from capturing any gains from underpayment through the imposition of penalties. In Bolton and Scharfstein (1990) and Hart and Moore (1989), managers pay outside investors to avoid liquidation.

The models reviewed above are inconsistent with ownership of equity claims by outside investors. Chang (1987) and Williams (1989) attempt to remedy this defect. These two models are similar to those of Townsend (1979), Diamond (1984), and Gale and Hellwig (1985) in that contracts may not depend directly on the value of the firm's assets. Chang also assumes that verification is possible at a cost as in Townsend and Gale and Hellwig. The models differ from the previous three, however, by postulating the existence of an asset or return that can be contractually allocated to outsiders. Chang assumes that one component of firm income can be included in the contract without cost. He shows that the optimal contract with investors involves debt just as in Townsend, Diamond, and Gale and Hellwig, and that all of the contractible component of firm income in excess of what is required to pay debtholders is assigned to outside investors. The manager keeps that part of the non-contractible component not used to pay debtholders. This is interpreted as a combination of debt and outside equity (whether these are held by the same or different investors is immaterial). Williams observes that often a firm possesses collateral, i.e., assets whose ownership can be assigned to outside investors even if their value cannot be verified.[15] Contracts can specify an allocation of such assets (in whole or in part) as well as cash flow assignments. Williams shows that, in an optimal contract, investors are assigned a *fixed* fraction of any collateral. He interprets this as outside equity. We discuss Williams' model in more detail after first describing Chang's comparative statics results briefly.

Chang's more interesting comparative statics results are the following. First, he shows that, in contrast to capital structure signaling models, more profitable firms have less debt. If returns are stochastically larger, debt becomes safer, and the promised payment on the debt can be reduced. This reduces the verification region (a similar result should follow from the Townsend model). Second, an increase in the fraction of income that is observable, holding the distribution of total income constant, also reduces the debt level. This is not surprising since such an increase also increases the expected payout, *ceteris paribus*.

Williams' model consists of a firm, a risk-averse manager, and risk-neutral outside investors. The firm has an investment opportunity requiring an initial investment. This investment creates assets whose value at the end of the single period is $x + c(x)$, where x is the value of the collateral at date one, and $c(x)$ is the value of a control benefit which is captured by the manager if he is in control at date one (in this, Williams' model is similar to control-based models that take securities as exogenous; see section 4). If the manager is not in control, the benefit is dissipated. For the manager to be in control at date one, he must retain at least the fraction $1 - \alpha$ of the collateral. The benefit $c(x)$ is strictly increasing in x.

The value of the collateral, x, is uncertain initially and is observed only by the manager at date one. After observing x, the manager reports a value y for x. Of course, y need not be truthful. Since the value x can be assigned, in whole or in part, to outside investors, feasible financial contracts must specify what fraction, $A(y)$, of the collateral and how much cash, $B(y)$, is transferred to the outside investors, as a function of the manager's report y. Thus the payoff to outside investors, $D(x,y)$, can depend on the unobservable value x provided it is linear in x: $D(x,y) = A(y)x + B(y)$. Using the Revelation Principle (Myerson, 1979 and Harris and Townsend, 1981), Williams restricts D to be incentive compatible, i.e., such that the manager will tell the truth.

Since the manager is risk averse, and investors are risk neutral, optimal risk sharing would involve the manager allocating the collateral entirely to the outside investors in return for a constant payoff. This, however, would result in the certain loss of the control benefits, $c(x)$. Consequently, Williams shows that the optimal contract assigns the entire asset, but no cash, to the outside investors only when the value of the asset and the control benefits are low. When x and $c(x)$ are high, the manager assigns to investors the maximum fraction of the asset that allows him to maintain control, α. Thus the optimal contract has $A(y) = 1$ for values of y less than some number, b, and $A(y) = \alpha$ for $y \geq b$. Incentive compatibility requires that the manager's *total cost* be continuous in the report. The total cost for $y \leq b$ is $x + c(x)$. Therefore, to make the total cost equal on the two branches at $x = b$, the payment to investors for $y > b$ must be $\alpha x + B(y)$ for some $B(y)$ with $B(b) = c(b) + (1 - \alpha)b$. The cash payment must be independent of the manager's report for $y \geq b$, however, for the same reason as in the other papers in this section. Therefore, the cash payment is $B(y) = c(b) + (1 - \alpha)b$ for $y \geq b$.[16]

To interpret the results, first note that, for values of the asset less than b, investors foreclose and acquire the entire collateral, x. For values of the asset greater than b, investors will receive $\alpha x + c(b) + (1 - \alpha)b = \alpha(x - b) + b + c(b)$. Williams interprets this payoff as the fraction α of the levered equity and debt of face value $b + c(b)$. There is a problem with this interpretation, however, since the term $\alpha(x - b)$ is not the payoff to levered equity if the face value of the debt is $b + c(b)$. While the optimal contract certainly has many of the features of debt and equity contracts, the correspondence is not perfect.

Except for Chang (1987), the papers in this subsection obtain only one result concerning capital structure, namely, the optimality of the debt and equity forms. Chang (1987) shows that more profitable firms and firms with a higher proportion of contractible cash flows will have less debt. Several avenues for further research on this type of model are suggested, however. First, Gale and Hellwig show that investment is smaller when verification costs are positive than when they are zero. This suggests that debt should be negatively related to verification costs. Second, Diamond's model depends on the ability to impose whatever penalty is necessary to make total cost to the manager independent of payout over a range. If penalties are limited, say to loss of reputation from bankruptcy, it may be the case that debt contracts are no longer optimal, or it may limit debt and hence investment. Third, it would be interesting to derive optimal contracts and comparative statics when, after defaulting on a promised payment, a firm had an option to liquidate or reorganize. Clearly, Hart and Moore (1989) have made a start in this direction (see also Harris and Raviv, 1990).

Most of the security design papers based on agency costs (Townsend, 1979; Diamond, 1984; Gale and Hellwig, 1985; Hart and Moore, 1989; Bolton and Scharfstein, 1990) assumed an extreme form of the investor–manager conflict, namely that managers can "consume" all income not paid out to investors. Chang (1987) and Williams (1989) considered a less severe agency cost by assuming that some returns or assets cannot be appropriated by the manager. All these models have ignored the asset substitution problem, replacing asset substitution as a cost of debt with other costs such as verification costs, deadweight penalties, or denial of future rents. These differences between the capital structure approach and the security design approach provide some ideas for further research, discussed in section 6.

1.3   Summary

Agency models have been among the most successful in generating interesting implications. In particular, these models predict that leverage is positively associated with firm value (Harris and Raviv, 1990; Stulz, 1991; Hirshleifer and Thakor, 1989), default probability (Harris and Raviv, 1990), extent of regulation (Jensen and Meckling, 1976; Stulz, forthcoming), free cash flow (Jensen, 1986; Stulz, 1991), liquidation value (Williamson, 1988; Harris and Raviv, 1990), extent to which the firm is a takeover target (Stulz, 1991; Hirshleifer and Thakor, 1989), and the importance of managerial reputation (Hirshleifer and Thakor, 1989). Also, leverage is expected to be negatively associated with the extent of growth opportunities (Jensen and Meckling, 1976; Stulz, 1991), firm profitability and the fraction of cash flows that are contractible (Chang, 1987), interest coverage, the cost of investigating firm prospects, and the probability of reorganization following default (Harris and Raviv, 1990). Some other implications include the prediction that bonds will have covenants that attempt to restrict the extent to which equityholders can pursue risky projects that reduce the value of the debt (Jensen and Meckling, 1976) and that older firms with longer credit histories will tend to have lower default rates and costs of debt (Diamond, 1989). Finally, the result that firm value and leverage are positively related follows from the fact that these two endogenous variables move in the same direction with changes in the exogenous factors (Harris and Raviv, 1990; Stulz, 1991; Hirshleifer and Thakor, 1989). Therefore, leverage increasing (decreasing) changes in capital structure caused by a change in one of these exogenous factors will be accompanied by stock price increases (decreases). Except for Chang (1987), the security design literature obtains only one result concerning capital structure, namely, the optimality of the debt and equity forms.

2   ASYMMETRIC INFORMATION

The introduction into economics of the explicit modeling of private information has made possible a number of approaches to explaining capital structure. In these theories, firm managers or insiders are assumed to possess private information about the characteristics of the firm's return stream or investment opportunities. In one set of approaches, choice of the firm's capital structure signals to outside investors the information of insiders. This stream of research began with the work of Ross (1977) and Leland and Pyle (1977). In another, capital structure is designed to mitigate inefficiencies in the firm's investment decisions that are caused by the information asymmetry. This branch of the literature starts with Myers and Majluf (1984) and Myers (1984). We survey the various approaches in the following subsections.[17]

2.1   Interaction of investment and capital structure

In their pioneering work, Myers and Majluf (1984) showed that, if investors are less well-informed than current firm insiders about the value of the firm's assets, then equity may be mispriced by the market. If firms are required to finance new projects by issuing equity, underpricing may be so severe that new investors capture more than the net-present-value (NPV) of the new project, resulting in a net loss to existing shareholders. In this case the project will be rejected even if its NPV is positive. This underinvestment can be avoided if the firm can finance the new project using a security that is not so severely undervalued by the market. For example, internal funds and/or riskless debt involve no undervaluation, and therefore, will be preferred to equity by firms in this situation. Even (not too) risky debt will be preferred to equity. Myers (1984) refers to this as a "pecking order" theory of financing, i.e., that capital structure will be driven by firms' desire to finance new investments first internally, then with low-risk debt, and finally with equity only as a last resort.[18]

To understand why firms may pass up positive NPV projects, suppose there are only two types of firms. The current assets of the firm are worth either H or $L < H$, depending on type. Initially, the firm's type is known only to the firm's managers whose objective is to maximize the true value of the current shareholders' claim.[19] Outside investors believe the firm is of type H with probability p and type L with probability $1 - p$. Both types of firm have access to a new project that requires an investment of I and has NPV of v (I and v can be assumed to be common knowledge). The firm must decide whether to accept the project. If the project is accepted, the investment I must be financed by issuing equity to new shareholders. Consider the following candidate equilibrium. A type H firm rejects the project and issues no equity while a type L firm accepts the project and issues equity worth I. Investors believe that issuance of equity signals that the firm is of type L. To verify that this is an equilibrium, first notice that investor beliefs are rational. Second, given these beliefs, the equity issued by type L firms is fairly priced by the market, i.e., current shareholders give up a fraction $\beta = I/(L+v+I)$ of the firm to new shareholders. Their payoff from taking the project and issuing equity is $(1-\beta)(L+v+I) = L+v$. Consequently, the current shareholders of type L firms capture the NPV, v, of the new project by issuing equity. They would not prefer to imitate type H firms since this would require passing up the project along with its positive NPV with no compensating gain in valuation of the existing assets, i.e., their payoff would be L. Third, if a type H firm passes up the project, the payoff to current shareholders is simply H. On the other hand, if a type H firm imitates a type L firm by issuing equity, this equity will be priced by the market as if the firm were type L. In this case, the current shareholders' payoff is $(1-\beta)(H+v+I)$. The underpricing of the new equity can be so severe that current shareholders of the type H firm give up claims to the existing assets as well as the entire NPV of the new project. They are thus worse off by taking the project. This will happen when the above expression is less than H, or $(H-L)\beta > v$. Consequently, for parameters satisfying this inequality, in equilibrium, only type L firms will accept the positive NPV project. The left-hand side of the inequality is the value transferred to the new equityholders who acquire the fraction β of the firm at the bargain price of L instead of the true value, H. The inequality then states that underinvestment occurs if this transfer exceeds the NPV of the project.

What are the empirical implications of Myers' "pecking order" theory? Probably the most important implication is that, upon announcement of an equity issue, the market value of the firm's existing shares will fall. Prior to the announcement, the firm's market value (of current shares) is $pH + (1-p)(L+v)$, reflecting prior beliefs about firm type and the equilibrium behavior of the firm. Upon announcement of an equity issue, investors realize that the firm is of type L, so firm value becomes $L+v$. For parameter values satisfying the above inequality, $pH + (1-p)(L+v) > L+v$, i.e., announcement of the equity issue results in a fall in the price of current shares. Moreover, financing via internal funds or riskless debt (or any security whose value is independent of the private information) will not convey information and will not result in any stock price reaction. A second implication is that new projects will tend to be financed mainly from internal sources or from the proceeds of low-risk debt issues.[20] Third, Korajczyk et al. (1990b,c) argue that the underinvestment problem is least severe after information releases such as annual reports and earnings announcements. Therefore equity issues will tend to cluster after such releases and the stock price drop will be negatively related to the time between the release and the issue announcement.[21] Finally, suppose firms with comparatively little tangible assets relative to firm value are more subject to information asymmetries. For such firms, then, the underinvestment problem will occur more often than for similar firms with less severe information asymmetries. These firms can be expected to accumulate more debt over time, other things equal.

A number of authors have extended the basic Myers–Majluf idea. Krasker (1986) allows firms to choose the size of the new investment project and the accompanying equity issue. He confirms the results of Myers and Majluf in this context and also shows that the larger the stock issue, the worse the signal and the fall in the firm's stock price.

Narayanan (1988) and Heinkel and Zechner (1990) obtain results similar to Myers and Majluf using a slightly different approach. They show that when the information asymmetry concerns only the value of the new project, there can be overinvestment, i.e., some negative NPV projects will be taken. The reason is that full separation of firms by project NPV is impossible when the only observable signal is whether the project is taken. The equilibrium involves pooling of firms with projects of various NPV with the equity issued by all such firms being priced at the average value. Firms whose projects have low NPV will benefit from selling overpriced equity. This may more than compensate for a negative project NPV. The result is a negative cut-off NPV such that all firms with project NPV above the cut-off accept the project. In Narayanan's model, because (risky) debt is less overpriced than equity, the cut-off level is higher when projects are financed by debt issues. In Heinkel and Zechner, existing debt makes investment less attractive (as in Myers, 1977) and increases the cut-off level. Thus new (Narayanan) or existing (Heinkel and Zechner) debt reduces the overinvestment problem relative to all equity financing. The models imply that when a firm accepts a new project, the firm's stock price will increase since the market discovers that the firm's new project's NPV is above the cut-off level. Narayanan shows that, when firms are allowed to issue either debt or equity, all firms either issue debt or reject the project. In this sense, his results are consistent with the "pecking order" theory. Since project acceptance is associated with issuing debt, debt issues are good news, i.e., result in an increase in the firm's stock price. This implication is the opposite of Myers and Majluf. Debt is not a signal in Heinkel and Zechner since it is issued before firms have private information. Also, internal funds can substitute for debt in Heinkel and Zechner. Note that it is crucial to the results of both Narayanan and Heinkel and Zechner that acceptance or rejection of the project is the signal. If investors could observe only whether the firm issues securities, firms with negative NPV projects could imitate good firms by issuing the same security but investing the proceeds in Treasury bills.

Brennan and Kraus (1987), Constantinides and Grundy (1989), and Noe (1988) cast doubt on the "pecking order" theory. These papers enrich the set of financing choices that a firm may make when faced with the situation modeled by Myers and Majluf.[22] They conclude that firms do not necessarily have a preference for issuing straight debt over equity and that the underinvestment problem can be resolved through signaling with the richer set of financing options.

Brennan and Kraus offer an example similar to those in Myers and Majluf. There are two types of firms, say L and H, as above. Here, each type of firm has debt outstanding initially. In equilibrium, firm type H issues enough equity to finance the new project *and* retire its outstanding debt at face value. Firm type L issues only enough equity to finance the new project. Investors infer the firm type correctly. The debt of type H firms is risk free in this example. Therefore, type H firms obtain a "fair" deal on both their equity issue and debt repurchase. Type H firms do not imitate type L firms, because by so doing the type H firm's equity would be underpriced. Type L firms do not imitate type H firms, because repurchase of their debt at full face value entails an overpayment (i.e., for type L firms, the debt is risky). The cost of this overpayment for the debt exceeds the benefits available from selling overpriced equity. Thus, in equilibrium, both types of firm issue equity and accept the positive NPV project. Obviously, the underinvestment result of Myers and Majluf does not obtain in this example. Moreover, firms are allowed to issue debt but do not. This is inconsistent with the "pecking order" theory. Finally, issuing equity in the Brennan and Kraus model is a negative signal, but simultaneously issuing equity and using *part* of the proceeds to repurchase debt is a positive signal.

Constantinides and Grundy (1989) allow firms to issue any type of security and to repurchase existing equity. Another variation from the basic Myers/Majluf setup is that managers are assumed to have an equity stake in the firm whose true value they maximize. Constantinides and Grundy show that there is a fully separating equilibrium (even with a continuum of firm types) in which all types of firm take the positive NPV investment financed by an issue of a security that is neither straight debt nor equity. The new security is issued in an amount sufficient to finance the new investment and repurchase some of the firm's existing equity. This issued security is locally convex in firm value at the true value and locally concave for at least some firm value below the true value (see their theorem 3). Constantinides and Grundy interpret these characteristics as being those of convertible debt. The basic idea is that the repurchase of equity makes it costly for firms to overstate their true value while the issuance of a security that is sensitive to firm value makes it costly to understate true value. Separation is attained by the design and size of the new issue so that, at the true value of the firm, these effects balance at the margin. In this model, the underinvestment problem is costlessly resolved. Although firms may issue some form of debt, the model does not support the "pecking order" rule. That is, there is no overriding reason to finance using internal funds or riskless debt.

Noe (1988) allows firms to issue either debt or equity. He presents an example with three firm types, say L, M, and H. In equilibrium all types accept the positive NPV project, but types L and H issue debt while type M issues equity. Investors revise their beliefs about firm type using Bayes' rule (e.g., they correctly identify type M). Either security issued by type L would be overpriced as a result of being confused either with type M or type H. Debt is less sensitive to firm type than equity but, since firm type H is much better than firm type M in this example, L's debt is more overpriced than its equity. Consequently, type L chooses to "imitate" type H. Debt issued by type M is actually risk free, but, if it is confused with debt of type L, will be perceived to be risky by investors. Consequently, if type M issues debt, the debt will be underpriced. Therefore, type M prefers to issue fairly priced equity. Either security issued by type H would be underpriced. In the example, firm type H's debt is less underpriced both because it is less sensitive to firm quality and because the probability that a firm is of type L (the only type whose debt is risky) is low. Consequently, type H prefers to "imitate" type L and issue debt. Notice that all three types accept the project, that one type actually prefers to issue equity, and that the equity issuing firm is not the lowest quality.[23]

Brennan and Kraus, Constantinides and Grundy, and Noe demonstrate that allowing firms a wider range of financing choices can invalidate the Myers–Majluf results in some cases. Whether the type of examples identified in these papers are more important empirically than those of Myers and Majluf is an open question. We note, however, that Noe shows that the average quality of firms issuing debt is higher in equilibrium than that of firms issuing equity. Therefore, like Myers and Majluf, Noe's model predicts a negative stock market response to an announcement of an equity issue. Noe also predicts a positive market response to an announcement of a debt issue. Moreover, when Constantinides and Grundy further extend the model to allow different firm types to have different optimal investment levels and assume that investment is observable, they show that firms can fully separate using investment and the size of a straight bond issue (with some share repurchase) as signals. Thus, in this situation straight debt is a preferred financing tool, although the reason here is that it helps to signal a firm's true type while in Myers and Majluf, debt is a device to avoid signaling. Also, in this variant of the model, the market reaction to a stock repurchase financed by debt is more favorable the larger is the transaction.

2.2   Signaling with proportion of debt

In the previous subsection, capital structure emerged as part of the solution to problems of over- and underinvestment. We turn now to models in which investment is fixed and capital structure serves as a signal of private insider information.

The seminal contribution in this area is that of Ross (1977). In Ross' model, managers know the true distribution of firm returns, but investors do not. Firm return distributions are ordered by first-order stochastic dominance. Managers benefit if the firm's securities are more highly valued by the market but are penalized if the firm goes bankrupt. Investors take larger debt levels as a signal of higher quality.[24] Since lower quality firms have higher marginal expected bankruptcy costs for any debt level, managers of low quality firms do not imitate higher quality firms by issuing more debt.

A simple formal model is the following. Suppose that the date-one returns, $\tilde{x}$, of a firm of type t are distributed uniformly on $[0,t]$. The manager is privately informed about t. He chooses the face value of debt, D, to maximize a weighted average of the market value of the firm at date zero and the expected value at date one, net of a penalty, L, for bankruptcy.[25] We denote by $V_0(D)$ the value assigned to the firm at date zero by the market if the debt level is D. The manager's objective function is then:

$$(1-\gamma)V_0(D)+\gamma(t/2-LD/t).$$

The parameter γ is a weight. The expected payoff at date one, given the manager's information is simply $t/2$. He evaluates the bankruptcy probability as D/t. If investors infer that $t = a(D)$ when the manager issues debt of face value D, then:

$$V_0(D)=a(D)/2.$$

Substituting this into the objective function and taking the derivative with respect to D gives the first-order condition. In equilibrium, investors correctly infer t from D, i.e., if $D(t)$ is the manager's optimal choice of debt level as a function of the firm type t, then $a(D(t)) \equiv t$. Using this in the first-order condition and solving the resulting differential equation gives:

$$D(t) = ct^2/L + b,$$

where c and b are constants.

The main empirical result is that firm value (or profitability) and the debt–equity ratio are positively related.[26] It is also easily seen from the above formula that increases in the bankruptcy penalty, other things equal, decrease the debt level and the probability of bankruptcy. Ross also shows that this probability is increasing in firm type, t. Thus firm value, debt level, and bankruptcy probability are all positively related in this model.

Heinkel (1982) considers a model similar to Ross but does not assume that firm returns are ordered by first-order stochastic dominance. Instead, the return distribution is assumed to be such that "higher" quality firms have higher overall value but lower quality bonds (lower market value for given face value), hence higher equity value. This allows firms to separate costlessly when insiders maximize the value of their residual claim subject to raising a given amount of external capital.[27] The reason is that any firm attempting to convince the market that it is a type other than its true type will gain from overvaluation of one security and lose from undervaluation of the other. In equilibrium, the amounts issued of the two securities for each type firm are such that the gains and losses balance at the margin. High value firms issue more debt. To imitate a high value firm, a lower value firm must issue more underpriced debt and reduce the amount of overpriced equity. Similarly, to imitate a low value firm, a higher value firm must issue less overpriced debt and more underpriced equity. Since higher quality firms have higher total value, the result that they issue more debt is consistent with Ross' result.[28]

Another model that uses debt as a signal is that of Poitevin (1989) which involves potential competition between an incumbent firm and an entrant. The entrant's marginal costs are privately known by the entrant.[29] In equilibrium, low cost entrants signal this fact by issuing debt while the incumbent and high cost entrants issue only equity. The cost to a firm of issuing debt is that it makes the firm vulnerable to predation by the other firm, possibly resulting in bankruptcy of the debt-financed firm. The benefit of debt is that the financial market places higher value on the debt-financed firm since it believes such a firm to be low cost. High-cost entrants will not issue debt since the resulting probability of bankruptcy due to predation by the incumbent renders the cost of misleading the capital market too high (incumbents prey equally on all debt-financed firms, even if thought to be low cost). The main result, like the other models in this subsection, is that issuance of debt is good news to the financial market. Since predation is used only to drive one's rival into bankruptcy, there will be predation only against debt-financed firms.

2.3   Models based on managerial risk aversion

Several studies exploit managerial risk aversion to obtain a signaling equilibrium in which capital structure is determined. The basic idea is that increases in firm leverage allow managers to retain a larger fraction of the (risky) equity. The larger equity share reduces managerial welfare due to risk aversion, but the decrease is smaller for managers of higher quality projects. Thus managers of higher quality firms can signal this fact by having more debt in equilibrium.[30]

A simple formal model based on Leland and Pyle (1977) is as follows. Consider an entrepreneur whose project returns $\tilde{x} = \mu + \tilde{\varepsilon}$ with $E\tilde{\varepsilon} = 0$ and who must raise I from external sources. The entrepreneur observes expected return, μ, but investors do not. He chooses the fraction of the equity he retains, α, and the face value of default-free debt, D, to maximize his expected utility of end-of-period wealth, $Eu(\tilde{W})$, where:

$$\tilde{W} = \alpha(\tilde{x} - D) + (1 - \alpha)(V(\alpha) - D) + D = \alpha\tilde{x} + (1 - \alpha)V(\alpha)^{31},$$

subject to the constraint that I of external funds must be raised:

$$(1 - \alpha)[V(\alpha) - D] + D = I.$$

Here $V(\alpha)$ is the market's assessment of the value of the firm given that the entrepreneur retains the fraction α of the equity. We have also assumed that there is no investment required ($K = 0$ in Leland and Pyle's notation) since this does not affect the results. Although the debt level, D, does not affect the entrepreneur's objective directly, his choice of α implies a debt level through the external-funds constraint.[32] It is clear from the formula for $\tilde{W}$ that increases in the entrepreneur's share, α, increase the riskiness of his portfolio (since $V(\alpha)$ is riskless cash) but also increase the amount he obtains for the share sold to outsiders through signaling (since V is increasing in α in equilibrium).

The first-order condition for α is obtained by differentiating $Eu(\tilde{W})$ with respect to α, substituting the equilibrium condition that $V(\alpha(\mu)) \equiv \mu$ (where $\alpha(\mu)$ is the entrepreneur's optimal ownership share if his expected return is μ), and setting the result equal to zero. It can be shown from this condition that the entrepreneur's equilibrium ownership share, α, increases with firm quality. To translate this into a capital structure theory, we must calculate the effect on the debt level D of changes in firm quality using the external-funds constraint. Increases in μ result in increases in α, as just shown, however, the increase in α has two opposing effects on D. The increased ownership of the entrepreneur, other things equal, would require that more funds be raised by debt. Firm value, V, is, however, larger for larger α, so that equityholders may pay more for the smaller fraction of the firm they receive. Consequently, D may not need to increase to finance the increased ownership share of the entrepreneur. Leland and Pyle (1977) derive some conditions on the parameters of an example that guarantee that debt increases with α. Under these conditions, firms with larger debt also have a larger fraction of the equity owned by insiders and are of higher quality.[33]

2.4   Summary

The main predictions of asymmetric information theories concern stock price reactions to issuance and exchange of securities, the amount of leverage, and whether firms observe a pecking order for security issues.

Stock price effects of security issues

> Debt: Myers and Majluf (1984) and Krasker (1986) predict the absence of price effects upon issuance of (riskless) debt. Noe (1988) and Narayanan (1988) predict a positive price effect of a (risky) debt issue.
>
> Equity: Myers and Majluf (1984), Krasker (1986), Noe (1988), Korajczyk, *et al.* (1990c), and Lucas and McDonald (1990) predict a negative price effect of an equity issue. This price drop will be larger the larger is the informational asymmetry and the larger is the equity issue. Moreover, Lucas and McDonald (1990) show that, on average, equity issues will be preceded by abnormal stock price increases.

Stock price effects of exchange offers

> Debt increasing offers: Constantinides and Grundy (1989) predict a positive stock price reaction that is larger the larger the exchange.
>
> Equity increasing offers: Brennan and Kraus (1987) predict a positive stock price reaction.

Is there a pecking order?

> Yes: Myers and Majluf (1984), Krasker (1986), and Narayanan (1988).

No: Brennan and Kraus (1987), Noe (1988); Constantinides and Grundy (1989) dispute the pecking order result in models similar to that of Myers and Majluf. Other signaling models, such as Ross (1977), Leland and Pyle (1977), and Heinkel (1982), do not obtain a pecking order result.

Leverage Myers and Majluf (1984) imply that leverage increases with the extent of the information asymmetry. Ross (1977), Leland and Pyle (1977), Heinkel (1982), Blazenko (1987), John (1987), Poitevin (1989), and Ravid and Sarig (1989) all derive a positive correlation between leverage and value in a cross section of otherwise similar firms. Ross (1977) also predicts a positive correlation between leverage or value and bankruptcy probability, while Leland and Pyle (1977) predict a positive correlation between value and equity ownership of insiders.

3   MODELS BASED ON PRODUCT/INPUT MARKET INTERACTIONS

Models of capital structure that use features of the theory of industrial organization have begun to appear in the literature. These models can be classified into two categories. One class of approaches exploits the relationship between a firm's capital structure and its *strategy* when competing in the product market. A second class of approaches addresses the relationship between a firm's capital structure and the *characteristics* of its product or inputs. These two literatures are surveyed in the next two subsections.[34]

3.1   Debt influences strategic interaction among competitors

Until recently, the industrial organization literature has assumed that, in choosing its competitive strategy, the firm's objective is to maximize total profits. The finance literature, on the other hand, has focused on maximization of equity value while generally ignoring product market strategy. The new literature linking capital structure and product market strategy adopts the finance view that managers generally have incentives to maximize equity value as opposed to profits or total value. In these papers, leverage changes the payoffs to equity and thus affects the equilibrium product market strategies.

One of the initial papers in this line of research was Brander and Lewis (1986).[35] They use the basic idea of Jensen and Meckling (1976) (see section 1) that increases in leverage induce equity holders to pursue riskier strategies. In the Brander and Lewis model, oligopolists increase risk by a more aggressive output policy. Thus, to commit to pursuing a more aggressive strategy in a subsequent Cournot game, firms choose positive debt levels.

To see how this process works in somewhat more detail, consider the following formal model based on Brander and Lewis. There are two firms, $i = 1, 2$. The two firms first commit simultaneously to a debt level, D_i, then choose simultaneously an output level, q_i. Profits to firm i are given by $R^i(q_i, q_j, z_i)$, where z_1 and z_2 are independent and identically distributed shocks to the firms' profits. We assume that firm i's profits are decreasing in the other firm's output and increasing in the random shock, z_i. Also, firm i's marginal profit $(\partial R^i / \partial q_i)$ is increasing in the random shock, z_i, and decreasing in either firm's output.

These assumptions are fairly standard in Cournot-equilibrium models except for the assumption that marginal profit increases with the random component.[36] This assumption states that the marginal "product" (profit) of output is larger in "good" states (when z is large). If the marginal product of output is high, the firm will optimally choose higher output than if it is low. But, in this model, the firm must choose output before its marginal product is known. Since levered equityholders receive payoffs only in good states (because of limited liability), however, they ignore the possibility that the marginal product of output is low. Consequently, leverage creates an incentive to increase output. Moreover, in Cournot oligopoly models, firms have an incentive to commit to producing large output since this causes their rivals to produce less. Leverage thus provides a device that allows firms to commit to producing more in the Cournot oligopoly. Therefore, in equilibrium, both firms will choose a positive debt level. Notice that the firms are worse off in this equilibrium than they would be in an all-equity Cournot equilibrium since, with leverage, firms produce more than the Cournot output.[37]

When oligopolies persist over time, tacit collusion is possible through the use of punishment strategies triggered when a rival deviates from the collusive output level. It is well known (see, e.g., Green and Porter, 1984) that the monopoly solution can be achieved in an infinitely repeated Cournot oligopoly by a subgame perfect equilibrium in which each firm reverts to the Cournot output forever in the period after any firm deviates from its share of the monopoly output. The condition that is required for this result is that the present value of monopoly profits exceeds the value of deviating for one period, then obtaining Cournot profits forever. If we denote monopoly profits per period by π_m, Cournot profits per period by π_c, the one-period profit from deviating by π_d, and the discount rate by r, the condition required for supporting the monopoly solution is:

$$\pi_m + \pi_m/r > \pi_d + \pi_c/r.$$

Maksimovic (1988) points out that if managers are assumed to maximize the value of equity (as opposed to the value of the firm) this condition must be modified. In particular, suppose the firm has issued debt that promises to pay b per period forever, where $b \geq \pi_c$ (otherwise, the debt has no effect since it will be paid even if the firm reverts to the Cournot equilibrium). Now, if the firm deviates, equityholders receive $\pi_d - b$ for one period, then nothing thereafter since the assets will be transferred to bondholders (who will then follow the Cournot strategy forever). The condition for supporting the monopoly solution is therefore:

$$\pi_m - b + (\pi_m - b)/r > \pi_d - b \text{ or } b < \pi_m + (\pi_m - \pi_d)r.$$

Maksimovic interprets this as a debt capacity, i.e., this is the maximum amount of leverage that firms in such industries can support without destroying the possibility of tacit collusion.

By modeling profits explicitly in terms of demand and cost functions and number of firms, Maksimovic is able to derive comparative static results on debt capacity as a function of industry and firm characteristics. He shows that debt capacity increases with the elasticity of demand and decreases with the discount rate. Assuming some advantage for debt (e.g., taxes), so that the firm's actual debt will be at capacity, makes these implications potentially testable.[38]

3.2   Debt influences interaction with customers and/or suppliers

The second industrial organization-based approach to capital structure determination is to identify product (input) or product market (input market) characteristics that interact in a significant way with the debt level. The examples included here are customers' need for a particular product or service, the need for workers to invest in firm-specific human capital, product quality, and the bargaining power of workers or other suppliers.

Titman (1984) observes that liquidation of a firm may impose costs on its customers (or suppliers), such as inability to obtain the product, parts, and/or service.[39] These costs are transferred to the stockholders in the form of lower prices for the firm's product. Consequently, the stockholders would like to commit to liquidate only in those states in which the net gains to liquidation exceed the costs imposed on customers. Unfortunately, when the firm's investors make the liquidation decision, they ignore these costs. Titman shows that capital structure can be used to commit the share-holders to an optimal liquidation policy. Specifically, capital structure is arranged so that stockholders never wish to liquidate, bondholders always wish to liquidate when the firm is in bankruptcy, and the firm will default only when the net gain to liquidation exceeds the cost to customers. It is shown that firms for which this effect is more important, e.g., computer and automobile companies, will have less debt, other things equal, than firms for which this effect is less important, e.g., hotels and restaurants. In general, for unique and/or durable products, the cost imposed on customers when a producer goes out of business is higher than for non-durable products or those made by more than one producer.

Maksimovic and Titman (forthcoming) show that producers of non-unique and non-durable goods may also be subject to a similar effect. Consider a firm that can produce goods of high or low quality in any period, and suppose that consumers cannot distinguish quality until after consuming the good. Even though high quality costs more to produce, it may be worthwhile for the firm to produce high quality if it can establish a reputation for being a high-quality producer. If, however, this reputation is lost (at least to stockholders) when the firm goes bankrupt, then the incentive to produce high quality is diminished by debt. Consequently, one would expect firms that can easily switch from high- to low-quality output but whose customers cannot distinguish quality without purchasing the good to have less debt, other things equal.

Another advantage of debt is that debt strengthens the bargaining position of equityholders in dealing with input suppliers. Sarig (1988) argues that bondholders bear a large share of the costs of bargaining failure but get only a small share of the gains from successful bargaining. That is, bondholders insure stockholders to some extent against failure of negotiations with suppliers. Increases in leverage increase the extent of this insurance and therefore increase the equityholders' threat point in negotiating with suppliers. As a result, debt can increase firm value. This implies that a firm should have more debt the greater is the bargaining power and/or the market alternatives of its suppliers. Thus Sarig predicts that highly unionized firms and/or firms that employ workers with highly transferable skills will have more debt, *ceteris paribus*.

3.3   Summary

Capital structure models based on product/input market interactions are in their infancy. These theories have explored the relationship between capital structure and either product market strategy or characteristics of products/inputs. The strategic variables considered are product price and quantity. These strategies are determined to affect the behavior of rivals, and capital structure in turn affects the equilibrium strategies and payoffs. Models involving product or input characteristics have focused on the effect of capital structure on the future availability of products, parts and service, product quality, and the bargaining game between management and input suppliers.

The models show that oligopolists will tend to have more debt than monopolists or firms in competitive industries (Brander and Lewis, 1986), and that the debt will tend to be long-term (Glazer, 1989). If, however, tacit collusion is important, debt is limited, and debt capacity increases with the elasticity of demand (Maksimovic, 1988). Firms that produce products that are unique or require service and/or parts and firms for which a reputation for producing high quality products is important may be expected to have less debt, other things equal (Titman, 1984 and Maksimovic and Titman, forthcoming). Finally, highly unionized firms and firms whose workers have easily transferable skills should have more debt (Sarig, 1988).

Models of capital structure based on industrial organization considerations have the potential to provide interesting results. For example, models similar to the ones surveyed above could delineate more specifically the relationship between capital structure and observable industry characteristics such as demand and supply conditions and extent of competition. In addition, it would be useful to explore the impact of capital structure on the choice of strategic variables other than price and quantity. These could include advertising, research and development expenditure, plant capacity, location, and product characteristics. Such research could help in explaining interindustry variations in capital structure.

4   THEORIES DRIVEN BY CORPORATE CONTROL CONSIDERATIONS

Following the growing importance of takeover activities in the 1980s, the finance literature began to examine the linkage between the market for corporate control and capital structure. This investigation evolved on two levels. In the traditional approach, securities are assumed to be non-voting debt and a single class of equity securities with one-share-one-vote. Changes in capital structure in these models affect the distribution of votes across securityholders. In the security design approach, voting rights and, in some cases, cash flows are derived endogenously.

4.1   Traditional corporate control models

These papers exploit the fact that common stock carries voting rights while debt does not. In this section, we discuss three contributions. In Harris and Raviv (1988a) and Stulz (1988), capital structure affects the outcome of takeover contests through its effect on the distribution of votes, especially the fraction owned by the manager. In Israel (1991), capital structure affects the distribution of cash flows between voting (equity) and non-voting (debt) claimants.

The first models to exploit the differential voting rights of debt and equity are those of Harris and Raviv (1988a) and Stulz (1988). These two models generate a relationship between the fraction of the equity owned by a firm's manager and the value of outside equity (equity held by non-contestants). This relationship follows from the dependence of firm value on whether the firm is taken over and, if so, how much is paid by the successful bidder. The manager's equity ownership is determined in part by the firm's capital structure. Thus capital structure affects the value of the firm, the probability of takeover, and the price effects of takeover. In what follows, we explain the models in more detail and compare their implications.

Harris and Raviv (1988a) focus on the ability of an incumbent firm manager to manipulate the method and probability of success of a takeover attempt by changing the fraction of the equity he owns. Since the incumbent and the rival have different abilities to manage the firm, the value of the firm depends on the outcome of the takeover contest. The manager's ownership share determines one of three possible outcomes: the rival takes over for sure, the incumbent remains in control for sure, or the outcome is determined by the votes of passive investors, and this results in the election of the better candidate. The optimal ownership share is determined by the incumbent manager who trades off capital gains on his stake against the loss of any personal benefits derived from being in control. Since the manager's ownership share is determined indirectly by the firm's capital structure, this tradeoff results in a theory of capital structure.

A simplified version of the Harris and Raviv model is the following. An incumbent entrepreneur/manager, I, owns an initial fraction α_0 of an all equity-financed firm. The remaining equity is held by passive investors who are not contenders for control. The incumbent obtains benefits of control of expected value B as long as he controls the firm. These benefits can be thought of as private control benefits or as the value of cash flows that he can expropriate from the firm if he is in control. The value of the cash flows (not including B) generated by the firm depends on the ability of the manager. There are two possible ability levels, 1 and 2, and the corresponding values of the cash flows are denoted Y_1 and Y_2, with $Y_1 > Y_2$.

In addition to the incumbent and passive investors, there is also a rival for control of the firm, R. If the rival takes over, he also obtains benefits of control. The abilities of the incumbent and rival are unobservable by all parties, but it is common knowledge that one is of higher ability than the other. That is, everyone knows that, with probability p, the incumbent has ability 1 and, with probability $1-p$, the rival has ability 1. The other has ability 2. Thus the value of the firm's cash flows if the incumbent controls is Y_I and if the rival controls is Y_R, where:

$$Y_I = pY_1 + (1-p)Y_2 \text{ and } Y_R = (1-p)Y_1 + pY_2.$$

When the rival appears, the incumbent first chooses a new fraction, α, of the equity of the firm (this change in ownership is the result of a change in capital structure; see below). The rival then acquires equity from the passive investors. The takeover contest is decided by a simple majority vote (ties go to the incumbent), where the two contestants each vote for themselves, and the fraction π of the passive investors vote for the incumbent (the rest vote for the rival).[40]

Depending on the choices of equity ownership by the incumbent and rival, the takeover contest can have one of three possible outcomes. First, the incumbent's stake may be so small that, even if the rival is of lower ability, he still succeeds in taking over. Harris and Raviv refer to this case as that of a *successful* tender offer. The value of the cash flows in this case is Y_R. Second, the incumbent's stake may be so large that, even if he is of lower ability, he still remains in control. This is referred to as the case of an *unsuccessful* tender offer, and the value of the cash flows in this case is Y_I. Finally, for intermediate values of α, the incumbent will win if and only if he is of higher ability. This case is called a *proxy fight*, since the identity of the winner is uncertain until the vote is actually taken. Note, however, that in this case the best candidate wins for sure, and hence the value of the cash flows is Y_1. The value of the firm's cash flows, $Y(\alpha)$, is determined by the incumbent's stake, α, through its effect on which of the above three cases prevails. Since Y_1 is larger than either Y_I or Y_R, if the objective were to maximize the value of the cash flow to outside investors, then α in the proxy fight range would be optimal. This would result in a model more similar to that of Stulz (1988) as will be seen below.

The objective in choosing the incumbent's share α is to maximize his expected payoff. This payoff is the value of his equity stake plus the value of his control benefits if he remains in control. The value of the incumbent's equity stake is $\alpha_0 Y(\alpha)$, where α_0 is his *initial* equity stake, since any transactions in which he engages to change his stake have zero net present value. Therefore, the incumbent's payoff, $V(\alpha)$, is $\alpha_0 Y_R$ if there is a successful tender offer (benefits of control are lost), $\alpha_0 Y_i + B$ if there is an unsuccessful tender offer (benefits retained for sure), and $\alpha_0 Y_1 + pB$ if there is a proxy fight (benefits retained with probability p). The optimal ownership share for the incumbent maximizes $V(\alpha)$. The tradeoffs are apparent from the description of V. In particular as α is increased, the probability that the incumbent retains control and its benefits increases. On the other hand, if α is increased too much, the value of the firm and the manager's stake are reduced.

In Harris and Raviv, α is determined indirectly through the firm's capital structure. In particular, the incumbent is assumed to have a fixed amount of wealth represented by his initial stake, α_0. He can increase his stake by having the firm repurchase equity from the passive investors, financing the repurchase by issuing debt. Debt decreases the value of the equity allowing him to purchase a larger fraction with his given wealth. Maximizing the manager's payoff is actually accomplished by choosing the debt level that determines the optimal share α. Since, Harris and Raviv assume that the expected benefits of control, B, decrease with the debt level, within any of the three cases described above, it is optimal to choose the lowest debt level consistent with that case.[41]

It follows from the above arguments that, if the case of successful tender offer is optimal, the firm will have no debt. It is also shown that generally, proxy fights require some debt, and guaranteeing that the tender offer is unsuccessful requires even more debt. Thus takeover targets will increase their debt levels on average and targets of unsuccessful tender offers will issue more debt on average than targets of successful tender offers or proxy fights. Also, firms that increase leverage either have unsuccessful tender offers or proxy fights. In the former case, firm value remains at Y_I on average, while in the latter it increases to Y_1. Thus, on average, debt issues are accompanied by stock price increases.

Finally, note that the fraction of passive investors who vote for the incumbent is determined by the information that these passive investors receive regarding the relative abilities of the two candidates. A larger fraction will vote for the incumbent if the passive investors' prior probability that he is more able, p, increases. Consequently, less debt is required to effect a proxy fight if the incumbent is more likely to be of higher ability. Since winning a proxy fight is positively related to the probability of being more able, the incumbent's winning is also associated with less debt. Therefore, in a sample of firms experiencing proxy fights, one would expect to observe less leverage among firms in which the incumbent remains in control.[42]

Stulz (1988) also focuses on the ability of shareholders to affect the nature of a takeover attempt by changing the incumbent's ownership share. In particular, as the incumbent's share, α, increases, the premium offered in a tender offer increases, but the probability that the takeover occurs and the shareholders actually receive the premium is reduced. Stulz discusses how the ownership share of the incumbent is affected by capital structure (as well as other variables).

The basic idea of Stulz's model can be presented simply as follows. As in Harris and Raviv, there is an incumbent manager of a firm, a potential rival, and a large number of passive investors. The incumbent owns the fraction α of the shares and obtains private benefits of control. Stulz assumes the incumbent will not tender his shares in any takeover attempt. The rival can obtain a random benefit of control, B, from taking over. Initially, B is unknown to all parties. The value of the benefit becomes known to the rival before he must decide what premium to offer shareholders. To acquire control, the rival must purchase 50 percent of the shares. These shares are purchased from the passive investors. This reflects the assumption that the passive investors vote for the incumbent in any takeover contest. The passive investors are assumed to have heterogeneous reservation prices for selling their shares. In particular, let $s(P)$ be the fraction of passive investors who tender if the total premium paid by the rival (above the value under the incumbent) is P. The supply function s is assumed to be increasing in P. Then, the minimum price that the rival must offer to purchase 50 percent of the votes, $P^*(\alpha)$, satisfies the condition:

$$s(P^*(\alpha))(1 - \alpha) = 1/2.$$

Since s is increasing in P, this condition implies that the offer premium P^* is increasing in the incumbent's share α. Intuitively, the larger the incumbent's stake, the larger the fraction of the passive investors' shares that must be acquired by the rival, hence the more he must pay. The rival will bid P^* if and only if his benefit B exceeds P^*. Therefore, the probability that the passive investors actually obtain the premium P^* is:

$$\Pr(B \geq P^*(\alpha)) \equiv \pi[P^*(\alpha)].$$

Since P^* increases with α and π is a decreasing function, the probability of a takeover declines with α. The expected gain to the passive investors is:

$$Y(\alpha) = P^*(\alpha)\pi[P^*(\alpha)].$$

The incumbent's share α is chosen to maximize Y. As mentioned above, increases in α increase the takeover premium given success but decrease the probability of success.

As in Harris and Raviv, α can be increased by increasing the firm's leverage.[43] Therefore, Stulz obtains the result that takeover targets have an optimal debt level that maximizes the value of outside investors' shares. Targets of hostile takeovers will have more debt than firms that are not targets. Since becoming a takeover target is good news, one would expect exchanges of debt for equity that accompany such an event to be associated with stock price increases. Moreover, the probability of a takeover is negatively related to the target's debt/equity ratio, and the takeover premium is positively related to this ratio.

A similar approach was taken by Israel (1991). In his model, as in Stulz (1988), increases in debt also increase the gain to target shareholders if a takeover occurs but lower the probability of this event. The reason that increases in debt increase the gain to target shareholders is different from that in Stulz (1988), however. Israel observes that debt commands a contractually fixed share of any gains from takeover. Target and acquiring shareholders bargain only over that portion of the gains that is not previously committed to debtholders. The more debt, the less gain is left for target and acquiring shareholders to split, and the smaller is the portion of the gain captured by acquiring shareholders. Moreover, target shareholders can capture the gains accruing to target debtholders when the debt is issued. Thus they capture all of the gain not going to acquiring shareholders. Since debt reduces the gain captured by acquiring shareholders, the payoff to target shareholders, given that a takeover occurs, is increased by increased debt levels. The optimal debt level is determined by balancing this effect against the reduced probability of takeover resulting from the reduced share of the gain that accrues to acquiring stockholders.

The essence of Israel's model is the following. Suppose that a takeover can generate a random total gain G in firm value, but the takeover costs T. Further, suppose the firm has issued risky debt of face value D, and, in the event of a takeover, this debt increases in value by $\delta(D,G)$. If the takeover occurs, the acquiring and target shareholders can then split the remaining net gain $G - \delta - T$. Assume that target shareholders obtain the fixed fraction $1 - \gamma$ of this net gain and acquiring shareholders capture the remaining fraction γ (γ can be thought of as measuring the acquirer's bargaining power). Thus, a takeover will occur if and only if $\gamma(G - \delta - T) > 0$ or $G - \delta(D,G) \geq T$, and the probability of a takeover is the probability of this event, denoted $\pi(D,T)$. In addition, when issuing the debt, target shareholders also capture the expected gain to debtholders. Consequently, target shareholders' total expected payoff is:

$$Y(D) = E[\{(1 - \gamma)[\tilde{G} - \delta(D,\tilde{G}) - T] + \delta(D,\tilde{G})\} | \tilde{G} - \delta(D,\tilde{G}) > T]\pi(D,T)$$
$$= E[\{(1 - \gamma)[\tilde{G} - T] + \gamma\delta(D,\tilde{G})\} | \tilde{G} - \delta(D,\tilde{G}) > T]\pi(D,T).$$

As can be seen from this last expression, target shareholders capture the fraction $1 - \gamma$ of the net total gains to takeover plus an additional fraction γ of the gain to target debtholders. The optimal debt level is obtained by maximizing $Y(D)$. This involves trading off the increase in amount extracted from the acquirer represented by the term in braces against the decrease in the probability that takeover occurs, π.[44]

Israel obtains several interesting comparative statics results. First, an increase in the cost of mounting a takeover contest, T, results in a decrease in leverage but an increase in the appreciation of target equity if a takeover occurs. Second, if the distribution of potential takeover gains shifts to the right, debt level increases. Such a shift could result from a *decrease* in the ability of the incumbent manager. Third, the optimal debt level increases, and the probability of takeover and the gain to target equity in the event of a takeover decrease with the rival's bargaining power, γ.

4.2   Security design based on corporate control

One of the most important aspects of security design is the specification of the extent to which the owners of each security are allowed to participate in corporate decisions. Perhaps the most critical decision for the firm is who controls the firm's assets. Consequently, it is natural to base security design on corporate control considerations. If conflicts of interest exist among the potential claimants to corporate resources, securities are designed to resolve the conflicts and maximize firm value.

Building on the work of Grossman and Hart (1988) and Harris and Raviv (1988b), Harris and Raviv (1989) develop a model of the cash flow characteristics and assignment of voting rights of corporate securities.[45] In this model, either the incumbent manager or a rival (but not both) has private benefits of control. As a result, each may have an incentive to acquire or maintain control even when his ability to manage the firm's resources is inferior to that of his opponent. Control is acquired by owning securities that confer on the owner sufficient voting rights. The cost to an inferior candidate of acquiring control, therefore, is the capital loss he suffers on these securities as a result of his lower ability to manage the firm. The extent of this loss depends on the way in which cash flows and voting rights are packaged. Securities are designed to maximize the cost to an inferior contestant of gaining control of the firm (or to extract control benefits). Obviously, such securities minimize the conflict between contestants for control and other claimants and hence maximize firm value. Three major insights follow from this approach: securities are a commitment device, securities should not allow a contestant to acquire "cheap votes," and securities may be designed to extract a rival's surplus. We now discuss each insight and its implications.

Securities serve as a commitment device
Since the entrepreneur bears the cost of inferior takeovers when he takes the firm public, it is in his interest to design securities to maximize firm value. Therefore, entrepreneurs will design securities in such a way that, to the extent possible, they will not later be able to resist a takeover attempt by a superior rival but can foil an attempt by an inferior rival. If an incumbent wants to commit not to oppose better rivals, he should maximize his cost of

retaining control. This cost is the capital gain he foregoes on the securities he retains as well as on those he purchases. Consequently, if the incumbent is inferior, he should retain no voting securities when the firm goes public, and any securities he retains should be risky (i.e., sensitive to who is in control). If the securities he retains have voting rights, this reduces the cost by reducing the amount of voting securities he must purchase. Moreover, the incumbent's cost of opposing a better rival can be increased if the incumbent's stake consists of securities that are more sensitive to firm performance.

No cheap votes

Firm value is increased if, to acquire voting rights, contestants for control must also acquire claims to cash flows that are as sensitive as possible to the outcome of control contests. Harris and Raviv (1989) refer to voting rights *not* attached to control-sensitive claims as "cheap votes." As stated in their paper, "Such [cheap] votes enable an inferior candidate to gain control without suffering from the consequent reduction in firm value."

A simple example will illustrate this point. Consider a firm financed by two securities, A and B, both of which are entirely owned by outside investors. Security $A(B)$ is entitled to cash flows worth 60 percent (40 percent) of the value of the firm (the pattern of cash flows is not important for this example).[46] Suppose that the current management has private benefits of control of $15. Consider a rival who can make improvements in the firm's operations worth δ. Assume that the incumbent must acquire 50 percent of the votes to remain in control. First suppose that security A is allocated *all* the votes. Thus votes are cheap in the sense that 50 percent of the votes can be acquired for only 30 percent of the value of the firm. By remaining in control, the incumbent foregoes a capital gain on his stake of 0.3δ. Since the incumbent's benefits of control are $15, the incumbent will defeat any rival with a value improvement less than $15/0.3 = $50. Now suppose that the votes are reallocated so that security A has 60 percent of the votes, and security B has 40 percent of the votes. Note that, in this case, each security is allocated votes in proportion to its fraction of firm value. Consequently, any portfolio of the two securities that carries 50 percent of the votes requires ownership of 50 percent of firm value. In this case, the two securities are essentially equivalent, i.e., there is really only one voting security. Harris and Raviv refer to this as one-share-one-vote even if the securities involved are not equity. Under one-share-one-vote, the cost of acquiring 50 percent of the votes is 0.5δ. Now, the incumbent can defeat only rivals with $\delta < $15/0.5 = $30. The reallocation of votes to a situation of one-share-one-vote allows improvements in value between $30 and $50 that were not possible before. Given a 50 percent majority rule for acquiring control, one cannot do better.[47]

This "no cheap votes" insight implies that having a single class of voting securities is optimal. If there is more than one class of voting securities, some classes will be less sensitive to firm value relative to their voting power than other classes. Such securities have cheap votes. It is also clear that issuing voting, riskless debt is suboptimal: such a security is the extreme form of cheap votes. Moreover, risky non-voting claims should not be sold to outside investors since these make the voting claims less sensitive to firm value and hence cheapen their votes.[48]

Extraction of rival's control benefits
Securities can be designed to extract from rivals their private benefits of control including any gains in the value of the firm that they might otherwise expropriate. If the rival has control benefits, but the incumbent is a better manager, it may be optimal for the incumbent to retain voting control when the firm goes public. In this case, he can use his monopoly power over the control rights to extract more of the rival's control benefits than could non-colluding individual shareholders if the value of the securities plus the rival's control benefits exceed the value of the securities under the incumbent.[49]

One feature of security design that was ignored in the literature just considered is allowing the control rights assigned to a security to be contingent on information regarding the firm's current financial condition. Zender (1990) considers securities that allocate control of corporate assets directly instead of through voting rights.[50] In his model, there are no contestants for control trying to capture voting rights from passive investors. The control issue is rather which group of claimants is allowed to make the firm's investment decision. It is well-known from the work of Jensen and Meckling (1976) and Myers (1977) that, when the decision-maker does not capture the entire return to the firm at the margin, his investment decision will not, in general, be optimal. Zender shows that an optimal resolution of this problem is to issue debt and leveraged equity and assign control to equityholders unless the firm's prospects are sufficiently poor.

In Zender's model, due to personal wealth constraints, a firm must raise funds for an initial investment from two risk-neutral investors. There are four dates. At date zero, the funds for the initial investment are raised by selling securities. At date one, income from the initial investment is realized. Investors observe only an imperfect signal regarding this income. At date two, control is awarded to one of the investors based on the date-one signal as specified in the security contracts. This investor chooses an additional investment financed by date-one income. All funds not invested are appropriated by the investor in control at date two. At date three, a second income is realized and is distributed according to the security contracts. The probability distribution of date-three income depends on date-one income and the investment made at date two. The object of the analysis is to design securities to maximize *ex ante* firm value. Each security specifies whether the holder makes the date-two investment decision as a function of the date-one signal and the cash flow that accrues to the security holder as a function of the signal and the realized date-three income.

The critical decision affected by the security design is the date-two investment. The investor in control bears the entire cost of the investment (since he keeps any date-one income not invested). The benefit of the investment (date-three income) is claimed by both investors, including the one not in control. The first best investment level can be obtained only if the investor in control captures the entire date-three income *at the margin*. Since it is not feasible for one investor to own the entire risky part of the date-three income, it follows that, to obtain first-best investment, control cannot be unconditionally vested in one investor. Zender assumes that the date-one signal allows investors to separate date-three income into two ranges. First-best investment can then be achieved by awarding control and all income except for a constant to a different investor in each range. For unfavorable date-one incomes, date-three incomes are known for sure to be in the lower range. In this case control and all date-three income is assigned to one investor called a bondholder. For favorable date-one incomes, date-three incomes are known for sure to be in the upper range. In this case control and all date-three income above a constant that is smaller than the smallest income in this range is assigned to the other investor called a stockholder. These names reflect Zender's interpretation of the two securities as a stock and a bond. Because of the fact that the signal allows separation of date-three outcomes into two ranges with probability one, the securities can be designed so as to allow the investor in control to capture the entire return to his investment decision at the margin.

Note that the bond specifies transfer of control to the bondholder based not on failure to make a required payment, but instead on some other event such as failure to meet an interest coverage ratio requirement. Also the bond allows bondholders to receive a payment when they are in control that may exceed the face value of their bond. A more important problem with Zender's model is that the firm must be financed by two investors (or small groups each of which acts as a single investor). Thus it applies more properly to proprietorships or partnerships than to large corporations.[51]

This subsection has outlined the early stages of research into questions involving the optimal design of securities focusing on the allocation of voting rights and corporate control. Two approaches have been taken. In Grossman and Hart (1988), Harris and Raviv (1988b), and Harris and Raviv (1989), any fraction of the voting rights can be allocated to any security, but the allocation is not allowed to depend on information that becomes known after securities are issued.

To contrast this literature with the related security design models, note that the models differ according to whose welfare is being maximized and the strategies available for achieving the goal. In the security design models, the objective is to maximize firm value. Because there is a conflict of interest between investors and insiders, the fact that securities can be used as commitment devices is an important consideration. In these models, however, insiders are not allowed to change the securities in the face of a takeover attempt (they may only change their own portfolios). In the capital structure literature, the use of securities as a commitment device is assumed away, and managers are allowed to change capital structure in response to a takeover attempt. In Harris and Raviv (1988a), intial capital structure was assumed to be all equity. In Stulz (1988) and Israel (1991), the issue of commitment does not arise since the objective is assumed to be shareholder welfare, i.e., there is no conflict of interest between management and shareholders. These differences between the capital structure approach and the security design approach provide some ideas for further research, discussed in section 6.

4.3   Summary

The papers discussed in this section provide a theory of capital structure related to takeover contests. The major results of the traditional capital structure literature are as follows. First, all three papers conclude that takeover targets will increase their debt levels on average, and this will be accompanied by a positive stock price reaction. Second, all three show that leverage is negatively related on average to whether the tender offer succeeds. Third, Harris and Raviv (1988a) also show that targets of unsuccessful tender offers will have more debt on average than targets of proxy fights. They also show that, among firms involved in proxy fights, leverage is lower on average when the incumbent remains in control. Fourth, with regard to the relationship between the fraction of the takeover premium captured by the target's equity and the amount of debt, Stulz (1988) and Israel (1991) obtain opposite results. In Stulz, the premium paid to target shareholders increases with increases in the target's debt level. In Israel, as the bargaining power of the target shareholders decreases, the target optimally issues more debt, and the fraction of the takeover premium captured by the target equity falls. Fifth, Israel shows that targets that are more costly to take over have less debt but capture a larger premium if a takeover occurs. Sixth, Israel predicts that firms that have greater potential takeover gains will have more debt.[52]

Two important observations should be noted here. First, the theories surveyed in this section should be viewed as theories of short-term changes in capital structure taken in response to imminent takeover threats, since the optimal capital structure derived in these models can be implemented in response to hostile takeover activity. As a result, theories based on corporate control considerations have nothing to say about the long-run capital structure of firms. Second, these papers take as given the character-istics of the securities issued by firms. In particular, both the cash flow aspects and the assignment of voting rights and other control-related features are treated as exogenous. This assumption is relaxed in the security design literature.

The main results of the design literature are that optimal securities involve a single class of voting security (one-share–one-vote) and that riskless debt should be non-voting. In Zender (1990), essentially all votes must be allocated to a single security, but this allocation may depend on information about the firm. Zender shows that optimal securities resemble debt and equity. The contracts specify that debtholders will control when the realization of a signal about future prospects is low.

5   SUMMARY OF RESULTS

The purpose of this section is to present the collected lessons of the literature surveyed. These lessons are presented in three subsections. In the first, we discuss the theoretical predictions of the models surveyed above. In the second, we briefly summarize the available empirical evidence. In the third, we compare the theoretical predictions with the evidence. Much of the material in this section is synthesized in tables. These tables are as follows:

Table 2.2: Summary of theoretical results
Table 2.3: Industry leverage rankings
Table 2.4: Determinants of leverage
Table 2.5: Comparison of theoretical and empirical results
Table 2.6: Other empirical results
Table 2.7: Summary of results by model type.

5.1   Summary of theoretical results

Those theoretical results that are potentially testable are summarized in table 2.2. Table 2.2 consists of four panels. Panel A contains implications regarding the relationship between leverage and exogenous factors that are not the result of decisions by agents in the model, e.g., profitability, characteristics of the product market, etc. Panel B contains implications regarding the relationship between leverage and endogenous factors that are the result of decisions by agents in the model. In this case, both leverage and the other factor are jointly determined by some third, exogenous factor. Typically, in these cases the endogenous factors are more readily observable than the exogenous driving factor. In panel C, we list results relating the firm's stock price response to announcements of capital structure changes. Panel D contains other results that do not fit into the above three groups.[53] In each panel, the first column contains the theoretical prediction; the second column indicates the type(s) of model(s) from which the result was derived and corresponds to the various sections of the survey; the third column provides the specific references for the result.

The table makes it clear that the literature provides a substantial number of implications. The other striking feature is that there are very few cases in which two or more theories have opposite implications (these are indicated by a grey background). Such conflicts can provide sharp tests capable of rejecting one or more theories in favor of another. The only instances of conflicting results are (i) Chang (1987) predicts a negative relationship of leverage and firm profitability, while several studies predict a positive relationship (see panel A), (ii) Myers and Majluf (1984) predict a negative relationship between leverage and free cash flow, while Jensen (1986) and Stulz (1991) predict a positive relationship (see panel A), (iii) Stulz (1988) predicts a positive relationship between leverage and the takeover premium captured by a target, while Israel (1991) predicts the opposite relationship (see panel B), (iv) Myers and Majluf (1984) and related papers predict the absence of a stock price reaction to a debt issue announcement, while numerous papers predict a positive reaction (see panel C), and (v) several papers argue against the pecking order theory of Myers and Majluf (1984) and others (see panel D). Since conflicting implications are rare, the large majority of the studies surveyed must therefore be considered as complements, i.e., any or all of the effects traced by these theories could be present simultaneously. The relative significance of these effects is an empirical issue.

The security design literature develops several basic insights. First, votes should not be attached to securities whose value is not sensitive to firm value, i.e., "no cheap votes" (Grossman and Hart, 1988; Harris and Raviv, 1988, 1989). Second, debt contracts are the only contracts capable of forcing managers to pay out cash flows (Townsend, 1979; Diamond, 1984; Gale and Hellwig, 1984; Bolton and Scharfstein, 1990; Hart and Moore, 1989). Third, securities can, and should, make control contingent on performance (Zender, 1990).

Table 2.2. *Summary of theoretical results*

The table shows, for each theoretical result, the type of model from which the result was derived and the specific papers that obtain the result. Model types also refer to sections in the paper. The shaded cells indicate results that are in conflict.

Panel A   Association between leverage and exogenous factors

Leverage increases with	Model	References
Extent of information asymmetry	Asymmetric info.	Myers and Majluf (1984)
Increases in profitability	Asymmetric info.	Ross (1977), Leland and Pyle (1977), Heinkel (1982), Blazenko (1987), John (1987), Poitevin (1989), Ravid and Sarig (1989)
Decreases in profitability	Agency	Chang (1987)
Extent of *strategic* interaction in the product market	Product/Input markets	Brander and Lewis (1986)
Extent to which product is not unique and does not require specialized service	Product/Input markets	Titman (1984)
Extent to which reputation for product quality is unimportant	Product/Input markets	Maksimovic and Titman (forthcoming)
Extent to which workers are unionized or have transferable skills	Product/Input markets	Sarig (1988)

Table 2.2 *Panel A (Cont.)*

Leverage increases with	Model	References
Extent to which the firm is a takeover target or lack of anti-takeover measures	Control	Harris and Raviv (1988a), Stulz (1988), Israel (1991)
	Agency	Stulz (1991), Hirshleifer and Thakor (1989)
Potential gains to takeover and reductions in their costs	Control	Israel (1991)
Fraction of cash flow that is unobservable	Agency	Chang (1987)
Lack of growth opportunities, extent of regulation	Agency	Jensen and Meckling (1976), Stulz (forthcoming)
Increases in free cash flow	Agency	Jensen (1986), Stulz (forthcoming)
Decreases in free cash flow	Asymmetric info.	Myers and Majluf (1984)
Increases in liquidation value	Agency	Williamson (1988), Harris and Raviv (1990)
Decreases in investigation costs	Agency	Harris and Raviv (1990)
Increases in the importance of managerial reputation	Agency	Hirshleifer and Thakor (1989)

Panel B   Association between leverage and endogenous factors

Result	Model	References
Leverage is positively correlated with firm value	Agency	Harris and Raviv (1990), Stulz (1991), Hirshleifer and Thakor (1989)
	Asymmetric info.	Ross (1977), Noe (1988), Narayanan (1988), Poitevin (1989)
	Control	Harris and Raviv (1988a), Stulz (1988), Israel (1991)
Leverage is positively correlated with default probability	Agency	Harris and Raviv (1990)
	Asymmetric info.	Ross (1977)
Leverage is positively correlated with the extent of managerial equity ownership	Asymmetric info.	Leland and Pyle (1977)
	Control	Harris and Raviv (1988a), Stulz (1988)
Leverage is positively correlated with target premium	Control	Stulz (1988)
Leverage is negatively correlated with target premium	Control	Israel (1991)
Leverage is negatively correlated with probability of successful takeover	Control	Stulz (1988)
Leverage is negatively correlated with the interest coverage ratio and the probability of reorganization following default	Agency	Harris and Raviv (1990)

Table 2.2   *Panel B (Cont.)*

Result	Model	References
Targets of an unsuccessful tender offer have more debt than targets of proxy fights or successful tender offers	Control	Harris and Raviv (1988a)
Targets of successful proxy fights have more debt than targets of unsuccessful proxy fights	Control	Harris and Raviv (1988a)
Targets of proxy fights have more debt than targets of successful tender offers	Control	Harris and Raviv (1988a)

Panel C   Announcement of security issues

Stock price	Model	References
Increases on announcement of debt issues, debt-for-equity exchanges, or stock repurchases	Agency	Harris and Raviv (1990), Stulz (1990), Hirshleifer and Thakor (1989)
	Asymmetric info.	Ross (1977), Noe (1988), Narayanan (1988), Poitevin (1989)
	Control	Harris and Raviv (1988a), Stulz (1988), Israel (1991)
Isn't affected by announcement of debt issue	Asymmetric info.	Myers and Majluf (1984), Krasker (1986), Korajczyk *et al.* (1990c)

Table 2.2   *Panel C (Cont.)*

Stock price	Model	References
Decreases on announcement of equity issue	Agency	Harris and Raviv (1990), Stulz (1991), Hirshleifer and Thakor (1989)
	Asymmetric info.	Ross (1977), Myers and Majluf (1984), Krasker (1986), Korajczyk et al. (1990c), Noe (1988), Narayanan (1988), Poitevin (1989), Lucas and McDonald (1990)
	Control	Harris and Raviv (1988a), Stulz (1988), Israel (1991)
Decreases more the larger is the informational asymmetry	Asymmetric info.	Myers and Majluf (1984), Krasker (1986), Korajczyk et al. (1990c)
Decreases more the larger is the size of the issue	Asymmetric info.	Krasker (1986)
Increases if some proceeds of equity issue used to repurchase debt	Asymmetric info.	Brennan and Kraus (1987)
Increases on announcement of issue of convertible debt in exchange for equity	Asymmetric info.	Constantinides and Grundy (1989)

Panel D   Other results

Result	Model	References
There is a pecking order: firms prefer internal finance, then issuing securities in order increasing sensitivity to firm performance	Asymmetric info.	Myers and Majluf (1984), Krasker (1986), Narayanan (1988)

Table 2.2   *Panel D (Cont.)*

Result	Model	References
There is no pecking order	Asymmetric info.	Brennan and Kraus (1987), Noe (1988), Constantinides and Grundy (1989)
Firms tend to issue equity following abnormal price appreciation	Asymmetric info.	Lucas and McDonald (1990)
Firms tend to issue equity when information asymmetry is smallest	Asymmetric info.	Myers and Majluf (1984), Korajczyk *et al.* (1990c)
Debt and equity are optimal securities	Agency	Townsend (1979), Diamond (1984), Gale and Hellwig (1985), Chang (1987), Williams (1989), Hart and Moore (1989), Bolton and Scharfstein (1990)
	Control	Zender (1990)
One-share-one-vote: a single class of voting security is optimal	Control	Grossman and Hart (1988), Harris and Raviv (1988b, 1989)
Low returns optimally entail change of control or ownership	Control	Aghion and Bolton (1988), Zender (1990)
Bonds can be expected to have covenants prohibiting "asset substitution"	Agency	Jensen and Meckling (1976)
Firms with longer track records have lower default probabilities	Agency	Diamond (1989)

The main results of these inquiries are:

to describe circumstances under which debt and levered equity are optimal means of allocating cash flows and control to investors, more profitable firms and those with a larger fraction of cash flows that are contractible will have less debt,

optimal securities involves one-share-one-vote (a single class of voting securities), and

debt (at least riskless debt) should be non-voting.

5.2   Summary of empirical evidence

The evidence fits into four categories. The first group contains evidence of general capital structure trends. The second group, event studies, generally measures the impact on stock value of an announcement of a capital structure change. The third group relates firm/industry characteristics to financial structure. The fourth group measures the relationship between capital structure and factors associated with corporate control. We discuss these four classes of empirical studies in the next subsections.

Before turning to this discussion, a word of caution is in order. The interpretation of the results must be tempered by an awareness of the difficulties involved in measuring both leverage and the explanatory variables of interest. In measuring leverage, one can include or exclude accounts payable, accounts receivable, cash, and other short-term debt. Some studies measure leverage as a ratio of book value of debt to book value of equity, others as book value of debt to market value of equity, still others as debt to market value of equity plus book value of debt. With regard to the explanatory variables, proxies are often difficult to interpret. For example, several studies measure growth opportunities as the ratio of market value of the firm to book value of assets. While firms with large growth opportunities should have large values of this ratio, other firms whose assets have appreciated significantly since purchase but which do not have large growth opportunities will also have large values of this ratio. In addition to measurement problems, there are the usual problems with interpreting statistical results. In what follows, we take the results reported at face value and compare results of various studies largely ignoring differences in measurement technique.

General trends

Firms raise funds for new investment both externally, through security issues, and internally from retained earnings. Internal sources, which add to total firm equity, have historically constituted a large but fairly steadily declining fraction of these funds. For example undistributed profits accounts for about 22 percent of total sources of funds for non-firm, non-financial corporate business in 1986. By comparison, the same figure averaged about 49 percent over the period 1946–66 (see Masulis, 1988, table 1.1, p. 3).

The second major trend in financial structure has been the secular increase in leverage. Taggart (1985) reports secular trends in leverage using a variety of different measurements. He concludes that leverage has increased steadily since the Second World War, but that current debt levels may not be high relative to those of the prewar period.

Event studies

Event studies have documented the stock price reaction to announcements of security offerings, exchanges and repurchases.[54] In some cases, the studies also document the reaction of earnings or earnings forecasts to the events. Generally, equity increasing transactions result in stock price decreases, while leverage increasing transactions result in stock price increases. Earnings and earnings forecasts react consistently with the stock price reactions.

With regard to security issues,[55]

> abnormal returns associated with announcements of common stocks are the most negative (about −3 percent according to Smith (1986)),
> abnormal returns associated with convertible bonds or convertible preferred stock are more negative than those associated with the respective non-convertible security,
> abnormal returns associated with straight debt or preferred stock are not statistically significantly different from zero,[56]
> abnormal returns associated with securities issued by utilities are less negative than those associated with the same securities issued by industrial firms.

Marsh (1982) finds that firms are more likely to issue long-term debt to the extent that their current long-term debt is below their target as measured by the average debt level of the previous ten years. He also finds that market conditions play a highly significant role in determining the probability that a firm will issue debt. Specifically, firms are more likely to issue debt (equity) when they expect other firms to issue debt (equity) and are more likely to issue equity to the extent that the previous year's share return exceeds that of the market portfolio. Korajczyk et al. (1990a) also document that a firm's stock price experiences significant abnormal rises on average prior to its issuing equity. In addition, Korajczyk *et al.* (1990b) find that equity issues are clustered after earnings announcements and the extent of the price drop at the announcement increases insignificantly with time since the last earnings announcement. Korajczyk *et al.* (1990a) examine the cross-sectional properties of the price rise and track debt ratios and Tobin's q around the time of equity issues. They find that debt ratios do not increase prior to equity issues "suggesting that strained debt capacity is not the main reason for equity issues." Tobin's q (the ratio of market to book value of assets) is observed to rise prior to an equity issue and fall following the issue. This suggests that equity is issued to finance new investments.

With regard to exchange offers, Masulis (1983) reports that:[57]

> debt issued in exchange for common stock results in a 14 percent abnormal stock return,
> preferred stock issued in exchange for common stock results in an 8.3 percent abnormal stock return,
> debt issued in exchange for preferred stock results in a 2.2 percent abnormal stock return,
> common stock issued in exchange for preferred stock results in a −2.6 percent abnormal stock return,
> common stock issued in exchange for debt results in a −9.9 percent abnormal stock return,
> preferred stock issued in exchange for debt results in a −7.7 percent abnormal stock return.

Further evidence on exchanges is offered by Lys and Sivaramakrishnan (1988), Cornett and Travlos (1989), and Israel *et al.* (forthcoming). Cornett and Travlos confirm Masulis' (1980, 1983) results that leverage increasing (decreasing) exchanges of securities are accompanied by positive (negative) abnormal common stock returns. They further document that abnormal price drops following leverage decreasing capital structure exchanges are positively related to unexpected earnings decreases. Finally they observe that abnormal price increases following leverage increasing capital structure exchanges are positively related to changes in managerial stock holdings. Lys and Sivaramakrishnan (1988) and Israel *et al.* (forthcoming) consider the effect of capital structure exchanges on the revisions of financial analysts' forecasts. In a study of leverage decreasing exchanges, they find that analysts revise their forecasts of net operating income downward and that these revisions are positively correlated with the size of the stock price reaction to the exchange announcement.

Stock repurchases via tender offers result in sharp stock price increases. Masulis (1980) reports a 21 percent abnormal stock return, Dann (1981) finds a 15.4 percent abnormal stock return, and Vermaelen (1981) documents a 13.3 percent abnormal stock return. Consistent with this evidence, Dann et al. (1989) document positive earnings surprises subsequent to tender offer stock repurchases (but not before).

Firm and industry characteristics

The most basic stylized facts concerning industry characteristics and capital structure are that firms within an industry are more similar than those in different industries and that industries tend to retain their relative leverage ratio rankings over time (Bowen et al., 1982; Bradley et al., 1984). Leverage ratios of specific industries have been documented by Bowen et al. (1982), Bradley et al., (1984), Long and Malitz (1985), and Kester (1986). Their results are in broad agreement and show that drugs, instruments, electronics, and food have consistently low leverage while paper, textile mill products, steel, airlines, and cement have consistently high leverage. Moreover, regulated industries (telephone, electric and gas utilities, and airlines) are among the most highly levered firms according to the study by Bradley et al. (1984). The evidence on industry leverage ratios is summarized in table 2.3.

Several studies shed light on the specific characteristics of firms and industries that determine leverage ratios (Bradley et al., 1984; Castanias, 1983; Long and Malitz, 1985; Kester, 1986; Marsh, 1982; Titman and Wessels, 1988). These studies generally agree that leverage increases with fixed assets, non-debt tax shields, growth opportunities, and firm size and decreases with volatility, advertising expenditures, R and D expenditures, bankruptcy probability, profitability, and uniqueness of the product. These results are summarized in table 2.4.

In addition to the evidence cited in table 2.4, Castanias (1983) also finds a negative correlation between leverage and default probability.

Corporate control considerations

Finally, since capital structure is used as an anti-takeover device (DeAngelo and DeAngelo, 1985; Dann and DeAngelo, 1988; Amihud et al., 1990), several studies of the market for corporate control have produced evidence about capital structure. First, leverage is positively correlated with the extent of managerial equity ownership (Kim and Sorensen, 1986; Agrawal and Mandelker, 1987; Amihud et al., 1990)[58] Second, Dann and DeAngelo (1988) find that hostile bidders rarely prevail in the face of capital restructuring. Indeed, Palepu (1986) finds that leverage is negatively correlated with the probability of being successfully taken over. Third,

Table 2.3. *Industry leverage rankings*

Industry	BJK	BDH	LM	Kester
Drugs	Low[a]		Low	Low
Cosmetics	Low		Low	Medium[b]
Instruments	Low		Low[c]	Low[d]
Metal mining	Low			
Publishing	Low			
Electronics	Low		Low[e]	Low
Machinery	Low			Medium[f]
Food	Low			Low[g]
Petroleum exploration	Medium			
Construction	Medium			
Petroleum refining	Medium	Low[h]	High	High
Metal working	Medium			
Chemicals	Medium	Medium		High
Apparel	Medium			Medium
Lumber	Medium			
Motor vehicle parts	Medium	Medium[i]	Low[j]	Medium
Paper	Medium		High	High
Textile mill products	High	Medium	High	High
Rubber	High			Medium
Retail department stores	High	Medium		
Retail grocery stores	High	Medium		
Trucking	High			
Steel	High	Low	High	High
Telephone	High			
Electric and gas utilities	High			
Airlines	High	High		
Cement			High	High
Glass				High

Notes:
[a] Drugs (SIC code 2830) and Cosmetics (SIC code 2840) are combined.
[b] Soaps and Detergents (SIC code 2841) part of Cosmetics (SIC code 2840) only.
[c] Photographic Equipment (SIC code 3861) part of Instruments (SIC code 3800) only.
[d] Photographic Equipment (SIC code 3861) part of Instruments (SIC code 3800) only.
[e] Radio and TV Receiving (SIC code 3651) part of Electronics (SIC code 3600) only.
[f] Construction Machinery, Agricultural Machinery and Machine Tools (SIC codes 3530, 3520, 3540).

[g]Confectionery and Alcoholic Beverages (SIC codes 2065 and 2082, 2085) part of Food (SIC code 2000) only.
[h]Oil-Integrated Domestic (SIC code 2912) part of Petroleum Refining (SIC code 2900) only.
[i]BDH split Motor Vehicle Parts (SIC code 3700) into Auto Parts and Accessories (SIC code 3714) and Aerospace (SIC code 3721). In their study, the former ranks consistently at or near the lowest leverage ratio while the latter ranks near the highest.
[j]Aircraft (SIC code 3721) part of Motor Vehicle Parts (SIC code 3700) only.

Rankings of industries by leverage ratio are reported based on four studies: Bradley et al. (1984, table 1) [denoted BJK], Bowen et al. (1982, Exhibit 1) [BDH], Long and Malitz (1985, table 3) [LM], and Kester (1986, Exhibit 2). We have listed industries from lowest to highest based on average debt-to-value ratio over the period 1962–81 using Bradley et al. The classification into "Low," "Medium," and "High," is our own and is somewhat arbitrary. The rankings in Bowen et al. are an average of rankings over the period 1951–69 based on long-term plus short-term debt divided by total assets. For Long and Malitz, "Low" ("High") means that the industry was one of the five lowest (highest) in leverage ratio (book value of long-term funded debt divided by total funded capital) out of a sample of 39 firms. The rankings for Kester are based on the average of net debt divided by market value of equity for a sample of 344 Japanese and 452 US companies in 27 industries over the period April, 1982 through March, 1983.

Table 2.4. *Determinants of leverage*

Characteristic	BJK	CN	FH/L	GLC	LM	Kest.	KS	Mar.[a]	TW
Volatility	−			−		−*	+		−*
Bankruptcy probability							−		
Fixed assets			+	+	+			+	+*
Non-debt tax shields	+	+					−		−*
Advertising	−[b]				−				
R & D expenditures	−				−				
Profitability		−	−*	−	−			−	

Table 2.4. (*Cont.*)

Characteristic	BJK	CN	FH/L	GLC	LM	Kest.	KS	Mar.[a]	TW
Growth opportunities		−*				+	−		−*
Size		−*	+*			−*	−*	+	−*
Free cash flow		−							
Uniqueness[c]									−

Notes:
[a]Marsh measures the probability of issuing debt conditional on issuing securities and on firm characteristics. The sign indicates the direction of change of this probability given a change in the indicated characteristic.
[b]Advertising and R & D expenditures are combined.
[c]This refers to the uniqueness of the product and is included specifically to test the model of Titman (1984).

The sign of the change in leverage as a result of an increase in the given characteristic is shown for each of six studies. Blank entry indicates that the specific study did not include the given characteristic. Asterisk (*) indicates that the result was either not statistically significantly different from zero at conventional significance levels or that the result was weak in a nonstatistical sense. The studies are Bradley *et al.* (1984) [denoted BJK], Chaplinsky and Niehaus (1990) [CN], Friend and Hasbrouck (1988) and Friend and Lang (1988) [FH/L], Gonedes *et al.* (1988) [GLC], Long and Malitz (1985) [LM], Kester (1986) [Kest.], Kim and Sorensen (1986) [KS], Marsh (1982) [Mar.], and Titman and Wessels (1988) [TW]. Comparisons suffer from the fact that these studies used different measures of the firm characteristics, different time periods, different leverage measures, and different methodologies.

stock price decreases following dual class recapitalization and other defensive strategies (Partch, 1987; Dann and DeAngelo, 1988; Jarrell and Poulsen, 1988). Fourth, claims with superior voting power command higher prices than similar claims with inferior voting power (Levy, 1983; Lease *et al.*, 1984; DeAngelo and DeAngelo, 1985). Fifth, high free cash flow is associated with higher probability of going private and larger premiums paid to stockholders upon going private (Lehn and Poulsen, 1989). Sixth, the distribution of equity ownership seems to play a role in both managerial behavior and capital structure. In particular, Agrawal and

Mandelker (1987) find that when managers own a larger share of the equity, they tend to choose higher variance targets. Also, Friend and Lang (1988) and Gonedes *et al.* (1988) find that leverage is lower in firms with dispersed outside ownership.

5.3   Comparison of theoretical predictions and empirical evidence

This subsection integrates the information described in the previous two subsections. Table 2.5 matches the empirical evidence with the theoretical results in table 2.2. Table 2.5 is organized exactly as table 2.2 except that columns two and three of table 2.2 are replaced by the evidence. Specifically, for each theoretical result, we list the relevant empirical studies divided into two groups: those consistent with the prediction (indicated by "Yes") and those inconsistent with it (indicated by "No").

The evidence cited in table 2.5 is either direct evidence about the particular result or, in some cases, represents an interpretation of the actual independent variable used in the study. In particular the following interpretations are embedded in table 2.5.

> Extent of regulation: telephone, electric and gas utilities, and airlines are all highly regulated and highly levered as indicated in table 2.3.
>
> Liquidation value: fixed assets and non-debt tax shields are generally regarded as proxies for the tangibility or liquidation value of assets. On the other hand, R and D and advertising expenditure can be interpreted as measuring the extent to which assets are intangible. See table 2.4.
>
> Firm value: in panel B, the studies cited document increases in earnings or earnings forecasts following leverage increases.
>
> Pecking order: the fact that leverage decreases with internal funds is interpreted as evidence that firms prefer to use internal financing before issuing debt (Chaplinsky and Niehaus, 1990). Also, Amihud *et al.* (1990) find that, in acquisitions, managers prefer to finance with cash or debt rather than equity, at least when they have a large equity stake. Finally, Korajczyk *et al.* (1990a) interpret the fact that debt ratios do not increase prior to equity issues used to finance investment as evidence that "strained debt capacity is not the main reason for equity issues."

Other evidence from table 2.3 (industry leverage ratio rankings) may conceivably bear on the predictions of the theory. For example, one might argue that the airline industry is marked by a high degree of strategic interaction across firms. If so, the fact that airlines are highly levered, is

Table 2.5. *Comparison of theoretical and empirical results*

The table lists, for each theoretical result in table 2.2, those empirical studies whose findings are either consistent (after the word "Yes:") or in consistent (after "No:") with the theoretical result. Blank cells indicate the lack of empirical evidence.

<table>
<tr><td colspan="2" align="center">Panel A   Association between leverage and exogenous factors</td></tr>
<tr><td>Leverage increases with:</td><td>Empirical evidence</td></tr>
<tr><td>Extent of information asymmetry</td><td></td></tr>
<tr><td>Increases in profitability</td><td>No: Kester (1986), Long and Malitz), Friend and Hasbrouck (1988), Friend and Lang (1988), Gonedes et al. (1988)*, Titman and Wessels (1988)</td></tr>
<tr><td>Extent of strategic interaction in the product market</td><td></td></tr>
<tr><td>Elasticity of demand for the product</td><td></td></tr>
<tr><td>Extent to which product is not unique and does not require specialized service</td><td>Yes: Titman and Wessels (1988)</td></tr>
<tr><td>Extent to which reputation for product quality is unimportant</td><td></td></tr>
<tr><td>Extent to which workers are unionized or have transferable skills</td><td></td></tr>
<tr><td>Extent to which the firm is a takeover target or lack of anti-takeover measures</td><td></td></tr>
<tr><td>Potential gains to takeover and reductions in their costs</td><td></td></tr>
<tr><td>Fraction of cash flow that is unobservable</td><td></td></tr>
<tr><td>Lack of growth opportunities</td><td>Yes: Kim and Sorensen (1986), Titman and Wessels (1988)*, Chaplinsky and Niehaus (1990)* No: Kester (1986)</td></tr>
</table>

Table 2.5   *Panel A (Cont.)*

Leverage increases with	Empirical evidence
Extent of regulation	Yes: Bowen, *et al.* (1982), Bradley *et al.* (1984)
Increases in free cash flow	No: Chaplinsky and Niehaus (1990)
Increases in liquidation value	Yes: Bradley *et al.* (1984), Long and Malitz (1985), Friend and Hasbrouck (1988), Friend and Lang (1988), Gonedes *et al.* (1988), Titman and Wessels (1988)*, Chaplinsky and Niehaus (1990) No: Kim and Sorensen (1986), Titman and Wessels (1988)*
Decreases in investigation costs	
Increases in the importance of managerial reputation	

Panel B   Association between leverage and endogenous factors

Result	Empirical evidence
Leverage is positively correlated with firm value	Yes: Lys and Sivaramakrishnan (1988), Cornett and Travlos (1989), Dann *et al.* (1989), Israel *et al.* (forthcoming)
Leverage is positively correlated with default probability	No: Castanias (1983)
Leverage is positively correlated with the extent of managerial equity ownership	Yes: Kim and Sorensen (1986), Agrawal and Mandelker (1987), Amihud *et al.* (1990) No: Friend and Hasbrouck (1988)*, Friend and Lang (1988)

Table 2.5   *Panel B (Cont.)*

Result	Empirical evidence
Leverage is positively correlated with target premium	
Leverage is negatively correlated with probability of successful takeover	Yes: Palepu (1986)
Leverage is negatively correlated with the interest coverage ratio and the probability of reorganization following default	
Targets of an unsuccessful tender offer have more debt than targets of proxy fights or successful tender offers	
Targets of successful proxy fights have more debt than targets of unsuccessful proxy fights	
Targets of proxy fights have more debt than targets of successful tender offers	

Panel C   Announcement of security issues

Stock price	Empirical evidence
Increases on announcement of debt issue	Yes: Kim and Stulz (1988) No: Dann and Mikkelson (1984)*, Eckbo (1986)*, Mikkelson and Partch (1986)*
Increases on announcement of debt for equity exchange	Yes: Masulis (1980, 1983), Cornett and Travlos (1989)
Increases on announcement of stock repurchase	Yes: Masulis (1980), Dann (1981), Vermaelen (1981), Dann et al. (1989)
Decreases on announcement of equity issue	Yes: Asquith and Mullins (1986), Masulis and Korwar (1986),

Table 2.5   *Panel C (Cont.)*

Stock price	Empirical evidence
	Mikkelson and Partch (1986), Schipper and Smith (1986)
Decreases on announcement of equity for debt exchange	Yes: Masulis (1980, 1983), Eckbo (1986), Mikkelson and Partch (1986), Cornett and Travlos (1989)
Decreases more the larger is the informational asymmetry	Yes: Korajczyk *et al.* (1990b)*
Decreases more the larger is the size of the issue	Yes: Asquith and Mullins (1986)
Increase if some proceeds of equity issue used to repurchase debt	
Increases on announcement of issue of convertible debt in exchange for equity	

Panel D   Other results

Result	Empirical evidence
There is a pecking order: firms prefer internal finance, then issuing securities in order of increasing sensitivity to firm performance	Yes: Chaplinsky and Niehaus (1990), Amihud *et al.* (1990) No: Korajczyk *et al.* (1990a)
Firms tend to issue equity following abnormal price appreciation	Yes: Marsh (1982), Korajczyk *et al.* (1990a)
Firms tend to issue equity when information asymmetry is smallest	Yes: Korajczyk *et al.* (1990b)
Low returns optimally entail change of control or ownership	

Table 2.5   *Panel D (Cont.)*

Result	Empirical evidence
Bonds can be expected to have covenants prohibiting "asset substitution"	Yes: Smith and Warner (1979)
Firms with longer track records have lower default probabilities	

Note: * = weak or statistically insignificant relationship.

consistent with the results of Brander and Lewis (1986). Similarly, if reputation for product quality is especially important in the drug industry, the fact that drug firms have low leverage is consistent with the results of Maksimovic and Titman (forthcoming). Also, to the extent that trucking is highly unionized, the high leverage found in this industry supports the model of Sarig (1988). Obviously, such inferences depend on detailed knowledge of the industries involved, knowledge we do not possess.

In addition to table 2.5, which matches the empirical evidence with the theoretical results, we also present, in table 2.6, those empirical findings that do not bear on any specific theoretical prediction. Some of these lend support to the assumptions of certain models. Others provide evidence to be explained.

Finally, in table 2.7, we reorganize the information in table 2.5 to present the theoretical results and the evidence by model type. In panels A and D we list, in turn, the implications of agency models (panel A), asymmetric information models (panel B), product/input market models (panel C), and corporate control models (panel D). The results are ordered, in each panel, so that those with evidence are listed first, followed by those for which there is no available evidence. Table 2.7 is useful for determining whether any model or class of models has been rejected by the evidence and what additional evidence would be useful for testing the models.

6   CONCLUSIONS

The theories surveyed here have identified a great many *potential* determinants of capital structure (in addition to taxes). These can be most easily seen in table 2.2, panels A and D. Since the theories are, for the most part, complementary, which of these factors is important in various contexts remains a largely unanswered empirical question.

Table 2.6. *Other empirical results*

This table lists empirical evidence not directly related to any theoretical result.

Empirical result	Source
The extent of external financing has increased over time	Masulis (1988)
Total leverage has increased steadily since World War II	Taggart (1985)
Capital structure is used to protect control	DeAngelo and DeAngelo (1985), Dann and DeAngelo (1988), Amihud *et al.* (1990)
Hostile bidders rarely prevail in face of capital restructuring	Dann and DeAngelo (1988)
Dual class recapitalization and other defensive strategies result in stock price decrease	Partch (1987)*, Dann and DeAngelo (1988), Jarrell and Poulsen (1988)
Stock price increases with voting power	Levy (1983), Lease *et al.* (1984), DeAngelo and DeAngelo (1985)
High free cash flow is associated with higher probability of going private and higher premiums	Lehn and Poulsen (1989)
Firms more likely to issue debt if current debt level is below target	Marsh (1982)
Leverage decreases with return volatility	Bradley *et al.* (1984), Kester (1986)*, Friend and Hasbrouch (1988), Friend and Lang (1988), Titman and Wessels (1988)*
Leverage increases with increases in operating risk	Kim and Sorensen (1986)

Table 2.6   (Cont.)

Empirical result	Source
Leverage decreases with increases in firm size	Yes: Kester (1986)*, Kim and Sorensen (1986)*, Titman and Wessels (1988)* No: Friend and Hasbrouck (1988)*, Friend and Lang (1988)*
High inside ownership is associated with return variance increasing investments	Agrawal and Mandelker (1987)
Leverage decreases with increases in dispersion of outside ownership	Friend and Lang (1988), Gonedes et al. (1988)

Note: * = weak or statistically insignificant relationship.

Table 2.7. Summary of results by model type

The table shows, for each model type, the main results [with sources in brackets] and the empirical studies whose findings are either consistent (after the word "Yes:") or inconsistent (after "No:") with the theoretical result.

Panel A Agency models	
Theoretical result [source]	Empirical evidence
Stock price increases on announcement of debt issues, debt-for-equity exchanges, or stock repurchases and decreases on announcement of equity issues or equity-for-debt exchanges [Harris and Raviv (1990), Stulz (forthcoming), Hirshleifer and Thakor (1989)]	Debt issues Yes: Kim and Stulz (1988) No: Dann and Mikkelson (1984)*, Eckbo (1986)*, Mikkelson and Partch (1986)* Debt-for-equity exchanges Yes: Masulis (1980, 1983), Cornett and Travlos (1989) Stock repurchases Yes: Masulis (1980), Dann (1981), Vermaelen (1981), Dann et al. (1989)

Table 2.7   *Panel A (Cont.)*

Theoretical result [source]	Empirical evidence
	Equity issues Yes: Asquith and Mullins (1986), Masulis and Korwar (1986), Mikkelson and Partch (1986), Schipper and Smith (1986)
	Equity-for-debt exchanges Yes: Masulis (1980, 1983), Eckbo (1986), Mikkelson and Partch (1986), Cornett and Travlos (1989)
Leverage is positively correlated with firm value [Harris and Raviv (1990), Stulz (forthcoming), Hirshleifer and Thakor (1989)]	Yes: Lys and Sivaramakrishnan (1988), Cornett and Travlos (1989), Dann *et al.* (1988), Israel *et al.* (forthcoming)
Leverage is positively correlated with default probability [Harris and Raviv (1990)]	No: Castanias (1983)
Leverage increases with lack of growth opportunities [Jensen and Meckling (1976), Stulz (forthcoming)]	Yes: Kim and Sorensen (1986), Titman and Wessels (1988)*, Chaplinsky and Niehaus (1990)* No: Kester (1986)
Leverage increases with decreases in profitability [Chang (1987)]	Yes: Kester (1986), Long and Malitz (1985) Friend and Hasbrouck (1988), Friend and Lang (1988), Gonedes *et al.* (1988)*, Titman and Wessels (1988)
Leverage increases with extent of regulation [Jensen and Meckling (1976), Stulz (forthcoming)]	Yes: Bowen *et al.*, (1982), Bradley *et al.* (1984)

Table 2.7   *Panel A (Cont.)*

Theoretical result [source]	Empirical evidence
Leverage increases with increases in free cash flow [Jensen (1986), Stulz (forthcoming)]	No: Chaplinsky and Niehaus (1990)
Leverage increases with increases in liquidation value [Williamson (1988), Harris and Raviv (1990)]	Yes: Bradley *et al.* (1984), Long and Malitz (1985), Friend and Hasbrouck (1988), Friend and Lang (1988), Gonedes *et al.* (1988), Titman and Wessels (1988)*, Chaplinsky and Niehaus (1990) No: Kim and Sorensen (1986), Titman and Wessels (1988)
Bonds can be expected to have covenants prohibiting "asset substitution" [Jensen and Meckling (1976)]	Yes: Smith and Warner (1979)
Debt and equity are optimal securities [Townsend (1979), Diamond (1984), Gale and Hellwig (1985), Chang (1987), Williams (1989), Hart and Moore (1989), Bolton and Scharfstein (1990)]	Consistent with casual observation
Leverage is negatively correlated with the interest coverage ratio and the probability of reorganization following default [Harris and Raviv (1990)]	
Leverage increases with fraction of cash flow that is unobservable [Chang (1987)]	
Leverage increases with extent to which the firm is a takeover target or lack of anti-takeover measures [Stulz (forthcoming), Hirshleifer and Thakor (1989)]	
Firms with longer track records have lower default probabilities [Diamond (1989)]	

Table 2.7   *Panel A (Cont.)*

Theoretical result [source]	Empirical evidence
Leverage increases with decreases in investigation costs [Harris and Raviv (1990)]	
Leverage increases with increases in the importance of managerial reputation [Hirshleifer and Thakor (1989)]	

Panel B   Asymmetric information models

Theoretical result [source]	Empirical evidence
Stock price increases on announcement of debt issues, debt-for-equity exchanges, or stock repurchases and decreases on announcement of equity-for-debt exchanges [Ross (1977), Noe (1988), Narayanan (1988), Poitevin (1989)]	Debt issues Yes: Kim and Stulz (1988) No: Dann and Mikkelson (1984)*, Eckbo (1986)*, Mikkelson and Partch (1986)* Debt-for-equity exchanges Yes: Masulis (1980, 1983), Cornett and Travlos (1989) Equity-for-debt exchanges Yes: Masulis (1980, 1983), Eckbo (1986), Mikkelson and Partch (1986), Cornett and Travlos (1989) Stock repurchases Yes: Masulis (1980), Dann (1981), Vermaelen (1981), Dann *et al.* (1989)
Stock price is unaffected by debt issues [Myers and Majluf (1984), Krasker (1986), Korajczyk *et al.* (1990c)]	See previous cell
Leverage increases with increases in profitability [Ross (1977), Leland and Pyle (1977), Heinkel (1982), Blazenko (1987),	Yes: Long and Malitz (1985)* No: Kester (1986), Friend and Hasbrouck (1988), Friend and

Table 2.7   *Panel B (Cont.)*

Theoretical result [source]	Empirical evidence
John (1987), Poitevin (1989)]	Lang (1988), Gonedes *et al.* (1988)*, Titman and Wessels (1988)
Leverage increases with decreases in free cash flow [Myers and Majluf (1984)]	Yes: Chaplinsky and Niehaus (1990)
Stock price decreases on announcement of equity issue [Ross (1977), Myers and Majluf (1984), Krasker (1986), Korajczyk *et al.* (1990c), Noe (1988), Narayanan (1988), Poitevin (1989), Lucas and McDonald (1990)]	Yes: Asquith and Mullins (1986), Masulis and Korwar (1986), Mikkelson and Partch (1986), Schipper and Smith (1986)
There is a pecking order: firms prefer internal finance, then issuing securities in order of increasing sensitivity to firm performance [Myers and Majluf (1984), Krasker (1986), Narayanan (1988)]	Yes: Chaplinsky and Niehaus (1990), Amihud *et al.* (1990) No: Korajczyk *et al.* (1990a)
Leverage is positively correlated with firm value [Ross (1977), Noe (1988), Narayanan (1988), Poitevin (1989)]	Yes: Lys and Sivaramakrishnan (1988), Cornett and Travlos (1989), Dann *et al.* (1989), Israel *et al.* (forthcoming)
Leverage is positively correlated with default probability [Ross (1977)]	No: Castanias (1983)
Leverage is positively correlated with the extent of managerial equity ownership [Leland and Pyle (1977)]	Yes: Kim and Sorensen (1986), Agrawal and Mandelker (1987), Amihud *et al.* (1990) No: Friend and Hasbrouck (1988)*, Friend and Lang (1988)
Firms tend to issue equity following abnormal price appreciation [Lucas and McDonald (1990)]	Yes: Marsh (1982), Korajczyk *et al.* (1990a)

Table 2.7   *Panel B (Cont.)*

Theoretical result [source]	Empirical evidence
Firms tend to issue equity when information asymmetry is smallest [Myers and Majluf (1984), Korajczyk *et al.* (1990)]	Yes: Korajczyk *et al.* (1990a)
Stock price decreases more the larger is the informational asymmetry [Myers and Majluf (1984), Krasker (1986), Korajczyk *et al.* (1990c)]	Yes: Korajczyk *et al.* (1990b)*
Leverage increases with extent of information asymmetry [Myers and Majluf (1984)]	
Stock price decreases more the larger is the size of the issue [Krasker (1986)]	Yes: Asquith and Mullins (1986)
Stock price increases if some proceeds of equity issue used to repurchase debt [Brennan and Kraus (1987)]	
Stock price increases on announcement of issue of convertible debt in exchange for equity [Constantinides and Grundy (1989)]	

Panel C   Product/input market models

Theoretical result [source]	Empirical evidence
Leverage increases with extent to which product is not unique and does not require specialized service [Titman (1984)]	Yes: Titman and Wessels (1988)
Leverage increases with extent of *strategic* interaction in the product market [Brander and Lewis (1986)]	
Leverage increases with elasticity of demand for the product [Maksimovic (1988)]	

Table 2.7   *Panel C (Cont.)*

Theoretical result [source]	Empirical evidence
Leverage increases with extent to which reputation for product quality is unimportant [Maksimovic and Titman (forthcoming)]	
Leverage increases with extent to which workers are unionized or have transferable skills [Sarig (1988)]	

Panel D   Corporate control models

Theoretical result [source]	Empirical evidence
Stock price increases on announcement of debt issues, debt-for-equity exchanges, or stock repurchases and decreases on announcement of equity issues or equity-for-debt exchanges [Harris and Raviv (1988a), Stulz (1988), Israel (1991)]	Debt issues Yes: Kim and Stulz (1988) No: Dann and Mikkelson (1984)*, Eckbo (1986)*, Mikkelson and Partch (1986)* Debt-for-equity exchanges Yes: Masulis (1980, 1983), Cornett and Travlos (1989) Stock repurchases Yes: Masulis (1980), Dann (1981), Vermaelen (1981), Dann et al. (1989) Equity issues Yes: Asquith and Mullins (1986), Masulis and Korwar (1986), Mikkelson and Partch (1986), Schipper and Smith (1986) Equity-for-debt exchanges Yes: Masulis (1980, 1983), Eckbo (1986), Mikkelson and Partch (1986), Cornett and Travlos (1989)
Leverage is positively correlated with firm value [Harris and Raviv (1988a), Stulz (1988), Israel (1991)]	Yes: Lys and Sivaramakrishnan (1988), Cornett and Travlos (1989), Dann et al. (1989), Israel et al. (forthcoming)

Table 2.7 *Panel D (Cont.)*

Theoretical result [source]	Empirical evidence
Leverage is positively correlated with the extent of managerial equity ownership [Harris and Raviv (1988a), Stulz (1988)]	Yes: Kim and Sorensen (1986), Agrawal and Mandelker (1987), Amihud *et al.* (1990) No: Friend and Hasbrouck (1988)*, Friend and Lang (1988)
Leverage is negatively correlated with probability of successful takeover [Stulz (1988)]	Yes: Palepu (1986)
Debt and equity are optimal securities [Zender (1990)]	Consistent with casual observation
One-share-one-vote: a single class of voting security is optimal [Grossman and Hart (1988), Harris and Raviv (1988b, 1989)]	Consistent with casual observation
Leverage increases with potential gains to takeover and reductions in their costs [Israel (1991)]	
Leverage is positively correlated with target premium [Stultz (1988)]	
Leverage increases with extent to which the firm is a takeover target or lack of anti-takeover measures [Harris and Raviv (1988a), Stulz (1988), Israel (1991)]	
Leverage is negatively correlated with target premium [Israel (1991)]	
Targets of an unsuccessful tender offer have more debt than targets of proxy fights or successful tender offers [Harris and Raviv (1988a)]	

Table 2.7   *Panel D (Cont.)*

Theoretical result [source]	Empirical evidence
Targets of successful proxy fights have more debt than targets of unsuccessful proxy fights [Harris and Raviv (1988a)]	
Targets of proxy fights have more debt than targets of successful tender offers [Harris and Raviv (1988a)]	

Note: * = weak or statistically insignificant relationship.

Although many potential factors emerge from the theory, a fairly small number of "general principles" are evident. The literature that takes debt and equity as given is based on four important properties of the debt contract:

Bankruptcy, i.e., debt provides for a costly takeover of the firm by debtholders under certain conditions. This fact is exploited in Ross (1977), Grossman and Hart (1982), Titman (1984), Jensen (1986), Harris and Raviv (1988a, 1990), Maksimovic and Titman (forthcoming), Poitevin (1989), Stulz (1990), and others.

Cash flow to levered equity is a convex function of returns to the firm. This fact leads to the asset substitution effect which is central in Jensen and Meckling (1976), Brander and Lewis (1986), Sarig (1988), Diamond (1989), and others.

Leverage increases the manager's equity ownership share. This effect works in two ways: it forces manager's payoffs to be more sensitive to firm performance, and, since debt is non-voting, it concentrates voting power. These properties are exploited in Jensen and Meckling (1976), Leland and Pyle (1977), Harris and Raviv (1988a), Stulz (1988), and others.

The value of debt is relatively insensitive to firm performance. Thus debt is priced more accurately than equity in situations involving asymmetric information. This fact is used by Myers and Majluf (1984) among others.

Two complementary rationales for debt are identified in the design literature:

The debt contract is an optimal response to a situation in which contracts cannot be based on income and firm managers can keep any income not paid out.

Debt is a method of splitting the cash flows and controls rights among more than one claimant while minimizing the distortion of the incentives of controlling managers to maximize firm value.

Since the survey shows that theory has identified numerous potential determinants, it is not surprising that the models have a wealth of different implications (very few opposing, however) (see table 2.2). Models within a given type (e.g., agency), however, have many common predictions (see table 2.7). Moreover, models of almost all types share the prediction that stock price will increase on announcement of leverage increasing capital structure changes (see table 2.2, panel B). This is probably because, since this effect is so well documented by event studies, the models were designed to produce this prediction. Although the event studies have generally been interpreted as evidence that announcements of security offerings, exchanges, and repurchases contain new information about the firm's future cash flows, i.e., as evidence for signaling models, in fact, they support at least three of the four types of models.

From tables 2.5 and 2.7 it is clear that the empirical evidence thus far accumulated is broadly consistent with the theory. It is perhaps unfortunate that there seem to be no significant empirical anomalies to guide further theoretical work. Indeed, it would be difficult to reject any models based on the available evidence.[59] Note, however, that many of the theoretical implications have not yet been tested (as evidenced by the empty cells in tables 2.5 and 2.7).

While recommendations for further work are always tentative, it seems clear that certain areas are unexplored. In our view, within the traditional approach, models that relate capital structure to products and inputs are the most promising. This area is still in its infancy and is short on implications relating capital structure to industrial organization variables such as demand and cost parameters, strategic variables, etc. On the other hand, it seems to us that models exploiting asymmetric information have been investigated to the point where diminishing returns have set in. It is unlikely that further effort in this area will lead to significant new insights. With regard to empirical work table 2.5 (or 2.7) provides a list of theoretical predictions that have not been tested. Of course, testing these results (or any of the others) is complicated by the wealth of *ceteris paribus* conditions each requires. Nevertheless, it is essential that empirical work be directed specifically at sorting out which effects are important in various contexts.

Security design models, despite explaining some of the features of observed financial contracts, have not rationalized subordinated debt or other more complex securities.[60] Even for the simple securities derived, few testable comparative statics results regarding capital structure are demonstrated. Also, models based on non-contractability of firm income have difficulty justifying simultaneously both debt and outside equity. Only Chang (1987) and Williams (1989) manage to derive securities that resemble debt and outside equity. The contract that is interpreted as outside equity in Williams' model has two features that do not correspond to actual equity. First, it specifies that "equityholders" do not receive the residual above the face value of debt when the firm is not bankrupt. Second, equityholders are entitled to a fraction of the *assets* of the firm, not its income. This claim corresponds to actual equity in a single period model in which the firm is liquidated at the end of the period but does not correspond well for ongoing firms.

Another shortcoming of the security design literature is that it has not fully addressed issues relating to corporate governance and bankruptcy law. As mentioned above, the corporate charter as well as the relevant bankruptcy statutes should be viewed as an implicit part of every financial contract. With respect to corporate governance, the security design approach might shed light on which issues should be decided by outside investors and how those issues should be decided. With respect to bankruptcy law, note that the debt contract is implicit in the term bankruptcy. In general, if the security design is endogenous, one must consider the law governing resolution of disputes resulting from default on the terms of the contract. Again, the security design approach may provide insights into socially optimal default resolution.

Security design modeling is still in its infancy. Further insights may be obtained either by enriching the current approaches (agency and control) or by finding new factors that determine security design. With respect to the agency approach, the discussion in section 1.2 implies an interesting direction for further research. If securities are issued before investment decisions occur, then security design must take into account the effect of the outstanding securities on the choice of investment project. That is, in this case, asset substitution or some other distortion of investment incentives can be an important determinant of optimal securities.

In the corporate control approach, our comparison of the security design models with the capital structure models suggests several interesting avenues. One important point from the capital structure literature is that managers can typically change the nature of the firm's financial securities to some extent in response to a takeover attempt as in Harris and Raviv (1988a). Allowing this in a security design setting will have significant implications for the optimal securities depending on the extent to which securities may be altered. Another idea suggested by the capital structure literature is that securities may be designed to maximize firm value with no conflict of interest between investors and managers as in Stulz (1988) and Israel (1991). In this case, securities will not be commitment devices but will instead be chosen to maximize the gain from potential takeovers.

One possible new factor driving security design is the desire to convey information through security prices. That is, what investor information is embedded in a security's price depends on the cash flow characteristics of the security. Paul (1989) has proposed this avenue. He observes that "vague" information possessed by investors may be difficult to use in an incentive contract, but that prices of a security are easily incorporated. Thus securities may be designed so that their prices serve as proxies in a compensation contract for information that is otherwise unusable in this context. This appears to be a promising avenue for future research. Another approach may be to examine the implications of various security designs for subsequent firm behavior in product or input markets (see the discussion of the interaction of capital structure and product markets in section 3).

Notes

* This chapter was prepared for the 6th World Congress of the Econometric Society, Barcelona, Spain, August 22–28, 1990. An abbreviated version that does not include the material on security design appeared in the *Journal of Finance*, March 1991. We gratefully acknowledge the financial support of the Bradley Foundation. Professor Harris wishes to acknowledge partial financial support from Dimensional Fund Advisors. We also thank our discussant, Patrick Bolton, seminar participants at the University of Chicago, UCLA, and Tel Aviv University, Michael Fishman, Robert Hansen, Ronen Israel, Steven Kaplan, Robert McDonald, Andrei Shleifer, René Stulz, Robert Vishny, and especially Vincent Warther whose tireless research assistance was invaluable.
1 Some other recent surveys include Allen (1990), Masulis (1988), Miller (1988), Ravid (1988), Taggart (1985), and comments on Miller (1988) by Bhattacharya (1988), Modigliani (1988), Ross (1988), and Stiglitz (1988). Masulis (1988) and Taggart (1985) are general surveys. Allen (1990) focuses on security design, and Ravid (1988) concentrates on interactions between capital structure and the product market.
2 This is less common in countries other than the United States. In many countries multiple classes of equity securities with differing voting rights prevail.
3 When control rights are included as part of the security design, the investigation of security design leads also to an investigation of corporate governance (e.g., majority rules). Since it is peripheral to our main interest, we will not pursue this topic here.
4 In addition to those surveys mentioned in note 1, see also Bradley *et al.* (1984).
5 Another benefit of debt financing is pointed out by Grossman and Hart (1982).

If bankruptcy is costly for managers, perhaps because they lose benefits of control or reputation, then debt can create an incentive for managers to work harder, consume fewer perquisites, make better investment decisions, etc., because this behavior reduces the probability of bankruptcy.

6 Obviously, conflicts between security holders do not arise if each investor holds all securities in proportion to their values, i.e., if each investor holds a "strip." Consequently, this literature assumes that equityholders and debtholders are disjoint classes of investors.

7 Myers (1977) points out another agency cost of debt. He observes that when firms are likely to go bankrupt in the near future, equityholders may have no incentive to contribute new capital even to invest in value increasing projects. The reason is that equityholders bear the entire cost of the investment, but the returns from the investment may be captured mainly by the debtholders. Thus larger debt levels result in the rejection of more value increasing projects. This agency cost of debt yields conclusions about capital structure similar to those of Jensen and Meckling.

8 Several authors have pointed out that agency problems can be reduced or eliminated through the use of managerial incentive schemes and/or more complicated financial securities such as convertible debt. See Barnea *et al.* (1985), Brander and Poitevin (1989), and Dybvig and Zender (1989). For a counter view, see Narayanan (1987) and the reply by Haugen and Senbet (1987).

9 Another approach that involves manager–investor conflicts is taken by Williamson (1988). In his view, the benefits of debt are the incentives provided to managers by the rules under which debtholders can take over the firm and liquidate the assets. The costs of debt are that the inflexibility of the rules can result in liquidation of the assets when they are more valuable in the firm. Thus Williamson concludes that assets that are more redeployable should be financed with debt.

10 A similar approach is taken by Hart and Moore (1990) with similar results. In particular, Hart and Moore (1990) also focus on the agency problem of overinvestment by managers. There are two major differences between the approach of Hart and Moore (1990) and that of Stulz (1990). First, Hart and Moore derive debt as an optimal security in this setting. Second, debt does not prevent overinvestment in the Hart and Moore approach by reducing available free cash flows. Instead, the existence of senior debt constrains the amount of external funds that can be raised since the outstanding debt represents a prior claim on all assets, including new investments. For a further discussion of the effect of seniority rules on the under and overinvestment incentives, see Berkovitch and Kim (1990).

11 Another literature considers factors that alleviate the underinvestment cost of debt pointed out by Myers (1977) (see note 7). Stulz and Johnson (1985) focus on collateral, John and Nachman (1985) focus on reputation, and Bergman and Callen (forthcoming) consider renegotiation with debtholders. Berkovitch and Kim (1990) and Kim and Maksimovic (forthcoming) show how debt can be used to trade off the overinvestment and underinvestment effects.

12 Green (1984) offers another method of mitigating this agency cost. He points out

that convertible bonds and warrants "reverse the convex shape of levered equity over the upper range of the firm's earnings" (p. 115) and therefore reduce the asset substitution problem.

13 Gale and Hellwig (1985) extend Townsend's model to allow for endogenous investment. The discussion that follows draws on both papers.

14 When the firm described above can be the target of predation by a firm with no external funding, it is shown that the optimal contract is similar except that funding is provided in the second period with probability less than one if payout is sufficiently high in the first period.

15 A similar model is offered by Lacker (1990).

16 If the expected net present value of the asset is sufficiently high (αEx exceeds the initial investment), then the manager can keep the control benefits for all outcomes and raise the required investment by assigning the investors the fraction α of the transferable asset for any report. This "all equity" solution is optimal in this case under certain conditions on the manager's risk aversion and the control benefits.

17 Interestingly, there are no security design models that focus on these considerations.

18 Strictly speaking, Myers and Majluf show only that debt whose value is not sensitive to the private information is preferred to equity (e.g., riskless debt). Moreover, if such debt is available, the theory implies that equity will never be issued by firms in the situation of extreme information asymmetry they model. Consequently, the "pecking order" theory requires an exogenous debt constraint in the Myers and Majluf model. Note also that there can be a pooling equilibrium in which all firms issue securities, because the project's NPV exceeds the worst underpricing. This equilibrium would not have the properties of the separating equilibrium mentioned in the text.

19 This objective function assumes that outside investors will discover the true value of the firm's existing assets soon after the decision to invest is made and that current shareholders will not sell their stakes before this occurs. Dybvig and Zender (1989) point out that optimal contracts with managers could completely resolve the underinvestment problem rendering capital structure irrelevant. The papers surveyed in this section thus implicitly assume that such contracts are ruled out.

20 For example, Bradford (1987) shows that, if managers are allowed to purchase the new equity issued by firms in the situation described by Myers and Majluf (1984), then the underinvestment problem is mitigated.

21 Lucas and McDonald (1990) consider a model in which Myers–Majluf type informational asymmetries are temporary and firms can delay the adoption of projects. They show that firms with private information that current earnings are low will not delay projects while firms whose current earnings are high will delay until this information becomes public. The result is that, on average, equity is issued after a period of abnormally high returns to the firm and to the market. They also obtain the result that, on average, stock price drops in response to stock issues.

22 Brennan and Kraus and Constantinides and Grundy use a method similar to

one first introduced by Heinkel (1982) to obtain costless signaling (see section 2.2).

23 Nachman and Noe (1989) consider a similar situation in which firms have private information about the value of a new investment. They assume, however, that firms can issue any monotone increasing security in a broad class. They show, under certain assumptions on the ordering of firm types, that the only equilibrium is one in which all firms issue debt.

24 An equivalent approach is to assume that managers can commit to paying dividends and suffer a penalty if the promised dividend is not paid. Ravid and Sarig (1989) consider a combination of debt and dividend commitment. They show that both dividends and debt level increase with firm quality.

25 This objective function reflects the implicit assumptions that the manager's welfare is increasing in the current and future stock price and decreases in the event of bankruptcy. This "bankruptcy penalty" could result from loss of reputation or search costs of finding a new position. The penalty is not a bankruptcy cost since it affects only the manager's welfare and not firm value.

26 This can be seen by calculating the value of the debt and equity as functions of $D(t)$ and t, taking the ratio, and showing that this ratio is increasing in t (see Ross, 1977, p. 37). As will be seen, below, many other models also imply a positive relation between firm profitability and leverage. Interestingly, Chang (1987), using an agency model, obtains the opposite result (see section 1.2).

27 See also Franke (1987) for a similar financial signaling model with costless separation of firms.

28 Another signaling model that obtains this result is John (1987).

29 Glazer and Israel (1990) also consider a model in which capital structure is used to signal costs of production. Unlike in Poitevin, in Glazer and Israel, an incumbent monopolist signals his cost to prevent entry. The incumbent's manager is assumed to be compensated based on the terminal value of equity, *not* including any dividends. Glazer and Israel assume that the proceeds of any debt issued are paid out in dividends. Therefore, leverage increases are costly for the manager. In equilibrium, potential entrants interpret more debt as indicative that the incumbent has lower marginal production costs. It is optimal for managers of low cost incumbents to issue more debt since for them the benefit of preventing entry exceeds the cost of debt. Managers of high cost imcumbents will not imitate since for them the value of entry prevention is lower. Note, however, that signaling could work equally well using dividends financed by retained earnings or preferred stock instead of by debt. The authors recognize this point and do not claim that their results constitute a theory of capital structure. Gertner *et al.* (1988) also consider a model in which firms use capital structure as a signal in the output market (as well as in the capital market). Their main result is that whether the equilibrium will involve pooling or separation depends on what is best for the informed firm.

30 In addition to the papers discussed below, see also Blazenko (1987).

31 This expression reflects the assumption that the amount raised externally, $(1-\alpha)[V(\alpha)-D]+D$ is invested in a riskless asset with zero return.

32 In fact, the debt level determined in the Leland and Pyle model is the total debt

issued by the corporation and the entrepreneur on personal account. The results can be interpreted as a theory of corporate capital structure only if personal debt is costly.

33 Darrough and Stoughton (1986) incorporate moral hazard into the Leland and Pyle formulation. The manager is assumed to choose an effort level after securities are issued. The marginal product of effect, μ, and the standard deviation of returns, σ, are known only to the entrepreneur, but investors know that $\sigma = \mu^2$. In this model, the fraction of equity retained by the entrepreneur is both a signal of μ and σ and an incentive device. The entrepreneur retains a smaller fraction the more risky are the returns. There are no specific results linking debt level or capital structure to observable characteristics of the firm.

34 With the exception of Bolton and Scharfstein (1990) discussed in section 1.2, security design models have not incorporated product/input market considerations.

35 Two other treatments that are contemporaneous with Brander and Lewis (1986) are Allen (1985) and Maksimovic (1986). For a similar treatment, see Maksimovic (1989).

36 Brander and Lewis consider both this case and the case in which the marginal profit is decreasing with z. They consider the increasing case to be the most important empirically, since, in the other case, firms will be unlevered in equilibrium.

37 Glazer (1989) shows that, when long-run considerations are taken into account in a Brander and Lewis type model, firms have an incentive to issue long-term debt which helps in enforcing a form of tacit collusion.

38 Maksimovic (1990) extends this analysis to the case in which firms are privately informed about their own productivity.

39 Allen (1985) also focuses on bankruptcy costs emanating from the product market. He points out that firms in financial distress may postpone investments thus giving an advantage to their competitors. See also John and Senbet (1988).

40 In the Harris and Raviv paper, π is derived from a model of passive investors' information.

41 Expected benefits may decrease with the debt level because the benefits are lost in bankruptcy, higher debt results in more monitoring by creditors, and/or less free cash flow allows the manager less discretion.

42 The model also has a number of other testable implications regarding stock price changes of takeover targets classified by the type of takeover attempt (proxy fight or tender offer) and the outcome (successful or unsuccessful).

43 Stulz also considers a number of other methods for changing α such as ESOPs, voting trusts, supermajority rules, and differential voting rights. Results derived from these considerations are not directly relevant to the topic at hand.

44 In a related paper, Israel (1989) notes that increases in leverage reduce the capital loss suffered by an incumbent manager if he resists a value increasing takeover. As a result, the manager can extract a larger share of the surplus for the firm's shareholders. Debt is limited by the amount of the surplus to be extracted.

45 In Harris and Raviv (1988b) and Grossman and Hart (1988), the cash flows of the securities are exogenously specified to be proportional to total cash flows,

i.e., the cash flow aspects of the securities are assumed to be unlevered equity. Bagwell and Judd (1989) also consider the allocation of voting rights to equity cash flow claims in a model of corporate control. They show that, when there is one-share-one-vote, controlling shareholders may choose strategies that involve dead-weight losses (e.g., paying tax-disadvantaged dividends instead of repurchasing shares) to stay in control. This behavior can be avoided by giving the controlling group shares with superior voting rights.

46 In fact, for this example the securities are assumed to command the same fractions of firm value regardless of who is in control of the firm. This will be true of equity but may not be for more complicated functions of the cash flows. In Harris and Raviv (1989), securities may be arbitrary non-decreasing, non-negative functions of the cash flows. The optimal forms of the functions are characterized.

47 From the point of view of maximizing total firm value, including benefits of control, one would want to defeat only those rivals with improvements less than $15. Obviously, in this example, requiring a larger majority would improve matters with 100 percent majority yielding maximal total firm value. If rivals also had benefits of control, such a supermajority rule might prevent incumbents from defeating inferior rivals. Harris and Raviv (1988b) show that, when both incumbents and rivals can have control benefits, the simple majority rule maximizes total firm value.

48 An exception to this rule may occur when the rival has control benefits and the incumbent has none. In this case, the incumbent may want to retain control on going public so as to extract the rival's benefits if a takeover occurs. If so, he may issue non-voting, risky securities.

49 Another method for extracting control benefits is to issue two "extreme" securities, one with only cash flows, the other with only votes. See Harris and Raviv (1988b).

50 Aghion and Bolton (1988) address a similar issue but do not focus on capital structure.

51 See Fama and Jensen (1983) for a discussion of what determines whether an activity is organized as a proprietorship or an open corporation.

52 Similar results are undoubtedly available from Stulz's model although he does not derive them. One can view B in Stulz's model as takeover benefits net of takeover costs. Then any increase in potential benefits or decrease in costs is simply a rightward shift of the distribution of B.

53 Other theoretical results not directly relating to capital structure are not included in this summary, even though they may be potentially testable.

54 Much of the literature is surveyed in Smith (1986). Masulis (1988) provides a more recent and comprehensive survey.

55 See Asquith and Mullins (1986), Dann and Mikkelson (1984), Eckbo (1986), Linn and Pinegar (1988), Masulis and Korwar (1986), Mikkelson and Partch (1986), and Schipper and Smith (1986).

56 Kim and Stulz (1988), however, found a significantly positive effect associated with Eurobond issues.

57 See also Masulis (1980), Eckbo (1986), Mikkelson and Partch (1986), Pinegar and Lease (1986), and Cornett and Travlos (1989).
58 Friend and Hasbrouck (1988) and Friend and Lang (1988) find evidence to the contrary, although in the former, the sign is insignificant.
59 Inspection of table 2.7 produces only the following candidates: the signaling models listed in panel B, line 3 (see also line 8); the free cash flow models listed in panel A, line 7, and Harris and Raviv (1990) (panel A, line 3). In each case, the empirical studies were not designed specifically to test the model and hence generally do not meet the *ceteris paribus* conditions demanded by the theory.
60 Ross (1989) proposes an agency model for explaining the demand for new financial instruments, even if these simply involve repackaging existing claims.

References

Aghion, Phillipe and Patrick Bolton (1988), "An 'Incomplete Contract' Approach to Bankruptcy and the Financial Structure of the Firm," Working Paper, MIT and Harvard University.

Agrawal, Anup and Gershon Mandelker (1987), "Managerial Incentives and Corporate Investment and Financing Decisions," *Journal of Finance*, 42: 823–37.

Allen, Franklin (1985), "Capital Structure and Imperfect Competition in Product Markets," Working Paper, The Wharton School, University of Pennsylvania.

(1990), "The Changing Nature of Debt and Equity: A Financial Perspective," in Richard W. Kopcke and Eric S. Rosengren (eds.), *Are the Distinctions Between Debt and Equity Disappearing?*, Boston: Federal Reserve Bank of Boston, Conference Series No. 33: 12–38.

Allen, Franklin and Douglas Gale (1988), "Optimal Security Design," *Review of Financial Studies*, 1: 229–64.

(1989), "Arbitrage, Short Sales and Financial Innovation," Working Paper 10–89, Rodney L. White Center for Financial Research, University of Pennsylvania.

Amihud, Yakov, Baruch Lev, and Nickolaos G. Travlos (1990), "Corporate Control and the Choice of Investment Financing: The Case of Corporate Acquisitions," *Journal of Finance*, 45: 603–16.

Asquith, Paul and David W. Mullins, Jr. (1986), "Equity Issues and Offering Dilution," *Journal of Financial Economics*, 15: 61–89.

Bagwell, Laurie Simon and Kenneth L. Judd (1989), "Transaction Costs and Corporate Control," Working Paper, Kellogg School, Northwestern University.

Barnea, Amir, Robert Haugen and Lemma Senbet (1985), *Agency Problems and Financial Contracting*, Englewood Cliffs, NJ: Prentice-Hall.

Bergman, Yaacov Z. and Jeffrey L. Callen (forthcoming), "Oportunistic Underinvestment in Debt Renegotiations and Capital Structure," *Journal of Financial Economics*.

Berkovitch, Elazar and E. Han Kim (1990), "Financial Contracting and Leverage Induced Over- and Under-Investment Incentives" *Journal of Finance*, 45: 765–94.

Bhattacharya, Sudipto (1988), "Corporate Finance and the Legacy of Miller and Modigliani," *Journal of Economic Perspectives*, 2: 135–48.

Blazenko, George (1987), "Managerial Preference, Asymmetric Information, and Financial Structure," *Journal of Finance*, 42: 839–62.

Bolton, Patrick and David S. Scharfstein (1990), "A Theory of Predation Based on Agency Problems in Financial Contracting," *American Economic Review*, 80: 93–106.

Bowen, Robert M., Lane A. Daly, and Charles C. Huber Jr. (1982), "Evidence on the Existence and Determinants of Inter-Industry Differences in Leverage," *Financial Management*, 11: 10–20.

Bradford, William (1987), "The Issue Decision of Manager-Owners under Information Asymmetry," *Journal of Finance*, 42: 1245–60.

Bradley, Michael, Gregg Jarrell, and E. Han Kim (1984), "On the Existence of an Optimal Capital Structure: Theory and Evidence," *Journal of Finance*, 39: 857–78.

Brander, James A. and Tracy R. Lewis (1986), "Oligopoly and Financial Structure: The Limited Liability Effect," *American Economic Review*, 76: 956–70.

Brander, James A. and Michael Poitevin (1989), "Management Compensation and the Agency Costs of Debt Finance," Working Paper, University of British Columbia.

Brennan, Michael and Alan Kraus (1987), "Efficient Financing under Asymmetric Information," *Journal of Finance*, 42: 1225–43.

Castanias, Richard (1983), "Bankruptcy Risk and Optimal Capital Structure," *Journal of Finance*, 38, 1617–35.

Chang, Chun (1987), "Capital Structure as Optimal Contracts," Working Paper, Carlson School of Management, University of Minnesota.

Chaplinsky, Susan and Greg Niehaus (1990), "The Determinants of Inside Ownership and Leverage," Working Paper, University of Michigan.

Constantinides, George M. and Bruce D. Grundy (1989), "Optimal Investment With Stock Repurchase and Financing as Signals," *The Review of Financial Studies*, 2, 445–66.

Cornett, Marcia and Nickolaos Travlos (1989), "Information Effects Associated with Debt-for-Equity and Equity-for- Debt Exchange Offers," *Journal of Finance*, 44: 451–68.

Dann, Larry Y. (1981), "Common Stock Repurchases: An Analysis of Returns to Bondholders and Stockholders," *Journal of Financial Economics*, 9: 113–38.

Dann, Larry and Harry DeAngelo (1988), "Corporate Financial Policy and Corporate Control: A Study of Defensive Adjustments in Asset and Ownership Structure," *Journal of Financial Economics*, 20: 87–127.

Dann, Larry, Ronald Masulis and David Mayers (1989), "Repurchase Tender Offers and Earnings Information," Working Paper, University of Oregon.

Dann, Larry Y. and Wayne H. Mikkelson (1984), "Convertible Debt Issuance,

Capital Structure Change and Financing-Related Information: Some New Evidence," *Journal of Financial Economics*, 13: 157–86.

Darrough, Masako and Neal Stoughton (1986), "Moral Hazard and Adverse Selection: The Question of Financial Structure," *Journal of Finance*, 41: 501–13.

DeAngelo, Harry and Linda DeAngelo (1985), "Managerial Ownership of Voting Rights: A Study of Public Corporations with Dual Classes of Common Stock," *Journal of Financial Economics*, 14: 33–69.

Diamond, Douglas (1984), "Financial Intermediation and Delegated Monitoring," *Review of Economic Studies*, 51: 393–414.

(1989), "Reputation Acquisition in Debt Markets," *Journal of Political Economy*, 97: 828–62.

Duffie, Darrell and Matthew O. Jackson (1989), "Optimal Innovation of Futures Contracts," *Review of Financial Studies*, 2: 275–96.

Dybvig, Philip and Jaime Zender (1989), "Capital Structure and Dividend Irrelevance with Asymmetric Information," Working Paper, Yale School of Organization and Management.

Eckbo, B. Espen (1986), "Valuation Effects of Corporate Debt Offerings," *Journal of Financial Economics*, 15: 119–51.

Fama, Eugene F. and Michael C. Jensen (1983), "Agency Problems and Residual Claims," *Journal of Law and Economics*, 26: 327–49.

Fama, Eugene F. and Merton H. Miller (1972), *The Theory of Finance*, New York: Holt, Rinehart, and Winston.

Franke, Günter (1987), "Costless Signalling in Financial Markets," *Journal of Finance*, 42: 809–22.

Friend, Irwin and Joel Hasbrouck (1988), "Determinants of Capital Structure," in Andy Chen (ed.), *Research in Finance*, vol. VII, New York: JAI Press, pp. 1–19.

Friend, Irwin and Larry Lang (1988), "An Empirical Test of the Impact of Managerial Self-Interest on Corporate Capital Structure," *Journal of Finance*, 43: 271–81.

Gale, David and Martin Hellwig (1985), "Incentive Compatible Debt Contracts: The One-Period Problem," *Review of Economic Studies*, 52: 647–63.

Gertner, Robert, Robert Gibbons and David Scharfstein (1988), "Simultaneous Signalling to the Capital and Product Markets," *Rand Journal of Economics*, 19: 173–90.

Glazer, Jacob (1989), "Live and Let Live: Collusion among Oligopolists with Long-Term Debt," Working Paper, Boston University.

Glazer, Jacob and Ronen Israel (1990), "Managerial Incentives and Financial Signalling in Product Market Competition," *International Journal of Industrial Economics*, 8: 271–80.

Gonedes, Nicholas J., Larry Lang and Mathias Chikaonda (1988), "Empirical Results on Managerial Incentives and Capital Structure," Working Paper, The Wharton School, University of Pennsylvania.

Green, Edward J. and Robert H. Porter (1984), "Noncooperative Collusion under Imperfect Price Information," *Econometrica*, 52: 87–100.

Green, Richard C. (1984), "Investment Incentives, Debt, and Warrants," *Journal of Financial Economics*, 13: 115–36.

Grossman, Sanford J. and Oliver Hart (1982), "Corporate Financial Structure and Managerial Incentives," in J. McCall (ed.), *The Economics of Information and Uncertainty*, Chicago: University of Chicago Press.

(1988), "One Share-One Vote and the Market for Corporate Control," *Journal of Financial Economics*, 20: 175–202.

Harris, Milton and Artur Raviv (1988a), "Corporate Control Contests and Capital Structure," *Journal of Financial Economics*, 20: 55–86.

(1988b), "Corporate Governance: Voting Rights and Majority Rules," *Journal of Financial Economics* 20: 203–35.

(1989), "The Design of Securities," *Journal of Financial Economics*, 24: 255–87.

(1990), "Capital Structure and the Informational Role of Debt," *Journal of Finance*, 45: 321–49.

Harris, Milton and Robert M. Townsend (1981), "Resource Allocation Under Asymmetric Information," *Econometrica*, 49: 33–64.

Hart, Oliver and John Moore (1989), "Default and Renegotiation: A Dynamic Model of Debt," Working Paper, MIT, August.

(1990), "A Theory of Corporate Financial Structure Based on the Seniority of Claims," Working Paper #560, MIT.

Haugen, Robert and Lemma Senbet (1987), "On the Resolution of Agency Problems by Complex Financial Instruments: A Reply," *Journal of Finance*, 42: 1091–5.

Heinkel, Robert (1982), "A Theory of Capital Structure Relevance under Imperfect Information," *Journal of Finance*, 37: 1141–50.

Heinkel, Robert and Josef Zechner (1990), "The Role of Debt and Preferred Stock as a Solution to Adverse Investment Incentives," *Journal of Financial and Quantitative Analysis*, 25: 1–24.

Hirshleifer, David and Anjan V. Thakor (1989), "Managerial Reputation, Project Choice and Debt," Working Paper #14–89, Anderson Graduate School of Management at UCLA.

Israel, Ronen (1989), "Capital and Ownership Structure, and the Market for Corporate Control," Working Paper, University of Michigan.

(1991), "Capital Structure and the Market for Corporate Control: The Defensive Role of Debt Financing," *Journal of Finance*, 46: 1391–1409.

Israel, Ronen, Aharon R. Ofer, and Daniel Siegel (forthcoming), "The Information Content of Equity for Debt Swaps: An Investigation of Analysts' Forecasts of Firm Cash Flows," *Journal of Financial Economics*.

Jarrell, Gregg and Annette Poulsen (1988), "Dual-Class Recapitalizations as Antitakeover Mechanisms: The Recent Evidence," *Journal of Financial Economics*, 20: 129–52.

Jensen, Michael C. (1986), "Agency Costs of Free Cash Flow, Corporate Finance and Takeovers," *American Economic Review*, 76: 323–39.

(1989), "Eclipse of the Public Corporation," *Harvard Business Review*, September–October, 61–74.

Jensen, Michael C. and William Meckling (1976), "Theory of the Firm: Managerial

Behavior, Agency Costs, and Capital Structure," *Journal of Financial Economics*, 3: 305–60.

John, Kose (1987), "Risk-Shifting Incentives and Signalling Through Corporate Capital Structure," *Journal of Finance*, 42: 623–41.

John, Kose and David C. Nachman (1985), "Risky Debt, Investment Incentives, and Reputation in a Sequential Equilibrium," *Journal of Finance*, 40: 863–80.

John, Kose and Lemma W. Senbet (1988), "Limited Liability, Corporate Leverage, and Public Policy," Working Paper, Stern School of Business, New York University.

Kester, Carl W. (1986), "Capital and Ownership Structure: A Comparison of United States and Japanese Manufacturing Corporations," *Financial Management*, 15: 5–16.

Kim, Moshe and Vojislav Maksimovic (forthcoming), "Technology, Debt and the Exploitation of Growth Options," *Journal of Banking and Finance*.

Kim, Wi Saeng and Eric H. Sorensen (1986), "Evidence on the Impact of the Agency Costs of Debt in Corporate Debt Policy," *Journal of Financial and Quantitative Analysis*, 21: 131–44.

Kim, Yong Cheol and René M. Stulz (1988), "The Eurobond Market and Corporate Financial Policy: A Test of the Clientele Hypothesis," *Journal of Financial Economics*, 22: 189–205.

Korajczyk, Robert A., Deborah Lucas and Robert L. McDonald (1990a), "Understanding Stock Price Behavior around the Time of Equity Issues," in R. Glen Hubbard (ed.), *Asymmetric Information, Corporate Finance, and Investment*, Chicago: University of Chicago Press, pp. 257–77.

(1990b), "The Effect of Information Releases on the Pricing and Timing of Equity Issues," *Review of Financial Studies*, 4: 685–708.

(1990c), "Equity Issues With Time-Varying Asymmetric Information," *Journal of Financial and Quantitative Analysis*, (forthcoming).

Krasker, William (1986), "Stock Price movements in Response to Stock Issues under Asymmetric Information," *Journal of Finance*, 41: 93–105.

Lacker, Jeffrey M. (1990), "Collateralized Debt as the Optimal Contract," Working Paper, Federal Reserve Bank of Richmond.

Lease, Ronald C., John J. McConnell, and Wayne H. Mikkelson (1984), "The Market Value of Differential Voting Rights in Closely Held Corporations," *Journal of Business*, 57: 443–67.

Lehn, Kenneth and Annette Poulsen (1989), "Free Cash Flow and Stockholder Gains in Going Private Transactions," *Journal of Finance*, 44: 771–87.

Leland, Hayne and David Pyle (1977), "Information Asymmetries, Financial Structure, and Financial Intermediation," *Journal of Finance*, 32: 371–88.

Levy, Haim (1983), "Economic Evaluation of Voting Power of Common Stock," *Journal of Finance*, 38: 79–93.

Linn, Scott C. and Michael Pinegar (1988), "The Effect of Issuing Preferred Stock on Common and Preferred Stockholder Wealth," *Journal of Financial Economics*, 22: 155–84.

Long, Michael and Ileen Malitz (1985), "The Investment-Financing Nexus: Some Empirical Evidence," *Midland Corporate Finance Journal*, 3: 53–9.

Lucas, Deborah and Robert McDonald (1990), "Equity Issues and Stock Price Dynamics," *Journal of Finance*, 45: 1019–43.

Lys, Thomas and Konduru Sivaramakrishnan (1988), "Earnings Expectations and Capital Restructuring: The Case of Equity-for-Debt Swaps," *Journal of Accounting Research*, 26: 273–99.

Maksimovic, Vojislav (1986), "Optimal Capital Structure in Oligopolies", Ph.D. thesis, Harvard University.

—— (1988), "Capital Structure in Repeated Oligopolies," *Rand Journal of Economics*, 19: 389–407.

—— (1989), "Optimal Financial Structure and Value Dissipation in Imperfect Product Markets," Working Paper, University of British Columbia.

—— (1990), "Oligopoly, Price Wars and Bankruptcy," Working Paper, University of British Columbia.

Maksimovic, Vojislav and Sheridan Titman (forthcoming), "Financial Policy and a Firm's Reputation for Product Qaulity," *Review of Financial Studies*.

Marsh, Paul (1982), "The Choice Between Equity and Debt: An Empirical Study," *Journal of Finance*, 37: 121–44.

Masulis, Ronald W. (1980), "The Effects of Capital Structure Change on Security Prices: A Study of Exchange Offers," *Journal of Financial Economics*, 8: 139–78.

—— (1983), "The Impact of Capital Structure Change on Firm Value: Some Estimates," *Journal of Finance*, 38: 107–26.

—— (1988), *The Debt/Equity Choice*, New York: Ballinger Publishing Company.

Masulis, Ronald W. and Ashok N. Korwar (1986), "Seasoned Equity Offerings: An Empirical Investigation," *Journal of Financial Economics*, 15: 91–118.

Mikkelson, Wayne H. and M. Megan Partch (1986), "Valuation Effects of Security Offerings and the Issuance Process," *Journal of Financial Economics*, 15: 31–60.

Miller, Merton H. (1988), "The Modigliani-Miller Propositions After Thirty Years," *Journal of Economic Perspectives*, 2: 99–120.

Modigliani, Franco (1988), "MM – Past, Present, and Future," *Journal of Economic Perspectives*, 2: 149–58.

Modigliani, Franco and Merton H. Miller (1958), "The Cost of Capital, Corporation Finance, and the Theory of Investment," *American Economic Review*, 48: 261–97.

Myers, Stewart C. (1977), "Determinants of Corporate Borrowing," *Journal of Financial Economics*, 5: 147–75.

—— (1984), "The Capital Structure Puzzle," *Journal of Finance*, 39: 575–92.

Myers, Stewart C. and Nicholas S. Majluf (1984), "Corporate Financing and Investment Decisions When Firms Have Information That Investors Do Not Have," *Journal of Financial Economics*, 13: 187–221.

Myerson, Roger B. (1979), "Incentive Compatibility and the Bargaining Problem," *Econometrica*, 47: 61–73.

Nachman, David C. and Thomas H. Noe (1989), "Design of Securities under Asymmetric Information," Working Paper, Georgia Institute of Technology.

Narayanan, M.P (1987), "On the Resolution of Agency Problems by Complex

Financial Instruments: A Comment," *Journal of Finance*, 42: 1083–90.

(1988), "Debt versus Equity under Asymmetric Information," *Journal of Financial and Quantitative Analysis*, 23: 39–51.

Noe, Thomas (1988), "Capital Structure and Signaling Game Equilibria," *Review of Financial Studies*, 1: 331–56.

Palepu, Krishna G. (1986), "Predicting Takeover Targets: A Methodological and Empirical Analysis," *Journal of Accounting and Economics*, 8: 3–37.

Partch, Megan (1987), "The Creation of a Class of Limited Voting Common Stock and Shareholder Wealth," *Journal of Financial Economics*, 18: 313–39.

Paul, Jonathan (1989), "Informationally Incomplete Markets and Capital Structure," Working Paper, Stanford University Department of Economics.

Pinegar, J. Michael and Ronald C. Lease (1986), "The Impact of Preferred-for-Common Exchange Offers on Firm Value," *Journal of Finance*, 41: 795–814.

Poitevin, Michel (1989), "Financial Signalling and the 'Deep-Pocket' Argument," *Rand Journal of Economics*, 20: 26–40.

Ravid, S. Abraham (1988), "On Interactions of Production and Financial Decisions," *Financial Management*, 8: 87–99.

Ravid, Abraham S. and Oded H. Sarig (1989), "Financial Signalling by Precommitting to Cash Outflows," Working Paper, Rutgers, The State University of New Jersey.

Ross, Stephen A. (1977), "The Determination of Financial Structure: The Incentive Signalling Approach," *Bell Journal of Economics*, 8: 23–40.

(1988), "Comment on the Modigliani-Miller Propositions," *Journal of Economic Perspectives*, 2: 127–34.

(1989), "Institutional Markets, Financial Marketing, and Financial Innovation," *Journal of Finance*, 44: 541–56.

Sarig, Oded H. (1988), "Bargaining with a Corporation and the Capital Structure of the Bargaining Firm," Working Paper, Tel Aviv University.

Schipper, Katherine and Abbie Smith (1986), "A Comparision of Equity Carve-Outs and Seasoned Equity Offerings: Share Price Effects and Corporate Restructuring," *Journal of Financial Economics*, 15: 153–86.

Smith, Clifford, Jr. (1986). "Investment Banking and the Capital Acquisition Process," *Journal of Financial Economics*, 15: 3–29.

Smith, Clifford and Jerold Warner (1979), "On Financial Contracting," *Journal of Financial Economics*, 7: 117–61.

Stiglitz, Joseph E. (1988), "Why Financial Structure Matters," *Journal of Economic Perspectives*, 2: 121–6.

Stulz, René M. (1991), "Managerial Discretion and Optimal Financing Policies," *Journal of Financial Economics*, 26: 3–27.

(1988), "Managerial Control of Voting Rights: Financing Policies and the Market for Corporate Control," *Journal of Financial Economics*, 20: 25–54.

Stultz, René M. and Herb Johnson (1985), "An Analysis of Secured Debt," *Journal of Financial Economics*, 14: 501–21.

Taggart, Robert A., Jr. (1985), "Secular Patterns in the Financing of U.S. Corporations," in B. Friedman (ed.), *Corporate Capital Structures in the*

United States, Chicago: University of Chicago Press, pp. 13–80.

Titman, Sheridan (1984), "The Effect of Capital Structure on a Firm's Liquidation Decision," *Journal of Financial Economics*, 13: 137–51.

Titman, Sheridan and Roberto Wessels (1988), "The Determinants of Capital Structure Choice," *Journal of Finance*, 43: 1–19.

Townsend, Robert M. (1979), "Optimal Contracts and Competitive Markets With Costly State Verification," *Journal of Economic Theory*, 21: 265–93.

Vermaelen, Theo (1981), "Common Stock Repurchases and Market Signalling: An Empirical Study," *Journal of Financial Economy*, 9: 139–83.

Williams, Joseph (1989), "Monitoring and Optimal Financial Contracts," Working Paper, University of British Columbia.

Williamson, Oliver (1988), "Corporate Finance and Corporate Governance," *Journal of Finance*, 43: 567–91.

Žender, Jaime (1990), "Optimal Financial Instruments," Working Paper, University of Utah.

CHAPTER 3

Collusion and the theory of organizations

Jean Tirole*

1 INTRODUCTION

1.1 Collusion and the social sciences

The phenomenon of collusion, and the concomitant concepts of "group," "power," "bureaucracy," and "politics" figure prominently in political science and sociology. Political scientists have always been concerned by the possibility that politicians and bureaucrats might identify with interest groups rather than serve the public interest. Montesquieu's plea for building a system of checks and balances among branches of government to limit the perversion of public policy, and the writings of the American federalists, in particular Madison, have deeply influenced the design of many constitutions. Later, Marx suggested that the State uses its coercive power to benefit large trusts. This vision of the capture of political life by interest groups was considerably enriched in the twentieth century by political scientists (Bentley, Truman) and especially by the political economists of the Chicago school (Stigler, Peltzman, Becker) and the Virginia school (Buchanan, Tollison, Tullock).

Concurrently, sociologists (Crozier, Dalton) and organization theorists (Cyert and March) have emphasized that behavior is often best predicted by the analysis of group as well as individual incentives. It would be naive to build incentives for individual members of an organization without considering their effect on collective behavior. In other words, incentive structures must account for the possibility that members collude to manipulate their functioning.

Collusive phenomena have been by and large ignored by economists, although there are many situations in which collusion is a concern besides the organization of political life and that of firms. (In labor economics, workers may worry that their union representatives strike deals with management that do not fit with their interests. In financial economics, collusion between the board of directors and management is well documented. In public economics, taxes and subsidies are not necessarily set to maximize a social welfare function, but may be motivated by the desire to benefit specific social classes; at a more micro level, the collection of taxes may be jeopardized by the possibility of collusion. In regulatory economics, the possibility of collusion between government agencies or politicians with industry or other interest groups strongly influences regulatory institutions and policies. Last, a substantial limitation of the theory of economic development is its neglect of corruption (Klitgaard, 1988).) Furthermore, collusive phenomena challenge the received theory of contracts. Contract design with multiple agents (e.g., Nash and Bayesian implementation, auctions and public goods mechanisms, moral hazard in teams, relative performance evaluation, hierarchical structures) is sensitive to the possibility of collusion among agents.

The main exception to this general neglect is the Chicago school approach to regulatory capture.[1] One of the fundamental contributions of Stigler (1971) was to apply Downs' and Olson's theory of interest groups to regulation. This theory implies that the power of an interest group depends on two factors, its stake and its organization cost. On the one hand, an interest group has more incentives to organize and to try and influence public policy if the policies considered by the government have substantially different impacts on their welfare. On the other hand, the interest group's cost of organizing is determined by two elements, the "mobilization cost" and the "transfer cost." The cost of mobilizing depends on the nature of the interest group. For instance, taxpayers are numerous and scattered; while their collective stake in policy is often substantial, their personal stake is generally negligible, so that most do not collect information and intervene about specific regulatory issues. In contrast, many industries (monopolized, cartelized, or even competitive) are well organized.

Transfer costs are related to the deadweight loss associated with the transfer of "income equivalent" from the interest groups to public decision-makers. In order to capture public policy, interest groups must be able to reciprocate favorable decisions. What interest groups can offer to public decision-makers takes many forms (many of which have counterparts in the other situations mentioned above). Bureaucrats of government agencies value jobs after their tenure in the agency, and the absence of complaint about their management of the industry; the political principal (executive, legislative) may receive votes, campaign contributions, or profitable contracts to their law or consulting firm; both can be offered monetary bribes, entertainment expenses (meals, stays in resorts), and friendly relationships. Most of these transfers of income equivalent involve deadweight losses in that the public decision-maker would prefer receiving direct monetary transfers if those were feasible.

The challenge for the economist is to build a theory of the role of collusion – existing or latent – in organizations. In this endeavor, it seems desirable to preserve the neoclassical precept that individuals act in their best interest. Collusion can then be viewed as the realization of gains from trade within groups of the organization. It also seems natural to build on the acquired knowledge of information economics. Indeed, collusion may not be a serious issue if there is full information. (To illustrate this point on the regulatory example discussed above, voters and courts would have little trouble controlling politicians in a world of perfect information; the latter would easily monitor government agencies, who in turn would perfectly regulate their industries; and it is hard to envision a role for interest groups and institutional checks and balances in such a world.) Furthermore, the introduction of informational problems is not only motivated by the theorist's search for coherence and aesthetics: As we will see, the consideration of information unveils a third determinant of the power of an interest group. Also, the structure of information plays a crucial role in the institutional response to the threat of collusion.

This chapter has two goals. The first is to describe the methodology and the insights existing in the literature on collusion, organizing the contributions along some main themes. The second is to list some open questions (there are many!).

Section 1.2 introduces the methodological divide between the "enforceable side contracts" and "self-enforcing side contracts" approaches to collusion. Almost all the literature has made the assumption that side contracts are enforceable, in that the promises are binding, and has not investigated the enforcement mechanism. We discuss the pros and cons of the assumption.

The second part of this chapter offers a critical review of the literature. Section 2.1 gives some broad themes. Section 2.2 develops a simple example in detail, with an emphasis on showing how one can solve organization design when the organization must be analyzed as a network of contracts rather than as a single, grand contract. In this example, collusion affects the organization, but does not arise in equilibrium. Section 2.3 analyzes the issues associated with coalition formation under asymmetric information. Sections 2.4 through 2.7 each relax an assumption of the example of section 2.2 to point at circumstances in which it is strictly optimal to let agents collude in equilibrium. Sections 2.8 through 2.10 summarize economic insights of the literature on collusion for several paradigms of organization design, and study the link between renegotiation and common agency models with collusion ones.

The third part of the chapter discusses the research agenda. Besides pursuing the applied theoretical research to derive economic insights for specific organizations, there is ample scope for more fundamental research. This research should proceed in two directions. The first consists in deriving general theorems for the enforceable side contract approach. Section 3.1 sets up a broad framework and section 3.2 discusses some difficulties in the derivation of such theorems. The second direction, introduced in section 3.3, is to develop a methodology to analyze organization design with self-enforcing side contracts and to relate the results to those of the enforceable side contracts approach. Section 3.4 and appendix 2 build two simple models to illustrate some facets of this construction. Making progress in these two directions is a formidable, but important task.

1.2   Enforceable versus self-enforcing side contracts

Collusion is driven by reciprocity. A member of an organization, agent 1, uses the discretion conferred on her by the organizational design to help another member, agent 2. This discretion may take the form of a task allocation, the choice of compensation or penalties, or reports to superiors. Its foundation is the information held by agent 1, but not the center. In exchange for the favor, agent 2 offers a side transfer or else uses his own discretion in the organization to benefit agent 1.

The large diversity of side transfers in practice, from monetary bribes to friendly relationships, makes it necessary to consider an array of "technologies" for side transfers. In general, the cost s of the side transfer for the donor differs from the value $\tilde{s}$ for the recipient. If $\tilde{s} < s$, the side transfer creates a deadweight loss. In section 1.1, we discussed two reasons why this may be the case. First, if the donor is a group of individuals, collecting $\tilde{s}$ may cost more than $\tilde{s}$ (mobilization cost). Second, non-monetary transfers may not be efficient. A \$100 lunch paid by an interest group to a civil servant may have value \$50 to him (in which case $s = 2\tilde{s}$). But there also exist cases in which $\tilde{s} > s$. For instance, the donor may at low time cost save a substantial amount of effort by the recipient by explaining how to use a new software. Such collusive activities are in general called cooperative activities. More generally, one can define a transaction technology that specifies the transfer $\tilde{s}(s)$ received by the recipient.

More elusive is the issue of how side contracts are enforced. Consider the situation in which agent 1 can use her discretion in the organization to increase agent 2's utility by Δ (the amount Δ, which we express in monetary terms, can be called agent 2's stake in agent 1's decision), and that the cost for agent 1 (in terms of effort, lower compensation, etc.) of doing so is lower than the maximum transfer $\bar{s}(\Delta)$ that she can receive from agent 2. Almost all the literature on collusion has assumed that in this situation the two agents agree on a side contract stipulating that agent 1 uses her discretion to benefit agent 2, who in exchange offers a side transfer sufficient to compensate agent 1, and that both agents abide by their commitment.

We call this the enforceability approach. It presumes that any gain from trade between parties (where the gains from trade are defined relatively to the transaction technology) is realized,[2] and does not investigate the mechanism that ensures compliance to the agreement.

Enforcement is a more serious issue for side contracts than for ordinary contracts. If collusion poses a threat to an organization, the latter may stipulate in its grand contract among all members that side contracts or some forms of potentially verifiable side transfers are prohibited. Indeed, organizations routinely do so. Administrative rules put constraints on (but do not fully prohibit) civil servants or representatives receiving money from interest groups. Similarly, employees in a firm are in general prevented from engaging in personal monetary transactions with other employees or customers. It is doubtful that courts would enforce side contracts that violate the letter or the spirit of the administrative rule or the corporate charter (in some instances of collusion, organized crime may substitute for a court, but fortunately such cases are not pervasive!).

The enforcement of side contracts in general relies on non-judicial mechanisms. One such mechanism is reputation: I do you a favor today because I trust you will reciprocate tomorrow. This leads to the view developed in sections 3.3 through 3.5 that collusion is linked with long-term relationships and is enforced by a sequence of favors and counterfavors.[3] We view reputation as an important enforcement mechanism. Yet it is not unique, as we do observe collusion in short-term relationships. The motorist who bribes the policeman in order not to be ticketed, the developer who builds a house at a low price for a city official in exchange for an adjustment in zoning, the interest group who pays a campaign contribution to a representative to obtain a favorable vote in Congress, the advisor who overstates the student's ability in exchange for having his name on the student's work need not be engaged in a long-term relationship with the colluding partner. Such one-shot exchange of favors seem to be enforced by one of the following mechanisms. First, a colluding party may have a "word of honor": once he has agreed (explicitly or implicitly) on a trade, he abides by his commitment. Second (and an elaboration on the theme that individuals care about respecting agreements), he may be worried that the other party would be upset by the breach of agreement and would seek revenge: a small probability that the motorist might shoot the policeman if the latter ticketed after receiving the bribe is likely to deter the policeman from cheating on the agreement. Third, the reputation mechanism may operate even if the relationship under consideration is one-shot, as long as at least one of the parties to the collusive agreement is a long-term player. I know of examples in which a mayor received bribes from individual citizens wanting to build on some tracts of land. While the relationship with each citizen was one-shot, it was known in some circles that the way to quickly and efficiently obtain desirable tracts was to bribe the mayor.

There are two ways of building a theory of side contracting. The first exogeneously assumes that side contracts are enforceable and the second traces the foundations of enforceability to repeated interaction and reputation. If, as is often the case, repeated interaction is indeed what enforces side contracts, the second approach is clearly preferable because it is more fundamentalist; it takes a more agnostic view of whether gains from trade are realized within groups, and, in doing so, it unveils an important control variable affecting the realization of collusion, i.e., the length of the relationship among the members of the group. More on this in sections 3.3 through 3.5.

The enforceability approach seems more innocuous when collusion is enforced by word of honor (which, we take, relieves parties from the need for court enforcement). When enforcement is ensured by repeated interaction and reputation, enforceable side contracts at best depict a polar case in which reputation mechanisms work well to enforce collusion (the word-of-honor paradigm can be viewed as an extreme case of a reputation model in which the prior probability of being trustworthy is equal to one). Yet, I would expect many insights obtained with the enforceability approach to carry over to self-enforcing side contracts. To this purpose, I invite the reader to ponder on the plausibility of the themes developed in the next sections (e.g., reduction in the stakes and in the power of incentive schemes, determinants of the power of a group or individual, generalized sufficiency results, role of information) in a self-enforceability framework.

These remarks may reflect some amount of cognitive dissonance since the literature has embraced the enforceability approach, and self-enforceability seems important in practice. The reason for this methodological choice is that the enforceability approach allows the use of classical contract theory by describing the organization as a nexus of contracts. In contrast, the self-enforceability approach requires the development of new techniques to deal with dynamic mechanism design with incentive constraints defined by equilibria of a game among the agents. I believe that the enforceability approach may offer a realistic description of side contracting, and that it still yields precious insights when it does not. I view the two approaches as complementary.

2 A REVIEW OF THE LITERATURE

2.1 The broad themes

This section introduces some broad themes of the literature. These themes are stated somewhat informally. Most of them will be illustrated in section 2.2. Section 2.8 describes more specific insights. Themes n° 1 and n° 2 relate to the occurrence of collusion in equilibrium.

THEME n° 1 (collusion proofness): Under some conditions, there is no loss in designing organizations which do not leave scope for collusion.

That is, the organization designer (the center, the principal) may anticipate collusion and give adequate incentives to the agents not to side contract. All transfers can take place between the center and individual members and not among agents; in other words, side transfers do not occur. This does not mean that collusion cannot occur in equilibrium; indeed, there are examples in which an alternative optimal organization design delegates, in that it gives aggregate incentives to a group of agents and lets them determine their internal contractual relationship.[4] The theory is then silent on whether collusion occurs in equilibrium. It only predicts the final outcome and not the contracting structure (collusion-free grand contract or delegation) that leads to this outcome. Yet, the possibility that collusion proofness involves no loss in welfare has fascinating implications. For, an outside observer would erroneously conclude from not observing collusive behavior that collusion is at best a minor phenomenon. This observer would overlook the institutional response to the threat of collusion. Casual empiricism suggests that actual collusive behavior is likely to be only the "tip of the iceberg" and to be less important than the effect of potential collusion on constitutions, corporate charters, organization design, and incentive schemes.

THEME n° 2 (equilibrium collusion): Yet, in other circumstances, letting members of the organization collude is optimal.

Cases in which side transfers among agents are desirable come readily to mind. Side transfers may be good for the organization if they are acts of cooperation (relatedly, direct transfers among members may be less costly than transfers channeled through a center). But equilibrium collusion may also arise when collusion is undesirable in the sense that the organization would be better off if side transfers were infeasible. Collusion then arises because it is too costly to fight. We later come back to these ideas in detail.

Themes n° 3 and n° 4 relate to two methods of fending off collusion, namely decreasing gains from trade and interlinking reward schemes.

THEME n° 3   (lack of discretion and bureaucratic behavior): The fear of collusion leads organizations to reduce stakes and to make less use of decentralized information.

The idea is simple: reducing the sensitivity of decisions to decentralized information, that is reducing the discretion of the agents, lowers the gains from collusion. For instance, the collusion between a foreman and a worker is less likely to occur if the foreman has little discretion over the worker's sake. The extreme case of lack of discretion is a rule whereby the center or statutes determine the course of actions without consulting the agents. Potential collusion is thus a crucial ingredient of a theory of bureaucracy.

THEME n° 4   (linkage of incentives): Standard sufficient statistics principles for rewarding agents do not hold in the presence of collusion.

That is, the rewards of members of an organization are not only based on variables that are informative about their individual performance.[5] Because agents are linked through potential side contracting, sufficient statistics results must be extended to the level of the group. For instance, Laffont (1990) shows that the reward of a team member may depend on the aggregate performance of the team even though a supervisor has information about individual performances (and shocks are uncorrelated, so that there is no role for relative performance evaluation). The point is that individual rewards that are less sensitive to individual performance and depend on team performance make it less likely that the supervisor will collude with particular team members to manipulate reports about individual performances. As another illustration, a supervisor must share a supervisee's reward or punishment even if he does not contribute to the supervisee's output and need not be induced to acquire supervisory information; the potential manipulation of his report about the supervisee's activity suffices to make them a team (Tirole, 1986).

Last, themes n° 5 and n° 6 relate to the question of which coalitions are effective. An agent (or group of agents) is said to have *power* if the possibility of his colluding with another agent (or group of agents) leads to a change in organization design and outcome. That is, the agent has power if he has an incentive to collude and if steps are taken to prevent his colluding. (As we will see, having power does not mean being better off. The institutional response to fend off collusion may actually hurt the agent.) We mentioned two determinants of power in section 1.1: to have power, an agent must have a stake in the other agent's decision (otherwise, he has no incentive to collude) and he must have means of payment (see the discussion on mobilization and transfer costs).

THEME n° 5   (determinant of power): The third determinant of power of an agent is the dissonance between the agent's and the organization's objectives. An agent has power when his interest lies in the center being poorly informed, i.e., in an inefficient organization.

In the next section, we give an example of an agent who has a stake in another agent's decision, has means of transferring income equivalent to him and yet has no power. A closely related theme is:

THEME n° 6   (effective coalitions): Only some coalitions are harmful to the organization even if all coalitions are *a priori* feasible (have stakes and can transfer income equivalent). That is, the organization can costlessly prevent other coalitions from forming.

2.2   An example

This section develops a simple model and illustrates all themes enunciated in section 2.1, but theme n° 2. In this model, the principal can without loss of generality focus on collusion-proof schemes. Theme n° 2, that equilibrium collusion may be desirable, will be illustrated in sections 2.4 through 2.7. The simplicity of the model sacrifices specific economic insights, but it allows a short exposition of its logical structure and of its variants.

2.2.1   The model

The model is a simplified version of the regulation model in Laffont and Tirole (1991a) (who also allow moral hazard, variable verifiable output, and more players). There are three parties: a principal (P), a supervisor (S) and an agent (A). A supplies 0 or 1 unit of a good to P. The agent's privately known cost of supplying 1 unit, β, takes value $\underline{\beta}$ with probability v and $\bar{\beta}$ with probability $(1-v)$. Let $\Delta\beta \equiv \bar{\beta} - \underline{\beta} > 0$. The gross surplus to P is S if A produces, and 0 otherwise. Let w denote the expected transfer from P to A, and let x denote the probability that the good is produced.

The two parties are risk neutral. A's utility is $U = w - \beta x$. He has reservation utility 0. In the absence of a supervisor, P's welfare is $W = Sx - w + \alpha_A U$, where $0 < \alpha_A < 1$. That is, P puts some weight on A's utility in his own objective function (α_A could be taken equal to 0 for most, but not all insights). There are two alternative justifications for this assumption. The first, which we will embrace here, is that W is a social welfare function, which weighs the utilities of consumers and the supplier. (Introducing prior contracting, together with risk aversion, supplies the second interpretation. If A is risk averse, his *ex post* rents are costly (which corresponds to $\alpha_A < 1$), but can to some extent be recouped by P in the initial contract (so $\alpha_A > 0$). This alternative justification requires a small change in the modeling, and we will not pursue the topic further.) Without a supervisor, the model is a slight variant of the classical monopoly pricing model. P chooses a price w, which A is free to accept or reject. Clearly the optimal price is either $\bar{\beta}$ or $\underline{\beta}$, and which one obtains depends on the probability distribution:

$$w = \bar{\beta} \quad \text{if}$$
$$S - \bar{\beta} + \alpha_A v \Delta \beta > v(S - \underline{\beta}) \tag{2.2.1}$$

and:

$$w = \underline{\beta} \quad \text{if}$$
$$S - \bar{\beta} + \alpha_A v \Delta \beta < v(S - \underline{\beta}). \tag{2.2.2}$$

If (2.2.1) holds, P prefers to have both types produce and does not try to screen for A's type by offering $\underline{\beta}$ and running the risk that A does not produce. In contrast, if (2.2.2) holds, P tries to "price discriminate." From now on we will assume that (2.2.1) holds. That is, P does not try to price discriminate in the absence of further information.

We now introduce a supervisor (S), whose role is to reduce the asymmetry of information between P and A. S learns a signal $\sigma \in \{\beta, \emptyset\}$. If $\beta = \underline{\beta}$, S learns it with probability ζ and learns nothing with probability $(1 - \zeta)$. If $\beta = \bar{\beta}$, S learns nothing. An interpretation of this information structure is that the basic production technology (known to everyone) costs $\bar{\beta}$, that the agent may or may not benefit from an improvement that reduces cost by $\Delta \beta$, and that the supervisor may or may not discover the improvement when it exists. We assume that the signal is hard information; that is, if $\sigma = \underline{\beta}$, and S reveals it to P, it is convincing evidence. The supervisor's report, r, belongs to $\{\sigma, \emptyset\}$. That is, if $\sigma = \emptyset$, S can only report that he has observed nothing. If $\sigma = \underline{\beta}$, S can either supply the evidence to P or hide it. Concealing information is S's degree of discretion. As we will see, there is no point considering other reports than σ and $\emptyset$.

Let s denote the supervisor's income. His utility is $V(s) = s$. The supervisor has reservation utility 0. The principal's welfare is $W = Sx - w - s + \alpha_A U + \alpha_S V$.

The timing is as follows: (1) A privately learns β. S learns σ, and for simplicity we will assume all along that A also learns σ.[6] (2) P offers S and A a grand contract, which is a mechanism specifying transfers w and s, and probability of production x as functions of messages sent by S and A, and S's report of hard information. (3) S and A can sign a side contract (we later allow other coalitions). A side contract specifies a side transfer which is a function of the messages and report made by S and A in the context of the grand contract, as well as, possibly, messages sent by S and A to each other. For concreteness, assume that S makes a take-it-or-leave-it offer of a side contract to A. (4) Contracts are implemented.

Remark This model is one of adverse selection, where the agents learn their informations before contracting. Alternatively, one could assume that the agents and P are symmetrically informed when signing the grand contract, that A and S later learn their information and that A and S are risk averse (see Tirole, 1986). Because insurance requires to extract *ex post* rents, the insights would be very similar in this alternative model.

For reference, we solve for the optimal grand contract for P when S and A cannot collude (stage 3 of the game is deleted). S is given a flat income $s \equiv 0$ and reports truthfully. If $r = \beta$, then $w = \beta$ and A's rent is extracted. If $r = \emptyset$, then (2.2.1) and the fact that posterior beliefs about β are $\hat{v} \equiv v(1-\zeta)/(v(1-\zeta)+1-v) < v$ imply that it is optimal to offer $w = \bar{\beta}$. Welfare is therefore:

$$W^d = v\zeta(S-\beta) + v(1-\zeta)(S-\bar{\beta}+\alpha_A\Delta\beta) + (1-v)(S-\bar{\beta}), \qquad (2.2.3)$$

where "d" stands for "price discrimination" (meaning that P uses supervisory information to screen for A's type. From (2.2.1), P does not price discriminate when receiving no information from S). Also for reference, we introduce the welfare under no price discrimination or uniform pricing:

$$W^u = S - \bar{\beta} + \alpha_A v\Delta\beta. \qquad (2.2.4)$$

Clearly $W^d > W^u$.

We now allow S and A to collude. We assume that A can transfer income equivalent to S at rate $k \in [0,1]$. That is, if A transfers t, S receives kt. The case $k = 0$ corresponds to a full deadweight loss in the transaction and yields the no-collusion case just studied.

2.2.2   Heuristics

When $\sigma = \emptyset$, S has no discretion and therefore collusion does not occur. When $\sigma = \beta$, giving the same wage to S as when $\sigma = \emptyset$ gives rise to collusion. Any positive bribe will convince S to conceal his information. Indeed, A is willing to pay up to $\Delta\beta$ for the retention of the signal, and therefore P must pay $s = k\Delta\beta$ to S when S reports $r = \beta$. Inducing S to reveal and offering the low price when he does so yields welfare:

$$\tilde{W}^d = v\zeta[S - \beta - (1 - \alpha_S)k\Delta\beta] + v(1 - \zeta)[S - \bar{\beta} + \alpha_A\Delta\beta] \qquad (2.2.5)$$
$$+ (1 - v)(S - \bar{\beta})$$
$$= W^d - v\zeta(1 - \alpha_S)k\Delta\beta.$$

Note that $\tilde{W}^d$ decreases with k. We call the policy of inducing revelation of supervisory information to extract the agent's rent the *incentive policy*.

In contrast, P can decide not to use S's information. He then offers $s \equiv 0$ and $w = \bar{\beta}$ (offering $w = \beta$ in the three states of nature is dominated from (2.2.1)). This yields welfare:

$$\tilde{W}^u = S - \bar{\beta} + \alpha_A v\Delta\beta \qquad (2.2.6)$$
$$= W^u.$$

This latter policy can be interpreted as eliminating S's discretion, i.e., destroying A's stake in a collusion with S, and is called the *bureaucratic policy*. Unlike $\tilde{W}^d$, $\tilde{W}^u$ is independent of k.

Note that for $k = 0$, $\tilde{W}^d = W^d > \tilde{W}^u = W^u$. Assume that $\alpha_A > \alpha_S$.[7] Then for $k = 1$, $\tilde{W}^d < \tilde{W}^u$, and there exists $k^* \in (0,1)$ such that P uses S's information to price discriminate if and only if $k < k^*$. This simple example illustrates a few of our themes:

THEME n° 3   (lack of discretion): When $k > k^*$, the threat of collusion leads P to reduce (actually eliminates) S's discretion. A no longer has a stake in colluding with S.

THEME n° 4   (linkage of incentives): When $k < k^*$, S's reward scheme depends on A's characteristics.

THEME n° 5   (determinant of power): A has power when $\sigma = \beta$ (for any $k > 0$) because his interest (concealment of information) is then dissonant with that of P (revelation of information).

Two comments about theme n° 5 are in order. First, whether A has power is information contingent: when $\sigma = \emptyset$, it has no power; that is, the allocation is the same as when $k = 0$. Similarly, if we allowed a signal $\sigma = \bar{\beta}$ (revealing to S that A is inefficient). A would have no power when $\sigma = \bar{\beta}$. Second, when $k < k^*$, A does not benefit from his power while he does when $k > k^*$ (for which P forgoes price discrimination). It is straightforward to build examples in which A's equilibrium utility decreases when k goes up.[8] This illustrates the importance of accounting for the institutional response to the threat of collusion.

THEME n° 6   (effective coalitions): The other coalitions (P/S and P/A) are not binding.

Let us sketch the proof of this fact. It suffices to show that the optimal scheme when only S and A can collude does not give rise to collusion between S and P or between P and A. Consider first the coalition between P and S. A necessary condition for this coalition to form is that A loses (we let the reader check this). But if the information $\sigma = \beta$ is retained, A is better off (if $k < k^*$) or as well off (if $k > k^*$) for the scheme that is optimal when only the coalition S/A is considered. Second, the coalition P/A does not arise either because S can guarantee himself his equilibrium utility ($s = k\Delta\beta$ or 0) in the absence of P/A coalition, regardless of A's announcement of his type.

Remark 1   The example above illustrates the difficulty of discriminating in the presence of collusion. In richer models, one can also say something about the form of the contract when A is employed. Assume that A's cost is observed by P, but depends both on an adverse selection parameter β and on A's unobservable effort. Then, the threat of collusion leads to *low-powered incentive schemes* (i.e., smaller effort) for the agent (Laffont and Tirole, 1988). To understand why this is so, take the two polar cases of contracts: the cost-plus contract in which P pays A's cost fully, and the fixed-price contract in which A is residual claimant for his cost savings. A cost-plus contract yields no rent (A's utility is independent of the technology because his cost is reimbursed anyway), and therefore there is no incentive to collude. In contrast, A derives substantial rents from a fixed-price contract.[9]

The threat of collusion seems an important factor for the widespread observation of low-powered schemes (cost-plus contracts in procurement or cost-of-service pricing in regulation, flat wages for employees). High-powered schemes like a fixed price contract for a supplier or a discriminating wage for an employee require fine evaluations of the appropriate reward levels and are prone to a perversion of the supervisory function.

Remark 2   Introduce a new player, the environmentalists who suffer (and are not compensated for) a loss due to pollution when the good is produced. Do they have power? Not in our example, because the concealment of $\sigma = \beta$ does not lead to the cancellation of the project. But if we introduce an extra signal $\sigma = \bar{\beta}$, then assuming that P wants to price discriminate when $r = \varnothing$, the environmentalists gain from the retention of signal $\sigma = \bar{\beta}$. They then have power. Like A when $\sigma = \bar{\beta}$, they gain from regulation being inefficient (i.e., from P being poorly informed).

Remark 3   S is here rewarded when he releases information that hurts A. An alternative incentive for truth-telling is the threat of being punished if caught colluding with A. Kofman and Lawarrée (1989) develop a model in which A is audited by an internal auditor and, possibly, by an external auditor. The internal auditor is more prone to collusion than the external one, but the external audit does not come for free. In Laffont and Tirole (1990c), a government agency in charge of overseeing a regulated firm is monitored by interest groups and is punished if evidence is found that it is lenient with the industry.

2.2.3   Collusion proofness

Let us sketch the proof of why there is no loss of generality in focusing on a collusion-proof contract as we have done in section 2.2.2 (theme n° 1). Suppose that P sets up a mechanism or grand contract specifying w, s, and x as functions of messages and reports, that may or may not give rise to coalition formation. The method of proof consists in considering the *final* allocation (transfers and production) as a function of the state of nature. The transfers may include side transfers and may be stochastic. One shows that this final allocation must satisfy some individual rationality and incentive compatibility constraints. Maximizing expected social welfare (which includes the deadweight loss associated with side transfers, if any) subject to these constraints yields an upper bound on social welfare. The last step consists in showing that this upper bound can be reached through the collusion-proof contract constructed in section 2.2.2.

Index the three states of nature in the following way: 1: $\sigma = \beta$; 2: $\sigma = \varnothing$ and $\beta = \underline{\beta}$; 3: $\sigma = \varnothing$ and $\beta = \bar{\beta}$. Let the final allocation be denoted by a hat. In state of nature i, A's and S's expected utilities, $\hat{U}_i$ and $\hat{V}_i$, must be non-negative (otherwise they would refuse to participate). Furthermore, because S and A can agree in state 1 to announce the messages they would announce in state 2, with high penalties in case of deviation:[10]

$$\hat{V}_1 - \hat{V}_2 \geqslant k(\hat{U}_2 - \hat{U}_1). \tag{2.2.7}$$

Second, when $\sigma = \varnothing$, S must get expected utility at least 0 and so must A whatever his type. Furthermore, because A is the only party to know β:

$$\hat{U}_2 \geqslant \hat{U}_3 + \Delta \beta \hat{x}_3. \tag{2.2.8}$$

Maximizing expected social welfare subject to the individual rationality constraints, the incentive compatibility constraint (2.2.8) and the coalition incentive compatibility constraint (2.2.7) shows that the upper bound on social welfare is max $\{\tilde{W}^d, \tilde{W}^u\}$.

2.3   Coalition formation under asymmetric information

In section 2.2, we assumed that, in the state of nature where he has discretion ($\sigma = \beta$), S knows A's private information. Collusion thus takes place under symmetric information between S and A. We now relax this assumption and illustrate some implications of coalition formation when the colluding parties are asymmetrically informed. Felli (1990), in a different model, makes the following points:

(a) Informational asymmetries may prevent colluding parties from realizing gains from trade. Even an allocation that is not interim efficient for the S/A coalition may not give rise to collusion.

(b) The classical revelation principle may not hold, in the sense that collusion may be prevented through the use of "augmented revelation mechanisms." Because parties learn information in the process of forming coalitions, the revelation principle must be interpreted in a broad sense, letting the parties announce not only their own information but also the information that they learn from others when bargaining for side contracts.

We first illustrate these two points in the context of our example, and then discuss mechanism design with asymmetrically informed colluding parties.

We change the model of section 2.2 in the following respect: S has one of two signals, $\sigma = \varnothing$ and $\sigma = \tilde{v}$, where $\tilde{v} > v$. That is, he may either learn nothing (in which case beliefs fall below v) or get (hard) evidence that A is likely to be efficient (meaning that the probability of $\beta = \underline{\beta}$ conditional on this signal is equal to $\tilde{v}$). The model of section 2.2 corresponds to the special case $\tilde{v} = 1$. Assume still that (2.2.1) holds so that P would not price discriminate when having no information, but that the signal $\sigma = \tilde{v}$ leads to a tougher stance:

$$\tilde{v}(S - \underline{\beta}) > S - \bar{\beta} + \alpha_A \tilde{v} \Delta\beta. \tag{2.3.1}$$

Consider the following mechanism: S has three potential reports $r \in \{\sigma, \varnothing, \underline{\beta}\}$ instead of two. The new report ($r = \underline{\beta}$) is a report of soft (unverifiable) information. A still has two possible announcements: $\hat{\beta} \in \{\underline{\beta}, \bar{\beta}\}$. S first reports r and then A announces $\hat{\beta}$. Rewards are as follows: S receives $s = 0$ unless he reports $r = \underline{\beta}$. If he announces $r = \underline{\beta}$, he receives $s = k\Delta\beta$ if $\hat{\beta} = \underline{\beta}$ (in which case $x = 1$ and $w = \underline{\beta}$) and $s = -\infty$ if $\hat{\beta} = \bar{\beta}$ (in which case $x = 0$ and $w = 0$). If $r = \tilde{v}$, then $x = 1$ and $w = \underline{\beta}$ if $\hat{\beta} = \underline{\beta}$, and $x = w = 0$ if $\hat{\beta} = \bar{\beta}$. If $r = \varnothing$, then $x = 1$ and $w = \bar{\beta}$ for all $\hat{\beta}$. In words, P price discriminates when beliefs are $\tilde{v}$ and does not when beliefs are lower than v, as is optimal from (2.3.1) and (2.2.1). He does not pay the supervisor. However, if S is sure that A has type $\underline{\beta}$, he can say so and obtain a reward; A then gets nothing.

Assume that A makes a take-it-or-leave-it-offer to S. This offer specifies a side transfer $t(r, \hat{\beta}, m)$ from A to S when reports and announcements to P are r and $\hat{\beta}$, and we allow S and A to exchange further messages m for generality.

We claim that *one* equilibrium is the no-collusion outcome, in which A offers the null side contract $t(.,.,.) \equiv 0$ and S and A report truthfully. For, suppose that $\sigma = \tilde{v}$ (that is, S has discretion). Let both types of A pool at the null side contract, and let any other (out-of-equilibrium) offer be interpreted by S as coming from type β. Because type β gains at most $\Delta\beta$ by having S conceal $\sigma = \tilde{v}$, any undominated offer by A is rejected by S, who can get $k\Delta\beta$ by reporting $r = \beta$.

If this equilibrium prevails, P does not suffer from the possibility of collusion. This example illustrates points (a) and (b). First, the outcome is not interim efficient (in the sense of Holmström and Myerson, 1983) for the S/A coalition. Consider the "side mechanism" M to be played between A and S when $\sigma = \tilde{v}$ before they play the mechanism offered by P: "A sends message $\tilde{\beta}$ or β to S; if the message is $\tilde{\beta}$, S reports $r = \tilde{v}$ and A transfers nothing to S; if the message is β, S reports $r = \emptyset$ and A transfers $t \in [0, \Delta\beta]$." The resulting allocation respects incentive compatibility given beliefs $\tilde{v}$ and Pareto dominates the no-collusion allocation for S and A. That is, the no-collusion allocation is not CIE (coalition interim efficient). Second, P uses an augmented revelation mechanism. The report $r = \beta$ is not used in equilibrium, but serves as a threat against the agent in case he were to try to collude with S.

Note that there exists another equilibrium of the collusion game in which A makes a take-it-or-leave-it offer and which yields the CIE outcome. When $\sigma = \tilde{v}$, both types of A pool to offer side contract M; and let any other offer be interpreted as coming from type β. Because his beliefs are still $\tilde{v}$ after the pooling offer is made, S accepts the offer and reports $r = \emptyset$.

This discussion raises the issue of the definition of collusion proofness when parties to a coalition are asymmetrically informed. An allocation is *weakly collusion proof* if there exists some equilibrium of the collusion game in which the null side contract is signed in all states of nature. It is *strongly collusion proof* if it is the only equilibrium allocation. Maskin and Tirole (1992), in their study of mechanism design by an informed party, show that the only strongly collusion proof allocations with two colluding parties and one-sided asymmetric information are the CIE allocations, that is, the allocations that are interim efficient for the two parties.

Note also that, if S made the offer for a side contract, only a CIE allocation is collusion proof (weakly or strongly), as there is no information leakage through bargaining for a side contract.

We conjecture that augmented revelation mechanisms are not needed if either S makes the collusive offer or one insists on strong collusion proofness. In either case, the allocation (as a function of β) must be CIE when $\sigma = \tilde{v}$. (Intuition: The grand contract defines a game between S and A. Define the set of incentive compatible allocations for all possible reports and announcements by S and A for $\sigma = \tilde{v}$. CIE allocations correspond to the efficient frontier of this set in the three-dimensional payoff space (one type for S and two types for A). Suppose that accounting for collusion, the final allocation is not CIE. Construct another equilibrium in which both types of A pool and offer to report type $\tilde{\beta}$ to S and the CIE allocation is then implemented. Last, try to show that the upper bound on welfare, subject to the CIE and individual rationality constraints, can be reached by a grand contract in which $r \in \{\sigma, \emptyset\}$ and $\beta \in \{\beta, \tilde{\beta}\}$.)

We summarize this discussion of the model with:

(c) When parties to a coalition are asymmetrically informed, there may be multiple equilibria of the coalition formation game and one is led to distinguish between weakly and strongly collusion proof allocations.

(d) Augmented revelation mechanisms may not be needed if one insists on strong collusion proofness.

2.4   Equilibrium collusion: unknown technology for side transfers

One of the ingredients of the collusion proofness principle in section 2.2.3 is that P can foresee collusion and make the transfer that induces revelation and deters collusion. Suppose now that P is uncertain about the transaction technology between S and A. To make sure that collusion does not arise, P must give the transfer that corresponds to the most efficient transaction technology. However, this "bunching mechanism" (that does not screen the transaction technology) may prove too costly. P may want to discriminate among the different types of transaction technologies. But the only way to do so is to allow collusion with positive probability in equilibrium (Kofman and Lawarrée (1990) make this point in a different model).

Modify the model of section 2.2 in a single respect: A can transfer income equivalent to S at rate k (with probability γ) or 0 (with probability $(1 - \gamma)$). Both S and A know which of k or 0 prevails, but P does not. One interpretation is that S may be dishonest (k) or honest (0). Assume that P wants to pay $\tilde{\beta}$ when $\sigma = \emptyset$ (otherwise collusion is not an issue). To obtain collusion proofness when $\sigma = \beta$, P must give income $s = k\Delta\beta$ when $r = \beta$. Welfare is then the same as in section 2.2:

$$W^{nc} = \tilde{W}^d, \tag{2.4.1}$$

where "nc" stands for "no collusion."

Suppose instead that P gives a flat transfer $s \equiv 0$ to S,[11] and offers $w = \beta$ when $r = \beta$ and $w = \tilde{\beta}$ when $r = \emptyset$. Collusion then occurs when the transaction technology is k. Welfare is then:

$$W^c = (1-\gamma)W^d + \gamma[S - \bar{\beta} + v\zeta\alpha_S k\Delta\beta + v(1-\zeta)\alpha_A\Delta\beta], \qquad (2.4.2)$$

where "c" stands for "collusion."[12] Using $W^d > \tilde{W}^d > [S - \bar{\beta} + v\zeta\alpha_S k\Delta\beta + v(1-\zeta)\alpha_A\Delta\beta]$, we conclude that $W^c < W^{nc}$ for γ high and $W^c > W^{nc}$ for γ low. If there is a very low probability of a dishonest supervisor, it is optimal not to pay attention to this possibility.

(e)   The only way to screen among different types of coalition transaction technologies is to allow equilibrium collusion.

2.5   Equilibrium collusion: non-separabilities

In the proof of collusion proofness in section 2.2.3, we used the fact that, if A wants to bribe S to report σ_0 instead of σ_1 (where report σ_0 is feasible given signal σ_1), then P can reward S by giving income differential $s_1 - s_0$ high enough to prevent collusion. Suppose now that σ_1 is a feasible report when the true signal is σ_2, and that A would like to bribe S to report σ_1 instead of σ_2 when the signal is σ_2. To prevent this collusion, P must create an income differential $s_2 - s_1$ high enough. We thus see that raising s_1 to prevent collusion when the signal is σ_1 makes it more costly to thwart collusion when the signal is σ_2. In such cases of non-separability among collusion proofness contraints it may be cheaper for P to allow collusion than fight it. There ought to exist several ways of creating and exploiting non-separabilities. The one we develop here is associated with a decreasing-returns transaction technology.

Consider the model of section 2.2 except that:

A's production cost can take one of three values: $\beta_2 = \beta = \bar{\beta} - \Delta\beta$ with probability v, $\beta_1 = \bar{\beta} - \dfrac{\Delta\beta}{2}$ with probability ε, and $\beta_0 = \bar{\beta}$ with probability $1 - v - \varepsilon$. The interpretation of this technology is that there are two potential improvements relative to the basic technology $\bar{\beta}$, each reducing cost by $\Delta\beta/2$. The number ε can be thought of as small (A is very likely to have benefited from two improvements conditional on having benefited from one).

S learns β perfectly. We can thus denote signals σ by the number of improvements: 2, 1, and 0. Furthermore S can report any $r \in \{0,1,2\}$ such that $r \leqslant \sigma$ (that is, he can conceal information about any observed improvement).

The transaction technology between S and A is non-linear:

$$k(t) = \begin{cases} kt & \text{for } t \leqslant \Delta\beta/2 \\ k\Delta\beta/2 & \text{for } t \geqslant \Delta\beta/2 \end{cases}$$

(the reader can check that the analysis carries over to the case in which $k(.)$ has a small positive slope beyond $\Delta\beta/2$). The interpretation of this transaction technology is that A can always do small favors for S but that larger favors are easily detected.

The gross consumer surplus is large enough (relative to ε) that it is not optimal for P to have no production in some state of nature. P puts more weight on S's welfare than on A's ($\alpha_S > \alpha_A$).

Let s_0, s_1 and s_2 denote S's salary when he reports he has observed 0, 1, and 2 improvements. Clearly $s_0 = 0$ is optimal. Suppose, first, that P extracts the agent's rent for each report. To prevent collusion when $\beta = \beta_2$, P must give salary s_2 to S that satisfies in particular:

$$s_2 - s_1 \geqslant k\Delta\beta/2$$

(were this inequality not satisfied, S would report $r = 1$, when $\sigma = 2$, and P would pay β_1 to A instead of β_2). Similarly preventing collusion when $\beta = \beta_1$ requires:

$$s_1 - s_0 \geqslant k\Delta\beta/2.$$

At the collusion-proof optimum, $s_2 = k\Delta\beta$ and $s_1 = k\Delta\beta/2$. Welfare is:

$$W^{nc} = v[S - \beta - (1 - \alpha_S)k\Delta\beta]$$
$$+ \varepsilon\left[S - \bar{\beta} + \frac{\Delta\beta}{2} - (1 - \alpha_S)k\frac{\Delta\beta}{2}\right]$$
$$+ (1 - v - \varepsilon)[S - \bar{\beta}].$$

The alternative way of preventing collusion in state β_1 is not to try to extract A's rent in that state of nature. P pays $\bar{\beta}$ to A and 0 to S. In state of nature β_2, P pays β to A and $k\Delta\beta/2$ to S (recall that, while A's stake in state of nature β_2 is $\Delta\beta$, P needs to give only $k\Delta\beta/2$ to S to prevent collusion, due to the non-linearity in the transaction technology). Welfare is then:

$$\tilde{W}^{nc} = v\left[S - \beta - (1 - \alpha_S)k\frac{\Delta\beta}{2}\right]$$
$$+ \varepsilon\left[S - \bar{\beta} + \alpha_A\frac{\Delta\beta}{2}\right]$$
$$+ (1 - v - \varepsilon)[S - \bar{\beta}].$$

(The linearity of the problem implies that one can restrict attention to these two ways of deterring collusion.)

Suppose instead that P "tries" to extract A's rent, but allows collusion when $\beta = \beta_1$: $s_1 = 0$, but pays $s_2 = k\Delta\beta/2$ (or slightly more to resolve indifferences). When $\beta = \beta_2$, collusion does not occur because A can channel at most $k(\Delta\beta) = k\Delta\beta/2$ to induce S to hush the information. Welfare is now:[13]

$$W^c = v\left[S - \beta - (1 - \alpha_S)k\frac{\Delta\beta}{2} \right]$$

$$+ \varepsilon\left[S - \bar{\beta} + \alpha_S k\frac{\Delta\beta}{2} \right]$$

$$+ (1 - v - \varepsilon)[S - \bar{\beta}].$$

For ε small, $W^c > W^{nc}$. Welfare is lower in state β_1 because collusion occurs, but higher in state β_2 because collusion is cheaper to prevent.

Next $W^c > \tilde{W}^{nc}$ if $\alpha_S k > \alpha_A$; that is, if it is more important to extract A's rent than S's rent and if the deadweight loss of side transfers in the range $[0, \Delta\beta/2]$ is small.

This example has an interesting interpretation. If a group can more easily exchange small favors than big ones, it may be optimal to tolerate minor expressions of collusion in order to deal with major expressions efficiently.

(f)   Equilibrium collusion may be optimal when collusion-proofness constraints are linked.

2.6   Equilibrium collusion: agents' comparative advantage in exchanging transfers

An important assumption in section 2.2 is that the transaction technology of coalitions is not more efficient than that between the center (principal) and the agents. One can think of situations where this assumption is invalid, so that P prefers side transfers across the hierarchy to fully centralized transfers (i.e., transfers that all originate or terminate with the center).

A notable case of an agent's comparative advantage in receiving transfers is the case of cooperation (Holmström and Milgrom, 1990; Itoh, 1989; Macho-Stadler and Pérez-Castrillo, 1989). If the transaction technology satisfies $k(t) > t$ over some range, side transfers are socially desirable.[14]

Even if they create no social surplus, side transfers may be socially desirable if centralized transfers are inefficient because P is a poor collector or distributor of funds. To illustrate this point, consider the case of a policeman (S) on a highway stopping a motorist (A) for speeding. The prominent method of levying the fine is to have the motorist pay the State (P) and, possibly, have the State reward the policeman through an incentive scheme. That is, transfers may be centralized. But one could think of situations in which centralization would not be optimal. For instance, the State could be a poor collector of funds (the motorist is very hard to locate once he leaves the policeman; or else the bureaucracy could be so corrupt that only part of the fine, if paid to the State, is used for useful purposes). In such a case, it may be optimal not to give the policeman a salary and let him be bribed.

Remark The conclusion that stakes should be reduced when collusion becomes feasible (theme n° 3) may no longer be valid when the principal values side transfers. Consider the following example: A can, at private cost c, help and provide S with a benefit v; P can recover enough of this benefit (e.g., through a prior contract with S) or else gets some other benefit from help (e.g., from an improved productivity in the shop) so that help is indeed desirable. Assume further that monetary or other transfers from S to A are either infeasible or inefficient (the foundations for this assumption ought to be studied in a larger model), so that the only vehicle for S to compensate A is the exercise of his supervisory discretion. It may then be optimal for P to raise the level of this discretion[15] in order for S to be able to compensate A for the cost c. High stakes then create the quid pro quo that allows side-trading and, thus cooperation.

2.7   Equilibrium collusion: incomplete grand contract

If the grand contract is incomplete, collusion may help to fill in the missing contingencies. The most obvious illustration of this point is the fact that the State does not determine all economic activity through a grand contract and that private contracting (which is an instance of collusion in the economic hierarchy with the State as a principal) is often socially beneficial. (Similarly, collusion may be socially desirable if the grand contract is socially suboptimal. According to political scientist Huntington (quoted in Klitgaard, 1988 and Kofman and Lawarrée, 1990), "In terms of economic growth, the only thing worse than a society with a rigid, overcentralized, dishonest bureaucracy is one with a rigid, overcentralized, honest bureaucracy"!)

In Itoh (1989), Holmström and Milgrom (1990) Macho-Stadler and Pérez-Castrillo (1989), Ramakrishnan and Thakor (1989), and Varian (1989), agents share information not available to the principal. These papers exclude the possibility of revelation of this shared information through "Nash implementation mechanisms."[16] Consequently, agents can sign agreements that are contingent on more information than the ones they sign with the principal. (Peer monitoring among borrowers or insurees gives rise to similar benefits from collusion, see Stiglitz, 1990a,b.) Similarly, in Laffont and Tirole's (1991a, section 7) example of cross-subsidization among consumer groups, the regulator can contract with a regulated firm, but cannot contract directly with the consumer groups. It may then be optimal to let some consumer group bribe the firm with whom it shares information.

A related situation in which the grand contract is incomplete is when (i) supervisory information is observable but not *ex ante* contractible (for instance, the supervisor may come up with a piece of information that everyone can interpret, but which could not have been contracted upon *ex ante*), and (ii) Nash implementation mechanisms are excluded. An illustration of this point[17] is the following: consider an organization with n owners and one agent. Suppose that the agent can divert an amount of money D. Each owner can spend his own money or time to obtain information that leads to the restitution of D, plus some fixed fine F paid by the agent, to the owners. Suppose that the owners cannot contract *ex ante* on the nature of the information that enables restitution; and that *ex post*, if a zealous owner reveals his information to receive a reward, the other owners use this information to recover the diverted money but don't pay him for supplying this public good. The zealous owner then enjoys only $(D+F)/n$. If n is large, no owner engages in monitoring because of free-riding and the agent can safely divert the money. Suppose in contrast that the owners allow any of them to sign a side contract with the agent. An owner who discovers information that enables restitution, bargains with the agent not to release this information (the information can be contracted upon *ex post*, and the owner does not suffer from showing it to the agent before contracting, while he does if he shows it to the other owners). This gives the owners more incentives to monitor and the agent less incentives to divert money.

2.8   Other hierarchical structures

Our development so far has focused on the principal/supervisor/agent paradigm. But collusion is a concern in any organization with more than two parties and it has been also studied in the context of a few alternative simple hierarchies.

2.8.1   Principal/multi agents

Itoh (1989), Holmström and Milgrom (1990) Macho-Stadler and Pérez-Castrillo (1989), Ramakrishnan and Thakor (1989), and Varian (1989) have studied the important issue of collusion among several agents against the principal. All papers analyze moral hazard frameworks and first show that, if the grand contract is complete, in the sense that the side contracts among agents are based on the same information as the grand contract, side contracting never makes the principal better off. The point is that side contracting does not enlarge the space of feasible contracts but adds additional constraints in the principal's optimization problem. For instance, agents who give insurance to each other impose conditions on their marginal rates of substitution. The papers then show that collusion based on shared information not held by the principal may be welfare improving. In particular, if two workers can observe each other's effort and can contract on their values, then the principal can use the workers to monitor each other. This literature obtains interesting insights about the determinants of the welfare effects of collusion: production externalities and team production (Itoh, 1989) degree of correlation between tasks (Ramakrishnan and Thakor, 1989), need for mutual help (Itoh, 1989; Macho-Stadler and Pérez-Castrillo, 1989). We refer the reader to the original papers and content ourselves with a brief discussion of one of them.

In Holmström and Milgrom, 1990 two observable outcomes depend on the two agents' actions (or vectors of actions). Rewards in the grand contract are contingent on the two outcomes, but the agents can observe each other's actions. Agents are risk averse and they have exponential utilities; utility is transferable, and in the "unrestricted side contracting" case, side transfers involve no deadweight loss ("$k=1$"). Holmström and Milgrom show that, without loss of generality, the principal can design a contract such that the side contract between the agents is contingent on their actions but not on the outcomes. This is a "partial collusion proofness" result: the principal can sign contracts contingent on outcomes, and does not need to let the agents coinsure each other.

Another interesting insight of their analysis is that the principal's optimal contract coincides with that offered to a single composite agent who is assigned the tasks of both agents, has disutility of effort equal to the sum of the two agents' disutilities of effort and has utility function with parameter of absolute risk aversion equal to the sum of the two agents' parameters. This result implies that, if each outcome depends on a single agent's effort (there is no team production and no help) and the noises in the two outcomes are independent (there is no motive for relative performance evaluation), side contracting always raises the principal's welfare. Given the sum of the two independent contracts that would obtain in the absence of collusion, the composite agent chooses the same actions and risk tolerance has improved. For more general technologies, side contracting is a mixed blessing. While it increases the set of contingencies on which contracts are based, it also constrains the feasible contracts (for instance, relative performance evaluation is difficult to perform if agents collude).[18]

A fairly distinct branch of the literature on collusion among several agents is that on bid rigging (Graham and Marshall, 1987; Mailath and Zemsky, 1989; McAfee and McMillan, 1988; Robinson, 1985; von Ungern Sternberg, 1988). Most (but not all) of this literature studies collusion in second-price auctions (in which the highest bidder wins and pays the second higher bid). It was pointed out that second-price auctions greatly facilitate collusion among bidders. To collude, bidders in a coalition with less than the highest valuation can suppress their bid (bid zero) and the highest valuation bidder can bid his valuation. The coalition members have no incentive to cheat on the agreement (if it is not enforceable) by submitting bids at the auction because they will lose anyway. The highest valuation bidder can be identified through a "pre-auction knockout" among colluding bidders (Graham and Marshall, 1987). Furthermore, second-price auctions to a large extent eliminate the difficult issue of inferences about valuations of bidders who offer to side contract or who refuse to participate in a coalition, because of the existence of a dominant strategy at the auction stage. (The issue of coalition formation is in general one of contract design by informed parties). Collusion in first-price auctions is much harder to analyze. More generally, an important practical and theoretical issue is that of optimal auction design under collusion.

2.8.2   Principal/supervisor/multi agents

In section 1.2, we mentioned Laffont's (1990) paper, which is concerned with the collusion of a supervisor having information about the agents' individual performances and engaging in collusion with particular agents. The supervisor can extort favors from the agents by organizing a competition among them for favorable reports. The paper's main focus is the extent to which the agents' incentive schemes can be personalized or must be based on aggregate rewards.

Laffont and Tirole (1991b and forthcoming) develop two regulation models in which the government agency (the supervisor) may favor one firm or one interest group over the others. The first paper studies the optimal design of a multidimensional auction when the government agency can collude with either one of the two bidding firms. Most procurement auctions involve the transfer of a complex object with price and quality dimensions. The government agency in general must use its information first to assess the firms' quality attributes and second to choose the appropriate weights between quality and price. This discretion gives rise to the threat of favoritism and indeed agencies are routinely constrained by their principals (administrative rules, Congress, European Commission . . .) to follow rigid auctioning procedures that are meant to restrict abuse. Optimal auctions make limited use of the agency's information about the relative merits of the bidders and privilege is given to tangible components of bids (price) over less tangible ones (quality).

The second paper revisits the old theme of cartelization by regulation. Suppose that entry of new firms in a regulated industry can be welfare improving (because of product diversity or because of the possibility of yardstick competition) or welfare decreasing (because of the duplication of fixed costs or more generally wasteful competition). Assume further that the government agency has information about the costs and benefits of entry not held by the political principal. Then the agency can take an anticompetition stance to raise the incumbents' informational rents or a procompetition stance to benefit the entrants and the industry's customers. Which behavior prevails depends on the information structure and on the relative organization costs. And, not surprisingly, the optimal institutional response is to reduce the agency's discretion in allowing or prohibiting entry.

2.9   Renegotiation as a form of collusion

The collusion paradigm turns out to be relevant for the study of contracting between two parties. It is known that optimal complete long-term contracts between two parties are generally not renegotiation-proof. That is, even though the long-term contract can be enforced if any party wishes so, the two parties are generally better off agreeing to alter the contract at some point in their relationship. The point is that optimal long-term contracts introduce allocational inefficiencies in order to influence the parties' decisions and that once these decisions are taken, the inefficiencies no longer serve an incentive purpose and therefore are removed.[19]

The reason why the collusion paradigm is relevant is that the two-party relationship can be viewed as a $2T$-party one if the relationship covers periods $\tau = 1, \ldots, T$. In period 1, a principal (P) and an agent (A), or rather their "first-period incarnations" P_1 and A_1, sign a long-term contract. At date 2, their second-period incarnations P_2 and A_2 renegotiate the initial contract, or equivalently add a new contract (one can assume either that they void the initial contract and write a new one, or, equivalently, that they leave the initial contract and possibly nullify its effects as part of the new contract. The second interpretation sheds more light on the link between renegotiation and collusion). In period 3, the incarnations P_3 and A_3 renegotiate the contract(s) in force, and so forth. Viewing the initial long-term contract as a grand contract linking the $2T$ parties, the renegotiation between P_τ and A_τ ($\tau \geqslant 2$) is nothing but their signing a side contract. Thus renegotiation is a special case of collusion, with the following specificities:

> only $(T-1)$ bilateral coalitions (of the type P_τ/A_τ for $\tau \geqslant 2$) are feasible (the transaction technology is $k = 1$ for these coalitions, and $k = 0$ for the others),
> the T incarnations of P have the same objective function; so do the T incarnations of A,
> coalition formation is sequential and furthermore the P_τ/A_τ coalition observes the side contracts of coalitions $P_2/A_2, \ldots,$ $P_{\tau-1}/A_{\tau-1}$.

The literature mentioned above assumes that a single party acquires private information, either before date 1 or during their relationship. When $T = 2$, there is a single renegotiation period and the renegotiation proofness (or collusion proofness) constraint takes a simple form if the uninformed party makes the renegotiation offer. The initial contract must be *interim efficient* at date 2 given the posterior beliefs about the informed party's type at that date. That is, there is no (type-contingent) allocation that is incentive compatible for the informed party and that makes the uninformed party and all types of informed party better off. Interim efficiency then fully characterizes the set of renegotiation proof allocations.

More generally, if the uninformed party makes the renegotiation offers at each period $\tau = 2, \ldots, T$, renegotiation proof contracts must be *sequentially interim efficient*. That is, given posterior beliefs at date T, the date-T allocation must be interim efficient. At $T-1$, the allocation for dates $(T-1)$ and T must be incentive compatible, i.e. implementable by a sequence of messages m_{T-1} and m_T by the informed party,[20] and there must not exist an alternative allocation for dates $(T-1)$ and T that is interim efficient at date T, is incentive compatible, Pareto-dominates it, and so forth. Sequential interim efficiency has strong consequences for organizational design (for instance, in Hart and Tirole (1988), it transforms the rental model of transaction between a seller and a buyer into the sale model).

When the informed party makes renegotiation offers, the issue of (side) contract design by an informed party mentioned in section 2.3 arises. One can distinguish between "weak renegotiation proofness" (the long-term contract is not renegotiated in some equilibrium) and "strong renegotiation proofness" (the long-term contract is renegotiated in no equilibrium).

Maskin and Tirole (1992) characterize the sets of weakly and strongly renegotiation proof contracts when there is a single period of renegotiation ($T=2$). For instance, strongly renegotiation proof contracts are those specifying interim efficient allocations at date 2. Thus, if strong renegotiation proofness is taken to be the criterion for contract design, it does not matter for the design of the initial contract who makes renegotiation offers. We conjecture that a similar result holds in the T-period framework.

2.10   Models with no grand contract

Equilibria in contracts have also been investigated in models in which some parties do not contract with each other, that is in which there is no grand contract. There are two branches of the literature in this direction.

2.10.1   Common agency

Common agency arises when n principals each sign a contract with a single agent but do not sign contracts among themselves. The models in general assume that each principal and the agent sign contracts simultaneously. For instance, the principals make a contract offer each to the agent, and the agent either is free to accept any set of contracts or must accept all or none. (Elaborations of this model also allow principals to offer contracts with exclusivity clauses.) The emphasis of the literature is on externalities in contracting. Each principal offers the contract that is best for him and does not internalize the other principals' welfare.

The systematic investigations of the common agency model are Bernheim and Whinston (1986) for moral hazard and Martimort (1990a) and Stole (1990) for adverse selection. Bernheim and Whinston show that, in a moral hazard framework, the agent's equilibrium effort is induced efficiently (that is, contracts are "cost minimizing"). However the level of effort differs from the one that would obtain if the principals joined forces to offer a single contract. Martimort and Stole study the inefficiencies associated with the multiple screening of the agent's private information by the principals. They show for example that common agency (relative to the situation where the principals merge) raises the efficiency of the allocation if the principals' screening variables are substitutes in the agent's utility function (and the equilibrium is symmetric) and lowers it when they are complements.

More specific studies have applied common agency ideas. Spiller (1990) uses a moral hazard framework to depict government agencies as a common agent for the government and the consumers. In an adverse selection context, Baron (1985) studies the conflict between two regulatory agencies, a Public Utility Commission and the Environmental Protection Agency, with different objectives for the regulation of a public utility. In Laffont and Tirole (1991c), one of the effects of the privatization of a public enterprise (that remains regulated after becoming a private firm) is to subject the firm to two masters, the regulator and the shareholders.

An objection to common agency models is that the principals would benefit from merging or from contracting among themselves to eliminate contracting externalities; that is, why is there no grand contract? One possible explanation for the absence of a grand contract is the existence of antitrust laws if the principals compete on the product market (for instance there might be two firms practicing non-linear pricing; or the agent could be a common retailer as in Bernheim and Whinston, 1985). A justification (not incorporated into the models) in the context of rival government agencies (or of legislative and executive control of a given agency) is the need for checks and balances in government. The foundations for this justification would require a more complex collusion model in which public decision-makers may identify with specific interest groups. Last, in the privatization example, public ownership (which eliminates common agency) has adverse consequences for the managers' incentive to invest because of future constraints on internal management[21] and also implies a different structure of monitoring of the firm by outsiders.

2.10.2   Competition among agents

Another branch of the literature has studied the following situation. There are two principals, P_1 and P_2, and two agents, A_1 and A_2, say. P_1 and P_2 simultaneously offer contracts to A_1 and A_2, respectively. P_i offers no contract to $A_j, j \neq i$ (no common agency) and neither the principals nor the agents contract among themselves, presumably for antitrust reasons. A_1 and A_2 play a game; for instance they compete on the product market. Vickers (1985) and Fertschman and Judd (1987) assume that the contract between a principal and his agent is observable by the other agent. The contracts can then serve as commitments and are strategically chosen to influence the other agent. For instance, if the agents compete in quantities, a wholesale price charged by P_i to A_i below P_i's marginal cost induces A_i to produce a high output and thus to behave like a "Stackelberg leader," inducing A_j to reduce his own output (P_i can recoup A_i's profit through a fixed payment).

This framework is subject to the criticism that P_i and A_i have an incentive to secretly renegotiate their initial (public) contract. In the Cournot example, it is optimal for P_i and A_i to sign a side contract specifying that the wholesale price is equal to P_i's marginal cost (i.e., to the internally efficient transfer price) after all. Anticipating this, A_j no longer believes A_i's commitment to a high output through a wholesale price below marginal cost. And, indeed, it can be shown that, in the absence of informational asymmetry, public contracts in general have no effect on the final outcome if they can be renegotiated.

Public contracts between principals and agents do however have some commitment power if P_i and A_i are asymmetrically informed (Dewatripont, 1988). In this case, renegotiation does not yield fully efficient outcomes. In particular, interim efficient contracts between P_i and A_i (which need not be *ex-post* efficient!) are not renegotiated. Caillaud, Jullien and Picard (1990) offer a systematic investigation of the commitment value of public contracts when principals have incomplete information about their agents.[22] Last, Martimort (1990b) analyzes the externalities among principal/agent contracts under adverse selection when the agents' informations are correlated, the agents compete on the product market, and there is no public contract at all.

3   THE RESEARCH AGENDA

3.1   Enforceable side contracts: a framework

The literature has focused on obtaining economic insights for specific models with enforceable side contracts. It would be worth taking a broader perspective and studying in a general framework some basic issues: what is the appropriate notion of "implementable allocation" in the presence of collusion? What are the general conditions under which the principal does not need to allow collusion on the equilibrium path? Under which the principal can content herself with revelation mechanisms? What is the link between collusion proof allocations and coalition interim efficient allocations? – and so forth. Sections 2.2 through 2.7 gave some insights on how to approach these questions, but many issues in providing general answers are left open. The goal of this section and the next is to list some of these issues.

Because the view of the organization as a nexus of contracts generalizes that of the organization as a single contract, it is worth starting with the grand contract approach (Myerson, 1982). In this formulation, there is a center or principal, $i = 0$, and n agents, $i = 1, \ldots, n$. Agent i has private information of type θ_i. Let $\theta \equiv (\theta_1, \ldots, \theta_n)$. The principal and the agents choose decisions $d = (d_0, d_1, \ldots, d_n)$. Utilities are $u_i(d, \theta)$ for $i \in I = \{0, 1, \ldots, n\}$. Decisions should be interpreted in a broad sense. They include for instance the hidden actions of the moral hazard literature or the revelation of informational parameters; decisions can be contingent on information acquired, etc. Myerson shows that, when the agents do not side contract, the following version of the revelation principle holds: the principal can content herself with mechanisms in which, first, the agents simultaneously and truthfully make reports $\hat{\theta} = (\hat{\theta}_1, \ldots, \hat{\theta}_n)$ of their types, second, the principal secretly recommends actions ($d_i(\hat{\theta})$ to agent i), and, third, the agents obey the recommendations.

Information

One can reinterpret the hard and soft information structures of our examples as special cases of the framework described above. Let Ω denote the set of states of nature with generic element ω. Type θ_i is nothing but the element (event) in agent i's information partition H_i. One way of formalizing soft information is to let the set of agent i's possible reports be the subset of all events in 2^Ω that belong to H_i. Agent i's hard information can be formalized by restricting possible reports to those elements θ_i' in H_i that contain θ_i.

While the notion of information of an agent is clear in a grand contract approach, we noted in section 2.3 that agents learn about each other in the process of forming coalitions. Similarly an agent may voluntarily disclose information or explain how to get it to another agent (as in Kofman and Lawarrée, 1989). It may then be necessary to define an agent's information as his total information, and not only his initial one. Of course, the mechanism built by the principal may have the agents announce any probability distribution over Ω^{23} (if their information is soft), but one might want to be more specific and, in the spirit of the revelation mechanism, restrict the set of possible messages by the agents. (As discussed in section 2.3, small message spaces may be more likely when we try to implement strongly collusion proof allocations.)

Grand contract

Consider the following timing:

> Stage 1: The principal offers a grand contract, which the agents accept or reject.
>
> Stage 2: Agents who accept engage in bargaining over side contracts according to some extensive form.
>
> Stage 3: The grand contract is implemented.

Following Myerson, we can define a grand contract as a multistage communication system among all parties. A multistage communication system results in a decision d_0 and messages $\tilde{m}_i$ received by the agents (through the center) as functions of the messages m_i sent by the agents. The agents then choose d_i as function of their type and the information received. We let κ_i denote the stage-3 strategy (contingent message transmission and decision) of agent i. Abusing notation let $u_i(\kappa,\theta)$ denote agent i's utility given strategies $\kappa \equiv (\kappa_1, \ldots, \kappa_n)$ in the implementation of the grand contract.

Let us identify the set of consequences with the set of vectors of consumptions of goods (money, time, effort, help, . . .) in some Euclidean space. Ignoring side transfers for the moment, let $\mu_{0i}(\kappa)$ denote the (possibility random) vector of goods for player i when strategies in the implementation of the grand contract are κ. Let $\mu_0 \equiv (\mu_{01}, \ldots, \mu_{0n})$. By a new abuse of notation, let $u_i(\mu_{0i},\theta)$ and $u_0(\mu_0,\theta)$ denote player i's and the principal's utilities, in the absence of side transfer.

One issue is whether the messages sent by the agents during the implementation of the grand contract are public information after stage 3 of the game is over. Assuming that they are public information is innocuous in the grand contract approach. It may not be in the presence of collusion. For instance there is a debate in industrial organization about whether disclosing bids after an auction promotes bid rigging. While disclosure keeps the principal from cheating or manipulating bids, it also makes deviations from agreements among bidders a bit easier to detect.

Transaction technology
Let x_{ij} denote the vector of gross transfers from party i to party j, where i, $j \in I$. Let μ_{ij} be a probability measure on x_{ij}. The transaction technology is defined by a set of functions $\{k_{ij}(.)\}$. Party j receives vector $\tilde{x}_{ij} = k_{ij}(x_{ij})$ when party i transfer x_{ij}. By abuse of notation, let $\tilde{\mu}_{ij} = k_{ij}(\mu_{ij})$ denote the random variable associated with μ_{ij}. We have:

$$\mu_i \equiv \sum_{\substack{j=1 \\ j \neq i}}^{n} (\tilde{\mu}_{ji} - \mu_{ij}) + \mu_{0i} \qquad \text{for } i = 1, \ldots, n.$$

Under side contracting, agent i's utility is $u_i(\mu_i,\theta)$. Let $\mu \equiv \{\mu_{ij}\}_{j=1,\ldots,n}^{i=0,\ldots,n}$. The principal's utility in the presence of side transfers is $u_0(\mu,\theta)$.

The transaction technology satisfies "*no comparative advantage*" if, for all μ and θ, there exists μ' such that $u_i(\mu_i',\theta) \geq u_i(\mu_i,\theta)$ for all $i \geq 1$, $u_0(\mu',\theta) \geq u_0(\mu,\theta)$, and $\mu_{ij} = 0$ for $i \neq 0$ and $j \neq 0$. That is, there is no technological cost involved in channeling transactions through the center (see section 2.6).

Implementable allocations
A final allocation μ is defined by an equilibrium of the bargaining-cum-implementation game among the agents (two remarks: first, an agent's strategy is bigger than κ_i because it includes the strategy in the

side-contracting stage 2. Second, we can allow the principal to renegotiate or collude by having her incarnation be as one of the agents).

We constrain the grand contract offered by the principal to be such that an equilibrium in the ensuing game of coalition formation and contract implementation exists. This requirement is not specific to side contracting. Classical contract theory already requires that agents have optimal strategies (for instance, that they do not face "open set problems"). The requirement may be more stringent in the presence of collusion. Myerson (1982) constructs an example with two principals offering one contract each to one agent, in which there is no equilibrium in contracts (because the set of incentive compatible mechanisms for a principal does not vary continuously with the contract offered by the other principal). Similar phenomena may well arise when several coalitions can form.

3.2   Enforceable side contracts: some issues

Implementable allocations
Like for traditional mechanism design (which is a special case in which side transfers are infeasible), a question logically prior to that of optimality is the characterization of the set of allocations that are implementable (i.e., that are feasible given the information structure and the possibility of collusion). This characterization of the set of implementable allocations may be side stepped with sufficient intuition, as shown in section 2.2. That is, one may guess necessarily binding constraints, optimize subject to this restricted set of constraints and then check that the optimal allocation is implementable. By proceeding in this manner, one has computed the optimal (implementable) allocation without solving for the whole set of implementable allocations. Yet it is interesting to derive this set.

There are two choices to be made in order to define the notion of implementable allocation:

> For a given extensive form for bargaining for side contracts, there may exist several equilibria (see section 2.3).[24] Thus the general issue of unique implementation that arises in classical contract theory at the implementation stage arises with a vengeance in this broader framework. Must an implementable allocation correspond to a unique equilibrium?
>
> Do we want allocations that arise for some extensive form for bargaining, or do we require them to be "robust" to the formulation of the extensive form? (As discussed in section 2.3, this question is not independent of the first one. There are circumstances under which, if we insist on unique implementa-

tion, the precise sequential bargaining form – unless it involves no proposal – is inconsequential.)

Remark 1 Once one has settled on a definition of implementable allocations, one ought to study the determinants of the set of implementable allocations in specific contexts. An important determinant seems to be the agents' degree of risk aversion. For instance, in principal/supervisor/agent structures, the reduction in the set of implementable allocations due to collusion is particularly large when S is very risk averse (Tirole, 1986). Suppose that the grand contract is signed prior to acquisition of information. A risk-neutral supervisor can be made residual claimant for the agent's performance; the hierarchy then becomes a two-tier structure and collusion does not arise. In contrast, when S is risk averse, his reward must be relatively insensitive to the information he acquires and reports. But such schemes are very prone to collusion because S has little to lose from misreporting.[25] For instance, in the limit where S is infinitely risk averse, no use can be made of supervisory information that may hurt A (but use can be made of supervisory information that does not: for instance, of the signal $\sigma = \bar{\beta}$ if such a signal exists and if the principal wants to price discriminate when $\sigma = \emptyset$. The supervisor can thus reduce the need for cost-reducing inefficiencies when A cannot supply verifiable information that $\beta = \bar{\beta}$ himself). S becomes a pure advocate for A.

Remark 2 As mentioned in remark 1, risk neutrality goes some way toward thwarting collusion. Cremer and Riordan (1987) consider a hierarchical organization of the following kind. It is set up as a tree. Each member of the tree trades goods with his immediate predecessor (if any) and with his immediate successors (if any). His utility function is quasi linear and his surplus depends on the net trade with his predecessor and successors, and on a private information parameter. Communications follow a hierarchical mechanism (see their paper for details). Cremer and Riordan show that, even if any predecessor–successor pair can secretly recontract, i.e., collude,[26] the first-best allocation can be *implemented* through Groves–d'Aspremont–Gerard Varet mechanisms. These mechanisms have each agent pay the expected externality on other agents. When a coalition forms (for this specific hierarchical structure and set of feasible coalitions), it internalizes the effect of its behavior on the welfare of agents outside the coalition, and therefore it cannot gain from inducing an allocation that is not the first-best one. This does not imply that the first-best allocation is *optimal* for P (after all, S and A are risk neutral in the model of section 2.2!). It is optimal when P's welfare is the sum of expected surpluses in society (in particular, P does not care about leaving informational rents). Cremer and Riordan thus identify a case in which the threat of collusion is harmless.

Collusion proofness

Can implementable allocations be implemented through a grand contract and an (the?) equilibrium in which no side transfer occurs on the equilibrium path ($\mu_{ij} = 0$ for $i \neq 0$, and $j \neq 0$)?

Sections 2.4 through 2.7 gave a few hints about conditions one might want to impose to derive the collusion-proofness principle: the technology $\{k_{ij}(.)\}$ should be known by the principal; the no-comparative-advantage condition stated in section 3.1 should hold; contracts should be complete (the agents might for instance announce everything they may have observed); and some sufficient condition for "separability" awaits to be found.

Link with efficiency notions

As discussed in sections 2.3 and 2.9, it is possible in simple models to characterize the sets of (weakly or strongly) collusion proof allocations in terms of efficiency notions. An open question is whether such characterizations are possible in the general framework.

We can define coalition interim efficient (CIE) allocations as follows. Consider a grand contract and strategies κ at the implementation stage giving rise to allocation $\mu_0(\kappa)$ in the absence of collusion. A coalition C is a subset of agents. θ^c is the vector of types of agents in the coalition[27] and θ^{-c} is the vector of types of agents outside the coalition; and similarly for other variables. In state of nature ω, let $M^c(\omega)$ denote the meet of the agents in C's information partitions (that is, $M^c(.)$ is the finest coarsening of their information structures).

The allocation $\mu_0(\kappa)$ is *coalition interim efficient* if one cannot find a state of nature ω, a coalition C, strategies $\kappa^c(\theta^c)$ in the implementation stage and side transfers μ^c within the coalition such that (i) for all $\omega' \in M^c(\omega)$, every member of the coalition is better off in expectation given that parties outside the coalition still play their strategies $\kappa^{-c}(.)$, (ii) side transfers respect the transaction technology, (iii) reporting truthfully to a center created by the coalition and obeying her recommendations is optimal for each member of the coalition.

That is, we envision the coalition as building a Myerson truthful and obedient submechanism whose phase of revelation is played among members of the coalition before stage 3.

An open question is whether coalition interim efficiency is a necessary condition for strong collusion proofness.

Other issues
It would be worth studying the issues of aggregation and delegation mentioned earlier.

3.3   Self-enforcing side contracts and controlled reputation games

In the last three sections of this paper, we depart from the assumption that side contracts are enforceable, and discuss the role of reputation in inducing parties to collude. Clearly the lack of enforceability imposes constraints on the side transactions between parties of an organization. In particular, allocations that are not coalition interim efficient may not give rise to collusion. The simplest illustration of this point is a one-period model of principal/supervisor/agent hierarchy. S may denounce A (report $\sigma = \beta$ in the model of section 2.2) or not. Simultaneously A chooses a transfer (money, help, ...) to S. If agreements between S and A cannot be legally enforced and if S and A are not of their word, the game between them is a prisoner's dilemma: S rats on A if he derives any small reward from doing so and A transfers nothing to S. In such a case, only repetition can allow collusion.

There are at least two important items on the research agenda:

(a) The first item is the derivation of general conditions under which the lack of enforceability does not prevent agents from colluding efficiently, i.e. from side contracting any time their allocation is not coalition interim efficient. More generally one would want to characterize what can be implemented by the principal in the presence of collusion sustained by reputational phenomena.[28] It seems that such results, if any, will be obtained only in the polar case where the colluding parties have long-run relationships and are patient.

For a given grand contract among the members of an organization, collusion enforced by reputation can be formalized along the lines of Kreps, Milgrom, Roberts, and Wilson (1982). The general result in this area is due to Fudenberg and Levine (1989), who show that a long-term player playing against a sequence of short-term players can obtain his "Stackelberg payoff" (i.e., the payoff he gets when his opponents are convinced he plays the strategy that elicits from them the response he likes best) if he is sufficiently patient. While Fudenberg and Levine identify one instance of a reputation phenomenon that works perfectly, their result is only a suggestion that similar ideas might be used to study collusion in organizations, and this for two reasons.

First, while some interesting situations involving collusion have a long-term player playing against a sequence of short-term players (as is the case for a mayor who receives bribes from individual citizens to deliver building permits, or of a supervisor or advisor who extorts generations of employees or students), many instances of collusion involve several long-term players. And general results on the level of efficiency of collusion among long-term players are harder to obtain, if only because the players have the conflicting objectives of developing the reputation they like best. My guess is that one is likely to make headway in this direction only by studying less general environments than those considered by Fudenberg and Levine.

Second, while one can study the set of reputational equilibria for a given game among agents, where the game is defined by a grand contract, optimal organizational design requires that one consider all possible grand contracts. That is, the principal, by choosing a grand contract, chooses among games to be played by the agents, the equilibria of which define the final allocations. While economists have some familiarity with contract design involving static Bayesian games among agents (see, e.g., the auctions and public goods literatures), nothing is known about the optimal design of dynamic Bayesian games. The design of such "controlled reputation games" is likely to be complex. Even in simple games like the supervisor/agent one mentioned above, the high degree of non-stationarity introduced by the endogenous choice of the timing of incentives and rewards by the principal is likely to complicate the analysis.[29]

(b) The second item on the research agenda is to develop economic insights from models with a couple of periods. One is unlikely to be able to develop general results from this approach, but the insights may end up being very suggestive for organization design. For instance one of the drawbacks of limit results of the Fudenberg and Levine type is that they require at least some long-term players. But an interesting question in organization design is the endogenization of the length of the relationship between two members of the organization. It is well-known that corps of civil servants or diplomats, and accounting firms rotate their personnel frequently in order to prevent collusion (stemming from an excessive development of trust) with the parties they interact (e.g., audited firms, contractors, host countries). Choosing a length for the relationship in a sense is one way of endogenizing the transaction technology (e.g., the parameter k introduced in previous sections).

The rest of this chapter discusses these two items with the use of simple principal/supervisor/agent models. Section 3.4 offers a very special example in which the enforceability and self-enforceability approaches yield exactly the same prediction. Section 3.5 discusses some potential ingredients of controlled reputation games, such as the optimal length of relationships; and appendix 2 develops a bare-bones example of the choice of optimal length. The design of controlled reputation games is quite complex. Section 3.4 and appendix 2 make restrictive assumptions to obtain the results. They are meant only to suggest the method of analysis and economic conclusions to be gleaned from the self-enforcing contracts approach.

3.4   Enforceable versus self-enforcing contracts

Consider the principal/supervisor/agent model of section 2.2, except that the relationship is repeated at dates $\tau = 0, 1, \ldots, \infty$. The agent's private cost of production, β_τ, (which, for simplicity, we assume "monetary" but non-verifiable) is identically and independently drawn from the same distribution over time. β_τ is equal to β with probability v and to $\bar{\beta}$ with probability $(1 - v)$. S learns β_τ and has hard evidence only when $\beta_\tau = \beta$, but not when $\beta_\tau = \bar{\beta}$ (this is the model of section 2.2, with a probability ζ equal to 1). When $\beta_\tau = \beta$, S can either denounce A($r_\tau = \beta$) or conceal the information ($r_\tau = \bar{\beta}$). We assume that P cannot dispense with either S or A in any period. S and A cannot save (that is, they consume what they receive immediately), and they are protected by limited liability (their monetary utility in each period cannot be negative). Let δ be the discount factor, and let w_τ, s_τ, t_τ denote the wages of A and S, and the side transfer from A to S at date τ (all are positive numbers). t_τ will be thought of as standing for help, friendship, or the like, i.e., as being non-monetary. Letting k denote the transaction technology parameter as in section 2.2, the intertemporal utilities of A and S are:

$$U = \sum_{\tau=0}^{\infty} \delta^\tau (w_\tau - \beta_\tau - t_\tau) \text{ and } V = \sum_{\tau=0}^{\infty} \delta^\tau (s_\tau + k t_\tau).$$

(where use is made of the fact that the agent is indispensable and thus produces in each period). The principal's utility is:

$$W = \sum_{\tau=0}^{\infty} \delta^\tau (S - w_\tau - s_\tau).$$

(that is, we assume that the coefficients α_A and α_S introduced in section 2.2 are equal to zero).

The timing is as follows: at the beginning of a period, A and S learn the technological parameter β_τ, and are offered a short-term contract specifying the reward $\{w_\tau, s_\tau\}$ to the agent and the supervisor as functions of the supervisor's report $r_\tau \in \{\beta_\tau, \bar{\beta}\}$. This contract satisfies $w_\tau(\bar{\beta}) = \bar{\beta}$ (when $\beta_\tau = \bar{\beta}, r_\tau = \bar{\beta}$ and the agent must get a non-negative monetary utility in each period by assumption), and $w_\tau(\beta) = \beta$.[30] After the contract is offered and accepted, A chooses a side transfer $t_\tau \geqslant 0$ to S. Then, S decides whether to "denounce" the agent, i.e., to report β (assuming that $\beta_\tau = \beta$. If $\beta_\tau = \bar{\beta}$, S can only report $\bar{\beta}$). If $\beta_\tau = \beta$ and $r_\tau = \bar{\beta}$, A enjoys flow rent $\Delta\beta \equiv \bar{\beta} - \beta$ (gross of the side transfer). If $\beta_\tau = \bar{\beta}$, or if $\beta_\tau = \beta$ and $r_\tau = \beta$, A has no flow rent (gross of the side transfer). Note that P is assumed not to be able to offer long-term contracts. We comment on this non-commitment assumption later. Note also that we rule out enforceable side contracts.

To formalize collusion, we use the technology developed by Kreps, Milgrom, Roberts and Wilson (1982). A's preferences are known (except for the realizations of the β_τ) and are described as above. S has two possible types. The "sane" type has the preferences described above and has probability $(1 - \eta)$. The "cooperative" or "Stackelberg" type has probability η and plays the following strategy: "as long as $t_{\tau-m} \geqslant \Delta\beta - \varepsilon$ for all $m \in \{0, \ldots, \tau\}$ such that $\beta_{\tau-m} = \beta$, I do not denounce A at date τ. Otherwise I denounce A at date τ (if $\beta_\tau = \beta$, of course)." That is, the Stackelberg type is willing to leave rent $\varepsilon > 0$ to A in periods of good draws. If A tries to appropriate more in some period, the Stackelberg type stops cooperating and denounces A forever.

PROPOSITION 1   For δ close to 1, there exists an equilibrium with payoff:

$$[S - \bar{\beta} + (1 - \eta)[v(1 - k)\Delta\beta + kv\varepsilon]]/(1 - \delta) \text{ for the principal.}$$

Note that when η and ε are small, the per-period welfare approximates that obtained for enforceable side contracts in equation (2.2.5) (recall that, to simplify notation, we took $\alpha_A = \alpha_S = 0$ and $\zeta = 1$). The intuition for proposition 1, which is proved in appendix 1, is straightforward: the agent operates the side transfer when he has not been denounced before, because his expected gain from colluding with the cooperative type is large for a long-horizon and a high-discount factor. The sane type of superior can thus enjoy a rent by never denouncing the agent. To break the collusion, the principal must compensate the sane type for the future lack of collusion, and thus must give reward $s^* = \delta vk[\Delta\beta - \varepsilon]/(1 - \delta)$ to the supervisor. While the intuition is straightforward, the analysis is quite involved, if only because the principal's and the agent's beliefs about the supervisor may differ. (This problem of different beliefs "disappears" when the principal can commit, as the game then becomes a two-player game. The principal's optimization however is then quite complex. In section 3.5, we assume commitment, fully characterize optimal contracts for one- and two-period relationships, and find sufficient conditions for one- and two-period relationships to be either optimal or dominated by longer relationships).

Remark 1   The Stackelberg or cooperative type extracts most of the surplus from collusion in this model if ε is taken to be small. One may think this is unrealistic. On the other hand, if ε is large, P can pay a per-period equivalent much lower than $vk\Delta\beta$ to break the collusion, a somewhat unpalatable conclusion. In this world of patient players, it may be the case that A and S succeed in colluding if P pays S much less than $vk\Delta\beta$ in per-period equivalent. Such collusion might be achieved for instance if the crazy type of S denounced A any time A does not operate a current transfer that will yield eventually an equal division of the gain from collusion between S and A. The complication of course is that this level of "fair side transfer" is obtained by backward induction and depends on future equilibrium behavior as well as the current reward for denunciation. Such reputations are very hard to work with, but may ensure that the principal must have to pay close to $vk\Delta\beta$ in per-period equivalent to break the collusion. (More generally, S might build a reputation for being less greedy than is presumed in this section).

Remark 2   We have assumed that the organization is run by a sequence of short-term contracts. It is easily checked that proposition 1 would be unaffected if we allowed commitment by P to a time-invariant reward s for the first period of denunciation (and 0 in other periods) and to confiscating A's rent after collusion is broken. Preliminary analysis however suggests that the restriction to such simple incentive schemes is not innocuous, at least with the two-type description of uncertainty about S used in the section. If both ε and η are small, A enjoys relatively little rent. Rather than paying S a large amount to break the collusion, P can commit not to confiscate A's rent for a finite (and small if ε and η are small) number of periods following a denunciation. A then has an incentive to refuse to pay the large side transfer and to break the collusion by triggering a denunciation. If this intuition is correct, then comments similar to those in remark 1 may apply to the commitment case.

Short-run principals versus long-run agents

We saw that a long-run principal finds it in his interest to prevent collusion. We can use this model to show why short-run principals (who belong to the organization for one period, and have utilities $S - w_\tau - s_\tau$) facing the long-run supervisor and agent do not break collusion and are in a weak position.

PROPOSITION 2   Assume short-run principals, and long-run supervisor and agent. For δ close to 1, in any equilibrium, the principals let the supervisor and the agent collude and have welfare $S - \bar{\beta}$.

The proof of proposition 2 is straightforward. The date-τ principal gains at most $\Delta\beta$ by having S denounce A. But even a salary equal to $\Delta\beta$ does not suffice to induce the sane S to denounce A as his gains from colluding are large if S and A are patient. That is, a principal benefits for only one period from breaking the collusion, but, to break the collusion, he must compensate the supervisor for the loss in collusive gain over the whole horizon. More generally, we would expect short-term players to be particularly vulnerable to collusion among long-term players in organizations.

3.5   Discussion

The model in section 3.4 is special in several respects. Let us discuss two extensions that are worth pursuing.

Principal's instruments
In section 3.4, the principal's only instrument to control the amount of collusion is the level of supervisory reward.

Another potential instrument was discussed in the context of enforceable side contracts and is ignored in section 3.4: the principal might choose the level of the agent's stake in collusion. Section 3.4 assumes that the agent's rent $\Delta\beta$ is confiscated in case of denunciation. More generally, the agent's incentive scheme determines his stake and therefore his incentive to collude.

There are still other instruments that, in specific contexts, would be worth introducing. The principal might control the information structure between agents by locating them in different buildings, or else by making reports anonymous (of course, a necessary condition for anonymity is the existence of several potential supervisors). The principal might also affect the extent of collusion by choosing the number of supervisors. Still another instrument is the length of relationship between the agents.

Desirability of collusion
Section 3.4, like most models of enforceable collusion (but the ones reviewed in sections 2.6 and 2.7), assumes that collusion is not desirable. As a consequence, the principal breaks collusion by giving the supervisor a reward that induces denunciation at the first opportunity. A similar use of other potential instruments is to be expected: to prevent collusion, the principal is likely to create very short relationships if those are not too costly; to ask for anonymous reports when there are several potential reviewers; and to bend over backwards to prevent any form of transfer between supervisor and agent.

In some contexts, some amount of collusion, while in itself detrimental to the principal, may foster cooperation and benefit the principal. For instance, the agent may supply socially desirable help to the supervisor if he expects that the supervisor will not denounce him in exchange. The principal's choice of supervisory reward then exhibits a tradeoff between high collusion and high cooperation and low collusion and low cooperation (assuming that the retention of information hurting the agent is the only favor the supervisor can offer in exchange for help).

Models of controlled reputation games are by no means easy to solve. This is particularly true when the principal wants to induce some amount of cooperation (and thus collusion), and structures history-contingent incentives for help and supervision. Appendix 2 develops an example in which the supervisor and the agent may collude in both useful and detrimental ways for the principal. The agent may help the supervisor (as wished by the principal), but the supervisor may protect the agent by not revealing information that would be useful to the principal. Because the principal cannot selectively intervene to eliminate one form of collusion but not the other, the optimal length of the relationship between the supervisor and the agent may be intermediate between one period (which limits both forms of collusion) and infinity (which promotes both forms of collusion).

Consequently, equilibrium collusion occurs, but is not perfect. The gain from long-term relationships is that they promote cooperation. That is, the principal can obtain more information without destroying cooperation. However, long relationships may not be optimal for two reasons. First, the supervisor may have large gains from collusion and it may become expensive to elicit his information. Second, once the supervisor has destroyed his reputation by informing on the agent, it becomes difficult to combine cooperation and elicitation of information. The supervisor–agent relationship has soured, and it is time to bring in new blood.

This example makes very strong assumptions (in particular, synchronized tenures of supervisor and agent, lexicographic preferences for the supervisor) and is meant only to suggest some of the many tradeoffs that enter the design of controlled reputation games. It is also not intended to describe all plausible reputational phenomena in organizations. For instance, the supervisor, if sane, does not develop a reputation for being cooperative, despite the fact that such behavior may be realistic in some organizations. The story told in appendix 2 is different: it is that of new agents in an organization who toe the line (cooperate) when they enter the organization; while they are uncertain of whether a cooperative relationship will develop, the relationship is sufficiently long that it is worth giving coworkers (here, supervisors) the benefit of the doubt and thus starting the relationship with a cooperative stance.

3.6   Concluding remark

The agency theory of group behavior is still in its infancy. Yet we hope to have demonstrated that tractable models in which agents abide by their agreements deliver substantial insights for the study of governmental and private organizations. We emphasized the reduction of externalities or stakes in collusion to respond to the threat of undesirable collusion. Other institutional responses, such as the use of secret committees or anonymous refereeing, the design of the production process, and the choice of the length of relationships, affect the agents' cost of colluding and ought to be further investigated. The relevance of group behavior to economic and political life makes the study of collusion full of potential rewards.

APPENDIX 1 Proof of proposition 1

Consider the following strategies:

P offers $s_\tau = s^* \equiv \delta v k[\Delta\beta - \varepsilon]/(1 - \delta)$ if S has not denounced A in the past; P offers $s_\tau = 0$ otherwise.

A transfers $t_\tau = 0$ if *either* he has been denounced in the past *or* $\beta_\tau = \bar\beta$ or there exists $m > 0$ satisfying *condition B*: $\beta_{\tau-m} = \beta$, $s_{\tau-m} < s^*\delta v/(\delta v + 1 - \delta), t_{\tau-m} < \Delta\beta - \varepsilon$ and S did not denounce A at $(\tau - m)$; A transfers $t_\tau = (\Delta\beta - \varepsilon)$ otherwise.

The sane S denounces A if $\beta_\tau = \beta$ and *either* $s_\tau \geqslant s^*$ *or* he has denounced A in the past *or* (there exists m such that condition B holds or $t_\tau < \Delta\beta - \varepsilon$) and $s_\tau \geqslant s^*\delta v/(\delta v + 1 - \delta)$; the sane S does not denounce A otherwise.

Suppose that δ is sufficiently large so that:

$$\frac{\eta\delta^2 v\varepsilon}{1-\delta} \geqslant (1+\delta)\Delta\beta.$$

Let us check the optimality of these strategies:

Principal: According to the equilibrium strategies, the principal never obtains information from the cooperative S, as A always transfers $(\Delta\beta - \varepsilon)$ until denounced. By offering $s_\tau < s^*$, P delays revelation of information by the sane S. Indeed, if $\beta_\tau = \beta$ (s_τ does not matter if $\beta_\tau = \bar\beta$) and S is sane, P loses:

$$\Delta\beta - s^* + s^*[\delta v + \delta^2 v(1-v) + \delta^3 v(1-v)^2 + \ldots]$$

$$= \Delta\beta - \frac{\delta v}{\delta v + 1 - \delta} k(\Delta\beta - \varepsilon) > 0,$$

for δ close to 1, using the fact that he will offer s^* in the future until denunciation occurs.

Agent: If the agent has been denounced in the past, both the cooperative and the sane S will denounce him today and in the future and there is no point operating any transfer. If there exists an m satisfying condition B, the agent knows from the equilibrium strategies that S is sane (this can be seen by taking the highest m if several such m exist). The equilibrium strategies then specify that S always denounces and A never transfers in the future. So it is indeed optimal for A not to transfer anything today. Next, suppose that there has not been any denunciation in the past, and that there exists no m satisfying condition B. Assume first, that $s_\tau \geqslant s^*$. The sane S denounces anyway. Because there has not been any denunciation in the past, the cooperative S will not denounce if and only if $t_\tau \geqslant \Delta\beta - \varepsilon$. The payoff when transferring $t_\tau < \Delta\beta - \varepsilon$ is thus $-t_\tau$. But, letting η_τ denote the posterior beliefs about S at date τ, A can guarantee himself $\eta_\tau \delta v\varepsilon/(1-\delta) - (\Delta\beta - \varepsilon)$ by always transferring $(\Delta\beta - \varepsilon)$ until denounced. Also, from the equilibrium strategies, and because there is no m satisfying condition B, $\eta_\tau \geqslant \eta$. Hence, A strictly prefers to transfer $(\Delta\beta - \varepsilon)$ today. Assume, second, that $s_\tau < s^*$. Then, $t_\tau < \Delta\beta - \varepsilon$ leads to either denunciation by both types (if $s_\tau \geqslant s^*\delta v/(\delta v + 1 - \delta)$), or to denunciation by the cooperative S and a zero continuation value with the sane S (because condition B will hold tomorrow) (if $s_\tau < s^*\delta v/(\delta v + 1 - \delta)$). So A's payoff is at most $-t_\tau + \Delta\beta$. In contrast, transferring $(\Delta\beta - \varepsilon)$ induces no denunciation today. Thus A can guarantee himself

$$\varepsilon + \delta\left[\eta_\tau\frac{\delta v\varepsilon}{1-\delta} - (\Delta\beta - \varepsilon)\right] \geqslant \Delta\beta \text{ as } \eta_\tau \geqslant \eta.$$

We thus conclude that the agent's strategy is optimal (from our assumption on δ).

Sane supervisor: If $s_\tau \geqslant s^*$, it is optimal for the sane S to denounce, because his continuation valuation if he does not is $(\delta v + \delta^2 v(1-v) + \delta^3 v(1-v) + \ldots)(k(\Delta\beta - \varepsilon) + s^*) = s^*$. If he has denounced in the past, A will never transfer anything again and P will never reward S again, and hence the sane S might as well denounce today. If there exists an m satisfying condition B or, if $t_\tau < \Delta\beta - \varepsilon$, then S has already revealed he is sane or reveals he is sane by not denouncing, and therefore will not receive transfers from A in the future. He can only get s^* in the future, and his continuation valuation after not denouncing is:

$$s^*(\delta v + \delta^2 v(1-v)^2 + \ldots) = s^*\delta v/(\delta v + 1 - \delta).$$

APPENDIX 2 Length of relationships, cooperation, and collusion[31]

We consider a variant of the models in sections 2.2 and 3.4, with the following features:

> the agent's side transfer can take one of two values: "help" or H, and "no help" or NH,
>
> the side transfer, help, is now socially valuable (an important difference with respect to section 3.4 will thus be that collusion may be desirable),
>
> the (training or disruption) cost of replacing s and A is no longer infinite (indeed, we will assume this cost is equal to zero. One of the foci of the analysis will be the optimal length of relationships within the organization),
>
> the principal can commit to an intertemporal reward scheme,
>
> (as in section 3.4) the agent's technological parameter, which takes value in $\{\beta, \bar{\beta}\}$ is identically and independently distributed over time.

The horizon is infinite. The stage game when $\beta = \beta$ is described in figure 3.1.

In each period τ of their relationship, A decides whether to help (H) or not (NH). S then decides whether to denounce A (D) or not (ND). The payoffs in parentheses are those of A, S, and P. Helping costs c to A, and yields v to S and h to P. Denunciation implies that A loses his rent $\Delta\beta$, that S receives reward s_τ (which is endogenous) from P, and that P gains g from having the information. We index the reward and the technology by the date within the S/A relationship and not by calendar time. $\tau = 0$ is the first period of the relationship and $\tau = T - 1$ is the last.

When $\beta = \bar{\beta}$, the stage game is the same except that $s_\tau = 0$ (there is nothing to reveal) and $\Delta\beta$ and g are replaced by 0.

As in section 3.4, S knows β_τ and can report β or $\bar{\beta}$ when $\beta_\tau = \beta$ and can only report $\bar{\beta}$ when $\beta_\tau = \bar{\beta}$. The principal cannot dispense with a supervisor and an agent in any period but he can change supervisor and agent over time. We assume that the supervisor and the agent are replaced at the same time. That is, the supervisor and the agent form a team for T periods, and then are replaced by a new supervisor and a new agent who team up for T periods and so forth, where $1 \leqslant T \leqslant +\infty$. An important topic for research is the effect on collusion and cooperation of having the tenures of supervisors and agents overlap rather than coincide.

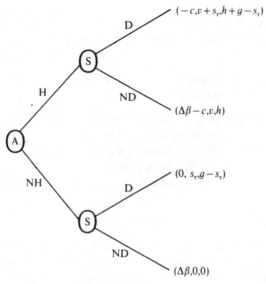

Figure 3.1

A and P have the stage game payoffs depicted in figure 3.1. As in section 3.4, S is one of two types. With probability $(1-\eta)$, S is "sane" and his payoff is as in figure 3.1. For technical reasons discussed below, we assume further that, *ceteris paribus*, the sane S prefers not to denounce A if A has always helped in the past when drawing β and prefers to denounce A otherwise. Among other things, this lexicographic preferences assumption simplifies the analysis as it implies that the sane S plays a pure strategy. With probability η, S is "cooperative"; that is, he does not denounce A as long as A has helped him in the past; if A stops helping him, S denounces A (every time that $\beta_\tau = \beta$) for the rest of their tenure.

We make the following assumptions:

A1: $c < \Delta\beta$ (helping is not a dominated strategy for A).

A2: $\eta\Delta\beta < c$ (the agent provides no help in a one-period relationship if the supervisor receives any reward from denouncing).

A3: $\eta(1+\delta)(\Delta\beta - c) > (1-\eta)c$ (this condition, which implies A1, will imply that helping is optimal for A in a two-period relationship).

A4: The probability v that $\beta_\tau = \beta$ is close to 1. Indeed in computations, we will take it equal to 1. (It cannot be equal to 1 because otherwise A would never enjoy a rent. If v is less than 1 and if A is indispensable, A receives rent $\Delta\beta$ as long as he is not denounced). That v be close to 1 is not crucial, but v cannot be too small for our analysis: if the probability that the agent has a potential rent in the future is small, collusion cannot be sustained at date τ if $\beta_\tau = \beta$.

A5: P commits to a tenure length T and to an intertemporal reward scheme $\{s_0, \ldots, s_{T-1}\}$ at the beginning of each S/A relationship.

We first study short-term relationships ($T = 1$) and distinguish two cases. We then analyze longer-run relationships.

$T = 1$: If S and A are engaged in a short-term relationship and $s_0 > 0$, the stage game has a unique equilibrium. The sane S denounces, the cooperative S denounces only if NH, and A does not help from assumption A2. Note also that an arbitrarily small reward guarantees this outcome. Hence the short-term and long-term welfares induced by positive rewards are:

$$w^S = g \text{ and } W^S = w^S/(1-\delta) = g/(1-\delta)$$

(note that there is an "openness problem" here, as reward $s_0 = 0$ does not yield denunciation. This problem disappears with a fine, but discrete reward space. For notational simplicity we identify the lowest strictly positive reward with 0).

Alternatively, P can offer $s_0 = 0$. The equilibrium is then for A to help and for (both types of) S not to denounce. Short-term and long-term welfares are then:

$$w^C = h \text{ and } W^C = w^C/(1-\delta) = h/(1-\delta).$$

Thus, in short-term relationships, P prefers not to create incentives for supervision if and only if help matters enough, or $h > g$. We will call the situation $w^S > w^C$ the *supervisory case* (S), and the situation $w^C > w^S$ the *cooperative case* (C). Let $w^1 \equiv \max\{w^C, w^S\}$.

$T = 2$: From assumption A3, A always helps as long as there are at least two periods to go. We first study two-period relationships. Two-period relationships may dominate one-period relationships. Suppose that P induces the sane S to denounce A in the first period of their relationship (if this is not the case, the two-period welfare is $h + \delta \max(h,g) \leqslant (1+\delta) \max(h,g)$, and thus P does not do better than with one-period relationships). P can either restore cooperation between the two in the second period by setting $s_1 = 0$ (recall that, for a given reward, the sane S prefers not to denounce when A has helped in the past); or P can induce denunciation, and therefore not help in the second period by setting an arbitrarily small but positive s_1. This second policy, however, imposes an extra cost $s_0 = \delta v$, as S loses the benefit of cooperation by denouncing in the first period. Therefore:

$$w^2 = \eta h(1+\delta) + (1-\eta)(h+g+\delta\max(h,g-v)).$$

Note that $w^2 > w^1(1+\delta)$, and therefore $W^2 > W^1$, whenever $h > g$. The two-period relationship allows P to obtain some information without foregoing cooperation; another way of explaining the result is to note that the two-period relationship allows P to capture some of A's rent under cooperation. We thus conclude that short-term relationships are non-optimal when help matters much.

When $g > h$, two-period relationships may still dominate one-period relationships if h is not too small and v is not too high. Two-period relationships then lead to more cooperation than one-period ones. They, however, involve two costs. First, A and the cooperative S collude; second, the sane S must be compensated for foregoing his future benefits from colluding. Let "SS" stand for the (purely supervisory) case in which P induces denunciation by the sane S in both periods and "SC" the (mixed) case in which he induces denunciation by the sane S only in the first period.

We now summarize the comparison between $T=1$ and $T=2$:

PROPOSITION 3 (comparison of $T=1$ and $T=2$): the principal's welfare is:

$$\frac{1}{1-\delta}\max\left\{g, h+(1-\eta)\frac{g}{1+\delta}, \ \eta h+(1-\eta)\left(\frac{h}{1+\delta}+g-\frac{\delta v}{1+\delta}\right)\right\}.$$

corresponding to regimes S, SC, and SS, respectively. Supervisory one-period relationships are optimal when g is high or h is low. Mixed supervisory-cooperative two-period relationships are optimal when h is large or g is small. Purely supervisory two-period relationships are optimal if g is close to, but greater than h and if v is sufficiently small.

$T > 2$: We now examine some features of longer-run relationships and show that:

(a)   If $c/\Delta\beta$ is close to 1, $T>2$ is not optimal. The intuition is that it becomes very hard to obtain any information from the sane S and still obtain help once A knows that S is sane. The worn-out relationship between S and A ought to be broken fast.

(b)   If $c/\Delta\beta$ is small, longer-term relationships ($T>2$) may be desirable. A is willing to help even if he knows that S is sane, as long as S is not induced to denounce all the time. The benefit of a longer-term relationship is that P can get even more information than with $T=2$ while fostering help.

We first derive an upper bound on the principal's welfare after the sane S has revealed his type by denouncing (recall that A always helps if S has not revealed his type and there are at least two periods to go). Suppose, without loss of generality, that the sane S denounces at date 0 (with probability 1: the sane S's lexicographic preferences ensure that he plays a pure strategy). Let $\{y_\tau\}_{\tau\in\{1,\ldots,T-1\}}$ and $\{z_\tau\}_{\tau\in\{1,\ldots,T-1\}}$ denote the unconditional probabilities (at the beginning of date 1, after S has denounced) that A helps, and that A is not denounced, respectively. Individual rationality of the agent implies that:

$$\left(\sum_{\tau=1}^{T-1}\delta^\tau z_\tau\right)\Delta\beta-\left(\sum_{\tau=1}^{T-1}\delta^\tau y_\tau\right)c\geqslant0.$$

An upper bound on P's welfare from 1 through $T-1$ (as viewed at the beginning of date 1) is:

$$\max_{(y_\tau,z_\tau)}\left\{\left(\sum_{\tau=1}^{T-1}\delta^\tau(1-z_\tau)\right)g+\left(\sum_{\tau=1}^{T-1}\delta^\tau y_\tau\right)h-\left[\sum_{\tau=1}^{T-1}\delta^\tau(1-y_\tau)\right]v\right\}.$$

The last term in this upper bound represents the date -0 salary to be paid to the sane S for him to denounce A at date 0. Using A's individual rationality constraint, this upper bound can be written as:

$$\left(\sum_{\tau=1}^{T-1}\delta^\tau\right)\left(\max\left\{h+g\left(1-\frac{c}{\Delta\beta}\right),\,g-v\right\}\right).$$

Next, because of the sane S's lexicographic preferences, there is some date m in $\{0,\ldots,T-1\}$ at which the sane S denounces with probability one at m. If S is sane, the principal gets h per period before m, $h+g$ at m (if $m\neq T-1$), and at most $\max\left\{h+g\left(1-\frac{c}{\Delta\beta}\right),\,g-v\right\}$ per period after date m. It is easily seen that $m=0$ is optimal if this long-term organization dominates the best one- or two-period organization. Assume that $h+g\left(1-\frac{c}{\Delta\beta}\right)\geqslant g-v$. With $T>2$, an upper bound on the per-period welfare is thus:

$$\eta h+(1-\eta)\left(\frac{h+g+(\delta+\ldots+\delta^T)\left(h+g\left(1-\frac{c}{\Delta\beta}\right)\right)}{1+\delta+\ldots+\delta^T}\right)$$

$$<\eta h+(1-\eta)\left(h+\frac{g}{1+\delta}\right),$$

if $\dfrac{c}{\Delta\beta}$ is close to 1.

Hence, if $\dfrac{c}{\Delta\beta}$ is close to 1, relationships with $T>2$ are dominated by SC relationships.

Conversely, let us show that for smaller values of $c/\Delta\beta$ may make $T>2$ optimal. Consider $T=+\infty$. Fix $\Delta\beta$, and choose integer m, or equivalently, cost c, such that:

$$(1+\delta+\ldots+\delta^{m-1})c=\delta^{m-1}\Delta\beta.$$

Then it is optimal for A to help even if he is denounced during $(m-1)$ periods, as long as he will not be denounced m periods from now. Let P offer $s_m=s_{2m}=\ldots=0$ and an arbitrarily small s_τ when $\tau\neq nm$ for $n\geqslant 1$. It is then optimal for A to help forever and for the sane S to denounce at dates $0,1,m-1,m+1,\ldots,2m-1,2m+1,\ldots$. For δ close to 1 and m large, the per-period welfare is approximately $\eta h+(1-\eta)(h+g)$, which exceeds the welfare for a sequence of two-period relationships.

Remark 1. It would be worth extending the analysis in several directions. First we restricted attention to synchronized relationships. Overlapping S/A relationships raise the interesting issue of how reputations carry over from one relationship to the next. Second, the length of the S/A relationship was fixed by P at the start. More generally, P could use history-contingent T. For instance, he could terminate the S/A relationship if he obtains no information; it is unclear, however, whether such contingent switching can substantially raise welfare, as it would lessen A's incentive to cooperate. Third, we have not exhibited an example in which the sane S builds a reputation for being cooperative (here, P does not need S to build a reputation for being cooperative because cooperation can be obtained simply by giving no incentives for supervision[32]). We would find such behavior plausible in some organizations. Fourth, our analysis ignores the possibility of blackmail. If S can report information that benefits A (for instance that one determinant of A's efficiency is low) and if there is a type of S who is "anti-agent" in that he never reports information that benefits the agent, the sane S may want to build a reputation for being that type and extort favors from A. Theme n° 5 of section 2.1 then does not hold, as A would want this kind of information to be released.

Remark 2. Let us comment on the sane S's lexicographic preferences. If, for reward 0, the sane S does not prefer not to denounce the agent when the latter has helped, then P can obtain as much information as is consistent with help in a one-period relationship, by offering $s_0=0$ and having the sane S randomize between denouncing and not denouncing in such a way that the overall probability of no denunciation is $c/\Delta\beta$. P's per-period welfare is then $h+g\left(1-\dfrac{c}{\Delta\beta}\right)$, and A's incentive constraint for help is binding. One can then show that P can restrict attention to one-period relationships. That P can obtain the maximum information consistent with help without paying S is, however, not robust. For instance, if the sane S strictly gained by denouncing A (denouncing for instance might allow S to reorganize the production process), the sane S would have to be paid not to denounce. Two-period relationships would then allow P to let the sane S denounce while still promoting help in the first period of their relationship. Lexicographic preferences allowed us to capture the trade-offs between the different objectives in an analytically simple way.

Notes

* The author is grateful to Patrick Bolton, Drew Fudenberg, Bengt Holmström, David Martimort and Lars Stole for useful comments on an earlier draft, and to Jean-Jacques Laffont for helpful discussions; to the Institut D'Economie Industrielle, Toulouse for its hospitality; and to the National Science Foundation and the MIT Center for Energy Policy Research for financial support.

1 See also Rose-Ackerman's (1978) analysis of corruption in political life.
2 As we will discuss in section 2.3, this statement must be qualified if the agents have asymmetric information when side contracting.
3 See Tirole (1986) for a more complete discussion of reputation.
4 See Tirole (1986) and Holmström and Milgrom (1989).
5 See Holmström (1979, 1982) and Shavell (1979) for sufficient statistics results in moral hazard models. There are also counterparts in aggregation results in adverse selection models (Laffont and Tirole, 1991a).
6 If σ is hard information, this is not as strong an assumption as one would think. For, if S wants to collude with A to conceal σ, he can show the evidence to A. A not knowing σ introduces the issue of coalition formation under asymmetric information, which we discuss in section 2.3.
7 That is, P puts more weight on A's welfare than on S's. An alternative interpretation for this assumption is that P signs a contract with S and A before they get their information and that S is more risk averse than A, so that it is more costly for P to leave *ex post* rents to S than to A.

   In more complex models, bureaucratic policies may be desirable even if $\alpha_S = \alpha_A$ and parties are risk neutral. For instance, in Laffont and Tirole (1991a), moral hazard on the agent's side implies that the agent's rent from private information is lower than the cost savings resulting from the disclosure of this information.
8 See Laffont and Tirole (1991a).
9 The low-powered incentives result holds when S has technological information, as is the case here. The effect of potential collusion becomes ambiguous when S's role is to audit cost padding (Laffont–Tirole, 1990b).

10 If the messages in state 2 are not deterministic, they can choose deterministic messages on the basis of a public randomizing device. Alternatively, they can deter deviations with stochastic penalities (recall that they are risk neutral). Inequality (2.2.7) assumes that $\hat{V}_1 \geqslant \hat{V}_2$. One can also consider the case where $\hat{V}_1 < \hat{V}_2$; the relevant constraint is then: $\hat{V}_2 - \hat{V}_1 \geqslant k(\hat{U}_1 - \hat{U}_2)$. But it is easy to show that this latter case is never optimal.

11 Or $s = \varepsilon$ small when $r = \beta$ to ensure truthful revelation when the transaction technology is 0.

12 In (2.4.2), we have assumed that S makes a take-it-or-leave-it offer to A. If A made the offer, the expression would be $W^c = (1 - \gamma)W^d + \gamma W^u$ The same comments would apply.

13 When $\beta = \beta_1$, we assume that A pays bribe $\Delta\beta/2$ not to reveal the improvement. Alternative divisions of the gains from trade in state of nature β_1 would lead to slightly different expressions for W^c, but would yield the same conclusion.

14 In some cases, like that of a software manual that would help an agent and whose existence or non-existence is known to another agent, transactions could still be centralized with P rewarding the second agent for the transfer of the manual. But, in most cases of interest, channeling cooperative activity through the principal is either infeasible or inefficient.

15 That is, to raise "$\Delta\beta$" in the model of section 2.2. Raising stakes can easily be done in the generalized version of this model that allows moral hazard for A: raising the stakes then is equivalent to giving higher-powered incentive schemes.

16 See Maskin (1977) and Moore and Repullo (1989) for demonstrations that information perfectly shared among agents is almost never private, in that it can be costlessly elicited by the principal, when agents do not collude. We are not aware of characterizations of the set of Nash implementable allocations in the presence of collusion.

For the model of section 2.2, section 2.2.3 shows that the revelation of S's signal by S only suffices, and, therefore, that P cannot gain by having A announce S's signal as well. The intuition there is that S and A can agree on their announcements to P and specify large penalties if one of them does not abide by the agreement. In contrast, for the models mentioned in this section, the grand contract does not elicit revelation of shared information (about respective efforts, say) by any of the agents. If they were feasible, Nash implementation mechanisms eliciting the shared information would not allow P to obtain the first-best allocation (because of collusion), but might increase welfare, for instance when side transfers are costly.

17 Taken from Vayanos (1990).

18 Holmström and Milgrom also study "regulated side contracts," in which the principal "taxes" side transfers at rate τ. The transaction technology for the coalition among agents is then characterized by $k = 1/(1 + \tau)$, but a difference with the previous sections is that there is no deadweight loss as the tax is collected by the principal (in a different version of their model, τ is equivalent to a cap on side transfers). Holmström and Milgrom point out that there is a tradeoff between preserving the beneficial aspects of collusion and eliminating the detrimental ones. In appendix 2, we will develop an example of self-enforcing

collusion in which the principal indirectly, rather than directly, controls the cost of side transfers.

19 See Dewatripont (1989), Dewatripont and Maskin (1989), Hart and Tirole (1988), Laffont and Tirole (1990d) for adverse selection models, and Fudenberg and Tirole (1990) for a model with moral hazard.

20 From the revelation principle, m_T can be taken to be the informed party's type, without loss of generality. This property however does not hold for $\tau = 1, \ldots, T-1$.

21 Public owners, unlike private ones, are likely to respond to unemployment, foreign trade, or other social concerns, and thus reduce the value of the private investment.

22 Katz (1991) and Caillaud-Hermalin (1989) are other examples of the strategic use of contracting when information is asymmetric.

23 Or more, if agents learn about each other's actions as in section 2.8.1.

24 Strong or unique implementation corresponds to the existence of a unique equilibrium in the overall game defined by the grand contract. (A distinct concept is that no player or coalition has a weak incentive to behave differently given the other parties' or coalitions' equilibrium behavior.)

25 The problem is even more acute if a risk-neutral party gives insurance to S beyond that provided by the grand contract (Felli and Villas Boas, 1990).

26 In Cremer and Riordan, a set of bilateral contracts is "collusion proof" if no predecessor–successor pair has an incentive to contract, given that other pairs do not either. Actually, they prove that the first best can be implemented even if the agents can collude under symmetric information (which maximizes the probability of collusion). See Cremer (1986) for a general analysis of collusion in Groves mechanisms.

27 The side transfers are contingent on types in the coalition, and also on whatever is observable at the implementation stage.

28 See Hart–Holmström (1987, section 3) for a good discussion of self-enforcing contracts between two parties.

29 Other issues are the potential multiplicity of equilibria (an issue that may also arise in the enforceability approach: see section 2.3) and the need to be confident about the actual information structure (see the Fudenberg and Maskin (1986) critique of the reputation approach).

30 One could allow the rewards to depend on reports by both S and A, and also allow the agent's wage to not extract his rent conditional on truthful reports. We have not investigated these possibilities.

31 This appendix is inspired by preliminary research on the topic with Drew Fudenberg. I am responsible for any error.

32 Aghion and Caillaud (1988) build a model with three types of supervisor. One of the types of supervisor always denounces, and therefore not rewarding denunciation does not necessarily suffice to promote cooperation. Reputation for being cooperative may then be needed to get cooperation.

References

Aghion, P. and B. Caillaud (1988). "On the Role of Intermediaries in Organizations," chapter 3 in B. Caillaud *Three Essays in Contract Theory: On the Role of Outside Parties in Contractual Relationships*, Ph.D. Thesis, MIT.

Baron, D. (1985), "Noncooperative Regulation of a Nonlocalized Externality," *Rand Journal of Economics*, 16: 533–68.

Becker, G. (1983), "A Theory of Competition Among Pressure Groups for Political Influence," *Quarterly Journal of Economics*, 98: 371–400.

(1985), "Public Policies, Pressure Groups, and Deadweight Costs," *Journal of Public Economics*, 28: 329–47.

Bernheim, D. and M. Whinston (1985), "Common Marketing Agency as a Device for Facilitating Collusion," *Rand Journal of Economics*, 16: 553–68.

(1986), "Common Agency," *Econometrica*, 54: 923–42.

Caillaud, B. and B. Hermalin (1989), "The Role of Outside Considerations in the Design of Compensation Schemes," mimeo, Cepremap and UC Berkeley.

Caillaud, B., B. Jullien, and P. Picard (1990) "Publicly Announced Contracts, Private Renegotiation and Precommitment Effects," mimeo, Cepremap, Paris.

Cremer, J. (1986), "Manipulations by Coalitions under Asymmetric Information: The Case of Groves Mechanisms," mimeo, VPI.

Cremer, J. and M. Riordan (1987), "On Governing Multilateral Transactions with Bilateral Contracts," *Rand Journal of Economics*, 18: 436–51.

Crozier, M. (1963), *Le Phenomene Bureaucratique* – Paris: Editions du Seuil. Translated by Crozier as *The Bureaucratic Phenomenon*. Chicago, University of Chicago Press, 1967.

Cyert, R. and J. March (1963), *A Behavioral Theory of the Firm*. Englewood Cliffs: Prentice-Hall.

Dalton, M. (1959), *Men Who Manage*. New York: Wiley and Sons.

Dewatripont, M. (1988). "Commitment through Renegotiation Proof Contracts with Third Parties," *Review of Economic Studies*, 55: 377–90.

(1989), "Renegotiation and Information Revelation Over Time: The Case of Optimal Labor Contracts," *Quarterly Journal of Economics*, 104: 589–619.

Dewatripont, M. and E. Maskin (1989), "Multidimensional Screening, Observability and Contracts Renegotiation," mimeo, Harvard University.

Downs, A. (1964), *Inside Bureaucracy*, Boston: Little, Brown and Co.

Felli, L. (1990), "Collusion in Incentive Contracts: Does Delegation Help?", mimeo, MIT.

Felli, L. and M. Villas Boas (1990), Unpublished Notes, Boston College and UC Berkeley.

Fertschman, C. and K. Judd (1987), "Equilibrium Incentives in Oligopoly," *American Economic Review*, 77: 927–40.

Fudenberg, D. and D. Levine (1989), "Reputation and Equilibrium Selection in Games with a Patient Player," *Econometrica*, 57: 759–78.

Fudenberg, D. and E. Maskin (1986), "Folk Theorems for Repeated Games with Discounting or with Incomplete Information," *Econometrica*, 54: 533–54.

Fudenberg, D. and J. Tirole (1990), "Moral Hazard and Renegotiation in Agency Contracts," *Econometrica*, 58: 1279–1320.

Graham, D. and R. Marshall (1987), "Collusive Bidder Behavior at Single-Object Second-price and English Auctions," *Journal of Political Economy* 95: 1217–39.

Graham, D., Marshall, R. and J.F. Richard (1989), "Differential Payments Within a Bidder Coalition and the Shapley Value," mimeo, Duke University.

Hart, O. and B. Holmström (1987), "The Theory of Contracts," in T. Bewley (ed.), *Advances in Economic Theory, 5th World Congress of the Econometric Society*, Cambridge University Press.

Hart, O. and J. Tirole (1988), "Contract Renegotiation and Coasian Dynamics," *Review of Economics Studies*, 55: 509–40.

Holmström, B. (1979), "Moral Hazard and Observability," *Bell Journal of Economics*, 10: 74–91.

(1982), "Moral Hazard in Teams," *Bell Journal of Economics*, 13: 324–40.

Holmström, B. and P. Milgrom (1990), "Regulating Trade Among Agents," *Journal of Institutional and Theoretical Economics*, 146: 85–105.

Holmström, B. and R. Myerson (1983), "Efficient and Durable Decision Rules with Incomplete Information," *Econometrica*, 51: 1799–820.

Itoh, H. (1989), "Collusion, Incentives, and Risk Sharing," mimeo, University of California, San Diego.

Katz, M. (1991), "Game Playing Agents: Contracts as Precommitments," *Rand Journal of Economics*, 22: 307–28.

Klitgaard, R. (1988), *Controlling Corruption*, Berkeley: University of California.

Kofman, F. and J. Lawarrée (1989). "Collusion in Hierarchical Agency," mimeo, University of California at Berkeley.

(1990), "On the Optimality of Allowing Collusion," mimeo, University of California at Berkeley.

Kreps, D., P. Milgrom, J. Roberts and R. Wilson (1982), "Rational Cooperation in the Finitely Repeated Prisoner's Dilemma," *Journal of Economic Theory*, 27: 245–52.

Laffont, J.J. (1990), "Analysis of Hidden Gaming in a Three Level Hierarchy," *Journal of Law, Economics and Organization*.

Laffont, J.J. and J. Tirole (1990a), "The Regulation of Multi-Product Firms, I: Theory," *Journal of Public Economics*, 43: 1–36.

(1990b), "Cost Padding, Auditing and Collusion," mimeo.

(1990c), "The Politics of Government Decision Making: Regulatory Institutions," *Journal of Law, Economics, and Organization*, 6: 1–32.

(1990d), "Adverse Selection and Renegotiation in Procurement," *Review of Economic Studies*, 57: 597–626.

(1991a), "The Politics of Government Decision Making: A Theory of Regulatory Capture," *Quarterly Journal of Economics*, 106: 1089–127.

(1991b), "Auction Design and Favoritism," *International Journal of Industrial Organization*, 9: 9–42.

(forthcoming), "Cartelization by Regulation," *Journal of Regulatory Economics*.

(1991c), "Privatization and Incentives," *Journal of Law, Economics and Organization*, supplement, 7: 84–105

McAfee, R.P. and J. McMillan (1988), "Bidding Rings," mimeo, University of Western Ontario.

Macho-Stadler, I. and D. Perez-Castrillo (1989), "Moral Hazard with Several Agents: the Gains from Cooperation," mimeo, Universidad del Pais Vasco, Bilbao.

Mailath, G. and P. Zemsky (1989), "Collusion in Second Price Auctions with Heterogeneous Bidders," CARESS Working Paper, 89-02.

Martimort, D. (1990a), "Multiple Principals and Asymmetric Information," mimeo, Université de Toulouse.

(1990b), "Optimal Contracts and Games between Principal-Agent Pairs," mimeo, Université de Toulouse.

Maskin, E. (1977), "Nash Equilibrium and Welfare Optimality," mimeo.

Maskin, E. and J. Tirole (1992), "The Principal-Agent Relationship with an Informed Principal, II: Common Values," *Econometrica*, 60: 1–42.

Moore, J. and R. Repullo (1989), "Subgame Perfect Implementation," *Econometrica*, 56: 1191–220.

Myerson, R. (1982), "Optimal Coordination Mechanisms in Generalized Principal-Agent Problems," *Journal of Mathematical Economics*, 10: 67–81.

Olson, M. (1965), *The Logic of Collective Action: Public Goods and the Theory of Collective Action*. Cambridge, MA: Harvard University Press.

Peltzman, S. (1976), "Toward a More General Theory of Regulation," *Journal of Law and Economics*, 19: 211–40.

Ramakrishnan, R. and A. Thakor (1989), "Cooperation vs Competition in Agency," mimeo, GSB, Columbia University and School of Business, Indiana University.

Robinson, M.S. (1985), "Collusion and the Choice of Auction," *Rand Journal of Economics*, 16: 141–5.

Rose-Ackerman, S. (1978), *Corruption: A Study in Political Economy*. New York: Academic Press.

Shavell, S. (1979), "Risk Sharing and Incentives in the Principal and Agent Relationship," *Bell Journal of Economics*, 10: 55–73.

Spiller, P. (1990), "Politicians, Interest Groups, and Regulators: A Multiple-Principals Agency Theory of Regulation (or 'Let Them Be Bribed')", *Journal of Law and Economics*.

Stigler, G. (1971), "The Economic Theory of Regulation," *Bell Journal of Economics*, 2: 3–21.

Stiglitz, J. (1990a), "Peer Monitoring and Credit Markets," mimeo, Stanford University.

(1990b), "Moral Hazard and Non-Market Institutions: Dysfunctional Crowding Out or Peer Monitoring?" mimeo, Stanford University.

Stole, L. (1990), "Mechanism Design under Common Agency," mimeo, MIT.

Tirole, J. (1986), "Hierarchies and Bureaucracies: on the Role of Collusion in Organizations," *Journal of Law, Economics and Organization*, 2(2): 181–214.

Varian, H.R. (1989), "Monitoring Agents with other Agents," mimeo, CREST Working Paper, University of Michigan.

Vayanos, D. (1990), "The Supervision Costs of Multi-Investor Projects: Free-Riding and Collusion," mimeo, MIT.

Vickers, J. (1985), "Delegation and the Theory of the Firm," *Economic Journal*, Conference Papers, 95: 138–47.

Von-Ungern-Sternberg, T. (1988), "Cartel Stability in Sealed Bid Second Price Auctions," *Journal of Industrial Economics*, 36: 351–8.

The theory of organizations: discussion of Harris and Raviv, and Tirole

Patrick Bolton

Harris and Raviv and Tirole have provided very comprehensive surveys of two branches of research dealing with the internal organization of firms. Newcomers into the field will find both papers essential reading. They both provide a fair and accurate account of the major achievements in the last fifteen years and they point toward several important avenues for future research. While there are clearly connections between the two fields covered by Harris and Raviv and Tirole, I shall not attempt to draw them here. I shall instead discuss each paper separately.

1   FINANCIAL CONTRACTING THEORY

In the last two decades or so the field of corporate finance has undergone a similar transformation to that witnessed in industrial organization. The application of the methods of game theory and incentive theory has opened up the way to the elaboration of a multitude of alternative theories on the choice of capital structure, dividend policy, acquisition strategies, and the like. Perhaps more so than in the field of industrial organization, this outburst of new theoretical investigations has also been accompanied by a considerable amount of empirical work. This combined research effort has substantially extended our knowledge and understanding of the determinants of corporate financial structure. For a long time after the publication of Modigliani and Miller's (1958) classic paper there was a dearth of coherent explanations of the firm's choice of capital structure; there is an abundance of alternative theories today. It is safe to say that the research agenda initially set by the Modigliani–Miller paper – of finding plausible explanations of the choice of debt/equity ratio in the light of their irrelevance theorem – has now largely been met. However, as in industrial organization, this remarkable development has given rise to the opposite concern that with a little imagination and skill in manipulating models with asymmetric information anything and its opposite could be explained in several different ways. At the same time, many of the recent models of the financial structure based on asymmetric information are highly stylized and it remains to be determined whether the main results in those models extend to richer settings.

Therefore, the challenge today is, in my view, to synthesize the major contributions of the last twenty years and to develop a unified framework within which the relative importance of the various existing explanations can be assessed.

In my opinion, some of the most recent research in security design just may provide the foundations of such a synthesis. If one imposes the requirement that the specific form of the financial instruments issued as well as the compensation packages of mangers be determined endogenously one is forced to construct the theory from first principles and to envisage all feasible alternatives that can be used to mitigate the incentive problem between the managers of the firm and its investors. This approach may not only lead to new insights but may also reveal similarities between two apparently distinct existing explanations. Perhaps more importantly, only a security design approach can:

1   account for the existence of many more complex securities than standard debt and equity;
2   assess the importance of the widely discussed shareholder–bondholder conflicts and/or the manager–shareholders and manager–debtholders conflicts;
3   explain financial innovation in response to changes in market conditions and/or changes in the tax system.

It has long been recognized that, if financial structure is mainly used as an instrument to mitigate the fundamental incentive problem between the managers of the firm and its investors, then a combination of standard debt and equity is generally not the most efficient incentive scheme. Take for instance the incentive towards excessive risk-taking of managers in highly levered firms. True enough, decreasing leverage does partly reduce these agency-costs – as Jensen–Meckling have suggested – but this incentive problem is more effectively mitigated by issuing warrants (see Green, 1984) or other kinds of securities that "concavify" the manager's objective function (for instance, the manager's compensation package may contain bond-options). The existence of securities other than debt and equity may thus be explained as an optimal response to an underlying agency problem. Alternatively, non-standard securities may be created to respond optimally to the corporate tax system. In a recent thought-provoking paper Bulow,

Summers, and Summers (1990) describe how several recent financial innovations like pay-in-kind securities or adjustable-rate convertible notes are basically attempts by firms at disguising equity as debt so as to take advantage of the more favorable tax treatment of debt.

In short, the security design approach to corporate structure can potentially explain both the existence of the wide variety of different financial instruments issued by firms and the observed prevalence of standard debt and equity. In addition it can test for the robustness of the theories based on conflicts between debtholders and equityholders arising from the specific form taken by standard debt and equity.

As the Harris–Raviv survey clearly indicates the recent literature on security design has already gone some way toward the elaboration of a theory of capital structure with endogenously determined securities. Situations in which standard debt is an optimal security have been identified; thus Townsend (1979) has shown in a bilateral contracting situation with a wealth constrained borrower, that when the lender faces *ex post* monitoring costs the investment contract minimizing expected monitoring costs is a standard debt contract; more recently Aghion and Bolton (1988) have shown that a standard debt contract may have optimal control allocation properties. In practice financial contracts are highly incomplete and the return on an investment depends in an important way on future decisions of the firm. Aghion and Bolton show that under certain conditions the best arrangement is for the borrower to take all the future decisions (i.e., to be in control) as long as he or she meets the repayment provisions on the loan; if these are violated then all the control rights should be shifted to the lender. This is basically the control-allocation arrangement specified in a standard secured debt contract or even in a leasing contract. Equally important insights have been gained recently about the optimality properties of common-stock arrangements. Harris and Raviv (1986) and Grossman and Hart (1988) have simultaneously and independently discovered the important "no cheap votes" principle which explains the optimality of one-share-one-vote arrangements.

All of these contributions, however, are cast implicitly or explicitly in a framework where the investors in a firm can be represented by a single investor, so that the contracting problem can be reduced to a simple bilateral problem. It remains to be determined how well these results extend to multilateral contracting settings. In order to make significant further progress toward the elaboration of a complete theory of capital structure one must move away from this bilateral contracting paradigm. In such a setting one can explain the design of one type of security, at most, not the coexistence of several different optimal securities.

In a multilateral contracting framework one can explain the coexistence of several different types of securities as a result of conflicts of interest between investors and as a result of the latter's preference for liquid securities. Conflicts of interest between investors create the need for individual investor protections, such as security interests, collated agreements, and the like. An optimal allocation of these protections among investors may be asymmetric. In other words, it may be optimal for some investors to have subordinated claims. Distinguishing among investors according to the seniority of their claims is one important way of introducing different types of securities and of elaborating a theory of capital structure. Secondly, investors' preference for liquid securities may explain why in a multilateral setting investors prefer a bilateral contract between the firm and themselves (together with multilateral rules determining the structure of individual claims) rather than a grand multilateral contract. One recent attempt in this direction by Hart and Moore (1990) illustrates some of the new difficulties one encounters when modeling the choice of capital structure as a multilateral contracting problem. But their work also illustrates the important new insights one can gain in following this approach.

To conclude, we are still far away from a complete theory of the corporate financial structure with endogenous securities. The research efforts of the past twenty years surveyed in this article have been important in identifying most of the many determinants of the firm's capital structure. The extent to which our understanding has improved is impressive, but I fear that an equally important effort is required in the future to make significant progress towards a completely endogenous theory of the firm's capital structure.

References

All the papers cited here can be found in the references of Harris and Raviv, except for:

Bulow, J., L. Summers, and V. Summers (1990), "Distinguishing Debt from Equity in the Junk Bond Era," in Shoven, J. and J. Waldfogel (eds), *Debt Taxes & Corporate Restructuring*, Washington, DC: Brookings Institute.

2   COLLUSION AND THE THEORY OF ORGANIZATIONS

The literature covered in this survey is very young and inevitably all the important issues concerning collusion in organizations are not yet precisely identified. Tirole pursues several different themes, some mainly methodological, others dealing with positive questions such as: "why does one observe collusion in organizations?" and another set of issues concerned with the more normative question of how the organization ought to respond to collusion. He is cautious enough not to take stock. I shall be rash and single out what I think are the main issues and achievements in this relatively new field.

The classic principal–agent paradigm has been applied successfully to many important economic problems. Harris and Raviv have shown the central role of agency theory in corporate finance. But equally important applications have been found in public finance, labor economics, regulation, etc. In many of these applications, however, the one principal–one agent representation of the problem is an oversimplification. A richer theoretical framework is often required to do justice to the full complexity of the problems considered. To take just two examples:

(i)   The modern theory of regulation of natural monopolies takes the view that the regulating agency acts in the "public interest" (see for example, Baron and Myerson, 1982 and Laffont and Tirole, 1986). But the public choice school and others have provided convincing evidence that this view is misleading. It is often more insightful to view the regulatory agencies as self-interested bodies reacting to external influences exerted by more or less well-organized pressure groups. Following this line of enquiry, however, requires a model with at least a principal–supervisor–agent structure (in many applications it is even necessary to consider a richer framework with multiple principals – one supervisor – one agent as in Laffont and Tirole [1988 and 1990c]);

(ii) the managerial firm is often represented as a principal–agent structure. Such a stylized representation may be appropriate in a macro-model (as in Holmström–Weiss [1985], for example) but is clearly inadequate as a theory of the managerial firm. A suitable foundation for a theory of the managerial firm has to be an "agency theory of group behavior" of which the basic building block is a principal–supervisor–agent structure.

In my view one of the major achievements of the recent literature surveyed by Tirole is the elaboration of this new principal–supervisor–agent paradigm in which one can address the problem of group incentives. Since most of the issues concerning collusion arise in this setup, I shall limit my discussion to this canonical model.

Undoubtedly, the key new conceptual difficulty arising in the principal–supervisor–agent framework is the specification of the side-contracting technology of any two parties. This explains why close to one third of the chapter is devoted to this issue (six sections out of seventeen). I should point out that much of this discussion is new material (in particular, sections 3.4,

3.5, and 3.6 contain original research). Roughly speaking, one can separate the problem of side contracting into two questions: first, when should the principal let the supervisor and agent write legally enforceable side contracts? (This is the problem of subcontracting.) Second, to what extent should the grand contract (between the principal–supervisor–agent) be structured in a way that all incentives to engage in hidden side contracting disappear? Relatively little has been written on subcontracting so I shall mostly discuss the second question. I shall also limit myself to the case where any form of hidden subcontracting is bad for the organization as a whole.

One can mitigate collusion by either removing its causes or by controlling its enforceability. As Tirole has clearly illustrated, the prescriptions for mitigating collusion may be sensitive to the specification of the enforcement technology of hidden side contracts. The early contributions have posited a perfect enforceability of side contracts. This assumption is clearly inadequate if one is interested in the methods by which the enforceability of side contracts can be undermined. In this respect, the sections on self-enforcing side contracts are important new developments. Some examples of the prescriptions emerging from these sections are:

(i)   Job-rotation in organizations and bureaucracies can prevent the creation of the long-run relations necessary for the enforcement of hidden side contracts;

(ii) The supervisor's reports about the agent ought to be kept secret so that the agent cannot verify whether the supervisor has complied with the hidden agreement; I presume that this is why letters of recommendation are secret or why some procurement contracts are assigned through sealed-bid auctions. In this respect it might perhaps be wise to have the votes of representatives be secret so as to impede lobbying activities. Of course, one of the limits of secret reports in practice is that they may permit false accusations . . . (note that this possibility is ruled out in most of the studies surveyed here, since only verifiable information is communicated);

(iii) The remuneration and promotion packages of the supervisor and agent ought to be kept secret; side contracting will then take place under asymmetric information so that all the gains from trade between the supervisor and agent may not be exploited.

All of these prescriptions and others deserve to be studied further.

To plead in favor of the earlier assumption of enforceable side contracts it is a useful shortcut when analyzing how the causes of collusion can be removed. In my opinion, the important insight on this question emerging from the literature is roughly speaking that the agent's compensation and promotion ought to be less sensitive to the supervisor's report about his performance than what standard agency theory would predict. This might explain why organizations seek to reduce the discretion of supervisors and rely instead on rules and why seniority, age, and other non-manipulable variables are important in determining promotions.

In sum, the literature reviewed in this discussion lays the foundations of both an economic theory of the internal organization of firms and an interest-group theory of regulation. Both of these areas have remained at the periphery of economics for too long and I hope that in the coming years we shall witness a rapid expansion of these fields.

References

The references to all the papers cited here can be found in the reference list of Tirole except for:

Baron, D. and R. Myerson (1982) "Regulating a Monopolist with Unknown Costs," *Econometrica*, 50: 911–30.

Holmström, B. and L. Weiss (1985) "Managerial Incentives, Investment and Aggregate Implications: Scale Effects," *The Review of Economic Studies*, 170: 403–26.

CHAPTER 4

The nature of incomplete security markets

Darrell Duffie

1   INTRODUCTION

Despite a spurt of progress on the theory of incomplete security markets over the past decade or so, there is relatively little yet in the way of testable implications or practical prescriptions. This essay presents a synopsis of some of the available models and points toward some of the important issues still standing in the way of the theory's fruition. This is not a general survey of the topic.

An incomplete security market is widely taken to be one in which certain contracts are not available for trade, a definition that is perhaps too rigid. The point is that active trading is observed only in contracts with satisfactory enforcement mechanisms, sufficiently low transactions costs, and enough incentive for exchange, relative to general market opportunities. Most economists would surely agree that markets will and do open in response to the emergence of these conditions. On the other hand, there is no well-understood reason to believe that the resulting constellation of traded contracts is therefore "appropriate" in some constrained sense of efficiency, or that "markets are as complete as they ought to be." There is also strong empirical evidence that security prices are not even approximately consistent with complete markets, at least under standard preference assumptions.

Most currently active security markets seem to have arisen in response to entrepreneurial incentives to provide markets for insurance, the need for corporations to raise capital in a convenient form, and historical accidents. The process of security market innovation, interesting in itself, also affects the pricing of securities and the allocation of contingent consumption. It is only beginning to be modeled. As yet, most of the theoretical attention of financial economists has been on complete markets models, for which we have a reasonably clear and elegant theory without much empirical basis, or to models with an exogenously fixed set of contracts. The theory's real success story has been the application of arbitrage-free restrictions to obtain relative prices for securities that are theoretically redundant, without saying much about the allocation of consumption or the pricing of the "primitive" set of underlying securities.

These comments are not designed to suggest a failure of the theory, but rather that it has not matured much beyond a way of organizing our thoughts.

Section 2 lays out a simple two-period security market model as a framework for the remainder. Section 3 is a brief review of results on the existence of equilibrium, which is surveyed in more depth by Geanakoplos (1990). Theories of the multiplicity of incomplete markets equilibria are reviewed in this volume by Cass (1990). Section 4 discusses the problem of security market innovation in a simple setting. Section 5 points to some of the available results on asset pricing with incomplete markets. Section 6 outlines the theory of the firm with incomplete security markets. An appendix shows some of the mathematical techniques that have been used to obtain existence of equilibria.

A standard treatment of general equilibrium with complete markets is given by Debreu (1953, 1959). Additional perspectives on general equilibrium with incomplete markets can be found in Geanakoplos (1990), Hahn (1990), and Magill and Shafer (1990b).

2   THE BASIC MODEL

The following restrictive model is more or less standard in the literature. There are two periods, denoted 0 and 1, and S states of the world, one of which will be publicly revealed to be true in period 1. There is no private information. With l commodities always available for trade on spot markets, we have the consumption space $L = \mathbb{R}^l \times (\mathbb{R}^l)^S$, with a typical consumption vector $x = (x_0, x_1)$ representing the commodity bundle x_0 at time zero and the bundle x_{1s} at time 1 in state s. There are m agents, with the preferences of agent i represented by a strictly increasing utility function $U_i : L_+ \to \mathbb{R}$ and the endowment of agent i given by a consumption vector e^i in L_+, the set of non-negative consumption vectors. So far, the primitives form an exchange economy $\mathcal{E} = \{(U_i, e^i) : 1 \leq i \leq m\}$ of the Arrow–Debreu (1954) variety.

Spot commodity prices are given by a non-zero vector $p \in L_+$. There are N securities defined by a function $D : L_+ \to \mathbb{R}^{S \times N}$. Given a spot price vector p, $D(p)$ is the matrix of dividends of the securities, with $D_{sn}(p)$ the dividend paid in units of account by security n in state s. For example, security n

could deliver the bundle $\delta_s \in R^l$ of commodities in state s, in which case $D_{sn}(p) = p_{1s} \cdot \delta_s$. Alternatively, as in the original general equilibrium model of security markets due to Arrow (1953), we could have $N = S$ and $D(p)$ equal to the identity matrix for all p, meaning that security n pays 1 unit of account if state n is revealed to be true, and 0 otherwise. Generalizing, we could have D an arbitrary constant $S \times N$ matrix as in Cass (1984) or Werner (1985), affine as in Duffie and Shafer (1986a), piecewise linear as in the options model of Krasa (1987), or some more general non-linear function as in the abstract model of Huang and Wu (1989).

To keep things simple, we'll assume, until introducing production in section 6, that there is no endowment of securities, which are traded in period 0. With a spot price vector p and a security price vector $q \in R^N$, this leaves agent i with the problem:

$$\max_{(x,\theta) \in L_+ \times R^N} U_i(x), \tag{1}$$

subject to:

$$p_0 \cdot (x_0 - e_0^i) + q \cdot \theta = 0, \tag{2}$$

and:

$$p_1 \square (x_1 - e_1^i) - D(p)\theta = 0, \tag{3}$$

where, for any p and x in L, $p_1 \square x_1$ denotes the vector in R^S whose s-th element is $p_{1s} \cdot x_{1s}$.

An equilibrium is a collection $(p,q,(x^1,\theta^1), \ldots,(x^m,\theta^m))$, where p is a spot price vector; q is a security price vector; for each $i,(x^i,\theta^i)$ solves problem (1)-(2)-(3); and markets clear: $\Sigma_i(x^i - e^i) = 0$ and $\Sigma_i \theta^i = 0$.

It is instructive to consider the alternative problem for agent i:

$$\max_{x \in L} U_i(x), \tag{4}$$

subject to:

$$p \cdot (x^i - e^i) = 0, \tag{5}$$

and:

$$p_1 \square (x_1 - e_1^i) \in \text{span}[D(p)]. \tag{6}$$

We define some $(p,x^1, \ldots,x^m) \in L_+^{m+1}$ to be an effective equilibrium for the economy $(\mathcal{E},D)$ if $\Sigma_i(x^i - e^i) = 0$ and, for all i, x^i solves (4)-(5)-(6).

PROPOSITION 1 $(x^1, \ldots,x^m) \in L_+^m$ is an effective equilibrium allocation if and only if it is an equilibrium allocation.

Proof Suppose $(p,x^1, \ldots,x^m)$ is an effective equilibrium. For each agent $i < m$, let θ^i solve the system (3) of linear equations. Let $\theta^m = -\Sigma_{i<m}\theta^i$. For each security n, let $q_n = \Sigma_{s=1}^S D_{sn}(p)$. Direct calculation verifies that $(p,q,(x^1,\theta^1), \ldots,(x^m,\theta^m))$ is an equilibrium. This proves the "only if" assertion. The reader is left the similar task of proving the other.

The proposition shows that it is enough for equilibrium to find an effective equilibrium, and also that securities affect allocations in this setting only by way of their span. In particular, in the case of complete markets, or $\text{span}[D(p)] = \mathbb{R}^S$, we have the efficiency properties of security markets observed by Arrow (1953).

3   EXISTENCE OF EQUILIBRIUM

This section is an overview of conditions for the existence of general equilibrium in the setting of the basic model.

3.1   History

An important check on the consistency of the model, and one of the more interesting technical achievements of the theory, is the demonstration of equilibrium under successively more general properties of the dividend function D. The story begins with Arrow (1953), who took $D \equiv I_{S \times S}$. Of course, this was even before Arrow and Debreu (1954) provided the required machinery for the existence of effective equilibrium, in this case the usual Walrasian equilibrium. The next important existence result is due to Radner (1972), who adjusted the model for linear D by placing a lower bound on portfolio choice. Among other important observations, Hart (1975) showed that an additional constraint such as this[1] lower bound is sometimes needed for existence.

In the models of Radner and Hart, as opposed to Arrow's, securities were defined as claims to bundles of commodities; that is, D was assumed to be linear. In 1984, Cass (1984) and Werner (1985) came up with a key observation: if securities are claims directly to units of account as in Arrow (1953), or in other words D is constant, then the existence of equilibrium[2] follows under typical and mild regularity conditions, complete markets or not. Repullo (1986), McManus (1984), and Magill and Shafer (1990a) all showed that Hart's counterexample to existence for linear D is not robust by providing a generic existence theorem for $N \geq S$. A generic existence theorem for $N < S$ was shown by Duffie and Shafer (1985), and then with more general techniques by Husseini, Lasry, and Magill (1990), Hirsch, Magill, and Mas-Colell (1990), and Geanakoplos and Shafer (1990).

In a slightly different model, Polemarchakis and Ku (1990) isolated a robust counterexample to existence for non-linear D, corresponding to an option. Krasa (1987), Kahn and Krasa (1990), and Krasa and Werner (1989) have variations on generic existence or non-existence with options. Huang and Wu (1989) have generic existence for smooth non-linear D.

3.2   Pseudo-equilibrium

The essential difficulty with existence, as pointed out by Hart, is that the span of $D(\cdot)$ is generally discontinuous. Even if D itself is continuous, its rank may drop suddenly at spot prices that, although extremely rare, cannot be ruled out as candidates for equilibrium. Geanakloplos (1990) has an excellent discussion of this problem. Duffie and Shafer (1985) proposed the following weakening of the definition of an effective equilibrium, from which a generic existence result emerges.

Let $\mathscr{G}_{NS}$ denote the set of N-dimensional linear subspaces of $\mathbb{R}^S$. If $D(p)$ is of maximal rank, which we hope to be true typically, then span $[D(p)]$ is in $\mathscr{G}_{NS}$. A pseudo-equilibrium for $(\mathcal{E},D)$ is a collection $(G,(p,x^1, \ldots,x^m))$ $\in \mathscr{G}_{NS} \times L_+^{m+1}$ such that:

(a) $\Sigma_i(x^i - e^i) = 0$.
(b)   For all i, x^i solves (4) subject to (5) and $p_1 \square (x_1 - e_1^i) \in G$.
(c)   span$[D(p)] \subset G$.

PROPOSITION 2   Suppose there is a pseudo-equilibrium $(G,(p, x^1, \ldots,x^m))$ whose dividend matrix $D(p)$ is of full rank. Then $(p,x^1, \ldots,x^m)$ is an effective equilibrium and there exists an equilibrium.

> *Proof*   Suppose $(G,(p,x^1, \ldots,x^m))$ is a pseudo-equilibrium. If $D(p)$ is of full rank, then condition (c) implies that span$[D(p)] = G$, so (b) is equivalent to optimality in the sense of (4)-(5)-(6). Thus $(p,x^1, \ldots,x^m)$ is an effective equilibrium, and an equilibrium exists by Proposition 1.

The general strategy for proof of generic existence of equilibrium is therefore:

> Step 1. For any economy $(\mathcal{E},D)$, demonstrate the existence of pseudo-equilibrium.
> Step 2. Show that, aside from an exceptional set of economies, at any pseudo-equilibrium $(G,(p,x^1, \ldots,x^m))$, the matrix $D(p)$ is of full rank.

We will not define "exceptional" precisely here because it depends on the set from which D is drawn, whether linear, affine, smooth non-linear, or other. For example, for linear D, we can identify each security with a matrix δ in $K \equiv \mathbb{R}^{S \times l}$ indicating the bundle δ_s of commodities that the security pays in state s. In that case, Duffie and Shafer (1985) take an exceptional set of economies to be a set of pairs (δ, e) of dividend commodity bundles δ and endowments $e = (e^1, \ldots, e^m)$ in a closed subset of Lebesgue measure zero of $K^N \times L_+^m$. (Bottazzi (1991) has just shown existence in this setting for fixed dividend bundles and generic endowments.)

Step 2 of the proof calls for conditions under which it is an exceptional accident to have linearly dependent security dividends. The proof relies on techniques introduced by Debreu (1972, 1976) that exploit smoothness and regularity properties of preferences, that is, the "differentiable approach" to equilibrium exposited by Mas-Colell (1985).

Step 1, however, relies only on regularity conditions that are typical for the existence of Walrasian equilibria with interior allocations. For example, consider:

(A)   Continuity: D is continuous and, for all i, U_i is continuous.
(B)   Convexity: for all i, U_i is strictly quasi-concave.
(C)   Interior endowments: for all i, $e^i \in \text{int}(L_+)$.
(D)   Monotonicity: for all i, U_i is strictly increasing.
(E)   Boundary behavior: for all i, the closure of A_i is a subset of $\text{int}(L_+)$, where:

$$A_i = \{x \in \text{int}(L_+) : U_i(x) = U_i(e^i), x \le e^1 + \cdots + e^m\}.$$

Condition D is already a maintained hypothesis, but is shown for completeness. Condition E means essentially that any consumption choice that includes each commodity in each state is strictly preferred to any choice that involves zero of some commodity in some state. This forces interior equilibria. The following result is shown[3] by Geanakoplos and Shafer (1990).

PROPOSITION 3   Under conditions A–E, an economy $(\mathcal{E}, D)$ has a pseudo-equilibrium.

The proof can be viewed as an application of degree theory; some of the required mathematical concepts are sketched out in the appendix.

It seems fair to summarize that the incomplete markets general equilibrium model as formulated here is consistent, with minor exceptions, in that equilibria usually exist.

4   INNOVATION OF SECURITY MARKETS

This section treats the endogenous formation of security markets, beginning with a general discussion and then turning to two specific models. The first model addresses the role of securities in spanning the risks in agents' endowments. The second model adds the additional consideration of liquidity in determining the resulting set of security markets.

4.1   The nature of innovation

As mentioned in the Introduction, the security markets that arise in our economy are partially a response by entrepreneurs to perceived gains from the active trading of currently untraded contracts. By the establishment of a security exchange, innovating entrepreneurs expect to profit from direct transactions fees charged to traders, the sale of "seats" (rights to trade and provide brokerage), and often by trading on the entrepreneurs' own accounts. Of course, seats are valuable because their holders can in turn charge brokerage fees, or themselves trade so as to profit on the bid–ask spread.

Modern futures, forwards, and options contracts are relatively clear examples of these motives for setting up markets; most are a direct response to an ongoing desire by economic agents to share risk and to speculate. The stockmarkets are somewhat poorer examples because the securities traded, the stocks themselves, are not originally designed to generate ongoing trade, but rather to meet the desires of the initial owners of a firm to obtain working capital and to diversify. It is usually an accident if a corporation's technology happens to generate dividends whose value spans relatively important risks in the economy, unless the corporation is so large that its dividends are themselves important to the economy. For example, shares of IBM are actively traded perhaps because they represent such a large fraction of the value of US equities, and also perhaps because their value is tied closely to the success of the important high technology component of the economy. It is also true, of course, that IBM is an obvious candidate for trades because of its high liquidity, but this is a circular claim to be discussed in section 4.3. Likewise, the nature of bond markets is colored by the need of the original debtors to raise funds, not necessarily in the form of a contract likely to generate active ongoing trading.

In short, many stocks, bonds, and other securities that are not specifically designed to generate active trading nevertheless do so because they happen to provide ongoing opportunities for spanning important economic risks. Such securities usually become traded in centralized security markets with standard procedures and a degree of competitive behavior. Other securities may not. It has become common, however, to decompose and repackage some primitive securities in forms that are likely to generate active trade. One example is the emergence of "baskets" of equities, possibly usurping the role of stock index futures contracts, single contracts that span the risk inherent in large portfolios of securities such as those represented in the Standard and Poors 500 and Nikkei indices. Most of the stocks making up these indices are themselves actively traded, so the emergence of these bundled contracts is a fairly subtle type of innovation related to transactions costs. Collateralized mortgage obligations are a better example; they are constructed by first packaging individual mortgages together into large pools and then decomposing the pools into various "tranches," each tied to a different type of interest-rate risk.

With only a sporadic need for trade in a given contract, it is unlikely that entrepreneurs would find it profitable to set up and maintain a security market. In that case, exchange could take place when the need arose between two parties, say by a one-time public auction or by direct negotiation. While such exchange is extremely important as a vehicle for sharing risk, including for example the lion's share of implicit and explicit labor contracts, it does not usually fit into the framework of security markets, and is not the subject of this section of this chapter.

4.2   A simple model of spanning and innovation

This subsection and the next present simple stylized models of innovation. There are no limits on the choice of contracts, and the innovating entrepreneur is motivated solely by the revenues to be generated from selling rights to trade.

The first of these models, adapted from Duffie and Jackson (1989), rests on a variation of the basic setup presented in section 2. The consumption space L is now taken to be the span of a collection of joint normal random variables on some probability space. A consumption choice $x \in L$ represents consumption, in each state in period 1, of some quantity of a single spot commodity. Agent i is represented by an endowment $e^i \in L$ and a utility function $U_i : L \to \mathbb{R}$ of the von Neumann–Morgenstern constant absolute risk-averse variety:

$$U_i(x) = E[-\exp(-r_i x)],$$

for some constant $r_i > 0$ representing risk aversion. There are N securities represented by their dividends $D = (D_1, \ldots, D_N) \in L^N$. We will treat these as futures contracts, with associated futures prices $q = (q_1, \ldots, q_N) \in \mathbb{R}^N$, so that a position $\theta \in \mathbb{R}^N$ in these contracts established in period 0 pays off the total consumption $\theta^\top (D - q)$ in period 1.

Given D and q, agent i then has the problem:

$$\max_{\theta \in \mathbb{R}^N} \quad U_i[e^i + \theta^\top (D - q)]. \tag{7}$$

Given some contract set D, an equilibrium is some $(q,\theta^1, \ldots, \theta^m) \in (\mathbb{R}^n)^{m+1}$ such that, for all i, θ^i solves (7) and markets clear: $\Sigma_{i=1}^m \theta^i = 0$. Given D, there is a unique equilibrium futures price vector:

$$q = E(D) - \gamma \mathrm{cov}(D,e), \tag{8}$$

where $e = e^1 + \cdots + e^m$, $\gamma = (r_1^{-1} + \cdots + r_m^{-1})^{-1}$, and $\mathrm{cov}(D,e)$ is the vector in $\mathbb{R}^N$ whose n-th element is $\mathrm{cov}(D_n,e)$. Assuming the contract payoffs are linearly independent, the equilibrium futures position of agent i is:

$$\theta^i = \mathrm{cov}(D)^{-1} \left[\frac{E(D)-q}{r_i} - \mathrm{cov}(D,e^i) \right]. \tag{9}$$

This is all standard. The interesting issue is the original choice D of futures contracts. If the contracts are chosen by a futures exchange, what incentives are at play? In practice, the members of a futures exchange have collective control of the choice of futures contracts to be made available for trade. Members, most of whom are traders, profit mainly from the supply of brokerage services to the public at large, either through direct commissions or indirectly by their willingness to make a market, adopting positions on their own accounts in ancitipation of offsetting trades to follow, effectively charging a bid–ask spread, albeit a risky one. If members also have endowments to hedge, or have differential skills in trading or brokerage, the choice of which contract to trade is a difficult bargaining problem. In a related model, Saloner (1984) has shown that Bertrand competition over brokerage fees among symmetrically defined floor brokers leads to equal shares of the trading volume and equal commissions. If we take this as a reasonable guideline, the members of a futures exchange would be close to unanimous in suport of that contract maximizing the volume[4] of trade.

Unfortunately, we are not able to deal directly with integer constraints on trade in combination with transactions costs, so the scaling of contracts is irrelevant, and the volume of trade is therefore indeterminate. Let us simplify as follows. First, we take the case of $N = 1$ contract to be chosen, and fix the scale of the contract to a standard deviation of 1. We can substitute the equilibrium futures price q from (8) into the agents' equilibrium futures positions in (9) and sum up the absolute values of these positions to obtain the total volume of trade:

$$V(D) = \gamma \mathrm{cov}(D, e_S \gamma_S - e_L \gamma_L), \tag{10}$$

where:

$e_S = \Sigma_{i: \theta^i < 0} \; e^i$, the sum of endowments on the short side.

$\gamma_S = (\Sigma_{i: \theta^i < 0} \; \gamma_i^{-1})^{-1}$, the "harmonic mean" of risk aversion on the short side.

$e_L = \Sigma_{i:\,\theta^i>0}\ e^i$, the sum of endowments on the long side.
$\gamma_L = (\Sigma_{i:\,\theta^i>0}\gamma_i^{-1})^{-1}$, the "harmonic mean" of risk aversion on the long side.

This leaves the innovation problem:

$$\max_{D\in L}\ V(D) \text{ subject to } \mathrm{sdev}(D)=1. \tag{11}$$

PROPOSITION 4   If D solves the innovation problem (11), and any trade occurs, then $\mathrm{corr}(D, e_S\gamma_S - e_L\gamma_L)=1$.

Interpreting, if a contract maximizes the volume of trade, fixing its scale, it must be perfectly correlated with the "target risk" to be hedged in endowments, the weighted sum of endowments on the two sides of the markets, with the weight on each side equal to the effective risk aversion of that side. This is consistent with an old maxim of Holbrook Working (1953) that the volume of trade in a futures contract is determined by hedging demand.

This characterization of optimal contract choice is incomplete in that the target risk $\eta(D) = e_S\gamma_S - e_L\gamma_L$ of the set D of contracts depends on the identity of long and short traders, which in turn depends on the contract D itself. The following complete characterization states that, in addition to designing a contract perfectly correlated with the target risk, a contract must single out the target risk that is as large as possible, in the sense of standard deviation.

PROPOSITION 5   A contract D^* with $\mathrm{sdev}(D^*)=1$ solves problem (11) if and only if $\mathrm{corr}[D^*,\eta(D^*)]=1$ and $\mathrm{sdev}[\eta(D^*)] \geq \mathrm{sdev}[\eta(D)]$ for all D in L.

A proof is given in Duffie and Jackson (1989). Empirical support for this sort of result can be found in Black (1986) and Johnson and McConnell (1989).

Now consider the multicontract case. Suppose $D_{-N} \equiv (D_1, \ldots, D_{N-1})$ forms the given $N-1$ contracts and that an exchange can choose any new contract D_N in L. We assume that D_{-N} has a non-singular covariance matrix. In this setting, it is only the portion of D_N orthogonal to D_{-N} that really matters as far as consumption allocations are concerned. We speak of orthogonality in the usual sense[5] of minimum variance projection, under which the portion of any x in L orthogonal to $(D_1, \ldots, D_{N-1})$ is defined as:

$$\Pi^\top(x|D_{-N}) = x - \mathrm{cov}(x, D_{-N})\mathrm{cov}(D_{-N})^{-1}D_{-N}.$$

For example, we define the innovation of a new contract D_N given D_{-N} to be the orthogonal component $\Pi^\top(D_N|D_{-N})$.

For reasons explained with examples in Duffie and Jackson (1989), it is natural to fix the scale of a new contract in terms of the standard deviation of its innovation. For any contract j, let $V_j(D)$ denote the volume of trade in the j-th contract in an equilibrium with given contracts $D = (D_1, \ldots, D_N)$. Assuming the innovator again has an incentive to maximize volume of trade in the new contract, given $D_{-j} = (D_1, \ldots, D_{j-1}, D_{j+1}, \ldots, D_N)$, this leaves the innovation problem:

$$\max_{D_j \in L} \quad V_j(D) \text{ subject to sdev}[\Pi^\top (D_j | D_{-j})] = 1. \tag{12}$$

This objective is unreasonable for an exchange with established contracts whose volume of trade is also to be considered as it introduces a new contract. There is nevertheless a theoretical lesson to be learned. The solution to (12) is the natural extension of that given by propositions 4 and 5. As before, given D, let $\eta_j(D)$ denote that "target risk" of the j-th contract, defined by:

$$\eta_j(D) = e_{S(j)} \gamma_{S(j)} - e_{L(j)} \gamma_{L(j)},$$

with $e_{S(j)} = \Sigma_{i \,:\, \theta^i_j < 0} e^i$, the sum of endowments on the short side of the j-th contract, and with $e_{L(j)}$, $\gamma_{S(j)}$, and $\gamma_{L(j)}$ analogously defined.

PROPOSITION 6   Suppose $D = (D_1, \ldots, D_N)$ is a set of linearly independent contracts normalized so that, for all j, sdev$[\Pi^\top (D_j | D_{-j})] = 1$. Then, for each j, the contract D_j solves (12) given D_{-j} if and only if corr$[D_j, \eta_j(D)] = 1$ and the standard deviation of $\Pi^\top [\eta_j(D) | D_{-j}]$ is maximal.

A (pure strategy) Nash equilibrium among N exchanges, each choosing a single futures contract, is a set $D = (D_1, \ldots, D_N)$ of contracts with the property that, for each j, the contract D_j solves (12) given D_{-j}. For example, consider the sequential innovation defined by D_1 solving (12) for $N = 1$, D_2 solving (12) given D_1 for $N = 2$, D_3 solving (12) given (D_1, D_2) for $N = 3$, and so on. Provided this results in a set D of linearly independent contracts, then D is a Nash equilibrium.

A set D of futures contracts is defined to be Pareto optimal if the resulting equilibrium allocation of consumption in L^m is not Pareto dominated by the equilibrium allocation, given any other set of N contracts. Duffie and Jackson (1989) show that, for the case $N = 1$, the contract choice is Pareto optimal. That is, in the simple monopolistic setting, the incentives of the innovating entrepreneur are aligned with social objectives, at least in the traditional sense of welfare economics. In the oligopolistic case $N > 1$, however, Duffie and Jackson (1989) show examples of both Pareto optimal and strictly suboptimal Nash equilibria. It is true, nevertheless, that, for given D_{-j}, any solution to (12) is Pareto optimal.

4.3   A simple model of spanning, liquidity, and innovation

This subsection is based on Cuny (1989), which extends the model of spanning and innovation discussed in the previous subsection to treat the issue of liquidity. The basic idea is that agents interested in reducing risk may turn away from a contract offering a superior hedge unless it offers reasonable liquidity. A famous example, but only one of many, is the failure of the North Pacific Coast wheat futures contract introduced in 1950 by the Chicago Board of Trade as an alternative to the standard hard wheat contract. Despite the fact that it offered hedgers of Pacific north-west wheat a better hedge than the standard hard wheat contract, the new contract's liquidity was judged to be much inferior, and the new contract failed from lack of volume. The liquidity judgment was of course self-fulfilling.

We will now examine a basic model in which hedgers consider both the hedging quality of a contract as well as the liquidity of the market in that contract, in terms of the slope of the supply function of the market. A large market order to buy in an illiquid contract, for example, is presumed to be executed at a higher average price than that of a small order to buy. A futures exchange, understanding the connection between liquidity, hedging quality, and volume of trade, chooses a contract as well as the price of membership conveying the right to trade that contract so as to maximize the total revenue from membership sales. For example, by setting relatively low membership prices, an exchange might hope to be compensated for from the reduced revenue on each seat by selling more seats, with a resulting higher level of liquidity that will in turn draw in additional hedging volume, justifying the price of a seat to broker–traders. An equilibrium is a set of contracts, seat prices, decisions by broker–traders of which exchange to join, market supply functions, and market-clearing utility-maximizing trades by hedgers and brokers. All of this is formalized below. Needless to say, the model is based on restrictive assumptions. It nevertheless delivers the sort of equilibrium behavior that one would expect based on the incentives of all agents.

The consumption space L, hedgers' endowments $e^1, \ldots, e^m$, and hedgers' utility functions $U_1, \ldots, U_m$ are exactly as specified in the previous subsection. For simplicity, all hedgers have the same risk-aversion coefficient, γ_H. There is also a continuum of brokers in one-to-one correspondence with an interval $[0,B]$. Like hedgers, brokers have utility functions of the von Neumann–Morgenstern constant absolute risk-averse variety, with coefficient γ_B of risk aversion. Brokers have zero endowments.

Hedger problem
Just as before, each hedger takes as given a set $D = (D_1, \ldots, D_N) \in L^N$ of futures contracts, but, rather than a fixed futures price q, hedger i takes as

given for each contract j an affine inverse market supply function p_{ij} defined by an intercept coefficient A_{ij} and slope coefficient with reciprocal l_j. That is, a market order by hedger i for a position of ϕ in contract j will be executed at the average futures price $p_{ij}(\phi) = A_{ij} + \phi/l_j$. Clearly, l_j is a measure of liquidity in the market for contract j; with infinite liquidity corresponding to the usual Walrasian model and zero liquidity making it impossible to effect a trade. The resulting inverse supply function for hedger i in all N contracts is denoted $p_i : \mathbb{R}^N \to \mathbb{R}^N$. This leaves hedger i with the problem:

$$\max_{\theta \in \mathbb{R}^N} \quad U_H(\theta \cdot [D - p_i(\theta)] + e^i). \tag{14}$$

Broker problem
A broker is allowed to trade only in that market, say j, in which the broker has purchased a membership. A broker is infinitesimal and therefore not concerned with liquidity in the execution of his or her own trades. Given a set D of contracts and corresponding futures prices given by $q \in \mathbb{R}^N$, a broker in market j therefore chooses a futures position ϕ_j solving the problem:

$$\max_{\phi \in \mathbb{R}} \quad U_B[(D_j - q_j)\phi]. \tag{15}$$

The certainty equivalent value of trading in market j is defined as that constant, denoted $V_j(D,q)$, with the property that the maximum defined by (15) is equal to $U_B[V_j(D,q)]$. Given D,q, and membership prices in the N markets, one for each contract, defined by a vector $k \in \mathbb{R}^N$, this leaves any broker with the maximum total certainty equivalent problem:

$$\max_{j \in \{0,1,\ldots,N\}} \quad V_j(D,q) - k_j, \tag{16}$$

where a choice of 0 is defined to give a total certainty equivalent of 0 and corresponds to membership in no markets at all.

Trading equilibrium
Given markets characterized by a set D of contracts with associated membership prices k, a trading equilibrium is a collection:

$$\{\theta^i, \phi_j, A_{ij}, l_j, v_j, q_j\}, i \in \{1, \ldots, m\}, j \in \{1, \ldots, N\},$$

such that:

1   For all i, the position θ^i solves (14) given the inverse supply function p_i characterized, for each contract j, by A_{ij} and l_j.

2 Given the futures price vector q, for all $j\in\{1, \ldots,N\}$, a subset of measure v_j of brokers solve (16) with j and (15) with ϕ_j, while a subset of measure $B-\Sigma_{j=1}^N v_j \geq 0$ solve (16) with 0.

3 Futures markets clear: for all j, $v_j\phi_j+\Sigma_{i=1}^m \theta_{ij}=0$.

4 Prices satisfy expectations: for all i and j, $q^j=A_{ij}+\theta_{ij}/l_j$.

In order to simplify the exposition, for some integer r we can take an orthonormal basis $z=(z_1, \ldots,z_r)\in L^r$ for the span of $\{e^1, \ldots,e^m, D_1, \ldots,D_N\}$, and represent total endowments by $e_1 + \cdots + e^m=\eta^T z$, for some $\eta\in\mathbb{R}^r$, and each security j by $D_j=\delta_j^T z$, for some $\delta_j\in\mathbb{R}^r$. In order to characterize a trading equilibrium, for each contract j let:

$$G_j=\left(I+\frac{\gamma H}{m+1}\sum_{n\neq j} l_n\delta_n\delta_n^T\right)^{-1}.$$

Cuny (1989) shows that, for any vector $\alpha\in\mathbb{R}^r$, $\alpha^T G_j z$ is the same as the orthogonal projection $\Pi^\perp(\alpha^T z|D_{-j})$ provided the liquidity l_n in each market n is infinite, and otherwise G_j corresponds to this projection operator corrected by weighting the effect of each contract by the liquidity in that contract's market. For example, $\eta^T G_j z$ is roughly speaking that portion of the total endowment that cannot be hedged in the contracts other than j, after correcting the hedging power of any market n by the liquidity l_n of that market.

PROPOSITION 6   Given membership prices $k\in\mathbb{R}^N$ and linearly independent contracts $D\in L^N$, there exists a constant β such that, if the measure B of brokers is greater than β, then there exists a trading equilibrium $\{\theta_i,\phi_j,A_{ij},l_j,v_j,q_j\}$ with the following properties:

1 The liquidity in market j is $l_j=v_j/\gamma_B$.

2 The measure of brokers in market j is:

$$v_j=s_j(\delta_j,k_j)\equiv\max\left(0,\frac{\sqrt{\gamma_B\delta_j^T G_j SG_j\delta_j/2k_j}-Q}{\delta_j^T G_j\delta_j}\right),\qquad(17)$$

where $S=\eta\eta^T$ and $Q=(m+1)\gamma_B/\gamma_H$.

Cuny identifies the constant β, proves this result, and provides several additional properties of a trading equilibrium. Property 1 shows that liquidity is directly proportional to the measure of brokers in a market.

Contract choice problem

The problem of exchange j in choosing (δ_j,k_j) is to maximize its revenue $k_j v_j$ from membership sales, given the formula (17) for v_j determined by the characteristics $\{(\delta_h, k_h, v_h) : h \neq j\}$ of the other exchanges. Without loss of generality, we restrict the choice of δ_j by exchange j to the unit ball $C = \{\alpha \in \mathbb{R}^r : \|\alpha\| = 1\}$. The following result is degenerate unless the rank of the total endowment matrix $S = \eta\eta^\top$ is r, which presents a problem, since, as defined, S clearly of rank 1. Cuny instead presents his results in a T-period setting, with i.i.d. futures contracts payoffs and endowments independently distributed across periods, but not identically distributed. That is, $\{z_t = (z_{1t}, \ldots, z_{rt})\}$ is i.i.d., each contract j is traded once each period with payoff $\delta^\top_j z_t$ in period t for fixed δ_j, and the total endowment in period t is $\eta^\top_t z_t$ for $\eta_t \in \mathbb{R}^r$ depending on t. In that case, all results go through replacing $S = \eta\eta^\top$ everywhere with $S = \Sigma^T_{t=1} \eta_t \eta^\top_t$, which can easily have rank r. Proposition 6 applies in this T-period setting with this definition of S; details are found in Cuny's paper.

PROPOSITION 7   Suppose the set D of contracts is linearly independent, $S = \Sigma^T_{t=1} \eta_t \eta^\top_t$ has full rank r, and the measure B of brokers is larger than $NQ\lambda^+_S / \lambda^-_S$, where λ^+_S and λ^-_S are the maximum and minimum eigenvalues of S, respectively. Then the problem:

$$\max_{(\hat{\delta}, \hat{k}) \in C \times \mathbb{R}_+} \hat{k} s_j(\hat{\delta}, kc)$$

of maximizing the total revenue from memberships sold to brokers is solved by letting $k_j = \gamma_B \delta^\top_j G_j S G_j \delta_j / (8Q^2)$ and by letting δ_j be any eigenvector of SG_j having its maximal eigenvalue.

The proposition implies that it is optimal for exchange j to choose a contract that, after factoring out with G_j the portion of endowments that can be efficiently hedged on other markets (accounting for liquidity effects), is the principal component of the remaining portion of endowment risk S, in the sense of maximal eigenvectors.

Finally, Cuny gives a theorem for the existence of an equilibrium:

$$\{(\delta_j, k_j), \theta^i, \phi_j, A_{ij}, l_j, v_j, q_j\}, i \in \{1, \ldots, m\}, j \in \{1, \ldots, N\},$$

defined by the properties that $\{\theta^i, \phi_j, A_{ij}, l_j, v_j, q_j\}$ is a trading equilibrium given $\{(\delta_j, k_j)\}$, and for each exchange j, (δ_j, k_j) maximizes sales revenue $v_j k_j$ from memberships in the sense of the last proposition. (The existence result is degenerate except in the multiperiod setting explained before the statement of proposition 7.) Cuny's proof is by construction.

In any equilibrium, no two exchanges choose the same contract, and for any two contracts D_h and D_j:

$$v_j \geq \frac{Q}{\sqrt{1 - [\text{corr}(D_h, D_j)]^2}}. \tag{18}$$

An examination of Cuny's results shows that exchanges in this model compete on two dimensions, liquidity and correlation with agents' endowments. In equilibrium, two exchanges choose contracts relatively highly correlated with one another only if there is a relatively large concentration of endowment risk nearby both contracts (measuring size and nearness in the sense of the standard deviation metric on L).

Other aspects of the innovation problem are studied by Allen and Gale (1988), Anderson and Harris (1986), Carlton (1983), Gale (1989), Ross (1989), and Miller (1986).

5   ASSET PRICING IN INCOMPLETE MARKETS

This section treats asset pricing in incomplete markets. The topic is covered in the literature and here mainly by example or empirical work, since there is little in the way of a general theory at this time.

5.1   The benchmark model

We consider the model $(\mathcal{E},D)$ of an economy from section 2, with a single consumption commodity ($l=1$). Under regularity conditions A–E of section 3.2, the existence of an equilibrium $(p,q,(x^1,\theta^1), \ldots,(x^m,\theta^m))$ with strictly positive spot commodity prices p and consumption allocation $(x^1, \ldots,x^m)$ is guaranteed. It is natural to take the single commodity as a numeraire in each state and date. We therefore normalize to the "real" prices $\hat{q}=q/p_0$ and real dividends $\hat{D}_s=D_s(p)/p_s$, state by state. If we assume that the utility function U_i has a vector $\partial U_i(x^i)\in L_{++}$ of partial derivatives in equilibrium, the first-order conditions for problem (1)-(2)-(3) give the well-known equation for real security prices as ratios of marginal rates of substitution:

$$\hat{q}^\top =\frac{1}{\partial U_i(x^i)_0} \partial U_i(x^i)_1 \hat{D}. \tag{19}$$

It is common to endow the set $\Omega= \{1, \ldots,S\}$ of states with the algebra $\mathcal{F}$ of all subsets and with a probability measure P, and to treat any vector in R^S as a random variable on $(\Omega,\mathcal{F},P)$. If it happens that there is a von Neumann–Morgenstern utility index $u_i: R_+ \to R$ with $U_i(x)=u_i(x_0)+ E[u_i(x_1)]$ (under this probability space), then (19) is equivalent to the familiar expression:

$$\hat{q}=\frac{1}{u_i'(x_0^i)} E[u_i'(x_1^i)\hat{D}], \tag{20}$$

with the obvious notational convention.

The traditional approach to asset pricing theory has been to assume either a single agent or complete markets. The two assumptions generate roughly the same asset pricing implications since both imply Pareto optimality of equilibria. For example, in the complete markets case, Pareto optimality is implied by the first welfare theorem, and from this the vectors $\partial U_1(x^1), \ldots, \partial U_m(x^m)$ are colinear. Defining, for given "utility weights" $\lambda \in \mathbb{R}^m_{++}$, the utility function:

$$U_\lambda(x) = \max_{y^1 + \ldots + y^m \leq x} \sum_i \lambda_i U_i(y^i), \tag{21}$$

it follows from Pareto optimality and regular preference assumptions (Debreu, 1972, 1976) that there exists λ such that $\partial U_\lambda(e)$ (which exists by the implicit function theorem) is colinear with $\partial U_i(x^i)$ for all i. From this, (p,q) is also an equilibrium set of prices for the one-agent economy with the same aggregate endowment e and the utility function U_λ. In particular, we have (19) in the form:

$$\hat{q}^\top = \frac{1}{\partial U_\lambda(e)_0} \partial U_\lambda(e)_1 \hat{D}. \tag{22}$$

In the above special case of expected utility representations for all utility functions (with a common probability measure):

$$\hat{q} = \frac{1}{u'_\lambda(e_0)} E[u'_\lambda(e_1)\hat{D}], \tag{23}$$

where $u_\lambda(x) = \max\{\lambda_1 u_1(y^1) + \cdots + \lambda_m u_m(y_m) : y_1 + \cdots + y_m \leq x\}$. Indeed, there are very few asset pricing models that are not effectively of the form of (23), and most of the exceptions are of the form (22) for a single agent having some non-separable utility function, such as the Epstein–Zin (1989) recursive utility model. For example (23) includes in effect the capital asset pricing model of Sharpe (1964) and Lintner (1965) and its extension to multiple periods (in various settings) by Rubinstein (1976), Lucas (1978), Breeden (1979), and Cox, Ingersoll, and Ross (1985). In a multiperiod setting, one replaces the dividend $\hat{D}$ in (23) with the total real payoff, price plus dividend, of the securities in the following period, and the utility functions usually incorporate some time-discounting effect.

5.2   The CAPM

A standard asset pricing model such as (23) is viewed as useful because it relates security prices (or returns) to the aggregate consumption e, which is arguably an observable macroeconomic variable. Such a relationship can be used to test various specifications of the model and to estimate equilibrium security prices. For example, if u_i is quadratic for all i (and strictly increasing at the equilibrium allocation), then u_λ is quadratic and (23) implies that there are constants k_1 and k_2 such that:

$$\hat{q}^\top = k_1 E(\hat{D}) + k_2 \text{cov}(\hat{D}, e_1). \tag{24}$$

One can alternatively derive (24) directly from (23), the assumption that u_λ'' exists and satisfies a growth condition, joint normality, and Rubinstein's identity: $\text{cov}[u_\lambda'(e_1)\hat{D}] = E[u_\lambda''(e_1)]\text{cov}(e_1, \hat{D})$. From (24) one has the CAPM: for each asset j with non-zero price q_j, the return $R_j = \hat{D}_j/\hat{q}_j$ satisfies:

$$E(R_j) - E(R_0) = \beta_j[E(R_*) - E(R_0)], \tag{25}$$

where:

R_0 is the return on a portfolio θ of securities whose total payoff $\hat{D}\theta$ is uncorrelated with aggregate consumption e_1.

R_* is the return on a portfolio θ of securities whose payoff $\hat{D}\theta$ has maximal correlation with aggregate consumption e_1.

$\beta_j = \text{cov}(R_j, R_*)/\text{var}(R_*)$ is the "beta" of security j.

With quadratic utility, the CAPM (25) applies whether or not markets are complete, and whether or not individual endowments are in the span of security dividends. If endowments are spanned, then the equilibrium consumption allocation is Pareto optimal and (23) applies. If not, then (20) still leads to (25). (Endowments are spanned in the original CAPM of Sharpe and Lintner because they are in the form of endowments of securities.) As shown by Breeden (1979), roughly the same CAPM applies without quadratic utility in a continuous-time setting, replacing moments with "infinitesimal moments," in the usual sense of Ito calculus.

5.3   The implication of Pareto inoptimality

Assuming stationarity, Hansen and Singleton (1982) tested the multiperiod analogue of (23):

$$\hat{q}_t = \frac{\rho}{u_\lambda'(e_t)} E[u_\lambda'(e_{t+1})(\hat{D}_{t+1} + \hat{q}_{t+1}) | \mathscr{F}_t], \tag{26}$$

where $\rho > 0$ is a constant discount factor, time subscripts indicate periods in the obvious fashion, and $\mathscr{F}_t$ is the σ-algebra representing information available at time t. This extension is justified by complete markets and restrictions on individual utility functions. Under the assumption that

$u_\lambda(c) = (c^{\gamma+1} - 1)/(\gamma + 1)$ for some constant $\gamma < 0$, Hansen and Singleton estimated the parameters ρ and γ using generalized instrumental variables. Their results, and many others to follow, show that the model does not conform well to consumption and security price data, at least for what are commonly felt to be reasonable choices of parameters. In particular, it has been asserted that expected returns on risky assets are exceptionally high, relative to less risky assets (Mehra and Prescott, 1985), and that (in a more restrictive setting) the volatility of security prices is in excess of that dictated by the model. On the "excess volatility" debate, see, for example, Shiller (1979, 1981), LeRoy and Porter (1981), LeRoy (1984), and Kleidon (1986).

Assuming that history has not been a misleading outlier, the representative–agent model (25) could perform in practice for any of a number of reasons, including:

1   incomplete markets (for example, Bewley, 1982; Mankiw, 1986; Weil 1990).
2   short sales and borrowing constraints (for example, Bewley, 1982; Scheinkman and Weiss, 1986).
3   transactions costs (for example, Grossman and Laroque, 1989).
4   misspecification of the representative utility function U_λ (for example, Constantinides, 1990; Epstein and Zin, 1989; Sundaresan, 1989).
5   non-stationarity of the relevant stochastic processes.
6   failure of "rational expectations behavior," by which we mean optimizing behavior relative to a common statistical model for uncertainty that is consistent with observations.
7   noisy data, especially incomplete or time-aggregated consumption series (for example, Grossman and Shiller, 1982; Hansen and Singleton, 1988; Heaton, 1988; and references therein).

Obviously, the first three are of the same variety, each implying that agents will not bring their utility gradients into colinearity because of limited access to markets. (It is worth noting that asymmetric information among agents and the absence of arbitrage implies incomplete markets, and that the converse is to be expected.)

Bewley (1982) has an excellent discussion, with examples, of the impact of the first three connected explanations for security price behavior in incomplete markets. The spirit of Bewley's approach can be found again in illuminating examples due to Mankiw (1986) and Weil (1990), on which we now focus.

5.4   The return premium puzzles

The following example of the impact of incomplete markets on asset prices is a simplified version of an example due to Weil (1990), who addresses the security return puzzles of Mehra and Prescot (1985). As with Mankiw's (1986) precursor example, Weil's premise is that these puzzles may arise from inappropriately assuming that agents have access to complete security markets.

In this example, agents are completely symmetrically defined. They have the same utility function U given by $U(x) = u(x_0) + E[u(x_1)]$, as in section 5.1, with u increasing, differentiable, and strictly concave. The endowment e^i of any agent i is $e_0^i = y_0 > 0$ in period zero. The endowments $\{e_1^1, \ldots, e_1^m\}$ in period 1 are symmetrically distributed and non-degenerate positive random variables with finite expectation. With complete markets, the efficiency of equilibrium allocations and symmetry imply an equilibrium in which all agents have the same consumption x^*, with $x_0^* = y_0$ and with $x_1^* = \bar{e} \equiv (e_1^1 + \cdots + e_1^m)/m$, providing some diversification of the second-period endowment risk.

For the incomplete markets case, suppose the N given securities have non-negative payoffs $D = (D_1, \ldots, D_N)$ such that $\{(e^1, D), (e^2, D), \ldots, (e^m, D)\}$ is symmetrically distributed. (In Weil's own example, $D = (1, d)$, where d is independent of $\{e_1^1, \ldots, e_1^m\}$, which is itself i.i.d., yielding our symmetry assumption[6].) In a symmetric incomplete-markets equilibrium with consumption allocation $\{x_1^1, \ldots, x_1^m\}$, the real security price vector is given by the first order conditions of any agent i as:

$$\hat{q} = \frac{E[u'(x_1^i)D]}{u'(y_0)}.$$

(We do not investigate the existence of symmetric equilibria. Under Weil's additional statistical assumptions, however, the autarchic symmetric equilibrium suffices for our purposes.) Adding up the previous equation across the set of agents and dividing by m:

$$\hat{q} = \frac{E[[u'(x_1^1) + \cdots + u'(x_1^m)]D]}{mu'(y_0)}. \tag{27}$$

We will compare this incomplete-markets security price vector $\hat{q}$ with its complete-markets counterpart:

$$q^* = \frac{E[u'(\bar{e}_1)D]}{u'(y_0)}. \tag{28}$$

PROPOSITION 8   If u' is convex, then $\hat{q} \geq q^*$.

The inequality given by this result holds strictly if u' is strictly convex and $x_1^i - \bar{e}_1$ is not in the span of D. The proposition states that, with convex marginal utility, the expected returns on all securities are higher in the complete markets setting. The proof is an easy application of Jensen's Inequality (but not as applied in Weil's example). Specifically, for each state s, the convexity of u' implies that:

$$\frac{u'(x_{1s}^1) + \cdots + u'(x_{1s}^m)}{m} \geq u'\left(\frac{x_{1s}^1 + \cdots + x_{1s}^m}{m}\right) = u'(\bar{e}_1).$$

Since this holds for all s, the positivity of D implies the result. The result extends beyond our given distributional assumptions under special utility assumptions such as $u(x) = x^\alpha, \alpha \in (0,1)$.

If one is willing to rest weight on this example, the puzzlingly low risk-free rate pointed out by Mehra and Prescott (1985) may be due to a misspecification of the model: Mehra and Prescott assumed the existence of a representative agent, or equivalently in this setting, the completeness of markets. The convexity of u' is also necessary for the price ordering given by this proposition if this same ordering is to apply to every possible choice for D. Of course, concave marginal utility would reverse the inequalities and rule out incomplete markets as an explanation.

As for the equity premium[7] puzzle of Mehra and Prescott (1985), Weil (1990) goes on to establish a sufficient condition on preferences for the same explanation: an inappropriate assumption of complete markets. In this case, the sufficient condition involves information about the fourth derivative of the utility function! Assuming enough smoothness, let $\mathcal{P}(\cdot)$ be defined by $\mathcal{P}(x) = -u'''(x)/u''(x)$, and be dubbed the "absolute prudence" of u. Under the assumption that $\mathcal{P}$ has a negative derivative, Weil shows that the equity premium is larger for incomplete markets than for complete markets (for sufficiently large m). He also points out that a HARA-class utility function that has decreasing absolute risk aversion also has decreasing absolute prudence.

5.5   The "volatility" of state prices

Hansen and Jaganathan (1990) address the excess volatility debate by estimating a lower bound on the variance of state prices, that is, the intertemporal marginal rates of substitution for wealth, state by state. Beyond their new econometric theory, Hansen and Jaganathan confirm that states prices are considerably more volatile than would be the case with a single representative agent using a classical additive separable utility function. While they examine more general utility models of the habit-persistence variety as an explanation for this "excess volatility," one may also explore the contributing role of market incompleteness. Is there a natural tendency for greater market incompleteness to lead to greater state-price volatility? We now look at two examples giving opposite hints on this question.

We are given security prices $q \in \mathbb{R}^N$ for security payoffs $D = (D^1, \ldots, D^N)$ as before, and take all random variables below to be of finite variance. Merely the linearity of pricing implies the existence of some unique portfolio payoff $\pi = \alpha^\top D$, such that $q = E(\pi D)$. Interpreting π as intertemporal marginal rates of substitution projected on to the span of security payoffs, Hansen and Jaganathan are interested in a lower bound on the standard deviation of π. They work in a multiperiod stationary setting; one should see their chapter for many important details neglected here. Figure 4.1 shows, for each possible level of $E(\pi)$ (the price of real discount bond, should one exist), an estimated lower bound on the standard deviation of π, based on the annual data on stocks and bonds for 1889 to 1985 used by Campbell and Shiller (1988). Also shown is a series of estimates of $(E(\pi), \text{sdev}(\pi))$ corresponding to a range of parameter choices for a single-agent model with additive-separable discounted power utility for consumption. Reasonable parameter choices bring one far below the lower bound on the standard deviation of π suggested directly by the security price data and the given representative agent.

The example of section 5.4 serves as one potential explanation of this apparent violation of the lower bound on state–price volatility. Returning to that example, and taking precisely the same symmetry assumptions, we assume for simplicity that there is a non-zero constant (riskless payoff) in the span of D. The first-order condition (20) implies that:

$$\pi = \Pi \left(\frac{u'(x_1^i)}{u'(x_0^i)} \middle| D \right), \tag{29}$$

where $\Pi(\cdot | D)$ denotes the L^2-projection on to the span of the security payoffs. More explicitly:

$$\pi = \frac{E[u'(x_1^i)D]^\top}{u'(x_0^i)} [E(DD^\top)]^{-1} D. \tag{30}$$

The corresponding projection of state prices for the complete markets case is denoted π^*. The identical arguments applied above in section 5.4 show that $\text{var}(\pi) \geq \text{var}(\pi^*)$ for convex u'. The required calculations are left to the reader, and are a bit easier if, without loss of generality, one takes $D_1, \ldots, D^N$ to be an orthonormal basis for the span of security payoffs. The

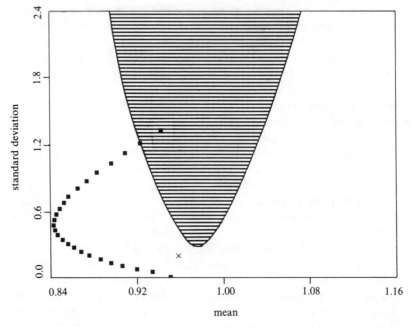

Figure 4.1 Variance bounds from Hansen and Jaganathan (1989)

ordering is strict with the non-degeneracies discussed after the statement of proposition 8. The intuition is that, by opening up enough markets to effectively diversify idiosyncratic endowment risk, the volatility of state prices is reduced.

While natural enough with convex marginal utility, this intuition would be almost completely overturned by examining the Hansen–Jaganathan volatility bounds under the CAPM model (24). With quadratic utility, we have:

$$\pi = \pi_D \equiv \Pi(\delta + k\delta e \,|\, D), \tag{31}$$

where δ is the risk-free discount (the price of a one-period real bond) and k is a constant that does not depend on D. It follows that the Sharpe Ratio sdev$(\pi_D)/E(\pi_D)$ is always increasing in the span of security markets with quadratic expected utility. The same is true with expected exponential utility and joint-normal distributions. In this sense, one estimates ever higher volatility bounds on state prices as markets are added, contrary to the intuition of the Weil example, and not suggesting the incompleteness of markets as an explanation of the Hansen–Jaganathan empirical results in a CAPM setting. (The same conclusion applies to the CAPM when one uses the Hansen–Jaganathan lower-bound estimator for state price volatility that incorporates the no-arbitrage restriction.)

Independently, Telmer (1990) has also proposed incompleteness of markets as a possible explanation for the results of Hansen and Jaganathan. He has constructed a simple two-heterogeneous-agent model in the spirit of Lucas (1978), solved it numerically, and compared the "volatility" of intertemporal marginal rates of substitution (IMRS) of this model and a corresponding one-agent model. He concludes: "while the incomplete-markets economies can account for approximately 7 times more of the variability in the equilibrium IMRS than the complete-markets model, the best case still results in a value that is roughly half of the most liberal Hansen–Jaganathan lower bound reported . . .. The reason for this is quite surprising. Despite a significant incompleteness in asset markets, agents are able to pool quite a substantial portion [of] their idiosyncratic risk using only a riskfree bond." Aiyagari and Gertler (1990), Marcet and Singleton (1990), Deborah Lucas (1990), Mace (1989), and Judd (1990) have also prepared numerical examples of heterogeneous agent incomplete-markets in the spirit of Lucas (1978). At this writing, it seems too early to summarize the implications of their work for asset prices.

Additional impressions of asset pricing in incomplete markets can be found in Hirshleifer (1988), Scheinkman (1989), Svennsson and Werner (1990), and the references therein.

6   THE FIRM IN INCOMPLETE MARKETS

This section[8] briefly reviews the firm's production and financial decisions in incomplete markets. The point of departure is the same Arrow–Debreu formulation of the Walrasian equilibrium model of section 2, augmented with endowments of shares of a firm defined as a production set $Y \subset L = \mathbb{R}^l \times (\mathbb{R}^l)^S$.

The competitive theory of the firm in incomplete markets is still unsatisfactory. We do not know how a firm could maximize its market value when it cannot infer from the available market prices the market values of all feasible production choices. Even if it could correctly infer value, it is not at all obvious that the firm's shareholders would support value maximization. Value maximization is unanimously supported provided shareholders ignore the spanning effect of the firm's payoffs (Makowski, 1980, 1983). Otherwise, one faces a difficult conflict of interest (Duffie and Shafer, 1986b). Within the Arrow–Debreu framework, the Modigliani–Miller theory of irrelevance of financial policy has been extended to a general setting with incomplete markets. This pushes the search for an explanation of financial transactions on the part of the firm (such as borrowing, financial hedging, share repurchase, and security investments) into rather difficult considerations such as taxes, transactions costs, credit constraints, asymmetric information, or non-competitive behavior (say, in a strategic context of corporate takeovers).

We will make a quick survey of the available theory, narrowly concentrating on the financial and production decisions of the firm, assuming incomplete markets for contingent claims in a competitive setting. We also touch briefly on issues of corporate control and the capital structure of the firm.

6.1   Shareholder agreement

In the Arrow–Debreu formulation of an economy, a "firm" is a subset Y of a consumption space L and the associated non-negative fractions $(\hat{\theta}_1, \ldots, \hat{\theta}_m)$ of the value of its production choice from Y that accrue to the m respective shareholders. Although this "anorexic" model (Oliver Hart's metaphor) neglects the formation and internal organization of the firm, it is adequate for a competitive theory of production choice in complete markets. Indeed, the following justification of value maximization by the firm with complete markets is so obvious and trivial that it does not seem to be credited to anyone. Fix a price vector ψ, a linear functional on L. A production choice y in Y is *value maximizing* if $\psi \cdot y \geq \psi \cdot y'$ for all y' in Y. Any consumer i, given control of the firm, would choose a value-maximizing production choice since an increase in $\hat{\theta}_i \psi \cdot y$ implies an expansion of the set of budget feasible choices for agent i. (If $\hat{\theta}_i > 0$ and consumer i is locally non-satiated, then consumer i would choose *only* a value-maximizing production choice.) In short, complete markets implies unanimity for value-maximizing production choices.

Wilson (1972) gave an example with incomplete markets in which no shareholder supports value maximization. This example can be generalized (Duffie and Shafer, 1986b). An even more general result seems possible, stating that for generic "smooth" economies, shareholders completely disagree with one another, in the sense that any two would prefer to adjust a given production choice in different directions. This difficulty rests with the fact that the span of markets is a strict subspace of the consumption space, and that this subspace can be moved by changing the firm's production choice. Even with identical preferences, shareholders would (generically) disagree on how to use the firm's production choice so as to insure themselves against their respective endowment risks. Of course, the problem can be circumvented by assuming that firms cannot affect the span of markets (Diamond (1967), Ekern and Wilson (1974), Radner (1974), Leland (1974)), or by supposing that at least shareholders assume so

(Makowski, 1983). Noteworthy is the fact that even a small firm, with unrestricted short sales of its stock, can in principle have a dramatic effect on the span of markets.

One may be brought to consider corporate control via some collective choice scheme, for example, a corporate charter that vests relative voting power according to the holdings of one or more classes of shares. The market for the firm's shares is then a natural mechanism for allocating corporate power, and leads toward (but need not arrive at) a relatively efficient production scheme, since an inefficient production choice would leave an incentive for profitable takeover. (Unfortunately, this is harder to model than my words here suggest.) The models of Grossman and Hart (1987) and Harris and Raviv (1988) indicate that the commonly observed one-share–one-vote decision mechanism has a natural place in supporting this efficient takeover mechanism. DeMarzo (1987) has shown that one-share–one-vote with majority rule (and non-strategic behavior) implies that the firm typically acts in the interests of its largest shareholder. We do not, however, have anything like general conditions for the existence of equilibrium with, say, a production choice that cannot be overturned by shareholders representing a majority of shares. (In fact, Gevers (1974) has an example of non-existence based on the well-known possibility of majority rule intransitivity.) A model of production choice with strategic share accumulation, extending for instance the work of Shleifer and Vishny (1986), may be called for; this would likely be quite complicated. The work of Aghion and Bolton (1988) deserves special mention, showing that the roles of equity shareholders and bondholders within the bankruptcy mechanism constitute a natural method of allocating control between an entrepreneur and an investor. Since their model has a single entrepreneur and a single investor, it does not, however, address how various holders of the same class of security would arrive at a common decision. Kihlstrom and Laffont (1982) went so far as to build a model in which firms arise in one-to-one correspondence with the types of consumers that invest in them, leading to an absence of conflict within each firm.

Further to the goals, efficiency, and control of the firm in incomplete markets, see Dreyfus (1984), Hart (1977), Leland (1973, 1978), Merton and Subrahmanyam (1974), and Stiglitz (1972, 1974).

6.2   Production indeterminacy and efficiency

We can illustrate some of the basic ideas of production indeterminacy with the model presented in section 2, adjusted slightly to include production. For simplicity, we take $l = 1$ commodity in each state, leaving the consumption space is $L = \mathbb{R} \times \mathbb{R}^S$ with a typical vector $x = (x_0, x_1)$ representing x_0 units of consumption (of a single commodity) at time zero, and x_{1s} units of consumption at time 1 in state s, for each state s in $\{1,2, \ldots,S\}$. There are N securities, defined by the vectors $y^1, \ldots,y^N$ in L. (Securities, here, pay dividends in both periods, as opposed to our earlier convention that dividends are paid only in the last period.) Let y_0 denote the vector $(y_0^1, \ldots,y_0^N)$ and y_1 denote the $S \times N$ matrix with (s,j)-element y_{1s}^j. Agent i is also endowed with θ_j^i units of security j. Given a vector $q \in \mathbb{R}^N$ for the *cum dividend* initial prices of the N securities, agent i then chooses:

$$(x^i,\theta^i) \in \arg\max_{(x,\theta) \in L_+ \times R^N} \quad U_i(x), \tag{32}$$

subject to:

$$x_0 - e_0^i - q \cdot (\hat{\theta}^i - \theta) - \theta \cdot y_0 = 0; \qquad x_1 - e_1^i - y_1\theta = 0,$$

generalizing (1)-(3).

The security price vector q is *arbitrage-free* if there is no portfolio $\theta \in \mathbb{R}^N$ with $\theta \cdot (q - y_0) \leq 0$ and $y_1\theta \geq 0$, with one of these two inequalities holding strictly. This is a necessary condition for the existence of a solution to (32), provided U_i is non-satiated. By the arguments of Ross (1978), if q is arbitrage-free, then there is some state price vector $\pi \in \mathbb{R}_{++}^S$ such that:

$$q = y_0 + y_1^{\mathsf{T}} \pi. \tag{33}$$

If y^j is to be chosen from a production set $Y_j \subset L$, one might therefore suggest that:

$$y^j \in \arg\max_{z \in Y_j} \quad z_0 + z_1^{\mathsf{T}} \pi. \tag{34}$$

An equilibrium is defined in the obvious way: a collection $(\pi,q,(x^i,\theta^i),(y^j))$ solving (32), (33), (34), and market clearing.

In complete markets the firm could infer the state price vector π from knowledge of the dividends and prices of all securities, and maximize the corresponding value of its production choice. With incomplete markets, however, the set of state prices (implied by y, q, and lack of arbitrage) has dimension $S - N$. Problem (34) is therefore indeterminate unless somehow the state prices are announced to the firm (perhaps as a function of endogenous parameters). Indeed, the set of equilibrium consumption allocations is (generically) S–N dimensional (contains an $(S - N)$-dimensional manifold) under regularity conditions described in Duffie and Shafer (1986b).

EXAMPLE (Duffie and Shafer, 1986b)   Consider an example with $m = 2$ agents, $S = 2$ states, and $N = 1$ firm. The agents' utility functions (restricted to $L_{++} \equiv \text{int}(L_+)$) are:

$$U_i(x) = \log(x_0) + \beta_1^i\log(x_{1,1}) + \beta_2^i\log(x_{1,2}), \qquad x \in L_{++},$$

for some $\beta^i \in \mathbb{R}^2_{++}, i \in \{1,2\}$. The production set is:

$$Y = \{y \in L : y_0 \le 0, \ y_1 \ge 0, \ y_1^\top y_1 - y_0\} - L_+.$$

That is, input of k units of consumption at time zero allows any output on the circle of radius $\sqrt{k}$ at time 1, with free disposal. The market maximizing production choice, given a state price vector π, is $y = (y_0, y_1) = (-\pi^\top \pi/4, \pi/2)$. The initial market value of the firm is thus $y_0 + \pi^\top y = \pi^\top \pi/4$. The problem of agent i is reduced to choosing the fraction θ^i of the firm to hold. It can be shown that the set of equilibrium allocations is generically a one-dimensional manifold. Consider the special case in which each agent is endowed with one unit of consumption at time zero, and none at time 1, with $\beta_1^i + \beta_2^i = 1$, and with $\theta^1 = \theta^2 = 1/2$. The set of equilibrium consumption allocations is in one-to-one correspondence with state prices $\pi \gg 0$ on the circle of radius $\sqrt{8/3}$. In figures 4.2 and 4.3, we graph the equilibria in terms of the monotonic transformation of utility:

$$u_i(x) = e^{U_i(x)}, \qquad i \in \{1,2\}.$$

The graph of equilibrium utilities for $\beta^1 = \beta^2$ is shown in figure 4.2. In this case, the equilibria are strictly Pareto ordered. The graph of equilibrium utilities for $\beta^1 = (\frac{1}{3}, \frac{2}{3})$ and $\beta^2 = (\frac{2}{3}, \frac{1}{3})$ is shown in figure 4.3 as the set of non-zero solutions to the cubic equation $u_1^6 + u_2^6 = k u_1^2 u_2^2$, for some scalar k. Only at point A in figure 4.3, does agent 2 agree with the production choice of the firm. [It also happens that A is the point of highest utility for agent 2 on the graph.] Similarly, agent 1 is in agreement with the firm's choice only at point B. This ends the example.

Drèze (1974) proposed a variation of the following scheme to eliminate the indeterminacy, ruling out short sales of securities. Suppose U_i is differentiable for all i, and at a given allocation $(x, \theta) = ((x^1, \theta^1), \ldots, (x^m, \theta^m))$ of consumption and shares, let $\pi^j(x, \theta)$ be a candidate state-price vector for firm j, defined by:

$$\pi^j(x, \theta) = \sum_{i=1}^{m} \theta_j^i \frac{\partial U_i(x^i)_1}{\partial U_i(x^i)_0}. \tag{35}$$

Firm j would then maximize "pseudo-value," using as state prices the share-weighted sum $\pi^j(x, \theta)$ of its shareholders' marginal rates of substitution. This is a uniquely defined objective for firm j (although different firms potentially apply different state prices) and leads to the existence of an equilibrium (with the obvious variation of the previous definition of equilibrium). Furthermore, in equilibrium, under typical convexity and monotonicity conditions:

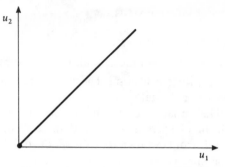

Figure 4.2 Equilibrium utilities for $\beta^1 = \beta^2$

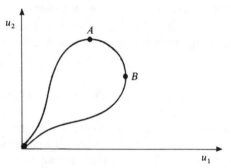

Figure 4.3 Equilibrium utilities for $\beta^1 \neq \beta^2$

For each firm j, $\pi^j(x,\theta)$ is indeed a state-price vector. In particular, the firm is not surprised, in that its maximal pseudo-value is equal to the stock price q_j commonly announced to agents.

For each firm j, fixing the production choices of other firms and the shareholdings of other agents, the production choice of firm j is Pareto optimal.

Fixing the production plans of all firms, the equilibrium distribution of shareholdings is Pareto optimal.

There are other schemes for defining state prices for each firm that result in an equilibrium with these properties. For example, one could replace the weight θ^i_j applied to agent i in the definition (35) of the state prices for firm j with some other agent weights. Grossman and Hart (1979), for example, use the pre-trade weights $\hat{\theta}^i_j$. (Kreps (1979) and Marimon (1987) give a more detailed discussion of this issue.) Drèze's criterion for the firm has the special property of treating the production choices of the firm as public goods (with fixed share holdings). If state prices are chosen somehow according to shareholdings, then one presumes that they would be rechosen in the following period (of a multiperiod model) according to the new shareholdings, but then the production choice of the firm would have to be revised in a manner inconsistent with the understanding of original shareholders. It seems that some form of sequential compatibility restriction would be called for, under which original shareholders understand the choice mechanism that will apply at each decision point, and tailor their own choice scheme accordingly. The modeling issues here seem daunting.

As far as providing the firm with a model for evaluating various production alternatives, a common tack often taken in the finance literature is the imposition of a restrictive asset pricing model that implies unique state prices, such as the Capital Asset Pricing Model, the consumption-based Capital Asset Pricing Model, or the single (or homogeneous) agent models of Lucas (1978) (extended to production by Brock (1979, 1982), Prescott and Mehra (1980), and others). This is the standard approach taught to financial managers, as, for example, in the popular corporate finance text by Brealey and Myers (1989).

In any case, the firm can only operate under the well-known restrictions of the principal–agent setting. If one treats managerial expertise as a factor input operating under an incentive compatibility constraint, the entire principal–agent interaction can be embedded within the definition of the set of feasible production alternatives (along with the associated non-convexities and incomplete information). If shareholder power is diffusely exercised (with many small shareholders, few of whom would optimally choose not to free-ride on the monitoring efforts of others) and if managerial control is sharply focused on its own interests and entrenchment, the conventional principal–agent view of corporate control, on its own, seems inadequate. As Hart (1987) explains, the potential for takeover places significant restrictions on the decisions of the firm. This weapon is blunt, however, and certainly does not provide a specific objective for the firm. It would seem wise to investigate the set of production choices ruled out by takeover threats, and to derive the corresponding notion of efficiency of stockmarkets (which must be fairly weak). Incidentally, it goes almost without saying that general equilibria of almost any natural variety will be Pareto inefficient. The search for a natural notion of constrainted efficiency continues. (For a notion of constrained efficiency that even equilibria with the Drèze objective fail to satisfy in a multicommodity setting, see Geanakoplos, Magill, Quinzii, and Drèze (1987).) The issues of corporate control and capital structure will probably receive more attention, and perhaps continue to draw more emphasis away from the decentralized treatment of production choices used in classical general equilibrium theory.

6.3   Financial indeterminacy and the Modigliani–Miller theorems

Quoting from Myers' 1984 Presidential Address to the American Finance Association,

> we know very little about capital structure. We do not know how firms choose the debt, equity, or hybrid securities they issue. We have only recently discovered that capital structure conveys information to investors. There has been little if any research testing whether the relationship between financial leverage and investors' required return is as the pure MM [Modigliani–Miller (1958)] theory predicts. In general, we have inadequate understanding of corporate financing behavior, and of how that behavior affects security returns.

First, the irrelevance of financial policy with complete markets is a triviality; nothing the firm does in a purely financial vein could possibly have any real effects. The interesting case is incomplete markets. We first take a look at indeterminacy in how the firm makes financial (as opposed to production) investments. Given a production plan, this determines the dividend process of the firm, and may be thought of as financial policy limited to the available set of securities. We later discuss the issue of innovation of new securities.

Suppose, in the model just described, that firms also hold portfolios of securities. Let $\beta^j \in \mathbb{R}^N$ denote the portfolio held by firm j, and let β denote the $N \times N$ matrix whose (j,k)-element is β_k^j. Is it possible for firm j to change its market value by changing the portfolio of shares that it holds? The answer would seemingly be "no," but some regularity is required. We must keep in mind that, if the securities' prices and dividends are jointly determined by mutual investments, then a change in the portfolio β^j affects the dividends received by any security, say k, that holds shares of j in its portfolio. But then the dividends of j are in turn affected (via its holdings of k) by the change in k's dividends, and so on. The answer is quite simple in this period setting. The total dividends $\Delta^j \in L$ *paid by security* j must satisfy:

$$\Delta_1^j = y_1^j + \sum_{k=1}^{N} \beta_k^j \Delta_1^k.$$

Letting Δ_1 denote the $S \times N$ matrix whose (s,j)-element is Δ_{1s}^j, we have:

$$\Delta_1 = y_1 + \Delta_1 \beta^\top. \tag{36}$$

Assuming that $I - \beta^\top$ is non-singular, $\Delta_1 = y_1(I - \beta^\top)^{-1}$. Taking a given state-price vector π, the initial dividends of the firm, net of the costs of securities, is $\Delta_0 = y_0 - \beta \Delta_1^\top \pi$. After simplification, the total initial market value of the firms is then $\Delta_0 + \Delta_1^\top \pi = y_0 + y_1^\top \pi = q$. That is, financial policy (in this sense) is irrelevant for the value of the firm. This is one part of the well-known Modigliani–Miller theorem.

The essence of the other part of the Modigliani–Miller theory is that shareholders are also indifferent to changes in the firms' financial policies. The following has been worked out in a multiperiod model by DeMarzo (1988). Suppose (x^i, θ^i) solves (32), and let $\bar{\theta}^i = (I - \beta)^\top \theta^i$. It follows that:

$$(x^i, \bar{\theta}^i) \in \arg\max_{(x,\theta) \in L_+ \times \mathbb{R}^N} \quad U_i(x) \tag{37}$$

subject to:

$$x_0 - e_0^i - q^\top (\bar{\theta}^i - \theta) - \theta^\top \Delta_0 = 0; \qquad x_1 - e_1^i - \Delta_1 \theta = 0.$$

This is merely (32), incorporating the effects of the purchases $\beta^1, \ldots, \beta^n$ of security portfolios by the respective firms. Furthermore, by a simple calculation, $\Sigma_i \theta^i = \Sigma_i \bar{\theta}^i + \Sigma_j \beta^j$. In short, for any equilibrium $(q, \pi, (x^i, \theta^i), (y^j, \beta^j))$ (with the obvious definition) and for any $\bar{\beta}$ (with $I - \bar{\beta}^\top$ non-singular) describing an alternative financial policy for the firms, there exists an equilibrium of the form $(q, \pi, (x^i, \bar{\theta}^i), (y^j, \bar{\beta}^j))$, having the original consumption allocation. In other words, both shareholders and firms are indifferent to financial transactions of this form. There are many other ways to view the Modigliani–Miller irrelevance principle, and not surprisingly, this principle does not apply with transactions costs, taxes, or short sales restrictions (see, for example, Hellwig, 1981; Gottardi, 1991).

There is a role for corporate financial policy in maintaining limited liability (positive dividends) and in effecting wealth transfers among the various claimants on the firm (Fama, 1978). But this is hardly an explanation of the particular financial policies adopted by firms. A flurry of research suggesting the use of financial policy as a signaling device (for example, Ross (1977) or Myers and Majluf (1984)) or as a managerial incentive scheme (for example, Jensen and Meckling, 1976) are successful on their own terms, but others have asked why financial policy is used, rather than more direct principal–agent control instruments (Hart and Holmstrom, 1987; Hart, 1987; Aghion and Bolton, 1988).

6.4 Corporation financial innovation

With incomplete markets, the firm can definitely induce real effects either by issuing or retiring securities. For the trivial example, the firm could issue a sufficient set of contingent claims to complete markets. With the price-taking assumption, and ignoring the costs of setting up and maintaining the additional security markets as well as the associated transactions costs, this would clearly be in every shareholder's favor. The rub, of course, is that one cannot ignore these market costs. There will come a point at which the value to the firm of innovating securities (of which it will have an initial monopoly) is exceeded by the cost of innovation. That, presumably, is a more encompassing notion of equilibrium that deserves far more attention. To quote a well-known textbook of corporate finance,

Proposition I [The Modigliani–Miller irrelevance principle] is violated when financial managers find an untapped demand and satisfy it by issuing something new and different. The argument between MM and the traditionalists finally boils down to whether this is difficult or easy. We lean toward MM's view: finding unsatisfied clienteles and designing exotic securities to meet their needs is a game that's fun to play but hard to win. (Brealey and Myers, 1989)

As long as markets are incomplete, there will be tension between the role of a firm as a producer of goods and services, and its role in supplementing the span of markets, the latter role being treated in section 4. Allen and Gale (1988) provide a model of this effect.

APPENDIX Degree and the existence of equilibria

This appendix[9] reviews some of the basic mathematical definitions and results used in recent applications of degree theory to the existence of incomplete markets equilibria, as well as other problems in economic theory. For general background, Guillemin and Pollack (1974) is suitable, but some of the material specifically on degree theory is in more advanced books such as Dold (1972) and (for the differentiable case) Hirsch (1976). Some of what follows is based on exposition in Duffie and Shafer (1985) and Geanakoplos and Shafer (1990). Other more extensive exposition on this topic can be found in Magill and Shafer (1990b).

A1   Manifolds

A "manifold" can be thought of as a space with the same "structure," in some sense, as a Euclidean space. To make this sense precise, let M be a topological space (a set with some subsets called "open" satisfying the usual conditions) which is Hausdorff (meaning distinct points have disjoint neighborhoods). Then M is an n-dimensional manifold if M has an open cover $\{U_\lambda : \lambda \in \Lambda\}$ such that for each λ there is a homeomorphism $\phi : U_\lambda \to V_\lambda$, where $V_\lambda \subset \mathbb{R}^n$ is open. (A homeomorphism is a continuous one-to-one function whose inverse is also continuous.) The pair $(\phi_\lambda, U_\lambda)$ is called a *chart*; the collection $\{(\phi_\lambda, U_\lambda) : \lambda \in \Lambda\}$ is an *atlas*.

EXAMPLE 1 (The unit interval) The unit interval $M = (0,1)$ is a one-dimensional manifold by the single-chart atlas $\{(\phi, U)\}$, where $U = M = V = (0,1)$ and ϕ is the identity $x \to x$. This ends example 1.

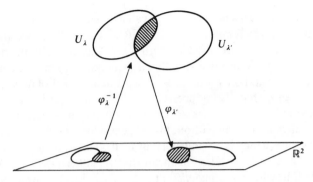

Figure 4.4 Coordinate changes

EXAMPLE 2 (The circle)   The unit circle $S = \{(x,y) \in \mathbb{R}^2 : x^2 + y^2 = 1\}$ is a one-dimensional manifold. Let ϕ_T map the top semicircle T onto $(-1,1)$ by $(x,y) \to x$; let ϕ_B map the bottom semicircle B onto $(-1,1)$ by $(x,y) \to x$; let ϕ_L map the left semicircle L onto $(-1,1)$ by $(x,y) \to y$; and let ϕ_R map the right semicircle R onto $(-1,1)$ by $(x,y) \to y$. These four charts form an appropriate atlas. Two charts are sufficient; one will not do. This ends example 2.

Both of the above examples are in some sense "smooth." More precisely, an atlas $\{(\phi_\lambda U_\lambda) : \lambda \in \Lambda\}$ for an n-dimensional manifold M is defined to be *smooth* (or C^∞) if, for every λ and λ' in Λ, the function:

$$\phi_\lambda \circ \phi_{\lambda'}^{-1} : \phi_{\lambda'}(U_\lambda \cap U_{\lambda'}) \to \phi_\lambda(U_\lambda \cap U_{\lambda'})$$

has continuous derivatives of every order. These compositions, illustrated in figure 4.4, are called *coordinate changes*. If the atlas $\Phi = \{(\phi_\lambda, U_\lambda) : \lambda \in \Lambda\}$ is smooth, the pair (M, Φ) is called a *smooth manifold*.

The previous two examples are fairly easy since the manifolds have an obvious Euclidean structure as Euclidean subsets. The following example, treating the space $\mathscr{G}_{N,S}$ of n-dimensional linear subspaces of $\mathbb{R}^S$, is a more interesting test of the definition of a manifold since $\mathscr{G}_{N,S}$ is not itself a subset of a Euclidean space. We also discuss $\mathscr{G}_{N,S}$ because it plays a central role in recent proofs of existence of equilibria with incomplete markets for state-contingent claims.

EXAMPLE 3 (The Grassmannian)   We will review how one can treat the space $\mathscr{G}_{N,S}$ of N-dimensional linear subspaces of $\mathbb{R}^S$ as a compact $[N(S-N)]$-dimensional manifold (for $1 \leq N < S$) with a smooth atlas. First we give $\mathscr{G}_{N,S}$ a Hausdorff topology. A particular subspace G in $\mathscr{G}_{N,S}$ is induced by a full rank $(S-N) \times S$ matrix A according to

$G = \{y \in \mathbb{R}^s : Ay = 0\}$. This defines an equivalence relation $\sim$ on the space X of full rank $(S - N) \times S$ matrices by: $A \sim B$ if A and B induce the same subspace. We can then identify $\mathscr{G}_{N,S}$ with $X/\sim$ endowed with the quotient topology. This is the same as saying that a sequence $\{G_N\}$ in $\mathscr{G}_{N,S}$ converges to a subspace G if and only if there exists a sequence $\{A_N\}$ of matrices in X with the property that A_N induces G_N and $\{A_N\}$ converges (in the usual Euclidean topology on matrices) to a matrix A that induces G. Since A_N can be taken to have unit norm without loss of generality, it follows that $\mathscr{G}_{N,S}$ is a compact space (which is obviously Hausdorff). The statement "$A \in G$," for a matrix A in X, will be taken to mean that A induces $G \in \mathscr{G}_{N,S}$. We next suggest the following *Grassmannian* atlas for $\mathscr{G}_{N,S}$. Let Σ denote the set of permutations of $\{1, 2, \ldots, S\}$. For each σ in Σ, let P_σ denote the $S \times S$ permutation matrix corresponding to σ. For example, if σ permutes the ordered set $\{1, 2, \ldots, S\}$ to the ordered set $\{2, 3, \ldots, S, 1\}$, then for any vector $x = (x_1 x_2, \ldots, x_S)$, we have $P_\sigma x = (x_2, x_3, \ldots, x_S, x_1)$, merely relabeling the coordinates. Let $\mathbb{R}^{(S-N) \times N}$ denote the space of $(S - N) \times N$ matrices, and for each E in $\mathbb{R}^{(S-N) \times N}$, let $[I|E]$ denote the $(S - N) \times S$ matrix with identity matrix in the left block. We see that $[I|E] \in X$ (that is, $[I|E]$ is full rank) automatically. For each permutation σ, let:

$$U_\sigma = \{G \in \mathscr{G}_{N,S} : \exists E \in \mathbb{R}^{(S-N) \times N}; [I|E]P_\sigma \in G\}.$$

We note that, for fixed σ, each matrix E in $\mathbb{R}^{(S-N) \times N}$ corresponds to a unique subspace in U_σ, and vice versa. Indeed, the function $\phi_\sigma : U_\sigma \to \mathbb{R}^{(S-N) \times N}$ defined by $[I|\phi_\sigma(G)]P_\sigma \in G$ is a homeomorphism, and $\{U_\sigma : \sigma \in \Sigma\}$ is an open cover of $\mathscr{G}_{N,S}$. It follows that $\mathscr{G}_{N,S}$ is an $[(S - N)N]$-dimensional manifold by the atlas $\Phi = \{(\phi_\sigma, U_\sigma) : \sigma \in \Sigma\}$. Finally, it is shown without much difficulty that the coordinate changes for this atlas Φ are smooth functions, implying that the atlas is smooth. That is, $(\mathscr{G}_{N,S}, \Phi)$ is a smooth manifold. This ends example 3.

There are other well known smooth atlases for a Grassmannian manifold, but there is a unique maximal smooth atlas Ψ which contains the atlas Φ defined in example 3. Such a maximal smooth atlas for a manifold is called a *differential structure*, and is uniquely defined by any atlas that it contains. The other well known smooth atlases for $\mathscr{G}_{N,S}$ are contained in the same differential structure Ψ. Whenever the choice of smooth atlas Φ for a manifold M is obvious or implicit, the terminology is often abused by referring to M itself as the smooth manifold (M, Φ).

A2   Degree

Here we review the most basic notions of mod 2 degree theory, leaving out the oriented degree theory for brevity. For the remainder of this section, let

X and Y be manifolds of the same dimension and let $f: X \to Y$ be continuous. The mod 2 degree $deg_2(f,y)$ of a map $f: X \to Y$ at a value $y \in Y$ (such that the inverse image $f^{-1}(y)$ is compact) is, roughly speaking, a notion of whether the number of points in $f^{-1}(y)$ is even or odd. Indeed, if $f^{-1}(y)$ is a set with n points, then (under conditions) $deg_2(f,y)$ is equivalent to 0 if n is even and equivalent to 1 if n is odd. In general, $f^{-1}(y)$ is not necessarily even a finite set, but the notion of degree extends to this case and (under conditions) $deg_2(f,y) \neq 0$ implies that $f^{-1}(y)$ is not empty. If f is an excess demand function, it then suffices to show that $deg_2(f,0) \neq 0$ in order to prove the existence of equilibrium. In the case of incomplete markets, this is one of the easy approaches to proving the existence of equilibrium. One of the reasons this approach is easy to use is the fact that degree is invariant (under conditions) to the choice of value y; that is $deg_2(f,y) = deg_2(f,\bar{y})$ for all y and $\bar{y}$ in Y. This is later stated more carefully.

As a preliminary to applications of the notion of degree, we review a few definitions. If X and Y are Euclidean spaces and $f: X \to Y$ is smooth, a value $y \in Y$ is *regular* if the Jacobian matrix $Df(x)$ of partial derivatives is of full rank at each point x such that $f(x) = y$. For general manifolds X and Y, we refer to the atlases $\{(\phi_\lambda, U_\lambda): \lambda \in \Lambda\}$ for X and $\{(\psi_\lambda, W_\alpha): \alpha \in A\}$ for Y for notions of smoothness and regular value[10] in terms of the obvious ("locally equivalent") functions defined on the corresponding Euclidean spaces. By default, if $f^{-1}(y)$ is empty, then y is a regular value. We recall that f is a *proper function* if the inverse image under f of any compact set is compact. The definition of a *connected manifold*[11] is a natural extension of the definition of a connected subset of a Euclidean space.

MOD 2 DEGREE THEOREM (Smooth version)   Suppose X and Y are smooth manifolds of the same dimension. If Y is connected and $f: X \to Y$ is smooth and proper, then one and only one of the following is true:

(i)   for any regular value y of f, $\#f^{-1}(y)$ is even;
(ii) for any regular value y of f, $\#f^{-1}(y)$ is odd.

The result states, under the given conditions, that the number of points $\#f^{-1}(y)$ in the inverse image of y, mod 2, is an invariant over regular values, and is denoted $deg_2(f)$ (figure 4.5). We will later extend this definition of the *mod 2 degree* of a smooth proper function to the general case of continuous proper functions.

EXAMPLE 4   Let Y be a set of economies, P a set of "equilibrators" (for example, prices), "p equilibrates y" be well defined, and $X = \{(p,y) \in P \times Y: p$ equilibrates $y\}$. Let $f: X \to Y$ be the projection $(p,y) \to y$. The following corollary gives the approach to demonstrating the existence of equilibria that was used in Duffie and Shafer (1985).

250   **Darrell Duffie**

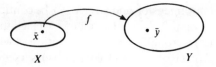

Figure 4.5 If $\bar{y}$ is regular and $f^{-1}(\bar{y})=\{\bar{x}\}$. Then $\deg_2 f = 1$

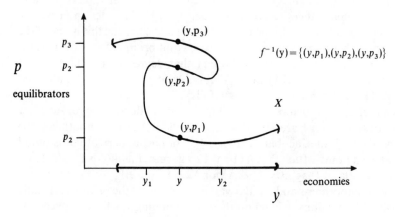

Figure 4.6 Counting equilibrium points

COROLLARY   Suppose f, X, and Y satisfy the conditions of the Mod 2 Degree Theorem, and there exists an economy $\bar{y}$ that is a regular value of f with a unique equilibrator (that is, $\#f^{-1}(\bar{y})=1$). Then every economy y has an equilibrator.

> *Proof* Any economy y without an equilibrator has $\#f^{-1}(y)=0$, and is therefore a regular value of f. By the theorem and $\#f^{-1}(\bar{y})=1$, every economy has a equilibrator.

The idea is illustrated in figure 4.6. As shown, for almost every point in the (one-dimensional) manifold Y of economies, the number of points in the manifold X of equilibria is odd. The values y_1 and y_2 at which this is not the case are indeed not regular values of the projection map of X onto Y. Nevertheless, these values y_1 and y_2 also have equilibria. This application tells us to look for a particular economy with a unique equilibrium. If that economy is regular, then every economy must have an equilibrium. In particular, every regular economy has an odd number of equilibria, which goes back to Dierker (1972, 1974). Balasko (1975) instigated the perspective of the "equilibrium manifold" and characterizing the set of equilibria in terms of the projection map into (in this case, onto) the space of economies. Many details may be found in Mas-Colell (1985) and Balasko (1989).

A3   Useful properties of smooth functions

We relate some useful properties of a smooth function $f: X \to Y$, where X is an n-dimensional smooth manifold and Y is an m-dimensional smooth manifold.

PRE-IMAGE THEOREM   If y is a regular value of f, then $f^{-1}(y)$ is an $(n - m)$-dimensional smooth manifold.

For $n < m$, one should read the result as stating that, for y regular, $f^{-1}(y)$ is empty. If X is compact and $n = m$, one should read the pre-image theorem as stating that (for y regular) $f^{-1}(y)$ is a finite set.

The next result, which makes the last quite useful, states that regular values are quite "typical." To say that *almost every* value is a regular value, if Y is a Euclidean space, means that the set of *critical values*, those that are not regular, is a subset of (Lebesgue) measure zero.[12]

SARD'S THEOREM   The set of critical values of f is of measure zero.

Our last result of this section is really just a simple consequence of definitions, but is the basis for many "genericity" arguments in economics. If $\dim(X) \geq \dim(Y)$ and every y in Y is regular for $f: X \to Y$, then we call f a submersion. In applications, we would take X to be the space of primitives defining an economy and $\bar{Y}$ to be a subset of well-behaved parameters (primitive or endogenous) in some set Y. The following lemma says that if f is a submersion, meaning that perturbation of the economy x always generates a full-dimensional perturbation of $f(x)$, then a generic set of economies has the property generically specified by $\bar{Y}$.

GENERICITY LEMMA   Suppose $f: X \to Y$ is a submersion and $\bar{Y} \subset Y$ is open with complement of measure zero. Then $f^{-1}(\bar{Y})$ is open with complement of measure zero.

A4   Existence of equilibrium in incomplete markets

We now sketch the proof of generic existence of equilibrium in the incomplete security market model of section 3, under conditions A–E of proposition 3, plus the additional simplifying assumptions that the utility functions are smooth (C^∞) and the dividend function D is linear. The method of proof is from Duffie and Shafer (1985), where many intermediate steps are shown in detail. We proceed in the two basic steps indicated in section A3: first show pseudo-equilibrium for any economy. Then show that, generically, a pseudo-equilibrium is an effective equilibrium. This implies the generic existence of equilibrium (proposition 2).

Let $L_{++} = \mathrm{int}(L_+)$. For any $(p,G,e) \in L_{++} \times \mathscr{G}_{N,S} \times L_{++}$ and any agent i, let $F_i(p,G,e^i)$ denote the solution x_i to problem (4) subject to (5) and $p_1 \square (x^i - e^i) \in G$. An argument shows that F_i defines a smooth function on $L_{++} \times \mathscr{G}_{N,S} \times L_{++}$ into L_{++}.

A pseudo-equilibrium for the economy $(\mathcal{E},D)$ is therefore reduced to a solution (p,G) to $\mathrm{span}[D(p)] \subset G$ and $Z(p,G,e) = 0$, where $Z(p,G,e) = \sum_{i=1}^m [F_i(p,G,e^i) - e_i]$. For technical reasons, however, we replace the excess demand function Z with $Z^*: L_{++} \times \mathscr{G}_{N,S} \times L_{++}^m \to L$, defined by:

$$Z^*(p,G,e) = \sum_{i=1}^{m-1} F_i(p,G,e^i) - \sum_{i=1}^{m} e^i + \left(\arg\max_{x \in L_{++} : p \cdot x \leq 1} U_m(x) \right),$$

that is, replacing the incomplete market demand function of agent m with the complete market demand function given a total budget of one unit of account. This is based on a trick introduced by Cass (1984), with the convenience that $(p,G,x^1, \ldots,x^m)$ is a pseudo-equilibrium with $p \cdot e^m = 1$ if and only if $\mathrm{span}[D(p)] \subset G$ and $Z^*(p,L,e) = 0$. This is implied by the fact that $p_1 \square (x_1^i - e_1^i) \in G$ for $i < m$ and $\sum_{i=1}^m (x^i - e^i) = 0$ together imply that $p_1 \square (x_1^m - e_1^m) \in G$.

By linear D, we mean that each security j is identified with a state-contingent commodity bundle δ_j in $K = \mathbb{R}^{S \times l}$ by $D_{sj}(p) = p_{1s} \cdot \delta_{js}$. For $\delta = (\delta_1, \ldots, \delta_N) \in K^N$, let D^δ denote the corresponding dividend function. Fixing utility functions, an economy is thus identified with a pair $(e,\delta) \in Y \subseteq L_{++}^m \times K^N$. We say that $(p,G) \in P \equiv L_{++} \times \mathscr{G}_{N,S}$ equilibrates $(e,\delta) \in Y$ if $Z^*(p,G,e) = 0$ and $\mathrm{span}[D\delta(p)] \subset G$. The equilibrium manifold, as in example 4, is:

$$X = \{[(p,G),(e,\delta)] \in P \times Y : (p,G) \text{ equilibrates } (e,\delta)\}.$$

PROPOSITION X and Y are smooth manifolds of the same dimension, Y is connected, and the projection map $f: X \to Y$ is smooth and proper.

The proof of this proposition is a tedious exercise in calculus to establish with the Pre-image Theorem that X is a smooth manifold of the same dimension as Y, plus an application of the boundary condition (E) on preferences to establish that f is proper. We are set for an application of the mod 2 degree theorem. Still needed is a regular value of f with an odd number of inverse image points, fixing the degree of f as odd, and assuring that every economy (e,δ) has a pseudo-equilibrium. In fact, there is an easy such candidate economy. Let $\bar{e}$ be a Pareto efficient interior allocation, let $\bar{p}$ be the Walrasian price vector for this allocation, scaled so that $\bar{p}\cdot\bar{e}^m = 1$. Let $\bar{\delta}\in K^N$ define any securities so that $D_{\bar{\delta}}(\bar{p})$ has full rank N. Finally, let $\bar{G} = \text{span}[D_{\bar{\delta}}(\bar{p})]$. It is easy to check that $(\bar{p}, \bar{G})$ is the unique equilibrator for $(\bar{e}, \bar{\delta})$. It is a bit more tedious to check that $(\bar{e}, \bar{\delta})$ is a regular value of f, but this is also true. Thus, by the smooth version of the Mod 2 Degree Theorem, every economy has a pseudo-equilibrium.

For generic existence of equilibria, we wish to show there exists a subset $\bar{Y}$ of Y whose complement is closed with Lebesgue measure zero such that, for every economy $(e,\delta)\in\bar{Y}$, there is an equilibrium. This can be argued as follows.

By Sard's Theorem, the subset $\hat{Y}\subset Y$ of regular values of Y has a complement of Lebesgue measure zero. Since f is proper, Y is open. Let us isolate a particular open subset $Y'\subset\hat{Y}$ on which there is a smooth function $\phi: Y'\to L_{++}$ assigning to each economy $(e,\delta)\in Y'$ one pseudo-equilibrium price vector $\phi(e,\delta)\in L_{++}$. The entire set $\hat{Y}$ can be covered with a countable number of open subsets having this property because of the Pre-Image Theorem. With the aid of proposition 2 in Section A3, the generic existence result is completed by showing that there is an open subset $\bar{Y}'\subset Y'$ whose complement has measure zero such that, for all $(e,\delta)\in\bar{Y}'$, the matrix $D_\delta[\phi(e,\delta)]$ has full rank. This last step has the following sub-steps.

1   An easy argument shows that $A = \{(p,\delta)\in L_{++}\times K : \text{rank}[D_\delta\ (p)] = N\}$ is open with complement of measure zero.

2   Let $\Psi: Y'\to L_{++}\times K^N$ be defined by $\Psi(e,\delta) = [\phi(e,\delta),\delta]$. A tedious calculation shows that the Jacobian of Ψ is everywhere of full rank. Since $\dim(Y')\geq\dim(L_{++}\times K^N)$, this implies that Ψ is a submersion.

3   Since Ψ is a submersion and A is open with complement of measure zero, the Genericity Lemma implies that $\bar{Y}'\equiv\Psi^{-1}(A)\subset Y'$ is open with complement of measure zero. This completes the sketch of the generic existence poof.

A5   General Mod 2 Degree Theorem

Geanakoplos and Shafer (1990) use the following extension of degree theory to show existence of pseudo-equilibrium for continuous D, and dropping the smoothness conditions on utility. This has both simplified and generalized the approach to existence of pseudo-equilibrium illustrated in the previous example, and allows for other applications.

One of the key parts of the following characterization of mod 2 degree is invariance of degree under homotopy. Two continuous functions $f: X\to Y$

and $g: X \to Y$ are *homotopic* if there is a continuous function $h: X \times [0,1]$ $\to Y$, such that $h(x,0) = f(x)$ and $h(x,1) = g(x)$ for all x in X. In this case, h is called a *homotopy* between f and g. In an informal sense, f and g are homotopic if they are equivalent up to continuous deformation of their graphs. We now extend the above given definition of mod 2 degree to the case of a continuous proper map $f: X \to Y$ between manifolds X and Y of the same dimension, where Y is connected. (The definition extends to weaker conditions.) Let F denote the space of all such functions, and let Z_2 denote the ring of integers modulo 2. [That is, in Z_2, we have $4 = 2 = 22$, and $1 = 7 = 69$, but $1 \neq 8$.]

MOD 2 DEGREE THEOREM   There is a function $\deg_2 : F \to Z_2$ with the following properties for any $f: X \to Y$ and $g: M \to N$ in F.

(a) If $X = Y$ and f is the identity map, then $\deg_2(f) = 1$.

(b) For open $U \subset X$ and open $V \subset Y$ such that $f(U) \subset V$, we have $\deg_2(f) = \deg_2(f|_U)$, where $f|_U : U \to V$ denotes the restriction of f to U.

(c) If $\{U_\lambda : \lambda \in \Lambda\}$ is a finite open partition of X, then $\deg_2$ $(f) = \sum_{\lambda \in \Lambda} \deg_2(f|_{U_\lambda})$.

(d) If there is a proper homotopy between f and g, then $\deg_2(f) = \deg_2(g)$.

(e) If $M = Y$, then $\deg_2(g \circ f) = \deg_2(f) \deg_2(g)$.

(f) If $\deg_2(f) \neq 0$ then $f^{-1}(y)$ is not empty for all $y \in Y$.

From this theorem, which can be improved, we have several key properties: (i) as in (d), degree is preserved under homotopy; (ii) from the fact that the degree of a composition is the product of the degrees (e), we see that the degree of a homoeomorphism is 1; and especially (iii) non-zero degree implies that every value has a non-zero inverse image. In particular, if f is an excess demand function for an economy (which could be defined on a general manifold of equilibrating parameters), then $\deg_2(f) \neq 0$ implies the existence of an equilibrium.

Notes

1 For existence, it would also be enough, however, to adjust the model instead with the more realistic imposition of transactions costs, say in the form of some technology set $T \subset \mathbb{R}^n \times L_+$, with $(\theta, z) \in T$ indicating that trading a portfolio θ can be accomplished with use of the consumption vector z. The objective (1) is then replaced with:

$$\max_{(x,(\theta,z)) \in L_+ \times T} U_i(x - z). \tag{1'}$$

The existence of equilibrium will follow if we adopt some typical regularity conditions, including convexity for T and semi-continuity for T and D, along with the natural property that: if $(\theta_n, z_n) \in T$ and $\|\theta_n\| \to \infty$, then $\|z_n\| \to \infty$. This line of attack is also suggested in Grodal and Vind (1986). This last assumption prevents the problem of "exploding portfolios" in Hart (1975). The objectionable convexity assumption on T could also be dropped by changing the set of agents to a non-atomic measure space, à la Hildenbrand (1974). The essential arguments and additional regularity assumptions could be deduced from the recent work of Yamazaki (1989).

2 The same conclusion follows if all securities are defined by claims to a single numeraire commodity in quantities depending on the state, as shown by Geanakoplos and Polemarchakis (1986) and Chae (1988).

3 This result appears in the penultimate, but not the ultimate, version of Geanakoplos and Shafer (1990).

4 In the variant of this model by Duffie and Jackson (1989), the exchange may also charge a transactions fee, in which case maximizing the volume of trade is equivalent to maximizing transactions revenues.

5 Formally, we are dealing with the inner product on L defined by covariance, and the corresponding Hilbert space sense of orthogonal projection.

6 In fact, Weil assumes that there is an uncountable number of agents with this i.i.d. endowment assumption, but that is mathematically problematic and in any case unnecessary, since his application of Jensen's Inequality can be replaced with the arguments given here in the finite-agent case.

7 The equity premium is, according to Weil (1990), the ratio of the rate of return on equity to the rate of return on the risk-free bond.

8 Portions of this section appeared as notes, purely for purposes of discussion, at the IMSSS Workshop on Incomplete Markets at Stanford University, 14 July 1987.

9 This appendix is a revised form of notes prepared solely for the IMSSS Workshop on Incomplete Markets, Stanford University, 17 July 1987.

10 In this case, f is *smooth* if, for each λ and at each point t in the image of ϕ_λ, the map $h_{\lambda\alpha}$ defined by $t \to \psi_\alpha[f(\phi_\lambda^{-1}(t))]$ (for an appropriate α) is smooth at t. Furthermore, $y \in Y$ is a regular value of f if the Jacobian $Dh_{\lambda\alpha}(t)$ is of full rank at each such (λ, α, t) satisfying $f(\phi_\lambda^{-1}(t)) = y$.

11 Two subsets A and B of a topological space are *separated* if $\bar{A} \cap B$ and $\bar{B} \cap A$ are both empty, where $\bar{A}$ denotes the closure of A. A topological space is *connected* if it is not the union of two non-empty separated subsets.

12 For a manifold M with atlas $\{(\phi_\lambda, U_\lambda) : \lambda \in \Lambda\}$, a subset $A \subset M$ is defined to be of measure zero if, for any λ, the set $\phi_\lambda(A \cap U_\lambda)$ is a subset of a set of measure zero.

References

Aghion, P. and P. Bolton (1988), "An 'Incomplete Contracts' Approach to Bankruptcy and the Optimal Financial Structure of the Firm," Unpublished, Harvard University.

Aiyagari, S.R. and M. Gertler (1990), "Asset Returns with Transactions Costs and Uninsured Individual Risk: A Stage III Exercise," Working Paper 454. Federal Reserve Bank of Minneapolis.

Allen, F. and D. Gale (1988), "Optimal Security Design," *Review of Financial Studies*, 1: 29–264.

Anderson, R. and C. Harris (1986), "A Model of Financial Innovation," Unpublished, City University of New York.

Arrow, K. (1953), "Le rôle des valeurs boursières pour la repartition la meillure des risques," *Econometrie*, pp. 41–7; discussion, pp. 47–8, Colloq. Internat. Centre National de la Recherche Scientifique, no. 40 (Paris, 1952) C.N.R.S. Paris, 1953; translated in *Review of Economic Studies*, 31 (1964): 91–6.

Arrow, K. and G. Debreu (1954), "Existence of an Equilibrium for a Competitive Economy," *Econometrica*, 22: 265–90.

Balasko, Y. (1975), "The Graph of The Walras Correspondence," *Econometrica*, 43: 907–12.

(1989), *Foundations of the Theory of General Equilibrium*. New York: Academic Press.

Bewley, T. (1982), "Thoughts on Volatility Tests of the Intertemporal Asset Pricing Model," Unpublished, Department of Economics, Northwestern University.

Black, D. (1986), *Success and Failure of Futures Contracts: Theory and Empirical Evidence*, Monograph 1986-1, Salomon Brothers Center for the Study of Financial Institutions.

Bottazzi, J.-M. (1991) "Note on the Algebraic Dimension of Critical Prices in Incomplete Markets," Unpublished, Laboratoire d'Econométrie de l'Ecole Polytechnique, Paris.

Brealey, R. and S. Myers (1989), *Principles of Corporate Finance (Third Edition)*, New York: McGraw-Hill.

Breeden, D. (1979), "An Intertemporal Asset Pricing Model with Stochastic Consumption and Investment Opportunities," *Journal of Financial Economics*, 7: 265–96.

Brock, W. (1979), "An Integration of Stochastic Growth Theory and The Theory of Finance, Part I: The Growth Model," in J. Green and J. Scheinkman, *General Equilibrium, Growth, and Trade*, New York: Academic Press.

(1982), "Asset Prices in a Production Economy," in J. McCall, *The Economics of Information and Uncertainty*, University of Chicago Press.

Campbell, J. and R. Shiller (1988), "Dividend-Price Ratios and Expectations of Future Dividends and Price Ratios," *Review of Financial Studies*, 1: 195–228.

Carlton, D. (1983), "Futures Volume, Market Interrelationships and Industry Structure," *American Journal of Agricultural Economics*, 65: 380–7.

Cass, D. (1984), "Competitive Equilibrium with Incomplete Financial Markets," Working Paper 84-09, Center for Analytic Research in Economics and the Social Sciences, University of Pennsylvania.

(1990), "Real Indeterminacy from Imperfect Financial Markets," Unpublished, Department of Economics, University of Pennsylvania.

Chae, S. (1988), "Existence of Competitive Equilibrium with Incomplete Markets," *Journal of Economic Theory*, 44: 9–18.

Constantinides, G. (1990), "Habit Formation: A Resolution of the Equity Premium Puzzle," *Journal of Political Economy*, 98: 519–43.

Cox, J., J. Ingersoll and S. Ross (1985), "An Intertemporal General Equilibrium Model of Asset Prices," *Econometrica*, 53: 363–84.

Cuny, C. (1989), "The Role of Liquidity in Futures Market Innovations," Unpublished, Graduate School of Management, U.C. Irvine.

Debreu, G. (1953), "Une Economie de l'Incertain," Unpublished, Electricité de France.

(1959), *Theory of Value*. Cowles Foundation Monograph 17, New Haven Connecticut: Yale University Press.

(1972), "Smooth Preferences," *Econometrica*, 40: 603–15.

(1976), "Smooth Preferences, A Corrigendum," *Econometrica*, 44: 831–2.

DeMarzo, P. (1987), "Majority Rule and Corporate Control: The Rule of the Dominant Shareholder," Unpublished, Stanford University.

(1988), "An Extension of the Modigliani-Miller Theorem to Stochastic Economies with Incomplete Markets," *Journal of Economic Theory*, 45: 353–69.

Diamond, P. (1967), "The Role of a Stock Market in a General Equilibrium Model with Technological Uncertainty," *American Economic Review*, 57: 759–76.

Dierker, E. (1972), "Two Remarks on the Number of Equilibria of an Economy," *Econometrica*, 40: 951–3.

(1974), *Topological Methods in Walrasian Economies*, Lecture Notes in Economics and Mathematical Systems Number 92, Berlin: Springer-Verlag.

Dold, A. (1972), *Lectures on Algebraic Topology*, Berlin: Springer.

Dreyfus, J.-F. (1984), "On the Modelling of Stock Market Economies: Definition, Existence and Optimality of Competitive Equilibria," CARESS Working Paper 84-17, University of Pennsylvania.

Drèze, J. (1974), "Investment under Private Ownership: Optimality, Equilibrium and Stability," in J. Drèze, *Allocation Under Uncertainty: Equilibrium and Optimality*, New York: Wiley, pp. 129–65.

Duffie, D. and M. Jackson (1989), "Optimal Innovation of Futures Contracts," *Review of Financial Studies*, 2: 275–96.

Duffie, D. and W. Shafer (1985), "Equilibrium in Incomplete Markets I: A Basic Model of Generic Existence," *Journal of Mathematical Economics*, 14: 285–300.

(1986a), "Equilibrium in Incomplete Markets II: Generic Existence in Stochastic Economies," *Journal of Mathematical Economics*, 15: 199–216.

(1986b), "Equilibrium and The Role of the Firm in Incomplete Markets," Research Paper 915, Graduate School of Business, Stanford University.

Ekern, S. and R. Wilson (1974), "On The Theory of the Firm in an Economy with Incomplete Markets," *Bell Journal of Economics and Management Science*, 5: 171–80.

Epstein, L. and S. Zin (1989), "Substitution, Risk Aversion, and the Temporal Behavior of Consumption and Asset Returns," *Econometrica*, 57: 937–69.

Fama, E. (1978), "The Effects of a Firm's Investment and Financing Decisions on the Welfare of its Security Holders," *American Economic Review*, 68: 272–84.

Gale, D. (1989), "Standard Securities," Unpublished, Department of Economics, University of Pittsburgh.

Geanakoplos, J. (1990), "An Introduction to General Equilibrium with Incomplete Asset Markets," *Journal of Mathematical Economics*, 19: 1–38.

Geanakoplos, J, M. Magill, M. Quinzii and J. Drèze (1987), "Generic Inefficiency of Stock Market Equilibrium When Markets are Incomplete," Working Paper M8735, University of Southern California.

Geanakoplos, J. and H. Polemarchakis (1986), "Existence, Regularity, and Constrained Suboptimality of Competitive Allocations when Markets are Incomplete," in W. Heller, R. Starr and D. Starrett, *Essays in Honor of Kenneth Arrow, vol. III*, Cambridge University Press.

Geanakoplos, J. and W. Shafer (1990), "Solving Systems of Simultaneous Equations in Economics," *Journal of Mathematical Economics*, 19: 69–95.

Gevers. L. (1974), "Competitive Equilibrium of the Stock Exchange and Pareto Efficiency," in J. Drèze, *Allocation under Uncertainty: Equilibrium and Optimality*, New York: Wiley.

Grodal, B. and K. Vind (1988), "Equilibrium with Arbitrary Market Structure," Unpublished, Department of Economics, University of Copenhagen.

Grossman, S. and O. Hart (1979), "A Theory of Competitive Equilibrium in Stock Market Economies," *Econometrica*, 47: 293–330.

(1987), "One Share/One Vote and the Market for Corporate Control," Unpublished, Princeton University.

Grossman, S. and G. Laroque (1989), "Asset Pricing and Optimal Portfolio Choice in the Presence of Illiquid Durable Consumption Goods," *Econometrica*, 58: 25–52.

Grossman, S. and R. Shiller (1982), "Consumption Correlatedness and Risk Measurement in Economies with Non-Traded Assets and Heterogeneous Information," *Journal of Financial Economics*, 10: 195–210.

Guillemin, V. and A. Pollack (1974), *Differential Topology*, Englewood Cliffs, NJ: Prentice-Hall.

Hahn, F. (1990), "Some Remarks on Missing Markets," Unpublished, Cambridge University.

Hansen, L. and R. Jaganathan (1990), "Implications of Security Market Data for Models of Dynamic Economies," *Journal of Political Economy*, 99: 225–62.

Hansen, L. and K. Singleton (1982), "Generalized Instrumental Variables Estimation of Nonlinear Rational Expectations Models," *Econometrica*, 50: 1269–86.

(1988), "Efficient Estimation of Linear Asset Pricing Models with Moving-Average Errors," Unpublished, Department of Economics, University of Chicago.

Harris, M. and A. Raviv (1988), "Corporate Control Contests and Capital Structure," *Journal of Financial Economics*, 20: 56–86.

Hart, O. (1975), "On the Optimality of Equilibrium when the Market Structure is Incomplete," *Journal of Economic Theory*, 11: 418–43.

(1977), "Takeover Bids and Stock Market Equilibrium," *Journal of Economic Theory*, 9: 53–83.

(1987), "Capital Structure as a Control Mechanism in Corporations," Research Paper 441, MIT.

Hart, O. and B. Holmstrom (1987), "The Theory of Contracts," in T. Bewley, *Advances in Economic Theory*, Cambridge University Press.

Heaton, J. (1988), "The Interaction Between Time-Nonseparable Preferences and Time Aggregation," Unpublished, Department of Economics, MIT.

Hellwig, M. (1981), "Bankruptcy, Limited Liability, and the Modigliani–Miller Theorem," *American Economic Review*, 71: 155–70.

Hildenbrand, W. (1974), *Core and Equilibrium of a Large Economy*, Princeton University Press.

Hirsch, M.D., M. Magill and A. Mas-Colell (1990), "A Geometric Approach to a Class of Equilibrium Existence Theorems," *Journal of Mathematical Economics*, 19: 95–107.

Hirsch, M.W. (1976), *Differential Topology*, New York: Springer-Verlag.

Hirshleifer, D. (1988), "Residual Risk, Trading Costs, and Commodity Futures Risk Premia," *Review of Financial Studies*, 1: 173–93.

Huang, P. and H.-M. Wu (1989), "Competitive Equilibrium of Incomplete Markets for Securities with Smooth Payoffs," Unpublished, Department of Economics, Tulane University.

Husseini, S., J.-M. Lasry and M. Magill (1990), "Existence of Equilibrium with Incomplete Markets," *Journal of Mathematical Economics*, 19: 39–68.

Jensen, M. and W. Meckling (1976), "Theory of the Firm: Managerial Behavior, Agency Costs and Ownership Structure," *Journal of Financial Economics*, 3: 305–60.

Johnston, E. and J. McConnell (1989), "Requiem for a Market: An Analysis of the Rise and Fall of a Financial Futures Contract," *Review of Financial Studies*, 2: 1–24.

Judd, K. (1990), "Minimum Weighted Residual Methods for Solving Dynamic Economic Models," Unpublished, Hoover Institution, Stanford University.

Kahn, C. and S. Krasa (1990), "Non-Existence and Inefficiency of Equilibria with American Options and Convertible Bonds," Unpublished, Department of Economics, University of Illinois at Urbana-Champaign.

Kihlstrom, R. and J. Laffont (1982), "A Competitive Entrepreneurial Model of a Stock Market," in J. McCall, *The Economics of Information and Uncertainty*, University of Chicago Press.

Kleidon, A. (1986), "Variance Bounds Tests and Stock Price Valuation Models," *Journal of Political Economy*, 94: 953–1001.

Krasa, S. (1987), "Existence of Competitive Equilibrium for Option Markets," *Journal of Economic Theory*, 47: 413–31.

Krasa, S. and J. Werner (1989), "Equilibria with Options: Existence and Indeterminacy," Unpublished, Department of Economics, University of Minnesota.

Kreps, D. (1979), "Three Essays on Capital Markets," Technical Report 298, Institute for Mathematical Studies in The Social Sciences, Stanford University.

Leland, H. (1973), "Capital Asset Markets, Production, and Optimality: A Synthesis," Technical Report 115, IMSSS, Stanford University.

(1974) "Production Theory and The Stock Market," *Bell Journal of Economics and Management Science,* 5: 125–44.

(1978), "Information, Management Choice, and Stockholder Unanimity," *Review of Economic Studies,* 45: 527–34.

LeRoy, S. (1984), "Efficiency and the Variability of Asset Prices," *American Economics Association Papers and Proceedings,* 74: 183–7.

LeRoy, S. and R. Porter (1981), "The Present-Value Relation: Tests Based on Implied Variance Bounds," *Econometrica,* 49: 555–74.

Lintner, J. (1965), "The Valuation of Risky Assets and the Selection of Risky Investment in Stock Portfolios and Capital Budgets," *Review of Economics and Statistics,* 47: 13–37.

Lucas, D. (1990), "Estimating the Equity Premium with Undiversifiable Risk and Short Sales Constraints," Unpublished, Kellogg School of Management, Northwestern University.

Lucas, R. (1978), "Asset Prices in an Exchange Economy," *Econometrica,* 46: 1429–45.

Mace, B. (1989), "Full Insurance in the Presence of Aggregate Uncertainty," Working Paper 197, Department of Economics, University of Rochester.

Magill, M. and W. Shafer (1990a), "Characterization of Generically Complete Real Asset Structures," *Journal of Mathematical Economics,* 19: 167–94.

(1990b), "Equilibrium in Incomplete Markets," in W. Hildenbrand and H. Sonnenschein (eds.), *Handbook of Mathematical Economics, Vol. IV*: 1523–1614.

Makowski, L. (1980), "A Characterization of Perfectly Competitive Economies with Production," *Journal of Economic Theory,* 22: 208–21.

(1983), "Competitive Stock Markets," *Review of Economic Studies,* 50: 305–30.

Mankiw, N.G. (1986), "The Equity Premium and the Concentration of Aggregate Shocks," *Journal of Financial Economics,* 17: 211–19.

Marcet, A. and K. Singleton (1990), "Private Communication," Unpublished, Graduate School of Business, Stanford University.

Marimon, R. (1987), "Kreps' Three Essays on Capital Markets' Almost Ten Years Later," *Revista Espanola de Economia.*

Mas-Colell, A. (1985), *The Theory of General Economic Equilibrium – A Differentiable Approach,* Cambridge University Press.

McManus, D. (1984), "Incomplete Markets: Generic Existence of Equilibrium and Optimality Properties in an Economy with Futures Markets," Unpublished, Department of Economics, University of Pennsylvania.

Mehra, R. and Prescott, E. (1985), "The Equity Premium: A Puzzle," *Journal of Monetary Economics,* 15: 145–61.

Merton, R. and Subrahmanyam, M. (1974), "The Optimality of a Competitive Stock Market," *Bell Journal of Economics and Management Science,* 5: 145–70.

Miller, M. (1986), "Financial Innovation: The Last Twenty Years and the Next," *Journal of Financial and Quantitative Analysis,* 21: 459–71.

Modigliani, F. and M. Miller (1958), "The Cost of Capital, Corporation Finance, and the Theory of Investment," *American Economic Review,* 48: 261–97.

Myers, S. (1984), "The Capital Structure Puzzle," *Journal of Finance,* 39: 575–92.

Myers, S. and N. Majluf (1984), "Corporate Financing and Investment Decisions when Firms Have Information that Investors do not Have," *Journal of Financial Economics*, 13: 187–221.

Polemarchakis, H. and B. Ku (1990), "Options and Equilibrium," *Journal of Mathematical Economics*, 19: 107–12.

Prescott, E. and R. Mehra (1980), "Recursive Competitive Equilibrium: The Case of Homogeneous Households," *Econometrica*, 48: 1365–79.

Radner, R. (1972), "Existence of Equilibrium of Plans, Prices and Price Expectations in a Sequence of Markets," *Econometrica*, 40: 289–303.

(1974), "A Note on Unanimity of Stockholders' Preferences Among Alternative Production Plans: A Reformulation of the Ekern–Wilson Model," *The Bell Journal of Economics and Management Science*, 5: 181–6.

Repullo, R. (1986), "On the Generic Existence of Radner Equilibria when there are as Many Securities as States of Nature," *Economic Letters*, 21: 101–5.

Ross, S. (1977), "The Determination of Financial Structure: The Incentive–Signalling Approach," *Bell Journal of Economics*, Spring, pp. 23–40.

(1978), "A Simple Approach to the Valuation of Risky Streams," *Journal of Business*, 51: 453–75.

(1989), "Institutional Markets, Financial Marketing, and Financial Innovation," *Journal of Finance*, 44: 541–56.

Rubinstein, M. (1976), "The Valuation of Uncertain Income Streams and The Pricing of Options," *Bell Journal of Economics*, 7: 407–25.

Saloner, G. (1984), "Self-Regulating Commodity Futures Exchanges," in R. Anderson, *Industrial Organization of Futures Markets*, Cambridge MA: Lexington Books.

Scheinkman, J. (1989), "Market Incompleteness and the Equilibrium Valuation of Assets," in S. Bhattacharya and G. Constantinides, *Theory of Valuation, Frontiers of Financial Theory, vol. I*, Totowa, NJ: Rowman and Littlefield, 45–51.

Scheinkman, J. and L. Weiss (1986), "Borrowing Constraints and Aggregate Economic Activity," *Econometrica*, 54: 23–45.

Sharpe, W. (1964), "Capital Asset Prices: A Theory of Market Equilibrium Under Conditions of Risk," *Journal of Finance*, 19: 425–42.

Shiller, R. (1979), "The Volatility of Long-Term Interest Rates and Expectations Models of the Term Structure," *Journal of Political Economy*, 87: 1190–209.

(1981), "Do Stock Prices Move Too Much to be Justified by Subsequent Changes in Dividends?" *American Economic Review*, 71: 421–36.

Shleifer, A. and R. Vishny (1986), "Large Shareholders and Corporate Control," *Journal of Political Economy*, 94: 461–88.

Stiglitz, J. (1972), "On the Optimality of the Stock Market Allocation of Investment," *Quarterly Journal of Economics*, 86: 25–60.

(1974), "On The Irrelevance of Corporate Financial Policy," *American Economic Review*, 64: 851–66.

Sundaresan, S. (1989), "Intertemporally Dependent Preferences and the Volatility of Consumption and Wealth," *Review of Financial Studies*, 2: 73–89.

Svennsson, L. and I. Werner (1990), "Nontraded Assets in Incomplete Markets:

Pricing and Portfolio Choice," Research Paper 2005, Graduate School of Business, Stanford University.

Telmer, C. (1990), "Asset Pricing Puzzles and Incomplete Markets," Unpublished, Department of Economics, Queen's University, Kingston, Ontario.

Weil, P. (1990), "Equilibrium Asset Prices with Undiversifiable Labor Income Risk," Unpublished, Department of Economics, Harvard University.

Werner, J. (1985), "Equilibrium in Economies with Incomplete Financial Markets," *Journal of Economic Theory*, 36: 110–19.

Wilson, R. (1972), "Comment on Stiglitz, 'On The Optimality of Stock Market Allocation of Investment'," Working Paper 8, IMSSS, Stanford University.

Working, H. (1953), "Futures Trading and Hedging," *American Economic Review*, 52: 431–59.

Yamazaki, A. (1989), "Monetary Equilibria in a Continuum Economy with General Transaction Technologies," Working Paper 89-39, Research Unit in Economics and Econometrics, Hitostubashi University.

CHAPTER 5

Incomplete financial markets and indeterminacy of competitive equilibrium*

David Cass

1   INTRODUCTION

The general conception of this line of inquiry is to broaden the canonical Walrasian or competitive equilibrium paradigm – a la Arrow-Debreu – to encompass (with regard to the economy's financial sector) **richer institutional structure** and **various market failures**. I believe that this is a very important undertaking for (somewhat) generalist-type theorists like myself: the Walrasian tradition is simply much too fundamental to be left to (purely) mathematical-type theorists with their excessive concern about existence in ever more abstract settings, or to (impurely?) macro- or finance-type theorists with their excessive reliance on non-robust or overly parametric examples. Be that as it may, the range of specific developments thus far has been quite modest, concentrating on inside (i.e., private) financial transactions within incomplete financial markets (using Arrow's famous reformulation of complete contingent goods markets as the benchmark), while maintaining the simplifications of perfect information, price-taking behavior, etc.

As one might have predicted, this research has focused on the three classical issues in general equilibrium theory: existence, optimality, and uniqueness or, better, determinacy. I will not have much to say about either existence or optimality – the first because I view it as primarily a technical issue (and, unsurprisingly, one which has received an inordinate amount of attention), the second because I cannot claim to be an expert on its intricacies. Fortunately, an excellent discussion of recent results on both problems can be found in John Geanakoplos' introduction to the special issue of the *JME* devoted to "Incomplete Markets" (Geanakoplos, 1990).

What I will expand on is the issue of determinacy, since I consider it to involve the most striking – as well as the most troublesome – property of these models: incomplete markets typically lead to significant price or **nominal** indeterminacy – that is, over and above that analogous to choosing a numeraire in the standard Walrasian model – which also naturally translates into substantial allocation or **real** indeterminacy.

While my primary objective is to present an overview of my own and others' past work on the analysis of indeterminacy, I also have two other important objectives in writing this chapter. First, specifically, in the appendix I attempt to explain – at a fairly informal level – what is essential in generating nominal as well as real indeterminacy when there are incomplete financial markets. Second, more generally, throughout the chapter I purposely attempt to emphasize my own considered opinions about the problem itself, which can be summarized in the following way:

> Nominal indeterminacy per se presents a severe practical hurdle for the rational expectations hypothesis. In short, is it plausible to maintain that households are capable of concentrating their beliefs (correctly) on one among a surfeit of possible market outcomes?

> Except in one very special situation – where all yields from financial instruments depend linearly homogeneously on future spot goods prices – competitive equilibrium with incomplete or, even more generally, otherwise imperfect financial markets exhibits pervasive real indeterminacy. Thus, in particular, this phenomenon does not depend on some very special feature of the means by which financial transactions take place.

> The degree of indeterminacy – nominal or real – depends on which financial parameters are treated as endogenous or **variable** (as opposed to exogenous or **fixed**). This means, taking a broad view, that the problems associated with indeterminacy will only be mitigated (and not eliminated) by elaborating the structure of the institutions and the behavior of the organizations (public or private) which constitute the financial sector.

Finally, at the outset I emphasize that – following most of the literature in this area – I will present the basic substantive results in the least conceptually complicated context possible (though then pointing out where important simplifications have been and should be examined further). Moreover, since this chapter is in the nature of a survey, in the text itself I will concentrate on results rather than proofs (though most of these, as the appendix tries to indicate, are pretty simple in conception, if also pretty complex in execution).

2   THE LEADING CASE

The basic model is essentially that described in Balasko and Cass (1989) or Geanakoplos and Mas-Colell (1989). There are C types of physical commodities (labelled by the superscript $c = 1, 2, \ldots, C$, and referred to as **goods**), and I types of credit or financial instruments (labelled by the superscript $i = 1, 2, \ldots, I$, and referred to as **bonds**). Both goods and bonds are traded on a spot market today, while only goods will be traded on a spot market in one of S possible states of the world tomorrow (these markets are labelled by the superscript $s = 0, 1, \ldots, S$, so that $s = 0$ represents today and $s > 0$ the possible states tomorrow, and are referred to as **spots**). Thus, altogether there are $G = (S + 1)C$ goods, whose quantities and (spot) prices are represented by the vectors:

$$x = (x^0, \ldots, x^s, \ldots, x^S,) \text{ (with } x^s = (x^{s,1}, \ldots, x^{s,c}, \ldots, x^{s,C})) \text{ and}$$
$$p = (p^0, \ldots, p^s, \ldots, p^S) \text{ (with } p^s = (p^{s,1}, \ldots, p^{s,c}, \ldots, p^{s,C})),$$

respectively. The quantities and prices of bonds are represented by the vectors:

$$b = (b^1, \ldots, b^i, \ldots, b^I) \text{ and}$$
$$q = (q^1, \ldots, q^i, \ldots, q^I),$$

respectively. [Note: It will be convenient, for example, in representing dollar values of spot market transactions, to treat every price or price-like (say, for instance, marginal utility) vector as a row. Otherwise I maintain the standard convention.] The typical bond, which costs q^i dollars at spot $s = 0$, promises to return a yield of $y^{s,i}$ dollars at spot $s > 0$. Let:

$$Y = \begin{bmatrix} y^{1,1} & & \\ & \ddots & \\ & & y^{s,i} \\ & & & \ddots \\ & & & & y^{S,I} \end{bmatrix} = \begin{bmatrix} y^1 \\ \vdots \\ y^s \\ \vdots \\ y^S \end{bmatrix}$$

$$= (S \times I) - \text{dimensional matrix of bond yields.}$$

Since, looking ahead, households are indifferent between having access to the whole array of bonds, or just a maximally linearly independent subset, there is no loss of generality in assuming that:

(A1)   Rank $Y = I$,   **no redundancy**

which implies that $I \leq S$. What gives the model its special character is assuming that, in fact:

(A2) $0 < I < S$.   **incomplete markets**

It will be convenient to let $D = S - I$, the **deficiency** in the bond market.

Finally, there are H households (labelled by the subscript $h = 1,2, \ldots ,H$) who are specified by (i) consumption sets $X_h = \mathbb{R}^{\mathbb{G}}_{++}$, (ii) utility functions $u_h : X_h \to \mathbb{R}$, and (iii) goods endowments $e_h \in X_h$. As in most of the literature on "smooth economies," I will assume throughout that:

(A3) u_h is C^2 (i.e., twice continuously differentiable), differentiably strictly increasing (i.e., $Du_h(x_h) \gg 0$) and differentiably strictly quasi-concave (i.e., $\Delta x \neq 0$ and $Du_h(x_h)\Delta x = 0 \Rightarrow \Delta x^T D^2 u_h(x_h)\Delta x < 0$), and has indifference surfaces with closure in X_h.

Let:

$$P = \{p \in \mathbb{R}^{G}_{++}\}$$
$$= \text{set of possible (no-free-lunch) spot goods prices,}$$
$$Q = \left\{ q \in \mathbb{R}^I : \text{there is no } b \in \mathbb{R}^I \text{s.t.} \begin{bmatrix} -q \\ Y \end{bmatrix} b > 0 \right\}$$
$$= \text{set of possible (no-financial-arbitrage) bond prices,}$$
$$\mathbf{Y} = \{ Y \in \mathbb{R}^{SI} : \text{rank } Y = I \}$$
$$= \text{set of possible bond yields, and}$$
$$E = \{ e = (e_1, \ldots ,e_h, \ldots ,e_H) \in (\mathbb{R}^{G}_{++})^H \}$$
$$= \text{set of possible goods endowments (as well as allocations).}$$

Then, given $(Y,e) \in \mathbf{Y} \times E$, $(p,q) \in P \times Q$ is a competitive equilibrium with incomplete financial markets, referred to hereafter as a **financial equilibrium**, if, when households optimize, i.,e.:

given (p,q,Y), $(x_h,b_h) = (f_h(p,q,Y,e_h),\phi_h(p,q,Y,e_h))$

solves the problem:

$$\begin{aligned}
&\text{maximize } u_h(x_h) \\
&\text{subject to } p^0(x_h^0 - e_h^0) = -qb_h, \\
&\qquad\qquad p^s(x_h^s - e_h^s) = y^s b_h, \text{ for } s > 0, \\
&\text{and} \qquad x_h \in X_h \qquad\qquad ,h = 1,2, \ldots ,H,
\end{aligned} \tag{1}$$

both spot goods and bond markets clear, i.e.:

$$\sum_h (x_h^{s,c} - e_h^{s,c}) = \sum_h (f_h^{s,c}(p,q,Y,e_h) - e_h^{s,c}) = 0, \text{ all } (s,c), \tag{2}$$

and

$$\sum_h b_h^i = \sum_h \phi_h^i(p,q,Y,e_h) = 0, \text{ all } i. \tag{3}$$

Remarks

1 Several specific aspects of this formulation greatly facilitate analyzing properties of financial equilibrium (though, as we shall see later on, are not necessarily crucial to establishing that real indeterminacy is pervasive). Most notable among these are the assumptions that: (i) There are only two periods, with no production (obviously, **the leading case**); (ii) The financial structure is exogenous (for instance, the number of bonds is given a priori), and all financial instruments are inside assets (that is, are issued and redeemed by households directly); (iii) The yields on financial instruments are specified in terms of units of account (which is certainly a polar case, usually contrasted to that in which yields are specified in terms of bundles of goods, representing a kind of generalized forward contract); [Note: In the literature the former are now commonly referred to as **nominal** assets, the latter **real** assets. I prefer the more specific terminology "bonds" and "forwards," partly because the obvious prototypes are in fact a bond or a forward, respectively, but mostly because this terminology avoids suggesting an exhaustive distinction. Many (if not most) financial instruments, for example (some types of) insurance policies, commodities futures or options, and, in my opinion, corporate stocks fit neatly into neither category.] (iv) The only market imperfection takes the form of a deficiency in the number of financial instruments (as opposed, in particular, to various restrictions on financial transactions, like quantity limits on short sales).

2 Analysis of financial equilibrium amounts to analysis of the solutions to the market clearing conditions (2) and (3). By virtue of the budget constraints in (1), however, $S+1$ of these equations are functionally dependent on the remainder (the analogue to Walras' law). Furthermore, there is some choice about which equations to treat as redundant. In particular, it is easily verified that (under assumption (A1)) those concerning the bonds together with a suitable selection of those for the first type of good at just $(S+1)-I$ spots are redundant, or, alternatively, that those concerning the first type of good at all $S+1$ spots are likewise redundant. An important implication of taking the first choice is that then variability of bond prices is not required for market clearing, and of taking the second that, again alternatively, then variability of spot prices for the first type of good is not required for market clearing. This means that, in addition to Y and e, either q (together with some household's marginal utilities of wealth at all spots) or $p^{\cdot,1} = (p^{0,1}, \ldots, p^{s,1}, \ldots, p^{S,1})$ can be viewed as parametric. These two possible approaches dictate the form in which I present the basic substantive results concerning real indeterminacy; they also correspond, respectively, to the central approaches taken in Balasko and Cass (1989)

(following Cass (1985)) and Geanakoplos and Mas-Colell (1989), where these results were first reported. (See also the paper by Werner (1986), which unifies the main results of both approaches by expanding on the first.) In the appendix I follow the second approach, since it survives generalizing the model to encompass additional impediments on the households' abilities to utilize financial markets for providing maximal or **full** wealth insurance.

3   THE BASIC RESULTS

Establishing the degree of real indeterminacy in this setting requires two further sorts of technical assumptions. The first concerns sufficiently flexible opportunities for exchange of credit (within the confines of incomplete markets), the second sufficiently disparate incentives for exchange of both goods and credit (in terms of numbers and also, implicitly, variety of households). So now assume that:

(A4′)   There is $b^+ \in \mathcal{R}^I$ **appropriately diverse yields**
          such that $Yb^+ \gg 0$; or

(A4″) Y is in general position; or

(A4‴) Y is variable; and

(A5) $H > D$.   **sufficiently numerous households**

Notice that, under either assumption (A4′) or assumption (A4″), Y is taken to be fixed. With various pairs of these additional assumptions (A4·) and (A5) – given the maintained assumptions (A1)–(A3) – one can demonstrate the following results.

THEOREM   Generically in endowments, the set of equilibrium allocations contains a smooth, D-dimensional manifold (with assumption (A4′)), or a smooth, $(S-1)$-dimensional manifold (with assumption (A4″)), or a smooth, DI-dimensional manifold (with assumption (A4‴)).

Remarks

1   The first and third results are Theorems 4.4 and 5.3 in Balasko/Cass, the second (essentially) Theorem 1 in Geanakoplos/Mas-Colell; the first obtains even when q is fixed (and thus, *a fortiori*, when q is variable). I find it quite elegant, but not really essential that the degree of real indeterminacy can be precisely measured in terms of the dimension of smooth manifolds. What is essential and important is what such measures reflect, namely, that any of a number of possible variables – or combinations of variables – can by themselves generate a continuum of economically distinct financial

equilibria. Thus, for instance, even when the particular spot goods prices $p^{s,1}$ (or, more generally, some weighted average of the spot goods prices, say, $\sum_c \alpha^{s,c} p^{s,c}$ with $\alpha^{s,c} \geq 0$, all c, and $\sum_c \alpha^{s,c} = 1$), all s, are fixed, variation in some or all of the bond yields $y^{s,i}$ can generate such a continuum. I will emphasize (and reemphasize) this point again, especially when I discuss the potential role of fiat or **outside** money in reducing real indeterminacy.

2 Assumptions (A4$'$) and (A4$''$) have the following interpretations (which persuade me that the first is somewhat more economic in flavor, the second somewhat more mathematic): on the one hand, since the households' financial opportunities are unaffected by replacing any particular bond with a fixed portfolio that includes that bond (a kind of mutual fund), while the choice of units of account is more or less arbitrary, (A4$'$) is basically equivalent to postulating the existence of **inside** money (or, a somewhat more misleading label, a "safe" asset), say, $y^{s,1} = 1, s > 0$. On the other hand, (A4$''$) means specifically that every I^2-dimensional submatrix of Y has full rank, which translates into the practical implication that – subject to the limitation of facing incomplete markets – households are capable of providing "full" wealth insurance (i.e., over any given subset of I future states).

3 Consider now just the case where q is variable (the one considered in some detail in the appendix). In this case, assumption (A4$'$) can be replaced by the weaker alternative:

(A4$'$a) $y^s \neq 0, s > 0$,

i.e., for every state there is some bond which has non-zero yield in that particular state. When (A4$'$a) is adopted as a maintained assumption, a defensible move, the Theorem can be interpreted to say that D is the **minimal** degree of real indeterminacy, and $S - 1$ (resp. DI) is the **maximal** degree of real indeterminacy with incomplete markets, when Y is fixed (resp. Y is variable). (Notice that these bounds only coincide when $I = 1$.) Both Geanakoplos/Mas-Colell and Werner (1990) provide fairly abstract characterizations of the intermediate possibilities (when Y is fixed), while Polemarchakis (1988) provides a more concrete characterization in terms of exchange-rate variability (when Y is variable).

4   VARIOUS REFINEMENTS AND EXTENSIONS

How robust is the phenomenon of extensive real indeterminacy? In this section I sketch an answer by briefly reviewing recent work which refines and extends the model and results described in the two previous sections.

While I have tried to mention all the work that I am aware of, I make no claim to being either completely comprehensive or even – from the various authors' viewpoints – particularly balanced.

For this discussion it is often useful to refocus attention from the separate variables bond prices q and bond yields Y to the overall variables bond **returns**, represented by $R = \begin{bmatrix} -q \\ Y \end{bmatrix}$. This manoeuver utilizes the fact that it is only properties of R which ultimately matter for household demand, and therefore for financial equilibrium itself as well.

Many periods

The only significant complication in going from two to many periods is that, with more than two periods, it is plausible to incorporate retrading markets for long-lived bonds. [Note: Under this generalization the spots correspond to enumerating the nodes in the standard date–event tree, while the bonds correspond to accounting for retrades as transactions in distinct financial instruments. I am also assuming that there are no constraints on retrading; in particular, households are presumed free to short-sell either original or retraded bonds.] The implication of this extension is that, in R, original or retraded bond prices may appear as entries in every row except those corresponding to the spots on the last date. Notice, however, that because the analysis in Balasko/Cass includes the case of fixed no-arbitrage bond prices and hence arbitrary fixed R, it again establishes the deficiency in the bond markets as the minimal degree of real indeterminacy under the obvious analogue of assumption (A4'). The situation with variable bond prices or yields is considerably more intricate; its analysis depends, in particular, on what sort of original bonds are available. Werner (1990) provides formulae for describing the degree of real indeterminacy in a three-period model with both (distinct) one- and two-period bonds, where the latter are originally traded today, and then retraded tomorrow.

Sunspots

I originally discovered the connection between incomplete markets and pervasive real indeterminacy while looking into the possibility of sunspots under various kinds of market failure (see Cass, 1989). My specific analysis involved the simplest leading example, i.e., where $C = 1$, $S = 2$, $I = 1$, and $H = 2$, with extrinsic rather than intrinsic uncertainty, i.e., where:

$$e_h^s = e_h^1, s > 0, \tag{4}$$

$$u_h(x_h) = \sum_{s>0} \pi^s v_h(x_h^0, x_h^s), \text{ with } \pi^s > 0, \text{ all } s \text{ and } \sum_{s>0} \pi^s = 1. \tag{5}$$

The Theorem doesn't cover the generalization of this leading example simply because the restriction (4) is non-generic in endowments. (The specialization (5) presents no problem.) Siconolfi (1990) has demonstrated that, in a general model of sunspots with incomplete markets, the set of equilibrium allocations contains a continuum, while Siconolfi and Villanacci (1991) have verified the minimal degree of real indeterminacy when (4) is weakened to rule out aggregate (but not individual) risk:

$$\sum_h e_h^s = \sum_h e_h^1, s > 0,$$

and the certainty utility functions in (5) are themselves additively separable, say:

$$v_h(x_h^0, x_h^1) = v_h^0(x_h^0) + v_h^1(x_h^1).$$

Fully extending the Theorem to cover sunspots remains a difficult open problem.

Inside instruments other than bonds

A common misconception is that the phenomenon of extensive real indeterminacy requires having bonds, that is, financial instruments whose yields are specified in units of account. Nothing could be farther from the truth – a point already emphatically underlined in both Balasko/Cass and Geanakoplos/Mas-Colell.

Consider yields which in principle depend on spot goods prices and other (as yet unspecified) parameters:

$$y^{s,i} = \Psi^{s,i}(p^s, \cdot). \tag{6}$$

For bonds (or so-called nominal assets), we have:

$$\Psi^{s,i}(p^s, \cdot) = \alpha^{s,i}, \text{ all } (s,i), \tag{7}$$

where $\alpha^{s,i}$ is simply a number of units of account, while for forwards (or so-called real assets):

$$\Psi^{s,i}(p^s, \cdot) = \sum_c \beta^{s,i,c} p^{s,c}, \text{ all } (s,i), \tag{8}$$

where $\beta^{s,i} = (\beta^{s,i,1}, \ldots, \beta^{s,i,c}, \ldots, \beta^{s,i,C})$ is simply a vector of quantities of goods. But there are obviously many other possibilities as well, for instance:

$$\Psi^{s,i}(p^s, \cdot) = \alpha^{s,i} + \sum_c \beta^{s,i,c} p^{s,c}, \text{ all } (s,i), \tag{9}$$

the general linear specification which encompasses both (7) and (8) as special cases.

For the time being, focus on just the three specifications (7), (8) and (9) (also taking, for the time being, the parameters $\alpha^{s,i}$ and $\beta^{s,i}$ as fixed). Appealing to the argument outlined in the appendix, intuitively the typical degree of indeterminacy under each of these specifications will be the same as the degree of **significant** nominal indeterminacy, which is determined by subtracting the maximum number of permissible price normalizations, say, N, from the total number of budget constraints, $S + 1$. Since the first budget constraint in (1) is linear homogeneous in spot goods and bond prices, it is always permissible to normalize, say, $p^{0,1} = 1$. The number of additional permissible price normalizations depends on the particular specification. Under (7) it is also permissible to normalize, say, $p^{s,1} = 1$ at any chosen spot $s = s' > 0$ (see the appendix), so that $N = 2$ and $(S + 1) - N = S - 1$; under (8) it is actually permissible to normalize, say, $p^{s,1} = 1$ at every spot $s > 0$ (since in this case each future budget constraint is linear homogeneous in its own spot goods prices), so that $N = S + 1$ and $(S + 1) - N = 0$; and under (9) there are in fact no additional permissible price normalizations, so that $N = 1$ and $(S + 1) - N = S$. In short, *only* the special case (8) entails that there is necessarily generic local uniqueness, and hence no extensive real indeterminacy; indeed, the general case (9) entails even *one more* degree of real indeterminacy than the special case (7) which has been the main focus of attention!

The formal analysis which validates my intuitive, "counting equations and unknowns" argument for the general case (9) can be found in Pietra (1988). Note that exactly the same sort of intuition suggests that, with an arbitrary specification of yields (6) (excluding the special cases (7) and (8)), the typical degree of real indeterminacy will be S. Express support for this conjecture is contained in Krasa and Werner (1991), who analyze a model of (potentially) incomplete markets with a variety of different financial instruments, including inside money, forwards and options written on the forwards.

Two other points are worth explicit mention. First, except in the special case (7), the rank of R – and hence the dimension of the wealth space it spans – may vary with p, which raises a problem for existence of financial equilibrium (and undoubtedly explains some preoccupation in the literature with the special case (8)). Usually, that is, for a typical specification of (6), the property of existence will (at best) *only* be generic (in both endowments and the parameters specifying yields). But also, to repeat for emphasis, usually the property of indeterminacy will *necessarily* be generic. (Pietra and Krasa/Werner both illustrate these two points very nicely.)

Second, even in the special case (8), when (some or all of) the parameters $\beta^{s,i,c}$ are treated as variables, there will be extensive real indeterminacy. More generally, suppose that the parameters in (6) reflect the characteristics of some particular array of financial instruments. Then, if various of these parameters are also taken as variable, this will usually contribute to increasing the degree of real indeterminacy beyond S. And there is just no convincing argument for taking all such parameters as fixed, since they essentially correspond – in abstract – to the terms on which credit is transacted between households.

Finally, I must surely note that, for the special case (8), Mas-Colell (1991) provides grounds for the assertion that, very roughly speaking, with "many" states of the world, it is not atypical that there will be commensurately "many" distinct financial equilibria. Thus, even in the most favorable circumstances, those holding to the rational expectations hypothesis may take only scant comfort from generic local uniqueness!

Outside money

A second misconception or, perhaps better, oversimplification concerning this issue is the belief that, since "the reason" for indeterminacy is that the future "price level" is not tied down, introducing the institution of outside money per se will eliminate the problem. While there is some basis for this conjecture, its validity depends on how one conceives the operation of a monetary system and, even more critically, on what one takes as variable in a monetary economy.

Consider first what difference the particular role assigned to outside money makes, in a setting where there are both inside and outside money, and where bond yields are fixed. At one extreme, when outside money is only required in order to pay terminal taxes (Villanacci, 1991), there is – for the same reason just previously explained – actually *one more* degree of significant nominal indeterminacy, and hence real indeterminacy. At the other extreme, when outside money is instead required in order to finance spot goods consumption now (Magill and Quinzii, 1988, 1991), or is simply assumed by households to have value to finance spot goods consumption later (Cass, 1990), there are in fact $S - 1$ less degrees of significant nominal indeterminacy, and hence no real indeterminacy. So, as conjectured, in these last two models – but of course, not the first – outside money *does* restore the generic local uniqueness associated with standard Walrasian equilibrium. [Note: The Magill/Quinzii model is somewhat cruder than most cash-in-advance models, since it amounts to imposing a very simplistic quantity theory of money spot-by-spot. But equally objection-able, the Cass model is just as crude as all such money-in-the-utility-function models. Nonetheless, both serve the useful purpose of showing that, in *some* monetary economies, outside money eliminates indetermin-acy.]

Consider next what happens when bond yields (excluding those on inside money) are variable, especially in the two models most favorable to monetarism. It turns out (again referring to my own work on monetary models) that now there is *absolutely no* reduction in the degree of significant nominal indeterminacy, and hence real indeterminacy; in this situation there are $D(S-1)$ degrees of real indeterminacy. (This formula differs from that given in the Theorem since it is derived under the hypothesis that $y^{s,1} = 1, s > 0$, is fixed, that is, that there is inside money.)

Since I find it quite reasonable (even compelling) to believe that, in a monetary economy, bond yields (as a proxy for the yields on a variety of financial instruments) as well as spot goods and bond prices are en-dogenous, I conclude the following (from the analysis of these extraordi-narily rudimentary models): the institution of outside money may reduce the degree of real indeterminacy. After all, it is likely that there is some connection (no matter how loose) between "monetary policy" and bond yields, so that these yields are not perfectly free to vary arbitrarily. However, at this time there are simply no acceptable grounds for asserting that outside money completely eliminates real indeterminacy.

Restricted participation on financial markets

While there might be some disagreement over whether, in a modern, developed economy, financial markets are actually incomplete, there can hardly be any disagreement over whether at least some economic agents are variously constrained in transacting on those financial markets. Without attempting a detailed explanation of how particular constraints come about (for example, in order to resolve problems arising from moral hazard), it is still possible to extend the model of section 2 to incorporate, in a very general way, their implications for financial equilibrium by adding a restriction of the form:

$$b_h \in B_h \subset \mathbb{R}^I$$

to the problem (1). Here B_h represents the **portfolio set**, the possible credit transactions available to the household. Balasko, Cass, and Siconolfi (1990) show that the Theorem of section 3 extends to the case where the portfolio set is defined by linear homogeneous equality constraints (so that B_h is an I_h-dimensional linear subspace, with $0 \le I_h \le I$). Just recently Cass,

Siconolfi and Villanacci (1991) have further extended these results to the case where the portfolio set is defined by smooth, quasi-concave inequality constraints. Either of these models with, say, **restricted participation** constitutes a bona fide generalization of the model with incomplete markets, but the latter potentially embodies far more interesting institutional features (and not just the flavor of restricted participation) since it permits, for instance, modeling short sales bounds or market margin requirements. Of course, in principle such constraints should themselves be determined endogenously.

Small imperfections in financial markets

An intriguing question is whether a "small" departure from complete markets results in a "small" amount of indeterminacy (or, closely related, a "small" departure from Pareto optimality). Obviously, the answer will depend on the choice of a more specific formulation of the question. Building on my joint analysis with Balasko and Siconolfi, I have provided one sort of basis for an affirmative response (Cass, 1990). Assume that there are complete markets, $I = S$, and that only some households are restricted:

$$B_h = \begin{cases} \mathbb{R}^I & ,h = 1,\ldots, H' < H \\ B_h \subset \mathbb{R}^I, \text{ otherwise.} \end{cases}$$

For instance, the households $h > H'$ might only have access to a subset of all the bond markets. Now consider the "improved participation" economy consisting of M replicas of the first H' (unrestricted) households, and N replicas of the remainder, with $M/N > 1$, and let $M/N \to \infty$. Then, the set of financial equilibria converges to that of the standard Walrasian economy consisting of just the unrestricted households. So, in this precise sense, indeterminacy – and also non-optimality – become (generically) insignificant as incompleteness becomes (relatively) insignificant.

Much caution is warranted here, however. Pursuing a quite different approach, Green and Spear (1989) and Zame (1988) formulate the idea of a "small" departure from complete markets by assuming that $I < S = \infty$, and then letting $I \to \infty$. They find – modeling financial instruments as forwards, and concentrating on the issue of optimality – that it is only under very restrictive conditions on the parametric structure of yields that equilibrium allocation converges to the set of Pareto optima. These results suggest that it is quite unlikely that under their formulation indeterminacy becomes (generically) insignificant.

Notice that, even under my formulation, since the argument concerns asymptotic behavior, the rational expectations hypothesis remains highly suspect: no matter how large the economy, a continuum remains a continuum!

Concluding comment

This review is almost as revealing for what it omitted as for what it included. For instance, I have said nothing at all about introducing firms or intermediaries, both of which create financial instruments – and the restrictions on their trade as well – endogenously. Obviously, I think that this undertaking, just now getting started, is an important and fascinating subject for future research. The same can be said about other possible projects that I have only alluded to earlier – for instance, incorporating a more tenable model of the institution of outside money, or elaborating the dependence of portfolio restrictions on endogenous variables.

APPENDIX

The purpose of this appendix is to provide some insight into the rationale for nominal indeterminacy, as well as the logic supporting its translation into a corresponding degree of real indeterminacy (barring exceptional circumstances).

Nominal indeterminacy

The central idea in establishing this result is pure and simply to "count equations and unknowns." That is, the essence of the analysis involves treating the market clearing conditions (2) and (3) as a system of equations in the whole collection of variables p,q,Y, and e and then – after verifying certain crucial prerequisites (by utilizing several basic techniques from differential topology) – employing the old workhorse of economic theory, the implicit function theorem. In following this program I intentionally give short shrift to the details of the underlying justification for treating particular price variables as being "dependent" (and the other price cum "fundamental" variables as being "independent") – the "certain crucial prerequisites" referred to just above.

Recall what, roughly, the implicit function theorem asserts: suppose that we are given a system of J (independent) equations in K (explicit) variables, so that necessarily $J \leq K$ (and the equations, being defined by sufficiently smooth functions of the specified variables, have Jacobian of full rank J at some particular solution). Then, locally, the system can be solved for J (distinguished) variables as continuously differentiable functions of the other $K - J$ variables. Thus, my task basically amounts to calculating J,K

and $K - J$ for the particular system of equations at hand. In carrying out this task it is quite instructive to begin by recalling a more familiar example, that arising from the standard Walrasian model.

So now suppose that, instead of trading on many spot goods and the bond markets, households trade on a single "overall" market for current and future contingent goods. For simplicity letting the previous notation also represent prices and allocations for such an economy, then, here, given $e \in E, p \in P$ is a **Walrasian equilibrium** if, when households optimize (according to the usual budget-constrained, utility-maximization problem), i.e.:

given $p, x_h = g_h(p, e_h)$ solves the problem

$$
\begin{aligned}
&\text{maximize } u_h(x_h) \\
&\text{subject to } p(x_h - e_h) = 0 \\
&\text{and} \qquad x_h \in X_h \qquad , h = 1, 2, \ldots, H,
\end{aligned}
\tag{A1}
$$

just the overall market for goods clears, i.e.:

$$
\sum_h (x_h^{s,c} - e_h^{s,c}) = \sum_h (g_h^{s,c}(p, e_h) - e_h^{s,c}) = 0, \text{ all } (s,c).
\tag{A2}
$$

In this setting, from the restriction imposed by the budget constraints in (A1) it follows that the market clearing conditions (A2) yield only $G - 1$ independent equations (Walras' law), while p and e constitute the only explicit variables. Thus, obviously $J = G - 1$ and $K = G + HG$, and (locally), say, the $K - J = 1 + HG$ variables $p^{0,1}$ and e uniquely determine the remaining prices p less $p^{0,1}$. In other words, there is one degree of nominal indeterminacy, the choice of the "price level" represented by $p^{0,1}$. Of course, from the linear homogeneity of the budget constraints in (A1) it also follows that such nominal indeterminacy is "insignificant," in the sense that it never engenders any real indeterminacy. For this reason it is conventional to normalize prices, for instance, by setting $p^{0,1} = 1$, and to maintain that equilibrium is locally unique (up to a "harmless" choice of numeraire), or that, say, there are no **significant** degrees of nominal indeterminacy in the Walrasian model. While I will also adopt this position in discussing the model with incomplete markets, I repeat for emphasis that it is, from a practical viewpoint, quite misleading; even such "insignificant" nominal indeterminacy raises havoc for presupposing rational expectations (a very important message, but one I will now take as having been fully delivered).

In applying similar reasoning to the model summarized by (1)–(3) it turns out that the only potential complication involves figuring out the number of significant price (or price-like) variables. So now returning to consideration of this system, we first recall that the restrictions imposed by the budget constraints in (1) render $S + 1$ of the market clearing conditions

(2) and (3) redundant, in particular, say, those concerning just the first type of good. Since these equations number altogether $G+I, J=G+I-(S+1)$, while clearly, since in general p,q,Y, and e are all variable, $K= G+I+SI+HG$. Thus (locally), say, the $K-J=(S+I)+SI+HG$ variables $p^{\cdot,1}$, Y, and e uniquely determine the remaining spot prices p less $p^{\cdot,1}$ and there are apparently $(S+1)+SI$ degrees of nominal indeterminacy. In order to explain why exactly 2 (when Y is fixed) or $(S+1)+S^2$ (when Y is variable) degrees of such nominal indeterminacy are "insignificant," it is very helpful (if not indispensable)) to digress a moment and reformulate the budget constraints in (1). The particular reformulation I have chosen to elaborate will also be very convenient for the discussion in the succeeding subsection.

Focus on the budget constraints of a typical household h:

$$p^0(x_h^0 - e_h^0) = -qb_h \text{ and}$$
$$p^s(x_h^s - e_h^s) = y^s b_h, \text{ for } s>0, \tag{A3}$$

and consider the following two-step transformation (both steps of which leave the household's consumption opportunities unaltered):

Step 1
Divide each of the budget constraints in (A3) by its own spot price for the first type of good:

$$\bar{p}^0(x_h^0 - e_h^0) = (-q/p^{0,1})b_h \text{ and}$$
$$\bar{p}^s(x_h^s - e_h^s) = (y^s/p^{s,1})b_h, \text{ for } s>0, \tag{A4}$$

where $\bar{p}^s = p^s/p^{s,1}, s=0,1,\ldots,S$.

Step 2
Assume, without loss of generality (by using assumption (A1) and relabelling spots appropriately), that the last I rows of Y are linearly independent, so that we can partition:

$$Y = \begin{bmatrix} \dot{Y} \\ \ddot{Y} \end{bmatrix} = \begin{bmatrix} y^1 \\ \vdots \\ y^D \\ \hline y^{D+1} \\ \vdots \\ y^{D+I} \end{bmatrix},$$

where again $D=S-I$ and thus $\ddot{Y}$ is an I^2-dimensional, full rank matrix. Then, reduce the right-hand side of (A4) by transforming the variables b^i to the variables $b^{i'} = (y^{D+i}/p^{D+i,1})b_h, i=1,2,\ldots,I$, as follows:

$$
\begin{bmatrix}
\dfrac{-q/p^{0,1}}{y^1/p^{1,1}} \\
\vdots \\
\dfrac{y^D/p^{D,1}}{y^{D+1}/p^{D+1,1}} \\
\vdots \\
y^{D+I}/p^{D+I,1}
\end{bmatrix} b_h =
\begin{bmatrix}
-(1/p^{0,1})q \\
\begin{pmatrix} 1/p^{1,1} & & 0 \\ & \ddots & \\ 0 & & 1/p^{D,1} \end{pmatrix} \dot{Y} \\
\begin{pmatrix} 1/p^{D+1,1} & & 0 \\ & \ddots & \\ 0 & & 1/p^{D+I,1} \end{pmatrix} \ddot{Y}
\end{bmatrix} b_h
\tag{A5}
$$

$$
= \left[\left(\begin{matrix} -(1/p^{0,1})q \\ \begin{bmatrix} 1/p^{1,1} & & 0 \\ & \ddots & \\ 0 & & 1/p^{D,1} \end{bmatrix} \dot{Y} \end{matrix} \right) \left(\begin{bmatrix} 1/p^{D+1,1} & & 0 \\ & \ddots & \\ 0 & & 1/p^{D+I,1} \end{bmatrix} \ddot{Y} \right)^{-1} \right] b_h'
$$

$$
= \begin{bmatrix}
-(1/p^{0,1})q\,\ddot{Y}^{-1}\begin{pmatrix} p^{D+1,1} & & 0 \\ & \ddots & \\ 0 & & p^{D+I,1} \end{pmatrix} \\
\begin{pmatrix} 1/p^{1,1} & & 0 \\ & \ddots & \\ 0 & & 1/p^{D,1} \end{pmatrix} \dot{Y}\ddot{Y}^{-1} \begin{pmatrix} p^{D+1,1} & & 0 \\ & \ddots & \\ 0 & & p^{D+I,1} \end{pmatrix} \\
I
\end{bmatrix} b_h'
$$

$$
= \begin{bmatrix}
-q' \\
\hline
\dot{Y}' \\
\hline
I
\end{bmatrix} b_h',
$$

where:

$$q' = q \ddot{Y}^{-1} \begin{bmatrix} p^{D+1,1}/p^{0,1} & & 0 \\ & \ddots & \\ 0 & & p^{D+I,1}/p^{0,1} \end{bmatrix}$$

and

$$\dot{Y}' = \begin{bmatrix} \omega^{1,1}(p^{D+1,1}/p^{1,1}) & \cdots & & \omega^{1,I}(p^{D+I,1}/p^{1,1}) \\ & \ddots & & \\ \vdots & & \omega^{j,k}(p^{D+k,1}/p^{j,1}) & \\ & & & \ddots \\ u^{D,1}(p^{D+1,1}/p^{D,1}) & \cdots & & \omega^{D,I}(p^{D+I,1}/p^{D,1}) \end{bmatrix} \quad (A6)$$

with $\Omega = - \dot{Y}\ddot{Y}^{-1}$;

the reason for the sign change in the definition of Ω will become clear below. [Note: It is easily seen that, if q are no-financial-arbitrage prices for bond yields $Y = \begin{bmatrix} \dot{Y} \\ \ddot{Y} \end{bmatrix}$, then q' are also no-financial-arbitrage prices for bond yields $Y' = \begin{bmatrix} \dot{Y}' \\ I \end{bmatrix}$. This means that, in (A5), for all practical purposes we can safely ignore the genesis of $q' \in \mathbb{R}^I$ – but of course, not that of $\dot{Y}' \in \mathbb{R}^{DI}$.]

Letting:

$$\bar{P} = \begin{bmatrix} \bar{p}^0 & & 0 \\ & \ddots & \\ 0 & & \bar{p}^S \end{bmatrix}$$

and $R' = \begin{bmatrix} -q' \\ \dot{Y}' \\ I \end{bmatrix}$,

and then substituting from (A5) into (A4) (while rewriting "b_h" for "b'_h") the budget constraints in (1) can be compactly reformulated as:

$$\bar{P}(x_h - e_h) = R'b_h. \quad (A7)$$

Now simply notice that, by virtue of the structure of $\dot{Y}'$ displayed in (A6), nothing significant is lost by assuming – when Y is fixed – that, for instance, $p^{0,1} = p^{D+1,1} = 1$ or – when Y is variable – that, for instance, $p^1 = 1$ and $\dot{Y} = I$ (so that, in (A6), $\dot{Y}' = -\Omega = \dot{Y}$, a $(D \times I)$-dimensional matrix): there are only $(S+1)-2=S-1$, or $[(S+1)+SI]-[(S+1)+I^2]=DI$ (significant) degrees of nominal indeterminacy, respectively.

Table 5.1 summarizes the foregoing enumeration, and should aid in digesting it.

Its translation into real indeterminacy

In order to see how the conclusions of the Theorem in the text follow from these two alternative degrees of (significant) nominal indeterminacy, it is convenient to introduce an additional piece of notation that permits concentrating on just significant price or yield variation.

Consider the transformed representation of bond yields in (A6), the matrix $\dot{Y}$. Since I will only be concerned with perturbing $p^{\cdot 1}$ (with $p^{0,1}=p^{D+1,1}=1$, for Y fixed) or Y (with $p^{\cdot 1}=1$ and $\ddot{Y}=I$, for Y variable), let:

$$\omega = (p^{1,1},\ldots,p^{D,1},1,p^{D+2,1},\ldots,p^{D+I,1})$$

as well as

$$\Omega = -\dot{Y}\ddot{Y}^{-1}.$$

Then, for simplicity suppressing the superfluous "'" (since q' depends only indirectly on ω and Ω under either hypothesis) we can rewrite $\dot{Y}'$ and R' as:

$$\dot{Y} = \dot{Y}(\omega,\Omega) = -\begin{bmatrix} \omega^{1,1}(1/\omega^1) & \cdots & \omega^{1,I}(\omega^{D+I}/\omega^1) \\ & \ddots & \\ \vdots & \omega^{j,k}(\omega^{D+k}/\omega^j) & \\ & & \ddots \\ \omega^{D,1}(1/\omega^D) & \cdots & \omega^{D,I}(\omega^{D+I}/\omega^D) \end{bmatrix} \qquad (A8)$$

and

$$R = R(q,\omega,\Omega) = \begin{bmatrix} -q \\ \dot{Y}(\omega,\Omega) \\ I \end{bmatrix},$$

respectively (with a corresponding simplification of (A7)).

At this point, the particular approach I prefer basically involves analyzing the overall implications of the households' personalized no-financial-arbitrage conditions (which derive from the Lagrangean characterization of the optimal solution to (1) after the budget constraints have been reformulated according to (A7); cf, again, Balasko/Cass). [Note: An

Table 5.1. *Nominal indeterminacy*

	Walrasian Equilibrium	Financial Equilibrium — Y fixed	Financial Equilibrium — Y variable
Equations	$\sum_h (g_h^{s,c}(p,e_h) - e_h^{s,c}) = 0$, all (s,c)	$\sum_h (f_h^{s,c}(p,q,Y,e_h) - e_h^{s,c}) = 0$, all (s,c) and $\sum_h \phi_h^i(p,q,Y,e_h) = 0$, all i	
no. of equations	G	$G+I$ — $s+1$	$G+I$ — $s+1$
interdependencies (no. of budget constraints)	1	$s+1$	$(S+1)+I^2$
$J = $ no. of independent equations	$G-1$	$G+I-(S+1)$	$G+I-(S+1)$
Variables			
no. of variables	p,e — $G+HG$	p,q,e — $G+I+HG$	p,q,Y,e — $G+I+SI+HG$
insignificancies (no. of price "normalizations")	1	2	$(S+1)+I^2$
$K = $ no. of significant variables	$(G-1)+HG$	$(G-2)+HG$	$[G-(S+1)]+I+DI+HG$
$K-J = $ no. of "independent" and significant variables	HG, say, e	$(S-1)+HG$, say, $p^{s,1},\ s>1$, and e	$DI+HG$, say, Ω and e
$K-J-HG = $ degree of (significant) nominal indeterminacy	0	$S-1$	DI

alternative approach involves analyzing the overall implications of the budget constraints themselves; cf, again, Geanakoplos/Mas-Colell. In my opinion this second approach is not nearly as efficient (or powerful) for drawing conclusions about properties of the mapping, say, for Y fixed, $f: M \to E$ such that:

$$(p,q,e) \to (x_1,. \ . \ .,x_h,. \ . \ .,x_H)$$
$$= f(p,q,Y,e)$$
$$= (f_1(p,q,Y,e_1),. \ . \ .,f_h(p,q,Y,e_h),. \ . \ .,f_H(p,q,Y,e_H)),$$

where $M \subset P \times Q \times E$ represents the equilibrium set, and thus $f(M) \subset E$ represents the corresponding allocation set.] Associating the Lagrange multipliers $\lambda_h = (\lambda_h^0,. \ . \ .,\lambda_h^s,. \ . \ .,\lambda_h^S) \in R_{++}^{S+1}$ with the constraints (A7), the first-order conditions for (1) become:

$$Du_h(x_h) = \lambda_h \bar{P} \tag{A9}$$

and

$$\lambda_h R = \dot{\lambda}_h \begin{bmatrix} -q \\ \dot{Y} \end{bmatrix} + \dot{\lambda}_h = \underline{0}$$

or

$$\lambda_h = \dot{\lambda}_h \left[I \begin{pmatrix} q \\ -\dot{Y} \end{pmatrix} \right], \tag{A10}$$

where, as before, I partition $\lambda_h = (\dot{\lambda}_h, \dot{\lambda}_h) = ((\lambda_h^0,. \ . \ .,\lambda_h^D),(\lambda_h^{D+1},. \ . \ .,\lambda_h^{D+I}))$. Substituting from (A10) into (A9) yields the fundamental construct for verifying generic existence of precise degrees of indeterminacy:

$$Du_h(x_h) = \dot{\lambda}_h \left[I \begin{pmatrix} q \\ -\dot{Y} \end{pmatrix} \right] \bar{P}, h = 1,2,. \ . \ .,H. \tag{A11}$$

The key mechanism for generating real from nominal indeterminacy, in principle, is quite simple. Perturbations of the $S-1$ spot prices ω (typically) or the, say, reduced form bond yields Ω (generally) alter the linear subspace orthogonal to that spanned by the columns of R (alternatively, and equivalently, the latter subspace itself). But this in turn (typically) changes the set of equilibrium allocations consistent with R according – in particular – to (A11) (alternatively, to (A7)). In order for this chain process to actually work out it must be the case, first, that R is sufficiently sensitive to price or yield variation, and second, that, as a whole, households are sufficiently sensitive to their altered financial opportunities. Assumption (A4) is designed to guarantee the former, and assumption (A5) (together with enough variety of endowments, given preferences) the latter. Before describing how these two assumptions operate, it is quite illuminating to look at several examples in which, though (significant) nominal indeterminacy is pervasive, it doesn't necessarily induce any real indeterminacy.

EXAMPLE 1   *Fully complete markets*: Suppose that $I = S$. Then (adapting previous usage in the natural way), $Y = \ddot{Y}$ and

$$R = \begin{bmatrix} -q \\ I \end{bmatrix},$$

and clearly, whether Y is fixed or variable, since R is essentially independent of both ω and Ω there is purely nominal indeterminacy. I must reemphasize, however, that, even in such an idyllic situation, households would still surely be in a real quandary about what prices they could reasonably expect in the future (as they surely are in any actual economic environment!).

EXAMPLE 2   *Fully incomplete markets*: Suppose that $I = 0$ or, to the same end, that $0 < I \le S$ but $Y = 0$. Then (again adapting previous usage in the natural way), necessarily $q = 0$, so that:

$$R = 0,$$

and we have exactly the same outcome as in the opposite case where there are fully complete markets.

EXAMPLE 3   *Incomplete markets with Arrow securities (for a subset of future spots)*: Suppose that $0 < I < S$ and:

$$y^{s,i} = \begin{cases} 1, & \text{for } s = D + i, i = 1, 2, \ldots, I \\ 0, & \text{otherwise.} \end{cases}$$

Then, $Y = \begin{bmatrix} 0 \\ I \end{bmatrix}$, so $\Omega = 0$ and

$$R = \begin{bmatrix} -q \\ 0 \\ I \end{bmatrix},$$

and again, clearly, for Y fixed, since R is independent of ω, there is purely nominal indeterminacy.

EXAMPLE 4   *Incomplete markets with inside money plus a subset of Arrow securities*: Suppose, slightly modifying the previous example, that bond 1 is inside money (rather than the Arrow security paying off at spot $D + 1$). Then:

$$Y = \begin{bmatrix} 1 & 0 \\ & I \end{bmatrix} = \begin{bmatrix} -/\dot{Y} \\ \ddot{Y} \end{bmatrix} = \begin{bmatrix} \overline{(1 \qquad 0)} \\ \left(\overline{(1,0,\ldots,0)} \right) \\ 1 \qquad I \end{bmatrix}$$

with

$$\ddot{Y}^{-1} = \begin{bmatrix} (1,0,\ldots,0) \\ -1 \qquad I \end{bmatrix},$$

so $\Omega = -\begin{bmatrix} 1 & 0 \end{bmatrix}$ and

$$R = \begin{bmatrix} -q \\ \begin{pmatrix} 1/\omega^1 \\ \vdots & 0 \\ 1/\omega^D \end{pmatrix} \\ I \end{bmatrix}.$$

In this example, for Y fixed, only perturbations of the first D elements of ω, say, $\dot\omega = (\omega^1, \omega^2, \cdots, \omega^D)$, affect R and therefore possibly generate real indeterminacy; Y satisfies assumption (A4′) but not (A4″). [Note: Generally, these two assumptions are not nested, so either can be satisfied when the other is not.]

EXAMPLE 5   Pareto optimality: Suppose that e is a Pareto optimal allocation (which is always true when $H = 1$). Then, clearly, since the only equilibrium allocation is autarky, the households' equilibrium behavior is independent of R, and there is, once again, purely nominal indeterminacy.

To see what can be learned from the first four examples – and understand why perturbations of ω and Ω alter the column span of R, say, for simplicity, **span** R, and thereby its orthogonal complement as well, that is, for short, why such perturbations are **effective** – it is important to bear in mind that, for this analysis, when Y is fixed, then $\Omega = -\dot{Y}\ddot{Y}^{-1}$ is also fixed, and only ω is perturbed, while when Y is variable, then $\omega = 1$ itself is fixed, and only Ω is perturbed.

From examination of the examples it is apparent that in each of the first three the difficulty is simply that no permissible perturbation is effective, while in the fourth, that only certain permissible perturbations (namely, of the subvector $\dot\omega$) are effective. More generally, and equally apparent from examination of R as displayed in (A8), is why assumptions (A4′) and (A4″) guarantee that perturbations of $\dot\omega$ and ω, respectively, are effective. In the first instance $Yb^+ \gg 0$ is equivalent to $(\dot{Y}\ddot{Y}^{-1})b^{+\prime} \gg 0$, where $b^{+\prime} = \ddot{Y}b^+$, and assumption (A4′) is tantamount to assuming that at least one element in each row of Ω is non-zero (which is, of course, why (A4′) can be replaced by (A4′a)). Hence, for $j = 1, 2, \ldots, D$:

$$\omega^{j,k} \neq 0 \ \& \ \omega^{j'} \neq \omega^{j''} \ (\text{with } \omega^{s'} = \omega^{s''} \text{ for } s = D + k, k = 1, 2, \ldots, I) \Rightarrow$$
$$R(q', \omega', \Omega) b \notin \mathrm{span} R(q'', \omega'', \Omega), \text{ for } b^i \neq 0, i = k, = 0, \text{ otherwise.}$$

In the second instance, assumption (A4″) implies that every element of Ω is non-zero. [Note: To say that "Y is in general position" means precisely that every I^2-dimensional submatrix of Y has full rank. This condition is violated if, for some (j,k), $\omega^{j,k} = 0$, because then replacing the kth row in $\ddot{Y}$ with the jth row in $\dot{Y}$ yields an I^2-dimensional submatrix with rank equal $I - 1$.] Hence, for $j = 1, 2, \ldots, D, k = 2, 3, \ldots, I$:

$$\omega^{j,k} \neq 0 \ (\text{resp. } \omega^{j,1} \neq 0), \omega^{j'} = \omega^{j''} \ \& \ \omega^{D+k'} \neq \omega^{D+k''} \ (\text{resp. } \omega^{j'} \neq \omega^{j''}) \Rightarrow$$
$$R(q', \omega', \Omega) b \notin \mathrm{span} R(q'', \omega'', \Omega), \quad \text{for} \quad b^i \neq 0, i = k \quad (\text{resp. } i = j), = 0,$$
otherwise.

It should now be more or less obvious why assumption (A4‴) works equally well:

$$\omega^{j,k'} \neq \omega^{j,k''} \Rightarrow$$
$$R(q', \omega, \Omega') b \notin \mathrm{span} R(q'', \omega, \Omega''), \text{ for } b^i \neq 0, i = k, = 0, \text{ otherwise.}$$

Finally, it is worthwhile mentioning again that while assumption (A4′) (but not (A4″)) has some economic content – and thus permits arguing for real indeterminacy without mathematical artifice – it also entails a weaker result than assumption (A4″), since it only provides a lower bound on the degree of real indeterminacy.

Once it has been determined that suitable perturbations of spot prices or bond yields are effective, the rest is easy (at least in conception). With enough households, as specified by assumption (A5), the property that:

$$\text{rank } [Du_h(x_h), h = 1, 2, \ldots, H] = \text{rank } [\dot{\lambda}_h, h = 1, 2, \ldots, H] = D + 1, \quad (A12)$$

which is its maximal value, is – like the property that $p^{\cdot,1}$, Y and e can be taken as "independent" variables – generic in endowments. That is, this "rank" property obtains (for some financial equilibrium) on an open, dense subset of E. [Note: Of course, example 5 illustrates the difficulty when (A12) fails, since, if x is a Pareto optimal allocation, then:

$$\text{rank } [Du_h(x_h), h = 1, 2, \ldots, H] = 1. \quad (A13)$$

This last result therefore also basically ratifies the intuition that, in the presence of incomplete markets, the coordination required by (A13) is most unlikely.] So, locally, variation in ω or Ω (by means of perturbing the overall returns exhibited in (A8)) must typically map diffeomorphically into variation in x (by virtue of satisfying the gradient restrictions exhibited in (A11)). As in the preceding subsection, I give short shrift to the argument supporting this last step – which again amounts to utilizing basic techniques from differential topology. For a detailed account, the interested reader is once more referred to Balasko/Cass.

Notes

* My endeavors on this and related topics have benefited greatly from interaction with many colleagues and students. I am especially indebted to my several co-authors, Yves Balasko, Paolo Siconolfi, and Antonio Villanacci. They, of course, bear no responsibility for the (occasionally idiosyncratic) opinions I express here. Research support from the University of Pennsylvania, CEPREMAP and the NSF is also gratefully acknowledged.

References

Balasko, Y. and D. Cass (1989), "The Structure of Financial Equilibrium with Exogenous Yields: The Case of Incomplete Markets," *Econometrica*, 57: 135–62.

Balasko, Y., D. Cass and P. Siconolfi, (1990), "The Structure of Financial Equilibrium with Exogenous Yields: The Case of Restricted Participation," *Journal of Mathematical Economics*, 19: 195–216.

Cass, D. (1985), "On the 'Number' of Equilibrium Allocations with Incomplete Financial Markets," CARESS Working Paper, University of Pennsylvania.

(1989), "Sunspots and Incomplete Financial Markets: The Leading Example," in G. Feiwel (ed.), *The Economics of Imperfect Competition: Joan Robinson and Beyond*, London: Macmillan.

(1990), "Real Indeterminacy from Imperfect Financial Markets: Two Addenda," CARESS Working Paper, University of Pennsylvania.

Cass, D., P. Siconolfi and A. Villanacci (1991), "A Note on Generalizing the Model of Financial Equilibrium with Restricted Participation," CARESS Working Paper, University of Pennsylvania.

Geanakoplos, J. (1990), "An Introduction to General Equilibrium with Incomplete Asset Markets," *Journal of Mathematical Economics*, 19: 1–38.

Geanakoplos, J. and A. Mas-Colell (1989), "Real Indeterminacy with Financial Assets," *Journal of Economic Theory*, 47: 22–38.

Green, R.C. and S.E. Spear (1989), "Equilibria in large commodity spaces with incomplete financial markets," Preliminary paper, Carnegie-Mellon University.

Krasa, S. and J. Werner (1991), "Equilibria with Options: Existence and Indeterminacy," *Journal of Economic Theory*, 54: 305–20.

Magill, M. and M. Quinzii (1988), "Real Effects of Money in General Equilibrium," MRG Working Paper, University of Southern California.

(1991), "The Non-neutrality of Money in a Production Economy with Nominal Assets," in W. A. Barnett et al. (eds.), *Equilibrium Theory and Applications*, Cambridge: Cambridge University Press.

Mas-Colell, A. (1991), "Indeterminacy in Incomplete Market Economies," *Economic Theory*, 1: 45–61.

Pietra, T. (1988), "Indeterminacy in General Equilibrium Models with Incomplete Financial Markets: Mixed Asset Returns," Preliminary paper, Rugers University.

Polemarchakis, H.M. (1988), "Portfolio choice, exchange rates and indeterminacy," *Journal of Economic Theory*, 46: 414–21.

Siconolfi, P. (1991), "Sunspot equilibria and Incomplete Financial Markets," *Journal of Mathematical Economics*, 20: 327–39.

Siconolfi, P. and A. Villanacci (1991), "Real Indeterminacy in Incomplete Financial Market Economies Without Aggregate Risk," *Economic Theory*, 1: 265–76.

Villanacci, A. (1991), "Indeterminacy of Equilibria, Taxes and Outside Money in Exchange Economies with Incomplete Financial Markets," CARESS Working Paper, University of Pennsylvania.

Werner, J. (1986), "Asset Prices and Real Indeterminacy in Equilibrium with Financial Markets," Discussion Paper, University of Bonn.

(1990), "Structure of Financial Markets and Real Indeterminacy of Equilibria," *Journal of Mathematical Economics* 19: 217–32.

Zame, W.R. (1988), "Asymptotic Behavior of Asset Markets, I: Asymptotic Inefficiency," Preliminary paper, SUNY at Buffalo (Department of Mathematics).

CHAPTER 6

Endogenous fluctuations

Roger Guesnerie and Michael Woodford

1 INTRODUCTION

Economic time series usually display deviations from their trends that, although irregular, have recurrent patterns. The explanation of such patterns of fluctuations is a subject that has received considerable attention from the economics profession.

Fluctuations may be generated by economic shocks that are due either to variations of private sector behavior originating in tastes or technological changes or to stochastic shifts in government policy. Under such an hypothesis, the variables subject to shocks will be modeled as exogeneous uncertain parameters. Typically, in exogenous shock models of economic fluctuations, the equilibrium is well defined, often unique – at least locally unique, in the terminology we will adopt later determinate – and stable: in the absence of recurrent exogenous shocks, the economy would tend to a steady state, but because of shocks a (possibly stationary) pattern of fluctuations will be observed.

Such a general structure of explanation is so familiar that some typologies of business cycle theories only refer to it, and classify models according, on the one hand, to the dominant type of "impulse" and, on the other hand, to the nature of "propagation mechanisms" that are posited. Textbook models, either "Keynesian" or "monetarist," describe exogenously generated fluctuations. Also, the recent theory of "real business cycles" is the last avatar of a popular exogenous shock theory.

There is however no logical reason to believe that exogenous shock models provide the only possible relevant explanation for business cycle and other fluctuations. It has been argued for a long time that the internal mechanics of a market economy might be responsible for (at least) part of observed variations even in the absence of any policy shock or shock to the economic fundamentals (tastes, technologies); see Hayek (1933), Schumpeter (1939), Wicksell (1898). In particular we know from the classic contributions of Goodwin (1951), Kaldor (1940), Kalecki (1935) that the interaction of the consumption multiplier and the investment accelerator in Keynesian macroeconomic models may generate cyclical paths, the origin of which is certainly not "exogenous," and hence has to be labeled endogenous.

The distinction between exogenous and endogenous fluctuations is in some contexts less straightforward than it may look, and we will make a more careful attempt at defining it in section 2. However, the work under review in the present chapter undoubtedly falls under the heading of endogenous fluctuations. But, in sharp contrast with the earlier literature on endogenous cycles just referred to, it relies on models in which the agents' behavior is derived from an explicit intertemporal optimization and in which agents are assumed to have rational expectations.

The adoption of the rational expectations hypothesis, together with the dominant neoclassical individual maximization hypothesis, is hardly surprising; indeed, the rational expectations hypothesis has taken over almost all fields of theoretical modeling in the last fifteen years. The present revival of interest in theories of endogenous fluctuations within this framework is reflected in a growing number of contributions; this fact is illustrated, for two examples among others, by the 1986 special issue of the *Journal of Economic Theory* (J.M. Grandmont, editor) and the 1989 volume on *"Economic complexity"* (edited by W. Barnett, J. Geweke, and K. Shell). The intellectual inspiration of this stream of reflection has not a single source, but several, among which the following three may be stressed.

1   The first source of inspiration has to be found in recent developments in the mathematical theory of dynamical systems. It has been more and more clearly realized that simple deterministic systems, such as those governed by time independent non-linear equations or by ordinary differential equations of the kind often found in economic models, may have very *complex dynamics*. The fact that a sequence of numbers (x_n) generated by an equation as simple as $x_{n+1} = 4x_n(1-x_n)$ may be indistinguishable from a random sequence from many points of view – a phenomenon called ergodic chaos – provides a striking example of this latter assertion. Indeed, the mathematical theory of dynamical systems, building upon the work of H. Poincaré at the beginning of the century, has been a subject of intense activity in the last thirty years and particularly in the last fifteen years. Recent work has significantly sharpened our understanding of complex (deterministic) dynamics. For one dimensional systems, the discoveries of Sarkovskii (1964) and Feigenbaum (1978) excited widespread interest.

Examples of most significant contributions to the understanding of multidimensional systems include those of Ruelle and Takens (1971) and Smale (1967). This mathematical breakthrough has had a considerable impact on several fields of scientific knowledge such as biology, physics, chemistry, and ecology. Early economic applications were the studies exhibiting deterministic chaos by Benhabib and Day (1981), Dana and Malgrange (1984), Day (1982, 1983) and Stutzer (1980).[1] Later, economic applications of dynamical systems theory have been of two main types. On the one hand are models, such as optimal growth models (e.g., Boldrin and Montrucchio, 1986), in which the state of the system at any time is uniquely determined by initial conditions, so that equilibrium dynamics are unique and (in the absence of exogenous shocks) deterministic. On the other hand are models, such as the overlapping generations (OLG) model, in which the state of the system at any given time is determined by expectations about its state at a later time. Here rational expectations equilibrium need not be unique (or even determinate), and need not be deterministic even in the absence of exogenous shocks. Nonetheless, deterministic (perfect foresight) equilibria are one class of possible equilibria, and dynamical systems theory can be employed to clarify the possibility of cyclical and chaotic trajectories among the possible perfect foresight paths (Grandmont, 1985a and b).

2   The second source of inspiration has come from the study of the possible *indeterminacy of rational expectations equilibrium.* As is discussed further in section 3, this issue quickly came to the fore once the hypothesis of rational expectations became a standard feature of models of economic dynamics. Let us, however, put the issue in a broader perspective. Economics, as a social science, has to face a coordination issue that is not present for example in physics. Economic agents' behavior depends not only upon past data but also upon agents' expectations of the future. Economic theory has therefore to explain how and to what extent expectations are being coordinated. Although the coordination of actions is already a delicate problem in a static Arrow–Debreu world (a problem which an hypothetical Walras tatonnement can solve only in good cases), the coordination of expectations in a multiperiod and *a fortiori* in infinite horizon models raises considerable difficulties. Even if one assumes that full coordination will be achieved, in the sense that the agents' image of the future will be, at least statistically, accurate, the reversal of causation between the present and the future that is involved in the rational expectations hypothesis may be a new source of multiplicity. For example, classic infinite horizon competitive models that have a steady state may also have a continuum of perfect foresight equilibria close to the steady state in some appropriate topology as soon as infinite lived agents coexist with enough finite lived ones (Muller

and Woodford, 1988). Also, the rational expectations hypothesis does not rule out that stochastic equilibria may exist in an otherwise non-stochastic economy. This has been known for some time in linear difference equations models (see for example the survey by Broze, Guriéroux, and Szafarz, 1991). Following an earlier suggestion of Shell (1977) (in an OLG context), Cass and Shell (1983) have formalized a concept of stochastic equilibrium in a finite horizon general equilibrium model, under the appealing terminology of *sunspot equilibrium*. Clearly in such equilibria the only shocks are shocks to beliefs. They can be viewed as triggered by what Cass and Shell called extrinsic uncertainty, generated by some outside coordinating device such as "sunspots," as opposed to the intrinsic uncertainty that affects tastes, endowments, and technologies in the exogenous fluctuations stories. More strikingly, the introduction of additional restrictions such as time independence or stationarity whenever they are compatible with the characteristics of the system under consideration does not succeed, in infinite horizon models, in eliminating sunspot equilibria. In OLG models, the examples of Azariadis (1981) and more systematically investigated by Azariadis and Guesnerie (1982, 1986) demonstrated that an otherwise non-stochastic stationary economy may experience stochastic fluctuations that are perfectly correlated with a stationary sunspot phenomenon. Furthermore, such equilibria are not locally unique and there is a continuum of candidate extrinsic phenomena that may trigger sunspot beliefs. Early work on this subject also includes Farmer and Woodford (1984), Spear (1984). Later work that is lengthily reported here has made clear that such sunspot equilibria will exist in more complex dynamical models without appealing to the somewhat special assumptions that were first considered (see Guesnerie, 1986; Woodford, 1986b; Chiappori and Guesnerie, 1989b).[2]

In fact, in many dynamic models without intrinsic uncertainty, sunspot equilibria appear to be the prototype rational expectations equilibrium (that include as limit cases steady states and periodic equilibria), and truly stochastic equilibria cannot be ruled out without proof. The importance of sunspot type multiplicity should not be underestimated. The fact that beliefs which are self-fulfilling leave significant ambiguity on what they are, questions still more acutely the significance of the axioms of philosophical determinism for economic modeling. Also, sunspot equilibria provide examples of the relevance of themes with a Keynesian flavor such as "animal spirits" and "expectations volatility" in a rational expectations framework. Finally, the fact that in systems otherwise immune to shocks of exogenous types, fluctuations that are uniquely based on beliefs cannot be a priori dismissed is an essential insight for any comprehensive understanding of fluctuations.

3   The third source of inspiration is research into the stability of rational expectations equilibrium. Whatever the equilibrium concept under consideration, the question of its "implementation," i.e., the process according to which the values of variables predicted by the equilibrium are reached, has to be faced. The emphasis of general equilibrium theory on tâtonnement and non-tâtonnement processes reflected the awareness of the "implementation" problem in the Walrasian theoretical tradition. The consideration of later temporal models raises not only the question of how equilibrium prices are found but also of how expectations are formed. This is a question that must be addressed by any ambitious theory of economic fluctuations. After all, fluctuations might be the temporary (resp. permanent) effects of agents' attempts to coordinate actions that turn out to be finally successful (resp. unsuccessful), even in a world that has, under some equilibrium concept, a unique equilibrium. In a rational expectations framework, the implementation issue amounts to understanding how expectations of the future become both fully coordinated and "true." Contrary to Muth's claim (Muth, 1961) according to which "the rational expectations hypothesis is nothing else than the extension of the rationality hypothesis to expectations," we need a theory of why the rational expectations equilibrium is reached. Analysis of *learning dynamics* provides a possible answer. It might be instantaneous learning taking place in people's minds[3] or learning based on processes that describe how expectations are revised as a function of past observations. Here, our attention will mainly focus on the latter type of learning procedures – as they have been assessed in the work of for example Evans (1985), Evans and Honkapohja (1990a and b), Grandmont (1985a), Grandmont and Laroque (1986, 1990a and b), Woodford (1990a). Most of these learning studies consider worlds in which the rational expectations equilibrium is indeterminate, so that learning convergence may be viewed as a selection procedure or a refinement device allowing one to choose among multiple equilibria. We also stress how outside intervention – e.g., by a government – can supplement mechanical procedures and aid coordination.

Hence *complex dynamics, sunspot equilibria*, and *learning* are three major themes that we associate here with a reflection upon *endogenous fluctuations*. These themes are either new in economic theory – as in the case of complex dynamics – or are being revived by current research – as is the case of learning. It is hardly surprising that the growing literature on such themes remains in an exploratory phase. Correspondingly, five warnings to the reader should be made at the outset.

(i)   The main and almost exclusive focus of the survey is on models in which there is no intrinsic uncertainty, i.e., on models in which the fundamentals are not subject to exogenous shocks. This means neither that our findings have no implication for a theory of "exogenous" fluctuations nor that we think that exogenous fluctuations are unimportant. On the one hand, as we stress later, certain results given here have a direct implication for a theory of purely exogenous fluctuations, as soon as this theory faces the (non-sunspot) multiplicity issue that may arise in a world with purely intrinsic uncertainty. On the other hand, the methodological option of looking at limit situations in which only extrinsic uncertainty may matter has allowed the present literature to bring attention to the essentials of the endogenous fluctuations argument and given strong foundations for the future task of merging the "exogenous" and "endogenous" viewpoints.

(ii)   Our review refers to many different models, which often have been built to answer different questions in different fields. This fact may disappoint the reader looking for a fully developed and general theory. This fact indeed reflects both the exploratory stage of economic reflection on many of the issues under scrutiny and also, in many cases, the mathematical difficulties generated by the analysis of more complex systems. It is hardly surprising, for example, that economic studies on chaos refer to the one dimensional case, the one for which mathematical theory is most advanced.[4] Modesty here is mainly a reflection of the state of mathematical knowledge.

(iii) Besides specific models, the literature has also tried to consider more general frameworks within which one could capture the common structure of a variety of specific arguments.[5] Such models have, as usual, to compromise between simplicity and generality. This compromise is particularly difficult to assess in an exploratory phase of the development of knowledge. We are aware that the compromise adopted in models attempting a more general analysis might appear later inappropriate. We are, however, convinced that both the techniques that are used and the main lines of argument that have been developed will be useful and relevant at later stages of modeling.

(iv)   Attention is almost exclusively focused on infinite horizon models. This option is self-explanatory for most of the models we are considering and is natural given our interest in the explanation of repetitive aggregate fluctuations. We are, however, aware that, at a more developed stage of knowledge, connections between long but finite horizon and infinite horizon problems should be better ascertained.

(v)   We have omitted any discussion of empirical tests of the importance of any of the theories of endogenous fluctuations presented
here as explanations of fluctuations in actual economies. This is
because there has as yet been little work attempting empirical tests.
Indeed, it seems unlikely that conclusive empirical tests can even
be proposed, in the absence of further theoretical understanding of
the conditions under which endogenous fluctuations are possible.
For it is not generally possible to distinguish time series generated
by an economy displaying endogenous fluctuations from those
generated by an economy with purely exogenous fluctuations,
without reference to some quite specific model in terms of which
the data are to be interpreted.[6] On the other hand, theoretical
studies thus far have considered only quite simple kinds of models
that plainly cannot be taken as literal descriptions of actual
economies, because of the limits of analytical tractability. It is to be
hoped that future work will give more attention to the issue of
empirical realism of specific models, perhaps through the use of
numerical solution methods to characterize the equilibrium dynamics of models that cannot be treated analytically.[7]

After these preliminary considerations we announce the plan of the
chapter.

Section 2 reviews the literature on complex dynamics in systems that
have a unique and determinate equilibrium. Special attention is given to
dynamics of optimal growth models.

Sections 2 to 6 are devoted to a review of the present knowledge on
sunspot equilibria – that may involve as limiting cases non-sunspot
periodic equilibria – in models in which equilibria are "indeterminate."
Section 3 provides a general discussion of the concept of sunspot
equilibrium. Section 4 presents the analytical methods that have been
developed to show the existence of sunspot equilibria, and the general
results available up to now. Sections 5 and 6 focus attention on sunspot
equilibria respectively in overlapping generations models (OLG models)
and in other infinite horizon models.

Sections 7 and 8 are concerned with the last theme evoked above. Section
7 reviews learning studies, while section 8 discusses stabilization policies.

2   ENDOGENOUS FLUCTUATIONS WITH
DETERMINATE EQUILIBRIUM DYNAMICS

In this section, we consider the possibility of endogenous equilibrium
fluctuations in models in which equilibrium dynamics are uniquely

determined. In such a model, all endogenous state variables can be written as a single-valued function of some vector x_t of predetermined endogenous state variables, and some vector z_t of exogenous (fundamental) state variables, representing stochastic shifts in the equilibrium conditions determining the endogenous variables. In particular, the values of the predetermined variables in the following period may be written as a function of the form:

$$x_{t+1} = f(x_t, z_t). \tag{2.1}$$

Given an exogenous process $\{z_t\}$, and an initial condition x_0, (2.1) suffices to uniquely determine the evolution of the predetermined state variables, which in turn determine the evolution of the other endogenous state variables. For purposes of determining whether or not a given system gives rise to endogenous fluctuations, it is generally sufficient to consider the dynamics (2.1).

If we assume that there are no exogenous shocks, (2.1) reduces to:

$$x_{t+1} = f(x_t) \tag{2.2}$$

and the dynamics are entirely determined by the initial condition k_0. We will generally be interested furthermore in systems for which there exists a compact set X such that $f(X)$ is contained in X, so that initial conditions in X imply dynamics restricted forever to that set. In such a case, we may say that the equilibrium exhibits *endogenous fluctuations* if the sequence $\{x_t\}$ does not converge asymptotically to some constant value x^*, despite its remaining forever bounded.

There is no way in which "sunspot" variables can affect the endogenous variables in such a model, and so, if exogenous shocks are neglected, equilibrium dynamics are deterministic. Hence the endogenous fluctuations just mentioned must consist of convergence to a *deterministic cycle*, or of *deterministic chaos*. But it would be a mistake, in our view, to identify this class of models as "models of deterministic cycles." On the one hand, deterministic equilibrium cycles can appear for very different reasons in models with multiple equilibria, and may be, as is discussed further below, essentially degenerate limiting cases of sunspot equilibria.[8] And on the other hand, the possibility of purely deterministic equilibrium fluctuations is not, in our view, the main point of the literature to be reviewed in this section. For no one can doubt that there exist significant exogenous shocks to the economy, that must be regarded as random, at least for purposes of economic modeling.

But there is no reason to define "endogenous cycles" as a concept relevant only to economies with no exogenous shocks. Suppose, more generally, that $\{z_t\}$ is a stationary, ergodic Markov process, taking values in some set Z, and that there exists a compact set X such that $f(X,Z)$ is contained in X, and let us consider the dynamics generated by (2.1) for given initial conditions $x_0 \in X$. We may say that the resulting fluctuations in $\{x_t\}$ are due entirely to the exogenous shocks $\{z_t\}$ if asymptotically the initial conditions cease to matter, in the sense that for t large enough it becomes possible to write the endogenous state variables as a function solely of the history of the exogenous shocks:

$$x_t = \phi(z_t, z_{t-1}, z_{t-2} \ldots),$$

where ϕ represents the limit of a recursive substitution of the form:[9]

$$\phi(z_t, z_{t-1}, z_{t-2} \ldots) = f(f(f(\ldots z_{t-2}), z_{t-1}), z_t).$$

On the other hand, if this fails to be true, and if not only the initial condition x_0, but also the number of elapsed periods t, continue to matter asymptotically, then we may say that the system exhibits *endogenous fluctuations*. In the case that there are no exogenous shocks, this criterion reduces to whether or not x_t converges asymptotically to some constant value (that might depend upon x_0). Hence the demonstration that cyclic or chaotic equilibria can occur in deterministic models is one, relatively straightforward, way of showing that endogenous fluctuations in this sense are possible, even when equilibrium dynamics are uniquely determined. But it should be clear that the criterion continues to be applicable, and of interest, even in the presence of exogenous shocks.

We confine our attention, for the remainder of this section, to the case of models with no exogenous shocks, as this is the case for which a substantial literature exists. An examination of the conditions under which endogenous fluctuations in the sense just described are possible in stochastic economies would seem to be an important topic for further research.

2.1   Possible types of asymptotic dynamics

As just explained, we are interested in systems in which a vector of predetermined state variables x_t evolves according to a law of motion of the form (2.2) given an initial condition x_0. It will be useful to summarize some of the mathematical possibilities for the behavior of such a system, before considering economic applications. We assume the existence of a compact set X such that $f(X)$ is contained in X, and that $f: X \rightarrow X$ is continuous, and continuously differentiable as many times as necessary (although this is often not essential). We assume that there exists at least one steady state $x^* \in X$, i.e., a point such that $f(x^*) = x^*$. (If X can be chosen to be convex, this is guaranteed by the Brouwer fixed point theorem.) We are interested in a classification of the possible *asymptotic* dynamics associated with (2.2),

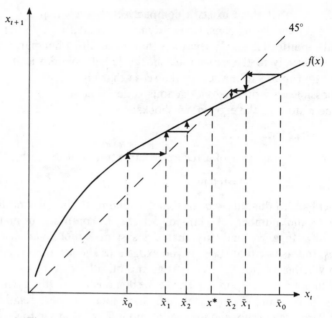

Figure 6.1a

since, as follows from the above discussion, the dependence of the transient dynamics upon the initial condition x_0 is irrelevant to the issue of whether "endogenous fluctuations" may be said to occur.

One possibility is that $x_t \to x^*$ asymptotically, regardless of the initial condition x_0. In this case, x^* is *globally stable*. A one-dimensional example with this property is shown in figure 6.1a; here the set X can be any interval $[\underline{x}, \bar{x}]$ with $0 < \underline{x} < x^* \le \bar{x}$. In such a case, endogenous fluctuations obviously do not occur; persistent fluctuations can be observed only in the case of recurrent exogenous shocks that repeatedly move the state vector away from the steady state.[10]

One case in which this fails to be so is when the steady state is not even *locally* stable, i.e., x_t does not converge to x^* even for most initial conditions in an arbitrarily small neighborhood of x^*. This occurs (the steady state is *unstable*) if $Df(x^*)$ has one or more eigenvalues of modulus greater than one. If all steady states contained in X are unstable, then almost all initial conditions in X must result in some kind of persistent fluctuations. While this is not a necessary condition for the occurrence of endogenous fluctuations (except for initial conditions near a steady state), because it is a sufficient condition that is easy to check, we will restrict attention here to this case. An example of a one-dimensional map with this property is given

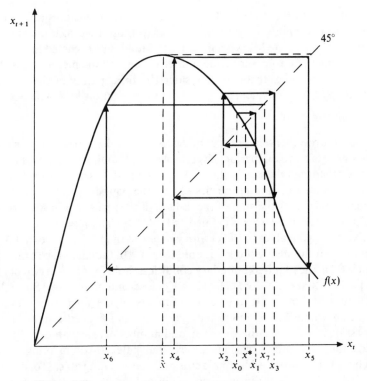

Figure 6.1b

in figure 6.1b. Here $X = [0, f(\tilde{x})]$, the two steady states are $(0, x^*)$, and $f'(0) > 1, f'(x^*) < -1$. It may be observed from the figure that in this case dynamics that begin near the steady state x^* rapidly spiral away from it.

The character of the asymptotic fluctuations in such a case cannot be so easily determined. It may be possible to show the existence of a deterministic equilibrium cycle, although this is not always true. By a *deterministic cycle of period k* is meant a sequence of vectors $(\bar{x}_1, \bar{x}_2, \ldots, \bar{x}_k)$, with $\bar{x}_1 \neq \bar{x}_2 \neq \ldots \neq \bar{x}_k$, such that if $x_o = \bar{x}_j$, for some $j \in \{1, \ldots, k\}$, then (2.2) implies $x_t = \bar{x}_{t+j(\mathrm{mod}\ k)}$, for all t. It then remains to ask for how many other initial conditions the dynamics converge to these perpetual oscillations. If the matrix:

$$Df(\bar{x}_1) \cdot Df(\bar{x}_2) \cdots Df(\bar{x}_k)$$

has all eigenvalues inside the unit circle, then the cycle is locally stable, i.e., there exist neighborhoods of each of the vectors $\bar{x}_j$ such that, if x_0 belongs to any of these neighborhoods, the dynamics implied by (2.2) converge asymptotically to the cycle.[11] Because the methods used to establish the existence of deterministic cycles are similar to those used to establish the existence of finite-state Markovian sunspot equilibria (discussed in section 4), it may be useful to describe them briefly here. [12] One method uses the Poincaré–Hopf index theorem. Consider the fixed points of the second iterate map f^2, or equivalently, the zeros of the function $h: X \to X$, where:

$$h(x) = f^2(x) - x.$$

Such points are either steady states or cycles of period 2. One can then show the existence of a cycle of period 2 by establishing that there must exist zeros of h in X other than the steady states. Assuming that X is a convex subset of R^n, and assuming certain properties of f on the boundary of X, the index theorem implies that the sum of the indices of the zeros of h in X must be $(-1)^n$; the index of a zero x is defined as $(-1)^\rho$, where ρ is the number of negative real eigenvalues of $Dh(x)$ with values less than 1. Suppose that X is chosen so that the steady state x^* is unique in X. (In the case of the example of figure 6.1b, the required boundary conditions hold for any interval of the form $[\underline{x}, \bar{x}]$ with $0 < \underline{x} < x^* < f(\tilde{x}) < \bar{x}$, and $\underline{x}$ close enough to zero.) Since the eigenvalues of $Dh(x^*)$ are the set of numbers of the form $(\lambda_i)^2 - 1$, for $i = 1, \ldots, n$, where $\{\lambda_i\}$ represent the eigenvalues of $Df(x^*)$, the index of the steady state is $-(-1)^n$ if there exist an odd number of eigenvalues of $Df(x^*)$ outside the unit circle. In such a case, the index theorem implies the existence of at least two additional zeros of h, representing at least one cycle of period 2.[13] Hence when $n = 1$, instability of the steady state (together with the proper boundary conditions, as in figure 6.1b) is a sufficient condition for the existence of a cycle of period 2.

It remains, of course, to determine the stability of the equilibrium cycle, and since the index theorem alone does not say much about the location of the cycle, even local stability is in general not easy to determine. The index theorem does guarantee the existence of at least two zeros (one cycle of period 2) with index $(-1)^n$. Since in the case of a two-cycle, the eigenvalues of Dh are the numbers of the form $\mu_i - 1$, where $\{\mu_i\}$ represent the eigenvalues of $Df(x) \cdot Df(f(x))$, there must exist at least one cycle for which the number of real eigenvalues $\{\mu_i\}$ less than 1 is odd. But the latter property is not enough to guarantee local stability, even when $n = 1$, for the single eigenvalue μ might be less than -1. (In the example of figure 6.1b, the unique cycle of period 2 is unstable if it consists of a point at which f is steeply upward sloping and another at which f is steeply downward sloping, with the product of the slopes below -1.) It is true that, when $n = 1$, instability of all cycles of period 2 implies the existence of at least one cycle of period 4, by a similar application of the Poincaré–Hopf theorem to the fourth iterate map f^4, and so on. But this infinite chain does not necessarily imply the existence of any locally stable equilibrium cycles. (See the discussion below of "everywhere expanding" systems.)

Another approach to proving the existence of cycles, that also gives results relating to their stability, involves studying the *bifurcations* that may result from smooth deformation of a map. Consider a family of smooth maps $f(.;\mu)$ of a one-dimensional interval X into itself, indexed by the parameter μ, and smoothly varying with μ. Suppose that for each μ, there exists a fixed point $x^*(\mu)$, and suppose the slope at the fixed point, $f'(x^*(\mu);\mu)$, passes through the value -1 as μ passes through some value μ^*, with a negative derivative of $f'(x^*(\mu);\mu)$ with respect to μ at this point. If in addition $f'''(x^*(\mu^*);\mu^*) + (3/2)(f''(x^*(\mu^*);\mu^*))^2 > 0$,[14] then one can show that as μ passes through the value μ^* from below, a *flip bifurcation* occurs, in which the steady state x^* loses its stability, and at the same time a locally stable cycle of period 2 is created. The locally stable cycle exists for all μ in some right neighborhood of μ^*, and is arbitrarily close to the steady state for μ close enough to μ^*. Such a purely local result might appear to be of only limited interest, but the technique suffices for the construction of robust examples of locally stable equilibrium cycles. Locally stable cycles of period 4 can also be created when a cycle of period 2 loses stability; the bifurcation argument is the same, as a cycle of period 2 of the map $f(.;\mu)$ can be regarded as a fixed point of the second iterate map $f(f(.;\mu);\mu)$. The process may continue through a succession of ever higher periods for the cycles; this occurs, for example, for a family of maps of the kind shown in figure 6.1b, satisfying certain regularity conditions, as the steepness of the hump is made progressively greater.[15]

This method also generalizes to higher-dimensional maps, in which case the bifurcation occurs when an eigenvalue of the matrix $Df(x^*(\mu);\mu)$ passes through the value -1 as μ passes through some value μ^*. In the case of higher-dimensional maps, stable equilibrium cycles near the steady state can also be created when a steady state loses stability due to a complex pair of eigenvalues of $Df(x^*(\mu);\mu)$ passing through the unit circle. (As in the one-dimensional case, the higher derivatives of f at the bifurcation point must satisfy certain side conditions, which are in fact satisfied by an open set of maps in the appropriate topology.) In this kind of bifurcation (a discrete-time *Hopf bifurcation*), for values $\mu > \mu^*$, the equilibrium dynamics come to possess a closed invariant curve near the steady state, to which invariant curve the dynamics are attracted for all initial conditions in a neighborhood of the steady state. The equilibrium dynamics on the closed curve need not be exactly periodic; instead, the asymptotic dynamics may be only *quasiperiodic*, in which case the same point is never visited twice, although the dynamics remain forever on the closed curve.[16]

Dynamics that fail to converge to a steady state need not, however, converge to any periodic orbit, or even to quasiperiodic motion on an invariant curve. It is possible that there may exist an uncountably infinite subset S of X with the property that:

$$\lim \sup |f^n(x) - f^n(y)| \geq \varepsilon$$
$$\lim \inf |f^n(x) - f^n(y)| = 0$$

for some $\varepsilon > 0$, and for all $x, y \in S$, with $x \neq y$. That is, nearby trajectories on this set always eventually wander apart (so that in particular there is never convergence to a steady state, nor do nearby trajectories remain forever nearby as in the case of a limit cycle), but all trajectories also always eventually pass arbitrarily close to one another (again unlike a limit cycle). This means both that small differences in initial conditions eventually mean completely different paths, and that knowing the initial conditions (even to very high, though not perfect, accuracy) is of little help in forecasting the state of the system in the sufficiently distant future. In this case, the dynamics associated with initial conditions in the set S are said to be *chaotic*. Such dynamics may well result from a map of the kind shown in figure 6.1b (as the complexity of the dynamics depicted is intended to suggest, though a demonstration is considerably more complex); for further discussion of why this is so, see Collet and Eckmann (1980), Devaney (1986), or May (1976). For example, Li and Yorke (1975) show that a continuous map of a compact interval that possesses a cycle of period 3 must exhibit chaotic dynamics in the sense just defined, and it is easily shown that if the hump in figure 6.1b is steep enough, such a cycle must exist.[17]

On the other hand, the definition given above does not rule out the possibility that the set S of initial conditions with this property may be of measure zero, so that chaos should not be observed except fortuitously. Conditions are known, however, under which there must exist a set S with positive Lebesgue measure. The following result for one-dimensional maps is useful in this regard.

THEOREM 2.1   Let X be a compact interval, and let $f: X \rightarrow X$ be piecewise C^2, and *everywhere expanding*, i.e., such that $\inf_{x \in X} |f'(x)| > 1$. Then f has at most a countable number of periodic points, and all periodic points (including steady states) are unstable. In addition, f has an absolutely continuous invariant measure, whose support S accordingly has positive measure, and the dynamics associated with f are chaotic for almost all initial conditions in S. Moreover, if f' has a single point of discontinuity, then the measure is ergodic, so that, for almost all initial conditions in S, this measure describes the long-run frequency with which different neighborhoods are visited.[18]

In such a case, one may say that the dynamics associated with f are characterized by *ergodic chaos*.[19] Note that the condition that the map be everywhere expanding, yet map a compact interval X on itself, implies discontinuity of f' at at least one point. However, the properties established will also hold for any map that is a topological conjugate of such a map, and this category includes smooth maps, such as $f(x) = 4x(1-x)$ for $0 \le x \le 1$ (see, e.g., Collet and Eckmann, 1980).

It might be useful to conclude with a brief discussion of why the possibility of "chaotic" dynamics should be considered an interesting theoretical result. This is principally because observed economic fluctuations are not so regular as to be modeled, even approximately, by exactly repetitive cycles; one "business cycle" is never of the same length as the one preceding it, nor are the relative sizes of or the phase relationships between the variations in different economic time series ever exactly the same across "cycles." The mathematical idea of chaotic dynamics shows that irregular fluctuations of this kind are consistent with a completely deterministic model of the evolution of economic time series, rather than proving the importance of random shocks. Indeed, chaotic deterministic systems are capable of generating time series which are indistinguishable (at least as far as linear econometric methods of data analysis are concerned, e.g., the autocorrelation function, power spectrum, etc.) from those generated by the autoregressive stochastic models used in empirical macroeconometrics.[20] Accordingly, more sophisticated analysis of observed fluctuations is needed in order to dismiss the hypothesis of (largely) endogenous fluctuations of the kind discussed in this section.[21]

However, the interest of the idea of deterministic chaos as an explanation of apparently random fluctuations is less obvious in economics than in the physical sciences. The laws of classical physics imply that the evolution of a system should be uniquely determined by initial conditions, so that if fluctuations are to be explained by those laws (rather than being attributed to exogenous random shocks that are not themselves explained by physical theory) they must be modeled as resulting from deterministic dynamics of the form (2.2). But, in economic dynamics, the mere requirement that a system be in equilibrium for all time often does not imply uniquely determined dynamics of this kind. As a result, in economic models of the kind discussed in subsequent sections, there is no difficulty in explaining how a truly stochastic equilibrium is possible, even in the absence of exogenous shocks – one need only assume that publicly observed random events may be used to coordinate people's expectations about which equilibrium possibilities will be realized.[22] And, as argued above, there is in any event no reason to restrict the hypothesis of "endogenous fluctuations" to mean that there are no important shocks to economic fundamentals.

2.2   Equilibrium fluctuations in optimal growth models

One class of models that have been much used in studies of economic dynamics, for which rational expectations equilibrium is necessarily unique, is the class of recursive infinite-horizon models with a representative consumer known as "optimal growth models." Here an intertemporal competitive equilibrium must involve an allocation of resources that maximizes the utility of the representative consumer, and an equilibrium price process that supports that allocation, so that the uniqueness of equilibrium follows (under quite weak regularity conditions) from the uniqueness of the solution to a social planning problem.

The mathematical results just sketched have shown that the type of dynamical laws needed to give rise to endogenous fluctuations are not particularly special; hence it might be expected that dynamic models of all types would be found to give rise to such behavior, for an appropriate choice of functional forms for technology, preferences, and the like. It is rather striking, then, that in the case of optimal growth models rather general conditions are known under which endogenous fluctuations are *not* possible. Suppose that the representative consumer seeks to maximize:

$$\sum_{t=0}^{\infty} \beta^t u(c_t),$$

where c_t represents a vector of m types of consumption in period t, and where $0 < \beta < 1$ is the discount factor. Feasible production programs are sequences of consumption vectors $\{c_t\}$ and n-vectors of capital stocks $\{k_t\}$ such that in every period t, the triple (k_t, c_t, k_{t+1}) belongs to a feasible set F. (This describes an $n+1$-sector technology, since the consumption good need not have the same production function as any of the n capital goods.) If we define D as the set of pairs (k_t, k_{t+1}) such that (k_t, c, k_{t+1}) belongs to F for some consumption vector c, and:

$$V(k_t, k_{t+1}) = \max_c u(c) \text{ s.t. } (k_t, c, k_{t+1}) \in F$$

then the equilibrium evolution of the capital stocks is the sequence $\{k_t\}$ that maximizes:

$$\sum_{t=0}^{\infty} \beta^t V(k_t, k_{t+1}), \tag{2.3}$$

subject to the constraints $(k_t, k_{t+1}) \in D$ for all $t \geq 0$, given an initial vector of capital stocks k_0. Under standard assumptions (A) on the preferences and technology, V is strictly concave, increasing in its first set of arguments and decreasing in the second set; D is convex and compact; and there exists a compact subset K of R^n, such that for any $k_t \in K$, the set of k_{t+1} for which $(k_t, k_{t+1}) \in D$ is a non-empty subset of K. Under these assumptions, the maximization problem has a unique solution for any $k_0 \in K$, and the solution is given by a dynamical system of the form (2.2), where $f: K \to K$ describes the optimal k_1 as a function of k_0. (Because of the recursive form of the maximization problem, the same function must give k_2 as a function of k_1, and so on.) We are then concerned to characterize the asymptotic dynamics associated with the map f.

THEOREM 2.2 ("Turnpike theorem")[23]   Let preferences and technology u and F (or equivalently, V and D) be fixed and satisfy (A). Then there exists a discount factor $\bar{\beta} < 1$ such that for any $\beta \in (\bar{\beta}, 1)$, the map f that solves the maximization problem (2.3) has a unique globally stable steady state $k^*(\beta)$. Hence for any discount factor in that range, in equilibrium the vector of capital stocks converges asymptotically to the same vector $k^*(\beta)$ for all initial conditions k_0.

Hence under reasonably general hypotheses one can show that, if people are sufficiently patient, the economy should converge asymptotically to a steady state, in the absence of any exogenous shocks. Roughly speaking, concavity of the utility function and convexity of the feasible set imply that an allocation involving perpetual oscillations attains a lower average level of the single-period utility $u(c)$ than would a constant allocation; and, if the rate of time preference is small enough, the representative consumer's objective is approximately the time average of $u(c)$.

However, it should be noted that a $\bar{\beta} < 1$ need not exist if V is not *strictly* concave. It is important to realize that strict concavity is *not* implied, in the multisector case, by the familiar assumptions of no risk-loving, no increasing returns to scale, and diminishing returns to capital due to the use of a fixed factor of production in each sector. For example, with a multisector constant returns technology, strict concavity does not hold in general, as long as the number of distinct capital goods exceeds the number of fixed factors, or the number of capital goods is as large as the number of fixed factors and utility is linear in consumption. This is the basis of a famous counter-example (in which an endogenous cycle exists for an arbitrarily low rate of time preference) due to Weitzman (see Samuelson, 1973). Of course, strict concavity can be achieved in any such example by introducing even a very small amount of strictly decreasing returns to scale; but, if the perturbation is small, the turnpike property will obtain only for very low rates of time preference.

Furthermore, the Turnpike Theorem places no restriction upon the asymptotic behavior in the case of lower discount factors (i.e., higher rates of time preference). In the case of a one-sector technology (i.e., a single produced good that is both capital good and consumption good), there continues to be a unique globally stable steady state, regardless of the discount factor, for in this case the map f is of the form shown in figure 6.1a (Dechert, 1984). But, if there are as few as two sectors (one capital good and one consumption good, with separate production functions), this ceases to be true. Benhabib and Nishimura (1985) describe conditions on preferences and technologies for a two-sector model, such that the map f describing evolution of the capital stock can be decreasing near the steady state. They show further that for a low enough rate of time preference, one must have $f'(k^*) > -1$, so that the steady state is locally stable (as required by the turnpike theorem), but that as β is made steadily lower, $f'(k^*)$ drops below -1, at which point a "flip bifurcation" occurs. Hence for a high enough rate of time preference, there exists a cycle of period 2. A similar bifurcation argument can be used to show the possibility of an equilibrium limit cycle in a continuous-time multisector model (Benhabib and Nishimura, 1979), and even in a one-sector model if the representative consumer's preferences are not additively separable between periods as assumed above (Ryder and Heal, 1973).[24]

In fact, in the case of high rates of time preference, the equilibrium dynamics of the capital stock can be of almost any sort, as the following result, due to Boldrin and Montrucchio (1986) shows.

THEOREM 2.3   Let $f: K \to K$ be any C^2 map, where K is a compact, convex subset of $\mathbb{R}^n$. Then there exists an $n + 1$-sector model described by a technology set D and a return function V (or, alternatively, a feasible set F and utility function u) satisfying (A), and a discount factor $0 < \beta < 1$, such that the solution to the problem (2.3) is described by the dynamical system (2.2), for any initial condition $k_0 \in K$.

Given the results of the previous subsection, this implies that a very large range of asymptotic behaviors are all theoretical possibilities. For example, it must be possible, in a two-sector model, for the map f to have the form shown in figure 6.1b. This hump shape results if the capital goods sector is more capital-intensive than the consumption goods sector when the aggregate capital–labor ratio is low enough, but the capital-intensities are reversed in the case of a high enough aggregate capital–labor ratio (Boldrin, 1989). Stable cycles of arbitrary periodicities are possible, as is ergodic chaos.[25] A similar result on the possibility of arbitrary dynamical behavior in continuous-time growth models is provided by Montrucchio (1987).

It should also be noted that the turnpike theorem does not establish that there are any rates of time preference that can be said to be so low as to rule out endogenous fluctuations.[26] The theorem says only that some $\bar{\beta} < 1$

exists for given V and D; this does not mean that for β arbitrarily close to 1, one cannot find a V and D satisfying (A) for which the steady state is unstable. One simply needs to find a V and D for which $\bar{\beta}$ is even higher. For discussion of why this is possible, see Boldrin and Woodford (1990); and for a demonstration of how to construct examples (in the case of a continuous-time model with two capital goods sectors and a consumption goods sector) see Benhabib and Rustichini (1989).

As a result it is not clear whether the technology and preference specifications needed for endogenous cycles in the case of an empirically realistic rate of time preference should be regarded as "extreme" and hence patently implausible or not. But it should be pointed out that known examples of an unstable steady state together with a large discount factor involve asymptotically periodic, rather than chaotic, dynamics; the explicit examples of chaotic models reported in the literature thus far involve quite low discount factors.

2.3   Market imperfections and endogenous fluctuations

It is worth noting that the conditions under which endogenous fluctuations are possible in models with market imperfections of various sorts are rather less special. In particular, if competitive equilibrium is not Pareto optimal, endogenous fluctuations may occur even in the case of arbitrarily low rates of time preference, and even in the case of a one-sector production technology. Since actual "business cycles" involve roughly contemporaneous co-movements of all sectors of the economy at once, and, since market real rates of return do not imply significant discounting over the time horizon of a typical "cycle," models with these properties are of particular interest.[27]

As a simple example (taken from Woodford, 1989), consider the consequences of modifying the one-sector optimal growth model to allow for heterogeneous ownership of factors of production (so that changes in factor rewards imply changes in the distribution of income), and imperfect financial intermediation (resulting in a greatly increased impact of the distribution of income upon the availability of funds to finance investment). It is only the imperfect financial markets that can allow us to avoid a "turnpike" result,[28] but this imperfection is of no significance unless people in the economy are sufficiently different for financial intermediation to serve some purpose. For the sake of concreteness, let there be two infinite-lived consumer types, "capitalists" and "workers," and suppose that only workers supply labor, while only capitalists have access to the production technology, and hence accumulate capital and organize production. Suppose furthermore that borrowing and lending is not possible between the two types; then workers' consumption spending each period will equal the wage bill, and the capital accumulated each period will equal the returns to capital minus capitalists' consumption. If, for example, capitalists seek to maximize:

$$\sum_{t=0}^{\infty} \beta^t \log c_t$$

then optimal consumption by capitalists each period is a fraction $(1 - \beta)$ of their wealth, regardless of expected future rates of return. If labor is supplied inelastically, and output each period is $F(k_t)$, where k_t represents the capital stock in period t, then (with full depreciation of the capital stock in each period's production) competitive factor rewards imply that capitalists' wealth at the end of period t will be given by $k_t F'(k_t)$, and so the capital stock evolves according to the relation:

$$k_{t+1} = \beta k_t F'(k_t). \tag{2.4}$$

Hence such an economy produces determinate equilibrium dynamics of the form (2.2).

Assuming that capital is essential in production, the returns to capital (that are bounded above by the total product) go to zero as the capital stock goes to zero; hence the right-hand side of (2.4) must be an increasing function of k_t at least for small k_t. On the other hand, if capital and labor are not too substitutable, the marginal product of capital will fall rapidly with increases in the capital–labor ratio, and the right-hand side of (2.4) may become a decreasing function, for large enough values of k_t, so that the map is of the hump shape shown in figure 6.1b. Specifically, if the elasticity of substitution between capital and labor (measured at the steady state capital–labor ratio) is less than half the share of labor income in total income (also measured at the steady state), then $f'(k^*) < -1$, as shown in figure 6.1b, and the steady state is unstable.[29] Hence some kind of persistent fluctuations will result, for almost all initial conditions. Note the role of imperfect financial intermediation in allowing this result; with perfect financial intermediation, desired aggregate savings (and hence capital accumulation) will depend upon aggregate income rather than only the returns to capital, and aggregate income will necessarily be a monotonically increasing function of the capital stock k_t (though the returns to capital need not be).

Among other possibilities, the system may generate ergodic chaos. Suppose that output per unit of labor input $F(k)$ falls smoothly as capital per unit of labor input k falls, except that below some minimal capital–labor ratio $\hat{k} > 0$, production becomes impossible. Then (normalizing the labor supply to equal one), if $k_t < \hat{k}$, labor will be in excess supply; output will equal $(k_t/\hat{k})F(\hat{k})$, and since the competitive wage will be zero, this will all represent returns to capital. Hence:

$$k_{t+1} = \beta(k_t/\hat{k})F(\hat{k})$$

for $k_t < \hat{k}$. For $k_t > \hat{k}$, there is full employment, and (2.4) again describes the dynamics of the capital stock. If we suppose that $F'(\hat{k}) = F(\hat{k})/\hat{k}$, we again obtain dynamics of the form (2.2) with f a continuous function; but, if $F''(\hat{k}) < 0, f'$ is not continuous at $\hat{k}$. Indeed, if the substitutability of capital for labor continues to be sufficiently low even when $k_t > \hat{k}$, f' will change sign (from positive to negative) at $\hat{k}$. If we assume that $F(\hat{k})/\hat{k} > 1$ (as is necessary in order for there to exist a steady state with a positive capital stock), and that for all $k > \hat{k}$, the elasticity of substitution between capital and labor is not too large, then $f'(k) > 1$ for all $k < \hat{k}$, and $f'(k) < -1$ for all $k < \hat{k}$. Hence the map f is everywhere expanding, and theorem 2.1 implies the existence of ergodic chaos.

Note that these results in no way depend upon a high rate of time preference for either capitalists or workers. The analysis of the dynamics associated with equation (2.4) goes through regardless of the size of β, and so holds for β arbitrarily close to 1. The rate of time preference of workers has no effect at all upon the dynamics of capital accumulation, given the assumption that they have no opportunity to invest in physical capital.

If labor supply is not completely inelastic, but workers' preferences are additively separable between periods, then (given the absence of opportunities to accumulate capital) labor supply will be a uniquely determined function of the current period's real wage, and hence (using this condition together with the marginal product condition) a function of the current period's capital stock. It is then again possible to obtain determinate equilibrium dynamics of the form (2.2), and similar results are again obtained, as long as the elasticity of labor supply is not too large. (The bounds stated above for the elasticity of substitution between factors become bounds that must be satisfied by the sum of the elasticity of substitution and the elasticity of labor supply.) Woodford (1989) shows that similar results also hold in the case of a competitive loan market, if firm-specific risk in the returns to investment is introduced, and it is assumed that loan agreements cannot be made contingent upon the firm-specific shock. In that case, capitalists will be unwilling to leverage themselves to too great an extent, even when the expected returns on capital exceed the real interest rate charged by lenders; and, if the elasticity of capitalists' leverage with respect to the excess returns on capital is not too great, similar dynamics result as in the case of no possibility of external financing.

Financial constraints are not the only kind of market imperfections that can give rise to endogenous fluctuations even with an arbitrarily low rate of time preference. Deneckere and Judd (1986) demonstrate the possibility of endogenous fluctuations in the rate of introduction of new products in an economy in which the creation of a new product involves a one-time fixed cost, and allows the innovator a one-period monopoly of production of the new product. Each period, new products are introduced to the point where the monopoly rents from the production of each new product are no greater than the fixed cost of creation of a new product. Deneckere and Judd show that, for a special parametric class of preferences, this makes the number of products N_t produced in any given period t a determinate function of the number of old products still in existence, and hence of the number of products produced in the previous period, N_{t-1}, and the function is completely independent of consumers' or producers' time preference. (The level of monopoly rents depends only upon consumers' elasticity of substitution between different products within a given period, and, because an innovator obtains monopoly profits only in the period in which the innovation is introduced, there is no intertemporal aspect to the innovation decision either.) The function mapping N_{t-1} to N_t can be non-monotonic. As long as the equilibrium rate of innovation is positive, it is decreasing in the number of old products (since the existence of such products reduces demand for the new products), and, if this effect is strong enough, N_t is a decreasing function of N_{t-1}. But once N_{t-1} exceeds a critical level, no innovation occurs, and N_t becomes an increasing function of N_{t-1}. If the decreasing part of the mapping is steep enough, endogenous cycles and ergodic chaos are possible.

One reason why it is particularly interesting to observe that market imperfections may make endogenous fluctuations possible even in models where preferences and technologies are such that, in the case of frictionless competitive markets, equilibrium would necessarily converge to a steady state, is that endogenous fluctuations of this sort might well justify interventions aimed at stabilizing the equilibrium dynamics. If endogenous fluctuations occur because of a high rate of time preference, or failure of the return function to be strictly concave (the possibilities discussed above in the case of optimal growth models), then there is no presumption that the occurrence of persistent fluctuations should represent an undesirable allocation of resources, *even though* the fluctuations are not associated with any shifts in preferences or technology. And indeed, when such fluctuations occur in an optimal growth model, they are obviously not undesirable; instead, any stabilization policy would have to lower the welfare of the representative consumer.

Models of endogenous fluctuations of the kind considered in this section have no general consequences for the desirability of interventions aimed at preventing equilibrium fluctuations. We have seen that equilibrium fluctuations can be optimal, even when not due to any shifts in preferences or technology, in the case of a representative consumer with a high rate of time preference, or in the case of constant returns to scale multisector technologies of certain kinds not covered by the classical "turnpike theorems." On the other hand, in a representative consumer model with a one-sector production technology, the optimal resource allocation necessarily converges asymptotically to a steady state; endogenous fluctuations can occur in such an economy only due to market imperfections, and the fluctuations in such a case are necessarily undesirable.

In the latter case, it might seem that the obvious implication of theory for policy is that microeconomic interventions, aimed at making markets function more efficiently, are the way to eliminate undesirable endogenous fluctuations. Such a conclusion must be taken with some caution, however. It has not been established that there is any monotonic relationship between the severity of fluctuations and the degree of the market imperfections (e.g., the severity of the constraints upon financial intermediation), so that partial elimination of market imperfections (e.g., opening a single new financial market) might have an ambiguous effect upon stability of the economy.

3   EXTRINSIC UNCERTAINTY: CONCEPTUAL ISSUES

This section discusses the concept of extrinsic uncertainty in the theory of general equilibrium with rational expectations. It is known that when expectations are rational the probabilistic beliefs of every economic agent should be identical to the true distribution of future variables (though the "true" probabilistic image of the future, conditional upon the information available to the agent, may differ from one agent to another). It was early realized that expectations could be garbled by "extraneous" noise while remaining rational so that many different beliefs might be equally self-confirming and hence equally rational. Indeed, the purpose of this section is to offer a brief conceptual review of this multiplicity issue which is in fact at the heart of the endogenous fluctuations problem that we are going to discuss. First, we recall how the multiplicity issue appeared in different segments of the literature. Second, we discuss a central question concerning the insurability of "extraneous" noise. Third, we present some comments on possible responses to the multiplicity issue. Fourth, we comment on the connections between the concept of sunspot equilibrium and several related but distinct notions.

3.1   Modeling extrinsic uncertainty in economics: an overview of recent trends

The concept of sunspot equilibrium, as proposed by Shell (1977) and Cass and Shell (1983) attracted the attention of the profession to the possible effects of "extrinsic" noise (*sunspots*) on the evolution of a general equilibrium system. In spite of the striking terminology which appealed attention and controversy, the concept is a variant of a rational expectations general equilibrium (which could be viewed more generally as a "correlated sunspot" equilibrium – see below), which recognizes the possibility that expectations may be garbled by extrinsic noise.[30] The recognition of such a possibility is neither specific nor even attributable to the general equilibrium literature. The idea appeared earlier in the macroeconomic literature on "linear rational expectations models"; also it has a counterpart in the game theoretical literature.

1   Linear rational expectations models have been widely used in macro-economics and in applied work in economic dynamics more generally, since the pioneer work of Muth (1961) on agricultural markets (for some of the more celebrated macroeconomic applications, see Lucas and Sargent, 1981, and Sargent, 1987). Important contributions to the analysis of such models include Blanchard and Khan (1980), Gouriéroux, Laffont, and Montfort (1982), Evans and Honkapojha (1984), and Broze, Gouriéroux and Szafarz (1991).

For our purpose, the nature of the influence of extrinsic noise on rational expectations solutions can easily be understood from the examination of the equation:

$$p_t = a\mathbb{E}_t p_{t+1}, \tag{3.1}$$

where p_t is a one-dimensional variable.

The equation describes the evolution of a system in which the state at time t is determined by averaging of stochastic expectations regarding the next period and these expectations describe the "true" random image of the future: $E_t p_{t+1}$ is the rationally expected value of p_{t+1}. The only deterministic solution is $p_t = 0\ \forall t p_t$. But any stochastic p_t such that $a^t p_t$ is a martingale is also a solution of the equation and all solutions are of this form. The noise that affects each of these many solutions may be viewed as the influence of noise on the history of the system and this noise is extraneous to the system, i.e., in previous terminology extrinsic.[31]

2   It may seem surprising that the question of the influence of parasite noise on equilibrium appeared significantly later in the general equilibrium

literature. The post-war history of ideas provides some partial explanation of this fact: the general and rigorous assessment of the Walrasian ideas led work to be concentrated on the abstract and static Arrow–Debreu world. In particular the generalization of normative ideas, through the introduction of dated commodities or contingent commodities, put emphasis on the role of atemporal markets – taking place at the beginning of time – for an optimal allocation of resources. Though it has been recognized since then that extrinsic uncertainty has a role in a static non-convex world (see subsection 4.2), the absence of time dimension and then the absence of need for expectations left the "garbling noise" issue out of the scene. However, the idea that the atemporal Arrow–Debreu solution has an intertemporal interpretation when agents had a correct forecast of prices was somewhat understood; it was precisely stated in the context of a 2-period model of the role of securities for the allocation of risk-bearing by Arrow (1953). But it was only through the introduction of the concept of equilibrium of plans, prices and price expectations by Radner (1972) that a formal apparatus allowing these ideas to be expressed with sufficient precision and generality become available.[32] Radner's concept assumes that economic agents have perfect foresight of future prices. Markets may be indexed by dates and/or by the realization of uncertainty (hence are associated with a "date-event") and perfect foresight prevails at each date-event for each future date-event. The questions raised by Shell (1977) and Cass and Shell (1983) can be viewed as the question of how uncertainty is chosen by the modeler. Naturally, uncertainty relative to technologies, initial endowments, preferences is unescapable. But besides such uncertainty, called "intrinsic", why should other uncertainty – although a priori irrelevant, i.e., "extrinsic" – be ruled out? Such extrinsic uncertainty is nothing else but the general equilibrium counterpart of the exogenous noise affecting the solution of linear rational expectations models.

3   Game theory is another domain where the role of "noisy" extrinsic variables for the determination of outcomes has been perceived and analyzed. Some game theorists such as Aumann (1987) stress the notion of correlated equilibrium as the central non-cooperative game-theoretic concept. A correlated equilibrium is in a fact a Nash equilibrium in which agents' actions are based on extrinsic noise. This extrinsic noise is generated by a correlating device from which players receive signals. These signals may be different but are all correlated to the true state of nature. Actions taken by players are functions of the received signals and are the best responses to the actions taken by others. In other words, a correlated equilibrium is a Nash equilibrium when the space of agents' actions is enlarged so that actions can be indexed by exogenous signals.

There are similarities as well as differences which are obvious between the linear model, general equilibrium and game-theoretical viewpoints. In stressing similarities, sunspot equilibria can be viewed, for example, as correlated equilibria arising in an economic context: the sunspot phenomenon is the correlating device and all agents receive the same signals (see Maskin and Tirole, 1987). However, an outside observer would probably be more struck by the strongly different emphasis of the three approaches. A comparison of the implicit or explicit assessment of harmfulness of noise provides a particularly striking reflection of the differences in perspectives and "cultures" of the subfields. Theorists educated in the Arrow–Debreu tradition are likely to argue that the introduction of extrinsic noise in the model should be accompanied by the introduction of claims contingent on this noise (in the same way as the presence of intrinsic noise justifies the introduction of contingent claims). In other words, if sunspots matter, then insurance against sunspots should be considered. (In an atemporal framework, insurance is achieved through an appropriate enlargement of the space of contingent commodities; in a sequential framework, it requires that enough claims on income contingent on sunspot events be tradeable.) We discuss this idea later. Let us point out now that it has no real counterpart elsewhere. In the linear models, although the idea that noise may be harmful is present (for example acceptability criteria have been devised which stress limitations on randomness of fluctuations: selection of equilibrium with minimum variance, etc.) the idea that noise could be eliminated by insurance markets has been rarely (if ever) expressed. The idea that noise is harmful is itself foreign to the pure game-theoretical tradition. On the contrary, a repeated argument in favour of correlated equilibria is that they are likely to be superior to pure Nash equilibria at least for some well-chosen correlating device. The game theoretrical discussions on correlated equilibrium gives no attention to the traditional economic argument according to which risk-sharing institutions may emerge in a system where individual agents face risk.

Clearly, the general equilibrium framework is the proper framework for the discussion of the economic issues which we are going to present: it has by definition a structure that is richer for our purpose than an unspecified game theoretical framework; also it allows one to face the important issue of existing markets which cannot be tackled in a linear partial equilibrium framework. However, the treatment of extrinsic uncertainty suggested by the Arrow–Debreu tradition needs to be subjected to a critical assessment aimed at clarifying both its consequences and its validity.

3.2   Insurability of extrinsic uncertainty

The first thorough discussion of this issue is due to Cass and Shell (1983). The so-called "ineffectivity theorem" that is the corner stone of their analysis can be presented in an informal way.

For the sake of simplicity let us consider an exchange economy with a finite number of commodities, which may possibly be "dated" or contingent. Consider a standard Arrow–Debreu competitive equilibrium with complete markets. Call it, for the sake of brevity, a complete competitive equilibrium. Assume now that some extrinsic noise appears in the system. Extend then the number of contingent claims in such a way that the set of markets is complete with respect to dates and contingencies (either intrinsic or extrinsic). Consider an Arrow–Debreu equilibrium with respect to the new set of markets and call it (following Guesnerie and Laffont, 1988) a *complete competitive equilibrium (read a sun-complete competitive equilibrium). The inefficiency theorem (Cass and Shell, 1983) can be stated as follows:[33]

THEOREM 3.1 Consider an Arrow–Debreu economy in which consumers' preferences are strictly convex. Then a *complete competitive equilibrium is a complete competitive equilibrium.

In other words, when claims contingent on sunspots are introduced, then sunspots do not matter.

The argument supporting the theorem has two distinct parts which can be described as follows:

1   First one has to note – and this only requires a careful comparison of the formal definitions that are not provided here – that a *complete equilibrium which determines a sunspot–independent allocation is necessarily a complete competitive equilibrium.
2   It remains to prove that a *complete competitive allocation is sunspot independent. Suppose it is not. Take the expected value of bundles across sunspots. Check that the set of individual bundles so computed defines a feasible allocation. Note that this allocation is Pareto superior (because of the averaging operation and of risk aversion) to the *complete competitive allocation. This latter fact contradicts the first welfare theorem (Pareto optimality of *complete equilibria with respect to the class of stochastic and deterministic allocations).

The above argument is both simple and general. In the setting under consideration sunspot noise can only be harmful and then will disappear with a market structure leading to efficient solutions. Such a market structure obtains with full insurance against sunspots.

Although the ineffectivity theorem makes a point which is central to our debate, its significance has to be carefully appreciated. Let us examine successively its explicit formal validity and its implicit requirements.

There are immense territories of models which are outside the domain of formal validity of the ineffectivity theorem: this includes models within the Arrow–Debreu tradition which however fail to meet one of the above conditions. For example, in economies with non-convex preferences, Guesnerie and Laffont (1988) give a simple example when a sunspot equilibrium (*complete competitive equilibrium) provides a socially desirable randomization of allocations.[34] Shell and Wright (1989) study simple economies with indivisibilities in consumption where some well-chosen extrinsic randomization device restores *ex-ante* efficiency. Sunspot equilibria may also be effective and in some cases beneficial in models with externalities: the existence results of Spear (1988), Kehoe, Levine, and Romer (1989), who consider models without insurance against sunspots would remain valid if this latter assumption was removed. Also, in infinite horizon competitive economies, the first welfare theorem does not necessarily hold, a fact that for example, the capital accumulation model of Diamond (1965) illustrates. More generally, independently of the horizon assumed, no general equilibrium model incorporating any kind of second-best constraint is covered by the ineffectivity theorem. This includes most of the directions of extension of classical Walrasian theory that have occupied theorists since the beginning of the seventies: (i) models with distorting taxes whether they are, or are not, inspired by second-best theory, (ii) models of monopolistic competition, (iii) models with incomplete markets, (iv) models including informational asymmetries (adverse selection or moral hazard), (v) models of sequential bargaining, (vi) models with rationing, and (vii) models with a transactions role for money.

In all these models, sunspot equilibria are not ruled out by the ineffectivity theorem and indeed have often been exhibited: Peck and Shell (1988) for (ii), Guesnerie and Laffont (1988), Hens (1990) for (iii). Also the analysis of Kehoe, Levine and Romer for (i), Woodford (1991) for (vi), Woodford (1988b) for (vii) is not basically modified if sunspot insurance is introduced.[35]

Besides its limited domain of validity, the ineffectivity theorem rests on a crucial implicit requirement: i.e., that sunspot events are insurable. This requirement raises a number of different objections that have to be carefully discussed.

(i)   The demographic structure, for example, appearing in an OLG model, may be inconsistent with the operation of full Arrow–

Debreu insurance markets: contrary to the assumption of atemporal participation, agents will only participate in markets open during their lifetime.

(ii)   As we shall see later, there are potentially many different extrinsic phenomena which could trigger sunspot beliefs. If all have to be insured, then there should be a considerable number of insurance markets which would be potentially active. Transactions costs make this assumption unrealistic.

(iii) The fluctuations associated with sunspot events in a given sunspot equilibrium often involve variations of economic activity which are not small. In the terminology of M. Allais (1943) they involve *"risques globalement inéliminables."* But the present theory of insurance has mainly developed for small risks (at least when equilibrium has to be found in the absence of the Walras–Arrow–Debreu auctioneer).

(iv)   The modern theory of contracts of which the insurance market is one of the favorite domains of application puts strong emphasis on the distinction between verifiability and observability. Contractible variables have to be not only observable by economic agents but also verifiable. Making sunspot events verifiable variables is a bold assumption, even if one does not accept the seductive but extreme position of C. Azariadis (1981) who interprets sunspots as states of mind rather than states of nature. The standard game-theoretic view is that any insurance markets that exist must be explicitly included among the set of strategies available to the players, while players remain free to randomize among those strategies using any randomizing device they wish. This does not allow full insurance against other players' actions (or equivalently, against the correlation device).

The observed split between two strands of literature, respectively concerned with finite horizon and infinite horizon models, also involves a difference of attitude *vis à vis* the insurance issue.

The literature on sunspot equilibria in finite horizon general equilibrium models sticks to the Arrow–Debreu tradition, by a priori considering the introduction of a complete set of contingent claims on sunspots. However, it recognizes that participation on these markets is restricted for demographic reasons (see Cass and Shell (1983), Balasko, Cass, and Shell (1988)) or that trading conditionally on sunspots, on a set of assets, that is initially incomplete, leaves us in an incomplete world (Guesnerie and Laffont (1988), Hens (1990)).[36]

In infinite horizon models, sunspots states are in general not assumed to be insurable. In an OLG model with a representative consumer, the assumption is not restrictive: because of the demographic structure, the insurance market would be inactive. In other models, however, the absence of insurance markets for sunspots expresses an implicit or explicit rejection of the idea that sunspot risks are insurable (we will see in section 5.2.7 how conclusions are modified when insurance is reintroduced in such models).

An intermediate attitude might be better. If the set of objections presented above suggest that direct insurance against sunspots is implausible, one may counter-object that indirect insurance can be found. A counter-objection to the counter-objection is that indirect devices rarely have a general focus: one can find options on the price of sugar not options based on the growth rate. The discussion at this stage leads to search for a satisfactory theory of existing markets that we have not. It is likely to remain inconclusive.

3.3   Refining sunspot equilibria

The preceding discussion suggests that rational expectations general equilibrium theory should indeed consider extrinsic noise. The ineffectivity theorem concludes the irrelevance of extrinsic noise in a general equilibrium setting only in special cases. In general, full insurance might attenuate rather than wipe out sunspot randomness. But the insurance hypothesis is itself a doubtful hypothesis.

One might conclude that sunspot equilibria are likely to be the rule rather than the exception in rational expectations general equilibrium models. More exactly, the above discussion suggests that the *burden of proof has to be reversed*; in all models outside the scope of the ineffectivity theorems, sunspot equilibria have to be considered, unless an explicit contrary proof is given;[37] in all models – whether or not the ineffectivity theorem holds – sunspot insurability is a strong assumption that has to be scrutinized and justified.

Hence rational expectations equilibria of the sunspot type will generate random fluctuations even in models without intrinsic uncertainty; the fluctuations, being only driven by beliefs, will be purely endogenous. Also, it will turn out that "many" – often a continuum of possible extrinsic beliefs will be candidates for equilibrium. Equilibria will not only be multiple but "indeterminate."

At this stage the theory seems to provide too many equilibria. Could it be the case that further considerations would allow us to eliminate some of them? In other words, can we refine the set of "sunspot equilibria"?

Two extreme and opposite type of reactions are possible.

On the one hand, one could argue that a theory which does not propose a unique outcome should be considered with suspicion or should be considered as incomplete. Such a position undoubtedly attracts broad support in our profession where the influence of philosophical determinism has been widespread. Taking this view seriously, not only should we look for refinements but for refinements possibly eliminating all outcomes but one.

This seductive project is however likely to be utopian. For example the recent literature on the refinements of Nash equilibria illustrates the difficulties of finding the appropriate refinement criterion: too loose restrictions will leave "too" many equilibria, more severe restrictions may lead to an empty solution in a broad class of models. The studies of refinements of sunspot equilibria in an OLG model based on learning considerations (see section 7) face a similar dilemma. Learning processes, such as those considered by Woodford (1990a) may leave many equilibria, while the more stringent criterion of Evans (1989) may leave none.

On the other hand, and at the other extreme, one could argue that the existence of too many equilibria signals some failure of the theory: too many consistent predictions makes no prediction at all. In other words, indeterminacy should be better interpreted as the absence of predictive power of the rational expectations construct; still in other words indeterminacy of rational expectations equilibrium would mean inadequacy of the concept of rational expectations as a predictive device.

Intermediate between these two extreme positions, we will adopt here a more pragmatic view. We will look for additional "reasonable" criteria which refine the set of RE equilibria without prejudging the "size" of the remaining REE. The fact that this pragmatic position has some merits is intuitively obvious. For example a perfect foresight equilibrium in the OLG model where the sequence of prices would be chaotic is unlikely to have descriptive value. More generally, an equilibrium which does not display minimal regularity through time – maybe stationarity – is unlikely to generate the coordination between agents that it assumes. A more complete discussion of the "refinement" issue is deferred to section 7.

3.4   Related concepts

Let us briefly discuss the connections between the literature on extrinsic uncertainty and several related literatures, namely the literature on speculative bubbles, the literature on multiplicity of equilibrium and the game-theoretic concept of *rationalizable* equilibria.

3.4.1   *Sunspot equilibria and bubbles*

Some authors have associated the random extrinsic fluctuations uncertainty in solutions of this kind with rational speculative bubbles. This is because economically equation (3.1) may represent the way in which the market-clearing price of an asset in one period depends upon the price at which it is expected to be saleable in the following period, in the presence of risk-neutral rational speculators. In this case p_t would represent the amount by which the asset's price at time t exceeds the discounted value of expected future dividends; solutions in which $p_t \neq 0$ would then correspond to speculative bubbles. But the use of the term "bubble solutions" to refer generally to solutions to linear rational expectations models in which extrinsic uncertainty affects the endogenous variables – or sometimes even to refer to any kind of multiplicity of rational expectations *equilibria* – is unfortunate in our view, since it encourages confusion between analytically distinct concepts. On the one hand, speculative bubbles – in the sense of equilibria in which some asset has a market value in excess of the value of the stream of dividends to which it represents a claim – need not involve extrinsic uncertainty, or even indeterminacy of rational expectations equilibrium. For example, in the overlapping generations model of fiat money, any deterministic monetary equilibrium involves a rational speculative bubble, in the sense that fiat money has a positive exchange value while yielding zero dividends in all periods (Tirole, 1985). Also, monetary equilibrium may be unique in such a model (Brock and Scheinkman, 1980). On the other hand, the existence of a multiplicity of rational expectations equilibria, possibly involving extrinsic uncertainty, need not imply speculative bubbles in any of these equilibria. Even when there exists a perpetual asset whose value is different in the different equilibria, its value may in each equilibrium equal the discounted value of future dividends – for the equilibrium real rate of return at which dividends should be discounted may itself be indeterminate, as in the example of Calvo (1978). And, as examples discussed below show, both indeterminacy of equilibrium and the existence of sunspot equilibria are possible in models in which no perpetual assets are traded at all. Hence the considerable literature that demonstrates that "rational speculative bubbles" are not possible under many conditions that might be considered empirically plausible, has little to say about the possible importance of equilibrium fluctuations due to extrinsic uncertainty.

3.4.2   Sunspot equilibria and the multiplicity of non-sunspot equilibria

The relationships between the sunspot equilibrium problem and the standard multiplicity issue when intrinsic uncertainty is only taken into account are well illustrated through a continuity argument.

Consider a sequence of economies when intrinsic uncertainty vanishes to zero; thus, if the equilibrium correspondence is continuous, the set of equilibria in the limit economy, that are sunspot equilibria, and the set of equilibria along the sequence, that are non-sunspot equilibria (since uncertainty, although small, is purely intrinsic), are close to each other, at least far enough in the sequence. In other words, the existence of true sunspot equilibria (in addition to non-sunspot equilibria) in an economy with purely extrinsic uncertainty, signals the existence of multiple (non-sunspot) equilibria in neighbor economies (where there is intrinsic – although small – uncertainty) (see Woodford, 1986b and Chiappori and Guesnerie, 1988b). Equilibria along the sequence close to the non-sunspot equilibrium of the limit economy reflect "normal reactions" of the economy to the small intrinsic uncertainty. Equilibria along the sequence close to the sunspot equilibria reflect "overreactions."

3.4.3   Sunspot equilibria and rationalizable equilibria

Game theorists (following the earlier suggestions of Luce and Raiffa (1957), Farqhason (1969), Moulin (1979)) have argued that the concept of rationalizable solutions (or still "correlated rationalizable" or "subjectively correlated") in the sense of Aumann (1987) is more basic (in the sense that it is the consequence of Bayesian rationality and of common knowledge of rationality; see Tan and Werlang (1985)) than the Nash concept. The application of this line of argument to expectations leads to the view of rational expectations as a special case of rationalizable expectations (see Guesnerie, 1989). A strong case for the rational expectations hypothesis obtains when the RE equilibrium coincides with a unique rationalizable expectations equilibrium. Outside this case, however, this view leads to skepticism about the predictive power of a rational expectations theory. Naturally the case of indeterminacy of RE falls in the bad case just mentioned.

Hence the view expressed above, i.e., that the existence of sunspot equilibria challenges the predictive power of the rational expectations hypothesis, is in line with the rationalizability viewpoint. However, the requirement that there is a unique (or locally unique) rationalizable equilibrium, is in general much stronger than the requirement of having a unique (or locally unique) rational expectations equilibrium. Closer connections between sunspots and rationalizability can nevertheless be observed either in the one-dimensional OLG model, or through learning criteria that implicitly refer to the "local rationalizability" argument.

4   SUNSPOT EQUILIBRIA IN INFINITE HORIZON ECONOMIES: GENERAL METHODS OF ANALYSIS

4.1   Sunspot equilibria in one-step forward-looking models

We are considering in this section a model in which the relationship between observable facts and expectations is particularly simple: the evolution of the system only reflects the interaction of state variables today and expectations of state variables tomorrow.

The state variables at time t are described by an n-dimensional vector x_t, the expectations of tomorrow's values are associated with a probability distribution of $\mathbb{R}^n$ denoted μ_{t+1} ($\mu_{t+1} \in \mathscr{P}(\mathbb{R}^n)$, where $\mathscr{P}(X)$ denotes the set of probability distributions over the set X).

Then, the evolution of the system is governed by some stochastic time independent "excess demand function" $\tilde{Z} : \mathbb{R}^n \times \mathscr{P}(\mathbb{R}^n) \to \mathbb{R}^n$ and a *temporary equilibrium* (x_t, μ_{t+1}) is associated with the equation

$$\tilde{Z}(x_t, \mu_{t+1}) = 0. \tag{4.1}$$

When expectations are no longer stochastic but reduce to deterministic "point expectations," $-x_{t+1}$ is expected with probability one, technically μ_{t+1} reduces to the Dirac measure $\delta_{x_{t+1}} - \tilde{Z}$ reduces to the deterministic excess demand function Z defined as follows:

$$Z(x_t, x_{t+1}) \overset{\text{def}}{=} \tilde{Z}(x_t, \delta_{x_{t+1}}), \tag{4.2}$$

i.e., deterministic excess demand is defined from the stochastic one by considering the Dirac measure that describes deterministic point expectations. The functions $\tilde{Z}$ and Z are the basic objects under consideration.

Using the deterministic function Z, the following formal definitions are classical:

> a *perfect foresight equilibrium* is a sequence $\{x_t\}$ s.t $Z(x_t, x_{t+1}) = 0, \forall t \geqslant 0$

> a *steady state* equilibrium is a state $\bar{x}$ s.t $Z(\bar{x}, \bar{x}) = 0$

> a *periodic equilibrium* of period k consists of k different states $\bar{x}_1 \ldots \bar{x}_k$ s.t $Z(\bar{x}_1, \bar{x}_2) = 0, Z(\bar{x}_2, \bar{x}_3) = 0, \ldots, Z(\bar{x}_k, \bar{x}_1) = 0$

Using the function $\tilde{Z}$, one can define, besides the already defined concept of temporary equilibrium, a number of other concepts. We will content ourselves with informal definitions, leaving it to the reader to make them precise.

> a *rational expectations equilibrium* is a sequence of (possibly stochastic) expectations that are self-fulfilling.

> a *sunspot equilibrium* is a rational expectations equilibrium which generates a time independent Markov process over the set of state variables.

a *stationary sunspot equilibrium* obtains when the Markov process in the definition of a sunspot equilibrium has an invariant measure.[38]

Consider the support $X_0 \subset \mathbb{R}^n$ of the Markov process and its transition probability $\mu_x, x \in X_0$. A sunspot equilibria is associated with a set of states X_0 and transition probabilities μ_x such that $\tilde{Z}(x,\mu_x) = 0, \forall x \in X_0$. When the support is finite (say with k elements), a sunspot equilibrium consists of k states and is associated with a Markov matrix $(k \times k)$ describing the probabilities of transition between the states. The sunspot equilibrium is said to be of *order k*. A standard interpretation of the Markov matrix, which also extends to the case of an infinite support, is that it describes the random evolution of a phenomenon extrinsic to the economy (sunspots) that can take k values. A (stationary) sunspot equilibrium is then nothing else than an equilibrium in which the k possible equilibrium states of the system are perfectly correlated to the k extrinsic states. (In other words, the theory according to which "sunspots determine equilibrium states," is self-fulfilling).

The early example of Azariadis (1981), Azariadis and Guesnerie (1982) describes the evolution of money prices (or real balances) of the unique good of an OLG model: prices fluctuate forever between two values (high or low) and the laws of stochastic motion are those of a two-state Markov process. Such a Markov process can be interpreted as an "extrinsic," universally observed, generator of prices and beliefs: its two possible realizations – sunspot, no sunspot – trigger different stochastic beliefs on the next period and then determine the economic state (high or low) that has to prevail. As anticipated by the agents, there is full correlation between the sunspot phenomenon and the level of economic activity.

Note that just as a perfect foresight equilibrium is a particular case of a rational expectations equilibrium, steady states or periodic equilibria are particular cases of stationary sunspot equilibria (SSE). However we shall stick to the convention that the word sunspot is used only for truly stochastic equilibria, so that neither steady states nor periodic equilibria will be considered, strictly speaking, as sunspot equilibria.

Note also that the present formulation rules out sunspot insurability a priori: an n-commodity system where "insurance" against a sunspot of order k is provided, should have nk markets today and nk^2 contingencies tomorrow, a fact incompatible with the constant state space dimension of our formulation. Our assumption here accordingly rules out sunspot insurability of the kind discussed in section 3.2 and below in section 6.1.[39]

Given the definition of sunspot equilibria, we have to face the questions: Do such equilibria exist? This is the *existence* question. What do they exactly look like? Or, more exactly, what are the stochastic characteristics of the endogenous fluctuations which they generate? By this we mean the properties of the Markov matrix, in the case of a finite order sunspot equilibrium, more generally, we mean characteristics of the transition probability and of the invariant measure. This is the *characterization* problem.

We are now going to review the main existing results concerning the *existence* and *characterization* problems for the model under consideration. This review closely follows and provides a quick and necessarily loose summary of the attempt at synthesis of Chiappori and Guesnerie (1989b). The exposition puts emphasis on intuition. Details as well as precise statements can be found in the just quoted article.

Throughout the section, we always assume that the functions Z and $\tilde{Z}$ meet a certain number of regularity requirements such as continuity for Z, closed graph for $\tilde{Z}$. We will refer to these requirements as (R).

Also, we assume that the derivatives of Z and $\tilde{Z}$ have some relationship around a "sure" situation x_t, x_{t+1}. This condition, called *consistency of derivatives* (CD), is normally a consequence of the fact that, in the underlying model, optimizing agents use the expected utility criterion.[40] We present now several categories of existence arguments.

4.1.1   The invariant set argument

The invariant set argument starts from the idea that one can find a set X_0 which is *invariant* in the following sense:

> Let $x_0 \in X_0$, then there exists $x' \in \operatorname{int} X_0$ (the interior of X_0)[41] such that $Z(x_0, x') = 0$.

We can also say in this case that the occurrence of x_0 today is "sustained" or "rationalized" or, here, "deterministically rationalized" by x' tomorrow.

Now, let us assume that $\tilde{Z}$ is such that, when some x_0 is deterministically rationalized by x', then it is also "stochastically" rationalized by some measure $\mu_{N(x')}^{x'}$ the support of which is $N(x')$, for as *small* as desired neighborhoods $N(x')$ around x' (an additional technical requirement that will not be precisely defined is that $\mu_{N(x')}^{x'}$ should not put too much weight on the immediate neighborhood of x'). This property, the description of which has just been sketched, reflects some kind of lower hemicontinuity for the rationalizability correspondence. Call it (LR).

The next assumption states that the rationalizability correspondence is convex valued, i.e., that the set $\{\mu \mid \tilde{Z}(x_0, \mu) = 0\}$ is convex $\forall x_0$. Call it (CVR).

Then the invariant compact set argument can be, roughly speaking, stated:

THEOREM 4.1[42]

Assume (R), (LR), (CVR). Assume that $\exists$ some compact set K of non-empty interior which is invariant in the above sense. Then, there exists a SSE with support on K.

The idea of invariance was explicitly exploited in one-dimensional OLG models by Farmer and Woodford (1984) and Grandmont (1986). Also, the example of Peck (1988) of a one-dimensional "invariant" open set in an OLG model shows that the conclusion of proposition 4.1 requires a compact set K. The above result is precisely stated and proved in Chiappori and Guesnerie (1989b). The Chiappori–Guesnerie proof relies upon the Duffie, Geanakoplos, Mas-Colell, and McLennan's (1988) version of a theorem of Blume (1982). Although the statement covers most of existing results based on invariance, it has the inconvenience of requiring (CVR) which, in specific versions of the model, normally holds only when there is a representative consumer.[43]

Naturally, the statement is intuitive enough and does not require many comments at this stage. We should however notice that, in our previous terminology, the proposition is more an "existence" result than a "characterization" result (although it provides some indication of the stochastic properties of sunspot phenomena).

4.1.2   Sunspot equilibria and stochastic equilibria in "tangent" linear systems

Consider some steady state $\bar{x}$ and consider the perfect foresight dynamics around this steady state. It is associated with the linearized equation:

$$(\partial_0 Z)_{(.)}(x_t - \bar{x}) + (\partial_1 Z)_{(.)}(x_{t+1} - \bar{x}) = 0,$$

where $(\partial_0 Z)_{(.)}, (\partial_1 Z)_{(.)}$ are straightforward notation for the Jacobian matrices of Z (with respect to x_t, x_{t+1} respectively) in the steady state $(\bar{x}, \bar{x})$. Assuming that $(\partial_0 Z)$ is invertible, we have:

$$(x_t - \bar{x}) = -(\partial_0 Z)^{-1}(\partial_1 Z)(x_{t+1} - \bar{x}). \tag{4.3}$$

Call $B \overset{\text{def}}{=} -(\partial_0 Z)^{-1}(\partial_1 Z)$. Assuming from now that B has no eigenvalue on the unit circle and dropping $\bar{x}$, rewrite (4.3) as:

$$x_t = B x_{t+1}. \tag{4.3'}$$

Let us recall at this stage that the perfect foresight dynamics associated with (4.3') is said to be determinate if there exists no sequence $\{x_t\}$ solution of (4.3′) that tends to zero. On the contrary it is said to be indeterminate if such a sequence exists.[44] It is straightforward and well-known that indeterminacy in this sense is equivalent to the fact that B has at least one eigenvalue outside the unit disk.

Consider now the stochastic version of the linear equation:

$$x_t = E[Bx_{t+1}], \tag{4.4}$$

where E designates the expected value operator.

Equations such as (4.4) are (part of) the subject of study of the literature on linear models with rational expectations which was evoked in section 3.1. (In fact this literature generally considers equations with an additional random exogenous perturbation of the right-hand side and often introduces a more complex memory structure – see references in section 4.2). Referring to Blanchard and Kahn (1980) in this literature, we have the following result:

> Equation (4.4) has a bounded stochastic solution if and only if the perfect foresight dynamics (4.3) is indeterminate if and only if B has at least one eigenvalue outside the unit circle.

Now, one can check that among the solutions of (4.4) there are SSE in the sense of the above definition and even SSE of "finite order."

Considering a k-state candidate SSE, let us introduce a Markov matrix M, the row-vectors of which may be written $M_i = (m_{i1} \ldots m_{ik})$, $\sum_k m_{ik} = 1$. Calling x the vector in $\mathbb{R}^{nk}$, with "components" in $\mathbb{R}^n, x^1 \ldots x^k$, equation (4.4) may be written:

$$x_i - \sum_j m_{ij} B x_{ij} = 0 \qquad \forall i,$$

or more compactly,

$$[I - M \otimes B]x = 0 \tag{4.5}$$

where I is the $(nk \times nk)$ identity matrix and $(M \otimes B)$ is the $(nk \times nk)$ matrix equal to the tensor product of M and B.

It can be shown that:

> (4.5) has a non-zero solution (i.e., there exists a SSE associated with M)[45] if and only if there exists m belonging to the spectrum of the M and b element of the spectrum of B such that $m = \dfrac{1}{b}$.

Again since the spectrum of a Markov matrix lies within the unit circle, this result implies that the existence of some SSE for some (possibly large) k requires the indeterminacy of the perfect foresight dynamics. But the indeterminacy of the perfect foresight dynamics is not enough to guarantee the existence of SSE of given order k. If B has one eigenvalue of modulus greater than one, then one can indeed show that SSE of any order exist, but if B has only complex eigenvalues of modulus strictly greater than one, then SSE of order k only obtain when $|b|\cos\dfrac{\pi}{k}>1$ (where $|b|$ is the modulus of the smallest eigenvalue greater than one).

What about SSE in the non-linear system? It is natural to conjecture that the phenomenon occurring in the tangent linear system has a counterpart in the non-linear system. More precisely, it can be shown that the non-linear counterpart of linear sunspot equilibria of order k should consist of SSE called "local," i.e., of SSE the support of which $\{x^1 \ldots x^k\}$ lies in a small neighborhood of the deterministic steady state. Furthermore this support is such that the directions $\dfrac{x^l-\bar{x}}{\|x^l-\bar{x}\|} l = 1 \ldots k$ are close to those of the solution to the tangent linear system.

Indeed Chiappori, Geoffard, and Guesnerie (1990) have shown the following:

THEOREM 4.2[46]
Assume conditions (CD) and (R). Then if $\bar{x}$ is an indeterminate steady state, for any neighborhood $v(\bar{x})$ of $\bar{x}$, there exists a SSE of order k with support in $v(\bar{x})$, for any k such that:

  (i) $k \geqslant 2$, if B has a real eigenvalue of modulus greater than 1; or
  (ii) $k \geqslant \bar{k}$, if the complex eigenvalue of B of largest modulus, b, is such that $|b|\cos\left(\dfrac{\pi}{\bar{k}}\right)>1$. is the smallest of the moduli greater than 1 among all the eigenvalues of B.

As in the prior analyses of Azariadis and Guesnerie (1986) and Guesnerie (1986), the proof of Geoffard, Chiappori and Guesnerie (1989) considers the space of Markov matrices as the basic parameter space:[47] a bifurcation occurs when an element of the spectrum of M "crosses" the inverse of one eigenvalue of the perfect foresight dynamics matrix. The bifurcation argument is standard in the case of real eigenvalues but intricate in the case of complex eigenvalues.

This result supports, and extends in the special case of finite-order SSE, Woodford's general conjecture that there should exist a close relationship between the indeterminacy of the perfect foresight equilibrium and the existence of "local" SSE. The present statement has indeed to be compared with Woodford's result (1986) that shows in a different way and in a model with predetermined variables that indeterminacy implies the existence of local SSE. The discussion of the application of Woodford's result to the present model, and its relationship with the present statement are postponed to section 4.2.

Also, the relationship of proposition 4.2 with proposition 4.1 can be briefly discussed. Naturally, their scope is different; proposition 4.1 is concerned with SSE the support of which need not be in a neighborhood of a steady state. However, proposition 4.1 will apply for compact sets that are in a close neighborhood of the steady state whenever *all* eigenvalues of the associated matrix B will be outside the unit circle, whereas proposition 4.2 only requires *one* such eigenvalue. Hence, so far as local SSE are concerned, proposition 4.2 is more powerful.

4.1.3   Sunspot equilibria detected by the Poincaré–Hopf method

The bifurcation argument evoked above only detects "local" SSE, the support of which is close to the steady state. The Poincaré–Hopf method is also based upon the analysis of the same Jacobian matrices as in the bifurcation study, i.e., those which describe the local behavior of the system around steady states. However, the argument exploits the discrepancies between the system's behavior around steady states and its boundary behavior and then crucially relies upon the non-linearities of the system. It detects sunspot equilibria that need not be local in the previous sense. The sufficient condition provided for the existence of "non-local" sunspot equilibria is a weaker one; in counterpart the characterization of the equilibrium – in fact of its support – is weaker as well.

The Poincaré–Hopf theorem is a powerful tool of analysis. In economics, it has been used for studying multiplicity of Walrasian equilibria (cf. for example Dierker, 1972). Its interest in analyzing deterministic cycles has been stressed in section 3.1. Its application as the Poincaré–Hopf method for detecting SSE was initially proposed by Azariadis and Guesnerie (1982) and then extensively used by Spear (1984), Guesnerie (1986), Chiappori and Guesnerie (1989a), Guesnerie and Laffont (1988), and Woodford (1990a).

The Poincaré–Hopf method for detecting SSE is closely similar to the PH detection method for cycles described in section 3.1. It can be explained as follows. SSE of order k obtain as zeros of a vector field in $\mathbb{R}^{nk}$ (or as zeros of a system of nk equations with nk unknowns). The steady state – or more exactly its k-replica – is a zero of this vector field. Now assume that (U) the steady state is unique and (B) the vector field has the "right" boundary behavior. Then one can compute the PH index ($+1$ or -1, depending on the sign of the determinant of the Jacobian matrix) of the vector field in the unique steady state. When this PH index differs from some characteristic number ($(-1)^{nk}$ when the vector field points inwards) then there must be other zeros of the vector field. Because of (U) these other zeros must be "true" SSE.

In the present context, this technology can be used to prove the following:

THEOREM 4.3[48]
Assume that (CD) (R) (B) and (U) are satisfied. Define as above $B = -(\partial_0 Z)^{-1}(\partial_1 Z)$. Then:

  (i) If matrix B has at least one real eigenvalue of absolute value greater than one, then for all $k \geqslant 2$, there exists a Markov matrix and a SSE of order $2 \leqslant j \leqslant k$ associated with it.

  (ii) In this case, if M is any Markov matrix let $SR(M)$(resp.$SR(B)$) denote the set of real eigenvalues of M(resp.B). If the two products:

$$P = \prod_{b \in SR(B)} (1-b)^k \text{ and } P_M = \prod_{\substack{b \in SR(B) \\ m \in SR(M)}} (1-bm)$$

have opposite signs then there exists a SSE of order j, ($2 \leqslant j \leqslant k$) associated with M.

Note that (i) results from the previous proposition 4.2 but that (ii) does not. In fact, statement (ii) allows "detection" of many phenomena triggering sunspot beliefs: in particular, for a given steady state of the system (and a given B), the set of Markov matrices detected by condition (ii) is open (in the space of Markov matrices). Intuitively, also it is "large": a number of examples of proposition 4.3 will confirm this intuition later. Also, a reasonable conjecture is that generically for matrices that fit the characterization condition of proposition 4.3, the sunspot equilibrium is exactly of order k[49] This assertion has been given a precise content only in the case of one-dimensional models (see Chiappori and Guesnerie, 1989a).

4.1.4   *Sunspot equilibria in systems with multiple steady states*

The existence of several deterministic steady states in the dynamical system under consideration will open original sources of self-fulfilling beliefs, which may not be captured by the previous techniques. Let us briefly examine the connections between multiplicity of steady states and the existence of sunspot equilibria.

(i) First assume that there exist two steady states $\bar{x}$ and $\bar{\bar{x}}$ and assume that there exists an intermediary state $\tilde{x}$ which is "stochastically" rationalized (in the sense defined at the beginning of the previous section) by $\bar{x},\bar{\bar{x}}$, i.e., by $\bar{x}$ with probability μ and $\bar{\bar{x}}$ with probability $1-\mu$.

Considering the Markov matrix $\begin{bmatrix} 1 & 0 & 0 \\ \mu & 0 & 1-\mu \\ 0 & 0 & 1 \end{bmatrix}$ one can note that $\bar{x},\tilde{x},\bar{\bar{x}}$

is a degenerate SSE (in the sense that the Markov matrix is degenerate). However, a *continuity argument* suggests that "generically" there will exist true SSE associated with non-degenerate Markov matrices. (This argument has been first exploited by J. Peck (1988) in the simple OLG model.)

(ii) Also, in systems with several steady states, a variant of the PH argument – as used in Guesnerie (1986) – shows that whenever each of these steady states satisfies the *uniqueness of Temporary Equilibrium Assumption* (i.e., the period t equilibrium associated with fixing the period $t+1$ expectations at their given steady state values is unique) then there exists SSE. Furthermore, such SSE may be associated with Markov matrices with equal rows, i.e., with time independent random processes. Guesnerie (1986) labeled such SSE non-informative: in contrast with what happens with time dependent processes, the self-fulfillment mechanism does not rely upon differential statistical information (that a sunspot believer would extract from sunspot realizations). Clearly, in such a case, the random process over state variables is also time independent.

(iii) Finally, sunspot equilibria may be associated with some kind of *random walk between two steady states*.

The *support* of this random walk is an infinite sequence of points, the two steady states being *accumulation points of this sequence*. The sunspot phenomenon triggering the corresponding beliefs is itself a random walk – as is the money supply for example in some monetary models. The actual movement of the system then is governed by the actual realization of the sunspot random variable but each state of the support is – according to the precise process under consideration – either "recurrent" with positive probability or with probability one (see Chiappori and Guesnerie, 1989).

The principle of the derivation of such sunspot equilibria can be more easily explained in the case where the random phenomenon is such that the process can reach only two values tomorrow from its present value today, i.e., an upper and a lower value, or $s+1$ and $s-1$ when starting from s. Then the equations which govern the equilibrium express a relationship between the corresponding elements of the support x^{s-1},x^s,x^{s+1}, that, for example, as in Chiappori and Guesnerie (1990) can be written:

$$\bar{x}^{s+1} = \Lambda(\bar{x}^s, \bar{x}^{s-1}). \tag{4.6}$$

This equation can also be rewritten as a dynamical system in $\mathbb{R}^{2n}$

$$\begin{pmatrix} \bar{x}^{s+1} \\ \bar{x}^s \end{pmatrix} = \phi\begin{pmatrix} \bar{x}^s \\ \bar{x}^{s-1} \end{pmatrix} \quad \text{or } y^{s+1} = \phi(y^s). \tag{4.7}$$

In the one-dimensional OLG model of Chiappori and Guesnerie (1988b), this system has two fixed points in $\mathbb{R}^2$ which are the points on the diagonal corresponding to the steady states ($\bar{x}$ and $\bar{\bar{x}}$) of the model. Under some conditions it can be shown that (4.7) has an heteroclinic orbit, i.e., an orbit linking (asymptotically) the two fixed points. Coming back to the original system, this implies that it has a family of solutions the support of which is such that $\lim_{s \to -\infty} \bar{x}^s = \bar{x}$, $\lim_{s \to +\infty} \bar{x}^s = \bar{\bar{x}}$, and the stochastic properties of which are those of a random walk.

Solutions of this kind obviously may exist independently of the dimension. They are called *heteroclinic* both because they correspond to heteroclinic orbits of the associated (higher dimensional) dynamical system and because their support has two accumulation points which are the steady states of the original system between which the system "oscillates." The method of construction of an associated dynamical system may indeed generalize from two-state random walks to random walks with any finite number of neighborhood states (see Chiappori and Guesnerie (1988b) who also propose a classification of solutions of systems of this type, which include, but do not reduce to, heteroclinic solutions).

4.1.5   Sunspots and cycles

As we already noted above, cycles are limit cases of SSE. Consider for example a deterministic periodic equilibrium of order 2, $\bar{x}_1, \bar{x}_2$ which satisfies:

$$Z(\bar{x}_1, \bar{x}_2) = 0 \qquad Z(\bar{x}_2, \bar{x}_1) = 0. \tag{4.8}$$

It can be viewed as a (degenerate) SSE associated with the (degenerate) Markov matrix $\begin{pmatrix} 0 & 1 \\ 1 & 0 \end{pmatrix}$; a similar argument applies for a periodic equilibrium of order k.

A continuity argument then suggests that there exist "generically" true SSE in the neighborhood of a periodic equilibrium (see Azariadis and Guesnerie, 1986).

THEOREM 4.4

Generically, SSE of order k exist in a neighborhood of a periodic equilibrium of order k.[50]

If proving the existence of cycles is a route toward proving the existence of truly stochastic SSE, it is also true that, conversely, existing results on SSE allow the detection of cycles. In fact, one way to show the existence of cycles in our framework is to apply proposition 4.3 for degenerate sunspot matrices. For example, a two-cycle is associated with a simple Markov matrix, the eigenvalues of which are $+1$ and -1. Then considering a system Z whose steady state and boundary behavior meet the assumptions of proposition 4.3, it can be seen that if the number of eigenvalues of the matrix B (which governs the perfect foresight dynamics around the steady state) outside $[-1, +1]$ is odd, a cycle of order 2 exists (see Guesnerie (1988) for a different but equivalent statement). However, given this fact, proposition 4.4 adds nothing to our knowledge of SSE that could not be deduced from proposition 4.3.

The case is different for one-dimensional systems, where our knowledge of periodic equilibria does not crucially rest on Poincaré–Hopf type arguments. Suppose for example that $Z(x_t, x_{t+1}) = 0$ can be solved as $x_t = \chi(x_{t+1})$ (as it is often the case in applications involving the OLG model, see section 5). Then the powerful machinery recently developed in mathematics for the study of one-dimensional dynamical systems is of direct use. A pioneer systematic application for the OLG model is due to J.M. Grandmont (1985). (See next section where existence results for cycles allow us, through proposition 4.4, to derive the existence of "neighborhood" SSE.)

Although the simple structure of the model under consideration allows a deeper understanding of the existence problem – and even though the model encompasses interesting multidimensional cases as the n-commodity OLG model with separable utility functions and representative consumers – it rules out many systems of economic interest with predetermined state variables. These include overlapping generations models with multiple goods per period (outside the special case just mentioned), or in which consumers live for more than two periods, as well as models with capital accumulation. The simplest case of a system with a predetermined variable is one in which the state variable determined at time t depends upon its value in the previous period (a predetermined variable at time t) as well as conditions about its value in the future. An economic example of this kind is discussed in Woodford (1986a). The study of such systems is the subject of the next subsection.

4.2   Sunspot equilibria in models with predetermined state variables

4.2.1   Local sunspot equilibria in models with memory

Assume that the stochastic dynamics (4.2) now depends upon a predetermined variable so that:

$$\tilde{Z}(x_{t-1}, x_t, \mu_{t+1}) = 0. \tag{4.9}$$

Similarly, the deterministic dynamics become:

$$Z(x_{t-1}, x_t, x_{t+1}) = 0. \tag{4.10}$$

And a steady state is now defined by:

$$Z(\bar{x}, \bar{x}, \bar{x}) = 0. \tag{4.11}$$

The study of the local perfect foresight dynamics of systems of this type (along the lines of the study of Kehoe and Levine, 1985) proceeds as follows. First, the linearization of the system around a steady state leads to the following set of equations:

$$B\begin{bmatrix} x_t \\ x_{t+1} \end{bmatrix} = \begin{bmatrix} x_{t-1} \\ x_t \end{bmatrix},$$

where (with straightforward notation):

$$B = \begin{bmatrix} -(\partial_{-1}Z)^{-1}(\partial_0 Z) & -(\partial_{-1}Z)^{-1}(\partial_1 Z) \\ I & 0 \end{bmatrix}.$$

Second, the study of the linear system can be made as in Blanchard and Kahn (1980). A converging perfect foresight path $\begin{pmatrix} x_{t-1} \\ x_t \end{pmatrix}$ necessarily belongs to the stable subspace generated by the eigenvectors of B associated with eigenvalues outside the unit disk. The question is then whether one can find, for any given x_{-1}, an x_0 such that the vector $\begin{pmatrix} x_{-1} \\ x_0 \end{pmatrix}$ belongs to the stable subspace. The answer depends on the dimension s of the subspace and, when matrix B is in a "generic position," leads us to distinguish three cases:

(i) $s < n$, then for almost all x_{-1}, no such x_0 can be found.
(ii) $s = n$, then for any x_{-1}, there exists exactly one such x_0.
(iii) $s > n$, then for any x_{-1}, there exists a continuum of such x_0.

Similar conclusions hold locally for non-linear systems as well, for by the stable manifold theorem (under certain regularity assumptions) there exists a stable manifold (to which $\begin{bmatrix} x_{-1} \\ x_0 \end{bmatrix}$ must belong if there is to exist a perfect foresight path remaining forever near, and converging to, the steady state), that is of the same dimension as, and indeed is tangent to, the stable subspace of the linearized system (see Kehoe and Levine, 1985). Also these conclusions have a counterpart for the stochastic linear dynamics that could be associated with (4.9), extending the result of section 4.1.3 concerning the relationship between indeterminacy and the existence of solutions to (4.4) (see Blanchard and Kahn, 1980). Following Woodford (1986), let us consider now the existence of local SSE around a steady state.

Consider a random process (u_t), and define $u^t = (u_t, u_{t-1} \ldots)$; u^t is the (infinite) history of the process at date t. The process is stationary, in the sense that the set of possible histories is endowed with an invariant measure. Assume that the stochastic excess demand $\tilde{Z}$ has Fréchet derivatives and that the deterministic excess demand Z fulfills a regularity condition (similar to that of the linear case). Now, a sunspot equilibrium is defined as a mapping Φ from the set of possible histories of the process to the set of state variables; i.e., $x_t = \Phi(u^t)$ for all t (we shall say that the corresponding SE is based upon the process (u_t)). Note that we do not rule out (and, in fact, we essentially consider) sunspots with infinite support (since the set of histories is infinite). Also, the autocorrelation structure of the (x_t) process may be quite complex (it depends on the structure of (u_t) and on the mapping Φ).

Woodford (1986b), at this stage, considers the sunspot equation $\tilde{Z}(.) = 0$ as an equation in Φ and investigates whether the solution Φ defined by $\Phi(u^t) = \bar{x}$ for all u^t is locally unique. It is clear that indeterminacy means that the above solution is *not* a locally unique solution (over the relevant set of sequences of x) of the (deterministic) equation $Z(.) = 0$. It turns out that indeterminacy has the same implication for $\tilde{Z}(.) = 0$, so that additional restrictions can be added to this equation up to the point where the implicit function theorem holds. Then, the extended system has a unique solution that, for almost all restrictions, does not coincide with the steady state solution, i.e., that is a sunspot solution.

If Woodford's argument relies on the simple principle just sketched, the key analysis of the derivative mapping associated with the basic functional equation is technically sophisticated. The following conclusion is established under weak regularity conditions:

THEOREM 4.5 (Woodford, 1986b)
For any given, stationary random process (u_t), stationary sunspot equilib-

ria based upon (u_t) exists in any neighborhood of the steady state if and only if the following, equivalent conditions are fulfilled:

(i)   the steady state is indeterminate for the perfect foresight dynamics;
(ii)   the matrix B has at least $n+1$ eigenvalues outside the unit disk.

A similar analysis applies to systems in which the number of predetermined state variables is $k \neq n$, with part (ii) of proposition 4.5 being modified to read "at least $k+1$ eigenvalues." The analysis therefore applies, as a special case, to the systems without predetermined state variables considered in section 4.1. In that case, indeterminacy requires only that matrix B have at least one eigenvalue outside the unit circle. As a result the conclusions of proposition 4.5 are very similar to those of proposition 4.2 for that case. In particular both imply that indeterminacy is a sufficient condition for the existence of local sunspot equilibria. However, the kind of sunspot equilibria that are exhibited differs in the two results. Proposition 4.2 exhibits local SSE with finite support, and relates the cardinality of the support to the properties of the matrix B. Proposition 4.5, by contrast, exhibits sunspot equilibria that are functions of the infinite history of some stationary random variable; since this infinite history has an infinite support (even when the stationary random variable (u_t) is a finite-state Markov process), there is no guarantee that (x_t) can have finite support in any of these equilibria.

Note also that both propositions provide necessary and sufficient conditions for the existence of local SSE *within* the class of processes that they consider. But the extent to which indeterminacy is thus shown to be a necessary condition for the existence of local SSE is different in the two cases (and rather limited in each). Proposition 4.2 says that for any order k, determinacy implies the existence of a neighborhood of the steady state in which there exist no SSE of order k. But it does not establish any relationship between the sizes of the neighborhoods for different values of k, and so does not guarantee the existence of any neighborhood such that there are no local SSE of any finite order in that neighborhood. Still less does it show that there may not exist SSE with infinite support arbitrarily close to the steady state (for an early discussion of this issue, see Laitner, 1985). Similarly, proposition 4.5 states for any *given* stationary variable (u_t), determinacy implies the existence of a neighborhood in which there exist no SSE measurable with respect to the infinite history of the variable (u_t). But it does not say anything about how the size of this neighborhood depends upon the particular variable (u_t) chosen. There exist representation theorems for Markov chains that allow one to show that all (ergodic) finite-state Markov processes, of arbitrary order, can be written as measurable functions of the infinite history of a single stationary process

(u_t), e.g., an i.i.d. random variable uniformly distributed on the unit interval. These results allow us to establish that determinacy precludes the existence of local SSE of any finite order, or indeed of any local SSE in which (x_t) is a Markov process of a kind to which such theorems apply. But even these results fall short of what would be needed to allow us to assert that no local SSE are possible.

The question of necessary and sufficient conditions for the existence of SSE globally (i.e., not simply in a neighborhood of a steady state) in these models is obviously even more difficult. No results exist of a generality of the kind that is possible in the case of one-dimensional systems with no predetermined state variables (see, for example, the discussion of overlapping generations models in section 5, or the discussion in Woodford (1988b)).

Counterparts of other results of section 4.1 also exist for the case of systems with predetermined state variables. For example, an invariant set argument can be used to prove a theorem similar to proposition 4.1. Such an argument is applied to a one-dimensional version of the model (4.9) in Woodford (1986a). Woodford's argument considers sunspot candidates which, as above, are functions of the infinite history of a random extrinsic process and which appear as fixed points of a contraction mapping. The existing analysis closest to an n-dimensional version of the invariant set argument (in the model under consideration in the present subsection) is that of Spear, Srivastava and Woodford (1990). Although Spear, Srivastava and Woodford consider an OLG exchange economy with (small) intrinsic uncertainty, their analysis can be better viewed (at least for the purpose of the present survey) as the combination of an existence result for sunspot equilibria preferences – in an exchange economy where nonadditive and heterogenous consumers make period t equilibrium conditions dependent upon realized states at $t-1$ – and of a continuity result – that links sunspot and non-sunspot equilibria, as explained below, when intrinsic uncertainty is small. Following Woodford (1986a), Spear, Srivastava and Woodford (1990) construct a contraction mapping (the existence of which implies the existence of an "invariant set") that operates on functions that take values in a neighborhood of the steady state when all relevant eigenvalues are outside the unit circle. Hence, as for the case of section 5.1, the existence of an invariant set near a steady state is deduced from conditions that are stronger than indeterminacy.

We may also consider the extension of proposition 4.4 to the case of predetermined state variables. Continuity arguments of the same kind again apply, but in this case additional regularity conditions are needed. It is also generally necessary to consider the periodic equilibrium of order k as a degenerate example of an SSE of order greater than k (so that the non-degenerate SSE constructed are also of that higher order). The regularity conditions needed for the continuity argument hold for an open set of parameterized models, but do not hold generically (i.e., for a set of parameters that is also dense). Thus the existence of a periodic equilibrium does not imply the existence of SSE with the same generality as is true for systems without predetermined state variables. (For a simple counter-example, see Woodford, 1986b.) One can also consider the existence of SSE near a periodic equilibrium, that share its periodicity. In this case the analysis used in proposition 4.5 applies, considering the periodic equilibrium as a steady state of a system with a larger number of state variables (and a redefined "period" length). Indeterminacy of perfect foresight equilibrium near the periodic equilibrium is then necessary and sufficient for the existence of local SSE of this particular kind.

Until now, attention has been limited to pure sunspot equilibria. Sunspot equilibria can be viewed as particularly dramatic examples of phenomena with broader scope. On the one hand, the effect of extrinsic uncertainty on equilibrium is not limited to economies without intrinsic uncertainty. On the other hand, even without any reference to extrinsic uncertainty, sunspot equilibria have counterparts in the form of multiple equilibria in economies with only intrinsic uncertainty. In particular, a continuity argument already evoked in section 3 suggests that economies with small intrinsic uncertainty may have intrinsic equilibria involving large fluctuations.

Although neither of the two lines of development just sketched is in the scope of the present survey, we should mention existing formalizations of the continuity argument.

Theorem 2 in Woodford (1986b) extends proposition 4.5 above, concerning the existence of local SSE around indeterminate steady states, to the case of small intrinsic uncertainty. Proposition 5.6 in Chiappori and Guesnerie (1988) provides a formal statement of the continuity argument starting from finite SSE (that need not be local) in a simple OLG model. Also, proposition 12 in Chiappori and Guesnerie (1988) shows the "sunspot connection" between their heteroclinic sunspot solution, discussed in section 4.1, and the "heteroclinic" solutions of a model with small intrinsic uncertainty of a random walk type. Manuelli and Peck (1988) discuss similar issues.

5   ECONOMIC APPLICATIONS: THE OVERLAPPING GENERATIONS MODEL

5.1   The model and its perfect foresight equilibria[51]

Consider an OLG model with two-period-lived agents. Let $U(c_1, c_2)$ be the utility of a consumer whose life cycle consumption program is (c_1, c_2) and whose life cycle endowment is (e_1, e_2). Faced with money price p_t today and expecting (some) p_{t+1} tomorrow, the consumer will have to decide upon m, the quantity of money which he holds. The first-order condition of his optimization program is:

$$\frac{1}{p_t}U_1\left(e_1-\frac{m}{p_t},e_2+\frac{m}{p_{t+1}}\right)-\frac{1}{p_{t+1}}U_2\left(e_1-\frac{m}{p_t},e_2+\frac{m}{p_{t+1}}\right)=0. \quad (5.1)$$

In a model with a representative consumer of this type, the reduced form equation associated with a perfect foresight equilibrium writes down under the form (4.2), i.e.:

$$Z(p_t,p_{t+1})=\frac{1}{p_t}U_1\left(e_1-\frac{M}{p_t},e_2+\frac{M}{p_{t+1}}\right)$$

$$-\frac{1}{p_{t+1}}U_2\left(e_1-\frac{M}{p_t},e_2+\frac{M}{p_{t+1}}\right)=0, \quad (5.2)$$

where M is the total quantity of money in the economy.

Without the representative consumer assumption, the equation determining the perfect foresight dynamics may be written down as:

$$Z(p_t,p_{t+1})=\frac{M}{p_t}-y\left(\frac{p_t}{p_{t+1}}\right)=0, \quad (5.3)$$

where $y\left(\frac{p_t}{p_{t+1}}\right)$ is total "real" savings from the young, obtained as the sum of individual "real" savings, i.e., the sum of $\frac{m_h}{p_t}$, where m_h would stand for household h money balances and would be implicitly determined by equation (5.1).

An alternative interpretation of equation (5.3) obtains if consumers have specialized functions in each period: they work when young and they only consume when old: in the reduced form (5.3), $y(p_t/p_{t+1})$ is then nothing else than the total labor supply of the young as a function of relative money prices p_t/p_{t+1}. In the following, we will mostly focus attention on the reduced form (5.3) and will essentially refer to the labor supply interpretation of the function y. We should however note, before going further, that many other different variants of OLG models fit the canonical formulation 5.3.

We shall give two more examples of the determination of equation (4.2) under alternative assumptions in the OLG model. For example, assuming as in Grandmont (1986) that government intervention in period $t+1$ combines a random shock x_{t+1} to money balances, an additional and proportional lump sum subsidy $S_{t+1}=(s-1)M_t x_{t+1}$ (where s is a given number), and government expenditures $G_{t+1} = (d-s)M_t x_{t+1}$ (where d is a fixed number), it can be checked that the consumer in the first period faces a (random) real income transfer $(s-1)\dfrac{M_t x_{t+1}}{p_{t+1}}$ and (random) terms of trade $\dfrac{p_t M_{t+1}}{dp_{t+1}M_t}$. His labor supply function incorporates in addition to the random terms of trade a random income term. But, under separability, equation (5.1) becomes:

$$U'_1\left(\frac{M_t}{p_t}\right) - \frac{p_t}{dM_t}E_t\left\{\frac{M_{t+1}}{p_{t+1}}U'_2\left(\frac{s}{d}\frac{M_{t+1}}{p_{t+1}}\right)\right\} = 0. \tag{5.1'}$$

Or as in Sargent (1984), consider the case where the interest rate on money balances is random but the real government expenditures are constant and financed through monetary policy. For young agents at period t the terms of trade are $\dfrac{p_t}{p_{t+1}}\dfrac{(M_{t+1}-gp_{t+1})}{M_t}$. Equation (5.1) becomes:

$$U'_1\left(\frac{M_t}{p_t}\right) = \frac{p_t}{M_t}E_t\left\{\left(\frac{M_{t+1}}{p_{t+1}}-g\right)U'_2\left(\frac{M_{t+1}}{p_{t+1}}-g\right)\right\}. \tag{5.1''}$$

After this quick overview of the different possible forms taken by equation (4.1) in the present context, let us return to the model with a representative consumer, the perfect foresight dynamics of which is given by equation (5.2). Figures 6.2 and 6.3 are used to visualize the dynamics of

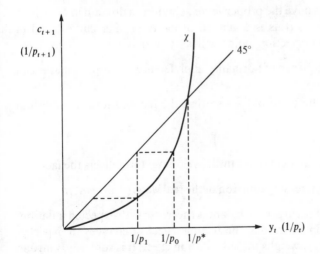

Figure 6.2

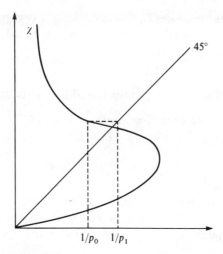

Figure 6.3

such a model. The main ingredient of such figures is the offer curve of the consumer, i.e., the locus of bundles chosen by the consumer when the price ratio varies. Consumption in old age is measured along the vertical axis, labor supply in youth is measured along the horizontal axis. If the total quantity of money is one, in a perfect foresight equilibrium ($\ldots p_t \ldots$) consumption and labor supply must be (respectively) $\dfrac{1}{p_{t+1}}$ and $\dfrac{1}{p_t}$.

Both offer curves have the properties of delimiting a domain in $\mathbb{R}^2_+$ which is star-shaped from 0 (this is a general property of offer curves) and of having only one intersection point with any horizontal line. This latter property is a consequence of normality in preferences; it implies that $\dfrac{1}{p_t}$ can be solved for as a function of $\dfrac{1}{p_{t+1}}$ so that the reduced form equilibrium equation can be written $\dfrac{1}{p_t} = \chi\left(\dfrac{1}{p_{t+1}}\right)$.

In figure 6.2, the offer curve is upwards sloping: this reflects the fact that labor supply is an increasing function of the real wage $\left(\dfrac{p_t}{p_{t+1}}\right)$ or, in another interpretation, that savings (real balances) decrease with expected inflation. On the contrary, in figure 6.3, the income effect of changes in expected returns on savings outweighs the substitution effect. It is sufficiently strong to generate a strongly backward bending offer curve: it intersects the diagonal with a slope smaller than -1.

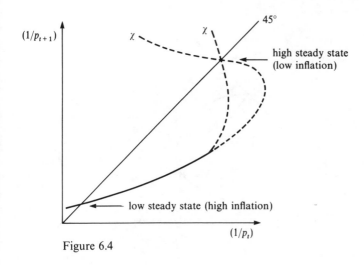

Figure 6.4

In both cases, there is a unique steady state associated with the money price of the good $\bar{p}$ such that $\frac{1}{\bar{p}} = y(1)$. However, the origin corresponds to a point $\left(\frac{1}{p} = 0\right)$, where money loses value and can be viewed as a pesudo-steady state. In fact, in the variant of the OLG model sketched above where a fixed amount g (real government expenditures) is financed through money creation, the model has two steady states, visualized in figure 6.4.

The question of *determinacy of the steady state* can now be considered either analytically or geometrically. The analytical results of the previous section apply. Matrix B reduces to the number $\frac{\partial_1 Z}{\partial_0 Z}$. Hence the steady state is determinate when $\left|\frac{\partial_1 Z}{\partial_0 Z}\right| < 1$ and indeterminate when $\left|\frac{\partial_1 Z}{\partial_0 Z}\right| > 1$. It is easily seen that the limit case $\left|\frac{\partial_1 Z}{\partial_0 Z}\right| = 1$ corresponds to the case where the offer curve intersects the diagonal with a slope -1, i.e., when elasticity of labor supply at the steady state is $-\frac{1}{2}$.[52] Hence, the steady state of figure 6.2 is "determinate" while the steady state of figure 6.3 (as well as the low steady state of figure 6.4) is indeterminate. Geometrically, in figure 6.2, starting from p_0 such that $\frac{1}{p_0} < \frac{1}{p^*}$ one can visualize an inflationary sequence

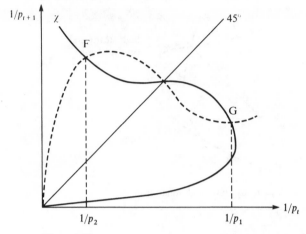

Figure 6.5

$\{p_0, p_1 \ldots\}$, where consumption converges to zero. In figure 6.3, a sequence converging to the steady state is visualized.

Let us now switch attention to the perfect foresight *periodic* equilibria. A first insight into the problem is provided by figure 6.5, where the offer curve of figure 6.3 is depicted together with its mirror image with respect to the first bisectrix. These mirror curves intersect at two symmetric points, F,G that define a periodic equilibrium of the order 2, or a two-cycle system, associated with money balances $\left(\dfrac{1}{p_1}\right), \left(\dfrac{1}{p_2}\right)$. Figure 6.5 then provides a diagrammatic proof of the fact that indeterminacy of the steady state, i.e., an offer curve intersecting the first bisectrix with slope smaller than -1, is a sufficient condition for the existence of a two-cycle system. When the reduced form equation can be written under the form:

$$\frac{1}{p_t} = \chi\left(\frac{1}{p_{t+1}}\right) \tag{5.4}$$

the analytical proof would easily follow, as explained in section 3.1, from the consideration of the boundary behavior and of the slope at the steady state of the second iterate of χ, χ^2.

J.M. Grandmont (1985) considers an OLG economy, where the representative consumer has an additively separable utility function so that its deterministic dynamics is governed by an equation of the type (5.4). Supposing that the second period coefficient of relative risk aversion (a

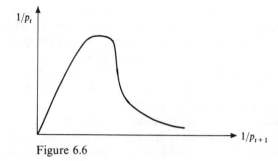

Figure 6.6

condition involving the first and second derivatives of the second period utility function) is increasing in wealth, then the function χ has necessarily the qualitative shape depicted in figures 6.2 or 6.3, i.e., it has at most one hump or is unimodal (see figure 6.6 for a picture analogous to figure 6.3 but with reversed axes).

With these assumptions, the function χ fits a category of functions for which powerful mathematical results (some of them having been sketched in section 3) have been derived in the last thirty years. (Note, however, that in the mathematical literature the χ function associates a future state to a past state, so that the forward dynamics there is the backwards dynamics of the present model and vice-versa).

Let us summarize some of the main applications of the mathematical literature to this OLG framework.

> First, if χ has a cycle of order k then it has any cycle of period k' with $k > k'$, where $>$ is Sarkovskii's preordering.[53] In particular if a cycle of period 3 exists (and proposition 4.4 in Grandmont, 1985, provides a sufficient condition for that), then there are cycles of any order.
>
> Theorem 4.5 in Grandmont (1985) introduces an additional condition concerning the coefficient of relative risk aversion, and assumes that the map χ that describes the offer curve of the representative consumer in the OLG model under consideration, has a negative Schwartzian derivative on an adequate interval – a condition that obtains in the constant elasticity case with a large enough second period risk aversion coefficient. Then *there exists at most one periodic orbit* that is weakly stable in the standard dynamics, i.e., for us in the backwards perfect foresight dynamics, *that is determinate* in our terminology (when determinacy has been conveniently redefined for periodic equilibria). Furthermore, if χ has a "determinate" periodic

orbit, the critical point of the graph of χ is attracted to it in the backwards perfect foresight dynamics. Grandmont notes that this latter property gives an "experimental" way, by iterating the critical point and checking whether the iterate converges, of checking for the existence of such a periodic equilibrium.

Third, for a well-chosen one-dimensional family of economies, parametrized by what can be thought of as the "height" of the hump in figure 6.6, something called a "Feigenbaum cascade" will be observed. As the height increases, a deterministic cycle of period 2 appears, followed by a cycle of period 4, and so on, in successively higher powers of 2, up to a value above which a cycle of period 3 exists. In this last area, a stable cycle may not exist, and "chaotic" dynamics appear. A computer experiment illustrating this period doubling bifurcation is run in Grandmont (1985) for a family of economies indexed by the old agent's coefficient of relative risk aversion.

5.2   Sunspot equilibria in the OLG model

The definition of sunspot equilibria first requires a description of the stochastic behavior of the system.

The representative consumer of subsection 5.2, facing random returns – because p_{t+1} is a random variable – on money holdings and maximizing expected utility will solve a problem, the first-order conditions of which are:

$$\frac{1}{p_t} U_1\left(e_1 - \frac{m}{p_t}, e_2 + \frac{m}{p_t}\right) - \mathrm{E}_t\left\{\frac{1}{p_{t+1}} U_2\left(e_1 - \frac{m}{p_t}, e_2 + \frac{m}{p_{t+1}}\right)\right\} = 0. \ (5.5)$$

More generally in a two-period-lived OLG model, the aggregate savings function instead of being a function of the real rate of returns $\dfrac{p_t}{p_{t+1}}$ will be a function of p_t and of the probability distribution μ_{t+1} over p_{t+1}. Then the stochastic dynamics will be described by:

$$\tilde{Z}(p_t,\mu_{t+1}) = \frac{M}{p_t} - \tilde{y}(p_t,\mu_{t+1}), \tag{5.6}$$

where $\tilde{y}$ will be the sum of individual savings functions implicitly defined by first-order conditions of type (5.5). With point (and thus deterministic) expectations, the function $\tilde{y}$ reduces to the function y of the preceding subsection 5.1.

Let us recall that a sunspot equilibrium is associated with a subset of prices $\mathscr{P}$, and a transition distribution probability μ_p with support on $\mathscr{P}$,

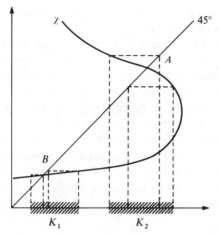

Figure 6.7

such that:

$$\frac{M}{p} - \tilde{y}(p,\mu_p) = 0, \ \forall p \in \mathcal{P} \tag{5.7}$$

and that it is stationary whenever there is an invariant measure on $\mathcal{P}$. A stationary sunspot equilibrium of order k consists of k (different) prices $p_1 \ldots p_k$ and a $k \times k$ Markov matrix $M^t = (m_1 \ldots m_k)$, where m_l is a row vector such that:

$$\frac{M}{p_l} = \tilde{y}(p_l, \{(p_1 \ldots p_k), m_l\}), \tag{5.8}$$

where $\{(p_1 \ldots p_k), m_l\}$ designates the probability distribution which puts the weights $m_{ll'}$ on $p_{l'}$.

Now the techniques developed in the previous section 4 have immediate applications:

5.2.1   The invariant compact set argument

In order to illustrate the application of the invariant compact set argument, let us adopt a diagrammatic argument appropriate for the representative consumer case. Two cases where one can easily exhibit an invariant compact set in the sense of proposition 4.1 are visualized in figure 6.7. When the offer curve is strongly backwards bending around a steady state A, the compact connected set such as K_2 is invariant and is a possible support of

SSE. In a "high inflation" steady state B (cf. figure 6.5 in section 5.1), a compact set such as K_1 is also invariant.

Note that, in both cases, figure 6.7 suggests that the compact set which is exhibited is centered around an indeterminate steady state. However, the reader will easily modify the offer curve around A to let K_1 remain invariant while having the steady state being determinate. Also it is evident in both cases that there are many Markovian transition probabilities that can sustain sunspot equilibria. However, the existence statement which we rely upon does not allow a complete characterization of sunspot beliefs.

Note here that an improvement of the invariant set argument allowed Grandmont (1986) to provide a necessary and sufficient condition for the existence of SSE with finite support in the OLG model with a representative consumer in each generation.[54]

5.2.2   *The linear tangent system argument and local SSE*

Proposition 4.2 tells us that there exist local SSE in the neighborhood of any indeterminate steady state. In fact as the relevant eigenvalue is real (because we are in a one dimensional system) part (i) of the proposition applies and local SSE of order 2 (and in fact in this case of any order superior to 2) do exist. Considering the case where the sunspot phenomenon consists of the past history generated by an infinite sequence of independent random variables with mean zero, one can see that the tangent linear system has a sunspot solution of the form:

$$p_t = \bar{p} + c \sum_{\gamma=0}^{+\infty} \left(\frac{\partial_1 Z}{\partial_2 Z} \right)^\gamma s_{t-\gamma},$$

where c is an arbitrary constant. This solution is indeed "tangent" to some local SSE of the kind under scrutiny in Woodford's (1986b) analysis.

A significant additional understanding of the structure of local SSE, in the case of the OLG model, where the eigenvalue governing the perfect foresight dynamics is close to -1, is provided by the analysis of Grandmont (1989). Grandmont considers the bifurcation of the equilibria of a family of OLG models when the parameter indexing the family crosses a value where the considered eigenvalue is -1. The bifurcation is a flip bifurcation. However, the situation differs according to whether the flip bifurcation is supercritical or subcritical (a fact which depends, as noted in section 3, on the sign of an appropriate Schwartzian derivative). In the former case, the union of the supports of the local SSE is, for values of the parameter beyond, but close enough to the bifurcation value, the interval bounded by the two-cycle. In the latter case, there exist SSE before and after the bifurcation; and again the union of their supports contains an interval bounded by two-cycles, which in this case exist both before and after the bifurcation.

5.2.3   Sunspots and cycles

As implied by proposition 4.3 above, all results on periodic equilibria and in particular the results derived by Grandmont (1985) in the OLG model and reported in section 5.1 have a "generically" valid counterpart for SSE "close" to the periodic solution.

Let us note, however, that, in the simple OLG model without government expenditures, the connections between periodic solutions and stationary sunspot equilibria is in fact much stronger than what the application of proposition 4.4 suggests. Azariadis and Guesnerie (1986) have shown that, in such a model, *a necessary and sufficient condition for the existence of SSE* of order 2 was *the existence of a periodic solution of order 2.* (See also Grandmont (1986), Woodford (1988b) who show in addition that the result extends to sunspot equilibria of a much broader class.)

Unfortunately this sharp characterization result is very unlikely to have a simple counterpart in multidimensional systems. We know that this equivalence result ceases to hold even in a one-dimensional OLG model with government expenditures. *A fortiori*, the derivation of conditions which instead of being sufficient (as each of our previous subsections indicate) would be necessary and sufficient for the existence of SSE is an open problem.

5.2.4   The Poincaré–Hopf method

The Poincaré–Hopf method applies here whenever there exists a unique steady state. Proposition 4.4 characterizes a set of matrices which are associated with SSE: as the matrix B is the real number $-\dfrac{\partial_2 Z}{\partial_1 Z} \overset{\text{def}}{=} b$, any $k \times k$ Markov matrix having an odd number of eigenvalues below $\dfrac{1}{b}$ is a candidate sunspot matrix (Chiappori and Guesnerie, 1989). In particular any 2×2 Markov matrix such that $m_{1,2} + m_{2,1} > +\dfrac{1}{b}$ is associated with a SSE of order 2 (Azariadis and Guesnerie, 1982, and Spear, 1984).

5.2.5   Sunspot equilibria in systems with multiple steady states

When the OLG model has two interior steady states, the continuity argument *à la* Peck (that has been presented in section 4) applies. Also the

Chiappori–Guesnerie (1988) heteroclinic solution, the general principle of which has been presented above, can be fully described in the context of the OLG model. The sunspot variable is a countably infinite Markov chain with a state space corresponding to the (positive and negative) integers. If the sunspot state is s in period t, in period $t+1$ it will be in state $s-1$ with probability α and in state $s+1$ with probability $1-\alpha$.

Consider the equilibria of the form $p_t = p_s$ whenever the sunspot state is s, for some fixed sequence of prices (p_s), s being any integer. Such an infinite sequence $\{p_s\}$ represents a rational expectation equilibrium if and only if (with straightforward notation):

$$\tilde{Z}(p_s,\{p_{s-1},p_{s+1}\},\alpha)=0$$
$$s = \cdots -2,-1,0,1,2\cdots \qquad (5.9)$$

As indicated in section 4, solutions to (5.9) can be viewed as the trajectories of a *two-dimensional* dynamical system: if the left-hand side is monotonic (here increasing because the substitution effect outweighs the income effect) one can solve p_{s+1} as a function of (p_s,p_{s-1}) – defining a "forward mapping" that associates (p_{s+1},p_s) to (p_s,p_{s-1})– and p_{s-2} as a function of (p_s,p_{s-1}) – defining similarly a "backward" mapping. If one is able to apply both mappings an unlimited number of times (so as to define a complete trajectory) without reaching a point where prices become negative or where the mapping ceases to be defined, then the corresponding sequence represents a rational expectations equilibrium. While the sequence $p_s = p^*, \forall s$, where p^* is the monetary steady state price level, is an equilibrium, there are also other (sunspot) equilibria.

In fact, Chiappori and Guesnerie show that the dynamics in the plane induced by the "forward" mapping can easily look like those of figure 6.8. The solid lines with arrows superimposed represent the stable and unstable manifold of the fixed point $(1/p^*,1/p^*)$. Now take for example a point $(1/p_1, 1/p_2)$ somewhere on the stable manifold that connects $(0,0)$ to $(1/p^*, 1/p^*)$. Applying the forward and the backward mapping repeatedly, one generates a sequence such that:

$$p^* < \cdots < p_{s+2} < p_{s+1} < p_s < p_{s-1} < p_{s-2} < \cdots < \infty.$$

In such a sunspot equilibrium, the price level fluctuates forever between p^* and infinity. With positive probability each point is visited a finite number of times, and in the limit case $\alpha = 1/2$ the number of such visits would be infinite with probability 1. The self-fulfillment mechanism, i.e., the fact that the price level increases (resp. falls), because the expected price level in the future increases (resp. falls), decreasing the current demand for real balances, rests on the standard Cagan effect of inflation expectations on money demand. The fact that such solutions exist is interesting in view of

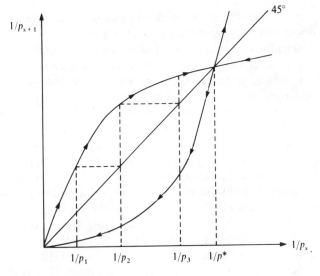

Figure 6.8

the frequent criticism that the backwards sloping offer curve (that is needed for having standard SSE in the present model) is unrealistic. Also, considering a solution lying on the stable manifold, and viewing the sunspot variable as the realization of an exogenous random money supply, Chiappori and Guesnerie interpret the sunspot solution as a Keynesian solution (where, as they show, the activity level increases with money supply) that is to be contrasted with the classical solution associated with the steady state. Although this interpretation has a rather illustrative purpose (the model is not quite Keynesian and there is as well an anti-Keynesian solution where activity level is negatively correlated with money supply), it provides a neat example of coexistence of self-fulfilling "theories."

Finally, the heteroclinic solutions persist when money has a small intrinsic impact on the economy, as well as when there is intrinsic uncertainty of the type considered by Lucas (1972). In a simple version of the Lucas model, Chiappori and Guesnerie (1990) compute an analytical solution of the Lucas equation that is reminiscent of one type of solution presented here (one on a manifold going from the fixed point to infinity).

5.2.6   *Sunspot equilibrium in more complex OLG models*

In the case of overlapping generations models with capital, heterogeneous consumers, or additively non-separable preferences, the analysis is made more difficult by the presence of predetermined state variables. Still, limited results may be obtained using the methods of section 4.2.

For example, Reichlin (1986) analyzes perfect foresight equilibrium dynamics in an OLG model with two-period lived consumers, endogenous labor supply by the young, and a one-sector production technology. The reduced form equilibrium equations involve the stocks of capital at periods $t-1, t, t+1$, so that they appear as a special case of equilibrium equations (4.9) and (4.10) associated with a (one-dimensional) system with predetermined variables. The results of section 4.2 then applys so that when the system determining the perfect foresight dynamics around the steady state has two eigenvalues of modulus greater than one, the steady state is indeterminate and there are local sunspot equilibria of the kind considered in proposition 4.5. The methods of Woodford (1986a) are also directly applicable in this case. Reichlin discusses the conditions (involving technology parameters and the elasticity of labor supply) under which the indeterminate steady state, and hence local SSE, occur. Farmer (1986) also discusses conditions for indeterminacy at the steady state in an OLG model with production, and local SSE can be shown to exist in his cases as well using similar methods.

An overlapping generations model with heterogeneous consumers, whose preferences need not be additively separable, is treated by Spear, Srivastava, and Woodford (1990). Although, as noted above, their explicit concern is with the multiplicity of stationary rational expectations equilibrium responses to intrinsic uncertainty (endowment shocks), their results apply equally in the case that endowments are unaffected by the random state (i.e., it is a sunspot variable). Thus conditions are exhibited under which SSE (characterized by a Markov process on a compact subset of $\mathbb{R}^n$) are possible in such a model.

5.2.7   The insurability issue

At this stage, we should discuss again the insurability issue that has been emphasized in section 3.

Consider first an OLG model with one consumer per generation, or equivalently with identical consumers within each generation. In a sunspot equilibrium, the young consumer faces some randomness in tomorrow's allocation. However, all the young consumers of this generation have the same marginal rates of substitution concerning future income in different states of nature tomorrow (since they face the same sunspot event today and they have the same probabilities about tomorrow's prices). As consumers of the old generation will not participate in an insurance market for sunspot risks tomorrow, such a market will be inactive: the only possible equilibrium prices of insurance are prices for contingent income that are proportional to the marginal rates of substitution associated with the initial SSE. Hence, in this model insurance against sunspot risk would be ineffective, leaving unaffected every SSE.

Clearly this conclusion is dependent upon the generational structure that prevents the agents from trading risks with agents whose lifetime has no overlap with their own lifetime. Indeed, in an OLG model, there cannot exist an SSE where money has positive value if a full insurance market is attended by all consumers at the beginning of time (see Burnell, 1989). However, the conclusion here does not follow from the Cass–Shell ineffectivity theorem (discussed in section 3.2), and even with an Arrow–Debreu market involving the participation of all agents at the beginning of history, non-monetary sunspot equilibria may exist, which, in the case studied by Cass–Shell (1989), Pareto dominate the autarkic equilibrium.

Also, the conclusion depends upon the assumption of homogeneity across consumers. With heterogeneous consumers, the insurance market against sunspot risks considered above would be active: since different young agents would have different marginal rates of substitution for second-period income contingent upon the sunspot state, they would trade, at least if the sunspot states were verifiable events. But it is intuitively clear that this would affect but not destroy the given SSE. Sunspot randomness would be attenuated rather than wiped out.

6   SUNSPOT EQUILIBRIA IN OTHER DYNAMIC MODELS

The overlapping generations model is hardly the only kind of dynamic economic model with a structure to which the methods surveyed in section 4 are applicable, and it is hardly the only type of model in which sunspot equilibria are known to be possible, although it is the example that has been most thoroughly studied. Other examples will be treated under two headings: other models of monetary economies, and examples involving market imperfections that are unrelated to the role of money in the economy.

6.1   Other models of monetary economies

Sunspot equilibria (of the various kinds discussed in the previous section, including finite-state Markov equilibria, and random walks on a countable state space) are also possible in monetary economies with a finite number of infinite-lived consumer types. Indeed, such models often give rise to equilibrium conditions that are mathematically quite similar to those associated with an overlapping generations model, insofar as the price level is determined by a demand for real balances that depends upon expected inflation.

As an example, consider a model in which money is held to allow smoothing of consumption in the face of income fluctuations (or equivalently, to allow variation in consumption in response to taste shocks) when borrowing against future income is impossible.[55] Suppose that there are equal numbers of two types of infinite-lived consumers, each seeking to maximize:

$$E\{ \sum_{t=0}^{\infty} \beta^t u(c_t) \}, \tag{6.1}$$

where $0 < \beta < 1$, u is an increasing, concave function, and c_t denotes consumption in period t. Suppose that the endowments of both types fluctuate between even- and odd-numbered periods, w_1 in one period and w_2 in the next, with one type having the high endowment (w_1) when the other's endowment is low (w_2) and vice versa. Suppose that borrowing against future endowment income is impossible, and consumers can save only by holding fiat money, that exists in a fixed positive supply $M > 0$. Consider the case of equilibria with valued fiat money in which the borrowing constraint binds in each period for the consumers who have a low endowment in that period, so that all money is held by consumers of the other type. Then a rational expectations equilibrium consists of a stochastic process for the price level p_t satisfying:

$$u'\left(w_1 - \frac{M}{p_t} \right) = \beta E_t \left\{ u'\left(w_2 + \frac{M}{p_{t+1}} \right) \frac{p_t}{p_{t+1}} \right\}, \tag{6.2}$$

$$u'\left(w_2 + \frac{M}{p_t} \right) \geq \beta E_t \left\{ u'\left(w_1 - \frac{M}{p_{t+1}} \right) \frac{p_t}{p_{t+1}} \right\} \tag{6.3}$$

for each period t, where E_t denotes the expectation conditional upon public information at time t. Note that (6.2) is a one-step-ahead forward-looking equilibrium condition of the form (4.1). Furthermore, this is exactly the equilibrium condition associated with an overlapping generations model in which each generation lives for two successive periods and has a utility function:

$$U(c_1, c_2) = u(c_1) + \beta u(c_2),$$

where c_i represents consumption in the ith period of life, and a life-cycle endowment of (w_1, w_2).

If only equation (6.2) were necessary for equilibrium, all of the results of section 5 would be directly applicable to this case as well. This is not always true, however, since a sunspot solution of (6.2) may violate (6.3) in some states. Nonetheless, certain of the results of the previous section have direct analogs here.

(i) In the unique steady state equilibrium of this model (with a constant price level), the inequality in (6.3) is strict. Hence there are equilibria of the present model corresponding to all equilibria of the overlapping generations model in which the price level remains forever close enough to the steady state price level. It follows from the results above that we can derive conditions for the indeterminacy of perfect foresight equilibrium near the steady state, i.e., the existence of a continuum of perfect foresight equilibria with price levels converging asymptotically to the steady state price level, as in figure 6.1b, and these conditions will also suffice for the existence of stationary sunspot equilibria in which the price level remains forever near the steady state price level, including (but not limited to) finite-state Markov equilibria. In the case of money supply growth at a rate sufficient to finance a constant positive real government deficit, one similarly obtains equilibrium conditions mathematically identical to those for the corresponding overlapping generations model, and in this case one finds that any non-zero endowment in the low-endowment periods suffices to guarantee the existence of stationary sunspot equilibria.

(ii) Theorem 4.4 (section 4.1.5) applies here as well. The conditions that suffice for the existence of equilibrium cycles in which the inequality constraint is always satisfied are more strict than those discussed in the case of the corresponding overlapping generations model (because of the additional constraint (6.3)); but it is known that such equilibrium cycles exist for open sets of preference and endowment specifications. For example, they exist for an open set of economies near a critical economy at which a "flip bifurcation" occurs, and the conditions under which such a bifurcation occurs are the same as for the overlapping generations model.

(iii) In the case that $u'(w_2 + m)m$ is a monotonically increasing function of m (so that desired real money balances are a monotonically decreasing function of expected inflation, in the case of point expectations), it can likewise be shown that there exists an equilibrium of the present model corresponding to every equilibrium of the overlapping generations model in which the price level remains forever greater than or equal to the steady state level, for in this case (6.3) is implied by $p_t, p_{t+1} \geq p^*$. It follows that under the conditions discussed in section 5.2(v) (with reference to the example of Chiappori and Guesnerie, 1988b), there can be shown to exist sunspot equilibria in which the price level follows a random walk on a countable sequence of price levels with no finite upper bound and with the steady state price level as a lower bound. (This sort of equilibrium corresponds to a "heteroclinic orbit" as discussed in section 4.1.4). Again, this is of interest because it shows that non-transient sunspot equilibrium fluctuations in the price level are possible even under the (empirically realistic) assumption that the demand for real money balances is a globally decreasing function of expected inflation.

Similar results are obtained in the case of a representative consumer economy in which the demand for money is due to the existence of a cash-in-advance constraint for certain goods purchases.[56] Consider a representative consumer economy in which endowments may be converted into either "cash goods" or "credit goods," two distinct types of goods as far as the preferences of the representative consumer are concerned, and suppose that a cash-in-advance constraint applies to purchases of "cash goods" but not to purchases of "credit goods"; this is a simple way of representing the possibility of substitution away from the use of money in response to an increase in the cost of holding money balances. Let the representative consumer seek to maximize:

$$E\left\{\sum_{t=0}^{\infty} \beta^t U(c_{1t}, c_{2t})\right\},$$

where c_{1t} represents "cash goods" consumption, and c_{2t} represents "credit goods" consumption, in period t, subject to the constraints:

$$p_t c_{1t} \leq M_t$$
$$M_{t+1} \leq M_t + p_t(e - c_{1t} - c_{2t}), \tag{6.4}$$
$$c_{1t}, c_{2t} \geq 0$$

where p_t represents the period t price level (the same for both goods and the endowment, because of the production technology), M_t represents money held at the beginning of period t, and e represents each period's endowment. Here the first constraint in (6.4) is the cash-in-advance constraint. Suppose also that there is a constant money supply $M > 0$, so that in equilibrium the choices of the representative consumer must satisfy:

$$M_t = M$$
$$c_{1t} + c_{2t} = e.$$

It can be shown that a rational expectations equilibrium of such a model corresponds to a stochastic process for the price level satisfying:

$$F\left(\frac{M}{p_t}\right) = \beta E_t\left\{G\left(\frac{M}{p_{t+1}}\right)\right\}, \tag{6.5}$$

where:

$$F(m) \equiv m U_2(\min(m, \hat{m}), e - \min(m, \hat{m}))$$
$$G(m) \equiv m U_1(\min(m, \hat{m}), e - \min(m, \hat{m}))$$

together with a "transversality condition" implying no excessive accumulation of wealth (due to explosive growth of real money balances). In the above, $\hat{m}$ denotes the solution to

$$U_1(\hat{m},e-\hat{m}) = U_2(\hat{m},e-\hat{m})$$

which is unique under standard monotonicity, concavity, and boundary assumptions on U. Again (6.5) is an equation for the price level that is of the form (4.1).

There are two possible technical difficulties with the application of our previous methods to this model. The first is the transversality condition. But this is in any event necessarily satisfied by any solutions in which the price level is forever bounded away from zero, such as finite-state Markov solutions or random walks on a countable sequence of price levels bounded below by a positive steady state price level. The second is the fact that the equilibrium conditions are non-differentiable at a single price level, that corresponding to a level of real balances just sufficient to result in a non-binding cash-in-advance constraint. However, it can be shown that the range of price levels over which the cash-in-advance constraint binds includes a neighborhood of the unique steady state price level, and also all price levels greater than or equal to the steady state price level. Hence the methods of section 4 involving local analysis near the steady state, or "heteroclinic orbits" between the monetary steady state and the steady state in which money has no value, are directly applicable to this model. Furthermore, for generic preferences and endowments, the failure of differentiability does not occur at a deterministic equilibrium cycle. Hence the methods involving local analysis near a deterministic cycle are applicable at least in the generic case. In fact, many of the results described earlier relating to existence of deterministic cycles depend only upon continuity of the equilibrium conditions, and so are fully applicable to the present model.

Hence results analogous to those obtained for the overlapping generations model in section 5 can be derived for this model as well. In fact, in the case that the preferences of the representative consumer are additively separable between "cash goods" and "credit goods," i.e., of the form:

$$U(c_1,c_2) = u(c_1) + v(c_2)$$

and restricting attention to equilibria in which the price level remains forever above the level at which the cash-in-advance constraint ceases to bind, conditions (6.5) are mathematically identical to those for an overlapping generations model with two-period-lived consumers with preferences:

$$U(c_1,c_2) = v(c_1) + \beta u(c_2).$$

Hence in this case many of the results of section 5 can be immediately translated into propositions regarding cash-in-advance economies, and, in particular, sufficient conditions are easily derived for the existence both of finite-state Markov sunspot equilibria and of sunspot equilibria that involve random walks on a countable set of price levels. However, the assumption of additive separability is quite inessential to these results; making direct use of the techniques in section 4, one may derive sufficient conditions for existence of both kinds of sunspot equilibria that do not depend upon additively separable preferences.[57]

Sunspot equilibria can also be shown to exist, using proposition 4.5 of section 4, in more complex monetary models, which will often involve predetermined state variables. An example of stationary sunspot equilibria in a monetary production economy is discussed in Woodford (1986a, 1988a). An interesting feature of this example, in contrast to those just discussed, is that stationary sunspot equilibria exist in which all state variables (including the level of real balances) remain forever within a compact set, even though consumer preferences satisfy the property of "gross substitutability" (and, in particular, the demand for real money balances is a decreasing function of expected inflation).

The existence of sunspot equilibria in monetary economies of these other sorts helps to clarify what is essential and what is inessential about the overlapping generations examples. For example, the suspicion of some (see, e.g., Sims, 1986 and Aiyagari, 1989) that the existence of endogenous equilibrum fluctuations in overlapping generations models with two-period lived consumers depends upon the assumption of lifetimes for consumers that are short compared to the period of the endogenous fluctuations, is clearly seen to be incorrect, insofar as the existence of market imperfections can result in optimization problems for long-lived consumers that are essentially equivalent to a sequence of independent short-horizon optimization problems. The examples just discussed also show that the properties of the overlapping generations model of fiat money that are responsible for the possibility of sunspot equilibria are unrelated to the features of the model that have often been criticized as making it an unrealistic model of the role of money in the economy (see, e.g., Tobin, 1980 and McCallum, 1983a), such as the fact that in equilibrium money must earn as high a rate of return as any other asset (because money is "only a store of value"), or the implication that money is held mainly for life-cycle saving purposes (so that changes in pension benefits should have a critical effect upon the demand for money).

These examples also allow us to reconsider an issue previously addressed, regarding whether the sunspot equilibria of the kinds discussed in section 5 depend upon the assumed non-existence of markets for insurance against sunspot risk. Even in the cases where the equilibrium conditions for monetary economies with infinite-lived consumers (in the absence of contingent claims markets) are formally identical to those of an overlapping generations model, the consequences of introducing markets for claims contingent upon sunspot realizations will in general not be the same. In the case of the representative consumer cash-in-advance model, one can allow trading in such claims without rendering irrelevant the cash-in-advance constraint. For this, one must assume that such claims are traded (against one another and against money) only in a market that is open between the times at which "cash goods" are purchased with money (Lucas and Stokey, 1987). The representative consumer's budget constraint (6.4) is now replaced by:

$$\tilde{M}_t + \Sigma_{s_{t+1}|s_t} q_t(s_{t+1}) x(s_{t+1}) \le M_t + x(s_t),$$

$$p_t c_{1t} \le \tilde{M}_t$$

(6.6)

where $q_t(s_{t+1})$ denotes the price in the period t securities market (prior to goods market trading) of a claim to one unit of money at the beginning of period $t+1$ contingent upon the occurrence of sunspot history $s_{t+1}, x(s_{t+1})$ denotes the number of such claims purchased in period t and carried into period $t+1$, and the sum in (6.6) is over all possible sunspot states that may occur in period $t+1$, given that the history up to period t is s_t. Here M_t denotes money held at the beginning of period t (before securities trading, and before the contingent claims are paid), and $\tilde{M}_t$ denotes money held in period t after securities trading (and so available for use in goods market purchases). In addition to the previous equilibrium conditions, it is also necessary that the markets for securities clear. But the securities markets clear at prices such that the representative consumer wishes neither to buy nor sell the contingent claims, and the equilibrium value of money is exactly the same as if the securities markets were closed. In particular (6.5) still characterizes equilibrium processes for the price level. It follows that the presence or absence of contingent claims markets has no effect whatsoever upon the conditions under which sunspot equilibria of the various kinds exist in this model.[58]

In the case of the Bewley model, the consequences of introducing insurance markets are less simple; because of the heterogeneity of consumer types, the existence of insurance markets will in general affect the equilibrium allocation of resources. Still, assuming that the contingent claims markets are constrained by the same informational imperfections that result in the borrowing constraints (that are the source of the "liquidity services" associated with money balances), it is possible to construct examples in which the character of the sunspot equilibrium fluctuations in the price level and in the allocation of resources are completely unchanged by the introduction of contingent claims markets. Consider again the case of two consumer types with alternating endowments, and monetary equilibria in which the entire money supply is held at the end of each period by the high-endowment type of consumers. Consumers can borrow only to the extent to which they have collateral in the form of money holdings, that is, they are still unable to borrow against future endowment income. We can write this constraint as:

$$M^j_{t+1} + x^j(s_{t+1}) \geq 0,$$

where M^j_{t+1} denotes type j's money holdings at the beginning of period $t+1$ (prior to payment of the contingent claims), and where the constraint must be satisfied in every sunspot history s_{t+1} that could possibly occur. Then the solutions to (6.2) described above continue to represent rational expectations equilibria, if they satisfy not only (6.3), but also a stronger version implying that low-endowment consumers do not wish to hold positive quantities of any of the contingent claims. In such equilibria, there is only one consumer type in any period that wishes to carry claims of positive value into any state in the following period; hence financial markets clear at prices such that no contingent claims are supplied or demanded. At least some of the equilibria previously discussed will satisfy these conditions; in particular, all equilibria (which include some stationary sunspot equilibria) in which the price level remains always within a small enough neighborhood of the steady state price level p^*. Hence one finds again that the introduction of insurance markets against sunspot risk need have no effect upon the possibility of sunspot equilibria.

Finally, we can also reconsider the question of whether sunspot equilibria involve "rational speculative bubbles." In the case of the overlapping generations model of fiat money, monetary equilibria all involve a speculative bubble, and so it might be suspected that the possibility of sunspot equilibria is somehow connected to this fact. But sunspot equilibria can exist in the Lucas–Stokey model as well, under similar conditions and for essentially the same reason. Yet in the latter model, valued fiat money does not represent a speculative bubble. Indeed, in all of the monetary equilibria described above (sunspot and non-sunspot equilibria alike), the value of money can be expressed as the present discounted value of future "dividends" received by holders of money, in the form of relaxation of the cash-in-advance constraint, without any additional "bubble" term:

$$\frac{1}{p_t(s_t)} = \sum_{j=0}^{\infty} \sum_{s_{t+j}|s_t} \left[\frac{p_{t+j}(s_{t+j})\tilde{q}_t(s_{t+j})}{p_t(s_t)} \right] \lambda_{t+j}(s_{t+j}).$$

Here $s_{t+j}|s_t$ denotes the set of states in period $t+j$ that may follow state

$s_t, \tilde{q}_t(s_{t+j})$ is the cost at time t of a securities trading plan that guarantees one dollar in state s_{t+j} if and when that state occurs, and $\lambda_{t+j}(s_{t+j})$ is the value of relaxation of the cash-in-advance constraint in state s_{t+j}, in units of state s_{t+j} cash goods, i.e.:

$$\lambda_t(s_t) = \frac{1}{p_t(s_t)} \left[\frac{G(M/p_t(s_t)) - F(M/p_t(s_t))}{G(M/p_t(s_t))} \right].$$

(Note that the "dividend" $\lambda_t(s_t)$ is positive in any state in which the cash-in-advance constraint binds, and zero in any state in which it does not.) In the case of sunspot equilibria, the value of money varies with the sunspot state, not because of variations in the size of a "bubble" term, but rather because (i) the "dividend" on money varies with the sunspot state in such equilibria, due to variations in the supply of real money balances, and (ii) the relevant discount factors vary with the sunspot state, due to variations in the consumption allocation and hence marginal rates of substitution.

6.2   Other types of market imperfections

Sunspot equilibria are also known to be possible in a variety of non-monetary dynamic models, which may involve a finite number of infinite-lived consumer types rather than overlapping generations. In particular, there are various ways in which sunspot equilibria may occur even in (infinite-lived) representative consumer economies, in which cases, as with the cash-in-advance model discussed above, the presence or not of markets for insurance against sunspot risk has no effect upon the set of possible equilibrium allocations of resources.

For example, the presence of technological externalities may make sunspot equilibria possible in an otherwise standard representative consumer growth model.[59] Instead of each firm's output per unit of labor inputs y being a function only of its own capital stock per unit of labor inputs k, suppose that it is given by a function $y = f(k,K)$, where K denotes the aggregate capital stock (or, equivalently, the capital stock per unit of labor for the aggregate economy, since we assume an inelastic labor supply normalized at one unit). For any given $K > 0$, the function $f(.,K)$ is an increasing, concave function as in a standard neoclassical growth model. It is assumed that each firm and each household takes as given the evolution of the aggregate capital stock in choosing its own consumption, accumulation, investment, and production decisions, and then imposed as an additional equilibrium condition that the stochastic process for the aggregate capital stock assumed by all agents is the one actually generated by their decisions, i.e., that $K_t = k_t$ at all times.

Let the representative consumer have preferences of the form (6.1). A rational expectations equilibrium can then be characterized by a pair of stochastic difference equations for the state variables $\{K_t, C_t\}$ of the form:

$$u'(C_t) = \beta r(K_t) E_t \{u'(C_{t+1})\}$$
$$K_{t+1} = y(K_t) - C_t,$$

where C_t represents consumption by the representative consumer at a time t, together with a transversality condition (that is necessarily satisfied in the case of any solution in which the state variables remain forever within a compact set). These equations have the same form as in the case of a standard one-sector optimal growth model, except that the aggregate capital–labor ratio is added as a second argument of the production function, and equated to the capital–labor ratio chosen by the representative producer. The equilibrium conditions depend upon the production function only through the two functions $y(K) = f(K,K)$ and $r(K) = f_1(K,K)$. The difference with the standard model is only that $r(K)$ need not equal the derivative of $y(K)$, and that the derivative of $r(K)$ need not be negative (since it is no longer equal to $f_{1,1}(K,K)$, which is necessarily negative).

Let us consider a steady state equilibrium, in which $K_t = K^*, C_t = C^*$ for all t. Using theorem 4.5 of section 4, we can in general determine whether there exist other nearby rational expectations equilibria by considering a linear approximation to the difference equations near the steady state values of the state variables. Let us assume that, near the steady state, $y' > 0$. We then find that the characteristic polynomial has one eigenvalue of modulus less than one and one of modulus greater than one if $r'(K^*) < 0$; that it has both eigenvalues of modulus less than one if $r'(K^*) > 0$ and $y'(K^*) < 1$; and that it has both eigenvalues of modulus greater than one if $r'(K^*) > 0$ and $y'(K^*) > 1$. In the absence of the externality, $r'(K^*) = f_{1,1}(K^*, K^*) < 0$, so that only the "saddlepoint" case is possible. In this case, since there is one predetermined state variable, perfect foresight equilibrium is locally stable and determinate near the steady state, and there exist no sunspot equilibria in which the state variables remain forever near their steady state values. This will continue to be true, by continuity, if the externality is sufficiently small. However, if the externality is sufficiently strong and if, in particular, there are external increasing returns, despite the internal diminishing returns to additional capital inputs, then one may have a steady state equilibrium with $r'(K^*) > 0$.

Perfect foresight equilibrium is indeterminate near the steady state, and so using theorem 4.5 there exist stationary sunspot equilibria near the steady state, in the case that both eigenvalues have modulus less than one, i.e., whenever $r'(K^*) > 0$ and $y'(K^*) < 1$. Now $y'(K^*) = f_1(K^*, K^*) + f_2(K^*, K^*)$. In the absence of the externality, one must have $y'(K^*) = r(K^*) = \beta^{-1} > 1$, so that the latter condition would also be impossible. But if $f_2(K^*,K^*)$ is sufficiently negative (which Hammour (1988) interprets as a congestion externality), then it is possible to have $y'(K^*)<1$. And, as above, if $f_{1,2}(K^*,K^*)$ is sufficiently positive (the case of external increasing returns), one may simultaneously have $r'(K^*)>0$. Hence strong enough externalities of the proper sort generate sunspot equilibria in economies of this kind.

Similar dynamics may also result from internal increasing returns to scale, even in the absence of technological externalities, if one assumes imperfect competition (e.g., monopolistic competition) so as to make possible an equilibrium with locally increasing returns.[60] In this case, the function $r(K)$ describing the rental price of capital as a function of the capital–labor ratio need not correspond to the derivative of $y(K)$, not because of an externality but because firms with market power do not equate the rental price to the marginal product of capital; and $r'(K)>0$ is possible in equilibrium for the same reason. Hence it is again possible to have a steady state equilibrium in which $r'(K^*)>0, y'(K^*)<1$, and again this implies indeterminacy of perfect foresight equilibrium and the existence of stationary sunspot equilibria near the steady state. Furthermore, Kehoe, Levine and Romer (1989) shows that growth models with distorting taxes can result in equilibrium conditions with a structure very similar to that of a growth model with production externalities; and here again, if the distortions are large enough, perfect foresight equilibrium may be indeterminate near the steady state, with the consequence that stationary sunspot equilibria exist near the steady state as well.[61]

Another type of market imperfection that can result in indeterminacy of equilibrium in a representative consumer economy is the existence of a fixed-price equilibrium with rationing, rather than market clearing, in firms' product markets. Woodford (1991c) provides an example of how this can occur. He shows how rationing leads to an equilibrium level of output y_t given by:

$$y_t = f(I_{t-1}, I_t), \qquad (6.7)$$

where I_t denotes investment in period t. Here past investment (which equals the period t capital stock, assuming complete depreciation each period, which although not necessary, will simplify the exposition) enters through the effect of the capital stock and hence capacity on equilibrium supply, while current investment enters through the "multiplier" effect of current investment spending upon aggregate demand. The returns r_t per unit of capital in period t depend upon the amount of capital in place and the level of output that is produced, which we may express:

$$r_t = r(I_{t-1}, y_t).$$

Due to the special form of preferences assumed for the representative consumer in Woodford's example, savers always insist on an expected real rate of return of r^*, so that the level of investment in period t is such that:

$$E_t[r(I_t, y_{t+1})] = r^* \tag{6.8}$$

given expectations about aggregate demand y_{t+1}. Substituting (6.7) into (6.8), we find that a rational expectations equilibrium is a stochastic process for investment that satisfies:

$$E_t[g(I_t, I_{t+1})] = r^* \tag{6.9}$$

for all t, where $g(I_1, I_2) \equiv r(I_1, f(I_1, I_2))$.

Condition (6.9) is again of the form (4.1), and, since there are no predetermined state variables in this example, all of the methods discussed in section 4 are applicable here. In particular:

$$|g_2(I^*, I^*)| > |g_1(I^*, I^*)| \tag{6.10}$$

is a sufficient condition for the existence of stationary sunspot equilibria, using proposition 2 of section 4.1.2, where I^* is the level of investment satisfying $g(I^*, I^*) = r^*$. Woodford discusses numerical values for the various technology and preference parameters of the model that will suffice for (6.10) to hold, and shows that they include values that are not unrealistic for the aggregate US economy. Hence this is not only a theoretical possibility in such an economy, but, granting the realism of the rationing equilibrium model, would appear to be a case of practical interest.[62]

Finally, it should be noted that the sort of borrowing constraints discussed in connection with the Bewley model in the previous subsection can also result in indeterminacy of equilibrium even in non-monetary economies. (This depends, of course, upon heterogeneity of consumer types, but only a finite number of types are needed.) For example, if in the Bewley example discussed above, fiat money is replaced by an asset that yields a constant positive stream of consumption good each period in perpetuity, an equilibrium is still possible in which the borrowing constraint binds in each period for the low-endowment consumer type, and the equilibrium conditions in this case are closely related to those given above. As a result, indeterminacy of equilibrium, deterministic cycles, and sunspot equilibria are also possible in an economy of this kind. In particular, given any equilibrium of the monetary economy (with a constant money supply) in which the price level is bounded forever, one can show that there exists a nearby equilibrium (in the sense that the allocation of resources, the real rate of return, and the time path of the value of the asset are at all times near their values in the case of the equilibrium of the monetary economy) for the economy with a productive asset, if the dividend on the total supply of the asset is small enough. (The continuity argument is essentially the same as the one made for the overlapping generations model by Azariadis (1981) and Woodford (1984).)[63] Equilibrium endogenous fluctuations are also possible in non-monetary models of this kind with a one-sector production technology, as is demonstrated by Bewley (1986).

7   EQUILIBRIUM SELECTION CRITERIA FOR MODELS WITH MULTIPLE EQUILIBRIA

The models discussed above in which sunspot equilibria are possible are all models in which there is a large multiplicity of equilibria – a large multiplicity of non-sunspot equilibria, as well as a large number of different types of sunspot equilibria. Such severe multiplicity of equilibria raises the question (as it has, for example, in the theory of repeated games) of whether the usual definition of equilibrium ought not be supplemented by additional "selection criteria," that narrow the set of equilibria that are considered to be possible outcomes for the economies described. The issue is of particular relevance to our inquiry into the possibility of endogenous fluctuations, insofar as some might find that an obvious place to begin winnowing is to ignore all equilibria involving sunspot variables. Such a conclusion, of course, would make the results of the previous sections of little importance for economic theory. Here we review some of the leading candidate approaches to equilibrium selection in economic dynamics.

7.1   Purely formal criteria: "minimum state variable" or "Markovian" equilibria

The issue of criteria for selecting among multiple rational expectations equilibria was first discussed in the literature on linear rational expectations models. Early discussions of the problem suggested a variety of purely formal criteria that might distinguish equilibria of particular interest, such as restricting attention to stationary or asymptotically stationary equilibria, or singling out the equilibrium in which the variance of some endogenous state variable is minimized.[64] The proposal that attention be restricted to stationary equilibria is of little concern to us here; we have shown that sunspot equilibria can often be of this form, and because we are interested here in models of more or less repetitive economic fluctuations, we have in any event emphasized stationary equilibria. The minimum-variance proposal derives from the view that equilibria that are better for the agents involved should be expected to occur;[65] in *ad hoc* linear macroeconomic models incorporating the "natural rate hypothesis," higher welfare for agents is often identified with a lower variance of output or employment. Since we consider explicit general equilibrium models, it makes more sense for us to directly consider the elimination of equilibria that are dominated in welfare terms. This might seem to imply ignoring sunspot equilibria, since in convex economies they are necessarily Pareto inefficient. But, in fact, sunspot equilibria need not be Pareto dominated by any of the possible non-sunspot equilibria, which (in economies of the kind in which sunspot equilibria are possible) are often not Pareto optimal either. Welfare comparisons between equilibria are taken up further in section 8.

A formal criterion that has received particular attention in the literature on linear models is McCallum's (1983b) notion of the "minimum state variable solution."[66] McCallum suggests that attention be restricted to those equilibria in which the endogenous state variables can be expressed as functions of the smallest set of predetermined variables. This criterion would seem always to rule out sunspot equilibria, insofar as there also exist equilibria in which the endogenous variables do not depend upon the sunspot states. While a general formulation of McCallum's principle (especially for non-linear models) is not available, it seems to be similar in spirit to an equilibrium refinement lately of interest among theorists of repeated games, known as "Markov perfect equilibrium" (Maskin and Tirole, 1988a, 1988b). In an equilibrium satisfying this refinement, the values taken by endogenous variables should be the same in all states that are equivalent. States are equivalent when, even if occurring at different times, the continuation economy from that point forward is the same for each state (in terms of endowments and tastes of agents, and conditional probability distributions over these quantities in the future).

The restriction of attention to "Markov" equilibria in this sense has some intuitive appeal; it is an extension of the requirement of stationarity that we have generally accepted here, and it is similar to the idea of considering symmetric equilibria when agents are all identical. But there seem to us to be some important reasons not to adopt it.[67] For one, such equilibria need not exist, even for economies for which a large number of non-Markov equilibria exist. A simple example may illustrate why. Consider a model with a temporary equilibrium relation of the form (4.9). In such a case, an equilibrium satisfies the Markov refinement only if it is given by iteration of a mapping of the form:

$$x_t = \phi(x_{t-1})$$

starting from any initial condition x_{-1}. If the matrix B (defined in section 4.2.1) has a pair of complex eigenvalues of modulus greater than one,[68] then there exists a large number of perfect foresight equilibria (as well as sunspot equilibria) remaining forever near the steady state, for any initial condition x_{-1} near the steady state value x^*. But none of these equilibria satisfy the Markov refinement. For, in order to satisfy that refinement, they would have to be perfect foresight equilibria described by a difference equation of the form above, where ϕ would be a map such that $\phi(x^*) = x^*$, and such that $\phi'(x^*)^{-1}$ would be an eigenvalue of B. But as B has by hypothesis no real eigenvalues, this is impossible.

Proponents of the "minimum state variable" selection criterion might classify such an economy as one in which the "minimal set" of state variables is in fact larger than just $\{x_{t-1}\}$; if one defines it as $\{x_{t-1}, x_{t-2}\}$, a time-invariant representation of the form:

$$x_t = \phi(x_{t-1}, x_{t-2})$$

becomes possible. But there is in such a case no compelling argument for the choice of one particular set of state variables rather than another, as there is in the case of the Markov principle. There is no reason why the second state variable should not be any exogenous state variable that has no effect on the equilibrium conditions but serves to coordinate expectations. In the case of the perfect foresight equilibria just discussed, such a variable could be time. But the model also possesses sunspot equilibria, and these may include equilibria of the form:

$$x_t = \phi(x_{t-1}, s_t),$$

where s_t is a Markovian sunspot variable. Hence there seems no obvious reason to regard sunspot equilibria as necessarily involving a larger set of state variables than other possibilities.

Both the "minimum state variable" criterion and the "Markov" criterion are subject to another objection, even in simpler examples. They do not rule out equilibria in which a variable which has only an extremely small effect on fundamentals (but, because of its effect, cannot be excluded from the canonical set of state variables) has a large effect on endogenous state variables. As discussed above in section 3.4.1 and section 4, such equilibria may be arbitrarily close to sunspot equilibria (in respects such as the stochastic properties of the endogenous variables). If these equilibria are to be regarded as possible outcomes, despite the existence of other equilibria in which the response of endogenous variables to the random disturbances is of the same order of magnitude as the disturbances, then it seems arbitrary, in the limiting case of no effect at all on fundamentals, to exclude the sunspot equilibria. Expressed more formally, it seems that a desirable equilibrium selection criterion should select a set of equilibria that is upper hemi-continuous in model parameters, and "minimum state variable" type criteria are not.

A general approach with which we have greater sympathy is to consider which rational expectations equilibria can be reached as the outcome of "learning" dynamics. Such approaches may seem to involve more arbitrary choices than a purely formal criterion of the kind discussed here; but at least the assumptions required for the specification of the learning dynamics are made fully explicit, and can be criticized on a variety of dimensions, such as consistency and efficiency of estimation under stronger or weaker maintained assumptions, computational simplicity, psychological realism, and so on. Such approaches also quite generally lead to selection criteria with the continuity property just mentioned. We turn now to a consideration of some of the main approaches that have been applied to the analysis of endogenous fluctuations.[69]

7.2   "Expectational stability"

An approach to equilibrium selection that is something of a hybrid between a formal selection criterion and an analysis of explicit (real time) learning dynamics is the criterion of "expectational stability" originally proposed by DeCanio (1979) and Lucas (1978), and extensively developed by Evans (1983, 1985, 1986, 1989) and Evans and Honkapohja (1990a, 1990b). The criterion has been offered both as a refinement of McCallum's principle (Evans, 1986) and as an approximation to the outcome of explicit learning dynamics (Evans and Honkapohja, 1990a, 1990b).

"Expectational stability" is not a single, uniquely defined criterion, but rather a general approach. One considers a finitely parametrized family M of possible models of the endogenous data, and then defines a map $T: M \rightarrow M$ that indicates the pattern $T(m)$ that the data will exhibit, if agents act on the basis of beliefs $m \in M$. Rational expectations equilibria then correspond to fixed points of the map T. The "expectational stability" (or E-stability) of such equilibria then depends upon the properties of the map T near the respective fixed points. According to the original De-Canio–Lucas definition (which we may call *iterative E-stability*), a fixed point $m^* \in M$ is E-stable if it is a stable rest point of the discrete-time dynamics:

$$m_{t+1} = T(m_t). \tag{7.1a}$$

According to a definition used more in the recent work of Evans and Honkapohja (*continuous E-stability*), a fixed point m^* is E-stable if it is a stable rest point of the continuous time dynamics:

$$\dot{m}_t = T(m_t) - m_t. \tag{7.1b}$$

The latter is easily seen to be a weaker condition, at least as far as local stability is concerned.[70]

The dynamics represented by equations (7.1) can be thought of as simple types of adaptive learning rules. In the iterative case, one might imagine that beliefs remain fixed at m_t for some long period of time, during which time data are generated that conform to the model $T(m_t)$. At the end of this period, beliefs are revised on the basis of observations during the period. If the previous beliefs are completely discounted, and the period is long enough to allow perfectly accurate determination of the data generating process $T(m_t)$, then the new beliefs m_{t+1} will be given by (7.1a). The continuous variant, instead, may be thought of as an adaptive process in which beliefs are continuously modified in the direction of the current discrepancy between beliefs m_t and the data generating process $T(m_t)$. Evans and Honkapohja (1990a, 1990b) show that continuous E-stability is closely related to stability under explicit learning dynamics based on recursive statistical estimation methods of the kind discussed in section 7.2. Alternatively, the iterative dynamics might be interpreted as representing "eductive" learning in the sense of Binmore (1987), i.e., taking place in people's minds in notional time.[71]

These criteria have some of the flavor of purely formal selection criteria, in that E-stability is defined simply in terms of the map T (that is also required, at least from one point of view, to define REE). There is no specification of a particular estimation procedure for agents' determination of the current data generating process $T(m_t)$; it is simply assumed that beliefs will adjust in proportion to the discrepancy $T(m_t) - m_t$, without any discussion of how the discrepancy manifests itself to agents. On the other hand, determination of E-stability does require more information than does the simple determination of REE points, since neither the space of possible models M nor the map T are uniquely determined by data (preferences, technology, etc.) that suffice to define REE. In fact, Evans (1985) introduces a distinction between "weak" and "strong" E-stability, accordingly as the class of models M is a narrower or a more inclusive class. Neither of these variants is unambiguously defined, as there is in general neither a unique minimal or maximal class of models containing a particular REE. This ambiguity is of course characteristic of any analysis of explicit learning dynamics: the dynamics derived (and the stability results obtained) always depend upon which variables agents are assumed to try to estimate, and which class of possible values they are willing to consider. A consideration of E-stability as opposed to more explicit learning dynamics has some obvious advantages; first, it is frequently much more simple to analyze, and second, the independence of the conclusions from any particular specification of the method by which agents estimate the parameters in question might be viewed as reducing the arbitrariness of the results obtained.

Evans (1986, 1989) has suggested that considerations of E-stability lead to a selection criterion closely related to McCallum's, and in particular that sunspot equilibria (or what he calls "bubble equilibria" of linear models) are never strongly E-stable, whereas non-sunspot equilibria sometimes are. It should be noted, however, that in Evans' (1989) discussion of sunspot equilibria in the overlapping generations model, conditions are exhibited under which sunspot equilibria are *weakly* E-stable.[72] In fact, for the class of economies, class of equilibria, and class of models M, considered in this analysis of weak E-stability, Evans shows that, whenever sunspot equilibria exist, at least some of them are weakly E-stable, while the monetary steady state (the "minimum state variable solution" in this case) is not even weakly E-stable. Hence E-stability as a selection criterion would not support the view that the monetary steady state represents the unique relevant prediction of the model, despite the theoretical possibility of sunspot equilibria.

Evans considers a special case of the Azariadis–Guesnerie model (section 5 above), in which the sunspot process is a two-state Markov process. The class of possible beliefs M is the two-parameter family of possible beliefs about what the price level will be in each of the two sunspot states, assuming that it is always the same whenever a given sunspot state occurs. (The price level process is indeed of this form in the stationary equilibria studied by Azariadis and Guesnerie.) Given any such beliefs m, there is an optimal action in each sunspot state, that then implies a market-clearing price level in each state, if people act upon those beliefs. The vector of market-clearing prices for the two states is then defined as $T(m) \in M$, and the monetary steady state and the stationary sunspot equilibria are both fixed points of the map T. In the case that stationary sunspot equilibria exist, the dynamics (7.1b) are of the form shown in figure 6.9. Note that, in the case shown, the monetary steady state is unstable, while both sunspot equilibria are locally stable, and almost all initial points in the plane are attracted to one sunspot equilibrium or the other.

Evans classifies the sunspot equilibria as not *strongly* E-stable, because these fixed points become unstable if one considers a broader class M, namely beliefs that the price level may depend upon the current values of *two* two-state Markov sunspot variables, the original one and another, independent process, with the transition probabilities for the latter Markov process chosen appropriately. But, of course, consideration of the broader class of theories can never make the monetary steady state stable. Furthermore, although Evans contrasts the "fragility" of the sunspot equilibria with the strong E-stability of the monetary steady state in the case of parameter values for which no stationary sunspot equilibria exists, the latter result surely depends upon having considered only a relatively restricted class of possible theories in the analysis of "strong" E-stability.

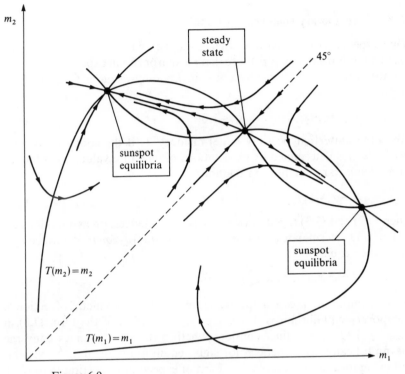

Figure 6.9

For example, the results of Grandmont and Laroque (1990b), discussed below, suggest that the monetary steady state would in all cases be unstable if the class of theories considered included divergent price paths of the right sort.[73]

Acceptance of strong E-stability as a selection criterion would mean that, in cases like that depicted in figure 6.9, there would simply be *no* equilibrium that could be regarded as a plausible state for the economy to remain in. Such a conclusion would hardly suggest that the theoretical existence of sunspot equilibria in such an economy is not a real source of instability for the economy; on the contrary, it would suggest the desirability of interventions that would allow the economy to have a strongly E-stable equilibrium (which would mean ruling out the possibility of sunspot equilibria).

7.3   Temporary equilibrium dynamics

One type of explicit learning dynamics that have been explored with particular thoroughness are those that result from point expectations about a future variable x_{t+1} given by a time-invariant *expectation function* of the form:

$$x^e_{t+1} = \psi(x_t, x_{t-1} \ldots x_{t-T}) \tag{7.2}$$

for some finite (but possibly large) memory T. If the endogenous state variable x_t is determined by expectations of its future value, according to some temporary equilibrium relation:

$$x_t = \chi(x^e_{t+1}) \tag{7.3}$$

then (7.2) and (7.3) together can be solved (under certain assumptions on ψ) to yield determinate *temporary equilibrium (t.e.) dynamics* described by a difference equation:

$$x_t = \phi(x_{t-1} \ldots x_{t-T}). \tag{7.4}$$

(For example, in the case of the overlapping generations model of section 5, temporary equilibrium is determined by a relation of the form (7.3), if $x_t = 1/p_t$.) One may then consider whether the t.e. dynamics converge asymptotically to a perfect foresight equilibrium or not.[74] Without allowing for a more complicated form of expectation function than (7.2), there is obviously no possibility of convergence to a sunspot equilibrium. One can, however, consider the possibility of convergence to a deterministic equilibrium cycle, which, as discussed above, represents endogenous instability of essentially the same sort in the case of a model of the form (7.3).

Let $(\bar{x}_1 \ldots \bar{x}_k)$ be a perfect foresight equilibrium cycle of period k, i.e., a sequence such that:

$$\bar{x}_j = \chi(\bar{x}_{j+1}), \qquad j = 1 \ldots k-1, \tag{7.5a}$$
$$x_k = \chi(\bar{x}_1). \tag{7.5b}$$

(If $k = 1$, this is a steady state equilibrium, and the results stated below apply to steady states as well.) Then Grandmont (1985) shows that sufficient conditions for the local stability of this cycle under the t.e. dynamics are that:[75]

(i) ψ is continuously differentiable;

(ii)   if $(x_1 \ldots x_{t-T})$ is any k-periodic sequence [i.e., if $x_{t-j} = x_{t-j(\text{mod } k)}$ for all $j = 0 \ldots T$], then:

$$\psi(x_t, x_{t-1} \ldots x_{t-T}) = x_{t-k+1}$$

(i.e., the expectation function extrapolates all cycles of period k);

(iii) $\partial\psi/\partial x_{t-j} \geq 0$ for all $j = 0 \ldots T$, evaluated at any k-periodic sequence $(x_1 \ldots x_{t-T})$; and:

$$\left| \prod_{i=1}^{k} \chi'(\bar{x}_i) \right| < 1 \qquad (7.6)$$

(i.e., perfect foresight equilibrium dynamics are *determinate* near the equilibrium cycle).

Conditions (i)–(iii) are intended to represent plausible properties of a forecasting rule, not involving any prior knowledge of the form of the equilibrium cycle $(x_1 \ldots x_k)$. (The willingness to extrapolate a cycle of period k is of course necessary if the cycle is to be consistent with the t.e. dynamics at all.) Condition (7.6), instead, does not involve the expectation function at all; and so this is the selection criterion with which Grandmont proposes to supplement the perfect foresight equilibrium conditions (7.5).

Grandmont and Laroque (1976) establish that (7.6) is also necessary for stability under the t.e. dynamics, assuming[76] (i) and that:

(ii′) the expectation function extrapolates all cycles of period $2k$.

Here (ii′) is simply a strengthening of (ii). Given the stronger condition on the expectation function, (7.6) becomes both necessary and sufficient for stability under the t.e. dynamics.[77]

It is evident that the selection criterion one thus obtains may single out fluctuating equilibria rather than any of the possible steady states. For example, consider a one-parameter smooth family of temporary equilibrium relations $\chi(.;\mu)$, that undergoes a *flip bifurcation* (as discussed in section 2.1) as μ passes through the critical value μ^*. (See section 5.1 for this possibility in the overlapping generations model.) Then for $\mu > \mu^*$, $\chi'(x^*(\mu);\mu) < -1$, and so the steady state $x^*(\mu)$ is unstable under t.e. dynamics of the Grandmont–Laroque sort (i.e., satisfying (i), (iii), and (ii′) for $k=1$). This may well be the unique steady state. (In the overlapping generations example, there is typically also a non-monetary steady state, but $\chi' > 1$ near it, so that it is also unstable under the t.e. dynamics.) Furthermore, for all μ in some right neighborhood of μ^*, there exists an equilibrium cycle of period 2, $(x_1(\mu), x_2(\mu))$, with:

$$\chi'(\bar{x}_1(\mu);\mu)\chi'(\bar{x}_2(\mu);\mu) < 1. \qquad (7.7)$$

Then since (ii′) for $k=1$ means that (ii) holds for $k=2$, the period two cycle is locally stable under the t.e. dynamics.

A simple example of an expectation function with these properties is:

$$\psi(x_t, x_{t-1} \ldots x_{t-T}) = x_{t-1}$$

in which case the t.e. dynamics are simply:

$$x_t = \chi(x_{t-1}).$$

These t.e. dynamics are graphed in figure 6.10, for the case of an overlapping generations economy with a unique two-cycle (as in figure 6.7) at which (7.7) holds. Note that the t.e. dynamics converge to the two-cycle, even from initial conditions close to consistency with the steady state equilibrium.[78]

Related results are obtained by Guesnerie and Woodford (1990), analyzing a class of generalizations of the familiar "adaptive expectations" rule. They consider recursive algorithms of the form:

$$x_{t+1}^e = x_{t-k+1}^e + \alpha(x_{t-k+1} - x_{t-k+1}^e)$$

for some $0 < \alpha \le 1$, and some integer $k \ge 1$. The idea of this specification is that expectations are revised in response to past forecasting errors, but that, because agents are prepared to extrapolate arbitrary cycles of period k, expectations regarding period $t+1$ are based solely upon past observations of periods s such that $s \pmod k = t + 1 \pmod k$. They show, for any $k \ge 2$, that an equilibrium k-cycle$(\overline{x_1} \ldots \overline{x_k})$ is locally stable under the resulting t.e. dynamics if and only if:

$$v(\alpha, k) < \prod_{i=1}^{k} \chi'(\overline{x_i}) < 1, \tag{7.8}$$

where $v(\alpha, k)$ is a function that they characterize in some detail; in particular, it is shown that:

$$v(\alpha, k) \le -1$$

for all α, k. In the case that $k = 1$, this condition is sufficient though not necessary. The selection criterion suggested by this analysis would be similar to that of Grandmont and Laroque, in that the only properties of the k-cycle or the t.e. relation that matter are the quantity $\prod_{i=1}^{k} \chi'(\overline{x_i})$.[79] And, for example, in the case of the flip bifurcation just discussed, if agents use an adaptive rule with $k = 2$, the steady state will be unstable and the two-cycle locally stable, just as for Grandmont and Laroque.

It should be emphasized, however, that stability under t.e. dynamics is far from providing an unambiguous selection criterion. While the Grandmont–Laroque conditions might seem relatively weak, condition (iii) in particular is not at all self-evident, as it rules out any willingness of agents to

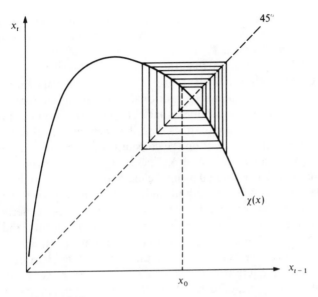

Figure 6.10

extrapolate explosively divergent paths. Grandmont and Laroque (1990b) show, in fact, that any steady state is always unstable under some kinds of t.e. dynamics; it is only necessary that the expectation function be able to extrapolate at least some paths that diverage exponentially from the steady state at a fast enough rate. This leads them to consider formation of expectations through linear regression of x_t on x_{t-1}, using the observations in periods $t - T$ through t to forecast x_{t+1} – a forecasting method that will extrapolate exponential convergence or divergence at any rate. They show that, with this type of expectation formation, any steady state is unstable, in the sense that any neighborhood of the steady state contains an open subset of initial conditions for which the t.e. dynamics diverge from the steady state.[80] Similar results presumably can be established for cycles of arbitrary periodicity.

From this point of view, it might be wondered in what sense steady states should be regarded as less likely outcomes after a flip bifurcation that creates a two-cycle than before such a bifurcation; or how robust are any results establishing conditions under which cycles are stable under t.e. dynamics. However, it is not clear to what extent the negative results of Grandmont and Laroque (1990b) extend to the case of economies subject to stochastic perturbation. Suppose that instead of (7.3) we have a stochastic t.e. relation:

$$x_t = \chi(x_{t+1}^e) + v_t,$$

where $\{v_t\}$ is a sequence of mean zero i.i.d. random variables with compact support, and suppose that expectations are again formed through linear regression of x_t on x_{t-1} (and a constant), but now with all observations up until period t being used, so that the number of observations used in calculating the regression coefficients grows with time.[81] Then a fixed point x^* of the map χ still corresponds to a rational expectations equilibrium (in the sense that, if expectations always equal x^*, they are always conditionally unbiased), and the learning dynamics described converge to this equilibrium if the regression coefficient on the constant converges to x^* while the coefficient on x_{t-1} converges to zero. The asymptotic behavior of these learning dynamics can be studied using the methods of Marcet and Sargent (1988, 1989a, 1989b).[82] These methods indicate that in the presence of any positive variance, however small, for the stochastic disturbance term v_t, a steady state x^* is locally stable in the sense of Marcet and Sargent if and only if $|\chi'(x^*)| < 1$, i.e., if and only if perfect foresight dynamics in the unperturbed system are determinate at the steady state.[83] Marcet and Sargent consider an equilibrium "locally stable" if there exists a compact set X, containing a neighborhood of the equilibrium values of the regression coefficients, such that if the estimated coefficients used to form expectations are never allowed to leave the set X (but the usual regression method applies whenever it yields coefficients in the interior of X), the estimated coefficients converge with probability one to the equilibrium values.

Grandmont and Laroque object that this sort of convergence result depends upon constraining the coefficient on x_{t-1} not to leave a certain region, and hence on not allowing agents to extrapolate divergent paths of certain kinds. But Marcet and Sargent's sense of local stability seems a reasonable one *in the case of a stochastic system*, even though that of Grandmont and Laroque is also reasonable in the case of the deterministic system that they consider. For, in the deterministic case, even once an economy has been in the steady state for an arbitrarily long time, it remains true that an arbitrary small perturbation of the observed data in a small number of periods (followed by no further perturbations) will suffice to cause the economy to diverge from the steady state; thus it is reasonable to consider the steady state an unstable equilibrium. But, in the stochastic case, once the economy has been in or near the steady state for a long enough time, the kind of perturbations that would have to occur in order to produce regression coefficients outside the set X are quite extreme; and, in fact, assuming stochastic perturbations each period with a compact support, as above, one can show (in the case of Marcet–Sargent "local stability") that with probability one the constraint on the regression coefficients ceases to bind after some finite time.

7.4   Learning dynamics based upon statistical estimation techniques

Various approaches to learning have also been analyzed in which agents' beliefs are assumed to derive from the application of one or another estimation technique used by statisticians. Such approaches, while in general more difficult to analyze, and, at least in the cases treated thus far in the literature, more special (and so, arguably, more arbitrary) in their assumptions than the approach described in the previous subsection, have nonetheless several advantages. One is that they make possible convergence to stochastic REE. This implies much more general applicability of such techniques, and, of particular interest in the present context, allows examination of the stability of stationary sunspot equilibria. Another is the arguable descriptive realism of a theory of expectation formation that assumes that economic agents use methods that people are in fact known (because taught) to use. A further advantage is the arguable "rationality" of methods of expectations formation that can be shown to possess desirable properties such as consistency of estimation in the case of some non-trivial class of statistical models.[84] Finally, we have seen in the previous subsection that consideration of temporary equilibrium dynamics in deterministic economies can yield stability results that are not robust to the introduction of even arbitrarily small stochastic disturbances. The statistical estimation procedures discussed here avoid this problem.

A simple example of such an approach is to assume that agents estimate the mean of the distribution from which some variable is believed to be drawn, using the sample mean of all observations of the variable thus far.[85] Lucas (1986) is an early example of the analysis of learning of this kind as a way of selecting among the multiple possible equilibria in an overlapping generations model. A generalization of this approach is to assume estimation of the sample mean using a recursive algorithm of the form:

$$x^e_{t+1} = x^e_t + \alpha_t(x_t - x^e_t),\qquad(7.9)$$

where $\{\alpha_t\}$ is a decreasing sequence of positive numbers that approach zero at a rate that is both slow enough to imply asymptotic independence of the estimate from its initial value and fast enough to imply asymptotic convergence of the estimate even when x_t is stochastic. This is equivalent to the use of the sample mean as an estimate in the case $\alpha_t = 1/t$.[86]

Evans and Honkapohja (1990b) apply this approach to the analysis of the stability of deterministic equilibrium cycles in economies where temporary equilibrium is determined by a relation of the form (7.3). Agents are assumed to believe that the mean of the distribution from which x_{t+1} is drawn is periodic with some period $k \geq 1$, and so to form their estimate x^e_{t+1} using only observations from periods s such that $s(\bmod k) = t + 1(\bmod k)$.

The obvious generalization of (7.9) is then:

$$x^e_{t+1} = x^e_{t+1-k} + \alpha_t(x_{t+1-k} - x^e_{t+1-k}).\tag{7.10}$$

Evans and Honkapohja show that with learning dynamics of the form (7.10), under certain conditions on the convergence of the sequence $\{\alpha_t\}$ to zero, a perfect foresight equilibrium k-cycle $(\overline{x_1} \ldots \overline{x_k})$ is locally stable under the learning dynamics if and only if:

$$\hat{v}(k) < \prod_{i=1}^{k} \chi'(\overline{x_i}) < 1,\tag{7.11}$$

where

$$\hat{v}(k) = \lim_{\alpha \to 0} v(\alpha,k)$$

and $v(\alpha,k)$ is the lower bound in (7.8) characterized by Guesnerie and Woodford (1990). As discussed above, this implies that cycles (with $k > 1$) can be stable and steady states unstable, and in particular that, in the case of the flip bifurcation, the steady state is unstable and the period-two cycle is locally stable.[87]

In the deterministic case, these results represent only a slight extension of the result of Guesnerie and Woodford (1990) for the case of α approaching zero. However, similar results obtain in the case of a stochastic temporary equilibrium relation of the form:

$$x_t = \chi(x^e_{t+1}) + v_t,$$

where $\{v_t\}$ is a sequence of independent mean zero random variables all taking values on the same compact interval, and where now x^e_{t+1} refers to the expectation at time t regarding the mean of the distribution from which x_{t+1} will be drawn.[88] Here a set of values $(\overline{x_1} \ldots \overline{x_k})$ satisfying (7.5) continue to describe a rational expectations equilibrium, in which:

$$x_t = \chi(\bar{x}_{t(\text{mod } k)+1}) + v_t.$$

And the learning dynamics generated by (7.10) can converge to such an equilibrium, since in the REE the expectations follow a deterministic cycle. Evans and Honkapohja show that (7.11) continues to be necessary and sufficient for local stability of the REE, where now, as for Marcet and Sargent, "local stability" means the existence of a compact set X containing a neighborhood of the k-cycle $(\overline{x_1} \ldots \overline{x_k})$, such that, if expectations are never allowed to leave the set X (i.e., (7.10) applies only if it yields an expectation in the set X), convergence to the k-cycle occurs with probability one, and (7.10) applies in all but a finite number of periods. Hence, as promised, this approach allows us to establish the robustness of certain results concerning stability of deterministic t.e. dynamics under the introduction of stochastic shocks.

Woodford (1990a) analyzes the stability of finite-state Markovian sunspot equilibria under learning dynamics of a related kind. Suppose that each agent i chooses his action x_t^i to maximize his expected value at time t of a payoff $U(x_t^i, x_t, x_{t+1})$, where x_t represents the action chosen on average by the population of agents (taken by agent i to be independent of his own action),[89] and where U is twice continuously differentiable, and concave in x_t^i. Let a sunspot variable be defined by a Markov process on the finite set of states S; then a stationary sunspot equilibrium is a set of values $\{x_s\}$, one for each sunspot state $s \in S$, such that:

$$\Sigma_{s'} \pi_{ss'} U_1(x_s, x_s, x_{s'}) = 0, \tag{7.12}$$

where $\pi_{ss'}$ is the probability of transition from s to s'. Now suppose that agents are unsure in what way their optimal action may depend upon the current sunspot state, but assume that it is always the same whenever a given sunspot state s occurs. One way that agents might seek to learn the set of optimal actions is to revise their estimates over time according to the "stochastic approximation" algorithm of Robbins and Monro (1951).[90] If $\hat{x}_s(m)$ represents an agent's estimate of the optimal action in state s, following m observations of aggregate conditions following occurrences of state s, then this estimate remains unchanged until the period following the next occurrence of state s, at which time it is modified according to the rule:

$$\hat{x}_s(m+1) = \hat{x}_s(m) + \frac{\gamma}{m+1} U_1(\hat{x}_s(m), x_t, x_{t+1}) \tag{7.13}$$

assuming that the $(m+1)$st occurrence of state s is in period t. (Here k is an arbitrary positive constant.)

This rule says that one's estimate is modified in proportion to the amount by which one learns, after the fact, that utility would have been increased had one's estimate been different in period t. The idea is that an agent's estimate will be systematically increased or decreased as further observations occur, unless it has attained a value for which the expected value of $U_1(\hat{x}_s, x_t, x_{t+1})$ is zero when the sunspot state in period t is s, which is to say that $\hat{x}_s$ is in fact the optimal action in state s. The adjustment in response to a given size utility gradient becomes smaller as the number of observations already incorporated in the estimate increases, so that convergence of the estimate is possible even in a stochastic equilibrium.[91] The rule (7.13) is a sort of generalization of the idea discussed above of estimating the mean of an unknown distribution using the sample mean of observations to date. For if $U_1(x_t^i, x_t, x_{t+1})$ takes the form $\chi(x_t, x_{t+1}) - x_t^i$, then the optimal action is just the conditional expectation of $\chi(x_t, x_{t+1})$ given that the sunspot state in period t is s, and (7.13) amounts, if $\gamma = 1$, to using as one's estimate the sample mean of the observed values of $\chi(x_t, x_{t+1})$ following previous occurrences of state s. The generalization provides a consistent estimator of the optimal action that is valid for general non-linear functions as well,[92] while preserving the simplicity of the Evans–Honkapohja scheme discussed above, in that only a single parameter need be estimated for each state. It also has the advantage of not requiring that agents restrict their beliefs about the possible processes generating the aggregate data to some finitely parameterized family, which would mean assuming a great deal of a priori knowledge, as well as possibly implying that a finite sequence of data could contradict agents' maintained beliefs.[93]

Suppose that all agents start out with common estimates and update them using (7.13), and that each period the action taken equals the current estimate of the optimal action given the current sunspot state. This then describes a stochastic process for the evolution of the estimates in response to the pattern of realizations of the sunspot states, and one may ask whether it is likely to converge to any of the stationary vectors of estimates satisfying (7.12), which set includes both steady state equilibria and stationary sunspot equilibria. Using the method of analysis of asymptotic dynamics developed by Ljung (1977, 1983), Woodford shows that the trajectories of this stochastic process for the estimates asymptotically approach the trajectories of a deterministic ordinary differential equation system, and it is in fact the system (7.1b) used in the analysis of continuous E-stability, where the map T is defined as in the Evans (1989) discussion of E-stability for sunspot equilibria in the overlapping generations model. Hence in the case of an overlapping generations economy with sunspot equilibria like those depicted in figure 6.9, the monetary steady state is unstable under the learning dynamics; even if all agents start with initial beliefs near the diagonal (i.e., not believing that the optimal action is much affected by the current sunspot state), or indeed near consistency with the monetary steady state, their beliefs will with probability one be driven away from the monetary steady state and toward different actions in the two sunspot states. Furthermore, with probability one, estimates converge to one or the other of the two stationary sunspot equilibria.[94] Hence one finds, again, little support for the view that the monetary steady state is the unique equilibrium likely to occur in such economies.[95]

This hardly means that we can, upon purely theoretical grounds, predict which equilibrium such an economy should end up in. Even under the conditions under which Woodford proves convergence with probability one to a sunspot equilibrium, there always exist at least two locally stable equilibria, to either of which the learning dynamics might converge. More importantly, convergence to certain particular sunspot equilibria is possible when agents consider the use of a particular sunspot variable in forecasting, but by the same token other sunspot equilibria would represent possible limit states if other sunspot variables were considered by agents. Indeed, even the stability of a particular sunspot equilibrium under the learning dynamics can change, depending upon what other sunspot variables (in addition to the one that matters in the equilibrium in question) are also considered by agents.[96] Hence the consideration of explicit learning dynamics cannot provide an actual equilibrium "selection criterion," or at least not a very strong one, in such models. Nonetheless, the demonstration that simple learning processes can end up at any of a variety of sunspot equilibria rather than at the steady state is important, in that it bears upon the issue of whether there is any need to design policy regimes so as to prevent the theoretical possibility of sunspot equilibria. This point is developed further in the following section.

Needless to say, our understanding of the asymptotic properties of sensible learning processes remains highly preliminary. It would be especially interesting to see further explored the consequences for learning of more sophisticated forms of rationality, such as the common knowledge of the structure of the economy and of other agents' objectives that is assumed in analyses of "rationalizable" outcomes in non-cooperative game theory. A number of recent results on learning in strategic situations suggest that the considerations involved in defining rationalizable outcomes are also of great relevance to defining the set of possible outcomes of learning processes.[97] The implications of these results for learning in the kinds of contexts of interest to us here are not yet known, but they suggest that strong connections may exist between the outcomes of "evolutive" and "eductive" learning (as suggested in our discussion of E-stability above).

8   STABILIZATION POLICIES FOR SUNSPOT EQUILIBRIA

A question of obvious interest if the models of sunspot equilibria are considered as possible explanations of observed fluctuations in economic activity is the implication of this type of model of fluctuations for the theory of stabilization policy. It is not useful to discuss stabilization in detail except in the context of a specific model of fluctuations that is regarded as empirically descriptive. Nonetheless, a few general remarks about the implications of sunspot theories as a class are possible.

8.1   The possibility of stabilization

Economic fluctuations due to self-fulfilling expectations are especially likely to be affected by government commitments to future policies that, if credible, will more or less directly affect agents' expectations. Such (possibly implicit) policy commitments that fully specify the government's response to all possible future contingencies are commonly referred to as *policy regimes*; while the importance of conceiving policy in these terms for purposes of analysis has been stressed in the literature on rational expectations generally (see, e.g., Sargent, 1986, chapter 1), the point is especially crucial in the present context. In most of the models discussed in the previous sections, with no exogenous variations in fundamentals, a steady state equilibrium, with no variation over time in the allocation of resources or in relative prices, is possible, and continues to be possible in the case of a wide variety of policy regimes that do not themselves introduce exogenous variations in fundamentals. For some policy regimes (including *laissez-faire*, in examples discussed above), however, the steady state is not the unique rational expectations equilibrium. But policy regimes may exist that succeed in making a non-fluctuating equilibrium the unique equilibrium; these can be referred to as *stabilization policies*. It is a striking feature of the kind of models considered here that stabilization may require no actual intervention, but only the threat of interventions that, if credible, will not have to be implemented.

This can be illustrated using some of the examples discussed earlier. A variety of types of stabilizing policies have been analyzed.

(i)   *Feedback rules for monetary policy.* We have discussed several types of monetary economies in which endogenous fluctuations in the price level are possible in the case of a constant money supply. Suppose now instead (following Grandmont, 1975) that the money supply is varied in response to current aggregate conditions, and that any variations in the money supply are achieved through transfers or taxes proportional to existing money holdings. (The latter stipulation is not essential, but makes it clear that in this case monetary policy is effective *only* because it succeeds in stabilizing expectations.) The equilibrium condition for determination of the price level, in each of the monetary models of sections 5 and 6, takes in this case the form:

$$E_t\left[Z\left(\frac{M_t}{p_t}, \frac{M_{t+1}}{p_{t+1}}\right)\right] = 0, \tag{8.1}$$

where M_t is the period t money supply, and where Z is the same function as in the case of a constant money supply. Note that the set of stochastic processes for real money balances that satisfy (8.1) are the same for all exogenous processes for the money supply $\{M_t\}$. Suppose, however, that the growth rate of the money supply is varied in response to the current rate of inflation, according to a rule of the form:[98]

$$\frac{M_{t+1}}{M_t} = \frac{p_{t+1}}{p_t} \, g\left(\frac{p_t}{p_{t-1}}\right). \tag{8.2}$$

To be precise, suppose that, at some date $t = 0$, a value is announced for M_0, and it is announced that (8.2) will determine the money supply in all periods $t + 1 \geq 1$. Substitution of (8.2) into (8.1) yields:

$$Z\left(\frac{M_t}{p_t}, \frac{M_t}{p_t} g\left(\frac{p_t}{p_{t-1}}\right)\right) = 0$$

for all periods $t \geq 0$. In the case of the overlapping generations model considered by Grandmont, and also (under weak conditions) for the other examples discussed in section 6, this implies a unique solution for M_t/p_t as a function of p_t/p_{t-1}. Substitution into (8.2) then gives M_{t+1}/p_{t+1} as a function of p_t/p_{t-1}, for all $t \geq 0$. Hence real balances are known with certainty in the previous period, and stochastic solutions to (8.1) are not possible equilibria. Thus sunspot equilibria are impossible. Grandmont furthermore exhibits conditions upon the policy function g, and upon the function Z describing the economy, under which the deterministic equilibrium dynamics are unique and converge asymptotically to a steady state with a constant rate of inflation, constant real balances, and the optimal stationary consumption allocation.

(ii) *Monetary policies without explicit feedback.* Stabilization is also possible other than through a feedback rule for the money supply, at least in certain of these models. For example, Woodford (1988b) shows that, in the case of the Lucas–Stokey model discussed above, a monetary policy that pegs the nominal interest rate on government bonds (letting the composition of outstanding government liabilities as between bonds and money be determined by the portfolio preferences of the private sector), coupled with a fiscal policy that sets the levels of government purchases and real tax collections at constant levels, results in a unique rational expectations equilibrium, namely, the deterministic steady state equilibrium (with a constant rate of growth of the money supply and a corresponding constant rate of inflation) associated with that level of nominal interest rates, government purchases, and tax collections. This is true even in the case of preferences such that, were the monetary policy instead to involve a commitment to the constant rate of money supply growth associated with that same steady state, leaving nominal interest rates to be determined so as to clear the bond market, there would exist sunspot equilibria among the possible rational expectations equilibria (as discussed in subsection 6.1). Here again (although in perhaps a less obvious way) the interest-rate pegging regime provides an anchor for expectations regarding the future price level; it is in particular critical in this example that a jump in the price level due to a sunspot realization, and accommodated by an expansion of the money supply in exchange for bonds, would result in a windfall gain to the government (due to reduced interest obligations on the government debt) that would not ever be distributed back to the private sector (e.g., through an eventual tax reduction).[99]

(iii) *Government spending to offset instability of private expenditure.* Another class of examples involve the use of variations in government purchases to offset changes in private spending, so as to insure an expectation of a constant demand for output.[100] For example, in the Woodford (1991) model of autonomous fluctuations in investment demand, allowance for variable government purchases changes equation (6.9) to:

$$y_t = f(I_{t-1}, I_t + G_t),$$

where G_t represents government purchases in period t, since the "multiplier" effect of government purchases on aggregate demand is the same as for investment purchases. As a result (6.11) becomes:

$$E_t[g(I_t, I_{t+1} + G_{t+1})] = r^*. \tag{8.3}$$

Now if government purchases are adjusted in response to variations in investment demand according to a rule of the form:

$$G_t = A - I_t$$

then (8.3) implies that investment demand in each period must satisfy:

$$g(I_t, A) = r^*.$$

This equation may well have a unique solution $I_t = I^*$, even if (6.11) admits sunspot equilibria as solutions, in which case the unique rational expectations equilibrium is one in which I_t (and hence y_t) never fluctuates. Note that, in equilibrium, G_t never fluctuates either; actual intervention is not needed, the credible commitment to engage in it being sufficient to stabilize expectations.

An alternative approach to stabilization, should this reliance upon the possibility of publicly and credibly commiting the government to a particular policy regime for the indefinite future seem undesirable, would involve an explicit analysis of the convergence of "learning" dynamics to a rational expectations equilibrium, as discussed in the previous section. In that case one would seek to design policies that made the desired steady state equilibrium an attractor for the learning dynamics, while insuring that no sunspot equilibria were. Since economic agents would be assumed to reach a rational expectations equilibrium through induction from past experience rather than by deduction of what is possible in the future, stabilization could occur as a result of having implemented the policy up until the present, rather than its depending upon anyone's understanding that it must be implemented in the future (although of course the nature of the policy regime is part of what agents would be learning about). This sort of approach would not necessarily reach the same conclusions as the approach illustrated above. For in some cases policy regimes that allow the existence of sunspot equilibria also make the steady state unstable under learning dynamics and result in convergence of the learning dynamics to certain of the sunspot equilibria, while alternative policies that eliminate the sunspot equilibria also insure convergence of the learning dynamics to the steady state (compare Grandmont (1986) with the analysis of learning dynamics in Grandmont (1985), Guesnerie and Woodford (1990), and Woodford (1990a)); but it is also possible that policy regimes that eliminate sunspot equilibria would make the steady state unstable under learning dynamics, while under a regime that allowed sunspot equilibria the steady state would nonetheless be an attractor for the learning dynamics (compare Howitt (1990) with the interest-rate pegging result of Woodford (1988b)).

8.2   Indeterminacy of equilibrium and welfare comparisons between policy regimes

In discussing the possibility of choosing a policy regime that implies the non-existence of sunspot equilibria, we have deferred discussion of why it is desirable to do so. While "stabilization" as such is often assumed to be an objective in discussions of macroeconomic policy, it is worth asking whether the types of economic structures identified as sources of instability in these models imply that stabilization of sunspot equilibria is to be desired.

One quite general result that bears upon this issue is, of course, the proposition discussed above in section 3.2 according to which the Pareto optima of convex economies do not involve any dependence of allocations upon sunspot states. This confirms the intuitive notion that fluctuations in the use of resources that are not motivated by any changes in "fundamentals" are undesirable. In fact, the proposition shows that this intuition is correct in the case of sunspot equilibria to a greater extent than is true for the sort of endogenous fluctuations associated with determinate but unstable dynamics (section 2). For the latter sort of endogenous fluctuations may be Pareto optimal, and indeed, may maximize the welfare of a representative consumer, as discussed above. In such examples, the allocation of resources fluctuates but is at all times optimal *given* the predetermined state variables (capital stocks) at that point in time, and the perpetual changes in the levels of those predetermined state variables are in turn a consequence of an optimal use of resources in earlier periods. Fluctuations in response to sunspot events (as opposed to mere variation over time) cannot have this kind of justification.

But the proposition just referred to does not imply that stabilization of the kind discussed in the previous subsection necessarily improves welfare. The mere fact that the sunspot equilibria that are possible in the absence of stabilization policy are not Pareto optimal (and hence are dominated by some feasible allocation) does not mean that they are Pareto dominated by any of the other possible equilibria. For example, in the model of self-fulfilling investment fluctuations of Woodford (1991), the fluctuations in consumption and labor supply by the representative household are such that the household's level of utility remains unchanged each period (the increased consumption exactly offsetting the reduced leisure); hence the level of utility of the representative household is the same in all of the equilibria, sunspot and non-sunspot equilibria alike. The sunspot equilibrium allocations are inefficient, but so is the steady state equilibrium allocation, because of the assumption of imperfect competition in the product market. Given that many of the kinds of economies in which sunspot equilibria are possible involve market imperfections that will typically imply that even non-sunspot equilibria are inefficient, one must use care in inferring from the Ineffectivity Theorem that it is desirable to stabilize sunspot equilibria.[101]

Nonetheless, in some cases one can show that the steady state equilibrium is Pareto superior to at least certain of the sunspot equilibria that are also possible. Consider again the Lucas–Stokey model of section 6.1, and as an example suppose that:

$$U(c_1,c_2) = ac_1 - (b/2)c_1^2 + c_2, \quad \text{if } c_1 \leq a/b,$$
$$= (a^2/2b) + c_2, \qquad \text{if } c_1 \geq a/b,$$

where $a > 3, b > 0$. Let us suppose furthermore that the money supply grows exogenously at a rate π, though lump sum transfers to consumers, received each period in time to allow the new cash to be used to satisfy the cash-in-advance constraint. (We may also allow for the case of $\pi < 0$, in which case consumers pay lump sum taxes, levied early enough each period to reduce the funds available for cash goods purchases in that period; but let us assume that $1 + \pi > \beta$.) In this case, equation (6.5) takes the form:

$$\frac{M_t}{p_t} = \frac{\beta}{1+\pi} E_t \left\{ \frac{M_{t+1}}{p_{t+1}} \left[a - b\min\left(\frac{M_{t+1}}{p_{t+1}}, \hat{m} \right) \right] \right\}, \tag{8.4}$$

where:

$$\hat{m} = \frac{a-1}{b}$$

and where the money supply process is $M_t = M_0(1+\pi)^t$. There exists a unique deterministic steady state equilibrium, with a constant level of real money balances:

$$m^* = \frac{a-\rho}{b},$$

where $\rho = (1 + \pi)/\beta$, and so with a constant rate of inflation π. The level of utility of the representative consumer in this equilibrium is:

$$W_{ss} = \frac{1}{1-\beta} \left\{ e + \left[\frac{a-2+\rho}{2} \right] \left[\frac{a-\rho}{b} \right] \right\}. \tag{8.5}$$

It can also be shown that there exists a unique two-period deterministic equilibrium cycle (in which the level of real balances alternates forever between two values, m_1 and m_2), in which the cash-in-advance constraint always binds, if and only if:

$$\frac{a}{3} > \rho > \frac{\sqrt{4a-3}-1}{2} > 1. \tag{8.6}$$

(The two-cycle bifurcates from the steady state at $\rho = a/3$, while at the lower bound for ρ, the cash-in-advance constraint ceases to bind in the high real-balance phase of the cycle, so that while a two-cycle continues to exist, the formulas given below do not apply.) In this equilibrium, the two alternating levels of real balances are given by:

$$m_{1,2} = \frac{a+\rho}{2b} \pm \frac{1}{2b} \sqrt{(a+\rho)^2 - 4\rho(a+\rho)}.$$

One possible welfare measure for this equilibrium is the average of the levels of utility of the representative consumer in the two possible cases, in which the first period is either a high real-balance or a low real-balance period. (This can be interpreted as the *ex ante* expected utility of the representative consumer, if an initial sunspot event determines which phase the cycle starts in, with probability one-half for each possibility.) By this measure, the level of welfare associated with the two-cycle is:

$$W_{2c} = \frac{1}{1-\beta} \left\{ e + \left[\frac{a-2+\rho}{2} \right] \left[\frac{a+\rho}{2b} \right] \right\}. \tag{8.7}$$

Comparison of (8.5) with (8.7) shows that $W_{ss} > W_{2c}$. This is accordingly an example of undesirable endogenous fluctuations. Furthermore, as explained in section 4.1.5, there exist non-degenerate stationary sunspot equilibria that are arbitrarily close to the equilibrium two-cycle, in which the level of welfare is arbitrarily close to the value (8.7); hence there exist non-degenerate stationary sunspot equilibria that involve a level of welfare lower than that associated with the deterministic steady state.

In such a case, a stabilization policy of either the Grandmont type or through interest-rate pegging would clearly result at least in an increase in the level of utility associated with the worst possible equilibria, without having any effect upon the desired equilibrium.[102] In fact, policies that improve in this sense can be constructed even under more general conditions, if one does not insist on stabilizing a steady state that is the same as one would have with no intervention. If, for example, in the Lucas–Stokey model one pegs the nominal interest rate at a lower positive value than that associated with the steady state equilibrium with a constant money supply, the resulting unique equilibrium involves a higher level of welfare for the representative consumer than in that steady state, and so may dominate sunspot equilibria that could exist in the case of a constant money supply, even if the constant money supply steady state does not. The Grandmont money supply rule (8.2) is similarly easily modified so as to lead to a steady state with a contracting money supply, by choosing the function g so that $g^{-1}(1) < 1$, which in the case of the Lucas–Stokey model would increase the utility of the representative consumer in the steady state.

In the event that there exist a sufficient number of policy instruments to insure that the first-best allocation is not just an equilibrium but the only equilibrium, the optimal policy will necessarily involve the suppression of sunspot equilibria (among other things), since, because of risk aversion, the first-best allocation must (under quite general assumptions) not involve fluctuations in response to extrinsic uncertainty. On the other hand, if only a restricted set of policy tools is available, this may not be possible, and in such a case there may be a conflict between the choice of policy so as to support as good as possible an equilibrium (looking only at the *best* equilibrium associated with each policy regime) and the choice of policy so as to suppress endogenous fluctuations.

Consider again the parametric example of a Lucas–Stokey economy just discussed, and consider the effect of variations in the exogenous rate of money growth π, for given parameters a, b, β, e. As shown above, for rates of money growth in the range (8.6), there exist stationary sunspot equilibria, in addition to the deterministic steady state, and these involve levels of welfare at least as low as that indicated in (8.7). On the other hand, one can show that no stationary sunspot equilibria exist if $\rho \geq a/3$; this can be shown by establishing, along the same lines as in Azariadis and Guesnerie (1986), Grandmont (1986), and Woodford (1988b), that stationary sunspot equilibria exist if and only if there exists a two-cycle. Hence if a high enough rate of money growth is chosen, so that $\rho \geq a/3$, the lowest level of welfare associated with any stationary equilibrium[103] is that given by (8.5); while for lower rates of money growth, in the range (8.6), the lowest level of welfare that may result is at least as low as that given by (8.7).

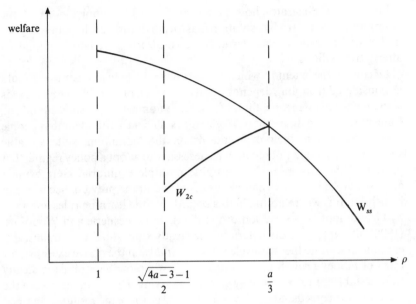

Figure 6.11

These two welfare levels, W_{ss} and W_{2c}, are plotted as functions of ρ (and hence as functions of the rate of money growth) in figure 6.11. One observes from (8.5) that:

$$\frac{dW_{ss}}{d\rho} = \frac{1-\rho}{b} < 0,$$

so that if one simply compares the level of welfare across steady states corresponding to different constant rates of money growth, one concludes that the lower the rate of money growth the better, all the way down to the rate of contraction ($\pi = \beta - 1$) called for by Friedman (1969). But this means abandoning the range of policies for which stationary equilibrium is unique, and entering the range in which endogenous fluctuations are possible. Furthermore, one observes from (8.7) that:

$$\frac{dW_{2c}}{d\rho} = \frac{a+\rho-1}{2b} > 0$$

as shown in the figure. It follows that the level of welfare associated with the *worst* possible stationary equilibrium is higher at $\rho = a/3$ than it is for any of the lower rates of money growth in the range (8.6),[104] and more generally, one observes that it can easily be higher for a higher value of ρ than it is for a lower. This illustrates how policy analysis that simply looks at the "minimum state variable solution" associated with each policy regime under consideration may result in a misleading welfare ranking of alternative policies.[105]

Of course, the extent to which the sort of problem just illustrated should be considered troubling depends upon how much of a problem one regards it to be if a policy regime allows for a large number of possible equilibria, some much worse than others. If one were sufficiently confident that people should coordinate their expectations on the "minimum state variable solution," one might not regard it as necessary to adopt a policy regime that prevented the existence of undesirable multiple equilibria. Here explicit analyses of "learning" dynamics, as discussed in the previous section, can be helpful. It is worth noting in this regard that the learning rules analyzed by Grandmont (1985), Woodford (1990a), and Guesnerie and Woodford (1990) all imply that the deterministic steady state should be an *unstable* equilibrium, while the two-cycle is locally *stable*, in the above example, for rates of money growth in the range (8.6), while the deterministic steady state is stable for rates of money growth satisfying $\rho \geq a/3$. In the case of the learning rule considered by Woodford (1990a), the same result is obtained in the case of a non-degenerate two-state Markovian stationary sunspot equilibrium that is *near* the two-cycle (in the sense explained above), although in this case, the critical value of ρ at which the stability of the steady state changes (and at which the stable sunspot equilibria come into existence) is near but not exactly equal to $a/3$. Furthermore, Woodford's results imply that, when the sunspot equilibria exist (generically, there are two of them), the learning dynamics converge asymptotically to one of them with probability one. Hence under these learning dynamics it is possible to argue that the stationary equilibrium that will result asymptotically, in the case of a lower rate of money growth, involves lower welfare than the stationary equilibrium that will result asymptotically, in the case of a higher rate of money growth.

CONCLUSION

We have stressed throughout the text a certain number of more or less provisional conclusions as well as directions for future research.

For the sake of conclusion, it may, however, be worthwhile to put the present survey contribution written for the occasion of the Econometric Society World Congress in Barcelona in the historical perspective of world congress surveys. In this series, the contribution closest to the present one is clearly the survey by Broze, Gouriéroux, and Szafarz (1991) written for the previous Boston Congress. In fact, the overlap is not so large but it is sufficient to illustrate continuity and discontinuity in economic modeling. Continuity because as we have stressed and as Woodford (1984) first conjectured, the analysis of stochastic equilibria in linear models is relevant to the analysis of a class of sunspot equilibria. Discontinuity because the general equilibrium perspective and the difficulties of the analysis of non-linear systems implies a very significant switch in economic and analytical emphasis. The comparison of the structure of both types of models however shows that the exogenous fluctuations aspects were integrated in a better way in linear models than they are now in our models. Continuity here suggests an obvious direction of future research.

Notes

1 The theory of bifurcations, a central theme in the mathematical theory of dynamical systems, appeared in economic theory in the seventies (Torre, 1977 and Varian, 1979 are early examples).

2 Other references are given in section 5.

3 This is discussed in sections 3 and 8.

4 Boldrin and Woodford (1990) provide a more comprehensive survey of this issue.

5 This part is based on Chiappori and Guesnerie (1990) to which the interested reader should refer for a more complete investigation.

6 Statistical techniques have recently been proposed to distinguish deterministic chaotic dynamics from "truly stochastic" time series under relatively weak assumptions about the two classes of processes. See Brock (1988) and Scheinkman (1990) for surveys of these techniques and applications to economic time series. However, these tests seem thus far to give little insight into how one might distinguish systems that would be stable in the absence of the exogenous shocks, and it is the latter comparison that is of relevance for economic systems.

7 Such methods have already become common in the analysis of real business cycle models (e.g., Kydland and Prescott, 1982). Illustrations of how numerical predictions regarding aggregate time series can be derived from theoretical models of endogenous fluctuations are provided in Woodford (1988a, 1990c).

8 Consequently, we defer discussion of deterministic equilibrium cycles in overlapping generations models until section 5.

9 For a more precise definition, see the discussion of "asymptotic strong determinacy" in Woodford (1990b). Such a representation is always possible, for example, in the case of a *linear* function f, if there exists a compact set X as assumed, and the set Z (and the dependence of f on z) is non-trivial. Hence the sort of endogenous fluctuations discussed here are inherently dependent upon the existence of significant non-linearities in the equilibrium conditions, unlike the endogenous fluctuations resulting from indeterminacy of equilibrium.

10 Of course, how large and how frequent the exogenous shocks must be, to

sustain persistent fluctuations of a given amplitude, depends upon how rapid the convergence is to the steady state in the absence of shocks. If convergence is slow, then relatively small or infrequent shocks suffice, and the statistical properties of the resulting fluctuations (e.g., their approximate "periodicity" as indicated by a peak in the power spectrum) will depend mainly upon the properties of the map f rather than upon statistical properties of the driving shocks. Such a system might then in a sense be said to have an endogenous tendency to produce fluctuations with a certain pattern, even if the fluctuations are eventually damped out in the absence of exogenous shocks; this is in fact Slutsky's (1937) idea of how business cycles should be modeled. It is perhaps not useful to insist upon a sharp distinction between systems of this kind and systems with purely endogenous cycles. But the study of systems with a tendency to fluctuate in Slutsky's sense means the study of systems with only very slow convergence to the steady state, and the study of endogenous cycles proper – insofar as it leads to attention to economic mechanisms that counteract the forces tending to produce convergence – probably leads to attention to much the same classes of models and ranges of parameter values.

11 In the one-dimensional case, and with further conditions on the global behavior of f, local stability of the cycle implies convergence to the cycle for all initial conditions in X except a subset of measure zero (Grandmont, 1985). Global convergence results of this kind are not generally available, for systems permitting the existence of cycles, for dimensions greater than one.

12 However, it must be recalled that the mere existence of a deterministic cycle is of little interest, for a cycle that is reached only from a set of initial conditions of measure zero should never be observed. Hence stability analysis is also an essential part of establishing the possibility of endogenous fluctuations of this kind. This is another important difference between the type of endogenous fluctuations considered in this section and those resulting from the indeterminacy of rational expectations equilibrium. In the case of the equilibria considered in subsection 4.1 below, it suffices to show the existence of a sunspot equilibrium as a solution to the equilibrium conditions (4.1) to establish that it may occur, since there are no predetermined state variables.

13 For further discussion and an economic application, see Guesnerie (1986).

14 This is the condition of a "positive Schwartzian derivative," used extensively in Grandmont (1985).

15 For a detailed analysis of the sequence of bifurcations that occur in such a case, and the types of cycles that may exist, see Collet and Eckmann (1980). Grandmont (1985) applies these results to the study of the kinds of cycles that may occur in an overlapping generations model, while Matsuyama (1989a) applies them to a representative consumer monetary economy of the kind originally studied by Brock (1974).

16 For the applications of this method to the study of equilibrium cycles in overlapping generations models, see Farmer (1986) and Reichlin (1986). In the case of a continuous-time system, a similar bifurcation leads to existence of a limit cycle. For an application to an optimal growth model, see Benhabib and Nishimura (1979).

17 For applications of this idea, see, e.g., Benhabib and Day (1980, 1982), or Day (1982, 1983).

18 This statement is taken from Woodford (1989); the crucial mathematical results are due to Lasota and Yorke (1973) and Li and Yorke (1978).

19 This notion is stronger than, but implies, the "thick chaos" of Melese and Transue (1986).

20 See Blatt (1978, 1983) for an early criticism of linear econometric analysis as a sufficient rebuttal of the hypothesis of endogenous fluctuations. On the spectral properties of the time series generated by chaotic maps, see, e.g., Sakai and Tokumaru (1980), and Brock and Chamberlain (1984).

21 Techniques that should be especially useful in distinguishing deterministic chaos from truly stochastic time series have recently been proposed by a number of authors, who have, on the whole, found little evidence suggesting deterministic chaos in economic time series. For reviews of this literature, see Brock (1988) and Scheinkman (1990).

22 For further development of this point, see Boldrin and Woodford (1990).

23 The variant cited here is due to Scheinkman (1976). For a survey of related results, see McKenzie (1986).

24 Sieveking and Semmler (1990) also emphasize the role of a high rate of time preference in generating endogenous cycles.

25 An early example of a two-sector model characterized by ergodic chaos was constructed by Deneckere and Pelikan (1986).

26 Sorger (1990) does, however, show that it is possible to put a lower bound on the rate of time preference that could possibly be consistent with any given map f. For example, in the case of the map resulting in ergodic chaos studied by Deneckere and Pelikan (1986), $f(k) = 4k(1-k)$, Sorger shows that this map cannot represent optimal capital accumulation dynamics in any economy with $\beta \geq 0.475$.

27 We will continue in this section to be concerned with explicit equilibrium models, in which case the role of particular market failures in generating dynamics different from those associated with an optimal growth model is clearly highlighted. Endogenous fluctuations despite determinate dynamics are also predicted by a variety of *ad hoc* "descriptive" models of macro-economic dynamics, as mentioned in the introduction. For a survey of this literature, see Lorenz (1989).

28 For "turnpike" results in models with (a finite number of) heterogeneous consumer types, see Bewley (1982) and Yano (1984).

29 On the other hand, if the elasticity of substitution exceeds the share of labor income, for all possible capital–labor ratios, then f is a monotonically increasing function, as shown in figure 6.1a, and the steady state is globally stable. In fact, Hernandez (1988) proves a "turnpike" theorem for a much more general class of economies in which consumers cannot borrow against future labor income, under this assumption on factor substitutability. See also the discussion by Becker and Foias (1989). But the degree of factor substitutability required for such results is not an obvious property of actual production technologies, at least over the relatively short horizons that are relevant for business cycle theory.

30 Against which (at least in the Cass–Shell original version) insurance is provided.

31 For an early discussion of the existence of the stochastic solutions in a model of this kind, the reader will refer to Shiller (1978).

32 Significantly enough, a rather general formulation of Arrow's ideas was not proposed until Guesnerie and Jaffray (1974).

33 Balasko (1983) shows that the theorem does not require the full strength of the expected utility hypothesis but only symmetry properties of the utility function defined on contingent commodities (see also Balasko, 1990). Prior work on large economies without aggregate uncertainty had emphasized, along lines of argument extremely close to that of Cass and Shell, that, in such economies, individual uncertainty was irrelevant in a Pareto optimal equilibrium (see Caspi, 1974).

34 However, Cass and Polemarchakis (1989) show that non-convexities in production alone would not destroy the ineffectivity theorem.

35 Note also that the second-best literature as well as the contracts literature have emphasized desirable randomizations (which are obviously assumed not to be insurable!). For a synthetical assessment of the second-best argument, cf. Arnott and Stiglitz (1985).

36 For a different approach to the sunspot problem in the case where there are "financial" assets, see Cass (1984). For a discussion of the ineffectivity theorem in this case, see Prechac (1990).

37 This assertion may be viewed as a (cautious) restatement of what Cass and Shell (1989) call the Pholk theorem, i.e., the fact that sunspot equilibria can be found in any class of models when the ineffectivity theorem does not hold.

38 We might want to distinguish the case where the measure is invariant from the case where it is, in addition, ergodic. For the purpose of the present section, this is not really necessary.

39 As illustrated in section 6, there exists, however, models (albeit of a relatively special kind) for which equilibrium conditions of the form 4.1 remain valid in the presence of insurance against sunspot uncertainty.

40 Again, the interested reader will find a precise definition of (CD) in Chiappori and Guesnerie (1989b). One should, however, note the close connection of this assumption with Woodford's assumption on the existence of Fréchet derivatives in Woodford (1986b).

41 It is only for technical reasons that the definition refers to int X.

42 Proposition 4.1 is precisely given as theorem 2 in Chiappori and Guesnerie (1989b).

43 However, it may be possible in specific problems with heterogenous agents to recover Proposition 4.1, although CVR does not hold for $\tilde{Z}$ as defined here. The trick consists of enlarging the state space, for example to include individual bundles. In the enlarged space, the expected utility hypothesis guarantees that CVR holds, for a "new" $\tilde{Z}$.

44 This is the terminology of, for example, Woodford (1984). We adopt it here.

45 Note that the fact that (4.5) has a non-zero solution does not imply the existence of a sunspot equilibrium of order k (two states in the support could be

identical) but only of order $j, 2 \leqslant j \leqslant k$. We are intentionally vague on this difficulty. Discussion and solution are in Chiappori, Geoffard, and Guesnerie (1989).

46 Proposition 4.2 follows from theorem 1 in Chiappori, Geoffard, and Guesnerie (1989).

47 Another bifurcation argument, with the space of economies as the parameter space, is presented in Grandmont (1986). We will come back to it in section 5.

48 Proposition 4.3 is theorem 4 in Chiappori and Guesnerie (1990).

49 Proposition 4.3(ii) does not assert that the matrix satisfying the properties under consideration "sustains" a SSE of order k: it only says that the SSE so detected is of cardinality k, i.e., of order at least equal to 2 and at most equal to k. However, for genericity reasons "most" SSE so detected are indeed of order k.

50 The one-dimensional genericity argument of Chiappori and Guesnerie (1989a) even suggests that there exist SSE of order k' in the neighborhood of a k-cycle for $k' \geqslant k$.

51 There is a considerable literature on the subject of this subsection (following Samuelson, 1958). We will mention here Gale (1973), Cass, Okuno, and Zilcha (1979), Balasko and Shell (1980, 1981) and the forthcoming survey by Geanakoplos and Polemarchakis (1991).

52 This can easily be checked by the reader.

53 Sarkovskii's preordering is:

$$3 > 5 > 7 \cdots$$
$$> 2.3 > 2.5 > 2.7 \cdots$$
$$\cdots \cdots \cdots \cdots \cdots \cdots$$
$$> 2^n.3 > 2^n.5 \cdots$$
$$> \cdots > 2^m > \cdots 8 > 4 > 2 > 1$$

54 Chiappori and Guesnerie (1990) provide a version of Grandmont's result, that although weaker is valid in one-dimensional systems.

55 Models of this kind are discussed by Bewley (1980, 1983), Kehoe, Levine and Woodford (1990), Levine (1986, 1987), Sargent (1987), and Townsend (1980). The discussion of sunspot equilibria follows Woodford (1988a). On indeterminacy and deterministic cycles in such a model see Boldrin and Woodford (1990).

56 Such models are analyzed by Grandmont and Younes (1972, 1973), Lucas and Stokey (1983, 1987), Svensson (1985a, 1985b), and Wilson (1979). The discussion here of sunspot equilibria follows Woodford (1988a, 1988c).

57 Indeterminacy of equilibrium and the existence of stationary sunspot equilibria can similarly be established in the case of a representative consumer monetary economy of the kind studied by Brock (1974), as is shown by Matsuyama (1989a, 1989b).

58 Contingent claims markets may be introduced into the overlapping generations model discussed in section 5 as well, without affecting the existence of sunspot equilibria, if participation in the markets for contingent claims is

suitably restricted; but in the present case no restrictions upon participation need be assumed.

59 Examples of the indeterminacy of rational expectations equilibrium and of the possibility of endogenous fluctuations due to technological externalities have been discussed by Drugeon (1990), Hammour (1988), Kehoe, Levine, and Romer (1989), Murphy, Shleifer, and Vishny (1989), and Spear (1988). Related phenomena are discussed in connection with a broader class of externalities in Howitt and McAfee (1988, 1990). Externalities also have been shown to result in endogenous equilibrium fluctuations and indeterminacy of equilibrium in a search economy by Diamond and Fudenberg (1989). The presentation here will follow that of Hammour.

60 Hammour (1988) also discusses a model of this kind, as do Matsuyama (1990) and Murphy, Shleifer, and Vishny (1989). The discussion here follows Hammour.

61 This provides a point of contact between the literature discussed here and the monetary examples described in the previous section, since the cash-in-advance constraint in the Lucas–Stokey model is closely analogous to an excise tax on sales of the "cash good."

62 Foley (1991) discusses deterministic equilibrium cycles in a related model. Another example of a dynamic rationing model (though not a representative consumer model) in which equilibrium is indeterminate and sunspot equilibria exist is the efficiency-wage labor market model discussed by Kimball (1989). In this case, however, it seems likely that introduction of realistic labor market frictions, that would prevent discontinuous jumps in the size of firms' workforces, will eliminate the sunspot equilibria. Other examples of imperfectly competitive market structures that result in the existence of multiple equilibria, including endogenous equilibrium fluctuations, are given by Shleifer (1986) and Aghion and Howitt (1990).

63 The possible indeterminacy of equilibrium in a model of this kind results from the combination of an infinite number of distinct goods (the fact that they are consumed at different dates is not essential) together with restrictions upon the set of possible exchanges of these goods for one another (due here to the borrowing constraints). For further discussion of this point and a different example, see Mas-Colell (1989).

64 See, e.g., Taylor (1977), Blanchard (1979), Burmeister (1980), Gouriéroux, Laffont, and Monfort (1982), and Pesaran (1987, section 5.3.2).

65 This is sometimes suggested as a selection criterion by game theorists. It appears, however, that the behavior of experimental subjects in laboratory simulations of non-cooperative games does not always conform to this criterion (Van Huyck et al., 1990). Considerations of stability under learning dynamics may better describe the equilibria that actually occur (Crawford, 1990). The latter approach to equilibrium selection is discussed at length below.

66 For further discussion, see Scarth (1985), Evans and Honkapohja (1984), Evans (1986), and Pesaran (1987).

67 The idea also remains controversial in game theory, since it would rule out

many types of equilibrium phenomena, such as the use of threats to sustain collusion, that are widely viewed as important in empirical applications of the theory of repeated games.

68 Examples of economic models in which this occurs are given in Reichlin (1986) and Woodford (1986a).

69 Because of our special concerns here we do not attempt to survey the entire literature on convergence of learning dynamics to rational expectations equilibrium, to say nothing of the growing literature on learning dynamics as an equilibrium selection criterion in game theory.

70 If one regards the dynamics described in (7.1a,b) as occurring in notional as opposed to real time (the perspective taken by most of the literature on E-stability), then there is no contradiction involved in applying both criteria to the same model. The economic model to which the criteria are applied might be discrete-time, continuous-time, or even a purely static equilibrium model.

71 Guesnerie (1989) argues that iterative E-stability is reminiscent of the mental iterative process involved in the definition of "rationalizable" outcomes in non-cooperative game theory. The idea is developed further in Evans and Guesnerie (1991).

72 Sunspot equilibria can also be weakly E-stable in linear rational expectations models, as is shown by Duffy (1990).

73 Evans and Honkapohja (1990b) find, contrastingly, that endogenous perfect foresight equilibrium cycles can be strongly E-stable in a similar model. A deterministic cycle of (lowest) period k is called "weakly E-stable" if it is stable when the class of theories M consists of all possible price level sequences of period k, and "strongly" stable if stable when the class M consists of all possible price level sequences of period nk, for all integers $n \geq 1$. Since the deterministic cycles considered are just degenerate cases of k-state stationary sunspot equilibria, it seems that the finding of strong E-stability in this case depends upon generalization of the class of theories M in a different way than is considered in Evans (1989).

74 Early analyses of this kind, with attention mainly to the stability under t.e. dynamics of steady state equilibria, include Fuchs and Laroque (1976), Fuchs (1976, 1979), Gouriéroux, Laffont, and Monfort (1983), Champsaur (1984), and Tillmann (1985).

75 We omit conditions needed to ensure existence of well-defined t.e. dynamics (7.4).

76 In addition to the conditions listed, Grandmont and Laroque assume that ψ does not depend upon x_t. This is simply a way of ensuring that the t.e. dynamics (7.4) are well-defined, and is not essential to their result.

77 This selection criterion is closely related to E-stability; it is in fact equivalent to weak iterative E-stability, or to strong (iterative or continuous) E-stability, in the sense defined above in footnote 9 (Evans and Honkapohja, 1990b). Grandmont and Laroque (1990a) provide a partial extension of their results to the case of a temporary equilibrium relation with a predetermined state variable.

78 Grandmont (1985) gives conditions upon the t.e. relation χ under which a

two-cycle satisfying (7.7) is converged to from almost all initial conditions under these dynamics (the "backwards perfect foresight" dynamics).

79 While the adaptive rule assumed is not exactly of the form (7.2), it satisfies conditions (i)–(iii), appropriately interpreted. And the results obtained are consistent with those of Grandmont and Laroque, in the sense that (7.6) implies (7.8), while for a cycle of period $k/2$, (7.8) also implies (7.6), since in that case:

$$\prod_{i=1}^{k} \chi'(\overline{x_i}) = \left[\prod_{i=1}^{k/2} \chi'(\overline{x_i}) \right]^2 \geq 0.$$

80 The convergence results are not the same for all initial conditions in a neighborhood of the steady state, no matter how small the neighborhood is, because this expectation function is not differentiable at the steady state.

81 This is necessary in order for convergence of the regression coefficients, and hence convergence to a "steady state" equilibrium – here understood as constant expectations rather than a constant value for x_t – to be possible in the stochastic case.

82 Marcet and Sargent show that learning dynamics of this kind can be described by a recursive stochastic algorithm of a type analyzed by Ljung (1977, 1983).

83 In addition to coinciding with the selection criterion suggested by Grandmont and Laroque (1976), this condition corresponds to weak continuous E-stability, when M is the two-parameter family of linear econometric models in which x_t equals a constant plus a multiple of x_{t-1} plus an orthogonal disturbance (Evans and Honkapohja, 1990a).

84 The "rationality" of such methods is necessarily of a strictly limited kind, insofar as the desirable properties of the estimators used hold only for data generated by processes in a certain class, and learning by means of such methods usually does not imply that the data observed by agents will in fact be generated by a process in that class.

85 Note that the formula:

$$x_{t+1}^e = \frac{1}{t} \sum_{s=1}^{t} x_s$$

is in many respects similar to an expectation function of the form (7.2). But there is an important difference, which is that the degree of dependence of the forecast upon particular recent past observations (e.g., the dependence of x_{t+1}^e upon x_{t-1}) decreases with time (as the number of past observations increases). This property is critical for the possibility of convergence of the estimate in the case that x_t is stochastic.

86 In a generalization of the weak law of large numbers, recursive algorithms of this sort can be shown to be consistent estimators of the mean under relatively weak assumptions about the distribution from which x_t is drawn each period (see, e.g., Ljung, 1977).

87 Evans and Honkapohja also show that (7.11) is necessary and sufficient for the k-cycle to be weakly continuously E-stable, in the sense defined in footnote 9.

This is an example of the close relation between continuous E-stability and stability under explicit learning dynamics, even though the latter are not defined in continuous time.

88 It is not very common in non-linear stochastic models derived from optimizing behavior for temporary equilibrium to depend only upon the conditional mean of the distribution in this manner. Evans and Honkapohja show, however, that similar results obtain when $\chi(x_{t+1}^e)$ is replaced by the conditional expectation of $\chi(x_{t+1})$, a specification of considerably broader application.

89 For example, in the overlapping generations model of section 5, a given agent's payoff from choosing a particular level of real money balances depends upon the price level now and in the following period, which in turn depend upon aggregate demand for real money balances now and in the following period.

90 See Ljung (1983) for discussion of numerous variants of this approach to stochastic optimization.

91 The fact that the weights decrease exactly as the reciprocal of the number of observations is not crucial to any of the results described below. It is only necessary that one have a sequence of decreasing weights $\{\alpha_m\}$ that converge to zero at a rate that is neither too fast nor too slow, as discussed above.

92 That is, one can show under quite weak assumptions that if (x_t, x_{t+1}) are in fact drawn independently from the same distribution whenever the sunspot state is s, then the stochastic approximation algorithm converges asymptotically with probability one to the optimal action in that state.

93 For example, in Evans' (1989) discussion of E-stability in the overlapping generations model, agents are assumed to consider only stochastic processes in which the price level is the same whenever a given sunspot state occurs. This type of belief implies a need to estimate only a finite number of parameters, but it has the disadvantage that agents should notice that their beliefs are disconfirmed after a finite number of periods, since until a stationary REE is reached, the price level will not in fact be the same each time a given sunspot state occurs.

94 Technically, this is proved under the assumption that the estimates are constrained not to leave a compact set with the property that the trajectories of the differential equation system (7.1b) point inward at all points on the boundary of the set. In a case like that shown in figure 6.9, this is not a strong restriction, since the compact set may include all combinations of estimates for the two states except those implying extreme actions.

Note that, as indicated by Evans (1989), E-stability analysis provides an approximation to the results obtained through an analysis of explicit dynamics. There are some important differences, however. The dynamics (7.1b) imply the existence of disjoint basins of attraction for the two sunspot equilibria, so that it might seem that initial beliefs uniquely determine which sunspot equilibrium will eventually be reached. In the case of the stochastic learning algorithm analyzed by Woodford (1990a), this is not true; there will in many cases be a positive probability of convergence to either sunspot equilibrium, although asymptotically the stochastic trajectory will approach a deterministic trajectory in one basin of attraction or the other. Similarly, the dynamics (7.1b) imply that an initial belief that the sunspot state is irrelevant will never be changed (dynamics starting on the diagonal remain on it forever), and will result in convergence to the monetary steady state. In the case of the stochastic learning algorithm, even agents whose initial estimates are identical for the two states will, with probability one, end up in one of the sunspot equilibria (as long as their initial beliefs are not exactly consistent with the monetary steady state). This is because the learning algorithm (7.13) does not lead agents to adjust the two estimates in an exactly coordinated fashion following subsequent observations.

95 See also Laffond and Lesourne (1990).

96 See Woodford (1990a, sec. 4). This is essentially the point made by Evans (1989) when he argues that sunspot equilibria in this model are weakly but not strongly *E*-stable.

97 For example, in games with a unique rationalizable outcome, a large number of reasonable learning processes converge to it (Gabay and Moulin (1980), Guesnerie (1989), Milgrom and Roberts (1990), Nyarko (1990)). More generally, Milgrom and Roberts have shown that learning by Bayesian agents leads to successive elimination of dominated strategies – in real time, when time is long enough – just as in the definition of the set of rationalizable outcomes. Nyarko also stresses the close connection between the set of rationalizable outcomes and the possible outcomes under Bayesian learning, and shows how a model with a large set of rationalizable outcomes may similarly have a large set of possible kinds of asymptotic behavior in the case of Bayesian learning, even when rational expectations equilibrium is unique. Furthermore, Cho (1990) shows that an extension of the common knowledge assumption from the rules of the game to the learning processes as well (even when these are not Bayesian) may drastically reduce the set of attainable equilibria.

98 It may be wondered what sort of operating procedures for the monetary authority make possible feedback of this kind from the current rate of inflation to current money growth. This is clearest in the case of the Lucas–Stokey model discussed in section 6.1, in the case where there exists trading in additional securities. For in that model, a policy rule of the Grandmont type is equivalent to a rule

$$i_{t+1} = f(i_t, p_t/p_{t-1})$$

specifying the nominal interest rate i_{t+1} (on some riskless one-period bond in terms of which the central bank conducts open market operations) in period $t+1$ (i.e., on bonds purchased in period $t+1$ and maturing in period $t+2$) as a function of the period t interest rate and the rate of inflation between periods $t-1$ and t. Accumulation of the one-period bond, together with (6.5), implies that $1+i_t = G(M_t/p_t)/F(M_t/p_t)$, where F and G are defined as in (6.5).

99 The consequences of interest-rate targeting versus money supply targeting for the existence of sunspot equilibria are also considered, in the context of a different model, in Smith (1989c). See also the discussion in Woodford (1990c, sections 3.2 and 3.3).

100 Examples of this kind include Reichlin (1986) and Woodford (1986a, 1990c).

101 The issue has, in particular, been neglected in the literature on stabilizing sunspot equilibria in the overlapping generations model, where the conditions required for a stabilization policy to bring about an actual Pareto improvement are particularly stringent owing to the differing interests of consumers in different generations. An important exception is the analysis of Chattopadhyay (1990).

102 Conditions for welfare improvement in monetary models of this type should probably not be taken too seriously, since the models omit the main reason why variable inflation is thought to be undesirable, namely distortions of supply decisions in the case of price level surprises as in the models of Lucas (1972, 1989). Sunspot equilibria ought to be studied in models of this kind; for an early exploration, see Chiappori and Guesnerie (1988a).

103 Further stipulations under which one may show that the steady state is the only equilibrium of any kind are explained in Woodford (1988b).

104 If one considers still lower values of ρ than those in the range (8.6), the level of welfare associated with the two-cycle becomes a decreasing function of ρ, and indeed, for low enough values of ρ, it comes to be higher than the level of welfare in the steady state with $\rho = a/3$. But it has at any rate been shown that the lowest level of welfare is not monotonic in the rate of money growth, and hence that greater care must be taken in concluding that a lower rate of money growth is better, as would be suggested by a simple comparison of steady states. Choosing a rate of money growth in just the right range to have a high level of welfare even in equilibria near the two-cycle may be difficult, in the absence of precise information about parameters, since too low a value for ρ may result in non-existence of monetary equilibrium (see Woodford, 1988b). Furthermore, the mere fact that the level of welfare associated with the two-cycle is not too low for ρ in this range does not establish that the *worst* possible sunspot equilibrium might not involve quite low welfare.

105 The association of lower rates of money growth with the existence of sunspot equilibria and endogenous cycles is in fact reasonably general in this class of models; Woodford (1988b) establishes general conditions under which sunspot equilibria necessarily exist for low enough rates of money growth, and under which the steady state is the unique equilibrium, for economies of the Lucas–Stokey type. These results are closely related to Brock's (1974) findings regarding the multiplicity of equilibria in representative consumer economies with money in the utility function, in the case of low rates of money growth. Grandmont (1986) also gives conditions, for a class of overlapping generations models, under which a high enough rate of money growth guarantees that the steady state is the unique stationary equilibrium, whereas cycles and stationary sunspot equilibria may be possible for lower rates of money growth. Here again a simple comparison of the steady states corresponding to alternative rates of money growth would lead one to prefer lower rates of money growth (at least in the range $\pi \geq 0$), since under quite weak assumptions, lower-money-growth steady states Pareto dominate higher-money-growth ones.

Additional cases where policies that increase the efficiency of the "minimum state variable solution" can result in existence of sunspot equilibria are provided by Smith (1988, 1989b), who analyzes economies in which sunspot equilibria become possible in the case of policies that increase the efficiency of financial intermediation. The consequences of monetary policy for the existence of sunspot equilibria are also analyzed in Smith (1989a, 1989c).

Bibliography

Aghion, P. and P. Howitt (1990), "A Model of Growth through Creative Destruction," mimeo, MIT, April.

Aiyagari, S.R. (1988), "Economic Fluctuations without Shocks to Fundamentals: Or Does the Stock Market Dance to its Own Music?" *Quarterly Review*, Federal Reserve Bank of Minneapolis, Winter.

(1989), "Can There be Short-Period Deterministic Cycles when People are Long Lived?" *Quarterly Journal of Economics*, 104: 163–85.

Allais, M. (1947), *Economie et Intérêt*, Paris: Imprimerie National.

Arnott, R. and J.E. Stiglitz (1985), "Randomization with Asymmetric Information: A Simplified Exposition," Queen's University Discussion Paper 59.

Arrow, K.J. (1953), "Le role des valeurs boursières pour la répartition la meilleure des risques," *Econometrie*, Paris, CNRS, pp. 41–8. English translation as "The Role of Securities in the Optimal Allocation of Risk-Bearing," *Review of Economic Studies*, 31: 91–6.

Aumann, R. (1987), "Correlated Equilibrium as an Expression of Bayesian Rationality," *Econometrica*, 55: 1–18.

Aumann, R., J. Peck, and K. Shell (forthcoming), "Asymmetric Information and Sunspot Equilibria: A Family of Simple Examples," in H.W. Kuhn (ed.), *Models of Incomplete Information and Bounded Rationality*, Springer-Verlag.

Azariadis, C. (1981), "Self-Fulfilling Prophecies," *Journal of Economic Theory*, 25: 380–96.

Azariadis, C. and R. Guesnerie (1982), "Prophéties créatrices et persistance des théories," *Review Economique*, 33: 787–806.

(1986), "Sunspots and Cycles," *Review of Economic Studies* 53: 725–36.

Balasko, Y. (1983), "Extrinsic Uncertainty Revisited," *Journal of Economic Theory*, 31: 203–10.

(forthcoming), "Equivariant General Equilibrium Theory," *Journal of Economic Theory*.

Balasko, Y., D. Cass, and K. Shell (1988), "Market Participation and Sunspot Equilibria," CAE Working Paper, Cornell University.

Balasko, Y. and K. Shell (1980), "The Overlapping Generations Model: I," *Journal of Economic Theory*, 3: 307–22.

(1981), "The Overlapping Generations Model: II," *Journal of Economic Theory*, 4: 112–42.

Becker, R.A. and C. Foias (1988), "A Characterization of Ramsey Equilibrium," *Journal of Economic Theory*, 44: 301–20.

Benhabib, J. and R.M. Day (1980), "Erratic Accumulation," *Economic Letters*, 6: 113–17.

(1981), "Rational Choice and Erratic Behavior," *Review of Economic Studies*, 48: 459–72.

(1982), "A Characterization of Erratic Dynamics in the Overlapping Generations Model," *Journal of Economic Dynamics and Control*, 4: 37–55.

Benhabib, J. and G. Laroque, "On Competitive Cycles in Production Economies," *Journal of Economic Theory*, 45: 145–70.

Benhabib, J. and K. Nishimura (1979), "The Hopf Bifurcation and the Existence and Stability of Closed Orbits in Multisector Models of Optimal Growth," *Journal of Economic Theory*, 21: 421–44.

(1985), "Competitive Equilibrium Cycles," *Journal of Economic Theory*, 35: 284–306.

Benhabib, J. and A. Rustichini (1989), "Equilibrium Cycling with Small Discounting: A Note," mimeo, New York University, May.

Bernheim, B.D. (1984), "Rationalizable Strategic Behavior," *Econometrica*, 52: 1007–28.

Bewley, T. (1980), "The Optimum Quantity of Money," in J.H. Kareken and N. Wallace (eds.), *Models of Monetary Economies*, Minneapolis: Federal Reserve Bank of Minneapolis.

(1982), "An Integration of Equilibrium Theory and Turnpike Theory," *Journal of Mathematical Economics*, 10: 233–68.

(1983), "A Difficulty with the Optimum Quantity of Money," *Econometrica*, 51: 1485–504.

(1986), "Dynamic Implications of the Form of the Budget Constraint," in H.F. Sonnenschein (ed.), *Models of Economic Dynamics*, New York: Springer-Verlag.

Binmore, K. (1987), "Modelling Rational Players," *Economics and Philosophy*, 3: 179–214.

Blanchard, O.J. (1979), "Backward and Forward Solutions for Economies with Rational Expectations," *American Economic Review Papers and Proceedings*, 69: May, 114–18.

Blanchard, O.J. and C.M. Kahn (1980), "The Solution of Linear Difference Models under Rational Expectations," *Econometrica*, 48: 1305–11.

Blatt, J.M. (1978), "On the Econometric Approach to Business-Cycle Analysis," *Oxford Economic Papers* 30: 292–300.

(1983), *Dynamic Economic Systems*, Armonk, NY: M.E. Sharpe.

Blume, L. (1982), "New Techniques for the Study of Dynamic Economic Models," *Journal of Mathematical Economics*, 9: 61–70.

Boldrin, M. (1989), "Paths of Optimal Accumulation in Two-Sector Models," in W.A. Barnett, J. Geweke, and K. Shell (eds.), *Economic Complexity: Chaos, Sunspots, Bubbles, and Nonlinearity*, New York: Cambridge University Press.

Boldrin, M. and L. Montrucchio (1986), "On the Indeterminacy of Capital Accumulation Paths", *Journal of Economic Theory*, 40: 26–39.

Boldrin, M. and M. Woodford (1990), "Equilibrium Models Displaying Endogenous Fluctuations and Chaos," *Journal of Monetary Economics*, 25: 189–222.

Brock, W.A. (1974), "Money and Growth: The Case of Long-Run Perfect Foresight," *International Economic Review*, 15: 750–77.

(1988), "Nonlinearities and Complex Dynamics in Economics and Finance," in P. Anderson, K. Arrow, and D. Pines (eds.), *The Economy as an Evolving Complex System*, New York: Addison-Wesley.

Brock, W.A. and G. Chamberlain (1984), "Spectral Analysis Cannot Tell a Macro-Econometrician whether His Time Series Came from a Stochastic Economy or from a Deterministic Economy," SSRI Working Paper 8419, University of Wisconsin, November.

Brock, W.A. and J.A. Scheinkman (1980), "Some Remarks on Monetary Policy in an Overlapping Generations Model," in J.H. Kareken and N. Wallace (eds.), *Models of Monetary Economies*, Minneapolis: Federal Reserve Bank.

Broze, L., C. Gouriéroux, and A. Szafarz (1991), *Reduced Forms of Rational Expectations Models*, Harwood Academic.

Burmeister, E. (1980), "On Some Conceptual Issues in Rational Expectations Modelling," *Journal of Money, Credit and Banking*, 12: 800–16.

Burnell, S. (1989), "Intrinsic and Extrinsic Uncertainty," mimeo, Emmanuel College, Cambridge University.

(1990), "Sunspots," in F.H. Hahn (ed.), *The Economics of Missing Markets, Information and Games*, Oxford: Oxford University Press.

Calvo, G.A. (1978), "On the Indeterminacy of Interest Rates and Wages with Perfect Foresight," *Journal of Economic Theory*, 19: 321–37.

Caspi, Y. (1974), "Optimum Allocation of Risk in a Market with Many Traders," in J. Drèze (ed.), *Uncertainty, Equilibrium, Optimality*, London: Macmillan.

Cass, D. (1989), "Sunspots and Incomplete Financial Markets: The Leading Example," in G. Feiwel (ed.), *The Economics of Imperfect Competition: Joan Robinson and Beyond*, London: Macmillan.

Cass, D., M. Okuno, and I. Zilcha (1979), "The Role of Money in Supporting the Pareto Optimality of Competitive Equilibrium in Consumption-Loan Type Models," *Journal of Economic Theory*, 20: 41–80.

Cass, D. and H. Polemarchakis (1989), "Convexity and Sunspots: A Remark," *Journal of Economic Theory*, 52: 433–9 (1990).

Cass, D. and K. Shell (1983), "Do Sunspots Matter?" *Journal of Political Economy*, 91: 193–227.

(1989), "Sunspot Equilibrium in an Overlapping Generations Economy with an Idealized Contingent Commodities Market," in W. Barnett, J. Geweke, and K. Shell (eds.), *Economic Complexity: Chaos, Sunspots, Bubbles and Nonlinearity*, Cambridge: Cambridge University Press, pp. 3–20.

Champsaur, P. (1984), "On the Stability of Rational Expectations Equilibria," CORE d.p. no. 8324, Université Catholique de Louvain, 1983. French version in *Cahiers du Séminaire d'Econométrie*, 26: 47–65.

Chatterjee, S., R. Cooper, and B. Ravikumar (1990), "Participation Dynamics: Sunspots and Cycles," NBER Working Paper 3438, September.

Chattopadhyay, S.K. (1990), "Optimal Improvement Policies for Stationary Sunspot Equilibria in an Overlapping Generations Economy: The Central Role of the Golden Rule Allocation," Institute for Decision Sciences Discussion Paper 90-21, SUNY Stony Brook, November.

Chiappori, P.-A., P.Y. Geoffard, and R. Guesnerie (1989), "Sunspot Fluctuations Around a Steady State: The Case of Multidimensional One-Step Forward Looking Economic Models," mimeo, DELTA, Paris. Forthcoming, *Econometrica*.

Chiappori, P.-A. and R. Guesnerie (1988a), "Lucas Equation, Indeterminacy, and Non-Neutrality: An Example," Doc. de travail no. 88-06, DELTA, Paris. Forthcoming in D. Gale and O. Hart (eds.), *In Honor of Frank Hahn*, Cambridge, MA: MIT Press.

(1988b), "Self-Fulfilling Theories: The Sunspot Connection," mimeo, EHESS, Paris.

(1988c), "Endogenous Fluctuations under Rational Expectations," *European Economic Review*, 32: 389–97.

(1989a), "On Stationary Sunspot Equilibria of Order k," in W. Barnett, J. Geweke, and K. Shell (eds.), *Economic Complexity: Chaos, Sunspots, Bubbles and Nonlinearity*, Cambridge: Cambridge University Press.

(1989b), "Sunspot Equilibria in Sequential Markets Models," mimeo, DELTA, Paris. Forthcoming in W. Hildenbrand and H. Sonnenschein (eds.), *Handbook of Mathematical Economics*, Volume IV, North-Holland.

(1990), "Anticipations, indéterminations et non neutralité de la monnaie,"*Ann. Economie et Statistiques*, 19: 1–25.

Collet, P. and J.-P. Eckmann (1980), *Iterated Maps on the Interval as Dynamical Systems*, Boston: Birkhauser.

Crawford, V.P. (1990), "An 'Evolutionary' Explanation of Van Huyck, Battalio, and Beil's Experimental Results on Coordination," UCSD Department of Economics Paper 89-28R, September.

Dana, R.-A. and P. Malgrange (1984), "The Dynamics of a Discrete Version of a Growth Cycle Model," in J.P. Ancot (ed.), *Analyzing the Structure of Econometric Models*, Amsterdam: Nijhoff.

Day, R.M. (1982), "Irregular Growth Cycles," *American Economic Review*, 72: 406–14.

(1983), "The Emergence of Chaos from Classical Economic Growth," *Quarterly Journal of Economics*, 98: 201–13.

DeCanio, S.J. (1979), "Rational Expectations and Learning from Experience," *Quarterly Journal of Economics*, 93: 47–58.

Dechert, W.D. (1984), "Does Optimal Growth Preclude Chaos? A Theorem on Monotonicity," *Z. Nationalokonomie*, 44: 57–61.

Deneckere, R. and K.L. Judd (1986), "Cyclical and Chaotic Behavior in a Dynamic Equilibrium Model, with Implications for Fiscal Policy," mimeo, Northwestern University, June.

Deneckere, R. and S. Pelikan (1986), "Competitive Chaos," *Journal of Economic Theory*, 40: 13–25.

Devaney, R.L. (1986), *An Introduction to Chaotic Dynamical Systems*, Menlo Park, CA: Benjamin Cummings.

Diamond, P.A. (1965), "National Debt in a Neoclassical Growth Model," *American Economic Review*, 55: 1126–50.

Diamond, P.A. and D. Fudenberg (1989), "An Example of Rational Expectations Business Cycles in Search Equilibrium," *Journal of Political Economy*, 97 606–19.

Dierker, E. (1972), "Two Remarks on the Number of Equilibria of an Economy," *Econometrica*, 40: 951–3.

Drugeon, J.-P. (1990), "An Equilibrium Model with Endogenous Cycles and Global Bifurcations in the Long Run," mimeo, Université de Paris I, December.

Duffie, D., J. Geanakoplos, A. Mas-Colell, and A. McLennan (1988), "Stationary Markov Equilibria," mimeo.

Duffy, J. (1990), "Convergence of Learning Rules as a Selection Criterion in Linear Rational Expectations Models with Multiple Equilibria," mimeo, UCLA, November.

Evans, G.W. (1983), "The Stability of Rational Expectations in Macroeconomic Models," in R. Frydman and E.S. Phelps (eds.), *Individual Forecasting and Aggregate Outcomes*, Cambridge: Cambridge University Press.

(1985), "Expectational Stability and the Multiple Equilibria Problem in Rational Expectations Models," *Quarterly Journal of Economics*, 100: 1217–33.

(1986), "Selection Criteria for Models with Non-Uniqueness," *Journal of Monetary Economics*, 18: 147–57.

(1989), "The Fragility of Sunspots and Bubbles," *Journal of Monetary Economics*, 23: 297–317.

Evans, G.W. and R. Guesnerie (1992), "Rationalizability, Strong Rationality, and Expectational Stability," mimeo, DELTA, Paris, no. 92–03.

Evans, G.W. and S. Honkapohja (1984), "A Complete Characterization of ARMA Solutions to Linear Rational Expectations Models," IMSSS Tech. Report no. 439, Stanford University.

(1990a), "Learning, Convergence and Stability with Multiple Rational Expectations Equilibria," STICERD Discussion Paper TE/90/212, London School of Economics, June.

(1990b), "Convergence of Recursive Learning Mechanisms to Steady States and Cycles in Stochastic Nonlinear Models," mimeo, London School of Economics, November.

Farmer, R.E.A. (1986), "Deficits and Cycles," *Journal of Economic Theory*, 40: 77–88.

(1989), "The Lucas Critique, Policy Invariance, and Multiple Equilibria," UCLA Department of Economics, Working Paper 551, March.

(1990), "Sticky Prices," mimeo, UCLA, January.

Farmer, R.E.A. and M. Woodford (1984), "Self Fulfilling Prophecies and the Business Cycle," CARESS Paper 84-12, University of Pennsylvania, April. Published in Spanish translation in *Cuadernos Economics de ICE*, Madrid, 35 (1989).

Farqharson, R. (1969), *Theory of Voting*, New Haven: Yale University Press.

Feigenbaum, M.J. (1978), "Quantitative Universality for a Class of Nonlinear Transformations," *Journal of Statistical Physics*, 19: 25–52.

Foley, D.K. (1991), "A Contribution to the Theory of Business Cycles," Barnard College Department of Economics Working Paper 91-03, May.

Friedman, M. (1969), "The Optimum Quantity of Money," in *The Optimum Quantity of Money and Other Essays*, Chicago: Aldine.

Fuchs, G. (1976), "Asymptotic Stability of Stationary Temporary Equilibria and Changes in Expectations," *Journal of Economic Theory*, 13: 201–16.

(1977), "Formation of Expectations: A Model in Temporary General Equilibrium Theory," *Journal of Mathematical Economics*, 4: 167–88.

Fuchs, G. and G. Laroque (1976), "Dynamics of Temporary Equilibria and Expectations," *Econometrica*, 44: 1157–78.

Futia, C. (1982), "Invariant Distributions and the Limiting Behavior of Markovian Economic Models," *Econometrica*, 50: 377–407.

Gabay, D. and H. Moulin (1980), "On the Uniqueness and Stability of Nash Equilibria in Non-cooperative Games," in Bensoussan, Kleindorfer, and Tatierd (eds.), *Applied Stochastic Control in Economics and Management Science*, North-Holland.

Gale, D. (1973), "Pure Exchange Equilibria of Dynamic Economic Models," *Journal of Economic Theory*, 6.

Galor, O. (1990), "A Two-Sector Overlapping Generations Model: A Characterization of the Dynamical System," Brown University Department of Economics Working Paper, 90-23, August.

Geanakoplos, J. and H. Polemarchakis (forthcoming), "Infinite Horizon Models," *Handbook of Mathematical Economics*, vol. IV, North-Holland.

Goodwin, R.M. (1951), "The Nonlinear Accelerator and the Persistence of Business Cycles," *Econometrica*, 19: 1–17.

Gouriéroux, C., J.J. Laffont, and A. Monfort (1982), "Rational Expectations in Dynamic Linear Models: Analysis of the Solutions," *Econometrica*, 50: 409–25.

(1983), "Révision adaptive des anticipations et convergence vers les anticipations rationelles," *Economie Appliquée*, 36: 9–26.

Grandmont, J.-M. (1985a), "On Endogenous Competitive Business Cycles," *Econometrica*, 53: 995–1046.

(1985b), "Cycles concurrentiels endogènes," *Cahiers du séminaire d'Econométrie*, 49-81.

(1986), "Stabilizing Competitive Business Cycles," *Journal of Economic Theory*, 40: 57–76.

(1989), "Local Bifurcations and Stationary Sunspots," in W. Barnett, J. Geweke, and K. Shell (eds.), *Economic Complexity: Chaos, Sunspots, Bubbles and Nonlinearity*, Cambridge: Cambridge University Press, 45–60.

Grandmont, J.-M. and G. Laroque (1986), "Stability of Cycles and Expectations," *Journal of Economic Theory*, 40: 138–51.

(1990a), "Stability, Expectations and Predetermined Variables," in P. Champsaur *et al.* (eds.), *Essays in Honor of Edmond Malinvaud*, vol. I, Cambridge, MA: MIT Press.

(1990b), "Economic Dynamics with Learning: Some Instability Examples," CEPREMAP Working Paper 9007, Paris, April.

Grandmont, J.-M. and P. Malgrange (1986), "Nonlinear Economic Dynamics: Introduction," *Journal of Economic Theory*, 40: 3–12.

Grandmont, J.-M. and Y. Younes (1972), "On the Role of Money and the Existence of a Monetary Equilibrium," *Review of Economic Studies*, 39: 355–72.

——— (1973), "On the Efficiency of a Monetary Equilibrium," *Review of Economic Studies*, 40: 149–65.

Guckenheimer, J. and P. Holmes (1983), *Nonlinear Oscillations, Dynamical Systems, and Bifurcations of Vector Fields*, New York: Springer-Verlag.

Guesnerie, R. (1986), "Stationary Sunspot Equilibria in an *n*-commodity World," *Journal of Economic Theory*, 40: 103–28.

——— (1989a), "Modern Economic Theory and the Multiplicity Issue," *Economic Record*, 77–81.

——— (1989b), "An Exploration of the Eductive Justification of the Rational Expectations Hypothesis," mimeo, DELTA, Paris. Forthcoming, *American Economic Review*.

——— (1989c), "A propos de la rationalité des anticipations rationelles," in *La théorie économique face aux fluctuations des marchés financiers*, Economica, 29-43.

Guesnerie, R. and J.Y. Jaffray (1974), "Optimality of Equilibria of Plans, Prices and Price Expectations," in J. Drèze (ed.), *Uncertainty, Equilibrium, Optimality*, London: Macmillan, pp. 71–86.

Guesnerie, R. and J.-J. Laffont (1988), "Notes on Sunspot Equilibria in Finite Economies," in P. Champsaur *et al.* (eds), *Volume en l'honneur d'Edmond Malinvaud*, Economica-EHESS, 118-43. (English edition: *Essays in Honor of Edmond Malinvaud*, Cambridge, MA: MIT Press, 1991.)

Guesnerie, R. and M. Woodford (1991), "Stability of Cycles with Adaptive Learning Rules," in W.A. Barnett *et al.* (eds.), *Equilibrium Theory and Applications: Proceedings of the Sixth International Symposium in Economic Theory and Econometrics*, Cambridge: Cambridge University Press.

Hahn, F.H. (1982), *Money and Inflation*, Oxford: Basil Blackwell.

Hammour, M. (1988), "Increasing Returns and Endogenous Business Cycles," mimeo, MIT, October.

Hayek, F.A. (1933), *Monetary Theory and the Trade Cycle*, New York: Harcourt Brace.

Hens, T. (1990), "Sunspot Equilibria in Finite Horizon Models with Incomplete Markets," mimeo.

Hernandez, A.D. (1988), "The Dynamics of Competitive Equilibrium Allocations with Borrowing Constraints," mimeo, University of Rochester.

Hicks, J.R. (1981), *Theory of the Trade Cycle*, Oxford: Oxford University Press.

Howitt, P. (1990), "Wicksell's Cumulative Process as Non-Convergence to Rational Expectations," Research Report 9004, University of W. Ontario, Department of Economics, February.

Howitt, P. and R.P. McAfee (1988), "Stability of Equilibria with Trade-Externalities," *Quarterly Journal of Economics*, 103:261–77.

——— (1990), "Animal Spirits," Research Report 9005, University of W. Ontario, Department of Economics, April.

Jullien, B. (1988), "Competitive Business Cycles in an Overlapping Generations

Economy with Productive Investment," *Journal of Economic Theory*, 46: 45–65.

Kaldor, N. (1940), "A Model of the Trade Cycle," *Economic Journal*, 50: 78–92.

Kalecki, M. (1935), "A Macroeconomic Theory of Business Cycles," *Econometrica*, 3: 327–44.

Kehoe, T.J. and D.K. Levine (1984a), "Intertemporal Separability in Overlapping Generations Models," *Journal of Economic Theory*, 34: 216–26.

(1984b), "Regularity in Overlapping Generations Exchange Models," *Journal of Mathematical Economics*, 13: 69–93.

(1985), "Comparative Statics and Perfect Foresight," *Econometrica*, 53: 433–54.

Kehoe, T.J., D.K. Levine, A. Mas-Colell, and W.R. Zame, "Determinacy of Equlibrium in Large-Square Economies," *Journal of Mathematical Economics*, 18: 231–62.

Kehoe, T.J., D.K. Levine, A. Mas-Colell, and M. Woodford (1991), "Gross Substitutability in Large-Square Economies," *Journal of Economic Theory*, 54: 1–25.

Kehoe, T.J., D.K. Levine, and P. Romer (1989), "Characterizing Equilibria of Models with Externalities and Taxes as Solutions to Optimization Problems," mimeo, Research Department, Federal Reserve Bank of Minneapolis, April.

Kehoe, T.J., D.K. Levine, and M. Woodford (forthcoming), "The Optimum Quantity of Money Revisited," in D. Gale and O. Hart (eds.), *In Honor of Frank Hahn*, Cambridge, MA: MIT Press.

Kimball, M.S. (1989), "Labor Market Dynamics when Unemployment is a Worker Discipline Device," NBER Working Paper 2967, May.

Kirman, A. (1983), "On Mistaken Beliefs and Resultant Equilibria," in R. Frydman and E.S. Phelps (eds.), *Individual Forecasting and Aggregate Outcomes*, Cambridge: Cambridge University Press, pp. 147–68.

Laffond, G. and J. Lesourne (1990), "Un modèle dynamique avec etats stables à taches solaires," mimeo, Paris.

Laitner, J. (1989), "Sunspot Equilibrium and Stability," *Journal of Economic Theory*, 47: 39–50.

Lasota, A. and J.A. Yorke (1973), "On the Existence of Invariant Measures for Piecewise Monotonic Transformations," *Transactions of the American Mathematical Society*, 186: 481–488.

Levine, D.K. (1986), "Borrowing Contraints and Expansionary Policy," mimeo, UCLA.

(1987), "Efficiency and the Value of Money," mimeo, UCLA.

Li, T.Y. and J.A. Yorke (1975), "Period Three Implies Chaos," *American Mathematical Monthly*, 82: 985–92.

(1978), "Ergodic Transformations from an Interval into Itself," *Transactions of the American Mathematical Society*, 235: 183–92.

Ljung, L. (1977), "Analysis of Recursive Stochastic Algorithms," *IEEE Trans. Auto. Control* AC-22: 551–7.

Ljung, L. and T. Soderstrom (1983), *Theory and Practice of Recursive Identification*, Cambridge, MA: MIT Press.

Lorenz, H.W. (1989), *Nonlinear Dynamical Economies and Chaotic Motions*, New York: Springer-Verlag.

Lucas, R.E., Jr. (1972), "Expectations and the Neutrality of Money," *Journal of Economic Theory*, 4: 103–24.

(1978), "Asset Prices in an Exchange Economy," *Econometrica*, 46: 1429–45.

(1986), "Adaptive Behavior and Economic Theory," *Journal of Business*, 59: S401–S426.

(1989), "Consequences of Monetary Surprises when Prices are Set in Advance," mimeo, University of Chicago, November.

Lucas, R.E., Jr. and T.J. Sargent (eds.) (1981), *Rational Expectations and Econometric Practice*, Minneapolis: University of Minnesota Press.

Lucas, R.E., Jr. and N.L. Stokey (1983), "Optimal Fiscal and Monetary Policy in an Economy without Capital," *Journal of Monetary Economics*, 12: 55–93.

(1987), "Money and Interest in a Cash-in-Advance Economy," *Econometrica*, 55: 491–514.

Luce, R.D. and H. Raiffa (1957), *Games and Decisions*, New York: Wiley.

Manuelli, R. and J. Peck (1988), "Sunspot-Like Effects of Random Endowments," mimeo, Northwestern University, July.

Marcet, A. and T.J. Sargent (1988), "The Fate of Systems with 'Adaptive' Expectations," *American Economic Review Papers and Proceedings*, 78, May, 168–72.

(1989a), "Convergence of Least Squares Learning Mechanisms in Self-Referential Stochastic Models," *Journal of Economic Theory*, 48: 337–68.

(1989b), "Convergence of Least Squares Learning in Environments with Hidden State Variables and Private Information," *Journal of Political Economy*, 97: 1306–22.

Mas-Colell, A. (1989), "Indeterminacy in Incomplete Market Economies," mimeo, Harvard University, August.

(1990), "Three Observations on Sunspots and Asset Redundancy," in D. Gale and O. Hart (eds.), *In Honor of Frank Hahn*, Cambridge, MA: MIT Press.

Maskin, E. and J. Tirole (1988a), "Models of Dynamic Oligopoly," *Econometrica*, 56: 549–69.

(1988b), "Models of Dynamic Oligopoly," *Econometrica*, 56: 571–99.

(1987), "Correlated Equilibria and Sunspots," *Journal of Economic Theory*, 43: 364–73.

Matsuyama, K. (1989a), "Endogenous Price Fluctuations in an Optimizing Model of a Monetary Economy," CMSEMS Discussion Paper 825, Northwestern University, March.

(1989b), "Serial Correlation of Sunspot Equilibria (Rational Bubbles) in Two Popular Models of Monetary Economies," CMSEMS Discussion Paper 827, Northwestern University, March.

(forthcoming), "Increasing Returns, Industrialization, and Indeterminacy of Equilibrium," *Quarterly Journal of Economics*.

May, R.B. (1976), "Simple Mathematical Models with Very Complicated Dynamics," *Nature*, 261: 459–67.

McCallum, B.T. (1983a), "The Role of Overlapping Generations Models in Monetary Economics," *Carnegie-Rochester Conference Series*, 18: 9–44.

(1983b), "On Non-Uniqueness in Linear Rational Expectations Models: An Attempt at Perspective," *Journal of Monetary Economics*, 11: 139–68.

McKenzie, L.W. (1986), "Optimal Economic Growth, Turnpike Theorems and Complex Dynamics," in K.J. Arrow and M.D. Intriligator (eds.), *Handbook of Mathematical Economics*, vol. III, Amsterdam: North-Holland.

Melese, F. and W. Transue (1986), "Unscrambling Chaos through Thick and Thin," *Quarterly Journal of Economics*, 51: 419–23.

Montrucchio, L. (1987), "Dynamical Systems that Solve Continuous Time Infinite Horizon Optimization Problems: Anything Goes," mimeo, Politecnico di Torino, October.

Moulin, H. (1979), "Dominance Solvable Voting Schemes," *Econometrica*, 47: 1337–351.

Muller, W.J. and M. Woodford (1988), "Determinacy of Equilibrium in Stationary Economies with both Finite and Infinite Lived Consumers," *Journal of Economic Theory*, 46: 255–90.

Murphy, K.M., A. Shleifer, and R.W. Vishny, "Building Blocks of Market Clearing Business Cycle Models," in O.J. Blanchard and S. Fischer (eds.), *NBER Macroeconomics Annual 1989*, Cambridge, MA: MIT Press.

Muth, J. (1961), "Rational Expectations and the Theory of Price Movements," *Econometrica*, 29: 315–35.

Nyarko, Y. (1990), "Bayesian Rationality and Learning without Common Priors," mimeo, New York University.

Peck, J. (1988), "On the Existence of Sunspot Equilibria in an Overlapping Generations Model," *Journal of Economic Theory*, 44: 19–42.

Peck, J. and K. Shell (1988), "Market Uncertainty: Correlated Equilibrium and Sunspot Equilibrium in Imperfectly Competitive Economies," CAE Working Paper 88-22, Cornell University, May.

(1989), "On the Non-equivalence of the Arrow-Securities Game and the Contingent-Commodities Game," in W. Barnett, J. Geweke, and K. Shell (eds.), *Economic Complexity: Chaos, Sunspots, Bubbles and Nonlinearity*, Cambridge: Cambridge University Press, pp. 61–85.

Pesaran, M.H. (1987), *The Limits to Rational Expectations*, Oxford: Basil Blackwell.

Prechac, A. (1990), "Etudes sur des extensions du modèle d'équilibre général," Thesis, University of Paris I.

Radner, R. (1972), "Equilibrium of Plans, Prices and Price Expectations," *Econometrica*, 40: 289–303.

Reichlin, P. (1986), "Equilibrium Cycles in an Overlapping Generations Model with Production," *Journal of Economic Theory*, 40: 89–102.

Ruelle, D. (1989), *Elements of Differentiable Dynamics and Bifurcation Theory*, New York: Academic Press.

Ruelle, D. and F. Takens (1971), "On the Nature of Turbulence," *Communications in Mathematical Physics*, 20: 167–92.

Ryder, H.E., Jr. and G.M. Heal (1973), "Optimum Growth with Intertemporally Dependent Preferences," *Review of Economic Studies*, 40: 1–32.

Sakai, H. and H. Tokumaru (1980), "Autocorrelations of a Certain Chaos," *IEEE Transactions in Acoustics, Speech and Signal Processing*, 28: 588–90.

Samuelson, P.A. (1939), "Interactions Between the Multiplier Analysis and the Principle of Acceleration," *Review of Economic Statistics*, 21: 75–8.

(1958), "An Exact Consumption Loan Model of Interest with or without the Social Contrivance of Money," *Journal of Political Economy*, 66: 467–82.

(1973), "Optimality of Profit, Including Prices Under Ideal Planning," *Proceedings of the National Academy of Sciences (USA)*, 70: 2109–11.

Sargent, T.J. (1986), *Rational Expectations and Inflation*, New York: Harper & Row.

(1987), *Dynamic Macroeconomic Theory*, Cambridge, MA: Harvard University Press.

Sargent, T.J. and N. Wallace (1984), "Exploding Inflation," mimeo, University of Minnesota, January.

Sarkovskii, A.N. (1964), "Coexistence of Cycles of a Continuous Map of the Line Into Itself," *Ukrain. Matem. Zhur.*, 16: 61–71.

Scarth, W.M. (1985), "A Note on Non-Uniqueness in Rational Expectations Models," *Journal of Monetary Economics*, 15: 247–54.

Scheinkman, J.A. (1976), "On Optimal Steady States of *n*-Sector Growth Models when Utility is Discounted," *Journal of Economic Theory*, 12: 11–30.

(1990), "Nonlinearities in Economic Dynamics," *Economic Journal*, 100: 33–48 (Conference).

Schumpeter, J.A. (1939), *Business Cycles*, New York: McGraw-Hill.

Shell, K. (1977), "Monnaie et allocation intertemporelle," mimeo, Séminaire d'Econométrie Roy-Malinvaud, Paris, November.

(1989), "Sunspot Equilibrium," in J. Eatwell, M. Milgate and P. Newman (eds.), *The New Palgrave: A Dictionary of Economics*, vol. IV, Macmillan, pp. 549–51.

Shell, K., and R. Wright (1989), "Indivisibilies, Contracts, Lotteries and Sunspots," mimeo.

Shleifer, A. (1986), "Implementation Cycles," *Journal of Political Economy*, 94: 1163–90.

Sieveking, M. and W. Semmler (1990), "Optimization without Planning: Economic Growth and Resource Exploitation with a Discount Rate Tending to Infinity," mimeo, Department of Mathematics, University of Frankfurt, May.

Sims, C.A. (1986), "Comments [on Grandmont paper]," in H.F. Sonnenschein (ed.), *Models of Economic Dynamics*, New York: Springer-Verlag.

Slutsky, E. (1937), "The Summation of Random Causes as the Source of Cyclical Processes," *Econometrica*, 5: 105–46.

Smale, S. (1967), "Differentiable Dynamical Systems," *Bulletin of the American Mathematical Society*, 73: 747–817.

Smith, B.D. (1988), "Legal Restrictions, 'Sunspots', and Peel's Bank Act: The Real Bills Doctrine versus the Quantity Theory Reconsidered," *Journal of Political Economy*, 96: 3–19.

(1989a), "Legal Restrictions, 'Sunspots,' and Cycles," *Journal of Economic Theory*, 47: 369–92.

(1989b), "Interest on Reserves and Sunspot Equilibria: Friedman's Proposal Reconsidered," mimeo, University of West Ontario.

(1989c), "Multiple and Sunspot Equilibria Under Interest Rate and Money Supply Rules," mimeo, University of West Ontario, October.

Sorger, G., (1990), "On the Minimal Rate of Impatience for Complicated Optimal Growth Paths," Forsch. bericht nr. 130, Universitat Technische Wien, September.

Spear, S.E. (1984), "Sufficient Conditions for the Existence of Sunspot Equilibria," *Journal of Economic Theory*, 34: 360–70.

(1985), "Rational Expectations in the Overlapping Generations Model," *Journal of Economic Theory*, 35: 251–75.

(1988), "Growth, Externalities, and Sunspots," mimeo, Carnegie-Mellon University, May.

(1989), "Are Sunspots Necessary?" *Journal of Political Economy*, 97: 965–73.

Spear, S.E. and S. Srivastava (1986), "Markov Rational Expectations Equilibrium in a Stationary Overlapping Generations Model," *Journal of Economic Theory*, 38.

Spear, S.E., S. Srivastava, and M. Woodford (1990), "On the Determinacy of Stationary Equilibrium in a Stochastic Overlapping Generations Model," *Journal of Economic Theory*, 50: 265–84.

Stutzer, M. (1980), "Chaotic Dynamics and Bifurcations in a Macro Model," *Journal of Economic Dynamics and Control*, 2: 353–76.

Svensson, L.E.O. (1985a), "Money and Asset Prices in a Cash-in-Advance Economy," *Journal of Political Economy*, 93: 919–44.

(1985b), "Currency Prices, Terms of Trade, and Interest Rates: A General Equilibrium Asset-Pricing Cash-in-Advance Approach," *Journal of International Economics*, 18: 17–41.

Tan, T. and S.R. Costa da Werlang (1985), "On Aumann's Notion of Common Knowledge: An Alternative Approach," CARESS Working Paper 88-09, University of Pennsylvania, February.

Taylor, J.B. (1977), "Conditions for Unique Solutions in Stochastic Macroeconomic Models with Rational Expectations," *Econometrica*, 45: 1372–85.

Tillmann, G. (1985), "Existence and Stability of Rational Expectations Equilibria in a Simple Overlapping Generations Model," *Journal of Economic Theory*, 36: 333–51.

Tirole, J. (1985), "Asset Bubbles and Overlapping Generations," *Econometrica*, 53: 1499–528.

Tobin, J. (1980), "Comments [on Wallace paper]," in J.H. Kareken and N. Wallace (eds.), *Models of Monetary Economies*, Minneapolis: Federal Reserve Bank of Minneapolis.

Torre, V., (1977), "Existence of Limit Cycles and Control in a Complete Keynesian System by the Theory of Bifurcations," *Econometrica* 45: 1457–66.

Townsend, R.M. (1980), "Models of Money with Spatially Separated Agents," in J.H. Kareken and N. Wallace, eds., *Models of Monetary Economies*, Minneapolis: Federal Reserve Bank of Minneapolis.

Van Huyck, J.B., R.C. Battalio, and R.O. Beil, (1980), "Tacit Coordination Games, Strategic Uncertainty, and Coordination Failure," *American Economic Revue*, 80: 234–48.

Varian, H. (1975), "A Third Remark on the Number of Equilibria of an Economy," *Econometrica*, 43: 985.

(1979), "Catastrophe Theory and the Business Cycle," *Economic Inquiry*, 17: 14–28.

Walliser, B. (1987), "Equilibre et anticipations," *Revue Economique*, 584–638.

Whiteman, C.H. (1983), *Linear Rational Expectations Models*, Minneapolis: University of Minnesota Press.

Whitesell, W. (1986), "Endogenous Cycles with Uncertain Lifespans in Continuous Time," *Economics Letters*, 22: 153–8.

Wicksell, K. (1898), *Interest and Prices*, 1898. Reprinted, New York: Augustus M. Kelley, 1962.

Wilson, C.A. (1979), "An Infinite Horizon Model with Money," in J.R. Green and J.A. Scheinkman (eds.), *General Equilibrium, Growth, and Trade*, New York: Academic Press.

Woodford, M. (1984), "Indeterminacy of Equilibrium in the Overlapping Generations Model: A Survey," mimeo, Columbia University, May.

(1986a), "Stationary Sunspot Equilibria in a Finance Constrained Economy," *Journal of Economic Theory*, 40: 128–37.

(1986b), "Stationary Sunspot Equilibria: The Case of Small Fluctuations around a Deterministic Steady State," mimeo, University of Chicago, September.

(1988a), "Expectations, Finance, and Aggregate Instability," in M. Kohn and S.-C. Tsiang (eds.), *Finance Constraints, Expectations, and Macroeconomics*, Oxford: Oxford University Press.

(1988b), "Monetary Policy and Price Level Indeterminacy in a Cash-in-Advance Economy," mimeo, University of Chicago, December.

(1989), "Imperfect Financial Intermediation and Complex Dynamics," in W.A. Barnett, J. Geweke, and K. Shell (eds.), *Economic Complexity: Chaos, Sunspots, Bubbles, and Nonlinearity*, New York: Cambridge University Press.

(1990a), "Learning to Believe in Sunspots," *Econometrica*, 58: 277–307.

(1990b), "Equilibrium Models of Endogenous Fluctuations: An Introduction," NBER Working Paper 3360, May.

(1990c), "The Optimum Quantity of Money," in B.M. Friedman and F.H. Hahn (eds.), *Handbook of Monetary Economics*, vol. II, Amsterdam: North-Holland.

(1991), "Self-Fulfilling Expectations and Fluctuations in Aggregate Demand," in N.G. Mankiw and D. Romer (eds.), *New Keynesian Economics*, Cambridge: MIT Press.

Yano, M. (1984), "The Turnpike of Dynamic General Equilibrium Paths and its Insensitivity to Initial Conditions," *Journal of Mathematical Economics*, 13: 235–54.

CHAPTER 7

Equilibrium in competitive, infinite dimensional, settings

Larry E. Jones

1   INTRODUCTION

Consider a small underdeveloped country. A new government is empowered and is looking for advice on how to speed the process of development. How might this government affect the quantity and types of foreign investment attracted through the explicit choice of its policies? Should they encourage this investment? Discourage it? Could and should this be done through explicit tax and spending policies? How would a policy of erecting tariff barriers to keep out imports of consumption goods affect their process of development? Should they undertake such a policy?

Does a government's "social security" policy adversely affect the incentives for private saving and the formation of capital? Should policies be adjusted because of this?

Is there "too much" trading in financial assets? Are the prices that these assets trade at too volatile? Should governments adopt explicit policies (such as transaction taxes) designed to reduce either the quantity of trading or the movements of prices in these markets?

Consider a one-dimensional beach along which bathers are uniformly distributed (more generally, a continuum of potential varieties and consumers with varying tastes). A local entrepreneur is considering opening a snack bar. Where along the beach should he locate? What if there are several entrepreneurs all competing for the same clientele, where will they locate? How would an omniscient social planner choose the locations and number of snack bars and how would this compare with the non-cooperative solution arrived at by the entrepreneurs? Should the government enter the picture and regulate entry and/or location of new snack bars? What should antitrust policy look like in this environment? Should something akin to patents be granted in this case? If so, for how long should they last?

This is a diverse set of substantive economic questions. One thing that they have in common is that the authors addressing them have used infinite dimensional modeling techniques. These techniques arise naturally in economics any time that the natural specification of the environment involves infinitely many goods. There are three primary examples of this in economic theory. The first is the modeling of decisions over time with an infinite horizon. These arise in connection with the first set of questions raised above. The second involves the modeling of static uncertainty with infinitely many states and arises naturally in connection with the second set of questions raised above. (Of course, combinations of these first two types of models can and have been constructed.) The third collection of examples arises in connection with economies with a continuum of either locations or qualities as primary decision variables. The third set of questions listed above have been discussed in this context.

Because of the importance of these examples in economic theory, the use of infinite dimensional techniques in economics has by now a long and distinguished history. It began over sixty years ago with the path-breaking work on optimal saving by Ramsey (1928). Other notable early works include Hotelling's theory of the optimal path of extraction of a natural resource (1931) and his model of the choice of location from a continuum by oligopolists (1929).

These works have spurred a continuing body of research reaching the present.

The most notable successors of Ramsey include Solow's model of growth (1956) and the resulting work on optimal growth initiated by Cass (1965) and Koopmans (1965). This has given rise to one of the most productive areas of research in modern macroeconomic theory. The recent book by Stokey and Lucas (with Prescott) (1989) contains a more complete bibliography than is possible here.

Similarly, Hotelling's work has led to a large amount of subsequent work. Notable examples include Lancaster's characteristics approach to modeling commodity differentiation (1971) (and a long list of successors) and the modern work on resource extraction. (References include Rosen (1974) and Dixit and Stiglitz (1977) on the commodity differentiation side and Solow (1974) and others on the resource extraction side.)

The works mentioned above share the property that they are all very special in terms of the specifications of preferences and technologies used by the authors. This is quite natural given that the goal of the papers is to obtain precise answers to policy questions. Correspondingly, however, the conclusions are quite restrictive. Because of this, it is quite natural that a parallel literature has emerged testing the limits of the special assumptions used in these works. This has given rise to the study of increasingly abstract generalizations of the models mentioned above to the point that there is now a small industry involved in the production of theorems concerning the properties of models with infinitely many commodities.

The aim in these notes is to give the reader a brief guide to this latter literature including an idea of the mathematical difficulties that arise and some hint of what I think are the most interesting open questions in this area. By necessity, this treatment must be incomplete. Since most of the work to this point concerns the existence of equilibrium with complete markets and price-taking agents, this will form the focus for most of the discussion. Most of the difficulties encountered can be conveniently exposited in this limited framework and it is to be expected that the techniques developed in this connection will be of use in less restrictive settings. Of course, this focus automatically limits the scope of these notes. (Other treatments of this topic include the recent monograph of Aliprantis, Brown, and Burkinshaw (1989a) and the survey by Mas-Colell and Zame (1990) which also give a more complete presentation of the mathematical methods used than is possible here.)

The remainder of the chapter is organized as follows. Section 2 is devoted to the exposition of some simple illustrative examples: the most common infinite dimensional model in economics (the basic Cass–Koopmans one-sector growth model) is laid out and it is shown how to interpret this as a general equilibrium model with infinitely many goods. Examples are presented building on this formulation to illustrate the main difficulties seen in the more general case. In section 3, general notation is introduced and the definitions of some familiar concepts are given in the infinite dimensional setting. In section 4, an outline of the solutions to the existence problem that have been discovered to this point is presented. Finally, in sections 5 and 6, areas of active new research are briefly discussed.

2   SOME EXAMPLES

In this section, I will lay out a simple (slightly modified) version of the Cass (1965) and Koopmans (1965) single-sector growth model, and show how it can be transformed into a standard general equilibrium model. Since this is both the simplest and most common form of infinite dimensional model found in practice, this will serve as motivation for the more general treatment discussed below.

Consider a country with many identical households each endowed with a time path of saleable labor services, $n^e(t), t = 0, , \ldots$ an initial stock of capital, $k(0)$, and an initial endowment of a time path of consumption, $c^e(t)$. There is a static "blueprint" for turning labor services and the flow of services of capital into usable output at each date, $y(t) = f(k(t), n(t))$, where f is non-negative, increasing, concave, and homogeneous of degree one.

This output can be used either directly for consumption at date t or indirectly for consumption in the future through augmenting the capital stock. Thus, the collection of technologically feasible activities (per capita) for this economy is:

(i) $c(t) + x(t) \leq f(k(t),n(t)) + c^e(t)$ $t = 0, \ldots$
(ii) $k(t+1) = (1 - \delta)k(t) + x(t)$ $t = 0, \ldots$
(iii) all variables are non-negative, $k(0)$ is fixed.

We have assumed the standard process for capital accumulation, $x(t)$ is investment, $n(t)$ is the amount worked each period, etc.

This is the complete description of the technological side of the model. For tastes, let us assume that they are of the form:

$$U(c(0),c(1), \ldots ;x(0),x(1), \ldots ;n(0),n(1), \ldots)$$
$$= \Sigma_t \beta^t u(c(t),1 - n(t)), \text{ where we have normalized } n^e(t) = 1 \text{ for all } t.$$

The simplest way to analyze this economic environment is what has become known as the planning approach. This is to assume that there is a benevolent social dictator or planner who can completely determine the activities undertaken. It is assumed that this planner acts to maximize the utility of the representative agent in this economy. In this example, the planner's problem is to maximize U subject to (i), (ii), and (iii) above.

This problem has been much studied over the years and a lot is known about its solution. One can show that, if u and f are continuous and concave, $f(k,1) - (1 - \delta)k + c^e(t)$ is bounded and $\beta < 1$, there is a solution to the problem above and it is unique. Moreover, one can show that, if $c^e(t)$ is constant, the solution to this planning problem has a stationary form. That is, $c(t) = c(k(t)), x(t) = x(k(t))$ and $n(t) = n(k(t))$ for some time invariant functions $c(\ ),x(\ ),n(\ )$ of the state variable k. Moreover, these functions are independent of the initial capital stock. Further, if $k(0) > 0$ and f is sufficiently productive, the time path of the variables converges to a unique positive steady state.

Comparative statics can be done on the "policy functions" (i.e., $c(\ ),x(\ ),n(\ )$), etc. Extensions to uncertainty are available. (See Stokey, Lucas, with Prescott (1989) for a detailed development of these points.)

This is a well-understood and obviously infinite dimensional model that has found many uses in economies.

As we are all aware, there is an alternative, positive, interpretation of the planning problem just described. This corresponds, through the second welfare theorem, to an alternative, market based analysis of the given economic environment. This interpretation features a large number of both firms and consumers interacting in markets and forms the basis for most of the use of this model as a tool in modern economic theory.

Following the notation of Debreu (1959), consider a production economy with many identical consumers with endowments and preferences as given above. Describe the production side of the economy via a production set of the form:

$$Y = \{(k(0); n(0), n(1), \ldots; z(0), z(1), \ldots) \mid k(0) \leq 0, n(t) \leq 0 \forall t,$$
$$\text{and } \exists k(1), k(2), \ldots \text{ with}$$
$$(-k(t-1) \leq -(1-\delta)k(t) - (f(-k(t), -n(t)) - z(t)\}$$

Define prices $p^k(0); p^c(0), p^c(1), \ldots; w(0), w(1), \ldots$ where $p^k(0)$ is the price of initial capital, $p^c(t)$ is the price of consumption goods at time t, and $w(t)$ is the wage rate at time t. Thus the firm buys capital at time 0 and hires labor at times $0, 1, \ldots$ which it uses to produce capital for investment and consumption for sale. (Investment is entirely internal to the firm in this formulation.)

Initial shareholdings are unimportant given our (standard) assumption that f is constant returns to scale.

An equilibrium is then a plan for labor sales and purchases by the consumer and firm respectively ($n^c(t)$ and $n^f(t)$), producer and consumer consumption goods decisions which clear the markets and:

(a)   firm's profits

$$p^k(0)k(0) + \Sigma_t z(t)p^c(t) + \Sigma_t w(t)n(t)$$

are maximized on Y, and

(b)   the consumer's utility, $\Sigma_t \beta^t u(c(t), 1 - n(t))$ is maximized subject to

$$\Sigma_t p^c(t)c(t) \leq p^k(0)k(0) + \Sigma_t w(t)n(t) + \Sigma_t p^c(t)c^e(t).$$

Then, the positive interpretation of the planning model presented above amounts to taking the allocation which solves the planning problem laid out above and finding prices as noted to "decentralize" it so that (a) and (b) are satisfied.

Given our assumptions, this amounts to finding prices and the resulting hyperplane which separates the upper contour set of the consumer from the set of technologically feasible possibilities. This is standard general equilibrium fare. Given our assumptions, both of these sets are convex and hence we should just invoke a separation theorem (e.g., Minkowski's would be the normal one) to get our equilibrium. Of course, as we have all seen many times before, $p^c(t)/p^c(0)$ is the marginal rate of substitution between consumption at dates t and 0 evaluated at the optimal quantities, etc.

As it turns out, the assumptions made above are strong enough to guarantee that this will work. That this is so follows roughly from the work of Bewley (1972). One doesn't have to go far from this simple example to encounter problems however.

In particular, a natural extension of the simple model described above is to allow for time dependent utility functions and (strong) intertemporal restrictions on the firm's production activities. Once this is done, the problems inherent in working, in infinite dimensional spaces begin to appear. To see this, consider the following simple example.

EXAMPLE 1
Consider a small deviation from the capital theoretic formulation described above with one consumer, one firm, and two goods per period. Denote by $(c_1(t),c_2(t))$ the time path of consumption of the two goods. Assume that preferences are of the form:

$$U(c_1(\ ),c_2(\ ))=\Sigma_t\beta^t u_1(c_1(t);t)+\Sigma_t\beta^t u_2(c_2(t);t),$$

where

$$u_1(c_1;t)=\begin{bmatrix}c_1 & \text{if } c_1\le 1\\ 2-e^{1-c_1} & \text{if } c_1>\end{bmatrix}$$

and

$$u_2(c_2;t)=\begin{bmatrix}\dfrac{1}{\beta^t}c_2 & \text{if } c_2\le\beta^t\\[2mm] 2-e^{\beta^t-c_2} & \text{if } c_2>\beta^t\end{bmatrix}$$

Assume that the consumer has an endowment given by:

$$c^e=(c_1^e(\ ),c_2^e(\ ))$$

where $0<c_1^e(t)<1, \lim_{t\to\infty}c_1^e(t)=0$ and $c_2^e(t)=\beta^t/2$.

Suppose that the production set of the firm is given by:

$$Y=\{(y_1(t),y_2(t))|\exists\lambda\ge 0\ni y_1(t)\le-\lambda\forall t \text{ and } y_2(t)\le\lambda\forall t\}.$$

Then, the first consumption good is an input each period and the second is an output each period. Note, however, that to get output at *any* date, a positive amount of good one must be input at *every* date. Thus, the decision to produce at date zero involves a commitment to use inputs forever (and promises output forever as well). One can think of this as describing a situation in which, once the technology is "started" (i.e., $y_1(t)<0$), inputs are required forever. (Perhaps nuclear containment is an example of such a technology.)

Is there an equilibrium for this simple economy? To find one, we follow the procedure outlined above. We will maximize U on the set of feasible allocations and assign prices according to marginal rates of substitution and transformation so that the decisions arising from the optimization problem are maximizing given those prices.

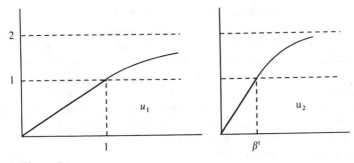

Figure 7.1

Suppose that there is an equilibrium. It follows from the form of endowments and the production set that no production is possible at all. Thus, if there is an equilibrium, it involves the agent consuming only his endowment. If this is the equilibrium, what must prices be? The usual marginal rates of substitution arguments imply that $p_1(t) = \beta^t p_1(0)$ for all t, $p_2(0) = p_1(0)$ and $p_2(t) = p_2(0)$ for all t with $p_1(0) > 0$. Without loss of generality, we can assume that $p_1(0) = 1$. It is straightforward to show that, with these prices, the consumer's endowment is his optimal choice given his budget constraint.

There is a problem with the firm, however. Notice that the plan in which one unit of good one is input forever with one unit of good 2 produced as output each period gives profits:

$$\pi = \Sigma_t p_1(t) \times (-1) + \Sigma_t p_2(t) \times 1 = -\Sigma_t \beta^t + \Sigma_t 1 = \infty.$$

It follows that the prescribed prices cannot be an equilibrium and hence no equilibrium exists.

As it turns out, there is a sense in which the initial endowment is a trivial quasiequilibrium. However, this requires that we allow prices which are not representable by sequences. In particular, Banach limits of sequences (see Dunford and Schwartz, 1988) will work. Note that in this case the value of the initial endowment is zero.

The point of this example is that you don't have to go very far from the simplest settings to find problems. For this example, every separating hyperplane (defined for all bounded sequences) gives value zero to the initial endowment. Hence, although there are separating hyperplanes, they give rise to quasiequilibria rather than full fledged equilibria.

The basic problem that this example is intended to highlight is one that is pervasive in infinite dimensional economics. This is the difficulty in finding meaningful (in an economic sense) separating hyperplanes. The reason for this difficulty is the difference between the sufficient conditions needed in the Separating Hyperplane Theorem (the relevant separation result in infinite dimensional spaces) and its finite dimensional counterpart, Minkowski's Theorem. In particular, to apply the Separating Hyperplane Theorem, it is necessary that one of the convex sets to be separated have a non-empty interior. This is not sensible without some notion of topology, of course.

The problem is, in most spaces of interest, the analog of the non-negative orthant (which contains the preferred set) has an empty interior. It follows that, as it is at least, this result cannot be applied.

There is a sense in which the fundamental problem in this example is a very old one in economics. The example given above has the flavor of an infinite dimensional example of what has become known as Arrow's exceptional case. This is a situation in which, because endowments are not interior to consumption sets, there are quasiequilibria but not equilibria. Although it is not obvious since $c_i^e(t) > 0$ for all $t, i = 1, 2$ in the example described above, the endowment of this one consumer exchange is on the boundary of the agent's consumption set.

As it turns out, in the context of capital theoretic examples, there is an easy way to fix this problem. This is to simply assume that the initial endowment is bounded below by a positive constant. This forces endowments to be interior and guarantees the existence of the desired, non-trivial, supporting prices. In a production context, an even more palatable solution exists. This is to assume that sufficient productive ability exists so that it is *possible* to produce in the interior (even if this is not what happens in equilibrium).

These insights come from the work of Bewley (1972) who provided the first general, equilibrium existence result covering models of the capital theoretic variety, although the difficulties caused by a lack of interiority were largely anticipated in the earlier work of Debreu (1954). (See also the early work on this subject by Gale (1967), McFadden (1967), and Radner (1967).)

Unfortunately, no easy fix for the problem exists in more general settings. This is because, as noted above, in general, the non-negative orthant of infinite dimensional spaces has an empty interior. It follows that without making further changes, we will never be able to invoke the Separating Hyperplane Theorem and solve the one consumer/one firm equilibrium problem in more general settings. As a result of this, there are settings in which there are not even quasiequilibria in one consumer/one firm settings. In fact, only small perturbations on the example presented are needed to generate examples of this more troublesome phenomenon as the reader can easily check.

This discussion highlights one of the main mathematical problems intrinsic to trying to do equilibrium theory in infinite dimensional settings. There is an important qualitative difference in the available separation results.

Examples similar to this one have appeared previously in Jones (1983) and (1984) and Mas-Colell (1986) in an exchange environment. Note that the work of Aliprantis, Brown, and Burkinshaw (1987a) shows that these earlier examples, although technically correct leave, in an important sense, something to be desired. This is because it can be shown (see Aliprantis, Brown, and Burkinshaw (1987a)) that in the exchange case the existence problem can be solved as long as one only requires that socially feasible consumption plans (i.e., those in the order ideal generated by the aggregate social endowment) be priced. The key to the example presented above is then that the presence of the possibility of production forces (through the profit maximization condition) socially infeasible production plans to be priced properly as well. The example shows that this cannot be done in general.

(Note that examples of a similar character can be constructed in which positive production does take place at the Pareto optimum. In this case, there are alternative plans available in the aggregate production set in which both costs and revenues are infinite when evaluated at the supporting prices.)

The second main problem that must be faced when studying economies in infinite dimensional spaces lies in compactness considerations. We will discuss three examples in this connection.

One of the main problems here is that there may not even exist Pareto Optima. Again, we will not have to go far from the simple capital theoretic setting to find problems.

EXAMPLE 2 (Araujo, 1985)
Consider a two-person exchange economy with initial endowments given by $c_1^e(t) = c_2^e(t) = 1$ for all t. Assume that preferences are given by:

$$U_1(c(\ )) = \Sigma_t \beta^t u(c(t)),$$

where $\beta < 1$ and u is strictly increasing, concave, and continuous, and $U_2(c(\ )) = \lim \inf_t c(t)$.

It is easy to see that no non-trivial Pareto optima exist for this economy. Given any candidate allocation that gives agent 2 positive consumption at any finite date, just delay his consumption further into the future. This allows for the increase of agent 1's utility with no lessening of agent 2's. Thus, this allocation cannot be Pareto optimal. It follows that no equilibrium can exist if agent 2 has a positive initial endowment. The problem here is that agent 2 is just too patient.

By analogy with the finite dimensional case, there are two potential reasons for this difficulty. These are either a lack of compactness of the set of feasible allocations or a lack of continuity of the utility functions. (Again, one needs a notion of topology for either of these to make sense!) Which of these causes the problem in this example? This is a difficult question to answer in this case. There is a topology (on the space of bounded sequences) such that both of these utility functions are continuous (the norm topology). Unfortunately, the set of feasible allocations is not compact in this topology. In this sense, there is a problem with compactness of the set of feasible allocations. On the other hand, there is a topology available (again, on the space of bounded sequences) such that the set of feasible allocations is compact. Unfortunately, in this topology, the second agent's utility function is not continuous. In this sense the problem is a lack of continuity of preferences.

This points out another problem that one must face in working in infinite dimensional spaces. This is that, in contrast to the situation in finite dimensional spaces, there is generally more than one reasonable candidate topology. Larger topologies give more continuous utility functions but fewer compact sets. Moreover, as is discussed in the next section, the choice among these alternative topologies sometimes has considerable economic "bite."

The other two examples that we will discuss in this regard are in continuous time. A simple reinterpretation of the index set in the discussion above is all that is required. Change sums to integrals where necessary.

EXAMPLE 3 (Hotelling's natural resource problem)
Consider a continuous time version of the natural resource extraction problem described in Hotelling (1931) and his successors. There is an initial stock $R(0)$ of the resource. There is one consumer who must choose a path of extraction, $r(t)$, over the interval $[0,T]$, to maximize utility $U(r(\ ))$ subject to the resource constraint:

$$\int_0^T r(t)dt \le R(0).$$

It is easy to see that, viewed as a set of time paths, this constraint set is not compact. For example, the sequence $r^n(t) = nR(0)\chi_{[0,1/n]}(t)$ is an infinite collection of time paths that has no accumulation point (at least not as a simple time path). Because of this, it is easy to construct examples where the corresponding one consumer, one firm economy has no competitive equilibrium. (For example, using $U(r(\ )) = \int u(t)r(t)dt$ will work for any strictly positive strictly decreasing function $u(t)$.)

What is even more unfortunate about this example is that it is easy to reinterpret the problem faced above as a budget problem for a consumer facing prices $p(t) = 1$ for all t with an initial wealth of $R(0)$. The result of this reinterpretation is that the example shows that consumer demand may not be well-defined for all prices! (This occurs because the consumer's budget set is not compact.)

It follows that one of the conclusions of any equilibrium existence result in an infinite dimensional setting is that there are prices such that consumer demand is well defined!

(Note that the problem uncovered by this example can be fixed in a variety of ways. Appeal to Inada conditions, bounding or restrictions on the class of utility functions through curvature restrictions can all do the trick.)

As a final example, one hope that one might hold out for from this line of research is the delivery of results giving general, strong properties of equilibrium behavior. Simple examples of this would include things like differentiability of the equilibrium consumption and/or production paths in a continuous time setting. To see that this will not work (at least in general) consider the following.

EXAMPLE 4

Consider a two-person continuous time finite horizon exchange economy on $[0,1]$. Assume that each of the two individuals has an initial endowment of the only good given by $c_1^e(t) = c_2^e(t) = 1$ for all t. Assume that preferences over time paths of consumption $c(t)$ are given by:

$$U_1(c(\ )) = \int_0^1 u_1(t)c(t)dt$$

and:

$$U_2(c(\ )) = \int_0^1 u_2(t)c(t)dt,$$

where u_1 is positive and strictly decreasing and u_2 is positive and strictly increasing. (If you like, you can think of this as a location model in which agent 1 "lives" at zero while agent 2 lives at one.)

Notice that each agent's endowment is continuous (in fact, they are C^∞) and hence the social endowment is as well. It would be nice, and not totally unreasonable to expect, to find an equilibrium allocation in which agent's consumption was continuous (or C^1 or C^∞). That is, can we, in this nicest of settings do equilibrium theory on the collection of continuous time paths?

It is easy to see that this example shows that this is not possible. To see this, note any equilibrium will have to be Pareto optimal. However, any Pareto optimal allocation in this setting *must* be of the form $c_1(t) = 2\chi_{[o,\tau]}(t)$, $c_2(t) = 2\chi_{(\tau,1]}(t)$ for some choice of τ. Of course, these do not give rise to continuous time paths.

As in the previous example, the basic problem here is a lack of compactness: the set of ways of decomposing a function which is continuous (resp. C^1, C^∞) as the sum of two functions which are each continuous (resp. C^1, C^∞) is not compact even though it is (norm) bounded.

Note that the conclusion here is not that one cannot do equilibrium theory in the setting of this example, rather that one cannot expect to get as much out of a general approach to the problem as one might have hoped due to compactness problems.

The example also shows that there are restrictions on how far one can go in getting nice properties of prices. To see this, note that equilibrium prices will necessarily be of the form $p(t) = \max(u_1(t), \alpha u_2(t))$ for some $\alpha > 0$. It follows that prices will not be differentiable even though marginal utilities (i.e., individual "internal" prices) are. This last example turns out to be quite important in the development of the general abstract approach to these problems. It shows two things. First, not all linear topological spaces are good candidates for models of consumption spaces. Second, not all linear topological spaces are good candidates for price spaces. We will return to this below in section 4.

The purpose of these examples is to illustrate the types of mathematical difficulties that can arise when trying to extend the results of equilibrium theory from finite to infinite dimensions. All of the examples above are pathological to some extent and have "fixes" that are economically acceptable in varying degrees. Thus, the interpretation of the examples should not be that one cannot take care of these economic situations. Rather, the interpretation is that to handle these types of environments we will have to add restrictions that played no role whatever in the finite dimensional theory.

In summary, the examples show that there are (at least) five potential significant mathematical problems that have to be dealt with. These are:

1   The collection of feasible allocations need not be bounded even in fairly nice settings. This follows from example 3.
2   Even if the collection of feasible allocations is bounded, it may not be compact. This follows from example 4.
3   Even if the collection of feasible allocations is compact in a nice topology, it need not be true that continuous utilities are "continuous enough." This is the essence of example 2.

4   Even if (1)–(3) are okay, it may not be possible to find prices separating production sets from the upper contour sets of consumers. Even worse, it may not be possible to separate consumption bundles from the upper contour sets of consumers in general. This is the content of example 1.

5   Even if (1)–(4) are okay, it may not be possible to simultaneously separate upper contour sets from allocations at Pareto optima. This follows from the second interpretation of example 4.

In subsequent sections, we will explore the ways in which these problems have been solved in the literature to date.

3   NOTATION

In order to address the problems suggested by the examples in the previous section, economists have turned to the existing mathematics literature for tools. The branch of mathematics that has proven most useful in this regard to this point is what is known as functional analysis (see Rudin, 1973 or Schaefer, 1971). This field involves the study of the topological properties of linear vector spaces. This is a natural fit for economics as the convexity structure we use so often is implicit in the vector space structure.

There are benefits and costs to this approach. The benefits come largely from the existing literature on these spaces including theorems characterizing compact sets and theorems guaranteeing the existence of separating hyperplanes. There are several costs as well. Among these is the requirement that one limit attention to a given infinite dimensional space from the start. Unfortunately, unlike the finite dimensional case, there are often many alternative spaces that are equally attractive from an economic point of view yet have very different mathematical properties. (See the discussion around example 4 on this point.)

In order to save on notation later, we will be very general now. Following Debreu (1959), we will consider an economy with finitely many consumers indexed by $i = 1, \ldots, I$ and finitely many firms indexed by $j = 1, \ldots, J$. In the background, there is a space containing the basic choice variables of all the agents in question. This will be denoted by X. It is assumed that X is a vector space over the reals (so that it makes sense to add elements in X and multiply them by scalars). Each consumer is assigned a consumption set $X_i \subset X$ and each producer has a production set $Y_j \subset X$. Each consumer has preferences $\geq_i$, an initial endowment e_i, and firm shares θ_{ij}. As is usual, a feasible allocation is an array of choices for all agents in the economy satisfying $\Sigma_i x_i = \Sigma_i e_i + \Sigma_j y_j$.

The first thing that sets the infinite dimensional treatment of equilibrium theory apart from its finite dimensional analog is the notion of prices. In the finite dimensional case, prices are just a list of numbers, one for each commodity. These carry the interpretation of the per unit purchase price of the good in question. At the level of generality being discussed here, the notion of a commodity is not even well defined (at least it is not obvious that it is). Because of this, we will have to generalize our notion of prices to some extent. Following Debreu (1954), the generalization that we will use is the notion of the value of a commodity bundle (i.e., an $x \in X$). The essential property of prices in a Walrasian setting is the view by the agents that they have no effect on them independent of what they do. That is, the bundle $2x$ costs twice as much as x, the bundle $x + x'$ costs as much as the bundle x plus the bundle x', etc. Formally, then the "value" of commodity bundles is a linear function defined on X. These will be denoted by x^* and are elements of X^* the set of all real valued linear functions defined on X (i.e., the algebraic dual of X). We will write the value of x when the prices are x^* alternatively as $x^*(x)$, (x,x^*), or xx^*. As we will see below, one question that we will want to address, when the notion of distinct commodities makes sense, is under what conditions this "valuation functional" can be interpreted as arising as a list of prices, one for each commodity.

A Walrasian equilibrium is then an array $(x_1, x_2, \ldots, x_I; y_1, \ldots, y_J; x^*)$ with $x_i \in X_i$ for all i, $y_j \in Y_j$ for all j and $x^* \in X^*$ such that:

(i)   For all i, x_i maximizes $\geq_i$ subject to the constraint – $x \in X_i$ and $(x,x^*) \leq (e_i,x^*) + \Sigma_j \theta_{ij}(y_j,x^*)$.

(ii) For all j, y_j maximizes (y_j,x^*) on Y_j.

(iii) $\Sigma_i x_i = \Sigma_i e_i + \Sigma_j y_j$.

Note that this definition is just the obvious generalization of the one now familiar from Debreu (1959).

In fact, the definition just given is a little too general to be useful. As in the finite dimensional case, proofs of the existence of a Walrasian equilibrium (this would not be much of a theory if one could not show at least this) rely on assumptions of continuity and convexity. This causes special problems in the infinite dimensional case for two reasons. First, given a choice of X, there is, in general, a multitude of topologies available which one could use to describe continuous preferences, closed consumption sets and closed production sets. (There is only one notion of convexity.) These different topologies capture different notions of what it means for two consumption bundles x and x' to be close. It follows that the assumption of continuity of preferences inherently places restrictions on the type of preferences allowed (as always). The second problem of this sort arising in the infinite dimensional case concerns the continuity of the function $x^*(x)$ where $x^* \in X^*$. That is, given an $x^* \in X^*$, for some choices of topology on X, the function

$x^*(\ )$ will be continuous, for others it will not be. (Without this continuity of x^*, the budget set need not be closed in the topology under which preferences are assumed to be continuous, and the objective function of the firm is not necessarily continuous.) Given this, when one is looking for an equilibrium, typically the search for prices is restricted to some subspace of X^* (it is straightforward to check that X^* is also a vector space over the reals) containing only functions that are continuous (on X) with respect to some preselected topology.

Given this notation, we can give the mathematical results that "solve" (at least partially) the difficulties noted in the previous section. Assume that τ is the topology on X. (There are some restrictions on this, it should be Hausdorff, addition and multiplication should be continuous, there should be a base of convex neighborhoods at 0, etc.) Let X' denote those elements of X^* that are τ continuous on X.

Then the infinite dimensional generalization of Minkowski's Theorem says that, if A and B are disjoint convex sets and A has a non-empty τ interior, there is a non-zero $x' \in X'$ separating A and B.

This result is known variously as the Separating Hyperplane Theorem and the Hahn–Banach Theorem.

To illustrate the potential usefulness of this result in our setting, consider a one consumer endowment economy. Let B be the set consisting of the endowment only and let A be the agent's utility upper contour set at the endowment. If A has a non-empty interior, the result cited above immediately gives rise to the desired supporting prices. Unfortunately, for most choices of X, the non-negative orthant, which contains A, has an empty interior in *all* topologies of interest. It follows that A has an empty interior as well. Hence, the result cannot be applied. Thus, without further restrictions, this result will not be useful in solving even the one consumer exchange problem. In the next section, the types of extra restrictions that have been used in the literature to date wil be discussed.

The second main result of interest deals with compactness. Let σ be the weakest (i.e., smallest) topology on X' such that each element $x \in X$, viewed as a linear function on X', is continuous. This topology is called the weak* topology on X' from the dual pairing (X, X'). Then, if V is any neighborhood of 0 in X and k is any real number, then:

$$V_k = \{x' \in X' \mid (x, x') \le k \forall x \in V\}$$

is σ compact. This is known as the Banach–Alaoglu Theorem.

The simplest example of the use of this result in the settings of interest here occurs if X is a Banach space with a Banach space "predual." That is, if X is the dual of a Banach space, Z. In this case, it is an implication of the Banach–Alaoglu Theorem that the closed norm unit ball in X is weak* compact. It then follows under mild assumptions that the set of feasible allocations is also weak* compact. From this, it can be seen that, if preferences are weak* continuous (actually upper semi-continuous is all that is needed), Pareto optima exist. This goes a long way in solving the problems described in examples 2 and 3.

4   EXISTING RESULTS

4.1   Early work

The presentation of the structure of infinite dimensional economic models given above follows closely the pioneering treatment given in Debreu (1954). At that time he showed that versions of the first and second welfare theorems hold in an abstract setting.

The proof of the first welfare theorem parallels the normal argument and depends only on weak properties (e.g., local non-satiation) of preferences and production sets.

The proof of the second welfare theorem is more troublesome, however. Given example 1 of section 2, this is only to be expected. Because of this, Debreu had to add one key, extra assumption to those that we normally see in the finite dimensional case. In this case, Debreu showed that every optimum can be supported as long as the aggregate production set contains what is known as an internal point. Example 1 shows that some extra assumption along these lines is indeed necessary.

Although this does give a positive result, the fact that the non-negative orthant has an empty interior in most infinite dimensional spaces implies that the result does not even cover the exchange case in general settings. As of yet, no systematic study of the types of production sets that this result allows has been undertaken. It is clear that it will be satisfied as long as the production set is defined by a continuous production function defined on all of X. (That is, if $Y = \{y \in X \,|\, F(y) \le 0\}$ for some continuous F.) It covers the capital theoretic example outlined in section 2 as well. (The reason for this will become clear in what follows.)

Although, Debreu did not show this in this original paper, it can be shown (see Duffie, 1986 and Jones, 1987b) that subject to solving the compactness problem as discussed above, this condition is sufficient to guarantee that equilibria exist as well. (Formally, the conditions that X have a Banach space predual, the feasible allocations are bounded, and that minus the aggregate social endowment lies interior to the aggregate production set are sufficient.)

4.2   Time and uncertainty

As noted above, the most common example of the structure outlined above found in the economics literature is when the elements of X correspond to paths of variables across time or states. This structure has been studied extensively in the mathematical economics literature. The first general treatment of the issues that arise in this connection came in the work of Bewley (1972) (see also Magill, 1981 and Brown and Lewis, 1981). Under Bewley's interpretation X becomes the collection of bounded measurable real valued functions defined on a σ-finite measure space, $X = L_\infty(\Omega, \mathscr{F}, \mu)$. Through the appropriate choice of the measure space $(\Omega, \mathscr{F}, \mu)$, this structure can capture many of the possibilities of interest in economics. Examples include:

1   Discrete time with an infinite horizon. Here choose $\Omega = N$, the natural numbers, $\mathscr{F} = P(N)$, the set of all subsets of N and $\mu =$ the counting measure on N.
2   Continuous time with either an infinite or finite horizon. Here choose $\Omega = [0, T]$, $T \leq \infty$, $\mathscr{F} =$ the Borel subsets of $[0, T]$ and $\mu = \lambda$, Lebesgue measure on $[0, T]$.
3   Static uncertainty. Here let $(\Omega, \mathscr{F}, \mu)$ be any probability space.

Further, through combining (1)–(3), dynamic structures under uncertainty can be captured as well. These examples cover the capital theoretic structures outlined in section 2 above (as well as the examples).

Given this choice for X, it is natural to identify each point $\omega \in \Omega$ as a commodity. Thus, $x(\omega)$ is the amount of the commodity ω being consumed, etc. Given this interpretation, it is natural to ask for prices to be interpretable as a list, one price for each commodity with value being calculated as simply the "sum" of price times quantity over commodities. Note that this does not follow automatically given the generality of the structure discussed to this point. If we were to require that the prices have this interpretation and that the value of every bundle x be finite, we would be led to searching for prices in $L_1(\Omega, \mathscr{F}, \mu)$ the space of summable (integrable) real-valued functions on $(\Omega, \mathscr{F}, \mu)$. (Without summability, $(x, x^*) = \infty$ for some $x \in X$.) Unfortunately, as it turns out this leaves out a large part of X^*. For example, if one were to adopt the norm topology on X (i.e., $\| x \| = \text{essup} | x(\omega) |$) the collection of continuous linear functionals on X is $ba(\Omega, \mathscr{F}, \mu)$, the collection of bounded additive set functions on $(\Omega, \mathscr{F}, \mu)$. This is exactly the space used by Bewley. (This is potentially an important distinction. Without it, the natural price space is not compact.)

In this connection, Bewley extended the classical equilibrium existence result to this setting. As the examples in section 2 show, this would not be possible without some important additional assumptions unfamiliar in the finite dimensional approaches to the theory. The key assumptions that Bewley had to make in this connection were:

1   Boundedness: The set of feasible production plans for any firm is bounded even using the outputs of other firms as inputs.
2   Adequacy: For each consumer, there is a production plan, feasible using only this individual's initial endowment, giving quantities of all goods that are bounded away from zero.
3   Monotonicity: There is a non-trivial set of goods (i.e., with positive μ-measure) along which preferences are strictly increasing. (Note that this is a joint restriction on preferences and consumption sets.)
4   Continuity: Production sets are weak* closed and preferences are weak* upper semi-continuous and norm lower semi-continuous.

In particular, the assumptions that he made were weak enough to cover the examples used in capital theory and outlined at the beginning of section 2.

In this setting, Bewley showed that an equilibrium exists in which $x^*\epsilon ba(\Omega,\mathscr{F},\mu)$. In addition, he explored the additional conditions necessary to guarantee that these prices could in fact be represented as elements of $L_1(\Omega,\mathscr{F},\mu)$ so that the interpretation as a price "list" is valid. He showed that, under relatively mild restrictions (from an economic point of view), this stronger result also holds (see also Prescott and Lucas, 1972).

How did Bewley handle the problems presented in the examples of section 2? As it turns out, L_∞ is the one case in which these problems are the least severe.

First, the non-negative orthant has a non-empty interior (in the norm topology). Thus, the Separating Hyperplane Theorem can be invoked directly to find supporting prices. This fact in conjunction with the Adequacy Assumption guarantees that the single consumer problem can be solved giving a non-trivial quasiequilibrium.

As noted above, the Banach–Alaoglu Theorem can be used to guarantee weak* compactness of the set of feasible allocations as long as they are bounded. This follows in this case directly because of the Boundedness Assumption.

The Continuity Assumption then insures that Pareto optima exist since preferences are upper semi-continuous in a topology in which the set of feasible allocations is compact.

Thus, example 1 is ruled out by the Adequacy Assumption, example 2 is ruled out by the Continuity Assumptions on preferences, and example 3 is ruled out by the Boundedness Assumption.

Given that bounded subsets are compact, example 2 may seem somewhat surprising. If the set of feasible allocations is compact why are there no Pareto optima? The answer to this question revolves around the technical topological notions in the background here. Thus, although the collection of feasible allocations is weak* compact, it is not norm compact. The trick in example 2 is that, although the preferences of consumer are norm continuous, they are not weak* continuous. Thus, to handle this problem the collection of preferences allowed is restricted according to the type of continuity properties possessed. This is the essence of the weak* qualification in the Continuity Assumption stated above.

It has been shown that this restriction on preferences amounts to the economically important notion of impatience on the part of consumers. Roughly speaking, in an infinite horizon discrete time setting, weak* upper semi-continuity of preferences guarantees that the tail of any sequence of consumptions has only a small impact on utility. Of course, this restriction is automatically satisfied in the additively separable discounted utility setting usually adopted in economics. This connection has been explored in detail in Brown and Lewis (1981) and Araujo (1985) and (as Bewley shows) is an important necessary ingredient to obtain prices that are representable as lists (i.e., in $L_1(\Omega,\mathscr{F},\mu)$). (See also the early work of Peleg and Yaari (1970) on this issue.)

Extensions of Bewley's result have been obtained in Bojan (1974), El'Barkuki (1977), Florenzano (1983), Yannelis and Prabhakar (1983), Khan (1984), and Toussaint (1984).

4.3   Differentiated commodities

Although Bewley's setting allows us to model many situations of economic interest, there is still some behavior that it does not adequately capture.

In the context of multiple product varieties, it is natural to think of there being a continuum of different varieties as allowed in Bewley's framework. However, in contrast to Bewley's approach, it seems reasonable to allow for individuals to concentrate their consumption on one or two goods. Similar considerations apply to firms. This cannot be handled with the Bewley framework since, by construction, consumption of any particular variety is of zero measure and hence of no consequence.

The way that this can be handled in a formal setting is to switch the basic space from L_∞ to $ca(K)$, the collection of countably additive measures on the set of commodity indices, K. One interpretation of this setting is that K describes the set of potential characteristics as in the Lancastrian formulation (1971). This model was first studied by Mas-Colell (1975) and then developed further in Jones (1984). It allows for specialization on the part of both consumers and firms through the choice of measures putting positive mass on distinct points. This model has also been analyzed in connection with imperfect competition in Hart (1979), Jones (1987a), and Ostroy and Zame (1988). (Note that this formulation will also handle the problem implicit in example 3 of section 2 by allowing the consumer to eat the entire resource at time zero.)

As is the case with L_∞, it is natural to place some restrictions on the types of prices that one will allow in an equilibrium. In this case, since the notion of distinct commodities still makes sense, it is natural to ask that prices be representable as a function on K. Moreover, if the notion of closeness of commodities is to make any sense, one would hope that nearby goods should sell for nearly the same prices. Thus, from an economic point of view, one would like to show that there is an equilibrium in which prices are continuous as a function of the commodity characteristics. (One might hope for more than this – every equilibrium can be supported by continuous prices, etc., see Mas-Colell and Zame (1990) in this regard.)

This space has very nice compactness properties as is the case with L_∞. In particular, bounded sets are weak* compact. Thus, the solution adopted in Jones (1984) to handle the analogs of the problems presented by the examples in section 2 is to assume boundedness and weak* continuity of preferences.

As in the case of L_∞ this continuity assumption has real economic consequences. In this case the assumption has the interpretation that nearby goods are good substitutes.

As in Bewley, consumption sets are assumed to be the non-negative orthant and preferences are assumed to be monotone.

Thus, the solution to the potential compactness problems in this setting are handled in much the same way as they were in Bewley's work.

Separation problems are another matter in this case however. Unlike the L_∞ case, there is no reasonable topology such that the non-negative orthant has a non-empty interior. It follows that the Separating Hyperplane Theorem cannot be of use in this setting without some further restrictions. One implication of this is that without these additional assumptions we will not even be able to solve the equilibrium problem for the one-consumer economy. Examples showing this difficulty can be found in Jones (1984) and Mas-Colell (1986). (If the set of varieties is uncountable it is an easy job to construct trivial quasiequilibria which are not equilibria in the exchange case in this setting.)

Rather than placing restrictions on endowments (which cannot work here), the solution adopted in this case is to restrict preferences to some degree. In addition to assuming that nearby goods are good substitutes, the stronger assumption that nearby goods are good substitutes at the margin is sufficient to guarantee that equilibria exist with prices that are a list, continuous as a function of product characteristics.

Formally, a sufficient condition is:

Smoothness: Assume that preferences are representable by a utility function such that the derivative

$$\frac{\partial U}{\partial \delta_k}(\mu)$$

exists and is a continuous function of both k and μ.

(Here δ_k is the Dirac measure at the point k, $\delta_k(B) = 1$ if $k \in B$ and 0 otherwise. Thus, $\partial U / \partial \delta_k(\mu)$ is the directional derivative of U in the direction δ_k, evaluated at the point $\mu \in X$.)

This condition is reminiscent of the early work of Debreu and Hildenbrand (1970) on the existence of equilibrium under uncertainty with a countable state space. There they show that equilibria exist assuming that preferences are of the von-Neumann/Morgenstern variety. In those notes, it is assumed that the state utility function is continuously differentiable and they use the derivatives of the utility function to bound the set of possible equilibrium prices. Much the same role is played in the existence proof by the Smoothness Assumption given above. (The work of Mas-Colell (1975) in this area handles the problems in quite a different way. This is to assume indivisibilities in the consumption sets of the individual agents. (Production economies were not studied.) The additional problems that these non-convexities created were then handled by introducing a continuum of agents.)

4.4   A more general approach

Given the models discussed in 4.2 and 4.3 above, it is natural to ask if there is something more general going on that can be exploited. In particular, it is natural to consider settings involving a mixture of the features of the two spaces described above. An example of this in a development context is discussed in Stokey (1991) where a model with a continuum of varieties is analyzed in an infinite horizon continuous time setting. For this reason, the approach taken by most recent authors in this area has been a more abstract one. The impetus in this work is to try and find results on the existence of equilibrium covering general classes of spaces.

In this regard, the spaces analyzed in the two previous sections share several common features. First, they are Banach (i.e., complete, normed) spaces. Moreover, they have Banach space "preduals." That is, they are the duals of Banach spaces. In the case of L_∞, the predual is L_1, the space of integrable functions defined on the same measure space. In the case of $ca(K)$, the predual is $C(K)$, the space of continuous real-valued functions on K. As pointed out above, this is a very useful property since it follows from this (by the Banach–Alaoglu Theorem) that norm bounded subsets are weak* compact. This goes a long way to solving the problems suggested in section 2.

The second main structural property that these two spaces share is the fact that they are ordered. That is, the notion of non-negativity makes sense. In most examples in economics, this notion plays a central role. Finally, they have the property that they are lattices (i.e., the max and min of any two elements are defined).

These three properties taken together mean that the spaces in 4.2 and 4.3 are what is known as Banach Lattices. Can the basics of equilibrium theory be extended to this class of spaces?

This is exactly the question addressed in an exchange environment in Mas-Colell (1986). (Actually, his result extends beyond this by covering what is known as topological vector lattices.) These spaces were first introduced into the economics literature in Aliprantis and Brown (1983) in an approach to the existence problem based on demand functions.

The problems suggested in the examples of section 2 are handled by four assumptions in this setting.

1   Closedness: The utility possibility frontier is closed.
2   Properness: There is a convex cone, C, with origin at zero and non-empty interior such that $C + \{x\}$ does not intersect the upper contour set at x.
3   Desirability: The aggregate social endowment is interior to $-C$, where C is the cone described in 2.
4   Consumption sets: The consumption set of all agents is the non-negative orthant of X.

We have seen in the examples how problems with compactness can arise in these settings. Here, this problem is handled by assumption 1. As above, sufficient conditions that this assumption is satisfied are that the space has a predual with the appropriate properties and that preferences are weak* continuous. Boundedness assumptions are not needed in the exchange case because of the fact that initial resources automatically bound the set of feasible allocations (given 4). This can be attained in the production case in much the way it was approached in Bewley. (Note that the assumption that the space have a Banach space predual is not essential. If one does not have this property, alternative routes for solving the compactness problem are possible, see Mas-Colell's paper for details.)

As noted above, the most serious difficulty in this setting is the fact that most infinite dimensional spaces have non-negative orthants with empty interiors. This means that one cannot even solve the one consumer exchange equilibrium problem without some additional assumptions.

The way that Mas-Colell handled this problem was a combination of the solutions adopted in Bewley and Jones. These are embodied in assumptions 2 and 3 above. First, the collection of allowable preferences was restricted enough to guarantee that separation results could be obtained for individual consumers. Since the upper contour set is a subset of the non-negative orthant, it will necessarily have an empty interior in most interesting cases. Thus, the separation will have to come in some other way. This is accomplished through the Properness Assumption given above. The essence of the assumption is to guarantee that, even if the (convex) upper contour set has a non-empty interior, there is a convex set lying *below* the preferred set that has a non-empty interior. It follows from this (from the fact that C has a non-empty interior) directly that supporting prices can be found at any allocation.

This is not quite enough to handle the multiple consumer case however. Additionally, one must guarantee that every Pareto optimum can be supported by prices in the polar of the properness cone first. This is exactly what Mas-Colell shows. This is the only place that the lattice properties of the space are used. It follows from an application of the Banach–Alaoglu Theorem (to X^*) that potential equilibrium prices can be confined to a compact subset of X^* (i.e., the polar of the properness cone).

Much work has been done since the first appearance of Mas-Colell's paper to try and understand the role of the properness assumption. Two papers deserve note in this regard. The first, by Richard and Zame (1986), shows that if preferences satisfy Mas-Colell's Properness Assumption they can be extended to a continuous preference ordering defined on an open set containing a non-empty interior. In particular, if preferences are proper, they can be extended so that upper contour sets have non-empty interiors. It follows from this that the necessary supporting prices can be found in the one consumer problem. Although, it would seem that this would provide a direct avenue to an alternative proof of Mas-Colell's theorem, there is one problem that still must be solved in adopting this approach. This is that, although this approach gives equilibria (e.g., apply Duffie (1986)) in the new economy (i.e., with the new, extended, preferences), there is no guarantee that an equilibrium in this new economy is an equilibrium in the original economy. The difficulty here is that, since preferences have been extended to a consumption set strictly containing the non-negative orthant (since it has non-empty interior), there is no guarantee that the equilibrium in the new economy has allocations that are feasible in the original economy.

A second result, contained in Jones (1987b), shows that an exchange economy on a Banach Lattice with proper preferences has exactly the same weak Pareto optima as an associated production economy with an aggregate production set with a non-empty interior. Given this, it can be shown (using the results in either Duffie (1986) or Jones (1987b)) that equilibria exist in the original economy.

Mas-Colell's result has been extended to cover the production case by Zame (1987) and to more general spaces in Mas-Colell and Richard (1991) and Richard (1989). The extension to the case of production requires a notion of properness for production sets mirroring that outlined above for preferences. See Zame's paper for details. The papers of Mas-Colell and Richard (1991) and Richard (1989) give existence results with weaker assumptions on the types of spaces allowed than outlined here. The important qualification that must be satisfied is that the price space have a lattice structure. (This includes the $(ca(K), C(K))$ pairing described in section 4.2 above.)

The necessity of this last property can be seen from example 4 in section 2. Recall that, in that case, individual marginal utilities are smooth functions of the commodity description (for both agents), and yet, equilibrium prices are not smooth. Because of this example, it follows that there are some essential restrictions on the choices of X and X^* that must be made. In particular, the example shows that choices of X^* without lattice properties (e.g., $X = L_\infty$ and $X^* = C^\infty$ in example 2) cannot work in complete generality. Here, the problem seems to be the way in which Walrasian theory constructs social equilibrium prices from those of individual consumers in situations in which consumption is not interior to the individual consumption sets.

4.5   A word about proofs

Three approaches have evolved for proving the existence of equilibrium in the papers cited above.

The first two were both initiated by Bewley in his work on L_∞. The first is to approximate the infinite dimensional space by finite dimensional spaces and then proceed with a limiting argument as the dimension of the space gets large. (A special case of this is to use truncation in an infinite horizon, discrete time setting.) This is also the approach adopted in both Mas-Colell (1975) and Jones (1984).

The second involves following the Negishi approach of searching through the Pareto frontier. This is the approach used in Mas-Colell (1986) and his successors.

A third, novel, approach to the problem has been developed by Aliprantis, Brown, and Burkinshaw (1987a). Their approach (based on the early work by Peleg and Yaari (1970)) is to do the equilibrium analysis on the order ideal generated by the social endowment. This is accomplished by searching through the core allocations for equilibria. Once this is done, prices are extended to all of the commodity space by invoking an argument using Mas-Colell's properness assumption.

5   EQUILIBRIUM WITH DISTORTIONS

Although this literature has progressed a great deal over the last few years, there is still much to be done. Looking back at the questions raised in the introduction, it is easy to see that the results surveyed to this point are not enough. The most obvious missing feature is that almost all of the questions listed in the introduction deal with issues of policy. It is not surprising that these are among the questions of most interest to economists.

There are several difficulties with trying to apply the results above to these more interesting economic settings. First, and most obvious, is the fact that the general formulations do not allow for the inclusion of policy variables. As it turns out, this is more than a simple convenience. As noted above, the structure of the proofs of these results in the general case is to conduct a search through the Pareto frontier for equilibria. (The advantage here is that the dimensionality of the problem is reduced to the finite case – almost.) Of course with distortionary government policies in effect, this approach cannot be applied. (It may be that something similar to this is possible, see Jones and Manuelli (1990) and Kehoe, Levine, and Romer (1988).)

Beyond this, in most real economies, consumption goods have complicated interactions in their use with both other consumption goods and with leisure. The normal way of handling this is to allow for more general consumption sets on the consumer side. Unfortunately, the lattice theoretic arguments used in the more general approaches rely heavily on the assumption that the consumption set is the non-negative orthant. It is not obvious how to extend the proofs from this more general work to cover this case. (See the counterexample in Back (1988) that shows that some restrictions are necessary in this regard.)

In recent work, an attempt to extend this line of research to explicitly include tax and spending policies in the Bewley setting has appeared in Jones and Manuelli (1989). This requires some adjustment in the approach outlined above. In particular, one must allow for different prices faced by different agents (e.g., before tax versus after tax prices), government production, and transfers. The formulation developed in Shafer and Sonnenschein (1976) for the finite dimensional case handles these considerations nicely. We will follow the notation introduced in section 3 closely. Let:

$$X^{\Delta} = X_1 \times X_2 \times \ldots \times X_I \times Y_1 \times \ldots \times Y_J$$

denote the set of socially feasible actions in this economy. A government policy is then a description of the taxing and spending plans that the government has contingent on the actions taken by all of the private agents in the economy and the prices that hold in the market (we will interpret x^* as the market prices henceforth). Formally, a government policy is a family of functions

$$\phi_i \text{ and } \mu_i \; i=1, \ldots,I; \text{ and } \psi_j, j=i, \ldots,J \text{ where:}$$

1   $\phi_i: X^\Delta \times X^* \to X^*$ is the prices consumer i must pay, after taxes, contingent on the action taken by the private agents in the economy and market prices.
2   $\mu_i: X^\Delta \times X^* \to \mathbb{R}$ is the lump-sum transfer (either positive or negative) consumer i receives from the government contingent on the actions taken by the private agents in the economy and market prices.
3   $\psi_j: X^\Delta \times X^* \to X^*$ is the prices that firm j receives, after taxes.

An equilibrium in this setting is then an array

$$(x_1, \ldots,x_I: y_1, \ldots,y_J; x^*)$$

such that:

(i) x_i maximizes $\geq_i$ subject to $x \in X_i$
      and $(x-e_i,\phi_i) \leq \mu_i + \Sigma_j \theta_{ij}(y_j,\psi_t)$ for all i.
(ii) y_i maximizes (y,ψ_j) for $y \in Y_j$ for all j.
(iii) $\Sigma_i x_i = \Sigma_i e_i + \Sigma_j y_j$.
(iv) $\Sigma_i \mu_i = \Sigma_i (x_i - e_i,\phi_i - x^*) + \Sigma_j(y_j,x^* - \psi_j)$.

Where the functions ϕ_i, μ_i and ψ_j are evaluated at the equilibrium quantities.

The first three of these conditions are the familiar ones where the market prices, x^*, have been replaced by their relevant after tax versions. Condition (iv) is new and requires that the government balance its budget in equilibrium. (Note that this means that the budget balances in present value terms if we interpret the x's and y's as sequences over time.)

Note that individuals (and firms) pay taxes only on their net trades. Thus, if a consumer makes net trade $x-e_i$, he pays $(x-e_i,\phi_i)$, in total, of which $(x-e_i,\phi_i-x^*)$ goes to the government. The remainder goes to the market. Government production and consumption is handled as the activity of one of the firms. Profit maximization on the part of this firm then amounts to cost minimization in government production (after prices have been distorted).

In order to prove that equilibria exist in this setting, in addition to the assumptions used in Bewley, Jones and Manuelli require that the government's policy satisfy the obvious analog of (iv) even out of equilibrium. Without this, Walras' Law is not satisfied in general. Note that this additional assumption puts strong restrictions on the types of policies this result can cover that are not obvious from the formulation. Thus, although it looks as if the government can charge zero prices for some goods and some individuals, this will not satisfy this restriction in general. Finally, it is required that the ϕ_i, μ_i, and ψ_j are continuous.

Despite this caveat, this result covers many cases of interest. For example, policies of the form: prices of consumption goods for firms are $1 - \tau$ times those in the market with all revenue being rebated lump-sum to consumers are obviously handled.

This result can be extended to cases in which there are certain types of externalities. In particular, one can allow for the dependence of individual preferences on the actions of other consumers and/or firms. There is a difficulty in extending this result to cover other externalities of interest. Formally, Shafer and Sonnenschein handle this problem by allowing the production sets (the dependence of consumption sets could be handled in a similar way) of producers to depend on the actions of the other agents in the economy. Of course, for decisions to be continuous in this case, it is necessary that this dependence have some continuity properties.

There are two issues that arise as a result of these considerations. First, the limiting arguments necessary in the proof seem to require that the correspondence describing the dependence of production sets on the actions of others need to be weak to norm lower hemicontinuous. (As it turns out, consumer's budget correspondences have this property when wealth is positive as long as the X_i satisfy the normal restrictions.) The reason for this is a mathematical difficulty that we have not touched on to this point. This is the lack of the (weak × weak) joint continuity of the map $E : X \times X^* \to \mathbb{R}$, defined by $E(x,x^*) = xx^*$. It should be expected that this problem will create difficulty in many further, more difficult problems in future research in infinite dimensional economies.

A second, more serious problem is that this condition, weak to norm lower hemicontinuity of the choice sets, is not satisfied in many examples of externalities of interest. There is still much work to be done here.

6   OTHER TOPICS

To this point, we have only scratched the surface of the topics that have been worked on in this area. In this section, I will briefly mention three further topics of active research in this area.

(A)   To this point, very little is known about the uniqueness of equilibria in infinite dimensional settings. Notable exceptions are the work of Kehoe, Levine, and Romer (1990) (in a capital theoretic setting with additively separable preferences) and the work on Hilbert spaces when consumption and price spaces have non-empty interiors by Kehoe, Levine, Mas-Colell, and Zame (1989). There is still much to be done here.

(B) An area of extremely active research in this connection is that of extending the·core equivalence theorem to infinite dimensional settings. Notable early examples of this line of research include Gabszewicz (1968), Bewley (1973), Mas-Colell (1975). More recently, this question has been treated extensively in the work of Aliprantis, Brown, and Burkinshaw. Their monograph (Aliprantis, Brown, and Burkinshaw (1988)) provides an excellent discussion of this topic.

(C) One of the more interesting possibilities presented in an infinite dimensional setting is the formal modeling of a situation in which, although each individual is small relative to the aggregate, some market power is still present. For example, consider a situation in which there is a continuum of goods indexed by the unit interval [0,1]. In this case, it is possible that even with an infinite number of producers, alternative models of competition will not give rise to the same allocations as would be seen in a Walrasian system. Clearly, whether or not this is true depends on the form of preferences for the goods.

Papers giving results on the equivalence of alternative theories to Walrasian equilibrium in settings like this include Mas-Colell (1975), Hart (1979), Jones (1987a), and Ostroy and Zame (1988) among others.

In addition, several examples have been constructed to show that in these situations equivalence theorems need not hold. Examples of this include Shaked and Sutton (1982), Jones (1987a), and Ostroy and Zame (1988). The essence of these examples is that, if nearby goods are not good substitutes, firms (or resource owners) can maintain important monopoly power even in the presence of a large number of nearby competitors. (Similar examples have been constructed with a countable number of commodities in Dixit and Stiglitz (1977) and Hart (1985a) and (1985b).)

This line of research holds out the interesting possibility of helping to define the limits to the applicability of Walrasian modeling.

References

Aliprantis, C. and D. Brown (1983), "Equilibria in Markets with a Reisz Space of Commodities," *Journal of Mathematical Economics*, 11: 189–207.

Aliprantis, C., D. Brown, and O. Burkinshaw (1987a), "Edgeworth Equilibria," *Econometrica*, 55: 1109–37.

(1987b), "Edgeworth Equilibria in Production Economies," *Journal of Economic Theory*, 43: 252–91.

(1989a), *Existence and Optimality of Competitive Equilibria*, New York: Springer-Verlag.

(1989b), "Equilibria in Exchange Economies with a Countable Number of Agents," *Journal of Mathematical Analysis and Applications*, 142: 250–99.

(1990), "Valuation and Optimality in the Overlapping Generations Model," *International Economic Review*, 31: 275–88.

Araujo, A. (1985), "Lack of Equilibria in Economies with Infinitely Many Commodities: The Need for Impatience," *Econometrica*, 53: 455–62.

Back, K. (1988), "Structure of consumption Sets and Existence of Equilibria in Infinite Dimensional Spaces," *Journal of Mathematical Economics*, 17: 89–99.

Bewley, T. (1972), "Existence of Equilibria in Economies with Infinitely Many Commodities," *Journal of Economic Theory*, 43: 514–40.

(1973), "Equality of the Core and the Set of Equilibria in Economies with Infinitely Many Commodities and a Continuum of Agents," *International Economic Review*, 14: 383–94.

Bojan, P. (1974), "A Generalization of Theorems on the Existence of Competitive Economic Equilibria to the Case of Infinitely Many Commodities," *Mathematica Balkanika*, 4: 490–4.

Brown, D. and L. Lewis (1981), "Myopic Economic Agents," *Econometrica*, 49: 359–68.

Cass, D. (1965), "Optimum Growth in an Aggregative Model of Capital Accumulation," *Review of Economic Studies*, 32: 233–40.

Debreu, G. (1954), "Valuation Equilibrium and Pareto Optimum," *Proceedings of the National Academy of Sciences*, 40: 588–92.

(1959), *Theory of Value*, New Haven: Yale University Press.

Dixit, A. and J. Stiglitz (1977), "Monopolistic Competition and Optimum Product Diversity," *American Economic Review*, 67: 297–308.

Duffie, D. (1986), "Competitive Equilibria in General Choice Spaces," *Journal of Mathematical Economics*, 15: 1–25.

Dunford, N. and J. Schwartz (1988), *Linear Operators Part I: General Theory*, New York: Wiley.

El' Barkuki, R.A. (1977), "The Existence of an Equilibrium in Economic Structures with a Banach Space of Commodities," *Akad. Nauk. Azerbaidjan, USSR Dokl.*, 33, 5: 8–12.

Gabszewicz, J-J. (1968), "A Limit Theorem on the Core of an Economy with a Continuum of Commodities," CORE working paper.

Gale, D. (1967), "On Optimal Development in a Multi-Sector Economy," *Review of Economic Studies*, 34: 1–19.

Hart, O. (1979), "Monopolistic Competition in a Large Economy with Differentiated Commodities," *Review of Economics Studies*, 46: 1–30.

(1985a), "Monopolistic Competition in the Spirit of Chamberlin, I: A General Model," *Review of Economic Studies*, 52: 529–46.

(1985b), "Monopolistic Competition in the Spirit of Chamberlin, II: Special Results," *Economic Journal*, 95: 889–908.

Hotelling, H. (1929), "Stability in Competition," *Economic Journal*, 39: 41–57.

(1931), "The Economics of Exhaustible Resources," *Journal of Political Economy*, 39: 137–75.

Jones, L. (1983), "Special Problems Arising in the Study of Economies with Infinitely Many Commodities," in H. Sonnenschein (ed.), *Models of Economic Dynamics*, New York: Springer-Verlag.

(1984), "A Competitive Model of Commodity Differentiation," *Econometrica*, 52: 507–30.

(1987a), "The Efficiency of Monopolistic Competition in Large Economies: Commodity Differentation with Gross Substitutes," *Journal of Economic Theory*, 41: 356–91.

(1987b), "Existence of Equilibria with Infinitely Many Commodities: Banach Lattices Revisited," *Journal of Mathematical Economics*, 16: 89–104.

Jones, L. and R. Manuelli (1989), "Notes on the Existence of Walrasian Equilibrium in Infinite Horizon Economies with Taxes and Government Spending," Northwestern University Discussion Paper.

(1990), "A Convex Model of Equilibrium Growth: Theory and Policy," *Journal of Political Economy*, 98: 1008–38.

Kehoe, T., D. Levine, A. Mas-Colell, and W. Zame (1989), "Determinacy of Equilibrium in Large Economies," *Journal of Mathematical Economics*, 18: 231–62.

Kehoe, T., D. Levine, and P. Romer (1988), "Characterizing Equilibria of Models with Externalities and Taxes as Solutions to Optimization Problems," University of Minnesota working paper.

(1990), "Determinacy of Equilibria in Dynamic Models with Fintely Many Consumers," *Journal of Economic Theory*, 50: 1–21.

Koopmans, T. (1965), "On the Concept of Optimal Economic Growth," in *The Econometric Approach to Development Planning*, Chicago: Rand McNally.

Lancaster, K. (1971), *Consumer Demand: A New Approach*, New York: Columbia University Press.

Magill, M. (1981), "An Equilibrium Existence Theorem," *Journal of Mathematical Analysis and Applications*, 84: 162–9.

Mas-Colell, A. (1975), "A Model of Equilibrium with Differentiated Commodities," *Journal of Mathematical Economics*, 2, 263–96.

(1986), "The Price Equilibrium Existence Problem in Topological Vector Lattices," *Econometrica*, 54: 1039–54.

Mas-Colell, A. and S. Richard (1991), "A New Approach to the Existence of Equilibria in Vector Lattices," *Journal of Economic Theory*, 53: 1–11.

Mas-Colell, A. and W. Zame (1990), "Equilibrium Theory in Infinite Dimensional Spaces," in the *Handbook of Mathematical Economics, Volume IV*, W.

Hildenbrand and H. Sonnenschein (eds), Amsterdam: North Holland.

McFadden, D. (1967), "The Evaluation of Development Programmes," *Review of Economic Studies*, 34: 25–50.

Ostroy, J. and W. Zame (1988), "Non-Atomic Economies and the Boundaries of Perfect Competition," UCLA Working Paper.

Peleg, B. and M. Yaari (1970), Markets with Countably Many Commodities," *International Economic Review*, 11: 369–77.

Prescott, E. and R. Lucas (1972), "A Note on Price Systems in Infinite Dimensional Spaces," *International Economic Review*, 13: 416–22.

Radner, R. (1967), "Efficiency Prices for Infinite Horizon Production Programmes," *Review of Economic Studies*, 34: 51–66.

Ramsey, F. (1928), "A Mathematical Theory of Saving," *Economic Journal*, 38: 543–59.

Richard, S. (1989), "A New Approach to Production Equilibria in Vector Lattices," *Journal of Mathematical Economics*, 18: 41–56.

Richard, S. and W. Zame (1986), "Proper Preference and Quasiconcave Utility Functions," *Journal of Mathematical Economics*, 15: 231–48.

Rosen, S. (1974), "Hedonic Prices and Implicit Markets: Product Differentiation in Pure Competition," *Journal of Political Economy*, 82: 34–55.

Rudin, W. (1973), *Functional Analysis*, New York: McGraw-Hill.

Schaefer, H.H. (1971), *Topological Vector Spaces*, New York: Springer-Verlag.

Shafer, W. and H. Sonnenschein (1976), "Equilibrium with Externalities, Commodity Taxation and Lump Sum Transfers," *International Economic Review*, 17: 601–11.

Shaked, A. and J. Sutton (1982), "Relaxing Price Competition Through Product Differentiation," *Review of Economic Studies*, 49: 3–13.

Solow, R. (1956), "A Contribution to the Theory of Economic Growth," *Quarterly Journal of Economics*, 70: 65–94.

——— (1974), "The Economics of Resources or the Resources of Economics," *American Economic Review*, 64: 1–14.

Stokey, N. (1991), "Human Capital, Product Quality and Growth," *Quarterly Journal of Economics*, 106: 587–616.

Stokey, N. and R.E. Lucas (with E. Prescott) (1989), *Recursive Methods in Economic Dynamics*, Cambridge, MA: Harvard University Press.

Toussaint, S. (1985), "On the Existence of Equilibria in Economies with Infinitely Many Commodities," *Journal of Economic Theory*, 13: 98–115.

Yannelis, N.C. (1985), "On a Market Equilibrium Theorem with an Infinite Number of Commodities," *Journal of Mathematical Analysis and Applications*, 108: 595–9.

Yannelis, N.C. and N.D. Prabhakar (1983), "Existence of Maximal Elements and Equilibria in Linear Topological Spaces," *Journal of Mathematical Economics*, 12: 233–45.

Yannelis, N.C. and W. Zame (1986), "Equilibria in Banach Lattices without Ordered Preferences," *Journal of Mathematical Economics*, 15: 75–110.

Zame, W. (1987), "Competitive Equilibria in Production Economies with an Infinite Dimensional Commodity Space," *Econometrica*, 55: 1075–108.

CHAPTER 8

Infinite-dimensional equilibrium theory: discussion of Jones*

Andreu Mas-Colell

There is little I can possibly add to the thorough account of the current state of equilibrium theory with infinitely many commodities that has been given in the chapter of L. Jones. But since the duty of the commentator is to offer comments I will oblige by touching on two points. The first concerns a contrast between the analytical treatment of exchange and of production economies, the second refers to the difficulties to extend the theory to environments where the first fundamental theorem fails and, in particular, to incomplete markets economies.

But before plunging into my specific comments perhaps I will be allowed a word on the purposes of the theory. The following observation is evident enough but it nonetheless bears repeating. While from a purely formal point of view an equilibrium model with infinitely many commodities includes, and therefore generalizes, the standard model with finitely many commodities, the justification of the theory is not generality but, on the contrary, concreteness. If all we wanted to know is, say, that an equilibrium exists we would do as well with the finite number of commodities model. After all the number of commodities can be arbitrarily large and since large can be very large indeed there can be no loss of substance in doing so. The problem, and the *raison d'être* of the infinite dimensional approach, is that proceeding in this way we neglect any preexisting regularities among the set of commodities (e.g., neighboring relations) and treat it as a finite, but otherwise undifferentiated, set. A considerable amount of information (on the structure of equilibrium prices, for example) is lost on the way. The point of view of infinite dimensional theory is that if there is more than a few commodities (I will not now commit myself to attach a number to this "few") it may altogether be more instructive to look at the infinite limit and proceed by deriving properties of equilibrium prices (e.g., summability, continuity in characteristics, stationarity, etc.) that, in the first place, exploit features of preferences, endowments, and technology best formalized in the limit case and, in the second place, would remain informative for the finite approximation if only one had the patience to carry out the ε,δ exercise. In summary: the infinite dimensional approach requires a heavier mathematical input than its finite counterpart. But it also gets answers to conceptually sharper questions.

1   EXCHANGE VERSUS PRODUCTION ECONOMIES

One of the reasons that so much of equilibrium theory has traditionally concentrated on the examination of exchange economies is that the incorporation of production (at least in the manner done by general equilibrium theory) presents no particular difficulty. Or perhaps it would be more precise to say that this is so once a few standard tricks have been learned.

It is possible that this will also be the eventual picture with infinite dimensional equilibrium theory. But for the sake of a discussion let me argue that exchange economies have one feature that from an infinite dimensional viewpoint makes them very particular. This feature is that the entire set of feasible allocations is contained in an order interval $\{(x_1, \ldots ,x_N) : 0 \leq x_i \leq \omega,$ all $i\}$, i.e., in a "box." The existence of an upper bound to the set of feasible allocations is given to us (by the initial endowments) in the exchange case but it may easily fail with production, except of course in a finite dimensional world where the boundedness of the feasible set does automatically imply that we can contain it in a box.

The order boundedness of the feasible set facilitates the analysis in at least three (related) respects.

The first is that it allows us to invoke the mathematics of vector lattices (or Riesz spaces) which seem, therefore, ideally fitted for the study of exchange economies. The order structure did not play any major role in the technical development of the finite dimensional theory. The reason is that the full power of the theory could be displayed by using only convexity structures (see, e.g., Debreu, 1962). To the extent that this does not appear to be so in general it has been most convenient to have at hand an alternative, and effective, tool. I refer to Aliprantis, Brown, and Burkinshaw (1989) that in all certainty will become the standard reference in economics for Riesz space applications.

The second respect is more specific. Knowing that the feasible set is contained in an order interval helps to establish its compactness for appropriate topologies. Some form of compactness is essential if, for example, we hope to prove existence.

The third respect is more conceptual and probably more important. The order boundedness property allows the neat separation of the equilibrium problem into two parts. First one searches for prices defined on the ideal generated by the total endowments. This is the program effectively pursued by Aliprantis, Brown, and Burkinshaw (1989). It turns out that the problem is then quite parallel to the classical contribution of Bewley (1972) (it can in fact be argued that the commodity space of Bewley is implictly nothing but the ideal of a larger universal commodity space). Second one then attempts to extend prices from the ideal to the, possibly much larger, entire space. I do not now want to discuss to what extent it is important to actually carry out the second step or if we can rest content with pricing any commodity bundle that could conceivably be marketed given the total endowments. I want to emphasize simply that in the exchange case the possibility for this clean separation in two steps exists and it is most useful.

2   DIFFICULTIES IN NON-CLASSICAL SET-UPS: INCOMPLETE MARKETS

The chapter by Larry Jones makes it patently clear that the extension of the classical Arrow–Debreu–McKenzie model to an infinite dimensional setting has been essentially achieved and that the mathematical techniques of functional analysis have proven to be tools extraordinarily effective for the task.

Equilibrium theory, however, is not exhausted by the classical model. Its practical use has required the consideration of many departures and the incorporation of many forms of "imperfections" and of market failure. Thus, there are equilibrium models with taxes, with externalities, without complete markets, with imperfect competition, etc. It would be comforting if we could assert that once the infinite-dimensional extension of the classical model is well understood the extension of the non-classical theory presents no particular difficulty. Unfortunately, this is not so. The point has already been made in Jones' chapter with reference to an equilibrium problem with externalities. I will discuss it further in the context of a model with incomplete markets. The issues raised are similar. In fact, they are likely to be similar in any situation where the first welfare theorem breaks down.

For concreteness take the simplest infinite dimensional incomplete market model (see the chapters of D. Cass and of D. Duffie). There is a set of states $S = [0,1]$. At each $s \in S$ there are spot markets for $l + 1$ commodities (having $l > 0$ is a way to capture some of the phenomena that can occur with more than two periods. We take the first commodity to be a numeraire). Final allocations $x = (x_1, \ldots, x_N), x_i \in (L_\infty^+([0,1]))^{l+1}$ and price functionals p are determined from utility functions $u_i(\cdot)$ and endowments ω_i in the usual way. The key restriction, reflecting the incompleteness of markets, is that there is a certain linear space (even possibly finite dimensional) of feasible net wealth transfers $L \subset L_\infty([0,1])$, that is, every individual optimization problem is subject to the constraint: "the function $s \mapsto p(s) \cdot (x_i(s) - \omega_i(s))$ belongs to L." This is a highly reduced description. It corresponds to the real numeraire asset case of Geanokoplos–Polemarchakis (1986) (the spot price of the numeraire being fixed to one).

For a state space S of finite cardinality a more general version of the above model was first formulated and studied by Radner (1972) who gave sufficient conditions for the existence of equilibrium prices p. He established existence by using the standard fixed point techniques of the classical theory. We will now argue, by means of two observations, that an attempt to follow a parallel approach for the case $S = [0,1]$ and to apply the functional analytical techniques of, say, Bewley (1972) or Aliprantis, Brown, and Burkinshaw (1989), to the existence problem will not work.

The first observation, already made in Mas-Colell and Zame (1988), has to do with the joint continuity of the evaluation maps. Typically, in attacking the problem along the suggested functional analytical lines one finds oneself at some stage with a double sequence (or net) x_n, p_n which, by appealing to suitably weak topologies, can be assumed to converge $x_n \to x, p_n \to p$. Moreover, by the nature of the sequences, the limits x, p would constitute an equilibrium if only $p_n \cdot x_{ni} \to p \cdot x_i$ for every i. There is no general mathematical reason for this joint continuity to hold for topologies weak enough to guarantee the existence of limits. But, as it was first shown by Bewley (1972), we may be rescued by the fact that the sequences x_n, p_n will not be arbitrary. In the first place, x_n will be alocations, that is $\Sigma_i x_{ni} = \Sigma_i \omega_i \equiv \omega$. Because the right-hand side does not depend on n this can be made to yield $\Sigma_i p_n \cdot x_{ni} \to p \cdot \omega = \Sigma_i p \cdot x_i$. In the second place, p_n will support, in an appropriate sense, the preferred sets to x_{ni}. To be specific, by an upper semicontinuity property on utility which is normally satisfied we will have $u_i(x_i + \varepsilon \omega) > u_i(x_{ni})$ for n large enough. If from this we could conclude that $p_n \cdot (x_i + \varepsilon \omega) \geq p_n \cdot x_{ni}$ we would be done since then $\limsup p_n \cdot x_{ni} \leq p \cdot x_i$ for every i and therefore $p_n \cdot x_{ni} \to p \cdot x_i$. The supporting property $p_n \cdot (x_i + \varepsilon \omega) \geq p_n \cdot x_{ni}$ obtains if markets are complete but may well fail if markets are incomplete because the net wealth trade function $s \mapsto p_n(s) \cdot (x_i(s) - (1 - \varepsilon) \omega_i(s))$ may not belong to L (compare with the externality model in Jones' chapter).

The second observation goes more to the heart of the matter because it shows that the joint continuity problem cannot be easily sidestepped. It has substantive implications. Indeed we will show that in the incomplete case with state space $[0,1]$ the equilibrium price set fails to be sequentially compact in the same sense that it is in the complete market case (the same remark can be made for the upper hemicontinuity of the equilibrium correspondence). Consider the following trivial example. Preferences (which are of the expected utility type) and endowments are state independent. Markets are as incomplete as they can be, i.e., $L(p) = \{0\}$ at all p. Suppose that spot markets clear at any of three (normalized) linearly independent price vectors $p', p'', p''' \in R_+^{l+1}$. Then an equilibrium of the incomplete market model is any price function $p : [0,1] \to \{p', p'', p'''\}$. There is no sense in which this set of equilibrium functions can be sequentially compact. Let p_n be the function such that $p_n(s) = p'$ (resp., $p_n(s) = p''$) if $\dfrac{j}{2n} \le s \le \dfrac{j+1}{2n}$ and j is even (resp. odd). Then, depending on the topology, either p_n has no accumulation point or if it has a limit function it cannot be other than $p(s) = \frac{1}{2}p' + \frac{1}{2}p''$, which is not an equilibrium price function. It should be evident that this spells trouble for any brute force attempt to prove the existence of an equilibrium by taking limits from finite state space approximations. Note that things are very different in the complete case. In the example the only equilibrium price functions would be the three constant functions. Thus the equilibrium price set, being finite, is necessarily compact.

What to do? One possibility is to recover the finite approximation techniques (more generally, the upper hemicontinuity of the equilibrium correspondence). There are at least two ways to do so. The first is to restrict the analysis to a countable state space. Existence theorems have then been obtained by Green and Spear (1987) and Zame (1988). The second is to extend the notion of equilibrium by allowing random prices (and allocations). We would now require as equilibrium conditions on p,x that for every s, $p(s),x(s)$ be a spot price equilibrium with probability one and that given the price expectations p,x_i be the random variable (jointly distributed with p) induced by utility maximization subject to the constraint: "for every s, $p(s) \cdot x(s)$ is non-stochastic (this is because asset trade comes before the realization of the random price) and the function $s \mapsto p(s) \cdot (x_i(s) - \omega_i(s))$ belongs to L." With this approach if we look again at the example of the previous paragraph then we see that the existence of equilibrium is restored (at any state randomize with equal weight between p' and p''). This is quite general. It is well known (at least since Hart, Hildenbrand, and Kohlberg, 1974) that equilibrium defined as distributions is very resistant to taking limits and it is thus more than likely that a distribution approach applied to the current problem will allow a comparatively simple extension of the Radner style proofs. However, this does not seem to have been done to date (see Duffie, Geanakoplos, Mas-Colell, and McLennan, 1988, for an application of distribution-like ideas to a related problem).

There are limitations to the two suggestions. Non-discrete, uncountable state spaces are non-pathological and are common in applications (e.g., in finance). As for the introduction of extraneous noise (sunspots after all) it is of course interesting to verify once more that it emerges "endogenously" as a natural closure of the equilibrium set. But one should realize that it brings with it a host of new problems. One is indeterminacy (the following is an informal conjecture: for the "typical" case either the model does not admit any equilibrium with random prices or there is a continuum of them). Another is suboptimality. Even if the underlying model is complete random prices can be self-sustaining and consequently Pareto optimality is not reached.

But perhaps the most serious limitation is that neither restrictions on the state space nor extensions of the equilibrium concept should be really necessary. It is the mathematical machinery, not the validity of the theory, that fails on us. It is in fact the strength of the functional analytical approach that proves at the end to be its shortcoming. That strength is abstraction. The time and uncertainty structures of the specific problems (the recursivities in time or the additivity properties implied by expected utility behavior) are all excised from models that once reduced to its bare essentials and free of "cluttering detail," are dealt with in a full blow. This works beautifully when applied to the classical Arrow–Debreu–McKenzie model. But, as we have seen, it does not in non-classical worlds. The way to proceed is clear. We should abstract less (or abstract differently). In particular, for the incomplete market existence problem it can be supposed that a positive solution will be obtained by not just remembering but actually building on time recursivities (broadly defined, no suggestion of stationarity) and the expected utility hypothesis. We will know in the next few years.

Note

* I thank L. Jones for his comments.

References

Aliprantis, C., D. Brown, and O. Burkinshaw (1989), *Existence and Optimality of Competitive Equilibria*, Springer-Verlag.

Bewley, T. (1972), "Existence of Equilibria in Economies with Infinitely Many Commodities," *Journal of Economic Theory*, 4: 519–40.

Debreu, G. (1962), "New Concepts and Techniques for Equilibrium Analysis," *International Economic Review*, 3: 257–73.

Duffie, D., J. Geanakoplos, A. Mas-Colell and A. McLennan (1988), "Stationary Markov Equilibria," mimeo, Stanford University.

Geanakoplos, J. and H. Polemarchakis (1986), "Existence, Regularity and Constrained Sub-Optimality of Competitive Allocations When the Asset Market is Incomplete," in *Uncertainty, Information and Communication*, W. Heller, R. Starr, and D. Starret (eds), Cambridge University Press.

Green, R. and S. Spear (1987), "Equilibria in Large Commodity Spaces with Incomplete Financial Markets," mimeo, Carnegie-Mellon.

Hart, S., W. Hildenbrand, and E. Kohlberg (1974), "On Equilibrium Allocations as Distribution in the Commodity Space," *Journal of Mathematical Economy*, 1 (2): 159–67.

Mas-Colell, A and W. Zane (1991) "Equilibrium Theory in Infinite Dimensional Spaces," in *Handbook of Mathematical Economics*, vol. IV, W. Hildenbrand and H. Sonnenschein (eds.), Amsterdam: North-Holland.

Radner, R. (1972), "Existence of Equilibrium of Places, and Price Expectations in a Sequence of Markets," *Econometrica*, 40: 289–303.

Zame, W. (1988), "Asymptotic Behavior of Asset Markets I: Asymptotic Inefficiency," mimeo, Department of Mathematics, SUNY at Buffalo.